AF572217

Xhosa Newspaper Reader and Lexicon

D. Julian Lloyd
Linda Murphy Marshall

African series editor: R. David Zorc

Xhosa Newspaper Reader and Lexicon

D. Julian Lloyd
Linda Murphy Marshall

2002
Dunwoody Press

Xhosa Newspaper Reader and Lexicon

All inquiries should be directed to:
Dunwoody Press
6564 Loisdale Ct., Suite 800
Springfield, VA 22150, USA

ISBN: 1-881265-90-0
Library of Congress Catalog Card Number: 2002113783
Printed and bound in the United States of America

Table of Contents

Readings

Translations

ACKNOWLEDGEMENTS

Having been engaged in the preparation of this reader for the last twenty months, my most lasting impression has been the recognition of the vast amount of work which had gone into the project before it was passed to me for completion. I understand that some of the people previously involved have had little or no exposure to the Xhosa language in its home territory and often no experience beyond their involvement with this reader. My task has been rendered so much easier by their linguistic skills and meticulous cataloging of the selections; they all have my gratitude.

My co-author, Dr. Linda Murphy Marshall, I have never met, but as time went on I was able to feel increasingly confident that where her hand had passed, there would be but little to change or improve. I owe her my thanks and my pleasure for co-authoring this project with me.

Others whom I have not met, but who played an important role in the early stages of the project with their assistance in the translations and glossing processes, also receive my praise. They are Mr. Khosi Mncube, Mrs. Naledi Tuswa Mncube, and Mr. Bam Siboto – **ndiyanibonga, ndiyanibulela, enkosi!**

For early work on the database, Mr. Drew Foerster needs mention, as indeed do all the staff of McNeil Technologies who work behind the scenes on projects like these – we know you're there and appreciate your contribution. Special mention of course must be made of Dr. R. David Zorc, the supervising editor of this reader whose friendly oversight and unfailing support certainly made my task easier.

Here in South Africa it was always comforting to know that I could call on the assistance of colleagues Dr. Tessa Dowling (who had a degree of involvement in the early stages of the project), Mr. Derek Gowlett, and Mr Zukile Jama, and, on occasion, Professor Sizwe Satyo, the co-author of the work selected to be the lexicon for this reader. To all of you, thank you for being there when I needed to 'bounce' a knotty idiom or piece of syntax from your able chests!

Mr. Zukile Jama was also responsible for reading all the selected readings so that a vocal record of our choices was available in a mother tongue as a further support for students of the language. Our warm thanks for his efforts.

Dr. Zorc has sometimes made exaggerated mention of my meticulousness. My wife Gillian, whose forbearance during the project is as usual appreciated and acknowledged, will say differently. Suffice it to say that any error of knowledge or judgement in this work is my fault alone, for which I accept full responsibility.

D. Julian Lloyd
Cape Town, South Africa
15 September 2002

PREFACE

This reader provides an advanced beginner or intermediate student of Xhosa with a variety of newspaper selections, complete with all grammatical and lexical information. It is intended for self study, but could also be used in a classroom situation.

Altogether there are four sections:

Front matter: including acknowledgements, preface, a list of abbreviations, the sources of the readings, resources, a frequency list, and a separate grammar sketch.

Part 1: the 37 reading selections

Part 2: English translations of the selections

Part 3: Xhosa lexicon (a composite glossary for all the selections and of forms or patterns treated in the grammatical outline, as well as an index of several Xhosa textbooks containing vocabulary not directly involved in this reader, but useful to the student.)

Some of the challenges one encounters when looking at the grammar of Xhosa are dealt with in the grammar sketch. The authors of previous readers in this series encountered frustration because the two major grammars currently available[1] treat various phenomena in drastically different ways. The numbering of noun classes is just one example. We have presented in summary form all productive affixes for each part of speech and all major grammatical patterns that occur in the reading selections, as well as some data on auxiliary verbs, conjunctives, and a list of all tenses in a series of tables after this section.

The 37 articles in Part 1 have been taken from two Xhosa periodicals published between 1994 and 1998: **Imvo** and **Xhosa Bona**. A full list of citations is presented later on in this introduction. The subject matter reflects the range and diversity of topics, genres, and styles encountered in the Xhosa press. Besides the expected news features – local (R18, R26, R27, R35) and international (R24), there are: advertisements (R1, R12, R15), opinion pieces (R2, R3, R9, R10, R11), personals or ISO's (R4a-d), an obituary (R5), medical advice – conventional (R6, R30) or alternative (R7, R15, R25), a recipe (R8),

---

[1] *These are: Herbert W. Pahl, IsiXhosa, 3rd ed. (Johannesburg: Educum, 1983); and Jan Adrian Du Plessis and M. W. Visser, Xhosa Syntax (Pretoria: Via Afrika, 1992). There is further discussion of this topic in Part 3.*

the South African national anthem (R13), advice (R14, R19), education (R16, R22), political issues (R17, R20), a government notice (R21), taxes (R23), a short story (R28), employment opportunities (R29), editorials (R31, R32), sports (R33), a horoscope (R34), an information piece on the effects of male rape (R36), and the language situation in South Africa (R37).

Most articles are within the range of Level 2 of the FSI/ILR (Foreign Service Institute / Interagency Language Roundtable) scale, except for R30 and later readings which go into Level 3 and beyond. The articles start out short and simple, and get progressively more complex. Additionally, one longer entry (R4) has been broken into smaller sections to avoid extensive vocabulary lists; R5-R16 are presented without breaks for practice at extended text interpretation. However, in the last 21, which represent the extensive prose so common in the Xhosa press, numbers have been introduced so that all notes can be found relatively quickly.

Every effort has been made to make this reader as self-contained as possible. All lexical and grammatical information is presented in the order of occurrence (i.e., not in alphabetical order). In each vocabulary section, the immediately relevant (usually literal) translation of each full word (or phrase) is in the margin. Indented underneath this can be found additional information about root words or affixes. The student who wishes only basic information should stick to what is presented on the left. Those who wish more details can use or study the indented material.

The selections are presented exactly as they occurred in the press. In those few instances where typographical errors were made, we have corrected the spelling.

Once a word is introduced, it is not re-glossed unless it has a significant change in meaning. However, if a (root) word occurs in a derived form or compound, it will be re-glossed at its individual appearance. Each word and affix can be looked up in the glossary, where one can review its meaning and find a reference to the reading(s) in which it occurs.

Part 2 consists of English translations for those who study without the benefit of a Xhosa teacher. Since literal translations of words and phrases are supplied in the individual vocabularies, the translations tend to be free, i.e., they have been rendered the way similar concepts would be rendered in the English press. Every element of the original Xhosa is accounted for, but using English word order and idiom. For example, the title of R2 is rendered "On the idle wandering of youth" although it literally reads "Little animals and children wander about." If such renditions are initially jolting, readers can go back to the original to see how such a translation is justified.

Part 3 is a Xhosa lexicon. While it includes glosses for all words, roots, and affixes used in the readings, we have added additional vocabulary and grammatical material from our research that are not in the currently available dictionaries in the hopes that it will carry the student further in his or her study of this fascinating language. The presentation of entries in the form in which they actually occur is in line with the need for a Beginner's Dictionary which ideally would list all possible forms in which a word may occur. The difficulty of achieving this ideal, however, is illustrated by the example of the word **abantu** which occurs 117 times in one form or other in the texts of this reader. Fifty-seven of these occur in the form shown, while the remainder have fourteen different kinds of prefixes which would make a comprehensive dictionary organized in this way a hefty tome indeed.

LIST OF ABBREVIATIONS

Note: Abbreviated references to publications (e.g., AXG, EAXZ, SG-3) are mostly limited to the Lexicon and are detailed in the Resources section.

~ or
/ sound change
// metathesis (sound switching)
zero or null (no affix when one might be expected)
«» insertions by the editors (e.g., paragraph numbers)
Δ root word (symbol)
1 first person *(I)*
2 second person *(you)*
3 third person *(he/she/they)*
abr abbreviation
abs abstract noun
adj adjective
adv adverb
Afr Afrikaans
AH: see American Heritage Dictionary.
Alt: alternate form
AM: see Munnik, Anne. 1994.
atr attributive (noun or verb functioning as an adjective)
aux auxiliary (verb)
AXG: see McLaren, James D. 1939.
ben benefactive (do s.t. for or to s.o.)
caus causative verb
CD1: see Dikeni, C. s.a.
CD2: see Dikeni, C. s.a.
CGB: see Pinnock, Patricia Schonstein. 1994.
cmp compound
col collective noun
conj conjunction
CTD: see Jennings, Lionel E. 1984.
deic deictic or demonstrative pronoun
dep dependent or participial verb form
dim diminutive
ditr ditransitive verb (takes two objects)
DNZ: see Dent, George Robinson and C. L. S. Nyembezi. 1984.
DZ David Zorc's personal analysis
EAXZ: see Uys, Isabel. 1996.
E&S: see Einhorn, E. and L. Siyengo. 1990.
emph emphatic; emphasis
Eng English
Ex: example
EXD: see Fischer, Arnold et al. 1985.
exis existential ('there is')
expr expression
ext extended meaning
EXXE: see Dictionary: English–Xhosa, Xhosa–English.
EZZE: see Doke, C. M. et al. 1990.
fig figurative meaning
fut future tense
GDX: see Pahl, Herbert W. 1989.
GX: see Gxilishe, D. S. s.a.
idiom idiomatic construction
imp imperative
IN: see Jordan, Archibald Currie. 1960.
inch inchoative (verb) = *becoming*
ind-rel indirect relative
inf infinitive verb form
instr instrumental = *with, by means of*
intens intensive verb

intj	interjection
intr	intransitive (verb)
inv	word order inversion
ir	irregular
ITX:	see Delport, Deon and Sandra Grobler. 1994.
ITXP:	see Finlayson, R. et al. 1993.
IX:	see Pahl, Herbert W. 1983.
JPD:	see Goodwill, J. S. et al. 1991.
KED:	see Kropf, Rev. Albert. 1915.
lit:	literally
LMM:	Entry made by Linda Murphy Marshall
loc	locative case (in, at)
LUMKO:	see Riordan, J. et al. 1969.
MI:	see Kirsch, Beverly A. and Silvia Skorge. 1995.
MOLO:	see Viljoen, André, Antoinette Daniel and Solomzi Madikane. 1995.
MQH:	see Mqhayi, S. E. K. 1929.
n	noun
n1	class 1 noun (**um**-/**aba**-)
nla	class la noun (#/**oo**-)
n2	class 2 noun (**um**-/**imi**-)
n3	class 3 noun (**ili**-/**ama**-)
n4	class 4 noun (**isi**-/**izi**-)
n5	class 5 noun (**in**-/**iin**-)
n6	class 6 noun (**ulu**-/**izin**-)
n7	class 7 noun (**ubu**-)
n8	class 8 verbal noun (**uku**-)
n9	class 9 locative noun (**pha**–)
nl0	class 10 locative noun (**uku**–)
NDK:	see Nabe, H. L., P. W. Dreyer, and G. L. Kakana. 1991.
neg	negative
NOM:	see Sinxo, G. B. 1922.
np	noun phrase
num	number/numeral
obj	object
Opp:	opposite, antonym
opt	optative
ord	ordinal number
part	participial or dependent verb form
pass	passive verb
past	past tense
PCX:	see Jordan, Archibald Currie. 1966.
perf	perfect or current relevance verb
pl	plural
pn	proper noun
pn-f	female personal name
pn-loc	place name
pn-m	male personal name
pol	polite or respectful
pos	positive (not negative)
poss	possessive verb ('having', 'to have')
pred	predicative verb ('being', 'to be')
prep	preposition
pres	present tense
prf	prefix
pro	pronoun
prog	progressive (is VERBing)
qw	question word interrogative
R**	Reading Selection number (from 1 upwards)
refl	reflexive (verb)
revers	reversative verb ('un-' or 'dis-')
recip	reciprocal verb (do s.t. to each other or one another)
red	reduction or contraction
refl	reflexive verb (do s.t. to oneself)
rel	relative construction
rw	root word
S1	subject of indicative verb
S2	subject of participial or dependent verb
S3a	subject of present subjunctive verb
S3b	subject of past subjunctive verb

S4 subject of potential or conditional construction
SAML: see South African Multi-Language Dictionary and Phrase Book.
sg singular
SG-1: see Finlayson, R. et al. 1991.
SG-2: see Finlayson, R. et al. 1990.
SG-3: see Gough, D. et al. 1989.
sneg subject negative
s.o. someone
s.t. something
st stative (verb)
sub subordinate or subjunctive verb form
subj subject (see S^1, S^2, etc.)
suf suffix
SXWU: see Dowling, Tessa et al. 1998.
Syn: synonym
SZZ: see Zotwana, Sydney Z. 1991.
TD: Dr. Tessa Dowling (personal communication)
tr transitive (verb)
UEX: see Wilken, Pam. 1994.
v verb
vn verbal noun
vp verb phrase
XEA: see Zotwana, Sydney Z. 1994.
XED: see McLaren, James D. 1994.
XFB: see Zotwana, Sydney Z. 1995.
XID: see Mahlasela, Benjamin Ezra Nuttall. 1977.
XNT: see Scheub, Harold Ernest. 1975.
XS: see Du Plessis, Jan Adrian and M. W. Visser. 1992.

SOURCES OF THE READINGS

1 ***Imvo***, 12 July 1995
2 ***Xhosa Bona***, July 1998, p. 8
3 ***Xhosa Bona***, August 1998, p. 8
4a ***Imvo***, 22 November 1995, p.6
4b ***Xhosa Bona***, September 1997, p. 147
4c ***Imvo***, 22 November 1995, p. 6
4d ***Imvo***, 22 November 1995, p. 6
5 ***Imvo***, 13 December 1995, p. 10
6 ***Xhosa Bona***, July 1998, p. 119
7 ***Imvo***, 13 December 1995, p. 10
8 ***Xhosa Bona***, July 1998, p. 97
9 ***Xhosa Bona***, January 1998, p.10
10 ***Xhosa Bona***, October 1997, p. 8
11 ***Xhosa Bona***, January 1998, p. 8
12 ***Xhosa Bona***, January 1998, p. 117 (advertisement)
13 Patricia Schonstein Pinnock's ***Xhosa: A Cultural Grammar for Beginners*** 1994, pp. 89–90
14 ***Xhosa Bona***, January 1998, p.11 (supplement)
15 ***Imvo***, 4 October 1995, p.12
16 ***Xhosa Bona***, January 1998, p. 8
17 ***Imvo***, 22 November 1995, p.6
18 ***Imvo***, *sine anno*
19 ***Imvo***, 22 November 1995, p.10
20 ***Imvo***, 22 November 1995, p. 6
21 ***Imvo***, 7 June 1995, p.13
22 ***Xhosa Bona***, January 1998, p. 18 (back insert)
23 ***Imvo***, 22 November 1995, p. 8
24 ***Xhosa Bona***, October 1997, p. 106
25 ***Imvo***, 23 August 1995, p.10
26 ***Imvo***, 25 February 1998
27 ***Imvo***, 25 February 1998
28 ***Xhosa Bona***, October 1997, p. 3 (supplement)
29 ***Xhosa Bona***, January 1998, p. 8 (back insert)
30 ***Xhosa Bona***, January 1998, pp. 80–82
31 ***Xhosa Bona***, December 1997, p. 6
32 ***Imvo***, 13 December 1995, p. 4
33 ***Xhosa Bona***, April 1998, pp. 60–61
34 ***Imvo***, 13 December 1995, p. 11
35 ***Xhosa Bona***, July 1998, pp. 120–21
36 ***Xhosa Bona***, July 1996, pp. 18–19
37 ***Bua!***, Vol. 10, No. 1, December 1995, pp. 18–19

RESOURCES

American Heritage Dictionary of the English Language. 1992. 3rd ed. New York: Houghton Mifflin.

Delport, Deon and Sandra Grobler. 1994. *An Introduction to Xhosa*. Pietermaritzburg: Shuter & Shooter.

Dent, George Robinson and C. L. S. Nyembezi. 1984. *Compact Zulu Dictionary: English–Zulu, Zulu–English*. Pietermaritzburg: Shuter & Shooter.

Dictionary: English–Xhosa, Xhosa–English. 1969. Cape Town: Via Afrika.

Dikeni, C. s.a. *Umfo waseLusuthu*. In preparation.

———. s.a. *Izinhanha ezisakhulayo*. In preparation.

Doke, C. M. et al. 1990. *English–Zulu Zulu–English Dictionary*. Johannesburg: Witwatersrand University Press.

Dowling, Tessa et al. 1998. *Speak Xhosa With Us*. Diep River, South Africa: African Voices.

Du Plessis, Jan Adrian and M. W. Visser. 1992. *Xhosa Syntax*. Pretoria: Via Afrika.

Einhorn, E. and L. Siyengo. 1990. *Xhosa: A Concise Manual*. Cape Town: Faircape Books.

Finlayson, R. et al. 1990. *Xhosa: Study Guide for XHS201-3*. Pretoria: University of South Africa Press.

———. 1991 *Xhosa: Only Study Guide for XHS302-8*. Pretoria: University of South Africa Press.

———. 1993. *An Introduction to Xhosa Phonetics*. Hout Bay: Marius Lubbe.

Fischer, Arnold et al. 1985. *English–Xhosa Dictionary*. Oxford: Oxford University Press.

Goodwill, J. S. et al. 1991. *The Oxford Junior Primary Dictionary for Southern Africa: An English Dictionary with Siswati, Xhosa and Zulu Words*. Oxford: Oxford University Press.

Gough, D. et al. 1989. *Xhosa: Study Guide for XHA100F*. Pretoria: University of South Africa.

Gxilishe, D. S. s.a. *Ulwimi nengqulelo*. In preparation.

Jennings, Lionel E. 1984. *The Concise Trilingual Dictionary: English, Xhosa, Afrikaans*. Rev. ed. Lovedale: Lovedale Press.

Jordan, Archibald Currie. 1960. *Ingqumbo yeminyanya*. Lovedale: Lovedale Press.

———. 1966. *A Practical Course in Xhosa*. Cape Town: Longmans.

Kirsch, Beverly A. and Silvia Skorge. 1995. *Masithethe IsiXhosa*. Kenwyn: Juta.

Kropf, Rev. Albert. 1915. *Kaffir–English dictionary*. Edited by Robert Godfrey. Lovedale: Lovedale Press.

Ladefoged, Peter. 1982. *A Course in Phonetics*. 2d ed. New York: Harcourt Brace Jovanovich.

Mahlasela, Benjamin Ezra Nuttall. 1977. *Some Xhosa Idioms and Expressions*. Occasional Paper No. 22. Grahamstown: Rhodes University Press.

McLaren, James D. 1939. *A Xhosa Grammar*. Edited by G. H. Welsh. Cape Town: Maskew Miller Longmans.

———. 1963. *A New Concise Xhosa–English Dictionary*. Cape Town: Maskew Miller Longman.

Mqhayi, S. E. K. 1929. *UDon Jadu*. Lovedale: Lovedale Press.

Munnik, Anne. 1994. *Learn Xhosa*. Pietermaritzburg: Shuter & Shooter.

Nabe, H. L., P. W. Dreyer and G. L. Kakana. 1991. *Xhosa Dictionary: English, Xhosa, Afrikaans; Xhosa, English, Afrikaans*. Johannesburg: Educum.

Pahl, Herbert W. 1983. *IsiXhosa*. 3rd ed. Johannesburg: Educum.

———. 1989. *The Greater Dictionary of Xhosa*. Vol. 3. Alice: University of Fort Hare Press.

Paulos, George and Sizwe C. Satyo. s.a. *A Linguistic Analysis of Xhosa*. In preparation.

Pinnock, Patricia Schonstein. 1994. *Xhosa: A Cultural Grammar for Beginners*. African Sun Press.

Riordan, J. et al. 1969. *Lumko Xhosa Self-Instruction Course*. Grahamstown: Rhodes University Press.

Scheub, Harold Ernest. 1975. *The Xhosa Ntsomi*. Oxford: Clarendon Press.

Sinxo, G. B. 1922. *UNomsa*. Alice: Lovedale Press.

South African Multi-Language Dictionary and Phrase Book. 1991. Cape Town: Reader's Digest Association South Africa.

Uys, Isabel. 1996. *The English Afrikaans Xhosa Zulu Aid*. Cape Town: Queillerie.

Viljoen, André, Antoinette Daniel, and Solomzi Madikane. 1995. *Molo–IsiXhosa Phrase Book*. Kenwyn: Juta.

Wilken, Pam. 1994. *Understanding Everyday Xhosa: A Vocabulary and Reference Book*. Cape Town: Maskew Miller Longman.

Zotwana, Sydney Z. 1991. *Xhosa in Context: From Novice to Intermediate*. Cape Town: Perskor.

———.1995. *Xhosa for Beginners (IsiXhosa Sabaqalayo)*. Cape Town: Vlaeberg.

———. 1994. *Xhosa Learner's Companion: A Xhosa–English–Afrikaans Phrase and Vocabulary Book*. Cape Town: Vlaeberg.

FREQUENCY LIST

The following 440 words are listed according to their frequency of occurrence in the reading selections. They are presented from highest down through three uses. Altogether, the 37 selections contain a corpus of 7,505 words (tokens) representing 4,315 lexical entries, i.e., many forms were used more than once. Those presented below are intentionally unglossed so as to provide a study tool, since their meanings and the articles in which they appeared can be found in the Lexicon. Note that most of the items towards the beginning of the list are grammatical forms, as is the case of just about any frequency study of any of the world's languages.

The Grammar section entitled "The Challenges of Learning Xhosa" discusses the problem of homographs which confront the student. In working through these high-frequency words, it is important to understand that many of the grammatical forms, e.g., **xa**, **kufuneka**, **le**, **kuba**, or **eli** can have different functions and/or different meanings.

abantu	57
xa	52
okanye	50
kufuneka	42
le	34
kuba	29
eli	25
kodwa	25
ukuze	24
oku	23
kwaye	21
ngabantu	21
apho	20
bhodi	20
ezi	20
yaye	20
ngoku	18
nto	17
amadoda	16
emva	16
afrika	15
i	15
indlela	15
into	15
izinto	15
ke	15
nje	15
imali	14
kule	14
ngayo	14
kunye	13
ngenxa	13
abantwana	12
inani	12
ithamsanqa	12
kakuhle	12
umbala	12
umntu	12
unobumba	12
zakho	12
ibe	11
ingaba	11
na	11
ukuba	11
uluntu	11
wakhe	11
apha	10
enye	10
indoda	10
ixesha	10

lo	10	ethekwini	7
ngaphandle	10	etyalwe	7
ngoko	10	ibhotile	7
njalo	10	inkxaso	7
oko	10	kukho	7
uthe	10	kwi	7
abagogekileyo	9	la	7
engama	9	m (= meters)	7
ikhondom	9	mali	7
kanti	9	mba	7
kokuba	9	msebenzi	7
kukuba	9	mthetho	7
kuphela	9	ngokuba	7
kweli	9	ntsapho	7
lokuba	9	sikelel'	7
lwimi	9	ube	7
yakho	9	ugqirha	7
yokuba	9	umntwana	7
zabantu	9	uya	7
bonke	8	aba	6
irayisi	8	amagama	6
isikolo	8	amakhosi	6
kakhulu	8	eluntwini	6
kulo	8	hewana	6
mandela	8	imveliso	6
nabo	8	inyama	6
nangona	8	khona	6
ngaphambili	8	kubalulekile	6
njani	8	kuya	6
nokuba	8	lindiwe	6
phantsi	8	lixesha	6
PObox	8	mna	6
R	8	nabantu	6
sele	8	ndifuna	6
umama	8	ngale	6
uninzi	8	ngalo	6
utshilo	8	ngokuthi	6
uza	8	osezantsi	6
wakho	8	phambili	6
ziko	8	umthetho	6
abanye	7	waza	6
after	7	yena	6
akukho	7	abahlali	5
care	7	abazali	5
centre	7	amanye	5
emelika	7	amathuba	5

aphantsi	5
aze	5
bakho	5
baya	5
bethu	5
de	5
ekufuneka	5
enkulu	5
entolongweni	5
ibhodi	5
iimbaleki	5
iinkokeli	5
incwadana	5
ingqondo	5
irhafu	5
iyeza	5
june	5
komzimba	5
kube	5
kuyo	5
kuzo	5
kwakhona	5
kwezentengiso	5
kwiindawo	5
lakhe	5
lakho	5
lobudoda	5
lokwenza	5
loo	5
mihla	5
nalo	5
nawo	5
nazo	5
ncwadana	5
ngexesha	5
ngo	5
njengoko	5
phakathi	5
siseko	5
ukutya	5
ukuya	5
ukwenza	5
umbulelo	5
umnu	5
umsebenzi	5
umzekelo	5
uncedo	5
utakalani	5
wonke	5
yazo	5
yesondo	5
yintoni	5
abakumgangatho	4
abantsundu	4
abe	4
abo	4
amaninzi	4
amapolisa	4
aseafrika	4
bafuna	4
bantu	4
baye	4
bill	4
ebalulekileyo	4
ekubeni	4
ematatiele	4
emininzi	4
eminyaka	4
emzantsi	4
eninzi	4
eyakuthi	4
eyiyo	4
ezifana	4
ezininzi	4
goniwe	4
guest	4
ilizwe	4
ilungu	4
imbiza	4
imfundo	4
impahla	4
inkokeli	4
inkqubo	4
ipansalb	4
isingesi	4
ithuba	4
izimvo	4
jabu	4
ka	4
khomishoni	4
koko	4
kubantu	4

kuwe	4	zethu	4
kwenzeka	4	zilandelayo	4
kwindawo	4	zimbini	4
leyo	4	zonke	4
line	4	abahlobo	3
linyanga	4	abaninzi	3
lizwe	4	abathi	3
lonke	4	amalungelo	3
lwabantu	4	amalungu	3
machel	4	amandla	3
manager	4	angamaxhoba	3
maziko	4	angasese	3
ml	4	apartheid	3
ngabahlali	4	april	3
ngakumbi	4	asetyenziswa	3
ngendlela	4	bakhe	3
ngohlobo	4	bathi	3
ngokubanzi	4	baza	3
ngokutsho	4	besithi	3
nguwe	4	bona	3
noluntu	4	championships	3
omkhulu	4	d	3
phambi	4	deadline	3
sahamba	4	ebantwini	3
sic	4	ebuhlungu	3
sikolo	4	ebusuku	3
ubomi	4	ekuphuculeni	3
ufuna	4	elawula	3
ukudlwengulwa	4	elide	3
unelson	4	entsha	3
uphando	4	esebenza	3
urhulumente	4	eyenza	3
uvuma	4	eyenziwa	3
uye	4	ezibhedlele	3
wam	4	fama	3
we	4	galela	3
wentlalo	4	gqatso	3
wenza	4	hayi	3
yabantu	4	iafrika	3
yakhe	4	ifoto	3
yile	4	iimbono	3
yiyo	4	iimpawu	3
yoluntu	4	iindawo	3
yona	4	imibutho	3
yonke	4	imisebenzi	3
zabo	4	ingakumbi	3

ingxowa	3
inxaxheba	3
inyanga	3
iphulo	3
iqabane	3
irhashalala	3
isebenzisane	3
isidanga	3
ithetha	3
ithi	3
iza	3
izifundo	3
izikolo	3
izilonda	3
kakubi	3
kaloku	3
kamnandi	3
kananjalo	3
koluntu	3
konke	3
kufuna	3
kugqatso	3
kuloo	3
kuma	3
kumalungu	3
kunjalo	3
kurhulumente	3
kuthetha	3
kuthi	3
kuyaphi	3
kuye	3
kuza	3
kwakhe	3
kwamadoda	3
kwe	3
kweelwimi	3
kwenzeke	3
kwezi	3
kwimisebenzi	3
labuschagne	3
leading	3
leli	3
lwabo	3
lwam	3
mabhele	3
makhe	3
malunga	3
maxa	3
minyaka	3
moya	3
nabanye	3
nale	3
nam	3
nangaphandle	3
nanjengoko	3
ndaba	3
ndlela	3
nemizuzwana	3
nezinye	3
ngako	3
ngamandla	3
ngaphakathi	3
nge	3
ngenjongo	3
ngenyanga	3
ngesixhosa	3
ngethuba	3
ngingqi	3
ngokwesondo	3
nkosi	3
noqeqesho	3
ntombazana	3
ntoni	3
nzima	3
onke	3
s	3
sakhe	3
samapolisa	3
sikelela	3
sishebo	3
sokuba	3
sonke	3
thina	3
thumela	3
together	3
u	3
ukuhla	3
ulwimi	3
umgaqosiseko	3
umoya	3
umvuzo	3
umyeni	3

ureginah 3
usebenza 3
usele 3
uyazi 3
wambi 3
wenze 3
wezi 3
x 3
xesha 3
xwebhu 3
yabo 3
yamapolisa 3
yase 3
yeelwimi 3
yethu 3
yezinto 3
yihla 3
yinto 3
zayo 3
zesondo 3
zinto 3
zokuziqeqesha 3

Grammar Sketch

1. The Challenges of Learning Xhosa

1.1. The Challenges of Xhosa Grammar

Learning a new language is challenging at any time, and is even more so when the language to be learned is from an unfamiliar language group.[2] This is because we tend to try to describe the target language in terms of the language which we know, and there may be many reasons why this leads to confusion and frustration.

For example, one sometimes sees the Bantu noun class prefixes referred to as 'articles', and compared to the articles which precede nouns in languages like English and French. In these languages, the article has the function of imparting the feature of definiteness, and in some cases (such as French) imparting the feature of sex gender as well, i.e., 'the boy, a girl; le garçon, une fille'.

These two features, however, are the features which are *not* imparted by the prefix in Xhosa or any other Bantu language, so it is easy to see how a learner can run into difficulty with a language like Xhosa.

This grammar sketch tries to avoid making such comparisons, and points out where possible any radical difference between English and Xhosa. The student will benefit most by carefully studying the readings and comparing them with the English renderings, together with, if possible, hearing the selected headings enunciated by a native speaker.

1.2. Different Writing Systems (Orthographies)

The Xhosa language was first produced in printed form in 1823 by Rev. J Bennie on a press imported from Scotland and installed at Tyhume in the Eastern Cape. Various shortcomings in spelling standards and word division as well as the use of additional symbols in the orthography were only addressed during a series of discussions which resulted in the adoption of a standard orthography in 1935. This orthography—which used 29 characters—prevailed until South Africa assumed responsibility for the education of

---

[2] *The languages of the world are divided by type into a number of language groups. English is a member of the Germanic subgroup of the large Indo-European group, while Xhosa is a member of the Bantu subgroup of the Niger Kordofanian (Niger Congo) group, one of the four groups found in Africa.*

indigenous African people for the first time in 1954. The principal change was the reversion to a standard 26-character orthography.

As a result of this, and the fact that many earlier Xhosa publications are out of print, the student may find him/herself working with a number of orthographies simultaneously. However, a fair amount of work has been republished using the new orthography, including McLaren's invaluable dictionary.[3]

The most comprehensive grammar to date is that of Pahl 1983[4] but as it is entirely in Xhosa it is of little value to the second-language beginner. A new definitive grammar of Xhosa is expected shortly as part of a series describing the Southern African Bantu languages.[5] This grammar is recommended to the users of this reader as the reference grammar for the language.

1.3. Difficult and Undifferentiated Sounds

As this reader is intended to deal with the written language, there is little scope for a detailed discussion of the sound system. A number of useful references will be found in most of the grammar books listed in the bibliography, in particular, Finlayson[6] gives a detailed overview of the Xhosa pronunciation system.

The student should be aware that certain areas will require special care and practice—notably the clicks, which are represented in the orthography as q, x, and c, respectively. Care should be taken to ensure that the symbols are not co-articulated with the clicks as if they were the same sounds as in the English orthography.

The orthographic 'h' occurring after the plosives p, t, and k, as well as after the affricate ts, is there to remind the speaker that the sound is not to be pronounced ejectively, but with aspiration. It is not to be confused with 'th' as in 'theater', 'thorough', and so on.

---

[3] *James D. McLaren, A New Concise Xhosa-English Dictionary (Cape Town: Maskew Miller Longman, 1963).*

[4] *Herbert W. Pahl, IsiXhosa, 3rd ed. (Johannesburg: Educum, 1983).*

[5] *George Poulos and Sizwe C. Satyo, A Linguistic Analysis of Xhosa (in preparation, s.a.).*

[6] *R. Finlayson et al, An Introduction to Xhosa Phonetics (Hout Bay: Marius Lubbe, 1993).*

Students should exercise care when pronouncing initial 'm' or 'n' when these sounds are part of a prefix. A common fault is to pronounce them as if there were a vowel in the syllable and to say 'em' or 'en'. Early missionaries similarly failed to notice the sounds at all, and wrote **di** for the first-person singular **ndi**.

Finally, a word about vowels. Xhosa is said to have a seven vowel system, of which the orthography only differentiates five. The student should refer to the Xhosa phonetic manual (Finlayson 1993) for information on the pronunciation of the vowel system. Note that under-differentiation of the vowel system is not unique to Xhosa—the English orthography also recognizes five vowels, although Ladefoged (1982:70) lists 16 American English vowels of which some are diphthongs, as found in words like 'bite' and 'boat', that are not indicated in the orthography.

1.4. Homographs (and Homonyms)

Xhosa is described as an agglutinating language with a degree of inflection. This means that the morphemes which comprise the elements of a grammatical structure are generally written in a conjoined way, thus:

ndi + ya + ba + bona	is written	**ndiyababona**
S^{1} + Asp + O + Verb		
'I them see'		

As a result, the number of small particles which appear in isolation in a language like Sotho, where generally each morpheme is written separately, is greatly reduced in the Xhosa language and the possibility of confusion is much less, particularly if careful attention is paid to context.

It must also be realized that Xhosa is a tonal language, and while this reader makes no attempt to indicate tonal differences,[7] a native speaker would have no difficulty in recognizing that similar apparently homographic constructs were in fact different. The simplest example is that of the pronominal prefix for the second- and third-person singular:

---

[7] *The standard tone markings for Xhosa are ´ for high tone, ` for low tone, and ^ for falling tone.*

u	**uyavúka**	you (sg) wake up
ú	**úyavúka**	he/she wakes up

Most grammars treat the phenomenon of homonymity somewhat lightly and usually only provide examples of noun or verb roots to illustrate the point. Two examples are shown here: the first, a noun, is homographic but not homophonic because of the tonal pattern; the second is a verb which exhibits true homonymity—it sounds and looks the same, regardless of which meaning applies.[8]

íthàngà	a pumpkin	**úkuthîya**	to give a name
îthângà	a cattle post	**úkuthîya**	to trap
íthàngá	a thigh	**úkuthîya**	to hate

Clearly, context is important in deciding the meaning of a particular homonym, and the student is urged to try to reach a solution based on the particular context rather that relying on a list which may not have anticipated all possible variants. For assistance in the early stages of the learning process, the lists given in Table 7 will be useful as they address four of the most frequently found forms.

1.5. Sound Changes

It is extremely important to understand the sound changes that occur in Xhosa as a key to a ready interpretation of the language. If the student can anticipate that a sound change will occur it will save much time in trying to identify the components of a particular construct.

Many sound changes occur when vowels juxtapose, and as a general rule students may assume that 'a' followed by 'i' will result in 'e', 'a' followed by 'u' will result in 'o', whereas 'a' followed by another 'a' produces a single 'a'. The adjectival concords are an example, being formed from 'a' and the regular class concord:

Class 1 (sg)	**a + um > om**	**omkhulu**
Class 5 (sg)	**a + in > en**	**enkulu**[9]

Another important sound change is that of palatalization, whereby certain bilabial sounds are palatalized, that is, they are articulated at

[8] *No marking on a vowel in a prosodic transcription presupposes low tone.*

[9] *Note loss of aspiration after the nasal 'n'.*

the palate instead of at the lips. The change is encountered in certain locative forms, in the passive form of verbs containing bilabial consonants, and in some diminutive forms:

umlambo	a river	**emlanjeni**	at the river
ukubamba	to catch	**ukubanjwa**	to be caught
iphaphu	a heart	**iphatshana**	a little heart

Attention must be paid to the possibility of sound changes when consulting a dictionary (see section 1.9 below).

While a list of sound changes is found in Table 8 that outlines many of the changes that may occur, try to make your own assessment before using the list for confirmation.

1.6. Learning Words Together

One learning approach which is sometimes assumed is that words of a Bantu language should be learned in sets. Thus, nouns are to be learned in pairs (singular and plural forms) together with the appropriate agreements for adjectives, relatives, and other qualificatives, while verb forms which should be memorized are the present indicative and perfect forms, as well as the positive and negative forms in each conjugation.

While there is some merit in such a system, it is preferred that the student should achieve a full understanding of the noun class system and the reasons behind the placement into different classes. It then becomes clear why the root **-ntu** can render **umntu, abantu, isintu, izintu, uluntu,** and **ubuntu** (person, people, human species (sg), human species (pl)[10], mankind, manhood, or humanity, respectively). Don't forget the diminutive form **umntwana, abantwana** (child, children), which comes from the same root too.

Verbs should present no difficulty once the basic structure is understood. Generally speaking, what goes before the verb root has to do with the people or things the verb is acting on, while the suffixes (those parts of the verb to the right of the root) deal with the how, why, and when of the verbal construct:

---

[10] *This class would be used if, for example, you were comparing* Homo sapiens sapiens *with* Homo sapiens neanderthalensis.

umama uyayiphikela indoda ukutya
Mother cooks food for her husband.

A typical verb is made up of the following parts:

u +	**ya** +	**yi** +	**phik** +	**el** +	**a**
Subj	Pres. Aspect	Obj	cook	for	V-Ind

Xhosa has the advantage over some of the Bantu languages in that its orthography is a conjoined system, that is to say that the component parts of the verbal form are all connected as in the above example rather than written separately as in the exploded explanation.

Adjectives and other qualificatives have to agree with the appropriate noun by adding the appropriate prefix. Again, an understanding of the class system will assist in determining this factor—remember that adjectives follow their nouns and may lose their pre-prefix in certain cases, such as when the demonstrative is present:

Umntu omhle	an attractive person
lo mntu mhle	this attractive person

Tables 1 and 2 will help you considerably to master these aspects of the grammar.

Preverbs (auxiliaries) and conjunctions may require a particular mood for the verb in the following verb phrase or clause. These are given in detail in Table 6.

1.7. Multiple Word Units

There are a few groups of words which combine to give a single meaning. When these are encountered it is better to learn the meaning as a whole rather than to probe the meanings of the separate forms, which may only serve to confuse. Here's an example:

maxa wambi sometimes
(Lit. (**a**)**maxa wambi** different times)

1.8. Differences in Terminology or Interpretation

Perhaps the most pertinent difference between the various approaches of academics to Xhosa grammar is that of the description of the Noun classes. It may appear to the casual or beginning student that academics do not agree on the number of classes, but this is not generally the reason for discrepancies. In the various grammars and dictionaries used in the preparation of this reader, the student will find two commonly used systems, namely, the system which allocates a class number to each noun form whether singular or plural, and the system which pairs singular and plural nouns together under one class number.

It is this latter system which has been adopted in this reader, and it is also the one used in McLaren's Xhosa–English dictionary which most students will find to be the most useful of those available. The dictionary does not mention noun classes beyond class 8 while this reader mentions classes 9 and 10 when appropriate, but this is not to be construed as an indication that no classes exist beyond those numbers, it is merely that a beginning student can get by quite satisfactorily without bothering about classes which are no longer used in Xhosa.

Serious students of Bantu languages would be advised to familiarize themselves with the full range of class numbers used in what is called the Meinhof system because its understanding will allow comparison with other languages in the group which may use classes not used by Xhosa speakers. The study of this system is beyond the scope of this reader, however.

1.9. Unexplained Grammatical Constructions

Some of the authors of Xhosa conversation or grammar books may indicate that a particular construction does not occur, nor have all phenomena been explained by all authors. One reason for this is that an author may have a particular target market in view and does not want to complicate the learning process. On the other hand, other works which have been consulted during the preparation of this reader may be considered as works which are intended to stand the scrutiny of the academic community and are therefore more likely to be all-embracing. Nevertheless, linguistic concepts change with the continual development of new theories, making some of the referenced works potentially outdated by later ones. It is for this reason that the authors of this reader have selected the latest work in the field and one that is a companion to a number of other works on related languages. This work, *A Linguistic Analysis of Xhosa* by George Poulos and Sizwe Satyo is, as mentioned above, in preparation at the time of writing, but should be available soon after this work is published.

1.10. Using a Xhosa Dictionary

Many students using a Xhosa dictionary for the first time are frustrated at the fact that they can rarely search for a word exactly as it appears in a text. This is because Xhosa is an agglutinative language, that is to say, a language in which prefixes and suffixes relating to the syntactic context are tacked on in front of and behind a conceptual root. It is the root that is usually found as the key word in dictionaries, with inflections and derivations following an initial explanation.

One of the dictionaries consulted during the preparation of this reader[11] has a very comprehensive section in the introduction which details very clearly what to discard in identifying the part of a word which will be listed. It is strongly recommended that students read this section before attempting to use any Xhosa dictionary. Particular attention should be paid to the notes on sound changes (and those referred to in section 1.5 above) as failure to recognize these will cause considerable difficulty.

1.11. Irregularities (or different rules)

All languages have apparent deviations from rules which are often described as irregular forms. Generally, however, these will turn out to be operating under a different rule rather than no rule at all. Such rules may not be apparent to any but the skilled Bantu philologist who has an understanding of the origins of these languages. For example, an observant student may note that the Xhosa word for 'people of European descent' is **abelungu** and the simple explanation is that **aba-** has become **abe-** because of the following high vowel **–u-**. But the word for 'learners', **abafundi**, also has a high vowel following the prefix and it does not cause assimilation. One has to go deeper than the scope of this book to find the reason. Students who wish to know more will find a stimulating career awaits them in researching the common origins of this widely spoken language family.

---

[11] James D. McLaren, A New Concise Xhosa-English Dictionary (Cape Town: Maskew Miller Longman, 1963).

1.12. Disjunctive vs. Conjunctive Writing Conventions

Xhosa is generally written in a conjunctive writing style, unlike, for example, Sotho, which follows a disjunctive convention. It should be remembered that the choice of writing style is somewhat arbitrary and probably evolved as a result of the preferences of those who first codified the language. The attachment of prefixes and suffixes to a central stem or root word is probably closer to the usual ways of writing Indo-European languages and thus the student may feel more at home with the conjunctive system.

This system does produce some unusually large constructions which make it difficult to decide whether they are words or sentences. For example, **bangasemlanjeni** means 'they are all down by the riverside'.

2. Overview of Xhosa Grammar

2.1. Characteristics of the Noun Classes

class 1	human nouns, ethnic affiliation, occupation, doer or agent noun
class 1a	personal names, kin terms, God, titles, -**so**- or -**no**- derivations, personified animal names
class 2	names of flora, mobile non-human things, some body parts, locality or position (in or near the earth), result nouns, periods of time
class 3	hard objects, fruits, voracious or dangerous animals, diseases, human characteristics, some parts of the body, Khoisan loanwords
class 3 plural	proper nouns with um-, diminutive or feminine plurals of noun class 5, things occurring in pairs or in quantity, liquid or viscous substances, classes of people having common characteristics, place or locality words, mental feelings or impressions
class 4	languages, useful things, personal traits, collective nouns, human characteristics, collective or abstract nouns, agent-object noun pairs, some parts of the body, ordinal numbers, result or abstract nouns, loanwords beginning with **s**-
class 5	animals, common objects, agent or doer, product, loanwords
class 6	long or high things, deprecatory, stative or abstract nouns
class 7	abstract or quality nouns, soft objects, time or place
class 8	infinitive, verbal noun, result of action
class 9	a few "frozen" or non-productive locative or time nouns; a few deictics (see 2.3)
class 10	a few non-productive locative or time nouns; frequently found in pronouns and deictics (see 2.3)

Table 1: Noun Class Agreement

class	prefix	subj / S1	obj	poss	pos-n1a	adj	rel / atr	enum
n1-sg	**um-**	**u-**	**-m-**	**wa-**	**ka-**	**om-**	**o-**	**wu-**
n1-pl	**aba-**	**ba-**	**-ba-**	**ba-**	**baka-**	**aba-**	**aba-**	**ba-**
n1a-sg	**u-**	**u-**	**-m-**	**wa-**	**ka-**	**om-**	**o-**	**wu-**
n1a-pl	**oo-**	**ba-**	**-ba-**	**ba-**	**baka-**	**aba-**	**aba-**	**ba-**
n2-sg	**um-**	**u-**	**-wu-**	**wa-**	**ka-**	**om-**	**o-**	**wu-**
n2-pl	**imi-**	**i-**	**-yi-**	**ya-**	**ka-**	**emi-**	**e-**	**yi-**
n3-sg	**ili-**	**li-**	**-li-**	**la-**	**lika-**	**eli-**	**eli-**	**li-**
n3-pl	**ama-**	**a-**	**-wa-**	**a-**	**ka-**	**ama-**	**a-**	**wa-**
n4-sg	**isi-**	**si-**	**-si-**	**sa-**	**sika-**	**esi-**	**esi-**	**si-**
n4-pl	**izi-**	**zi-**	**-zi-**	**za-**	**zika-**	**ezi-**	**ezi-**	**zi-**
n5-sg	**iN-**	**i-**	**-yi-**	**ya-**	**ka-**	**en-**	**e-**	**yi-**
n5-pl	**iiN-**	**zi-**	**-zi-**	**za-**	**zika-**	**eziN-**	**ezi-**	**zi-**
n6-sg	**ulu-**	**lu-**	**-lu-**	**lwa-**	**luka-**	**olu-**	**olu-**	**lu-**
n6-pl	**izin-**	**zi-**	**-zi-**	**za-**	**zika-**	**eziN-**	**ezi-**	**zi-**
n7-sg	**ubu-**	**bu-**	**-bu-**	**ba-**	**buka-**	**obu-**	**obu-**	**bu-**
n8-vn	**uku-**	**ku-**	**-ku-**	**kwa-**	**kuka-**	**oku-**	**oku-**	**ku-**
n9-loc	**pha-**							
n10-loc	**uku-**			**kwa-**	**ko-**	**oku-**	**oku-**	

*Subject agreement forms are quite similar except that both nasals [**m**, **n**] and initial ("weak") vowels drop, e.g., **um**- > **u-**, **imi**- > **i-**, **ama**- > **a-, in**- > **i**-, **izin**- > **zi**-; **ili**- > **li**-, **isi**- > **si**-, **izi**- > **zi**-

For more information, see:
CGB:102ff; 117
SAML:372
XED:xv–xvi

2.1.1. Strong vs. Weak Noun Classes

If a noun prefix consists of a single vowel or if it has a nasal, then it is called a weak class noun and is subject to different rules from the strong class nouns. These result in shorter prefixes which tend to apply across the Xhosa grammatical system. Thus:

Table 2: Strong vs. Weak Noun Classes

weak noun	prefix	subj	n1a-sg-poss	rel/atr
n1-sg	**um-**	**u-**	**ka-**	**o-**
n1a-sg	**u-**	**u-**	**ka-**	**o-**
n2-sg	**um-**	**u-**	**ka-**	**o-**
n2-pl	**imi-**	**i-**	**ka-**	**e-**
n3-pl	**ama-**	**a-**	**ka-**	**a-**
n5-sg	**iN-**	**i-**	**ka-**	**e-**

2.1.2. Variations in Noun Classes (usually due to phonological changes)

n1-pl	**ab-**	instead of aba-	reduction in front of vowel-initial root
n1-pl	**abe-**	instead of aba-	assimilation of following high vowel i or u.
n3-sg	**i-**	instead of ili-	full prefix used only with monosyllabic roots
n3-pl	**ame-**	instead of ama-	assimilation of following high vowel
n4-sg	**is-**	instead of isi-	reduction in front of vowel-initial root
n4-pl	**iz-**	instead of izi-	reduction in front of vowel-initial root
n5-pl	**iziN-**	instead of iiN-	full prefix used only with monosyllabic roots
n6-sg	**ul-**	instead of ulu-	reduction in front of vowel-initial root
n6-sg	**u-**	instead of ulu-	full prefix used only with monosyllabic roots
n6-sg	**ulw-**	instead of ulu-	reduction and insertion of semivowel
n7-sg	**ub-**	instead of ubu-	reduction in front of vowel-initial root
n8-vn	**uk-**	instead of uku-	reduction in front of vowel-initial root
n8-vn	**ukw-**	instead of uku-	reduction and insertion of semivowel
n10-loc	**ukw-**	instead of uku-	reduction and insertion of semivowel

2.2. Pronouns

Note: Students should pay attention to the fact that these agreement concords do not always have a pronominal function—this is only true when the noun to which the concord is anaphorically related is NOT present in the sentence. Under all other conditions these constructs are agreement concords only.

Table 3: Xhosa Pronoun Agreement (David Zorc)

Person	abs	S1	sneg	S2	S3a	S3b	rel1Atr	rel2*	Pred
1sg I	mna	ndi- nd-	andi-	ndi-	ndi-	nda-	endi-	ndi-	ndim-
1pl we	thina	si- s-	asi-	si-	si-	sa-	esi-	si-	sithi-
2sg you	wena	u- w-	aku- †	u-	u-	wa-	o-	u-	nguwe-
2pl you	nina	ni-	ani-	ni-	ni-	na-	eni-	ni-	nini-
3sg he/she	yena	u-	aka- †	e- †	a- †	wa-	o-	u-	ngum-
3pl they	bona	ba-	aba-	be- †	ba-	ba-	aba-	ba-	ngaba-
Classes									
n1sg	yena	u-	aka- †	e- †	a- †	wa-	o-	u-	ngum-
n1pl	bona	ba-	aba-	be- †	ba-	ba-	aba-	bà-	ngaba-
n1a-sg									ngu- †
n1a-pl									ngoo- †
n2-sg	wona	u-	awu- +	u-	u-	wa-	o-	u-	ngum-
n2-pl	yona	i-	ayi- +	i-	i-	ya-	e-	i-	yimi-
n3-sg	lona	li-	ali-	li-	li-	la-	eli-	li-	lili-
n3-pl	wona	a-	aka- †	e- †	a-	wa-	a-	a-	ngama-
n4-sg	sona	si-	asi-	si-	si-	sa-	esi-	si-	sisi-
n4-pl	zona	zi-	azi-	zi-	zi-	za-	ezi-	zi-	zizi-
n5-sg	yona	i-	ayi- +	i-	i-	ya-	e-	i-	yin-
n5-pl	zona	zi-	azi-	zi-	zi-	za-	ezi-	zi-	zizi-
n6-sg	lona	lu-	alu-	lu-	lu-	lwa-	olu-	lu-	lulu-
n6-pl	zona	zi-	azi-	zi-	zi-	za-	ezi-	zi-	zizi-
n7-abs	bona	bu-	abu-	bu-	bu-	ba-	obu-	bu-	bubu-
n8-vn	kona	ku-	aku-	ku-	ku-	kwa-	oku-	ku-	kuku-
n10-loc	khona	ku-	aku-	ku-	ku-	kwa-	oku-	ku-	kuku-

* Reduced prefix set used after demonstratives.
† These are the only forms that differ within this set (column).
\+ A corresponding semivowel is added (y before i, w before u).
Only indicative forms have different (SNEG) subject agreement, participials and subjunctives have identical subjects.

References:
XED:xv-xvi
CGB:115; 119; 158; 167 [S3a]; 189 [S3b]; 191 [S2]
E&S:18 [SNEG]
PCX:82 [S2], 61f,81 [S3a], 81 [S3b]
AM:163

Table 4: Possessive Pronouns

Root	-am	-ethu	-akho	-enu	-akhe	-abo
English	my	our	your [s]	your [p]	his/her	their
n1-sg	**wam**	**wethu**	**wakho**	**wenu**	**wakhe**	**wabo**
n1-pl	**bam**	**bethu**	**bakho**	**benu**	**bakhe**	**babo**
n2-sg	**wam**	**wethu**	**wakho**	**wenu**	**wakhe**	**wabo**
n2-pl	**yam**	**yethu**	**yakho**	**yenu**	**yakhe**	**yabo**
n3-sg	**lam**	**lethu**	**lakho**	**lenu**	**lakhe**	**labo**
n3-pl	**#am**	**#ethu**	**#akho**	**#enu**	**#akhe**	**#abo**
n4-sg	**sam**	**sethu**	**sakho**	**senu**	**sakhe**	**sabo**
n4-pl	**zam**	**zethu**	**zakho**	**zenu**	**zakhe**	**zabo**
n5-sg	**yam**	**yethu**	**yakho**	**yenu**	**yakhe**	**yabo**
n5-pl	**zam**	**zethu**	**zakho**	**zenu**	**zakhe**	**zabo**
n6-sg	**lwam**	**lwethu**	**lwakho**	**lwenu**	**lwakhe**	**lwabo**
n7-abs	**bam**	**bethu**	**bakho**	**benu**	**bakhe**	**babo**
n8-vn	**kwam**	**kwethu**	**kwakho**	**kwenu**	**kwakhe**	**kwabo**
n10-loc	**kwam**	**kwethu**	**kwakho**	**kwenu**	**kwakhe**	**kwabo**

See CGB:181–183
See E&S:22 for complete table

Table 5: Relative Possessive Pronouns

Root	-am	-ethu	-akho	-enu	-akhe	-abo
English	of mine	of ours	of yours	of yours	of his	of theirs
n1-sg	**owam**	**owethu**	**owakho**	**owenu**	**owakhe**	**owabo**
n1-pl	**obam**	**obethu**	**obakho**	**obenu**	**obakhe**	**obabo**
n2-sg	**owam**	**owethu**	**owakho**	**owenu**	**owakhe**	**owabo**
n2-pl	**eyam**	**eyethu**	**eyakho**	**eyenu**	**eyakhe**	**eyabo**
n3-sg	**elam**	**elethu**	**elakho**	**elenu**	**elakhe**	**elabo**
n3-pl	**awam**	**awethu**	**awakho**	**awenu**	**awakhe**	**awabo**
n4-sg	**esam**	**esethu**	**esakho**	**esenu**	**esakhe**	**esabo**
n4-pl	**ezam**	**ezethu**	**ezakho**	**ezenu**	**ezakhe**	**ezabo**
n5-sg	**eyam**	**eyethu**	**eyakho**	**eyenu**	**eyakhe**	**eyabo**
n5-pl	**ezam**	**ezethu**	**ezakho**	**ezenu**	**ezakhe**	**ezabo**
n6-sg	**olwam**	**olwethu**	**olwakho**	**olwenu**	**olwakhe**	**olwabo**
n7-abs	**obam**	**obethu**	**obakho**	**obenu**	**obakhe**	**obabo**
n8-vn	**okwam**	**okwethu**	**okwakho**	**okwenu**	**okwakhe**	**okwabo**
n10-loc	**okwam**	**okwethu**	**okwakho**	**okwenu**	**okwakhe**	**okwabo**

Extrapolated from E&S:23

Table 6: Enumerative Pronouns

Root	Enum pronouns
English	all, every
n1-sg	**wonke**
n1-pl	**bonke**
n2-sg	**wonke**
n2-pl	**yonke**
n3-sg	**lonke**
n3-pl	**#onke**
n4-sg	**sonke**
n4-pl	**zonke**
n5-sg	**yonke**
n5-pl	**zonke**
n6-sg	**lonke**
n7-abs	**bonke**
n8-vn	**konke**

Root is either **-onke** (AM: 163) with a thematic consonant or **-nke** with a unique series of affixes (**wo-**, **bo-**, etc.) or an archaic formative **-o-** + root **-nke**.

2.3. Demonstrative Pronouns or Deictics

Note: Entries marked with double asterisk (**) are as follows: n6-pl is the same as n5-pl. The three fossilized locative classes above n8-vn all use **ku-** as their concord. Only remnants of these classes still appear in Xhosa, e.g., **phakathi** (inside), **ukwindla** (autumn) and **umva** (behind) (now in n2-sg) and the **apha-apho-phaya** set.

Table 7: Basic set

Class	Position		
	this	that (near)	that (yonder)
n1-sg	**lo**	**lowo**	**lowa** or **laa**
n1-pl	**aba**	**abo**	**abaya** or **abaa**
n2-sg	**lo**	**lowo**	**lowa** or **laa**
n2-pl	**le**	**leyo**	**leya** or **laa**
n3-sg	**eli**	**elo**	**eliya** or **elaa**
n3-pl	**la**	**lawo**	**lawa** or **laa**
n4-sg	**esi**	**eso**	**esiya** or **esaa**
n4-pl	**ezi**	**ezo**	**eziya** or **ezaa**
n5-sg	**le**	**leyo**	**leya** or **laa**
n5-pl	**ezi**	**ezo**	**eziya** or **ezaa**

n6-sg	**olu**	**olo**	**oluya** or **olaa** or **olwaa**
n6-pl	**	**	**
n7-sg	**obu**	**obo**	**obuya** or **obaa**
n8-vn	**oku**	**oko**	**okuya** or **okwaa**
n9-loc	**apha**	**apho**	**phaya**
n10-loc	**oku**	**oko**	**okuya** or **okwaa**
Sources: CGB:163, E&S:26, PCX:86			

Table 8: Predicative set

Class	**Position**		
	it is this	it is that (near)	it is that (yonder)
n1-sg	**ngulo**	**nguloo**	**ngulaa**
n1-pl	**ngaba**	**ngabo**	**ngabaa**
n2-sg	**ngulo**	**nguloo**	**ngulaa**
n2-pl	**yile**	**yiloo**	**yilaa**
n3-sg	**leli**	**lelo**	**lelaa**
n3-pl	**ngala**	**ngaloo**	**ngalaa**
n4-sg	**sesi**	**seso**	**sesaa**
n4-pl	**zezi**	**zezo**	**zezaa**
n5-sg	**yile**	**yiloo**	**yilaa**
n5-pl	**zezi**	**zezo**	**zezaa**
n6-sg	**lolu**	**lolo**	**lolwaa** ** **lolaa**
n6-pl	**	**	**
n7-sg	**bobu**	**bobo**	**bobaa**
n8-vn	**koku**	**koko**	**kokwaa**
n9-loc	**	**	**
n10-loc	**koku** **	**koko** **	**kokwaa** **
Sources: E&S:26			

Table 9: Conjunctive set

Class	**Position**		
	and this	and that (near)	and that (yonder)
n1-sg	**nalo**	**naloo**	**nalaa**
n1-pl	**naba**	**nabo**	**nabaa**
n2-sg	**nalo**	**naloo**	**nalaa**
n2-pl	**nale**	**naloo**	**nalaa**
n3-sg	**neli**	**nelo**	**nelaa**

n3-pl	**nala**	**naloo**	**nalaa**
n4-sg	**nesi**	**neso**	**nesaa**
n4-pl	**nezi**	**nezo**	**nezaa**
n5-sg	**nale**	**naloo**	**nalaa**
n5-pl	**nezi**	**nezo**	**nezaa**
n6-sg	**nolu**	**nolo**	**nolwaa**
n6-pl	**	**	**
n7-sg	**nobu**	**nobo**	**nobaa**
n8-vn	**noku**	**noko**	**nokwaa**
n9-loc			
n10-loc	**noku**	**noko**	**nokwaa**
Sources: E&S:26			

Table 10: Comitative set

Class	**Position**		
	with this	with that (near)	with that (far)
n1-sg	**nalo**	**naloo**	**nalaa**
n1-pl	**naba**	**nabo**	**nabaa**
n2-sg	**nalo**	**naloo**	**nalaa**
n2-pl	**nale**	**naloo**	**nalaa**
n3-sg	**neli**	**nelo**	**nelaa**
n3-pl	**nala**	**naloo**	**nalaa**
n4-sg	**nesi**	**neso**	**nesaa**
n4-pl	**nezi**	**nezo**	**nezaa**
n5-sg	**nale**	**naloo**	**nalaa**
n5-pl	**nezi**	**nezo**	**nezaa**
n6-sg	**nolu**	**nolo**	**nolwaa**
n6-pl	**	**	**
n7-sg	**nobu**	**nobo**	**nobaa**
n8-vn	**noku**	**noko**	**nokwaa**
n9-loc			
n10-loc	**noku**	**noko**	**nokwaa**
Sources: E&S:26			

Table 11: Instrumental set

Class	**Position**		
	using this	using that (near)	using that (far)
n1-sg	**ngalo**	**ngaloo**	**ngalaa**
n1-pl	**ngaba**	**ngabo**	**ngabaa**

n2-sg	**ngalo**	**ngaloo**	**ngalaa**
n2-pl	**ngale**	**ngaloo**	**ngalaa**
n3-sg	**ngeli**	**ngelo**	**ngelaa**
n3-pl	**ngala**	**ngaloo**	**ngalaa**
n4-sg	**ngesi**	**ngeso**	**ngesaa**
n4-pl	**ngezi**	**ngezo**	**ngezaa**
n5-sg	**ngale**	**ngaloo**	**ngalaa**
n5-pl	**ngezi**	**ngezo**	**ngezaa**
n6-sg	**ngolu**	**ngolo**	**ngolwaa**
n6-pl	**	**	**
n7-sg	**ngobu**	**ngobo**	**ngobaa**
n8-vn	**ngoku**	**ngoko**	**ngokwaa**
n9-loc	**	**	**
n10-loc	**ngoku** **	**ngoko** **	**ngokwaa** **
Sources: E&S:26			

Table 12: Relational set

Class	Position		
	about this	about that (near)	about that (far)
n1-sg	**ngalo**	**ngaloo**	**ngalaa**
n1-pl	**ngaba**	**ngabo**	**ngabaa**
n2-sg	**ngalo**	**ngaloo**	**ngalaa**
n2-pl	**ngale**	**ngaloo**	**ngalaa**
n3-sg	**ngeli**	**ngelo**	**ngelaa**
n3-pl	**ngala**	**ngaloo**	**ngalaa**
n4-sg	**ngesi**	**ngeso**	**ngesaa**
n4-pl	**ngezi**	**ngezo**	**ngezaa**
n5-sg	**ngale**	**ngaloo**	**ngalaa**
n5-pl	**ngezi**	**ngezo**	**ngezaa**
n6-sg	**ngolu**	**ngolo**	**ngolwaa**
n6-pl	**	**	**
n7-sg	**ngobu**	**ngobo**	**ngobaa**
n8-vn	**ngoku**	**ngoko**	**ngokwaa**
n9-loc	**	**	**
n10-loc	**ngoku** **	**ngoko** **	**ngokwaa** **
Sources: E&S:26			

Table 13: Basic locative set (with *ku*)

Class	Position		
	at, in, or to this	at, in, or to that (near)	at, in, or to that (yonder)
n1-sg	**kulo**	**kuloo**	**kulaa**
n1-pl	**kwaba**	**kwabo**	**kwabaa**
n2-sg	**kulo**	**kuloo**	**kulaa**
n2-pl	**kule**	**kuloo**	**kulaa**
n3-sg	**kweli**	**kwelo**	**kwelaa**
n3-pl	**kula**	**kuloo**	**kulaa**
n4-sg	**kwesi**	**kweso**	**kwesaa**
n4-pl	**kwezi**	**kwezo**	**kwezaa**
n5-sg	**kule**	**kuloo**	**kulaa**
n5-pl	**kwezi**	**kwezo**	**kwezaa**
n6-sg	**kolu**	**kolo**	**kolwaa**
n6-pl	**	**	**
n7-sg	**kobu**	**kobo**	**kobaa**
n8-vn	**koku**	**koko**	**kokwaa**
n9-loc	**	**	**
n10-loc	**koku** **	**koko** **	**kokwaa** **
Sources: E&S:27			

Table 14: Domain locative set (with *kwa*)

Class	Position		
	to, in, or from this	to, in, or from that (near)	to, in, or from that (yonder)
n1-sg	**kwalo**	**kwaloo**	**kwalaa**
n1-pl	**kwaba**	**kwabo**	**kwabaa**
n2-sg	**kwalo**	**kwaloo**	**kwalaa**
n2-pl	**kwale**	**kwaloo**	**kwalaa**
n3-sg	**kweli**	**kwelo**	**kwelaa**
n3-pl	**kwala**	**kwaloo**	**kwalaa**
n4-sg	**kwesi**	**kweso**	**kwesaa**
n4-pl	**kwezi**	**kwezo**	**kwezaa**
n5-sg	**kwale**	**kwaloo**	**kwalaa**
n5-pl	**kwezi**	**kwezo**	**kwezaa**
n6-sg	**kolu**	**kolo**	**kolwaa**
n6-pl	**	**	**
n7-sg	**kobu**	**kobo**	**kobaa**

n8-vn	**koku**	**koko**	**kokwaa**
n9-loc	**	**	**
n10-loc	**koku** **	**koko** **	**kokwaa** **
Sources: E&S:27			
Note that **ku** and **kwa** merge, becoming **kw**- before **a** or **e**, and **k** before **o**.			

2.4. Adjectives

True adjectives in Xhosa are a closed class; it is not a productive category as no more adjectives may be added. Generally it is assumed that the list totals 18 (see SG-3:62), but various authorities add some variants. The list below, based on Jordan 1966 (PCX:119–120), indicates such variants with markers.

Table 15: Adjective Class

-bi	bad, evil; ugly	AM:193f, CGB:171f, E&S:30, PCX:120, R2
-bini	two	AM:76, CGB:171, E&S:30, PCX:29,120, R16, R37
-dala	old, aged, adult; senior; eldest; stale	CGB:171, E&S:30, PCX:118ff, SAML:378, XED:27, R30, R37
-de	long; tall, high	CGB:171,179, E&S:30, PCX:120
-fuphi	short, squat	CGB:171, E&S:30, PCX:120, XED:41, R10x
-futshane	short, very short	CGB:171, E&S:30, PCX:120, XED:41, R10
-hlanu	five	AM:76, CGB:171, E&S:30, PCX:120
-hle	good, nice; beautiful	AM:193, CGB:171,179, E&S:30, PCX:120
-khulu	big, large, great	AM:115, CGB:171f,179, E&S:30, PCX:120
-ncikane	little, small	PCX:120*
-ncinane	small (very small), little, slight, tiny; young	CGB:171,179, E&S:30, PCX:120
-ncinci	small	CGB:171, E&S:30, PCX:120
-ne	four	AM:76, CGB:171, E&S:30, PCX:120
-nga **-ngaphi**	so much, of such a number (unnamed) how much?	E&S:30, PCX:120† SG-3: 62; XED:99
-ninji	much, many	PCX:120*

-nintshi	much, many	PCX:120*
-ninzi	many, a lot or plenty (of), much, abundant, plentiful	AM:193, CGB:171,179, E&S:30, PCX:120, SAML:400, XED:104, R10, R37
-nje	of this number (usually specified by raising the appropriate number of fingers)	PCX:120, KED:272 †
-nye	one; single, individual; some; other, another (of the same kind)	AM:76, CGB:171, E&S:30, EXD:425, PCX:120, R9, R14, R11
-thandathu	six	AM:76, CGB:171, E&S:30, PCX:120
-thathu	three	AM:76, CGB:171, E&S:30, PCX:120, XED:158
-tsha	new; young; fresh; recent; modern	CGB:171, E&S:30, PCX:120, SAML:405;102, XED:163, R37
* Dialectal variation		
† Adverbial rather than adjectival		

2.5. Auxiliary Verbs

2.5.1. Auxiliary Verbs Used in the Conjugation of Verbs

Group 1.

These are auxiliaries which are affixal, and placed between Subject Concord and stem, or between stem and terminative (**isincedisi**). (Pahl's first group.)

Table 16:

Verb	Usage	Construction	Meaning
-ya-	Long form, Present tense	SC + **-ya-** + stem **ndiyahamba**	Aspect or referential
-wa-	Together with **-ya-** to give inchoative but derogatory meaning.	SC + **-ya-** + **-wa-** + stem **Suka, uyawanxila.**	Inchoative / derogatory. You are becoming a drunkard.
-sa-	With Indicative and Participial moods, most tenses - progressive.	SC + **-sa-** + stem Still (Neg. no longer) **Ndisathetha**	I am still speaking.

-ka-	Negative form of Progressive	NEG + SC + **-ka-** + stem **Andikaboni nto**	I do not yet see anything.
-â-	Remote Past Tense formative	SC + **-â-** + stem (with coalescence) **Ndâfûnda**	I learnt.
-nga-	Potential affix	SC + **-nga-** + stem **Ndingahamba**	I may go.
-nge-		Neg. - **andingehambi**	I may not go.
-kwa-	Inclusive aspect	SC + **-kwa-** + stem **AmaGqunukhwebe akwabusa kumaRharhabe**	Even, the same, that very. Those very Gqunukhwebe people pay homage to the Rharhabes.

Group 2.

These are auxiliaries which may be conjugated as separate constructions, or prefixed to the main verb (**iintsiza-senzi**) and followed by the infinitive, participal (Pahl's groups 2 & 3), or the subjunctive.

Table 17:

Verb	Usage	Construction	Meaning
-ba/ -be	in continuous tenses	SC + **-be** + participial	was
-ya/-ye	in Future tenses (**-ya**)	SC + **-ya** + infinitive	will
	in remote past continuous (**-ye**)	SC + **-ye** + participial	was
	in narrative past (**-ye**)	(see SG-3 for XHA100-F:123)	were used to
-za/ -ze	in near future tense	SC + **-za** + infinitive	will
se (le)	all indicative tenses	SC + **-se** + participial	already
nge-	Perfect tense (**nge-**)	**nge-** + SC + root **Ngendivuyile** (< **Ndinge ndivuyile**)	should / ought / wish I should have been glad.
ma-	Hortative	**ma-** + SC + subjunctive	let / cause to

musa	Negative imperative		do not

2.5.2. Auxiliary Verbs Not Used in the Conjugation of Verbs

These auxiliaries do not have any part to play in the formation of tenses or the conjugation of the verb. (Pahl's group 4.)

Group 1. Auxiliary Verbs with No Corresponding Independent Verbs.

Table 18:

Verb	Usage	Construction	Meaning
-kha/ -khe	As a prefix, e.g., **khawuzize**	**kha-** + subjunctive	just bring
	conjugable, as aux.	e.g., **akhe athethe**	speak a little
		SC + **-khe** + participial	
-da/ -de	conjugable, as aux.	**sada safika**	Eventually we arrived.
	in subjunctive	**(lu)de luthambe**	until it is soft
	negative subjunctive	**akafiki engadange afunde**	He will not come before he has learnt.
-phantsa /e	followed by subjunctive	**uphantse awe**	He nearly fell.
	followed by infinitive	**uphantse ukuwa**	He nearly fell
-tyapha/ e	followed by subjunctive	**tyaphe amkele ukutya**	It is a good thing that he has received food.

Group 2. Auxiliary Verbs with Independent Meanings. (Pahl's group 5.)

Table 19:

Verb	Usage	Construction	Meaning
fika/e	conjugable, foll. by subjunctive	**usana lusaya kufika lufunde**	The child will soon learn.
-hla/e	followed by narrative	**sahla salwa**	We suddenly fought.

	followed by subjunctive	**sihle silwe**	We suddenly fight.
-suka/e	followed by subjunctive	**usuke wayityala imbewu**	He had hurriedly planted seed.
	followed by participial	**usuka ungabikho namhla**	It happens that he is not here.
-buya/e	followed by subjunctive	**babuye bayitshise ngca**	They burnt the grass again.
-phinda/e	followed by subjunctive	**ubephinde wafumane umbona omninzi.**	He has again had a good crop of mealies (corn).
-fana/e	followed by subjunctive	**wafana waphosisa**	He just told a lie.
-fumana/e		**ufumane aphendule**	He just replies without thinking.
	followed by participial	**ufumana ethetha**	He is speaking in vain.
-hlala		**ehlela ephekele indoda yakhe ukutya.**	She is always cooking food for her husband.
-sala		**kusala kufika...**	As soon as he arrived...
-kade	all followed by participial	**bekade behamba apha.**	They used to walk here.
-mana/e		**ubemane esiba iigusha.**	He repeatedly stole sheep.
-soloko		**usoloko ehamba.**	He is always walking.
		andisoloko ndithenga iinkomo.	I don't always buy cattle.
-fuda/ula		**ifudula isakha amanzi.**	She is used to drawing water.
-sanda, -sandula, -andula		**usandul'ukuxhel a inkomo**	He has just slaughtered a beast.
		ndandul'ukuham ba	And then I left.
		akandule ahambe.	He no longer runs.
-fanele, -melwe		**ufanele ukuthandaza**	He ought to pray.
-kholisa, andisa, -dla		**ukholisa ukulima.**	He ploughs satisfactorily.

		ndandisa kuya edolophini	I go to town often.
		badla ngokuba babi	They are usually bad.
-funa, -thanda		**umlambo ufuna ukuphuphuma**	The river is about to overflow.
-thi	used with ideophone	**ukuthi cwaka.**	ideophone supplies meaning
	as auxiliary	**uze uthi ekuseni ubavuse**	You must waken them in the morning.

2.6. Conjunctives in Xhosa

2.6.1. Conjunctives Followed by the Indicative Mood

Table 20:

Xhosa conjunctive	English gloss	Remarks	Example
okokuba ukuba ukuthi	that	no purpose, desire, wish may be expressed	**undixelele ukuba bafikile** 'He told me they had arrived'
kodwa	but		**besiya kubabona kodwa uyagula** 'We would have seen them but he is ill'
kanti	and yet, on the other hand		**akubathandi kanti ufuna ukubabona** 'You don't like them yet you want to see them'
kuba ngokuba	because	also used in other moods	**kodwa kuba abantu bayazazi iinkokeli zabo** '...but because the people know their leaders...'

2.6.2. Conjunctives Followed by the Participial Mood

Note: Some conjunctives may be followed by either the common participial mood or the relative participial mood; those followed by the relative can also use the common form.

Table 21:

Xhosa conjunctive	English gloss	Remarks	Example
xa **xenikweni** **xeshikweni** **mhlenikwezeni**	when, if the time that... the day that...	many related forms with similar meaning	**xa afikileyo/xa efikileyo** 'when she has arrived'
ngangoko	as much as		**uthetha ngangoku athandayo/ethanda** 'he says what he wants'
njengoko	like		**ndenza njengoko ndithanda** 'I do as I like'
nangona	although		R10
noko	even though		R26
okukhona	the more		**okukhona alisukelayo lamshiya ihashe lakhe** 'the more he chased it, the further his horse left him behind'
kuba **ngokuba** **ngakuba**	because after negative		**kuba engenayo imali yesikolo** 'because there's not enough school money'
njengokuba **ngangokuba**	just like, as much as		**simnceda njengokuba ethanda** 'we help him as much as he wants'

2.6.3. Conjunctives Followed by the Subjunctive Mood

Table 22:

Xhosa conjunctive	English gloss	Remarks	Example
ukuba	that	when the main verb expresses wish, want, or desire	**ndifuna ukuba ndihambe** 'I want to go'
ukuze	so that		**ufunda ukuze aphumelele** 'He studies so that he may succeed'
hleze	lest		**mabahambe hleze bafike kuvaliwe esikolweni** 'Let them go lest the school be closed on their arrival'
phambi kokuba	before	main clause in pluperfect	**bahambe phambi kokuba ndifike** 'They went before I arrived'

2.7. Summary of Tenses in the Indicative Mood

Table 23:

Name of Tense	Xhosa Structure	English meaning
Present Short Positive	**ndibona**	I see
Present Long Positive	**ndiyabona**	I see
Present Negative	**andiboni**	I do not see
Near Future Positive	**ndiza kubona**	I shall see
Near Future Negative	**andizi kubona**	I shall not see
Remote Future Positive	**ndiya kubona**	I shall see
Remote Future Negative	**andiyi kubona**	I shall not see
Continuous Future Pos.	**ndiya kuba ndibona**	I shall be seeing
Continuous Future Neg.	**ndiya kuba ndingaboni**	I shall not be seeing
Perfect Long Positive	**ndibonile**	I have seen
Perfect Short Positive	**ndibone**	I have seen
Perfect Negative	**andibonanga**	I have not seen
Remote Past Positive	**ndabona**	I saw
Remote Past Negative	**zange ndibone**	I did not see

Near Past Cont. Pos.	**ndibe ndibona**	I used to see
Near Past Cont. Neg.	**ndibe ndingaboni**	I used not to see
Remote Past Cont. Pos.	**ndabe ndibona**	I used to see
Remote Past Cont. Neg.	**ndabe ndingaboni**	I used not to see
Past Perfect Positive	**ndibe ndibonile**	I had seen
Past Perfect Negative	**ndibe ndingabonanga**	I had not seen
Future Contingent Pos.	**ndibe ndiza kubona**	I should have seen
Future Contingent Neg.	**ndibe ndingazi kubona**	I should not have seen

2.8. Sound Changes

Table 24:

#	change (loss) of -I before vowel. Ex: Ndazi 'I know' = nd(i)-azi; ndonwaba 'I am happy' = nd(i)-onwab-a. CGB:119
#	change of aa (loss of -a) before another a. Ex: babanye 'of individuals' [= ba-(a)-ba-nye] CGB:119,120, R11
#	change (loss) of -a or -e before suffix -eni Ex: PCX:68, R11
e	change (coalescence) of –a + i- to e Ex: nekati 'and cat' = na-i-kati CGB:120
ee	change (coalescence) of –a + ii- to ee Ex: neekati 'and cats' = na-ii-kati CGB:120, R9
j	change of bh to j CGB:142, PCX:103,196
k	change of kh to k Ex: inkokeli 'leader' [= in-khok-el-i], inkosi 'chief' [= in-khosi] E&S:51, R4b, R16
kc	change of ch to kc Ex: inkcaza 'comb' [= in-kc/chaz-a] (change induced by nasal) ITXP:69
kq	change of qh to kq Ex: inkqubo 'program; progress' [= in-kq/qhub-o] (change induced by nasal) ITXP:69, R16, R22, R37
l	consonant added to n9 roots apha and apho Ex: balapha CGB:179, R37
nj	change of mb to nj CGB:142, PCX:103,196, R37
nts	change of mp to ntsh CGB:142, PCX:103,196
ny	change of m to ny Ex: -menywa 'be invited' [= -mem/ny-w-a], entanyeni 'on the neck' [= e-(i)ntam/ny-eni], emlonyeni 'in the mouth' [= e-(u)m-lom/ny-eni] CGB:142, PCX:103,196
o	change (coalescence) of –a + u- to o Ex: notata 'and father' = na-u-tata CGB:120, R14
p	change of ph to p Ex: impendulo 'answer' [= im-phendul-o], impilo 'health' [= im-phil-o], impatho 'treatment' [= im-phath-o] E&S:51
t	change of th to t Ex: iintuthu 'ashes' [= iin-thuthu], intobeko 'humility' [= in-thobek-o], izinti 'sticks' [= izin-thi] (change

	induced by nasal) E&S:51
tl	change of hl to tl Ex: intlumo 'growth' [= in-hlum-o], izintlu 'rows' [= izin-hlu], wentlalo 'of living' [= wa-in-hlal-o] E&S:51, R37
ts	change of s to ts Ex: iintsiba 'pens' [= iin-siba], iintsuku 'full days' [= iin-suku] SG-2: 67
tsh	change of ph to tsh Ex: -hlonitshwa 'be respected' [= hloniph/tsh-w-a]; futshane 'very short' [= fuph(i)/tsh-ane]; elusatsheni 'in the family' [= e-lu-saph/tsh-eni] CGB:142, PCX:103,196, R10, R11
ty	change of b to ty Ex: -setyenziswa 'be used' [= sebenz /ty-is-w-a] CGB:142, PCX:103,196, R4B, R9
ty	change of tyh to ty Ex: intyafo 'weakness' [= in-tyhaf-o] E&S:51
w	change of o or u to w before a vowel Ex: abantwana 'children' [= aba-ntu-ana]; wenza 'you do' [= u-enz-a]; esikolweni 'to school' CGB:119,125, PCX:30, R4b, R9, R10
y	change of i to y before a vowel Ex: yoyika 'it fears' [= i-oyika] CGB:119
y	addition of y before i- after a vowel-final prefix Ex: mayinyanzelwe [= ma-y+i-nyanz-el-w-e] R10

Readings

Amandla Meats

i-MEAT MARKET
Inyama kubantu bonke
Sithengisa inyama yodidi.
Amaxabiso ethu aphantsi onke
Inyama yethu ihlala ibukeka.
Zikhona nazo izisulu zempela-veki.
MARKET SQUARE, KING WILLIAMS TOWN.

Vocabulary

Amandla (name)
Cf: **amandla** strength, energy, power; biceps [n3-pl-mass]
i-meat market [n5-sg] {Eng}
i- [group 5 (Bantu class 9) singular noun prefix]
inyama meat [n5-sg]
Note: The n5 prefix **iN-** is subject to and causes many sound changes because of following sounds. See the grammar reference section for more discussion.
kubantu for people
ku- at, in, to, from, with, of, among [locative prefix for a named person, kin term, pronoun or deictic]
Contrast: **e**- [simple locative], **kwa**- [domain locative]
bantu people [n1-pl-red]
abantu people; persons [n1-pl; sg: **umntu**]
bonke all; every [pro-enum-n1-pl]
b- [n1-pl thematic consonant prefix]
onke all, every, the whole (of) [pro-enum-root = o-nke]
-**nke** all, every, the whole (of) [pro-enum-root]
sithengisa we sell [= si-theng-is-a]
si- we [pro-1pl-S1]
-**theng**- buy, purchase [v-tr]
-**is**- cause to VERB, make VERB [v-caus or v-trans suf]
-**thengis**- sell [v-caus]
-**a** [short v-pres suf; Structure: S1-#-Δ-a]
inyama yodidi premium meat
yodidi of pedigree [= ya-u-didi]
yo- [combo form indicating that n6-sg (**u**-) is possessed by a n5-sg (**ya**-)]
ya- of [group 5 singular possessive agreement prefix]
u- [group 6 (Bantu class 11) singular noun prefix]
udidi sort, kind, type, category; pedigree, breed; class; caste, rank; row; stamp [n6-sg; pl: **iindidi**]
amaxabiso prices [n3-pl]
ixabiso bar; limit; worth, value, price; importance [n3-sg]
ama- [group 3 (Bantu class 6) plural noun prefix]
-**xab**- lay across, bar (entrance); thwart, hinder, obstruct; oppose; reprove [v-tr]
-**xabis**- set across, set awry; reach the mark; make hostile; be worth [v-tr]
-**o** [noun-forming suffix]

ethu our [pro-1pl-poss-n3-pl = a-ithu or #-ethu]
a- of [group 3 plural possessive agreement prefix]
-**ithu** our, ours; our own [plural possessive root]
(zero) [n3-pl zero thematic consonant prefix]
-**ethu** our, ours; our own [plural possessive root]
aphantsi are lower [atr-n3-pl]
a- [group 3 plural relative or attributive agreement prefix; here used attributively]
phantsi down, below; place on the ground; [atr] low, lower; elementary [n9-loc; adv-loc]
onke all; every [pro-enum-n3-pl]
yethu our [pro-1pl-poss-n5-sg = ya-ithu or y-ethu]
y- [group 5 singular thematic consonant prefix]
ihlala it is always VERB [v-aux-n5-sg]
i- he, she, it [group 5 singular subject (S1) agreement prefix]
-**hlal**- always VERB; do VERB continually or constantly [v-aux]
Cf: -**hlal**- sit, get seated; live, reside, dwell; stay, be still; be awake; be well or healthy [v-intr]
ibukeka it is admired or liked [= i-buk-ek-a]
-**buk**- admire, like, look at (with pleasure or admiration); prize; take care of; conserve, be sparing with; browse (through a book), watch (TV), see (a movie) [v-tr]
-**ek**- -able, -ible; be or become VERB [v-st or v-atr suf]
-**bukek**- be admired or liked; [perf] admirable, exquisite, comely [v-atr]
zikhona they are
zi- they VERB [group 4 plural subject (S1) agreement prefix]
-**khona** be present or there [v-exis]
nazo there are (not far or just mentioned) [deic-2-n4-pl-pred-loc]
izisulu bargains [n4-pl]
izi- [group 4 (Bantu class 8) plural noun prefix]
isisulu windfall, piece of good luck; easy prey, s.t. easily come by; [ext] bargain [n4-sg]
-**sul**- wipe off or away, blot out; clean, polish; wipe out, obliterate [v-tr]
-**u** [noun forming suffix]
zempela-veki on the weekend [= za- (i)m-p/phel-a-veki]
za- of the [n4-pl-poss-n5-sg]
impela end, ending; [adv] entirely, completely, thoroughly [n5-sg]
Cf: **impelo** end, ending, termination; the end [n5-sg]
-**phel**- stop, cease, finish, come to an end, terminate [v-intr]
CHANGE of **ph** to **p**
-**a** [noun forming suffix]
iveki week [n5-sg-time]

Izilwanyana Nabantwana Abayabulayo

Kwizilwanyana akuvumeleki ukuba amantshontsho ayabule ebusuku nasemini kuba anokwenzakala. Abazali abangabahoyi abantwana babo babi kunezilwanyana babangela abantwana babo bayabule ebusuku, besiba bezifaka ezinkathazweni.

Vocabulary

izilwanyana small animals (lit: little fighters) [n4-pl-dim = izi-lw(a)-anyana]
 isilwanyana animal (small or noxious), vertebrate, insect [n4-sg-dim]
 lwa- fight, struggle [v-intr]
 -anyana tiny, very small [diminutive noun suffix]
nabantwana and children [= na-(a)ba-ntu-/w-ana]
 na- and [conjunctive prefix before the final noun in the linked series]
 aba- [group 1 (Bantu class 2) plural noun prefix]
 umntwana baby, infant, child; young (person); pupil [n1-sg; dim: um-ntu-ana little person; pl: **abantwana**]
 CHANGE of O or U to W before a vowel
 -ana little, small; somewhat [diminutive noun suffix]
abayabulayo they who wander [= aba-yabul-a-yo]
 aba- they who [group 1 or 1a plural relative or attributive agreement prefix]
 -yabul- roam about aimlessly, wander (around) [v-intr]
 -a VERBing [present tense participial construction]
 -yo [v-rel suf, used attributively]
kwizilwanyana in the animal kingdom [= kw(a)-izi-lw(a)-anyana]
 kw- to, in, at, from [short form of **kwa** before another vowel]
 kwa- to, in, at, from [locative prefix for the domain, residence or property of s.o.]
akuvumeleki it is not allowed
 aku- there is no VERBing [group 10 locative or impersonal negative present subject prefix]
 a- **-i** do(es) not VERB [negative present tense construction]
 ku- it is; one VERBs; they VERB [impersonal verb marker]
 -**vum**- consent, agree, accede; assent to; admit, confess; suit, agree with s.o.; fall in with the leader (in singing) [v-tr]
 -**el**- do VERB for or to s.o. [benefactive or applied verb suffix indicating that the action is carried out for, on behalf of, or to the detriment of s.o. or s.t.]
 -**vumel**- allow, agree to, approve of [v-ben]
 -**vumelek**- be approved of, be allowable [v-atr]
 -**i** [negative verb suffix, not past]
ukuba that [conj followed by sub]
amantshontsho pups, cubs, chicks, fledglings, the young (of animals) [n3-pl]
 intshontsho disgusting thing, s.t. ugly, fowl-smelling; pup, cub, chick, fledgling [n3-sg]
ayabule that they should roam [= a-yabul-e]

a- [group 3 plural present subjunctive verb subject (S^{3a}) agreement prefix]
-**e** that ~ should VERB [present subjunctive verb suffix]
ebusuku at night [n7-sg-loc-time = e-(u)bu-suku]
e- in, at, to [locative prefix which replaces initial vowel of class prefix]
LOSS of noun class article after **e**- locative prefix
ubu- [group 7 (Bantu class 14) singular noun prefix]
ubusuku night(time) [n7-sg-time]
Cf: **usuku** day (24 hour period), a day and a night [n6-sg-time; pl: **iintsuku**]
nasemini and during the day [= na-s-e-(i)mini]
-**s**- being in [copulative or predicative locative, occurs after the predicative prefix and before the **e**- locative prefix, probably derived from *sala >sele > se* 'stay, remain,' thus 'those who remain in the locations']
emini during the day, in the daytime [n5-sg-time-loc]
imini day (-time) [n5-sg-time]
kuba because [conj] (lit: it being)
-**ba** be; become [v-pred]
anokwenzakala they could get hurt [= a-na-uku-enz-akal-a]
S1-#-Δ-**a** VERBs, is VERBing [short present tense verb construction]
a- they [group 3 plural subject (S1) agreement prefix]
-**noku**- can or could VERB, be able or willing to VERB [= na-uku-; Structure: S1 **noku**-Δ-a]
-**enz**- do, make; perform; execute; cause [v-tr]
-**akal**- -able, -ible; become VERB [attributive or neuter verb suffix]
-**enzakal**- be done to; get hurt or injured [v-st]
abazali parents [n1-pl]
aba- -**i** -ers, -ors [plural agent noun circumfix]
-**zal**- beget, generate, bear (child); lay (eggs) [v-tr]
Cf: **umzali** parent (male), father, progenitor [n1-sg]
Cf: **umzalikazi** parent (female), mother [n1-sg-fem]
abangabahoyi who are not concerned about them [= a-ba-nga-ba-hoy-i]
-**nga**- not [negative dependent verb (participial, relative, or subjunctive) prefix]
Note: subject is RELATIVE, otherwise the S2 subject would be **be**-
-**ba**- them [group 1 plural object agreement prefix]
-**hoy**- mind, be concerned about; attend to; obey [v-tr]
babo their (own); theirs [pro-3pl-poss-n1-pl]
ba- of [group 1 plural possessive agreement prefix]
-**bo** their (own); theirs [n1-pl possessive root]
babi kunezilwanyana they are worse than the animal parents
babi they are bad
ba- they are ADJ [group 1 or 1a plural adjective agreement prefix used predicatively]
-**bi** bad, evil, ugly [adj-root]
kunezilwanyana than the ones having small animals [= ku-na-izi-lw-anyana]
ku- than, in comparison with [comparative]
nezi- they have [n4-pl-obj; combo = na- + izi-]
na- have, own, possess [v-poss]
babangela they give
ba- they [group 1 or 1a plural subject (S1) agreement prefix]
-**bang**- cause, occasion, bring on, produce [v-tr]
-**bangel**- cause for; bring upon; give to [v-ben]

Cf: -**bangel**- claim s.t. for s.o.
bayabule (that) they should roam
ba- (that) they VERB [group 1 or 1a plural present subjunctive verb subject (S^{3a}) agreement prefix]
besiba they stealing (c.f. Eng. they roam about stealing)
be- they [group 1 or 1a plural participial subject (S2) agreement prefix]
-**si**- [prefix added to positive participial form of monosyllabic verbs]
-**ba** steal; cheat, deceive, get the better of [v-tr]
bezifaka they getting themselves involved
-**zifaka e**- get oneself involved in, meddle with [v-refl-cmp]
-**zi**- VERB oneself [reflexive verb prefix]
-**fak**- insert, enclose, put in [v-tr]
ezinkathazweni in troubles [= e-(i)zin-k/khathaz-o/w-eni]
iziN- [group 5 (Bantu class 10) plural noun prefix]
inkathazo trouble, annoyance [n5-sg]
CHANGE of **kh** to **k**
-**khathaz**- bother, perturb, annoy, distress; hinder; trouble, pester, plague; wear s.o. out, fatigue [v-tr]
CHANGE of **o** to **w**
-**eni** at, in, to [locative suffix]
Note: -**ini** is the Bantu locative suffix, and it is subject to change of its initial vowel depending on preceding sounds.
nguM.S.W. by M.S.W.
ngu- by (done or produced by) him or her [marker of n1a-sg agent of passive verb]
eBarkly East from Barkley East {Eng}

Hloniphani Ootitshala

Lifikile ixesha lokuba sihlonele abazali kwanootitshala. Ndicinga ukuba ootitshala ngabona bantu babalulekileyo kuluntu. Ngaphandle kootitshala, khawutsho ngebekho oogqirha, amagqwetha, abongikazi, 'abaguquli' nabanye abantu abafunekayo ukuze isizwe sibe nenkqubela?

nguS.M., eReitz

Vocabulary

hloniphani (you all) respect! [v-tr-imp-pl]
 -hloniph- respect, pay or show respect to; revere; observe name or word taboo [v-tr]
 -ani do VERB! [positive imperative plural verb suffix]
 -hlon- be shy or bashful {obsolete}; this root is connected both to **-hloniph-** and to **-hlonel-** BELOW

ootitshala teachers [n1a-pl]
 oo- [group 1a (Bantu class 2a) plural noun prefix]
 utitshala teacher [n1a-sg; Alt: **ititshala** n5-sg]

lifikile it has arrived
 li- he, she, it [group 3 singular subject (S1) agreement prefix]
 -fik- arrive [v-intr]
 -ile has VERBed [long perfect or recent past tense suffix; denotes current relevance on stative verbs]

ixesha time; period (of time); clock, watch, timepiece [n3-sg; pl: **amaxesha**]

lokuba that [conjunctive; = la-uku-ba] (lit: of being)
 loku- [combo n3-sg poss n8-vn]
 la- of [n3-sg poss prefix]
 uku- [group 8 (Bantu class 15) verbal noun prefix]

sihlonele we should respect
 si- (and) we VERB [S^{3a} present subjunctive subject pronoun]
 -hlonel- fear, respect, reverence; show deference to [v-tr]

abazali kwanootitshala parents and teachers
 kwanoo- [combo kwa 'even' + n(a)- 'and' + oo- n1a-pl]
 kwana- even, and even [emphatic prefix combination]
 kwa- even [adv-prf]
 LOSS (ELISION) of **-a** before **oo-**

ndicinga I think
 ndi- I [pro-1sg-S1-prf]
 -cing- think, imagine, suppose; intend to (do) [v-intr]

ukuba that [conj introducing a statement of fact followed by indicative]

ngabona they are
 nga- is ..., are ... [predicative copulative element]
 bona they [group 1 plural absolutive pronoun]

babalulekileyo who are important [= ba-balul-ek-ile-yo]
 ba- they who are [group 1, 1a plural relative, attributive agreement prefix used predicatively]
 -balulekileyo important, distinguished [v-perf-rel]
 -balul- pick (out), choose, select; distinguish, specificy; make an exception of [v-tr]

-balulek- get selected; become good; be distinguished, notable, important [v-st]

kuluntu to society [= ku-uluntu; Cf: kwa-uluntu the place of...]

ku at, in, to, from, with, of, among [locative prefix for a named person, kin term, pronoun or deictic]

uluntu people, population; community, society; humanity, the human race; the common people [n6-sg; no plural]

ngaphandle kootitshala without teachers [= nga-pha-ndle kwa/k-oo-titshala]

ngaphandle kwa except (for); without [prep-expr]

Cf: **ngaphandle** on top; outside [adv-loc]

nga- at, on, in, into [unspecified place or vague location]

pha [group 9 (Bantu class 16) locative noun prefix]

ndle out (in the open) [root]

Cf: **indle** open field, veld [n5-sg; usually loc **endle** 'in the open']

kootitshala to/from teachers [= kwa-/k-oo-titshala]

CHANGE (merger) of **ku** and **kwa** to **k** before **o**

khawutsho would you ever say? [= kha-w+u-tsho]

kha- do VERB sometimes, ever, a little, at all [v-aux]

-**w**- addition of **w** before **u**- after a vowel-final prefix

u- you [pro-2sg-S1-prf]

-tsho assert, say so, declare so, do thus; how are you? [for a greeting, usually among males] [v-ir]

ngebekho there would not be [there would be no...]

nge- there is/are not [negative marker in predicative constructions]

bekho [Subj form of **ukuba** 'to be' + **kho** loc 'there, in that place']

oogqirha doctors [n1a-pl]

ugqirha doctor (medical); medicine man; any medical practitioner [n1a-sg]

amagqwetha lawyers [n3-pl]

igqwetha lawyer, attorney, advocate [n3-sg] (lit: distorter)

-gqweth- turn upside down; distort, misrepresent, pervert [v-tr]

abongikazi nurses [n1-pl]

umongikazi nurse [n1-sg]

ab- [reduced form of group 1 (Bantu class 2) plural noun prefix before vowel-inital root]

-ong- use sparingly, frugally, economically; avoid waste; give food a little at a time; [ext] nurse, take care of the sick [v-tr]

abaguquli translators [n1-pl]

umguquli translator, interpreter [n1-sg]

-guqul- turn s.t. back; change, convert, revolutionize; translate; say in reply [v-tr]

nabanye and others [= na-(a)ba-nye]

abanye some, others [adj-num-n1-pl]

aba- [group 1, 1a plural adjective agreement prefix]

-nye one; single, individual; some; other, another (of the same kind) [adj-root-num]

abafunekayo who are needed [= aba-fun-ek-a-yo]

aba- they who [group 1, 1a plural relative, attributive agreement prefix]

-fun- need; want , wish, desire; seek, search, look for [v-tr]

-funek- be sought, wanted, desirable or necessary [v-atr]

ukuze that, so, in order that [conj, followed by present subjunctive]

isizwe nation [n4-sg]

sibe nenkqubela that it might have progress [si-b-e na-in-kq/qhub-el-a]
sibe that it might become
si- (and) he, she, it VERBs [n4-sg present subjunctive verb subject (S^{3a}) agreement prefix]
-**be na**- that [S^{3a}] might have
-**be** that [S^{3a}] be; that it (should) become [v-pred-sub]
nenkqubela have progress
nen- [combo = na- 'have' + in- n5-sg]
in- [group 5 (Bantu class 9) singular noun prefix]
inkqubela progress [n5-sg]
-**qhub**- drive (animal ~ vehicle); push on with; move s.t. along; press, urge, exhort, drive (people) on; make steady progress [v-tr]
-**qhubel**- drive (animal, vehicle) for/to; make steady progress on [v-ben]
CHANGE of **qh** to **kq**
eReitz from Reitz

Part A

Ndifuna iqabanekazi elineminyaka engama-20, mna ndineminyaka engama-22. Anditshayi kwaye andiseli, ndihamba icawa. Ndabanjwa ngoJuni. Ndicela lindithumele ifoto.

Mncedisi Nethi, Stutterheim Prison P/Bag X 5, Stutterheim 4930

Vocabulary

ndifuna I am looking for, I want
iqabanekazi female friend ~ partner [n3-sg-fem = i-qab-an-e-kazi]
iqabane intimate friend; companion, mate, partner [n3-sg]
i- [group 3 (Bantu class 5) singular noun prefix]
-**qab**- smear the body with red clay ~ ochre mixed with fat; paint [v-tr]
-**an**- each other, one another [reciprocal ~ mutual verb suffix]
-**qaban**- paint ~ smear each other with red clay ~ ochre mixed with fat; [ext] be intimate [v-recip]
-**e** [noun forming suffix]
-**kazi** -ess, -ine, female- [feminine noun suffix]
Cf: -**kazi** largish, very big [augmentative noun suffix]
elineminyaka who has years [= eli-na-imi-nyaka]
-**neminyaka engama**-NUM who is NUM years old
eli- [group 3 singular relative or attributive agreement prefix]
-**neminyaka** has years
nemi- [combo of na- + imi-]
e- CHANGE (coalescence) of -**a** + **i**- to **e**
imi- [group 2 (Bantu class 4) plural noun prefix]
umnyaka year [n2-sg-time; pl: **iminyaka**]
engama-20 which are 20
e- [group 2 plural relative, attributive agreement prefix referring to **iminyaka**]
ngama- they are ... [class 3 plural copulative ~ predicative prefix construction, broken up as]
-**ng**- is/are [predicative/copulative prefix; See: **ngaba**- [n1-pl], **ngama**- [n3-pl], **ngoo**- [n1a-pl], **ngu**- [n1a-sg], **ngum**- [n1-sg, n2-sg]
amashumi [n3-pl] 'tens' is involved in any number from **amashumi amabini** '20' upwards]
mna I; myself; as for me [pro-1sg-abs]
ndineminyaka engama-22 I am 22 years old
anditshayi I don't smoke
andi- I not
-**tshay**- smoke (tobacco) [v-intr]
-**i** do(es) not VERB [negative present tense verb suffix]
kwaye and even [conj links coordinate verb clauses together; Alt: **yaye**]
-**ye** and; (and) also [conj-root]
andiseli I don't drink
-**sel**- drink (s.t. cold) [v-tr]
Cf: -**phung**- drink (s.t. hot) [v-tr]
ndihamba I go (to)
-**hamb**- go, walk, move, travel; go (away, from), depart, leave;

proceed, advance; flow (water); [fig] behave [v-intr]

icawa religious service, church (worship) [n5-sg]
Cf: **iCawa** Sunday [n5-sg-time]

ndabanjwa I was arrested [= nda-bamb/nj-w-a]
nda- I [Note: this is Remote Past as the sentence has a main clause only – Past Subjunctive would be subordinate]
-**bamb**- hold, grasp; seize, catch; keep, retain, hold for; arrest, apprehend, take prisoner; [ext] regard as [v-tr]
-**w**- be VERBed [passive verb suffix]
-**banjwa** be arrested
CHANGE of **mb** to **nj** in passive
-**a** did VERB, had VERBed [past verb suffix]

ngoJuni in June [= nga-u-Juni]
ngo- [combo]
nga- on, by [date]; at, in [time]
uJuni June [n1a-sg-time]

ndicela I request
-**cel**- ask for s.t., request, beg [v-tr]

lindithumele that she should send me
li- she VERB [S^{3a} present subjunctive subject pronoun; (refers to **iqabanekazi**, which is rather far away]
-**ndi**- me [pro-1sg-obj-prf]
-**thum**- send [v-tr]
-**thumel**- send s.t. to s.o., dispatch to ~ for [v-ditr-ben]

ifoto photograph, picture [n5-sg] {Eng}
-**fot**- photograph, take a picture of s.o. [v-tr] {Eng}

Mncedisi (personal name)

Nethi (family name)
Cf: **intolongo** prison, jail [n5-sg]

Part B

UEdward Matyana unama-27 eminyaka engathanda ukubhalelwa ngamagqiyazana aneminyaka ephakathi kwe-18 nama-35. Uthanda ukudlala ibhola ekhatywayo, intenetya, ukuphulaphula umculo, ukufunda nokubhala nokuya enkonzweni. Khanimbhalele ngesiXhosa isiBhulu okanye isiNgesi nize nifake ifoto. Idilesi yakhe ithi Correctional Services, Private Bag X2, Patensie, 6335.

Vocabulary

UEdward Edward (personal name) [n1a-pn]
  u- [group 1a (Bantu class 1a) singular noun prefix]
Matyana Matyana (family name)
unama-27 **eminyaka** he is 27 years old [= u-na-(a)ma-27] (lit: he has 27 of years)
  u- he, she [group 1, 1a singular subject (S1) agreement prefix]
  -**nama**-NUM **eminyaka** SUBJ is NUM years old
eminyaka of years; [atr] years old [n3-pl-poss-n2-pl = a-iminyaka]
  emi- [combo = a- + imi-]
  a- of [group 3 plural possessive agreement prefix]
engathanda he would like
  e- he ~ she [group 1 ~ 1a singular participial subject (S2) agreement prefix]
  -**nga**- may, can, would [potential ~ conditional]; would you mind if ... ? [permissive preverb]
  -**thand**- love, like; adore [v-tr]
ukubhalelwa to be written to [v-ben-pass = uku-bhal-el-w-a]
  uku-Δ-**a** to VERB; VERBing [positive infinitive ~ gerund verb construction]
  -**bhal**- write [v-tr]
  -**bhalel**- write to s.o. [v-ben]
ngamagqiyazana by young single women [n3-pl-agent]
  ngama- by (done ~ produced by) [marker of class 3 plural agent of passive verb]
  igqiyazana young single woman [n3-sg; pl: **amagqiyazana**] {respect}
  Cf: **gqi** happen suddenly [ideophone]
  Cf: **gqi** look!, behold! [intj]
  Cf: **iqhiya** kerchief, head covering; handkerchief [n5-sg]
  -**azana** [diminutive noun suffix]
aneminyaka who have NUM years [= a-na-iminyaka]
ephakathi which are between
  phakathi between, among
kwe- from [combo = kwa- + i-]
nama- and [= na-ama]
uthanda he likes
ukudlala to play
  -**dlal**- play [v-tr]
ibhola ekhatywayo soccer [n5-sg-cmp]
ibhola ball [n5-sg] {Eng}
  i- [n5-sg prefix]
ekhatywayo which is being kicked [v-n5-sg-pass-part-rel = e-khab/ty-w-a-yo]
  e- [group 5 singular relative ~ attributive agreement prefix]
  -**khab**- kick (ball); [v-intr] shoot, sprout (plant)

CHANGE of **b** to **ty** in passive constructions
intenetya tennis [n5-sg]
Cf: **intenetya** rock hare [n5-sg]
ukuphulaphula to listen to [v-inf]
-**phulaphul**- listen (to), hearken; attend; obey [v-tr]
umculo singing, concert; [ext] music [n2-sg]
um- [group 2 (Bantu class 3) singular noun prefix]
-**cul**- sing [v-intr]
ukufunda reading, to read [n8-vn]
-**fund**- study, learn; read [v-tr]
nokubhala and writing [n8-vn = na-uku-bhal-a]
noku- and to VERB; and VERBing [combo]
nokuya and going [n8-vn = na-uku-ya]
-**ya** go (to), travel [v-intr]
enkonzweni to church service [n5-sg-loc = e-(i)n-k/khonz-o/w-eni]
inkonzo service; religious ~ church service [n5-sg]
-**khonz**- serve, do service [v-intr used with locative]
CHANGE of **o** ~ **u** to **w** before a vowel
khanimbhalele won't you write to him
khani- won't you all [plural]
kha- won't you just VERB [hortative preverb used with the second person, followed by the present subjunctive; Structure: kha-S^{3a}-Δ-e]
ni- (and) you (all) VERB [S^{3a} present subjunctive subject pronoun]
-**m**- him, her [group 1 singular object agreement prefix]
ngesiXhosa in Xhosa [n4-sg-instr = nga-isi-Xhosa]
ngesi- [combo = nga- + isi-]
nga- with, through, by means of [instrumental prefix]
isi- [group 4 (Bantu class 7) singular noun prefix]
isiXhosa Xhosa (language) [n4-sg]
isiBhulu Afrikaans [n4-sg]
okanye or [conj]
isiNgesi English [n4-sg]
nize you (all) should
ni- (and) you (all) VERB [S^{3a} present subjunctive subject pronoun]
ze should, shalt [v-aux-imp]
za should, shalt [v-aux; Structure: S^{3a}-ze S^{3a} Δ-e]
Cf: **zeni-Δ-e** you [plural] ought to VERB
nifake you should enclose
-**fak**- insert, enclose, put in [v-tr]
idilesi address [n5-sg]
yakhe his, her, its [pro-3sg-poss-n5-sg]
ithi is as follows [v-pres-n5-sg]
i- he, she, it [group 5 singular subject (S1) agreement prefix]
-**thi** say, mean, think [v-tr-ir]

Part C

Ndiyintombazana eneminyaka engama-26, ndifuna iqabane elidiniweyo zizinto zomhlaba. Mna andiseli, anditshayi kodwa yena nokuba angatshaya angaseli ulungile. Ndithanda ukubukela ezemidlalo kumabonakude nokumamela umculo wegosipile. Onomdla afake ifoto yakhe kwileta yokuqala. Nam ndiya kwenza njalo. AbaseBhayi bancede bangazihluphi bandiphoxa kwanele.

Doris Roberts, P.O. Box 2352, Port Elizabeth

Vocabulary

ndiyintombazana I am a (single) girl
ndi- I am ... [copulative or predicative prefix construction]
-**y**- addition of **y** before **i**- after a vowel-final prefix
intombazana young, single girl [n5-sg-dim = in-t/thomb-azana]
intombi girl; maiden, virgin; daughter [n5-sg]
eneminyaka engama-26 who is 26 years old
elidiniweyo who is tired [v-pass-perf-rel = eli-din-iwe-yo]
-**dinwa** be ~ get tired, become fatigued [v-pass; perf: **diniwe**]
-**din**- tire, fatigue [v-tr]
-**iw**- be VERBed [passive verb suffix on monosyllabic and vowel verbs]
-**e** -ed [short past ending]
Note: do not confuse with -**iwe** was ~ were VERBed [long form passive past verb suffix]
zizinto by the things [n5-pl-agent]
zizi- by (done/produced by) them [marker of class 5 plural agent of passive verb]
izinto things [n5-pl]
into thing, item, article, object; element, substance; phenomenon; subject matter [n5-sg]
zomhlaba of the world [= za-um-hlaba]
zom- [combo of za- + um-]
za- of [group 5 plural possessive agreement prefix]
umhlaba earth, ground, soil; world, the Earth [n2-sg]
kodwa but [conj]
yena he, she; himself, herself; as for him, her [pro-3sg-abs; same as n1-sg-abs-pro, but without an antecedent]
nokuba even if, even though [calls attention to the extreme nature of what follows, usually followed by S1 and indicative mood (see R7), but here by the potential]
angatshaya he may smoke
a- [n1-sg-S4 potential]
angaseli he may not drink [neg potential or subjunctive]
-**nga**-Δ-**i** not VERBing [negative present subjunctive construction]
ulungile he is OK
u- he, she [group 1, 1a singular subject (S1) agreement prefix]
-**lung**- be right, good, suitable, fitting, becoming, OK [v-st]
-**ile** has VERBed [long perfect or recent past tense suffix; denotes current relevance on stative verbs]
ndithanda I like

ukubukela to watch
-**buk**- admire, like, look at (with pleasure ~ admiration); prize; take care of; conserve, be sparing with; browse (through a book), watch (TV), see (a movie) [v-tr]
-**bukel**- watch (TV, etc. for one's own enjoyment) [v-ben; note here the benefactive suffix plays an autobenefactive role, i.e., for oneself]
-**a** [v inf suf]

ezemidlalo at those sports [= eze-mi-dlalo (from eza +imi)]
e- which [group 2 plural relative, attributive agreement prefix]
imidlalo games; sports [n2-pl]
umdlalo play; game; sport [n2-sg]

kumabonakude on TV [= ku-(u)-ma-bona-kude]
umabonakude telescope, binoculars; [ext] television [n1a-sg] (lit: allows to see far)
ma- let VERB, may it be so [hortative preverb]; had better VERB [implicative preverb]
bona see, behold; perceive; find [v-tr]
kude far off ~ away; [atr] distant, remote [adv-loc]

nokumamela and to listen [= na-uku-mamel-a]
noku- and to VERB; and VERBing [See: na- + uku-]
-**mamel**- listen [v-tr]

umculo music [n2-sg]
-**cul**- sing [v-intr]

wegosipile of the gospel [= wa-i-gosipile]
we- [combo]
wa- of [group 2 singular possessive agreement prefix]
igosipile gospel [n5-sg] {Eng}

onomdla whoever is interested [= o-na-um-dla] (lit: who has interest)
o- who [group 1, 1a singular relative, attributive agreement prefix]
umdla appetite, relish (for); delight (in); [ext] interest, enthusiasm [n2-sg]

afake he should enclose [v-pres-sub]
a- (and) he, she VERBs [group 1, 1a singular present subjunctive verb subject (S3a) agreement prefix]
-**fak**- put in, on, among ~ into; insert, enclose

yakhe his, her [pro-3sg-poss-n5-sg]

kwileta in the letter [n5-sg-loc = kw(a)-i-leta]
ileta letter [n5-sg] {Eng}

yokuqala of starting; [atr] beginning, first [= ya-uku-qal-a]
yoku- [combo of ya- + uku-]
-**qal**- begin, start, commence; do s.t. for the first time; do s.t. ahead of s.o. else; be the first (to do), take the lead, pioneer; start (a fight) [v-tr]

nam and I; and as for me [pro-1sg-conj = na-m(na)]
-**m** I; my, mine; my own [reduced absolutive pronoun/short possessive root; See: **mna**]

ndiya kwenza I will do
-**ya**- will ~ shall VERB [proposed ~ remote future positive preverb with structure: S1-ya-ku-Δ-a]

kwenza to do [short infinitive]
kw- [group 8 verbal noun object agreement prefix before vowel initial verb (other than o); Alt: **ku**-]

njalo so, thus, like that; in that way; the same [atr-root, adv]

abaseBhayi those who are from Port Elizabeth [= aba-s-e-(i)Bhayi]
aba- they who ... [pro-3-pl, relative, without an antecedent]
iBhayi Port Elizabeth, Algoa Bay [n5-sg-pn-loc]

bancede they should please

ba- they should VERB [group 1 ~ 1a plural present subjunctive verb subject (S3a) agreement prefix]
-nced- please [preverb with structure: **nceda** S3a Δ-**e** (used with second person forms and the present subjunctive)]

bangazihluphi they should not waste their time [neg pres sub]
S3a-**nga-**Δ-**i** (that) not VERB [negative present subjunctive verb construction]
-**zi**- VERB oneself [reflexive verb prefix]
-**hluph**- inconvenience; cause anxiety; waste s.o.'s time [v-tr]
-**zihluph**- trouble oneself; get anxious; waste one's own time [v-refl]
-**i** [negative present subjunctive verb suffix]

bandiphoxa they have made a fool of me
ba- they VERBed [group 1 ~ 1a plural past subjunctive verb subject (S3b) agreement prefix]
-**ndi**- me [obj]
-**phox**- shame, put to shame, make a fool of s.o.; deride, mock [v-tr]
-**a** [past subjunctive suf]

kwanele and it is enough
kw- [n10-loc impersonal construction]
ku- it is; one VERBs; they VERB [impersonal verb marker]
-**anel**- be enough (for); suffice
Cf: **ngokwaneleyo** enough [adv]

Part D

Ndifuna iqabanekazi eliza kuba ngumakoti, libe neminyaka esukela kuma-38 ukuya kuma-42. Ongemhle kodwa akhuthalele ukuba ngumama wekhaya, sinakane, sihambisane, sikhulisane, sithembane ngomsa kaThixo. Mna ndingumyeni opheleleyo kodwa oosisi bathi ndisathandana ngolwathando lwakudala. Bathi bafuna umntu onemali. Ndifuna umntu ozimisele ngothando lwenyaniso, namava nothando lwentliziyo nomoya.

Bongane Mashilwane, P.O. Box 391 Warrenton 8530

Vocabulary

eliza kuba who will become
za will ~ shall VERB; going to VERB [near future positive preverb]
kuba to be [reduced infinitive in future construction]
ku- [shortened form of infinitive prefix used in future constructions]
ngumakoti be my wife [n1a-sg copulative]
ngu- he, she, it is ... [group 1a singular copulative or predicative prefix construction]
umakoti my wife [n1a-sg-kin; pl: **oomakoti**]
libe who may be [relative + subjunctive]
li- (and) he, she, it VERBs [group 3 singular present subjunctive verb subject (S3a) agreement prefix]
esukela (years of age) which are/starting from
-**suk**- start (off); go away, leave; rise, get up, arise [v-intr]
-**sukel**- get up for; start from [v-ben]
kuma-38 from 38 (years)
ukuya to go to; going to; up to
-**ya** go (to), travel [v-intr]
ongemhle who (need) not be pretty
-**nge**- not [negative marker in relative constructions]
-**m**- [group 1, 1a singular adjective agreement prefix used predicatively]
-**hle** beautiful, pretty, elegant; good, fine, nice, pleasing [adj-root]
akhuthalele she should be hard-working [pres sub]
-**khuthal**- be active, industrious, diligent [v-st]
-**khuthalel**- be active for s.o.; be industrious, diligent, hard-working at s.t. [v-st-ben]
Cf: -**khuthele** was active; [atr] industrious, diligent, hard-working
ukuba as long as, so long as, provided that [conj marking the statement of a condition]
ngumama she is a mother [n1a-sg copulative]
umama (my) mother [n1a-sg]
wekhaya of the home [= wa-i-khaya]
wa- of [group 1, 1a singular possessive agreement prefix]
ikhaya home, (one's own) residence, domicile, abode [n3-sg]
sinakane we should meet [present subjunctive]
-**nakan**- glimpse, see from afar, have a distant view of s.t.; guess (at), form an idea of; get an inkling

of, begin to comprehend, perceive; understand a little [v-tr]
Contrast: -**nakan** accuse one another; get each other into trouble [v-recip]
Cf: -**nak**- accuse s.o. falsely; get s.o. into trouble [v-tr]
sihambisane and we would go out together [subjunctive]
-**hambis**- cause to go; walk; make s.o. move (on); forward; deliver; dispatch, send off; circulate; proceed with (a speech) [v-caus]
-**hambisan**- move forward together, make mutual progress [v-caus-recip]
sikhulisane and we would grow together [v-pres-sub]
-**khul**- grow (up), become big; increase [v-inch]
-**khulis**- cause to grow; raise, bring up; increase, magnify, make great; extol [v-caus]
-**khulisan**- cause each other to grow, nurture one another [v-caus-recip]
sithembane and we would rely on each other [present subjunctive]
-**themb**- expect, hope; trust, rely (on, upon) [v-tr]
-**themban**- trust one another, rely on each other [v-recip]
ngomsa in the love, with the affection [instrumental]
ngom- [combo form indicating that the instrumental preposition (nga-) is linked to n2-sg (um-)]
umsa love, affection, tenderness (of a mother) [n2-sg]
kaThixo of God [n1a-sg-poss]
ka- of [personal possessive prefix ~ marker for noun group 1a singular]
uThixo God [n1a-sg]
ndingumyeni I am a husband
ngum- he, she, it is ... [group 1 singular copulative or predicative prefix construction]
um- [group 1 (Bantu class 1) singular noun prefix]
umyeni husband, bridegroom; male relative (by marriage) [n1-sg]
opheleleyo who is perfect [v-perf-rel-atr = o-phel-el-e-yo]
-**phelel**- be complete, intact, perfect; be a virgin [v-ben]
-**phelele** perfect; complete, intact; fully; implicit [v-perf-atr]
-**e** (who) VERBed [short participial perfect/recent past relative tense suffix]
oosisi women [n1a-pl, term of respect or endearment]
usisi woman; sister [term of respect for a girl or woman older than oneself; term of endearment used by elders for a female of any age]
bathi they say
ndisathandana I still fall in love (in an old fashioned way – see below)
-**sa**- still; [neg] no longer [progressive aspect preverb]
-**thand**- love, like; adore [v-tr]
-**thandan**- be in love with, fall in love with [v-recip]
ngolwathando by means of that love [instrumental = nga-oluya-thand-o] (agreeing with **lwakudala**)]
nga- by [instrumental]
oluya- that [deic-3-n6-sg]
uthando love [n6-sg-abs; no plural]
lwakudala old-fashioned [n6-sg-atr-poss]
lwa- of [group 6 singular possessive agreement prefix]
-**kudala** old-fashioned; [adv] of old; long ago [atr using possessive agreement markers]
-**dala** old, aged, adult; senior; eldest; stale [adj-root]
bafuna they want

umntu person, individual, human being; [pro] someone, somebody [n1-sg; pl: **abantu**]

onemali who has money [= o-na-i-mali]

ne- [combo form indicating that the possessive verb (na-) has a n5-sg object (i-)]

imali money, coin, cash, currency; price, value [n5-sg]

ozimisele who is serious [= o-zi-m-is-el-e]

-**zimisele** sincere, serious [v-refl-perf-atr]

-**ma** stand, be standing; stop; wait; live, inhabit, dwell, occupy [v-st]

-**mis**- make stand; institute, set up, erect; establish, ordain; appoint (to a position); restore, make restitution; stop (a vehicle) [v-caus]

-**misel**- set up, establish; appoint s.o. for/to (a position); restore, compensate for; substantiate [v-ben]

ngothando about love [= nga-u-thand-o]

ngo- [combo form indicating that the relational preposition (**nga**-) is linked to n6-sg (**u**-)]

nga- about, over, concerning, regarding [prep relational or topical]

lwenyaniso of the truth

lwe- [combo indicating that a n5-sg (i-) is possessed by a n6-sg (lwa-)]

inyaniso truth [n5-sg]

-**nyanis**- speak the truth; be true; be sincere (in speech), correct, upright (in conduct) [v-intr]

namava and experience [n3-pl-conj = na-(a)ma-va]

amava impressions; convictions; [col] experience [n3-pl]

-**va** perceive by sense: hear, taste, feel; understand; obey; be vigorous ~ fruitful [v-ir; latent root -**iva**]

iliva thorn; [ext] impression, s.t. felt; conviction [n3-sg]

Cf: **ameva** thorns [n3-pl-ir]

nothando and the love [= na-u-thand-o]

no- and [combo form indicating that the conjunctive prefix (**na**-) is linked to a noun prefixed with the article **u**-]

lwentliziyo of the heart [= lwa-i-ntliziyo]

intliziyo heart (the organ, or in a moral sense); [ext] mind, disposition, feeling; conscience [n5-sg]

Cf: **iphaphu** heart, liver, lungs (of an animal) [n3-sg]

nomoya and soul [= na-um-oya]

nom- [combo form indicating that the conjunctive (na-) is linked to a n2-sg (um-)]

umoya air; wind; the atmosphere; breath; spirit, soul [n2-sg]

Bongane (personal name)

Mashilwane (family name)

Warrenton (town in Northern Cape Province)

Umbulelo

Umzi wakwa-Mabhele KwaMasele wenza umbulelo kubo bonke abathe baza kulilisana nabo xa bebe kwilifu elimnyama lokushiywa ngutata wekhaya u-J.D. Mabhele, ngakumbi aba NoBible, Mrs. Mnamata, Magingxa, Xayiya, Sonjani, Gwayi, noTokoyi. Sithi nangomso zihlobo. Sikhutshwa ngu-Lottie Mabhele, uNoBible nosapho KwaMasele.

This is a thank-you note from the wife of the deceased especially addressed to fellow "NoBible." The **NoBible** are usually older women in a church who join a guild and wear the uniform of that particular church—this uniform is different depending on the religion. In South Africa they are called NoBible (lit: mother of the Bible), not so much because they study the Bible, but because they are always seen carrying a Bible on their way to church, a funeral, a wake, etc.

Vocabulary

umbulelo thank you; thanks, gratitude, thankfulness [n2-sg]
 -**bul**- confess, admit [v-intr]
 -**bulel**- admit an obligation to; be grateful, give thanks to ~ for [v-ben]
umzi home (institution), household; extended family; homestead, group of huts belonging to a single owner; village; kraal; [ext] tribe, nation, people [n2-sg]
wakwa-Mabhele of the Mabhele family
 Mabhele (family name)
kwaMasele from ~ of Masele
 Masele (town, village of that name)
wenza it is making
 w- him, her ~ it [group 2 singular short object form before vowel initial verb]
kubo with, to, from them [n1-pl-pro-loc]
bonke all; every [pro-enum-n1-pl]
 b- [class 1 plural thematic consonant prefix]
abathe who said
 aba- they who [group 1, 1a plural relative, attributive agreement prefix]
 -**the** said [v-tr-irreg-past of **thi**]
 -**thi** say, mean, think [v-tr-irreg]
baza kulilisana they would share in the mourning
S1-**za ku**-Δ-**a** will VERB; going to VERB [near future positive preverb]
baza they will
 ba- they [group 1, 1a plural subject (S1) agreement prefix]
 -**za**- will ~ shall VERB; going to VERB [near future positive preverb]
kulilisana to make each other cry
 -**lil**- cry, weep, shed tears; mourn; crow (of rooster); ring (of bell) [v-intr]
 -**lilis**- make s.o. cry, cause to weep; ring (a bell) [v-caus]
 -**lilisan**- make each other cry, cause one another to mourn [v-caus-recip]
nabo with them
 na- with, together with, accompanied by [comitative]
xa when, whenever; while, as [temporal conj]

bebe they were being [class 1 plural recent past participial predicative]
-be was being [past participial form of predicative verb **ba** 'to be']
kwilifu in the cloud [= kw(a)-ili-fu]
ili- [group 3 (Bantu class 5) singular noun prefix]
ilifu cloud [n3-sg]
elimnyama which is dark
-mnyama black; dark [atr-root]
lokushiywa of being left by [= la-uku-shiy-w-a]
loku- [n3-sg poss n8 vn combo]
la- of [group 3 singular possessive agreement prefix]
-shiy- leave (behind), abandon, forsake, desert; omit, leave out
ngutata by father
utata father, my father [n1a-sg-kin]
u-J.D. Mabhele (name)
u- [group 1 ~ 1a singular relative ~ attributive agreement prefix used predicatively]
ngakumbi all the more, especially [adv]
nga- -ly [adverb-forming prefix]
-mbi other, some other, another (of a different kind); [neg] no other [enum-pro-root]
aba NoBible these Bible Holders
aba these [deic-1-n1-pl]
(zero) [group 1a plural reduced noun prefix]
uNoBible Bible Holder (female helper associated with a church) [n1a-sg]
uno- (lit: mother of) [noun forming prefix; reduction of **unina wo**–, a female personifying prefix, even if the noun so formed may have a masculine meaning]
Mnamata (family name)
Magingxa (name)
Xayiya (name)
Sonjani (name)
Gwayi (name)
noTokoyi and Tokoyi
uTokoyi (name)
sithi we say (like Eng. let's say)
si- we [pro-1pl-S1]
nangomso even tomorrow
na- equates to Eng. even
ngomso tomorrow
zihlobo friends, buddies [n4-pl-red]
zi- they are [group 4 plural relative or attributive agreement prefix used predicatively]
isihlobo friend, buddy [n4-sg]
sikhutshwa [= si-khuph/tsh-w-a]
si- it is Cf: **S'ithi** it is we...
-khutshwa be taken out, withdrawn [v-pass]
CHANGE of **ph** to **tsh**
-khuph- take out, withdraw; send out [v-tr]
ngu-Lottie by Lottie
nosapho and family [= na-u-sapho]
usapho family; offspring [n6-sg; pl: **iintsapho**]

Ukusetyenziwa Kwamayeza

• Imiyalelo yifunde ngocoselelo usele (okanye useze) ngokwemiyalelo.

• Sela iyeza elilungiselelwe wena - musa ukulipha abanye okanye usele awabanye.

• Xa ulunyukiswa ngokungaseli, ungaqhubi okanye usebenzise umatshini, xa usebenzisa iyeza elithile, wuthobele lo myalelo. Ukungawuthobeli kunokukufak' engozini.

• Xa ukhulelwe, mbuze ugqirha wakho phambi kokuba usele naliphi na iyeza angakunikanga lona.

• Watshixele amayeza.

> Be aware of what may be called NEGATIVE CARRYOVER in this selection. There are two instances where a negative in the first clause is to be implied in the second, although the verb in the second is in the positive (not negative) mood. While this construction is just like that of English and offers no problems in translation, one must remember this when translating into Xhosa. Thus: **musa ukulipha abanye okanye usele awabanye** 'don't give/refrain from giving it to others or take that of others;' **ungaqhubi okanye usebenzise umatshini** 'you should not drive or operate [lit: use] machinery'

Vocabulary

ukusetyenziwa usage [= uku-/ty-sebenz+i-w-a] (lit: to be used)
- **uku-** **-a** to VERB; VERBing [positive infinitive ~ gerund verb construction]
- **sebenz-** work, labor (at); operate; use [v-tr]
- **+i-** addition of vowel to break up a consonant cluster (Not given in most dictionaries, but fairly common practice)

kwamayeza of medicines [n3-pl-poss = kwa-(a)ma-yeza]
- **kwama-** [combo form indicating that n3 pl (**ama-**) is possessed by a n8 vn (**kwa-**)]
- **kwa-** of [group 8 verbal noun possessive agreement prefix]
- **amayeza** medicines [n3-pl; sg: **iyeza** BELOW]

imiyalelo directions [n2-pl = imi-yal-el-o]
- **umyalelo** instruction, direction [n2-sg]
- **-yal-** instruct (a novice in his duties), exhort, admonish, warn, charge, command [v-tr]
- **-yalel-** direct, instruct, order [v-tr]

yifunde read them [v-obj-imp = yi-fund-e]
- **-yi-** [group 2 plural object agreement prefix]
- **-e** VERB it! [positive object-oriented imperative singular verb suffix]

ngocoselelo with care; [adv] carefully [n6-sg-instr = nga-u-coselel-o]
- **ngo-** [combo form indicating that the instrumental preposition **nga-** is linked to n6-sg **u-**]

ucoselelo carefulness, close attention, interest [n6-sg]
-**coselel**- attend to closely, take interest in [v-tr]

usele you should drink [v-pres-sub]
u- (that) you (singular = thou) VERB [S3a present subjunctive subject pronoun]
-**sel**- drink (s.t. cold); take (medicine) [v-tr; See: **andiseli** in R4a, R4c]

Note use of -**e** [subjunctive] in sequence of commands

useze you should give it to s.o. to drink [v-pres-sub]
-**sez**- give s.o. s.t. to drink; make drink; water; drench [v-tr; irregular causative of -**sela**]

ngokwemiyalelo according to the directions [= ngokwa-imi-yal-el-o]
ngokwa- according to (lit: through that of; usually results in an adverb of manner)

sela take! [v-imp-sg]
-**a** do VERB! [positive imperative singular verb suffix with structure: #-Δ-a]

iyeza medicine [n3-sg]

elilungiselelwe which is right for [= eli-lung-is-elel-w-e]
-**lungis**- make right, good, suitable, ready; outfit, fit out; repair, mend; do the right thing; [ext] reward s.o. [v-caus]
-**elel**- do VERB to, for, on behalf of [double benefactive verb compound suffix]
Contrast: -**elel**- do VERB completely, thoroughly, efficiently ~ well [perfective ~ intensive verb suffix]
-**lungiselel**- make s.t. right for s.o.; transact s.t. for another; do service to [v-diben]
-**we** was/were VERBed [short form passive past verb suffix]
-**e** VERBed [short indicative perfect ~ recent past tense suffix]

wena you; yourself [pro-2sg-abs]

musa ukulipha don't give it!
musa uku-**Δ-a** do not VERB!, stop or refrain from VERBing [negative imperative singular]
-**li**- [group 3 singular object agreement prefix]
-**pha** give s.t. to s.o., present to, bestow upon [v-tr]

abanye others [adj-num-n1-pl]

Contrast: -**mbi** (another of a different kind) in S5

awabanye that of others
awaba- [combo form showing that n1-pl (**abanye**) is possessed by a n3-pl (**amayeza**)]

ulunyukiswa you are warned [= u-lumk/nyu-is-w-a]
u- you [S2]
-**lumk**- be prudent, careful, wary; take care [v-st]
-**lumkis**- make s.o. prudent, careful, wise; instruct, teach a lesson to; warn; [fig] take advantage of, cheat [v-caus]
CHANGE of **m** to **nyu** (because **m** is syllabic, i.e., **u** is latent)
-**lunyukisw**- be warned; get instructed [v-pass]

ngokungaseli about not drinking [inf-neg-relat = nga-uku-nga-sel-i]
ukunga- -**i** not to VERB; not VERBing [negative infinitive ~ gerund verb construction]
-**i** not to VERB; not VERBing [negative infinitive ~ gerund verb suffix]

ungaqhubi you should not drive [v-sub-neg-pres = u-nga-qhub-i]
-**qhub**- drive (animal ~ vehicle); push on with; operate, move s.t. along; press, urge, exhort; make steady progress [v-tr; See: **nenkqubela** in R3]

usebenzise and you should (not) operate [v-pres-sub denoting sequence]

-**sebenzis**- make s.o./s.t. work; employ, give work to; use, utilize, make use of; apply, make work; operate s.t. [v-caus]

umatshini machine [n1a-sg] {Eng}

usebenzisa you use

elithile a particular [atr-n3-sg]
-**thile** certain, particular; some [atr-root]

wuthobele obey it! [object-oriented imperative]
wu- [group 2 singular object agreement prefix agreeing with **umyalelo** BELOW]
-**thob**- bend, bow, stoop down [v-st]; depress, lower [v-tr]
-**thobel**- bow to/under; submit to; obey [v-ben]

lo this [deic-1-n2-sg]

myalelo instruction, direction [n2-sg-red – a noun following a deictic is in its REDUCED form, i.e., without the initial vowel article]
m- [group 2 singular reduced noun prefix]

ukungawuthobeli not obeying it [neg-inf = uku-nga-wu-thob-el-i]

kunokukufak' it can put you [v-abil = ku-noku-ku-fak(a); Note: ELISION of final vowel of verb before a word beginning with a vowel]
ku- he, she, it [n8-vn subject (S1) agreement prefix]
-**ku**- you (thee) [pro-2sg obj]

engozini in danger [e-(i)-ngoz(i)-ini]
ingozi danger, peril, risk; accident, misfortune; injury [n5-sg]
-**ini** at, in, to [loc suf used in conjunction with **e**- prefix on nouns that end in -**i** or -**u**]
Cf: **ubungozi** misfortune; peril, state of danger [n7-sg]

xa ukhulelwe if you are pregnant [= u-khul-el-w-e]
-**khulel**- grow up in a certain place; grow up with/among s.o.; become large for; [ext] be too big/strong for s.o. [v-ben]
-**khulelw**- be full of, get filled with s.t.; be big with; [fig] be pregnant [v-pass-ben]
See: **sikhulisane** in S4d

mbuze ask him! [v-imp-obj]
-**buz**- ask, question, enquire, interrogate; examine, investigate [v-tr]

ugqirha doctor [n1a-sg; pl: **oogqirha** – see R3]

wakho your [pro-2sg-poss-n2-sg]

phambi kokuba before [conj-expr followed by present subjunctive (no matter what mood or tense of the main verb)]

phambi ahead, in front (of) [adv spatial]; before [adv temporal]
ko- of [personal possessive prefix/marker for locative noun group 10]
kuba being [n8-vn red of **ukuba**]

naliphina whatever, whichever [pro-indef-n3-sg]
liphi which (one)? [qw-n3-sg]

na is it? [question particle put after a verb or another question word]

angakunikanga which he did not give you [= a-nga-ku-nik-anga]
-**nik**- give, hand s.t. to s.o.; deliver; bestow upon [v-tr]
-**anga** did not VERB, have not VERBed [neg perfect verb suffix]

lona he, she, it [n3-sg absolutive pronoun]

watshixele lock them up!
-**wa**- them [n3-pl object]
-**tshix**- lock, bolt, bar; turn the key [v-tr]
-**tshixel**- lock s.t. up in; turn the key on [v-ben]

Uyafuna ukutyeba?

Fundela ubuxhwele ngembalelwano

Izifundo zethu zilula ungazilandela nokuba akufundanga kuyaphi. Izifundo zethu zibhalwe ngesiXhosa, isiSuthu, isiNgesi nesiZulu. Ebomini akukho msebenzi unokukutyebisa njengobuxhwele.

Xa sele uligqirha okanye ixhwele singakufumanisa icertificate sokuba lilungu lombutho wamagqirha namaxhwele. Ukufumana inkcazelo epheleleyo kunye nezifundo zakho zokuqala, thumela i-R80.00 ngeRegister kule Address.

A.H.C.C. P.O. Box 254, Butterworth 4960.

Vocabulary

uyafuna do you want?
 u- you [pro-2sg-S1]
 See: **khawutsho** in R3
 -**ya**- does VERB, is/are VERBing [long present verb prefix with structure S1-ya-Δ-a]
 -**funa uku**- want to VERB, like VERBing [v-aux followed by inf when the subject of both clauses is the same]
ukutyeba to become rich [v-inf]
 -**tyeb**- be fat; be ~ become rich; be valuable [v-inch]
fundela learn for/at, study about [v-ben]
ubuxhwele herbal medicine; state of being a herbalist or medicine man [n7-sg]
 See: **ixhwele** BELOW
ngembalelwano by correspondence [= nga-im-bhal-el-w-an-o] (lit: by each other being written to)
 ngem- [combo indicating that the instrumental preposition (**nga**-) is linked to n5-sg (**im**-)]
 nga- with, through, by means of [instrumental]
 im- [group 5 (Bantu class 9) singular noun prefix]
 imbalelwano correspondence [n5-sg]
 -**bhal**- mark, make a mark; write [v-tr]
 Cf: -**bhalelan**- correspond with, write to one another [v-recip]
 CHANGE of **bh** to **b**
izifundo lessons [n4-pl]
 isifundo lesson; lecture [n4-sg]
zethu our [pro-1pl-poss-n4-pl]
zilula they are easy [atr-n4-pl]
 zi- they are/which are [group 4 plural relative 2 construction, attributive agreement prefix used predicatively]
 -**lula** light; easy [atr-root]
ungazilandela you can follow them [v-pot-pres = u-nga-zi-land-el-a]
 u- you can VERB; you may VERB [second person singular potential/conditional verb subject (S4) agreement pronoun]
 -**zi**- them [group 4 plural object agreement prefix]
 -**land**- follow (by scent), track, trace, pursue, follow up [v-tr]
 -**landel**- follow up, go/come after, chase, pursue; be after, come next [v-ben]

akufundanga you have not studied
aku- you not VERB [second person singular negative subject prefix]
kuyaphi to any point; anywhere; [ext atr] at all
ku- [loc] // [impers]
-**ya**- do VERB [factitive auxiliary]
-**phi** any [pro-indef-root]
Cf: -**phi** which? [qw-enum-root]
zibhalwe they were written [= zi-bhal-w-e]
zi- [n4-pl-S1]
isiSuthu Sotho (language) [n4-sg; known as **Sesotho**]
isiNgesi English [n4-sg]
nesiZulu and Zulu
nesi- [combo indicating that the conjunctive (**na**-) is linked to a n4-sg (**isi**-)]
isiZulu Zulu (language) [n4-sg]
ebomini in life [n7-sg-loc = e-(u)b-om(i)-ini]
ubomi life [n7-sg-abs]
akukho there is none [v-exis-neg-n10-impers]
aku- there is no VERBing [neg-pres-n10-loc-prf]
-**kho** exist, be present [v-exis]
msebenzi work, occupation [n2-sg-red; REDUCED NOUN FORM in negative clauses]
umsebenzi work, job, employment; labor, task; duty; trade, occupation; use, service [n2-sg]
unokukutyebisa which can make you rich [v-pot-pres]
u- [n2-sg relative 2 construction, attributive agreement prefix used predicatively]
noku- can ~ could VERB, be able ~ willing to VERB
-**ku**- you [pro-2sg-obj]
-**tyebis**- fatten, cause to become fat; enrich, make s.o. rich [v-caus]
njengobuxhwele like a medicine man, such as being a herbalist
njenga- as, like, such as [comparative conj prefix]
xa sele whenever, at such time that [conj-expr followed by a participial construction] (lit: when already)
sele already [v-aux-perf followed by S2 + participial]
uligqirha you being a witch doctor
u- you (singular = thou) VERB-ing [S2 participial subject]
li- he, she, it is ... [group 3 singular copulative ~ predicative prefix construction on polysyllabic roots]
igqirha witch doctor, medicine man [n3-sg]
ixhwele herbalist, medicine man [n3-sg]
Cf: **ixhwele** ankle joint, foot and ankle, fetlock [n3-sg]
singakufumanisa we can help you get [= si-nga-ku-fuman-is-a]
si- we can VERB; we may VERB [first person plural potential/conditional verb subject (S4) agreement pronoun]
-**ku**- you [pro-2sg-obj]
-**fuman**- find; get [v-tr]
-**fumanis**- make s.o. get s.t.; help s.o. to find [v-caus]
icertificate certificate (isatifiketi) [n4-sg] {Eng}
sokuba of that, of being
soku- of [combo indicating that n8 vn (**uku**-) is possessed by n4-sg (**sa**-)]
sa- of [group 4 singular possessive agreement prefix]
lilungu be a member [n3-sg-pred]
ilungu joint (of body); node (of plant), knot; member (of a group); [fig] genitals [n3-sg]
lombutho of the association [n2-sg-poss]
lom- of [combo form indicating that n2-sg (**um**-) is possessed by a n3-sg (**la**-)]

umbutho assembly, gathering; organization, society, association [n2-sg]
wamagqirha of witch doctors
wama- [combo form indicating that n3 pl (**ama**-) is possessed by a n2-sg (**wa**-)]
amagqirha doctors, witch doctors, medicine men [n3-pl]
namaxhwele and herbalists [n3-pl-conj]
amaxhwele herbalists, medicine men [n3-pl]
ukufumana to get, to find [v-inf]
inkcazelo explanation [n5-sg]
Zulu spelling: **incazelo** [Dent & Nybembezi:419]
-**chaz**- comb; straighten out, unravel; make incisions in the skin, scarify; [ext] explain [v-tr]
-**chazel**- unravel ~ straighten s.t. out for s.o; [ext] explain s.t. to s.o. [v-ben]
CHANGE of **ch** to **kc**
epheleleyo which is complete [v-perf-rel = e-phelel-e-yo]
See: **opheleleyo** in R4d
-**phel**- stop, cease, finish, come to an end, terminate [v-intr]
-**phelel**- be complete ~ intact; be a virgin [v-ben]
-**phelele** perfect; complete, intact; implicit [v-perf]
kunye na- and, as well as, together with [conj-expr]
Cf: kwanootitshala in R3
nezifundo and lessons [n4-pl-conj = na-izi-fund-o]
nezi- [combo indicating that the conjunctive (**na**-) is linked to a n4 pl (**izi**-)]
zakho your, yours; thy; your own [pro-2sg-poss-n4-pl]
zokuqala first [n8-vn-poss-n4-pl]
zoku- [combo indicating that n8 vn (**uku**-) is possessed by n4 pl (**za**-)]
i-R80.00 80 rand
R rand (unit of South African currency) [abr]
ngeRegister by registered mail [n5-sg-instr = nga-i-Register] {Eng}
kule at, on, to this [deic-n5-sg]
Butterworth (coastal town)

Ispicy Lamb Sishebo

30 ml yeoyile
500 g yelamb chops okanye iiknuckles
2 amatswele, anqunqwe
2 iitumato, zinqunqwe
3 iminqathe, ichutywe isikwe ibe zizangqa
2 iitapile, zisikwe
250 ml yechopped green beans
60 ml yeJikelele Sishebo Mix with Rajah
250 ml yamanzi

Yenza shushu ioyile, qhotsa inyama ibe nombala omdaka. Galela itswele, liqhotse de lithambe. Galela iitumato, iminqathe, iitapile neegreen beans. Galela iJikelele Sishebo Mix namanzi. Ntyontyisa kwisitovu esikubushushu obuphantsi ama-45 emizuzu ukuya kwiyure okanye de inyama ithambe. Baphe nerayisi, umngqusho okanye umqa.

Recipes tend to follow the structure and often the word order of English, thus **2 amatswele**, rather than **amatswele amabini**, etc. When numbers are borrowed into Xhosa, they are often inconsistently assigned among several classes, thus u100 [n1a-sg], i100 [n5-sg], or i100 [n3-sg]. Note that they are treated as singular even if they clearly designate more than one. In this article, most of the numerals are in group 5 singular, hence the agreement 500 g yelamb chops, 250 ml yechopped green beans, 250 ml yamanzi. The one exception is **ama-45 emizuzu**, where **ama-** refers to numerals above twenty (see R4a).

Vocabulary

iSpicy Lamb Sishebo Spicy Lamb Mix {Eng}
sishebo flavoring, mix [n4-sg-red] {Zulu}
Cf: **isishebo** {Zulu} mixed meal, mixed grill < **-sheb-** 'eat a mixed meal; flavor (with sauce, etc.)'
30 ml 30 milliliters {Eng abr} [the phrase is here interpreted as **i-** n5-sg]
30 (amashumi amathathu)

Cf: **ilitere** liter [n5-sg]
yeoyile of oil
ye- of [combo form indicating that n5-sg (**i**-) is possessed by a n5-sg (**ya**- NUMERAL)]
ioyile oil [n5-sg; Alt: **ioli**]
500 (amakhulu amahlanu)
g gram {Eng abr }
Cf: **igraam** gram [n5-sg]
yelamb chops of lamb chops {Eng}
iiknuckles knuckles [n5-pl] {Eng}
ii- [group 5 (Bantu class 10) plural noun prefix]
2 (properly amatswele amabini; rw: **-bini**)
amatswele onions [n3-pl]
See: **itswele** BELOW
anqunqwe they should be chopped [v-pres-sub = a-nqunq-w-e]
a- they [n3-pl S3a]
-**nqunq**- chop (up), mince, dice, cut fine; chop (firewood) [v-tr]
2 (properly iitumato ezimbini)
iitumato tomatoes [n5-pl] {Eng}
zinqunqwe they should be chopped [v-pres-sub = zi-nqunq-w-e]
zi- (and) they VERB [group 5 plural present subjunctive verb subject (S3a) agreement prefix]
3 (properly iminqathe emithathu; rw: **-thathu**)
iminqathe carrots [n2-pl]
umnqathe wild carrot [n2-sg]
ichutywe they should be peeled [v-pres-sub = i-chub/ty-w-e]
i- (and) they VERB [group 2 plural present subjunctive verb subject (S3a) agreement prefix]
-**chub**- peel, pick (grains off a corn cob), pick out (kernel of a nut); [fig] select the best (of s.t.); [ext] train, civilize [v-tr]
isikwe they should be cut [pres-sub = i-sik-w-e]
-**sik**- cut (off/out); supplant; [ext] kill, murder
ibe they should be; that they be; that they might become [n2-pl-S3a v-pred-pres-sub]
-**be** that [S3a] be; that it (should) become [v-pred-pres-sub]
zizangqa they are circles [n4-pl-pred = ziz(i)-angqa]
zizi- they are ... [group 4 plural copulative ~ predicative prefix construction]
LOSS of final vowel of prefix before vowel-initial root
isangqa circle; halo [n4-sg]
2 (properly iitapile ezimbini; rw: -**bini**)
iitapile potatoes [n5-pl] {Afr}
zisikwe they should be cut [pres-sub = zi-sik-w-e]
250 ml 250 milliliters {Eng abr} [interpreted as **i**- n5-sg]
yechopped green beans of chopped green beans {Eng}
60 ml 60 milliliters {Eng abr} [interpreted as **i**- n5-sg]
yeJikelele Sishebo Mix of Jikelele Sishebo Mix
Cf: **jikelele** [atr] all around, universal; [adv] universally
Rajah curry powder (brand)
yamanzi of water [n3-pl-poss-n5-sg = ya-(a)manzi]
amanzi water; [atr] wet, damp, moist [n3-pl-mass; no singular]
yenza make! [v-imp = y-enz-a]
y-Δ-a do VERB! [positive imperative singular verb construction, on vowel-initial verb stems and latent-I monosyllabic stems]
shushu warm, hot [atr-root]
qhotsa fry [v-imp]
-**qhots**- cook s.t. dry; bake; fry [v-tr]
ibe na- it should have [n5-sg-S3a v-poss-pres-sub]

ibe it should be/become [n5-sg-S3a v-pred-pres-sub]
i- (and) he, she, it VERBs [n5-sg present subjunctive verb subject (S3a) agreement prefix]
nombala have a color [v-poss-n2-sg-obj = na-um-bala]
nom- [combo form indicating that the possessive verb (**na**-) has a n2-sg object (**um**-)]
umbala color [n2-sg]
omdaka which is dark brown [rel1]
o- [group 2 singular relative, attributive agreement prefix]
-**mdaka** dirty, unclean, untidy, muddy; dun, mud-colored, dark earth brown; dark (of color); [fig] evil [atr-root]
galela mix in [v-ben-imp]
-**gal**- pour [v-tr] {archaic}
-**galel**- pour out; mix in; join with; throw stones at; attack [v-ben]
itswele onion [n3-sg]
liqhotse fry it! [v-obj-imp]
li- [group 3 singular object agreement prefix]
de until VERB [v-aux; perf of **da**; takes present subjunctive complement]
lithambe it should become soft [v-pres-sub = li-thamb-e]
li- (and) he, she, it VERBs [n3-sg present subjunctive verb subject (S3a) agreement prefix]
-**thamb**- soften, become soft, supple, pliant, tender; be tame, civilized; be gentle [v-inch]
neegreen beans and green beans {Eng}
nee- [combo form indicating that the conjunctive prefix **na**- is linked to n5-pl **ii**-]
iJikelele Sishebo Mix (brand name)
namanzi with water
ntyontyisa simmer [v-imp]
-**ntyonty**- whistle continuously [v-intr]
-**ntyontyis**- do s.t. for a while, do for a long time, prolong; simmer [v-caus]
kwisitovu on the stove [= ku/w-isi-tovu]
kw- in, among [alternate form of the specific locative prefix before the vowels **e** and **i**]
isitovu stove [n4-sg] {Afr, Eng}
esikubushushu which is at a temperature
esi- which is [n4-sg relative 1, attributive agreement prefix]
ku- in, on, among [specific loc for noun groups 2 and above]
ubushushu heat; temperature [n7-sg-abs]
obuphantsi which is low
obu- [n7-sg relative prefix]
ama-45 [See: **engama-20** in R4a for numbers from 20 upwards]
emizuzu of minutes
umzuzu a while, short time; brief space; minute (60 seconds) [n2-sg; pl: **imizuzu**]
ukuya going to; up to, until
-**ya** go (to), travel [v-intr]
kwiyure to an hour [= ku/w-i-yure]
iyure hour [n5-sg] {Afr uur}
ithambe it should become tender [v-pres-sub]
baphe serve them! [v-obj-imp]
ba- [n1-pl-obj]
-**pha** give s.t. to s.o.; serve (food to) [v-ditr]
nerayisi with rice [n5-sg-comit = na-i-rayisi]
ne- [combo form for **na**- linked to a noun prefixed with the article **i**-]
irayisi rice [n5-sg] {Afr rijs, Eng rice}
umngqusho corn meal, mush, pulverized maize [n2-sg]
umqa porridge, mush; Kaffir-corn porridge [n2-sg]

Abantwana Basetyenziswa Ekunyuseni Ingxowa-mali

Ndikhathazwa kokwenziwa zizikolo zamabanga aphantsi ngegama lokuba zinyusa ingxowa-mali yazo. Abantwana bethu bathunywa ezitratweni nasemakhayeni ukuba bayongqiba imali. Abazi ukuba abantwana bethu babachanaba enini? Izidlwengu nabantu ababaphatha kakubi abantwana baxhaphakile kule mihla, kufana nje nokuphosa igusha kwiingonyama. Oku kuthetha ukuba umntwana wam kufuneka athembele nakuwuphi na umntu angamaziyo! Zinqununu neetitshala khanisebenzisane nathi -- abantwana bethu babalulekile, masibakhusele. Masizame eny'indlela yokunyusa imali yezikolo.

nguL.S., eZimbabwe

Vocabulary

basetyenziswa they are being used [= ba-sebenz/ty-is-w-a]
Note: while this is perhaps homographic with the narrative past form, modern journalese uses a present tense form in headlines.
ba- they [n1-pl-S1]
-**setyenzisw**- be used [v-caus-pass]
-**sebenz**- work, labor (at); operate; use [with **nga**-] [v-tr]
CHANGE of **b** > **ty** because of following velar labial -**w**- (palatalization)

ekunyuseni in raising [n8-vn-loc = e-(u)ku-nyus(a)-eni]
ukunyusa raising [n8-vn]
CHANGE/LOSS of initial vowel of agreement concord after **e**- (locative prefix)
-**nyus**- raise, rise [v-caus]
-**nyuk**- ascend, go up ~ higher [v-intr]
-**s**- make VERB, cause to VERB [causative verb suffix on verbs ending in -**k**-]
CHANGE/LOSS of -**a** ~ -**e** before suffix -**eni**

ingxowa-mali money bag; fund (for a special purpose)
ingxowa bag, sack, case [n5-sg]
CHANGE of **n** to velar place of articulation

ndikhathazwa I am troubled [v-pass = ndi-khatha(l)-z-w-a]
-**khathaz**- bother, perturb; hinder; trouble, pester [v-tr]
-**khathal**- be troubled, vexed, anxious [v-st]
-**z**- make VERB, cause to VERB [causative verb suffix on verbs ending in -la]
-**khathazw**- be bothered, troubled, perturbed [v-pass]

kokwenziwa on account of being made [v-pass = **-uku-enz+i-w-a**]
kokw- = kwa- [loc]
CHANGE of **u** > **w**
-**enziw**- be made; be done [v-pass]

zizikolo by schools [n4-pl-agent = zizi-kolo]
zizi- by (done/produced by) them [marker of group 4 plural agent of passive verb]
izikolo schools [n4-pl]

isikolo school; mission station [n4-sg]
zamabanga of grades [n3-pl-poss-n4-pl = za-(a)ma-banga]
zama- [combo form indicating that n3 pl (**ama**-) is possessed by a n4 pl (**za**-)
za- of [group 4 plural possessive agreement prefix]
amabanga grades (school levels) [n3-pl]
ibanga interval, space; grade (in school); step, pace; ground, reason [n3-sg]
ngegama in the name, using the name [n3-sg-instr = nga-i-gama]
nge- [combo form indicating that the instrumental preposition (**nga**-) is linked to n3-sg (**i**-)]
igama name; kind, sort; letter (of the alphabet); word {ling} [n3-sg]
lokuba of that [= la-uku-ba]
loku- [combo]
la- of [group 3 singular possessive agreement prefix]
ukuba that [complementizer; statement of situation followed by participial]
zinyusa they raising [= zi-nyusa]
zi- [n4-pl-S2 (situational clause) agreeing with **izikolo**]
yazo for them; their; of them [n4-pl-poss-n5-sg]
-**zo** they; their [group 4 plural reduced root]
bethu our [pro-poss-n1-pl]
bathunywa they are sent [v-pass-pres = ba-thum/ny-w-a]
-**thunyw**- be sent [v-pass]
CHANGE of **m** to **ny** before **w** [passive]
ezitratweni on the streets [n4-pl-loc = e-(i)zi-trato/w-eni]
izitrato streets [n4-pl]
nasemakhayeni and to homes [n3-pl-conj-loc = na-s-e-(a)ma-khay(a)-eni]
amakhaya homes, residences [n3-pl; See: **wekhaya** in R4d]
ukuba so that [conj; statement of fact followed by indicative]
bayongqiba they will beg for it [= ba-y-o-ngqib-a]
-**y**- it [group 5 singular short object form before vowel initial verb]
-**o**- will VERB [contracted/short future prefix]
-**ngqib**- beg (s.t. from s.o.); ask alms (of s.o.); sponge (off s.o.) [v-tr]
abazi they do not know [= ab(a)-azi]
ab- they do not VERB [group 1 plural negative present subject prefix before vowel-initial verb]
-**azi** know, know how to, be versed in; understand; be aware of; be acquainted with; be conscious of; [fig] be guilty of [v-tr-ir]
babachanaba they are exposing them
-**chanab**- expose (s.o. to great heat, public view) [v-tr]
enini to what (kind)? [qw-loc = e-n(i)-ini]
ni what (kind)?, of what sort? [qw-adj-root]
Contrast: -**nini** when? [qw-adv]
izidlwengu rapists [n4-pl]
-**dlwengul**- treat with violence; rape, ravish, violate [v-tr]
isidlwengu violent person, rapist, ravisher [n4-sg]
nabantu and people [n1-pl-conj]
ababaphatha who handle them [v-pres-rel]
aba- who [n1-pl-rel]
-**phath**- touch, handle, treat [v-tr]
kakubi badly, poorly, abusively [adv]
kaku- -ly [limited adverb-forming prefix on roots -**bi** and -**hle**]
ka- -ly [adverb-forming prefix]

ku- [impers]
-**bi** bad, evil, ugly [adj-root]

baxhaphakile they are all over the place [v-st-perf = ba-xhaph-ak-ile]
-**xhaphak**- be plentiful, abundant; be present in great numbers, quantities; be all over the place; be regular, occur often; frequent, be a frequent visitor (to a place) [v-st]
Cf: -**xhapha** bubble (up, when boiling); boil over; froth, foam at the mouth; sound of animal lapping up (water) [ideophone]
Cf: -**xhaph**- lap up (as dog); eat carelessly [v-tr]; [v-st] be smeared around the mouth (with food, fat, blood, foam); boil over, bubble up (when boiling)
-**ile** VERBed [long perfect/recent past tense suffix; denotes current relevance on stative verbs]

kule mihla nowadays [n2-pl-cmp-time] (lit: in these days)

kule at, on, to these [deic-n2-pl-loc]
ku [locative prefix for a named person, kin term, pronoun, or deictic]
le these [deic-1-n2-pl]

mihla days [n2-pl-time-red; Cf: **imihla**]
mi- [group 2 plural reduced noun prefix]
umhla day, date; point in time [n2-sg-time]
-(**i**)**hla** go down, descend [v-intr-latent]

kufana na it is the same as; it is just like
-**fana na** resemble, be like, appear similar to [vp]

nje thus, such, like this; in this way, in this manner, so [atr, adv, also used for marking emphasis]
Cf: **nje** just, only [adv]

nokuphosa (like) throwing [n8-vn-comparative = na-uku-phos-a]
-**phos**- throw, hurl, cast, fling [v-tr]

igusha sheep; sheepskin coat [n5-sg]

kwiingonyama to the lions [n5-pl-loc]
kwiin- [combo form indicating that the specific locative (**ku**-) is joined to n5 pl (**iin**-)]
ingonyama lion [n5-sg; pl: **iingonyama**]
-**gony**- act with great force [v-intr]

oku kuthetha this means, this is to say

oku this (place, situation, time) [deic-1-n10]

kuthetha it means
ku- it [group 10 locative noun subject 1 agreement prefix]
-**theth**- say, talk, speak; talk of; mean [v-tr]

wam my, mine; my own [pro-1sg-poss-n1-sg]

kufuneka must, need to, ought to, should [v-aux-impers] (lit: it is necessary)

athembele he should trust [v-pres-sub]
a- he, she [n1-sg-S3a]
-**themb**- expect, hope; trust, rely (on, upon)
-**thembel**- hope for; trust in, rely upon; confide in [v-ben]

nakuwuphina in anyone; in whomever [pro-indef-n1-sg-loc = na-ku-wu-phi-na]
na- -**na** any-, -ever [indefinite pronoun circumfix]

Note: The first **na** is necessary because of the applicative form of the verb -**themb**-, the second is an interrogative form imparting the meaning of 'whomever' mentioned above. Also too, also, as well [adv-prf] vs. even [emphatic-prf]
wuphi which (one)? [qw-n1-sg]

wu- [group 1, 1a singular enumerative agreement prefix]
-phi any- (as in anything, anyone); -ever (as in whatever, whichever) [indefinite pronoun root]
phi which? (of two or more) [enumerative interrogative root]
-na is it? [qw]
umntu person, individual, human being; [pro] someone, somebody [n1-sg]
um- [n1-sg-prf]

angamaziyo whom he does not know [ind rel = a-nga-m-azi-yo]
a- he [indirect relative]
-**nga**-Δ-**i** not VERBing [negative present participial construction]

zinqununu principals! [vocative]
ziN- [n5-pl prefix without initial vowel when used as vocative]
inqununu principal (of a school) [n5-sg; pl: **iinqununu**]

neetitshala and teachers
nee- [combo conj-prf]
iititshala teachers [n5-pl; sg: **ititshala**]
Cf: **ootitshala** [n1a-pl] in R3

khanisebenzisane won't you work together with
khani- won't you [hortative preverb; not negative – English uses "won't" as a more polite hortative than "will you"]
-**ni**- (and) you (all) VERB [S3a present subjunctive subject]
-**sebenzisan**- cooperate, work together [v-caus-recip]

nathi with us
thi we; us [first person plural pronoun root in copulative and prepositional expressions]

babalulekile they are important
-**balul**- pick (out), choose, select; distinguish, specificy; make an exception of
-**balulek**- get selected; become good; be distinguished, notable, important
-**ile** VERBed [long perfect/recent past tense suffix; denotes current relevance on stative verbs]

masibakhusele let us protect them [v-hort]
si- we [pro-1pl-S3a]
-**khus**- keep off/out (rain, wind, danger) [v-tr]
-**khusel**- screen, shelter, protect [v-ben]

masizame let us try [v-hort]
-**zam**- shake, move (as a tree in the wind); struggle (with), strain, strive, try, exert oneself; persevere; urge, press [v-tr]

eny'indlela another way
Note: **e**- is not locative here
enye another [atr-n5-sg]
e- that which [n5-sg direct relative 1 attributive prefix in positive or negative construction]
indlela path, road, street; direction, route; way, method, means, system, mode; way of life [n5]

yokunyusa of raising

yezikolo of/for schools
yezi- [combo form indicating that n4 pl (**izi**-) is possessed by a n5-sg (**ya**-)]

eZimbabwe in Zimbabwe
Zimbabwe (country) [n5-sg-pn]

Mayinyanzelwe Ngumthetho Imfundo

Imfundo ayinyanzelwa ngumthetho eMzantsi-Afrika. Oko kwenzeka nangona kusithiwa makangagxothwa umntwana esikolweni kuba engenayo imali yesikolo. Nangona eli ilinyathelo eliya phambili, kungani urhulumente exhasa amabanga aphantsi kuphela, aze angayixhasi imfundo yamabanga ephakamileyo apho kuhlawulwa imali eninzi ngexesha elifutshane.

Yinto eyaziwa nanguthathatha ukuba abantu basezilalini abanayo imali efunwa kumaziko emfundo ephakemeyo. Uninzi lwabo alusebenzi, kanti abanye basamkela imivuzo ephantsi nanamhlanje. Ngaphezu koko, urhulumente wethu woyisakele ukukhusela nokuvula amathuba emisebenzi.

NguT.J.Z., eElandsfontein.

Vocabulary

mayinyanzelwe let it be forced; it should be compulsory [= ma-y+i-nyanzel-w-e]
+y addition of **y** before **i-** after a vowel-final prefix
i- [n5-sg-S3a]
-nyanzel- press, squeeze, crumple up; [ext] force, compel, constrain [v-tr]
-nyanzelw- be forced ~ compelled [v-pass]
ngumthetho by law, under the law [n2-sg-agent]
ngum- by him, her ~ it [marker of class 2 singular agent (agentive copulative) of passive verb]
umthetho law, rule, regulation [n2-sg; pl: **imithetho**]
imfundo education, learning [n5-sg]
ayinyanzelwa it is not forced [v-n5-sg-SNEG-neg-pres-pass]
a-SNEG-Δ-**w**-**a** is not VERBed [negative present tense passive verb construction]
ayi- he, she, it does not VERB [class 5 singular negative present subject prefix]
Note: negative of the passive is -**a** (not -**i**) [CGB:188]
eMzantsi-Afrika in South Africa
uMzantsi-Afrika South Africa [pn2-cmp]
umzantsi lower part; bottom; south [n2-sg]
-zantsi south, southern; low [n-root, atr]
Afrika Africa [pn5-loc-root]
oko that (time, place, situation not far ~ just mentioned) [deic-2-n10-loc]
kwenzeka it happens
kw- [group 10 locative noun S1 subject agreement prefix before vowel initial verb (other than o)]
-enzek- happen, occur; get done; be possible [v-st]
Cf: **-zek-** take to oneself; marry; obtain, receive, incur; grip, hold fast to [v-tr]
nangona although, even if; even supposing [conj, followed by participial construction]
kusithiwa it is being said
makangagxothwa he/she should not be turned away

maka- he must, she should, let him/her [hortative preverb]
-gxoth- drive away; defeat [v-tr]
esikolweni from school [n4-sg-loc = e-(i)si-kolo/w-eni]
engenayo he who does not have
yesikolo of/for school [ya-i-si-kolo]
ya- [n5-sg poss]
-(i) -si- [n4 sing] [a- + -i- > ye- by coalescence]
nangona although, even if; even supposing [conj, followed by relative construction]
eli this [deic-1-n3-sg]
ilinyathelo it is a step
inyathelo step, footstep; step forward [n3-sg]
-nyathel- step on, tread upon, trample; run over [v-tr]
eliya which goes
eli- he, she who/that which [group 3 singular direct relative 1 attributive agreement prefix positive or negative construction]
Contrast: **eliya** that (far) [deic-3-n3-sg]
phambili ahead, in front , forward [n9-loc; adv-loc]
kungani why?; why is it? [qw-expr = ku-nga-ni]
-ni what (kind)?, of what sort? [qw-adj-root]
ngani (na) why?
urhulumente government [n1a-sg]
exhasa it supporting [v-pres-part]
-xhas- prop, stay up; support, maintain, assist [v-tr]
kuphela only [adv]
aze auxiliary verb, when complement is negative, gives emphasis, thus here 'never'
-ze auxiliary verb, derived from '**ukuza**, to come
angayixhasi it does not support it [pres sub showing sequence]
-yi- [group 5 singular object agreement prefix agreeing with **imfundo**]
imfundo yamabanga ephakamileyo at higher education standards (lit: those standards catering for higher education)
yamabanga of grades
yama- = ya- + (a)ma- [n5-sg poss n3 pl combo]
ephakamileyo which is higher ~ advanced [= e-phakam-ile-yo]
-phakam- stand up ~ erect, rise, be elevated; stand out [v-intr]
apho there, that place (not far) [deic-2-n9-loc-adv] ; also like Eng. where [ind-rel]
kuhlawulwa it is paid [= ku-hlawul-w-a]
-hlawul- pay, settle; expiate [v-tr]
eninzi lots, much [adj-n5-sg]
eN- [adj-n5-sg]
-ninzi many, a lot ~ plenty (of), much, abundant, plentiful [adj-root]
ngexesha elifutshane in a very short period of time
ngexesha in time [n3-sg = nga-i-xesha]
nge- combo = nga- + i-
Cf: **ngexesha** early [adv-time]
elifutshane very short [adj-n3-sg]
-futshane short, very short [adj-dim-root]
fuphi short, squat [adj-root]
CHANGE of **ph** to **tsh**
-ane [diminutive suffix]
Yinto eyaziwa nangutha-thatha ukuba It is common knowledge that ...
yinto it is a thing [n5-sg pred]
yi- he, she, it is ... [class 5 singular copulative ~ predicative prefix construction]
eyaziwa which is known [v-pass = e+y-azi-w-a]

-**ya**- long form pres. indicative tense.
nanguthathatha and even by a little child
na- even [emphatic adv-prf]
uthathatha trifle, s.t. of little or no significance; simpleton, person of little intelligence; kid, small child who still has an immature mind [n1a-sg]
basezilalini those who are in rural areas [= ba-s-e-(i)zi-lal(i)-ini]
ilali location, settlement; ward; rural area [n5-sg; pl: **iilali**]
abanayo who do not have
efunwa which is needed [v-pass-n5-sg-rel]
-**funw**- be needed [v-pass]
kumaziko ku maziko of/for households
amaziko hearths; households [n3-pl]
emfundo in education [n5-sg-loc]
ephakemeyo which is raised, i.e., higher. Note: the perf short form is not common in Xhosa; *ephakamileyo* would have been more likely. The form is Zulu, but it cannot be assumed that it is a borrowing on just one occurrence — it is thus considered to be interference; the writer is either a second-language Xhosa speaker or has many Zulu friends!
ASSIMILATION of **a** to **e** before perfect suffix -**e**
uninzi majority; the most [n6-sg]
lwabo of them; their (own); theirs [pro-3pl-poss-n6-sg]
alusebenzi does not work
alu- he, she, it does not VERB [class 6 singular negative present subject prefix]
kanti and yet, on the other hand; nevertheless, notwithstanding; whereas [conj]
basamkela they still receive [= ba-s(a)-amkel-a]
-**s**- [consonant added to positive participial form of vowel-initial verbs]
sa still [progressive form affix, derived from *–sala* remain]
-**amkel**- receive, accept; adopt; welcome; agree [v-tr]
imivuzo wages [n2-pl; sg: **umvuzo**]
-**vuz**- reward; pay [v-tr]
nanamhlanje and today, of the day, currently
namhlanje today, nowadays [adv-time]
ngaphezu koko moreover, in addition [conj-expr]
ngaphezu over, exceeding; upon; than [adv]
koko that [dem]
k- [loc prefix following **–phezu** (normally ku-)]
-**oko** [locative demonstrative, of that place]
wethu our, ours; our own [pro-1pl-poss-n1-sg]
woyisakele [= w-oyis-akal-e] it is fearful of
-**oyis**- fear [v-tr] (lit: cause to fear)
-**oyisakal**- be fearful of
-**ele** [perf, stative]
nokuvula and to open [conj + v-inf = na-uku-vula]
-**vul**- open [v-tr]
amathuba opportunities, chances [n3-pl]
ithuba moment; opportunity, occasion; turn, chance; [atr] interim [n3-sg]
emisebenzi in jobs [n2-pl-loc = e-(i)mi-sebenz-i]
imisebenzi jobs [n2-pl]
eElandstontein in Elandstontein (town) [loc]

Khuselani Abamsulwa

Abuhlonitshwa ubomi babanye abantu elizweni lethu. Abantu babulala kungekho sizathu. Izaphuli-mthetho ziyazi ukuba azohlwaywa ngezenzo zazo, yiloo nto ulwaphulo-mthetho lwandile nje. Zenza nokuba yintoni na. Iintolongo zibukeka zintle kuba zifana nemizi yazo. Ngokwendlela mna endibona ngayo uMzantsi Afrika kufuneka ube nemithetho engqongqo njengakwamanye amazwe. Ababulali, izidlwengu nezinye izaphuli-mthetho kufuneka zohlwaywe kalukhuni, ukuze nezinye zoyike. Ndithetha oku kungekuko ukuba ndiyabazonda abantu abophula umthetho, bangabantakwethu. Bona siyabathanda kodwa sizonda indlela le baziphethe ngayo.

nguO.F., eKwaeng

Vocabulary

khuselani you (all) protect! [v-imp-pl]
-ni [v-suf-imp-pl]
NOT: **-ani** [imp-pl] (non-morphemic)

abamsulwa those who are innocent [n1-pl-rel = aba-m-sul-w-a]
-msulwa pure, innocent, faultless [atr-root]
-m- [archaic attributive prefix]
-sul- wipe off ~ away, blot out; clean, polish; wipe out, obliterate [v-tr]

abuhlonitshwa it is not respected [v-neg-pass-pres-n7-sg = a-bu-hloniph/tsh-w-a]
abu- it does not VERB [class 7 singular negative present subject prefix]

babanye of some/individual [= ba-(a)ba-nye]

elizweni in the country ~ land [n3-sg-loc = e-(i)li-zwe-(e)ni]
ilizwe land, region, country; [ext] a great deal; a large number; very often [n3-sg]
CHANGE /LOSS of **-a** ~ **-e** before suffix **-eni**

lethu our, ours, our own [pro-1pl-poss-n3-sg]

babulala they kill ~ are killing
-bulal- kill, murder; hurt; destroy [v-tr]

kungekho there not being any [v-exis-neg-part]
-ngekho be absent, not be there [v-exis-neg]
nge- may not, cannot, would not [negative potential/conditional preverb expressing inability, lack of permission, unwillingness, impossibility]

sizathu reason [n4-sg-red]
isizathu reason, cause; proof [n4-sg; pl: izizathu]

izaphuli-mthetho criminals, lawbreakers [n4-pl-cmp]
isaphuli-mthetho lawbreaker [n4-sg-cmp]
iz- [n4-pl-prf]
-aphul- break; break down [v-tr~intr]
mthetho law, rule, regulation [n2-sg-red; See: **umthetho** and **–theth-**]

ziyazi they know [= zi-y-azi]

-**y**- is ~ are VERBing [long present verb prefix on vowel-initial verb stems]
azohlwaywa they will not be punished
az- they will not VERB [class 4 plural negative future subject prefix before vowel-initial verb] (shortened form – see Lexicon)
-**ohlway**- find fault with; rebuke, reprove; punish, fine [v-tr]
ngezenzo for deeds ~ actions [n4-pl-instr = nga-iz-enz-o]
ngez- = nga- + iz-
isenzo deed, act, performance [n4-sg; pl: **izenzo**]
zazo their [n4-pl-poss-n4-pl] agreeing with izenzo
yiloo that is [deic-2-n5-sg-pred]
nto something [n5-sg-red]
ulwaphulo-mthetho crime, breaking the law [n6-sg-cmp]
ulw- [group 6 (Bantu class 11) singular noun prefix]
lwandile it has increased
lu- [n6-sg-S1]
CHANGE of **o** ~ **u** to **w** before a vowel
-**and**- become larger, extend, expand, increase [v-inch]
zenza they do
z- they VERB [n4-pl S1 prefix before vowel-initial verb]
nokuba even if, and that, and if, whether; or [= na+ukuba]
yintoni is it something ? (lit: what is this thing?)
na and, with; has/have here - is it [qw]
iintolongo prisons, jails [n5-pl; sg: **intolongo**] {Afr tronk}
zibukeka they are admired/liked
Note: Adjectives can be coordinated with zero [DuPlessis & Visser 1992:327]
zintle they are pretty
ziN- [n5-pl-atr]
zifana nemizi yazo they are just like their homes
zifana they are similar to/like
nemizi with homes [= na-imi-zi]
yazo their [n5-pl-poss-n2-pl]
ya- of [group 2 plural possessive agreement prefix]
ngokwendlela in such a way
ngokwa indlela according to my way [of thinking]
ngokwa- according to [instr]
endibona as I see (it) [v-pres-ind-rel] (lit: me whom)
endi- I who [pro-1sg-ind-rel1]
Note: indirect relative because the subject is not the same
ngayo through it, by means of it [n5-sg-instr = nga-yo]
uMzantsi Afrika South Africa [pn2-cmp-loc]
ube that it be ~ (should) become [n2-sg-S3a-v-pred-sub]
nemithetho having laws [= na-imi-theth-o]
engqongqo which are hard [rel-n2-pl]
-**ngqongqo** hard, severe [atr]
njengakwamanye just like in others [= njenga-kwa-(a)ma-nye]
amazwe countries [n3-pl; sg: **ilizwe**]
-**zwe** country, nation [noun root]
ababulali killers, murderers [n1-pl]
aba-Δ-**i** -ers, -ors [plural agent noun circumfix; Sg: **um**-Δ-**i**]
umbulali killer, murderer [n1-sg]
nezinye and other [= n(a)-ezi-nye]
ezi- [n4-pl-adj]
zohlwaywe they should be punished
kalukhuni hard; harshly, strictly, severely [adv]
-**lukhuni** hard (as a rock); difficult, tough; enduring; strict; harsh, severe, hard-hearted [atr]
Cf: **ukhuni** wood; log [n6-sg; pl: **iinkuni**]
zoyike they should fear [v-sub]

-**oyik**- fear, dread, be afraid of [v-tr]
ndithetha I say, I am talking (about)
oku this [deic-1-n8-vn]
kungekuko it could be it;
-**ko** [loc. deic] place there
ndiyabazonda I feel strongly about them [= ndi-ya-ba-zond-a]
-**zond**- have a strong feeling (for ~ against); desire, long for, dote on, be very fond of; hate, loathe, abhor, detest [v-tr]
abophula those who break it [= aba-wu-aphul-a]
bangabantakwethu they are our children [= ba-ngaba-nta-kwa-ithu]
ngaba- they are ... [class 1 plural copulative (full form) ~ predicative prefix construction]
banta children [n1-pl; sg: **umnta**; red: **bantwana**]
kwethu our (place); our own (domain) [pro-1 n9 (loc)-poss-n1pl]
siyabathanda we love them [= si-ya-ba-thand-a]
sizonda we feel strongly (about, for, against)
le this [deic-1-n5-sg] agreeing with **indlela**
baziphethe they have behaved [= ba-zi-phath/e-e]
-**ziphath**- behave, carry oneself [v-refl; perf: -**ziphethe**]
-**phethe** touched; held; treated, dealt with; took charge of, managed; commanded, ruled [perf of: -**phatha**]
eKwaeng from Kwaeng

Irayisi Etyalwe Emelika Ikunika Amandla

Ukuze indoda ibe nezihlunu ezomeleleyo ibe namandla kangangoko, ifuna ukutya okuphambili ehlabathini - irayisi yekhwalithi etyalwe eMelika. Kuba irayisi etyalwe eMelika iqulethe okuthile okusisipesheli, esingathi ngumxube wee carbohydrate. Oku kuthetha ukuba xa usitya irayisi etyalwe eMelika ufumana oko kwaneliseka kukodwa - kuba uhluthi ngenene, kodwa ungengompatsiya. Kananjalo uyakufumanisa ukuba unamandla nokomelela okugqithisileyo ukujongana nosuku olude emsebenzini okanye kwezemidlalo.

Irayisi etyalwe eMelika kananjalo iqulethe i vitamin B, i protein, i calcium ne iron.

Ngoko, rhoqo xa uthenga irayisi, biza amagama anerayisi yekhwalithi etyalwe eMelika.

Amagama aphambili kwirayisi aqulethe irayisi etyalwe eMelika kuphela.

Ewe! Ndicela ninndithumelele incwadana yee resiphi yasimahla.

Irayisi inceda abantwana bakho bahlale bekrelekrele bedlamkile.

Vocabulary

irayisi rice [n5-sg] {Afr rijs, Eng rice}
etyalwe which was planted [v-rel-pass-short-past]
-tyal- plant (with the hand) [v-tr]
eMelika in America [n5-sg-pn-geog-loc]
iMelika America [n5-sg-pn-geog]
ikunika it gives you [v-pres]
amandla strength, energy, power; force; biceps [n3-pl-mass; no singular]
indoda man, male; husband [n5-sg; pl: **amadoda**]
ibe nezihlunu that he might have muscles [= i-b-e na-izi-hlunu]
-be na- that he might have [v-poss-pres-sub]
nezihlunu having muscles
isihlunu muscle; flesh; lean (meat) [n4-sg; pl: **izihlunu**]
ezomeleleyo which are strong [v-st-perf-rel = ez(i)-om-elel-e-yo]
ez- they who/those which [group 4 plural direct relative 1 attributive agreement prefix positive or negative construction before a vowel verb]
-om- become dry, hard; get ripe; [perf] dried up, paralyzed [v-st]
-omelel- dry out; harden; ripen; [perf] be strong, vigorous, robust, healthy [v-st]
ibe namandla and that he be strong
namandla strong, powerful, forcible [v-poss-atr] (lit: having force)
kangangoko therefrom, arising from this [= ka-nga-ng-oko]
ngoko therefore, because of that

Cf: **nga ngokuba** as much as [conj-expr]
Cf: **kangaka** so greatly
ifuna he wants [v-pres-n5-sg-S1]
ukutya to eat [v-inf]
-ty- eat, consume, devour; [ext] cheat s.o. out of s.t. [v-tr]
okuphambili that which is foremost [n8-vn-rel1]
oku- the VERBing which [group 8 verbal noun direct relative 1 attributive agreement prefix positive or negative construction]
ehlabathini in soil; [ext] around the world
ihlabathi sand, soil; [ext] the world (as a whole) [n3-sg]
yekhwalithi of quality
ikhwalithi quality [n5-sg] {Eng}
iqulethe it contains [v-st-perf-part]
-quleth- contain, hold; [fig] have (within oneself) [v-tr]
okuthile certain, particular [n8-vn-rel1]
okusisipesheli which is being special [n8-vn-rel1-n4-sg]
isipesheli specialty [n4-sg] {Eng}
esingathi which can be said, in other words
ngumxube it is a mixture [n2-sg-pred]
umxube mixture [n2-sg]
-xub- mix (s.t. up); [perf st] be different, be of different sorts [v-tr]
wee carbohydrate of carbohydrates {Eng} [Note: if this interpretation is correct, there should be no space between **wee** and **carbohydrate**, which justifies the alternative parsing BELOW]
wee possessive formative [n2-sg-poss + n5 –pl] (u + a > wa + ii > wee)
wee carbohydrate called carbohydrate {Eng}
wee- called [abbreviated form of **wathi**, often used when **ukuthi** is functioning as an auxiliary]
iicarbohydrate [n5-pl] carbohydrates {Eng}
usitya you eating [v-part-pres = u-si-ty-a]
ufumana you find [v-tr-pres]
kwaneliseka it is satisfying, sufficient, enough [= ku/w-anel-is-ek-a]
kwa- it [group 8 noun subject 1 agreement prefix before vowel initial verb (other than **o**)]
kukodwa it is alone; all by itself [v-pred-n10-pro-quant]
-odwa only, alone, by oneself [pro-quant-root]
uhluthi you get full [v-part-perf]
-hluth- become sated, satisfied; [perf] have enough, be full (after eating) [v-inch; perf: -hluthi]
ngenene truly, in truth, in reality; absolutely [adv = nga-i-nene]
inene truth, reality; [atr] real, true; [adv] truly, indeed [n5-sg]
Contrast: **inene** nobleman, gentleman; upright reliable person; right-hand man, principal councillor of a chief [n3-sg]
ungengompatsiya you won't get bloated [= u-nge-nga +(u)>o-m-patsiya]
-ngo- not being, not becoming
umpatsiya bloated stomach [n2-sg]
kananjalo so, in that way [adv]
uya kufumanisa you will discover
unamandla you have energy [v-poss = u-na-mandla]
Note: **-fuman-** takes S1 independent clause or S2 participial
nokomelela (and) can be vigorous
nok- can, could VERB; be able, willing to VERB [reduced form of **noku-** used before **o** verb]

okugqithisileyo which has surpassed; beyond measure [=oku-gqith-is-ile-yo]
-gqith- pass (by), go past; surpass, excel; be in great numbers; [ext] trespass, transgress [v-tr]
-gqithis- make pass; pass s.t. on; surpass [v-caus]
ukujongana nosuku to face a day [v-cmp-expr]
-jong- look (at fixedly), watch, stare [v-tr]; [intr] glare, look fierce
-jongan- stare at each other [v-recip]
-jongana na- face (the day, a problem, death)
nosuku with a day [n6-sg-comit = na-u-suku]
olude long [adj-n6-sg]
olu- [group 6 singular adjective agreement prefix]
-de long; high, tall [adj-root]
emsebenzini at work; to work [n2-sg-loc]
kwezemidlalo in sporting events [= ku-e-za-imi-dlal-o]
See: **ezemidlalo** in R4c
kweze- in (lit: in those...)
zemi- [indicates that n2 pl (**imi**–) is possessed by a n5 pl (**za**-)]
i vitamin B [n5-sg] {Eng}
i protein [n5-sg] {Eng}
i calcium [n5-sg] {Eng}
ne iron and iron {Eng}
ngoko therefore, so [conj]
rhoqo do often, always, continually [preverb; alt sp: **roqo**]
uthenga you buying [v-part]
biza ask for! [v-imp]
-biz- call, summon, name; ask for, demand [v-tr]
amagama words; names; brands (commerial products) [n3-pl]
anerayisi which have rice [= a-na-i-rayisi]
aphambili ahead, in front; [atr] foremost [n3-pl-atr]
kwirayisi among rice [n5-sg-spec-loc]
kwi- [combo form indicating that the specific locative prefix (**ku**-) is linked to a noun prefixed with the article **i**-]
aqulethe they contain; they have [v-st-perf current relevance]
ewe yes! [intj]
incwadana booklet [n5-sg-dim]
incwadi book [n5-sg; pl: **iincwadi**]
yeeresiphi of recipes
yee- [combo (non morphemic – there are two morphemes here) form indicates that n5 pl (**ii**-) is possessed by a n5-sg (**ya**-)]
iresiphi recipe [n5-sg] {Eng}
yasimahla for free [n5-sg-poss]
-simahla free, gratis, for nothing [atr-adv]
inceda it helps
-nced- help, aid, assist [v-tr]
bakho your [pro-2sg-poss-n1-pl]
bahlale that they always VERB
bekrelekrele being bright, intelligent [v-st-n1-pl-S2]
-krelekrele shine, be bright; [ext] be smart ~ intelligent [v-st]
Cf: **ubukrele-krele** brilliance [MI:198]
bedlamkile being lively [v-st-n1-pl-S2]
-dlamk- be merry, lively, frolicsome, in good spirits [v-st]

Nkosi sikelel' iAfrika

«1»
Nkosi sikelel' iAfrika
Maluphakamis' uphondo lwayo
Yiva nemithandazo yethu
Usisikelele.
«2»
Yihla Moya, yihla Moya
Yihla Oyingcwele.
«3»
Sikelela iinkosi zethu
Zikhumbule umDali wazo
Zimoyika zezemhlonele.
Azisikelele.
«4»
Sikelel' amadoda esizwe
Sikelela kwanomlisele
Ulithwal'ilizwe ngomonde
Uwusikelele.
«5»
Sikelel' amakhosikazi
Nawo onk'amanenekazi
Phakamisa wonk'umthinjana
Uwusikelele.
«6»
Sikelela abefundisi
Bemvaba zonke zeli lizwe
Ubathwese ngoMoya Wakho
Ubasikelele.
«7»
Sikelel' ulimo nemfuyo
Gxotha zonk' indlala nezifo
Zalisa ilizwe ngempilo

Ulisikelele.

«8»

Sikelel' amalinga ethu
Awimanyano nokuzakha
Awemfundo nemvisiswano
Uwasikelele.

«9»

Nkosi sikelel' iAfrika
Cima bonk' ubugwenxa bayo
Nezigqitho nezono zayo.

At the time of writing, the official National Anthem of South Africa comprises the first verse as shown above, followed by a verse in Sotho (which is unlike any of the verses herein), then a verse in Afrikaans, and concluding with the English verse shown at the end of the translation. It is more correct to say that this version is closer to the original hymn written by Enoch Sontonga.

Vocabulary

«1»

Nkosi lord
sikelel' bless! [imperative]
 sikelela bless, confer favors on; cut into, for, on behalf of [v-tr]
iAfrika Africa
maluphakamis' let it be exalted
 -lu- it, [OC] referrring to Class 6 noun
 -phakanyisw- be exalted [pass]
uphondo horn; tusk; tower, turret, steeple; wing (of an army) [n6-sg]
lwayo his, her, its; of him, her, it [n5-sg-poss-n6-sg]
yiva hear
nemithandazo the prayers [na+n2-pl]
 umthandazo prayer [n2-sg]
usisikelele you should bless us [v-sub; because an imp (**yiva**) appears in the same clause, a sub occurs, not **sisikelele**]

«2»

yihla go down, come down [imp]
moya spirit [n2-sg]
oyingcwele who is holy
 -ngcwele holy, pure, bright, saintly

«3»

iinkosi chiefs, lords [n5-pl]
zethu our [pro-1pl-poss-n5-pl]
zikhumbule keep in mind, remember [v-subj +OC]
umDali creator (God) [n1-sg]
 -dal- create, make s.t. new; cause, originate; ordain [v-tr]
wazo their [n5-pl-poss-n1-sg, agreeing with iinkosi and umdali]
zimoyika they (the chiefs) (should) fear him
zezemhlonele and they should just respect him (Note: **zezimhlonele** is given in an early translation, which seems to indicate a typo here)
 ze [aux.verb derived from **ukuza**] should come to VERB

-hlonel- respect, fear, show deference to, reverence
«4»
amadoda men [n3-pl]
esizwe of the nation [n4-sg.loc]
kwanomlisele even/also the youth
umlisela the youth, the young men, prime, of an army or nation, flower
ulithwal' you should carry [v-subj +OC] Note: the translation from the original article says "that they carry…" which is incorrect ; the author is exhorting God to bear the nation with patience!
ngomonde with patience or perseverance [adv+n7-abstr]
umonde perseverance, patience [n7-abs]
«5»
amakhosikazi women [n3-pl]
nawo and them
onk'amanenekazi all the ladies
onk'(e) all [n3-pl-enum]
inenekazi lady [n3-sg; pl: **amanenekazi** ladies]
wonk'umthinjana all young maidens
wonk'(e) all [n1-pl-enum]
-thinjana maiden (Cf: **inthonjane** coming-of-age ceremony for girls)
«6»
abefundisi preachers [n1-pl]
bemvaba of missionaries
imvaba skin milksack; [ext] source of supply; [fig] missionary society [n5-sg]
zonke all [n5-pl-enum]
zeli of this [deic-1-n3-sg poss n5-pl]
ubathwese you should crown them
-thwes- crown, put on the head, supply with, initiate (a young doctor), instruct
ngoMoya with the spirit
«7»
ulimo the crops [n7-abstr]
Cf: **isilimo** a crop [n4-sg]
nemfuyo and livestock [conj+n5-sg]
imfuyo stock, property [n5-sg]
gxotha expel, drive away; defeat [v-tr]
indlala hunger, famine, drought; dearth, scarcity [n5-sg]
nezifo and illness [conj+n4-pl]
zalisa help in childbirth (generate) [v-caus]
Contrast: **-zalis-** make full, fill (up) [v-caus]
ngempilo with life [conj+n5-sg]
«8»
amalinga attempts [Class3-pl-agr+n3-pl]
-ling- attempt, try, make an effort [v-tr]
awimanyano of union (should be **awomanyano**) [n3-pl-poss-emph-n6-sg]
umanyano association, combination, union [n6-sg]
nokuzakha and to build [conj+verbal noun n8]
-akh- build [v-tr]
awemfundo of education [class3-pl-agr+n6-abstr]
nemvisiswano and mutual understanding [conj+n5-sg]
imvisiswano agreement, accordance [n5-sg]
«9»
cima extinguish, put out, give an enema, shut your eyes – here 'blot out'
bonk' all [n7--sg-enum]
ubugwenxa wrongness, perversity, crookedness [n7-abstr]
bayo its [n5-sg-poss-n7-sg]
nezigqitho and the transgressions [n4-pl-conj]
isigqitho trespass, transgression [n4-sg]
nezono and sins [conj+n4-pl]
isono sin [n4-sg; pl: izono]

zayo its [n5-sg-poss-n4-pl referring to **iAfrika**]

Abahlobo

Abahlobo babalulekile ebutsheni bakho.

Abahlobo banokukuhenda ukuba wenze izinto ongekazilungeli. Banokukwenza ungazithandi kwawena. Ngamaxesha anje kubalulekile ukwenza isigqibo sokuba ubagcine na abo bahlobo okanye hayi.

Yintoni eyenza umntu abe ngumhlobo olungileyo? Makhe sijonge:

... baya kukuxhasa ngamaxesha obumnandi nawobunzima. Baya kuba kunye nawe xa wonwabile. Abayi kukulibala xa uselusizini yaye abakuhleki.

... baya kukuphulaphula okutshoyo. Maxa wambi nokungavumelani nokutshoyo. Oko akunakuguqula indlela abakuthanda.

... baya kukuxolela. Ngamanye amaxesha unokuxabana nabahlobo bakho. Umona nokuxabana kubakho maxa wambi. Funda ukuxolisa nokwamkela abantu abaxolisayo.

... ngabantu onokuthetha nabo ngeengcinga zakho. Funda ukutyhileka kubafundi bakho. Baxelele okucingayo neemvakalelo zakho.

Nabo banike ithuba lokwenza oko.

Vocabulary

abahlobo friends [n1-pl]
  -hlobo [n-root (non-verb derived)]
  umhlobo friend, intimate [n1-sg]
  ubuhlobo friendship, intimacy, mutual attachment [n7-abs]
babalulekile they are important
  -balulek- be distinguished, notable ~ important [v-st]
ebutsheni in youth [n7-sg-loc = e-(u)bu-tsh(a)-eni]
  ubutsha newness, freshness; youth [n7-sg-abs]
banokukuhenda they can tempt ~ entice you [= ba-na-uku-ku-hend-a]
  -noku- be willing ~ able to VERB [CGB:150: "When **na-** is prefixed to the infinitive of a verb, it indicates an ability or willingness to act"]
  -hend- tempt (to do evil) [v-tr]
wenze you might do [v-sub]

ongekazilungeli (things) which are not appropriate for you [ind-rel]
-ka- yet (not yet) [punctual aspect prefix, negative only]
-lungel- be right ~ good for; be better for; suit, fit [v-ben]
banokukwenza they are able to make you [= ba-na-uku-kw-enz-a]
ungazithandi that you (should) not like yourself
kwawena for yourself; as a person
ngamaxesha in/at times [= ng(a)-ama-xesha]
amaxesha times, instances [n3-pl]
anje such [atr-n3-pl]
kubalulekile it is important [v-atr-perf]
isigqibo decision [n4-sg]
-gqib- finish, end, complete; end by saying; resolve [v-tr]
ubagcine you should keep them [v-sub]
-gcin- keep, take care of, preserve; defend, protect [v-tr]
abo those [deic-2-n1-pl]
bahlobo friends [n1-pl-red]
hayi not [intj-neg]
eyenza that makes
abe that he ~ she become [n1-sg-S3a + v-pred-sub]
ngumhlobo he is a friend
olungileyo [= a-u-lung-ile-yo] who is right, good, ready
makhe sijonge let us take a little glimpse
makhe let's do VERB a little
sijonge we should look at
-jong- look (at ~ fixedly), watch, stare; [intr] glare, look fierce [v-tr]
baya kukuxhasa they will support you
baya they will
kukuxhasa to support you [v-red-inf-pro-2sg-obj] S1-ya-ku-Δ-a will ~ shall VERB [proposed ~ future positive verb construction]
-xhas- prop, stay up; support, maintain, assist [v-tr]
obumnandi of joy/pleasure [= a-ubu-mnandi]
ubumnandi sweetness; delight, joy, pleasure, jubilation [n7-sg]
-mnandi nice, good, pleasant, delightful, a pleasure; fine, smooth, soft; fun; sweet, delicious; refined, civil, polite [atr-root]
nawobunzima and of difficulty [= n(a)-a/w-ubu-nzima]
ubunzima difficulty, hardship; sadness [n7-sg]
-nzima heavy, weighty; difficult, hard [atr-root]
baya kuba they will be
nawe with you [conj-abs.prn]
wonwabile you are happy
-onwab- be happy [v-st]
abayi kukulibala they will not forget you
abayi they won't
a-SNEG-yi-ku-Δ-a will not VERB [proposed ~ future negative construction]
-yi- will not VERB [proposed ~ future negative preverb]
-libal- neglect, forget [v-tr]
uselusizini you in sadness [= u + se + lusizini]
se still/-s- + e- [loc]
lusizi sad, sorrowful, miserable [adj]
yaye and also [conj]
abakuhleki they don't laugh at you [= a-ba-ku-hlek-i]
-hlek- laugh, laugh at
baya kukuphulaphula they will listen to you
kukuphulaphula to listen to you [v-red-inf-pro-2sg-obj]
-phulaphul- listen (to), hearken; attend; obey [v-tr]
okutshoyo oku + tsho + yo that which you say
oku- o- [rel] + ku- (you) + VERB

maxa wambi sometimes; [cmp] sometimes ... other times [adv-time]
maxa when [conj]
wambi others, some others (of a different kind) [enum-pro-n3-pl]
wa- [group 3 plural enumerative agreement prefix]
nokungavumelani not agreeing with (what you say) [= na-uku-nga-vumela-ni]
nokutshoyo ...what you say (see above) [= na-uku-tsho-yo]
Oko then, at that time; when
akunakuguqula they do not turn away from you/change the way (-**ku**- is temporal form) [= a-ku-na-ku-guqul-a]
-**guqul**- turn s.t. back; change, convert; translate; say in reply [v-tr]
abakuthanda a + ba + ku + thanda they like you
baya kukuxolela they will forgive you
kukuxolela to forgive you [v-red-inf-pro-2sg-obj]
-**xolel**- be appeased towards; forgive, pardon; be satisfied ~ content with [v-ben]
-**xol**- become satisfied, appeased ~ reconciled; [perf] be at peace ~ satisfied [v-st]
ngamanye amaxesha sometimes [adv-cmp-time]
ngamanye in other
ma- [n3-pl-red]
unokuxabana nabahlobo bakho you can quarrel with your friends
-**xabana na** quarrel with [vp-recip]
-**xaban**- obstruct one another, be at cross-purposes; [ext] disagree, quarrel [v-recip]
-**xab**- lie across, bar, thwart, hinder, obstruct, oppose [v-tr]
nabahlobo with friends [= na-(a)ba-hlob-o]
umona you wrong him/her [v-tr]
kubakho towards/with you, is yours [loc+bakho]
ukuxolisa satisfy, appease, put at peace
nokwamkela and to accept [= na-uku-amkel-a]
abaxolisayo who are peaceful
ngabantu there (they) are people [n1-pl-pred]
onokuthetha who can say
ngeengcinga zakho [= ng(a)-iing-cing-a] about your ideas
ingcinga thought, idea [n5-sg; pl: **iingcinga**]
zakho your [pro 2sg poss n5 pl]
ukutyhileka to be open, disclosed ~ revealed [v-st-inf]
-**tyhil**- uncover, lay bare; reveal, disclose, expose; narrate [v-tr]
-**tyhilek**- be disclosed ~ revealed; be open ~ manifest [v-st]
kubafundi to students
baxelele tell them! (-**ba**-**xel**-**el**-**e**)
-**xel**- tell, say, mention; order, command; be like, resemble [v-tr]
-**xelel**- inform, tell s.o. s.t., mention s.t. to s.o. [v-ditr]
okucingayo what you are thinking [REL = a-uku-cing-ayo]
neemvakalelo and the things you feel [= n(a)-iim-va-kal-el-o]
iimvakalelo feelings, emotions [n5-pl]
-**vakal**- be audible, sensible ~ perceptible; be clear ~ intelligible
banike you must give them [obj-imp]
lokwenza of doing [= la-uku-enz-a]
oko that [deic-2-]

Unompumelelo

(Inyanga yase Mozambique)

P.O. Box 12922

Jacobs 4026

Phone (031) 420413

Ingaba unenkinga ngekhaya lakho?

Awutholi bantwana? Uwelwa ngumzi (induku ayivuki)?

Imali iphelela ezandleni, ungayiboni into oyenzileyo ngayo?

Ingaba ufuna umcebo? Uma kunjalo bonana no-Nompumelelo inyanga yase-Nampura kwelase Mozambique. Yelapha ngezindlela ezininingi ezahlukene. Ungashaya ucingo ngale nombolo yocingo engenhla kumbe ubhalele kuleyo dilesi engenhla, uma wenze njalo usulutholile usizo okade walifuna.

> This article is an example of mixing of Zulu and Xhosa, which is called "Township Xhosa" and is very common in many South African urban areas. These words have been underlined in the article. In the vocabulary, the Zulu words are followed by their Xhosa equivalents.

Vocabulary

uNompumelelo (Nguni female personal name) (lit: success)
inyanga healer {Zulu}
See: **inyangi** or **umnyangi** XED:116
yase Mozambique from Mozambique [= ya-s-e-Mozambique]
yase- of in [combo locative indicating that a predicate locative (-s-e-) is possessed by n5-sg]
Jacobs (town in Mozambique)
ingaba maybe, perhaps, it may be, it seems [conj]
unenkinga you have a problem [= u-na-in-kinga]
inkinga difficulty, problem; perplexity; source of astonishment or surprise [n5-sg]
ngekhaya at home [n3-sg- = nga-i-khaya] (lit: by way of...)
lakho your [pro-2sg-poss-n3-sg]
awutholi {Zulu} = Xhosa **akufumani** you don't get
-**wu**- you [pro-2sg-SNEG; often used instead of -**ku**- after the negative formative **a**-; Alt: **aku**-]
-thol- obtain, get, pick up, receive; come upon, find; adopt [v-tr] {Zulu} Note Xhosa does use **isithole**, 'young plant, seedling' showing semantic affinity with the entry below.
-thola umntwana give birth [v-cmp] {Zulu}
uwelwa ngumzi your house is falling apart {idiom} (lit: you are fallen upon by the household)
uwelwa you are fallen on [= u-w-el-w-a] (from **ukuwa** 'to fall')

-**wa** fall
-**wel**- fall on/into, befall, overtake [Note affective passive]
ngumzi by the household
induku club, knobbed stick, knobkerrie; [euphemism] penis [n5-sg]
Contrast: -**duk**- wander away, get lost, disappear
ayivuki does not get up, awaken
-**vuk**- get up, wake up, arise [v-intr]
imali iphelela ezandleni money disappears in your hands {idiom}
iphelela it is the last of; it ends in nothing [v-pres]:
-**phelel**- end (for), expire; be the last of s.t.; end in nothing [v-ben]
See: -**phelel**- be complete, intact, perfect; be a virgin in R4d, R7
ezandleni in/from the hands [n4-pl-loc = e-(i)z-andl(a)-eni]
iz- [group 4 (Bantu class 8) rare alternate plural noun prefix before a noun root beginning with a vowel]
izandla hands [n4-pl]
isandla hand; [ext] agent, assistant, clerk; instrument, tool [n4-sg]
ungayiboni and you cannot see it [v-pot-sub]
-**nga**- [potential; note the negative pot should be -**nge**-]
oyenzileyo which you do [= o-y-enz-ile-yo]
ngayo with it/about it
ufuna you want/seek
umcebo wealth, riches, possessions [n2-sg] {Zulu}
See Xhosa: **utyebo** wealth, riches [n6-sg]
uma if {Zulu} // = Xhosa xa
Cf: (but don't confuse with): -**ma** stand, be standing; stop; wait; live, inhabit, dwell, occupy [v-st]
kunjalo it is so, it is like that
bonana noNompumelelo consult Nompumelelo [= na-u-Nompumelelo]
-**bonan**- see one another
-**bonana na**- visit, see, consult with [v-cmp]
yase-Nampura from Nampura
kwelase-Mozambique in Mozambique
kwela(a)-s-e- [kwa+elaa+s-e] in
yelapha she cures {Zulu} = Xhosa inyanga fr. Xh. **ukunyanga**
y- here, 'she', the inyanga
-**elapha** {Zulu} cure [v-tr]
inyanga she cures
-**nyang**- cure
ngezindlela {Zulu} Xhosa
ngeendlela by ways/means
nga + eziN + [in]dlela by means of/through these means
ngeendlela by ways/means [n5-pl-instr = nga-iin-dlela]
ngeen- by +n5
iindlela ways, means [n5-pl]
eziningi many {Zulu} = Xhosa
ezininzi many [adj-n5-pl]
ezahlukene which are different from one another {Zulu}
-**ahlukene** different/separate from one another [DNZ:69]
ez- [n5-pl-rel before a verb beginning with a vowel]
-**ahlul**- separate, sever, part, divide [v-tr] [XED:1]
-**ahluk**- be separate, parted; differ [v-intr] [XED:1]
-**ahlukan**- separate, part with, go in different ways, be severed from; lose one another; differ from; disagree with [v-recip]
CHANGE of -**ane** to -**ene** in perfect tense
ungashaya {Zulu} = Xhosa
ungabetha you can reach
-**shaya ucingo** phone, send telegram {Zulu} [DNZ:477]
ungabetha you can reach
-**beth**- hit, beat, strike; assault; punish; reach [v-tr]

ucingo wire (metal); wire fence; telegraph line; [ext] telegraph; telegram; telephone [n6-sg]
-**betha ucingo** telegraph [NDK:368] [evolved to mean telephone as well as telegraph; "betha" also has many idiomatic meanings (Cf: Eng., 'hit the road')]
ngale by means of this, with (using) this one [deic-1-n5-sg-instr]
nombolo number [n5-sg-red] {Eng, Afr}
yocingo of telephone [= ya-ucingo]
yo- [combo]
engenhla {Zulu} above [adv-loc]
-**ngenhla** {Zulu} = Xhosa **ngentla** above, on the upper side, on the North
Cf: **intla** upper side, the higher part of a hill or valley; [ext] north [n5-sg]
kumbe {Zulu} = Xhosa **okanye** or [conj]
ubhalele you should write to
kuleyo to that [= ku-leyo]
ku- Note that it binds with demonstratives
leyo that (not far, just mentioned) [deic-2-n5-sg]
dilesi address [n5-sg-red] (elided prefix after demonstrative)
usulutholile {Zulu} Xhosa **usalufumene** you would have already received
-**thola usizo** receive help {Zulu} [DNZ:213]
-**thol-** get, obtain, find, come upon {Zulu}
-**salufumene** have already received it (**usizo**)
-**ene** [perf suf of -**an**-]
usizo {Zulu} Xhosa **uncedo** help [n6-sg]
okade {Zulu} Xhosa -**kade** already, as soon as [EZZE:11]
walifuna you needed it

Isikolo Seenkokeli ZaseAfrika

Inkoliso yeenkokeli zamazwe aseAfrika kufuneka zifunde kwinkokeli yaseMzantsi aAfrika, uNelson Mandela. Ungumntu obalulekileyo, onenkathalo nothanda abantu. I-Afrika iphela nelizwe ngokubanzi liyamhlonipha. Ndibongoza ubaw' uMandela ukuba aseke isikolo sokufundisa iinkokeli zaseAfrika. Sinentlaninge yeengqondi kwiipolitiki ezinokufundisa ngemibandela enjengokuhlonipha umthetho. umgaqo-siseko nokusetyenziswa kwawo, unyulo olukhulekileyo, inkqubo yomthetho kwanokukwazi ukusebenzisa igunya. Iimeko ezimbi kwinkoliso yamazwe aseAfrika ibangelwe ngoozwilakhe abalambele isikhundla, kwanobunkokeli obonakeleyo kumazwe aseAfrika. Inkokeli enyulwe ngedemokhrasi ifanele ifunde kubaw' uNelson Mandela oye wavavanywa. Abaphathi bemikhosi kumakhulu eminyaka kufuneka bafunde kuGerry Rawlings waseGhana. Ezi nkokeli zimbini zinomdla kwizilangazelelo zabantu. Ndingavuya ukuba ubaw' uNelson Mandela unokuvula isikolo esinje phambi kokuba ayeke kwiipolitiki.

nguA.M., eKeetmanshoop, eNamibia.

Vocabulary

seenkokeli of leaders [n5-pl-poss-n4-sg = sa-iin-k/khok-el-i]
 inkokeli leader [n5-sg]
 -**khok**- draw out; lead out [v-tr]
 -**khokel**- go in front of; lead [v-ben]
 Cf: **umkhokeli** guide; leader [n1-sg]

zaseAfrika African, of (those) in Africa [= za-s-e-Afrika]

inkoliso most, greater part, majority [n5-sg = in-k/khol-is-o]
 -**khol**- satisfy, content; convince [v-tr]
 -**kholis**- satisfy, please, give satisfaction to s.o.; inspire confidence in s.o. [v-caus]

yeenkokeli of leaders [n5-pl-poss-n5-sg = ya-iin-k/khok-el-i]

zamazwe of countries [= za-(a)ma-zwe]

aseAfrika African, of (those) in Africa [= a-s-e-Afrika]

kufuneka it is necessary; need to, must, should [followed by subjunctive]

zifunde that they should learn

kwinkokeli from the leader [= ku-in-k/khok-el-i]
 kwin- = ku- + in-
 inkokeli leader

yaseMzantsi of (those) in the south [= ya-s-e-m-zantsi]

aAfrika of Africa (Cf: **UMzantsi-Afrika** South Africa)
 a- [possessive formative n3-pl]

uNelson Mandela Nelson Mandela

ungumntu he is a person

obalulekileyo [who is] important

onenkathalo who has interest or concern [= o-na-in-kathal-o]
inkathalo interest, concern, care (for s.o.), attention (to s.t.); anxiety [n5-sg; root: –**khathal**-]
nothanda na uthanda and loves/love of
no- expresses possession of an attribute
iphela i phela all [of]
nelizwe na ilizwe and the [his] country
ngokubanzi at large; broadly
banzi wide
liyamhlonipha it respects him [= li-ya-m-hlon-iph-a]
Ndibongoza I implore
-**bongoz**- beseech, implore, entreat
ubaw' father
uMandela Mandela
aseke that he establish [subjunctive = a-sek-e]
-**sek**- found, establish [v-tr]
sokufundisa for training, teaching [= sa-uku-fund-is-a]
iinkokeli leaders [n5-pl]
Sinentlaninge we have plenty
si na intlaninge [1 pers pl + possessor + n5-sg]
intlaninge abundance, plenty; a great number [n5-sg]
yeengqondi of minds [= ya-iing-qond-i]
inqondi mind [n5-sg; pl: **iinqondi**]
kwiipolitiki kwi ipolitiki political
ezinokufundisa which can teach [= e-zi-na-uku-fund-is-a]
ngemibandela about additional topics
umbandela fibula (bone attached to the shinbone); addition, supplement; graft, amendment; crowd of hangers-on [n2-sg: pl: **imibandela**]
enjengokuhlonipha how to respect [= e njenga uku hlonipha]
umgaqo-siseko constitution
nokusetyenziswa usable; useful [= na-uku-sebenz/ty-is-w-a] here 'and its uses'
kwawo its, of it [n2-sg-poss-n8-vn]
unyulo election
olukhulekileyo o lu khulekileyo [which is] free
inkqubo yomthetho due process
inkqubo program, procedure, proceedings
yomthetho [ya umthetho] of the law
kwanokukwazi for being able to know how
ukusebenzisa to use
igunya authority, right (given to s.o.) [n3-sg]
iimeko qualities; circumstances, situations [n5-pl]
imeko quality, circumstance, situation [n5-sg]
ezimbi which are bad
kwinkoliso kwa inkoliso in the majority
inkoliso majority
yamazwe of countries
ibangelwe have been caused
ngoozwilakhe nga uzwilakhe by dictators
uzwilakhe dictator [n1a-sg]
abalambele they were hungry for
-**lambel**- hunger for [ben]
-**lamb**- get hungry; [perf] be hungry [v-st]
isikhundla situation, place, position [n4-sg; pl: **izikhundla**]
kwanobunkokeli kwa na ubunkokeli by leadership (becoming the kind of leadership...)
ubunkokeli leadership
obonakeleyo which are left destitute
-**bonakalel**- be transparent, be visible, be seen to be; suffer a loss, be left destitute [v-atr-ben]

kumazwe ku [a]mazwe in countries
amazwe countries
enyulwe e nyulwe elected
-nyul- choose, select, elect
ngedemokhrasi democratically [= nga idemokhrasi] (lit: by democracy)
ifanele it is proper, suitable, right, fitting; ought, should
i- refers to inkokeli
ifunde i funde [subj] that he/leader study
kubaw' ku baw' from father
oye o ye [subj] that he [inkokeli] be
wavavanywa he has been tested [v-past-sub]
-vavany- test, try (out), examine, inspect, investigate [v-tr]
Abaphathi rulers
bemikhosi military [= ba imikhosi]
umkhosi military [n, atr]
kumakhulu ku [a]makhulu for many
eminyaka in years [= e-(i)mi-nyaka]
unyaka year
bafunde they should study [= ba-fund-e pres sub]
kuGerry ku Gerry with Gerry
Rawlings Rawlings (proper name)
waseGhana wa se Ghana of Ghana
nkokeli leaders
zimbini two
zinomdla they have interest [= zi na umdla]
umdla appetite, relish (for); delight (in); [ext] interest, enthusiasm [n2-sg]
kwizilangazelelo [= kwi zi langazelelo] in the desires
isilangazelelo longing, desire [n4-sg; pl: **izilangazelelo**]
zabantu of people
ndingavuya [= ndi nga vuya] I would be glad, grateful
-vuy- be glad, joyful, delighted
unokuvula he is able to open
-vul- open
esinje e si [isikolo] nje such [a]
phambi kokuba before
ayeke he might leave [v-pres-sub]
-yek- leave (off, alone); cease, stop; spare; give in, yield [v-tr]
kwiipolitiki kwa ipolitiki [from] politics
nguAM by AM
eKeetmanshoop e Keemanshoop in Keetmanshoop
eNamibia e Namibia in Namibia

Izimvo Zaba ... Masijonge kuMadiba

«1»

Mhleli, Indiphatha kakubi into eyenziwa ngabantu abathi bafundile ngokwenza izinto ezingafaniyo nale nto bayiyo.

«2»

Izolo eli, izifundiswa bezihleli phantsi, sixhuma-xhuma, besithi thina singamaqaba kuba behlonipha amaBhulu.

«3»

Namhlanje xa ilungile le nto esasiyifuna, bona ngoku bafuna ukuphazamisa. Ukuba nditsho, ayiphucukanga into eyenziwa ngoonesi ezibhedlele ukuyeka abantu besifa ngenjongo zokufuna ukuphila bona.

«4»

Imbi kakhulu lo nto iya sinyelisa kwizizwe ezinenjongo zokusixhasa ekuzameni ukusiphucula kobu bugxwayiba sikubo.

«5»

Amazwi athethwa ngoonesi ayandigulisa, ubawo uMadiba masimhlonipheni, singafane silibize nje igama lakhe.

«6»

Kufuneka sicinge ukusifukama kwakhe esesiqithini. Makhe sinyamezele khe sikhangele, sijonge kuMadiba negqiza lakhe mhlawumbi kuza kulunga.

«7»

Xa nditshoyo sanukungxama midaka yakowethu.

Fuzile Mxoli, Western Holdings, D24, Welkom

Vocabulary

izimvo opinions, ideas, feelings [n6-pl]
zaba of these (people) [deic-1-n1-pl-poss-n6-pl]
masijonge ma si jonge let's look at
kuMadiba to Madiba [tribal name for Nelson Mandela]
«1»
mhleli editor! [voc]
umhleli editor [n1-sg]
indiphatha it seems to me
-phath- feel, touch
eyenziwa e yenz iwa which is being done
ngabantu by people [n1-pl-agent]
abathi a ba thi who (they) say
bafundile ba fundile (they are) learned, educated
ngokwenza ngo kwenza by doing
ezingafaniyo ezi nga fan iyo which are not similar, like

nale na le with this
le this [dem-class5-sg]
bayiyo which they are [rel cop]
«2»
izolo yesterday [n3-sg-time, adv]
izifundiswa the educated, learned
bezihleli hlala phantsi sit down 'they sat down'
sixhuma-xhuma we rattling, prancing
xhuma-xhuma clank, rattle, prance
besithi be sithi we said, saying (participial)
thina we [pro-1pl-abs]
singamaqaba si nga maqaba we are not educated (lit: we are 'red' people)
maqaba 'red' people, uneducated people [n3-pl]
behlonipha be hlonipha they respected
amaBhulu white people, ususally Afrikaner
«3»
namhlanje today, nowadays [adv-time]
ilungile it is ok
esasiyifuna (the thing) (which) we still want
ngoku now [adv-time]
ukuphazamisa uku phazamisa hinder, impede, obstruct, interrupt
nditsho ndi tsho I say so
ayiphucukanga it is not civilized
-phucuk- slip off, come completely out; get rubbed, abraded, chafed, bruised; become smooth, polished; [ext] become civilized [v-intr]
eyenziwa which is being done
ngoonesi by nurses
ezibhedlele in the hospitals
izibhedlele hospital
ukuyeka to abandon, leave alone [v-inf]
-yek- leave, leave alone [XED:188]
besifa they being sick, they dying
fa be sick, die
ngenjongo on purpose, purposely; for the purpose (of)
injongo aim, object, purpose, goal; meaning [n5-sg]
zokufuna wanting
za ukufuna (poss) of wanting
ukuphila to be in [good] health
«4»
imbi it is bad
iN- he, she, it is ADJ [group 5 singular adjective agreement prefix used predicatively] i.e., copulative form
kakhulu much, very, a lot, greatly [adv]
iya it is going to
sinyelisa abuse, slander, revile us
-nyelis- abuse, slander, revile
kwizizwe in countries
izizwe countries
ezinenjongo which have the purpose
zokusixhasa za uku si xhasa of supporting us
ekuzameni e ku zam eni in the effort, in trying
ukusiphucula to civilize us
-phucul- to civilize [v-trans]
kobu in this [deic-1-n7-loc]
bugxwayiba (u) bu gxwayiba this country overgrown with bush
ubugxwayiba bushland, country overgrown with bush [n7-sg] [XED:54]
sikubo we are in
«5»
amazwi words
athethwa a theth wa [which are] spoken
ayandigulisa a ya ndi gulisa they [the words] make me sick
gulisa to make sick
ubawo father [n1a-sg]
uMadiba Nelson Mandela's tribal name
masimhlonipheni we should respect him

masi we should [hortative.aux-1pers-pl]
singafane si nga fane we cannot just
fana here, as aux 'just'
silibize si li bize (that) we call/invoke it [name] [subjunctive]
lakhe his [pro-3sg-poss-n3-sg]
«6»
sicinge that we think [present subjunctive]
ukusifukama here, to sit, in the sense of being in prison; a euphemism widely understood in S. Africa
-**fukam**- brood, sit on, lie in; digest (prey, of a snake)
kwakhe his, her [pro-3sg-poss-n8-vn]
esesiqithini while still on the island [locative]
-**se**- still
isiqithi island [n4-sg]
makhe let's do VERB a little
-**khe**- should VERB sometimes; might VERB a little
sinyamezele si nyamezele we must be patient, persevere, endure, bear
nyamezela endure, bear, be patient, persevere
sikhangele we should look at
-**khangel**- look (at), behold
sijonge we should look up to [v-1pl-pres-sub]
kuMadiba at Nelson Mandela
negqiza and a small group [n3-sg-conj]
igqiza small group, small number (of people) [n3-sg]
mhlawumbi perhaps [adv] (lit: another day)
kuza [it] is going to
kulunga to be all right [v-red-inf]
«7»
nditshoyo I say so
sanukungxama don't rush!
sanuku- -**a** don't (you all) VERB! [negative imperative pl]
-**ngxama**- rush, be impetuous
midaka common people; black people [n2-pl-red]
umdaka very dark person [n2-sg]
yakowethu our (lit: of ours)
Fuzile name
Mxoli name
Welkom location

Izikrelemnqa Zitshise Iincwadi Zesikolo

«1»

Isikolo seMfundo ePhakamileyo iNonceba kwilokishi yakwaZwelitsha ngaseQonce sisengxakini enkulu kunye nabazali babafundi besi sikolo ngokuthi sivula nje unyaka sitshiselwe iincwadi zizikrelemnqa ezingaziwayo.

«2»

Oku kwenzeke kwelinye lamagumbi elizaliswe ziincwadi ezisisipho sikarhulumente weli phondo nekungakhange kuvakale nomkhondo nakwimizi ekufutshane nesi sikolo.

«3»

Kuphando olwenziwe leli jelo kwinqununu yesi sikolo uNkosk. S.M. Mtika uthe intelekelelo yelahleko eyenzeke kwesi sikolo ifikelele kuma R50 000.

«4»

Uthe eyona ngxaki banayo kukuba iSebe leMfundo lazisa ukuba akukho ziincwadi zizakukhutshwa leli sebe kulo nyaka. UNkosk. Mtika ukwathe bafikelele ekubeni kubizwe intlanganiso yabazali ngokukhawuleza.

«5»

Kwakhona eli jelo xa belidlana indlebe noNtsumpa Clive Nkopo wesikhululo samapolisa kwaZwelitsha ungqinile ukuba kwenzeke umonakalo omkhulu nangona benganakwazi ukuba ungakanani ngenxa yophando oluqhutywayo ngabakwantsasana.

«6»

Uthe bafuna nabanina onolwazi eze ngaphambili kwaye ukhuselekile iyakuba ziindaba zakwamkhozi.

Vocabulary

izikrelemnqa vandals, criminals [n4-pl]
isikrelemnqa criminal (evildoer operating under cover of night), thief, burglar, vandal [n4-sg]
zitshise they burned
-tshis- burn [EXD:75]
iincwadi books [n5-pl]
zesikolo of school
«1»
seMfundo se Mfundo (of) education
ePhakamileyo e Phakamileyo which is high
phakamileyo high, in this sense, higher education
iNonceba (name of the school)
kwilokishi kwi lokishi located (in)] [EXD:353]
kwi in

lokishi location
yakwaZwelitsha ya kwa Zwelitsha (of) (at the place of) Zwelitsha
yakwa of
Zwelitsha noun
ngaseQonce near Qonce (King Williamstown)
ngase- nearby, near, close to, in the vicinity of [loc-cmp-prf]
Qonce King Williamstown
sisengxakini si (isikolo) se ngxak(a) ini it (sikolo) is in/has problems
ingxaki/iingxaki problem/s
enkulu big [adj-n5-sg]
-**khulu** big, huge, large [EXD:332]
nabazali and parents
abazali parents
babafundi of students
abafundi students [n1 pl]
besi of this [deic-1-n4-sg-poss-n1-pl]
ngokuthi because (here, auxiliary linking clause about age of school to main dialogue)
sivula it opens, is open
vula open
unyaka year [n1a-sg-time]
Alt: **umnyaka** [n2], **inyaka** [n5]
sitshiselwe it was burned [n4-sg-burn-appl-pass]
zizikrelemnqa by vandals
zizi by the [agent copulative following passive]
- **krelemnqa** vandals, thieves [prob. compound noun – see note in Lexicon]
ezingaziwayo unknown [rel; lit: which they not they are known]
«2»
kwenzeke happened
-**enzek**- happen
kwelinye in one
ilinye one [c3sg.enum]
lamagumbi of the rooms
igumbi room [n3-sg]
elizaliswe which were filled
zalisa fill
zala become full
ziincwadi by books [n5-pl-passive agent]
ziiN- by them [group 5 plural passive agent prefix construction on polysyllabic roots]
ezisisipho which are donated, which are gifts
pha donate [v-tr]
isipho gift, donation [n4-pl]
sikarhulumente by [lit: of] the government
sika of [n4-sg-poss-prf]
weli phondo of this province
weli of this [deic-1-n3-sg poss n1-sg]
phondo region (in SA: province)
iphondo province, region
nekungakhange that did not/were not ever
-**khange** not at all; never [preverb followed by **aux kha** in present subjunctive]
kuvakale to hear
nomkhondo with a trace, but rendered negative by -**khange**, thus, without a trace, not even a trace
na- here, without [**na**- following negative means 'not even']
umkhondo footprint, track, trace, trail; lead, clue; class, row [n2-sg]
nakwimizi na kwi mizi in the homes (**umzi/mizi**) [EXD:279]
ekufutshane near
nesi in this [AGR: sikolo]
«3»
kuphando in the investigation
phando investigation
olwenziwe olu wenziwe that it be done/carried out (imperative of passive)
leli by this [deic-1-n3-sg-pass-agent]
jelo source [n3-sg-red]

ijelo tube, pipe, spout; barrel (of gun); telescope; [fig] source (of information) [n3-sg]
kwinqununu kwi to , nqununu principal
uNkosk [Abr: uNkosikazi] Mrs., Miss, Ms.
S.M. Mtika (name)
uthe he/she said
intelekelelo estimate [EXD:195, NDK-91:99]
yelahleko of the loss
ilahleko loss [XED:80]
eyenzeke that happened
ey- that
enzeke happened
kwesi in this [deic-1-n4-sg-loc] kwa-esi [E&S:27]
ifikelele it reached
-**fikelel**- attain, reach [v-intens]
fikelele reached, amounts to
kuma ku [a]ma to [plural]
R50 000 50,000 Rands (S.A. currency)
«4»
eyona the real one, that very one; the most [group 5 singular emphatic pronoun]
ngxaki problem [n5-sg-red]
banayo they have
kukuba ku kuba is that
iSebe branch, department [EXD:67]
lazisa it announced, made known
lazisa la (leMfundo) azisa (it/Board of Education)
azisa make known (caus. form of **azi** 'to know')
akukho there is not; there are none [v-exis-neg-n10-impers]
ziincwadi they are books [pred]
zizakukhutshwa that will be released
ziza that will be
-**kukhutshwa** released
kulo in this [deic-1-n2-sg-loc]
ukwathe u kwa the also said
bafikelele they reached
ekubeni seeing that, in as much as, in that, whereas
kubizwe to be called
bizwe be called [v-pass]
intlanganiso meeting, assembly, congregation of people [n5-sg]
yabazali of parents
ngokukhawuleza right away, quickly, in a hurry
-**khawulez**- hurry, quickly, fast
«5»
kwakhona again
belidlana they were conferring
-**dla** eat, consume [v-tr]
-**dlana indlebe** confer (lit: to eat one another's ear) [v-recip; used to refer to s.o. having a discussion with s.o. else]
indlebe ear
noNtsumpa with Superintendent
no with
ntsumpa principal, head, superintendent
Clive Nkopo (name)
wesikhululo of the station
wesi- of [combo]
isikhululo station (railway, bus, police)
samapolisa of the police
amapolisa police
kwaZwelitsha in Zwelitsha
ungqinile he/she gave testimony/testified
ubungqina testimony, evidence [NDB-91:510-511]
ukugqina confirm, witness, testify
umonakalo damage
omkhulu big, large, huge; major [adj-n2-sg]
nangona although; even though [conj. followed by participial]
benganakwazi they cannot know
ngenxa because, on account of
yophando of the investigation
oluqhutywayo which is being conducted

-**qub**- push forward, drive, proceed in, push on with work [KED:361]
ngabakwantsasana by the police
ngaba by the members of...
kwantsasana of the police (lit: of the little branch of...)
«6»
nabanina anyone, anybody
na- -**na** [See note in Lexicon]
nabani anyone
onolwazi o na ulwazi (he/she) who has knowledge/knows
eze e ze that he/she come (subjunctive)
ngaphambili forward
ukhuselekile it is protected
-**khuselekile** protected
iyakuba it will be
ziindaba they are news
iindaba news, tidings; information; intelligence [n6-pl]
udaba report, message, item of conversation [n6-sg]
zakwamkhozi lit: confidentially; in this context **indaba zakwa-mkhozi** confidential information
Note: If the response to a request for information is **Zindaba zakwamkhozi** (in short **zezakwamkhozi**), it simply means that the information is confidential.
zakwa of
umkhozi eagle [n2-sg]

uThandi uphendula iingxaki zakho

«1»

Thandi: Ndingumfana oneminyaka engama-22, ingxaki yam, ngexesha ndisesikolweni ndaye ndathandana nentombazana eneminyaka engama-24 eyandifihlelayo ukuba itshatile, kwaye inomntwana oyintombazana.

«2»

Ekuhambeni kwexesha le ntombazana ibe nzima umntwana wam. Kungelo xesha apho waqala ukundixelela ukuba kanti utshatile. Kwanyanzeleka ukuba sohlukane, kodwa emva kokuba umntwana lo wam ezelwe baye bohlukana nomyeni wakhe.

«3»

Le ntombazana ibuyele kum indixelela ukuba ayinakwenza ngakumbi ngaphandle kwam. Into endikhathazayo kukuba umyeni lo wayo uye wathatha kunye nalo mntwana ungowam kuba engayazi ukuba asingo wakhe.

Okhathazekileyo, eMonti.

«4»

• Ingaba isazela sale ntombazana sona sithini? Okokuqala uthandane nawe kwakhona wabuyela emyenini wakhe enzima umntwana ongowakho.

«5»

Kwakhona wohlukane nomyeni wakhe wabuyela kuwe ngaphandle komntwana lowo. Wena okanye yena makamxelele umyeni lo wakhe ukuba umntwana asingowakhe.

«6»

Lindela inkathazo nakanjani kuba kaloku kunyanzelekile ubonakalise ubungqina bokuba asingomntwana wakhe.

Vocabulary

uThandi proper name
uphendula answers, replies to
iingxaki problems
ndingumfana I am a young man
umfana young man
oneminyaka who is NUM years old
  one o na he/she who has/is
engama-22 22 (years)
ndisesikolweni I was still in school [= ndi-s-e-(i)si-kol(o)/w-eni]
ndaye I did VERB [remote past compound tense preverb]
ndathandana I fell in love (with)
nentombazana with a girl
eyandifihlelayo who (from) me was someone who hid

-**fihlel**- conceal for/from, hide
itshatile she is/was married
-**tshat**- marry (said only of a woman) [v-trans & v-intr]
inomntwana has a child
oyintombazana who is a girl
Ekuhambeni in (the) going
kwexesha of time
ntombazana young single girl [n5-sg-dim-red]
ibe i be she became (from **ba**)
nzima 'pregnant'; heavy, difficult
Kungelo ku ngelo at that [neut-adv-dem]
waqala she began
ukundixelela to tell me, mention to me
utshatile she was married
kwanyanzeleka it forced (us)
-**nyanzelek**- be forced, compelled
sohlukane that we would separate [v-fut-sub]
so- we will VERB [contracted positive future pronoun prefix]
emva kokuba after
emva after [loc] in the rear
kokuba [lit: of being]
ezelwe it had been born, having been born
baye [aux compound tense]
bohlukana and they would separate (from)
bo- [short fut]
nomyeni with husband
umyeni husband [n1-sg]
ibuyele she returned
-**buyel**- return
kum with, to, from me
indixelela (and) told me
ayinakwenza she cannot ever do
ayi- he, she, it does not VERB [n5-sg neg present subject prefix]
-**nakw**- -naku- **na** here has sense of 'never'; **ku** because of vowel verb
ngakumbi all the more, especially [adv]
ngaphandle except for, without
kwam my (place); mine; my own (domain) [pro-1sg-poss-n10-loc]
endikhathazayo that which bothers me
-**khataz**- worry, bother, trouble
kukuba it is that
wayo of hers [poss]
uye he even
wathatha he took
-**thath**- -take [v-tr]
nalo with this
ungowam who is mine
engayazi that he does not know
asingo- he, she, it is not ... [group 1a singular negative copulative ~ predicative prefix construction]
okhathazekileyo one who is troubled
-**khathazek**- [Verb-troubled]
eMonti in East London (place name)
ingaba it seems, perhaps, maybe
isazela conscience; consciousness [n4-sg]
sale of this [deic-1-n5-sg-poss-n4-sg]
sona he, she, it [group 4 singular absolutive pronoun]
sithini what is it (conscience) saying?
-**thini** do something, do anything; [qw] do what?; [dummy] do whatever action is implied [v-intr = -thi + -ni]
okokuqala to start with
uthandane she fell in love
nawe with you
kwakhona again, in the same way [adv]
wabuyela she returned
emyenini to the husband
enzima being pregnant
ongowakho which is yours
wohlukane and she would separate [fut sub]
wo- [short fut]
nomyeni with the husband
kuwe to you

komntwana to the child
lowo that [deic-2-n1-sg]
makamxelele must tell him [v-hort]
asingowakhe it is not his
lindela wait expectantly for [v-ben]
inkathazo problem
nakanjani anyway
kaloku of course
kunyanzelekile it's compulsory
ubonakalise that you show
-**bonakalis**- show, reveal, make visible [v-atr-caus]
ubungqina evidence; testimony [n7-sg]
bokuba of that
asingomntwana it's not a child

Abantu Bayazazi Iinkokeli Zabo

«1»

Mhleli,

Ndithi makhe ndiseke kwelijikayo ngabantu aba babizwa nje ngeenkokeli zemveli.

«2»

Hayi zinto zikabawo ukuba aniwazi amakhosi anisokuze niphinde niwazi. Inkokeli ikhethwa ngabantu, ke abantu bayayazi inkokeli yabo, kanti inkosi iyinkosi ngabantu, xa bengekho abantu asokuze ibe yinkosi.

«3»

Amaninzi amakhosi ayetsho ngezisu eziphaya esondliwa lucalucalulo, kwakubanjwa abantu ngamaDlagusha ngenxa yawo amakhosi.

«4»

Amakhosi amaninzi ayengafuni ukwahlukana nobandlululo kuba ayezii-"baas boy." Xa unokucinga mlesi kwakusenziwa yintoni ukuba bonke oorhulumente bonomgogwana baphathwe ngamakhosi?

«5»

Jonga KwaZulu, kwaVenda, Bophuthatswana, Transkei, Ciskei nakwaNdebele, kwakuphethe amakhosi esitya kakuhle ngenxa yobandlululo.

«6»

Asimangalanga xa sibona bengafuni kuyiwe elugqatsweni, besenza umfelandawonye namaDlagusha, kodwa kuba abantu bayazazi iinkokeli zabo bawaqhawula loo matyathanga.

«7»

Nakule ke ngoku nango eshumayela lo vangeli. Kutheni amakhosi xa efuna amalungelo awo esebenzisa uluntu? Asenzele ntoni isizwe yonke le minyaka iinkokeli ziseziseleni, elubhacweni? Phantsi ngamaveletshona!!

Paulos Tshatshu,

P.O. Box 324

Isipingo

4110

Vocabulary

bayazazi they know
iinkokeli leaders [n5-pl]
-kokel- lead, guide
zabo theirs [pro-3pl-poss-n5-pl]
«1»
ndithi I am saying
ndiseke that I support
kwelijikayo of this turnabout [= kwa-ili-jik-a-yo]
-jik- change, turn around, turn about, rotate, crooked, wire [v]
babizwa who are called [v-pass]
nje ngeenkokeli as leaders
zemveli of the time
imveli origin, the old time, nature [n-5sg]
«2»
zinto things—here means 'children' [vocative]
zikabawo of the father, of my father
zika- of [personal possessive prefix/marker for noun group 5 plural]
aniwazi you don't know
amakhosi chiefs [n3-pl; sg: **inkosi**]
-khosi an army, regiment, force, chieftainship, lordship, chief [here – n-5sg]
anisokuze you won't (will never) [a-ni-sa-ukuze]
-**s(a)** exclusive form, 'never'
-**(u)kuze** never VERB [preverb (aux) taking S3a + fut. subjunctive]
niphinde you again
-phind- do VERB again [v-aux] Cf: -phind- fold over, turn a thing over itself; revenge [v]
niwazi you know
ikhethwa he, she, it is chosen
-kheth- select, pick out, choose
ke well, but, now, then, and so [conj-adv/embellishment]
bayayazi they know
yabo their [pro-3pl-poss-n5-sg]
iyinkosi he is a chief
xa bengekho abantu if there were no people
bengekho they being absent [v-pred-neg-part]
-kho there, from [prn-abs 'khona']
«3»
amaninzi there are many
ayetsho who said (who had)
aye- they had VERBed [group 3 plural contracted remote past compound tense]
ngezisu with a stomach
su belly, stomach, abdomen, the muscle of the side, large tripe of an animal [n-4sg]
eziphaya that are over there
phaya beyond, over there, yonder, on the other side of [n-loc/adv]
esondliwa that is fed
-ondla bring up, feed, nourish, cherish, provide for, rear [v]
lucalu-caluIo by distinction; Apartheid
-calul- make distinction, distinction, partiality [v]
kwakubanjwa when they were arrested [pass impersonal temporal]
kwaku- when it VERBs/VERBed [group 10 locative/impersonal noun temporal construction]
ngamaDlagusha by the sheep eaters [pass-agent] – here 'the Boers' (the Afrikaner government of the time)
dla eat, consume [v-tr mono]
gusha merino sheep, sheepskin cloak; derived from the verb, to speak frankly, conceal, hide [n-5sg]
yawo their [n3-pl-poss-n5-sg]

«4»
ayengafuni they had not wanted
aye- they had VERBed [group 3 plural contracted remote past compound tense]
ukwahlukana to part with
-**ahlul**- lose, part with, be severed from, differ from each other, disunion, separate, divide [v]
nobandlululo and/with/from Apartheid [n-2sg]
baas boy Uncle Tom, White Man's lackey, fink (collaborator during the Apartheid era)
baas master, overlord {Afr}
unokucinga you can think
-**noku**- can
Contrast: -**cinga** wheat, anything thin; elope, run away
mlesi reader
lesa read {Afr lesen} [v; uncommon usage]
kwakusenziwa what was causing
kwaku- [remote past]
oorhulumente governments [n1a-pl]
bonomgogwana ba-u-no-(u)m-gog-(w)-ana puppet [atr]
baphathwe they are ruled
ngamakhosi by chiefs
«5»
kwaZulu (province in South Africa, former homeland)
kwaVenda (province in South Africa, former homeland)
Bophuthatswana (province in South Africa, former homeland)
Transkei (province in South Africa, former homeland)
Ciskei (province in South Africa, former homeland)
nakwaNdebele and Ndebele (province in South Africa, former homeland)
kwakuphethe they were ruled
kwaku- neuter form of concord
Cf: **kwakufika inkwenkwe** a boy arrived
esitya they eating
kakuhle nicely [adv]
yobandlululo (on account) of Apartheid [poss-n1a-sg]
«6»
asimangalanga we were not surprised
-**mangal**- be astonished, wonder, marvel, accuse, complaint, amazing [v]
sibona we see
kuyiwe to go, be part of
-**iya** go, move [v]
elugqatsweni in the race
-**gqats**- make hot, race for, scorch, a race [v]
umfelandawonye supporter, staunch member of a specific group [n1-sg-cmp; lit: one who (with others) dies at one place]
namaDlagusha the Boers
bawaqhawula they cut short
-**qhawul**- snap short, break short, cut short, rupture [v-tr]
loo those [deic-2-n3-pl]
matyathanga eaters of pumpkin [n-3pl]
ithanga pumpkin, gourd; the thigh [n3-sg]
«7»
nakule and to this (in the sense of 'moving on')
nango here it is [conj+cop]
eshumayela he/she preaches [v-part]
-**shumayel**- report, proclaim, preach [v]
vangeli sermon [n-5sg] {Afr}
kutheni why? [qw-adv]
xa efuna when they want
amalungelo advantages, benefits; rights, privileges [n3-pl]
awo their [n3-pl-poss-n3-pl]
esebenzisa they use [v-part]
asenzele they did
yonke all [pro-enum-n2-pl]
minyaka years [n-2pl]
ziseziseleni they are in cells
seleni prison cell [n-loc]{Eng}

elubhacweni in exile [n6-loc]
ubhaco destitution [n6-sg]
-**bhac**- wander about in a destitute state; be homeless; go without having any definite object in view [v-intr]
Cf: -**bhac**- cut a skin dress [v]

ngamaveletshona!! with Westerners! (lit: with those who come from the West)
-**tshon**- go down, disappear, sink, drown; become bankrupt; set (of celestial body) [v-intr] hence, West

Paulos (personal name)

Tshatshu (family name)

Isipingo (city in South Africa)

Sichazele Ngawakho Amazwi Imo Yezinto Ezisezakwenzeka

«1»

Lisekhona ixesha lokuba ubenezwi ekwenziweni ko Mgaqosiseko. Besithanda ukuva kuwe malunga nale mibandela ebalulekileyo.

I-Volkstaat/Ukuzibalula Koluntu

«2»

• Ingaba umgaqosiseko kufuneka ukuqwalasele ukuzibalula koluntu oluzithethe zifanayo?

«3»

• Ukuba ucinga okokuba umgaqosiseko lo mawukuqwalasele oku ingaba ke oku makube kwimo yamaphandle i-volkstaat umzekelo - okanye ingaba ikhona enye indlela yokuphuhlisa?

«4»

• Luhlobo luni lolulunto ekungathiwa luhlangene ngezithethe ukuze kuqinisekiseke ubume balo?

«5»

• Kufuneka ibekwiliphi ibanga inkxaso yoluntu njengesikhokelo sokuzibalula? Deadline 4 June 1995

«6»

Inkqubo Yonyulo

«7»

• Ingaba amalungu ePalamente kufuneka anyulwe njani?

«8»

• Ingaba inkqubo yethu yonyulo kufuneka isekelwe kuludwe lwamaqela njengoko bekwenziwe kunyulo luka 1994 - okanye kufuneka ihlanganiswe nomgaqosiseko? Deadline 19 June 1995

«9»

Inguqu Kumgaqosiseko

«10»

• Wakuba uMgaqosiseko wokugqibela wamkelwe, ingaba kufuneka inguqu zenziwe njani? Deadline 20 June 1995

«11»

Veza izimvo zakho ephepheni kwaye unike iimbono zakho okanye iziphakamiso ku Mlawuli Omkhulu, Indlu yowiso mthetho, P.O. Box 15, Cape Town 8000, okanye thumela nge fax (021) 24 1160/1. Sincede ekubeni sibumbe ikamva lethu sonke.

Vocabulary

Sichazele explain to us
ngawakho with yours, your own, by means of your...
imo status; derived from **-ma** stand, stop, stand beside each other
ezisezakwenzeka that are still to happen [e-zi-se-za-k(u)w-enz-ek-a]
lisekhona it [n3-sg] is there
ubenezwi you have a voice [= u-be-na-i-zwi]
ekwenziweni in the making [= e-kw-enz-iw-eni]
ko of [personal possessive prefix ~ marker for n10-loc]
umgaqosiseko constitution [n2-sg-cmp]
umgaqo regulation, class, ruler, standard [n2-sg]
-sek- foundation, support, base, stand, a circle for a hut [n-4sg]
besithanda we would like
ukuva to hear [v-inf]
malunga towards; about, concerning, regarding, with regard to [adv]
mibandela amendments, grafts, supplement [n-2pl-red]
ebalulekileyo that is important
-balul- notable, distinguished, make an exception, distinction [XED:7]
Contrast: selection, a choice; pick out
Volkstaat (a People's State in South Africa)
ukuzibalula to select for oneself; self-determination [= uku-zi-balul-a]
ukuqwalasele to observe attentively
-qwalasel- watch, view, look at intently, observe attentively; address (an issue) [v-tr]
koluntu of mankind
oluzithethe which is traditional [atr-n-4pl]
isithethe traditional custom, tradition [n-4sg]
Contrast: **-thetha** the derivative of such words as speak, orator, captain, a speech, a law, an advocacy
zifanayo alike
-fan- like, resemble, fitting, proper [v]
ucinga you think
okokuba ukuba that
makube let there be
kwimo the state
yamaphandle the country outside, external
phandle outside, out, without, the outside of anything [old locative noun]
umzekelo example; pattern [n2-sg]
yokuphuhlisa come up well
-phuhl- grow well, be full of sap, come up well, healthy, be energetic, vigorous [v-tr]
luhlobo it is a kind [n6-sg pred]
uhlobo sort, kind, type; [atr] choice, pedigree [n6-sg]
luni what kind?, of what sort? [qw-n6-sg]
ekungathiwa that can be said
luhlangene it is joined with
-hlangan- assemble, meet together, join with, meet with [v-recip]
kuqinisekiseke be confirmed [= ku-qin-is-ek-is-ek-e]

-**qin**- firm, steadfast, confirm, establish, convinced, sure [v-tr]
Contrast: -**qina** rendering, melting
ubume position, state, status, condition [n7-sg]
balo its, of it
ibekwiliphi be where
ibanga interval, reason [n3-sg]
-**bang**- bring on, space, cause, interval, claim, pace, ground, step, reason [XED:8]
inkxaso support, maintenance; subsidy [n5-sg]
yoluntu of the community
njengesikhokelo as the lead
isikhokelo lead [n4-sg]
sokuzibalula to select, to self-determine
inkqubo procedure; program (radio, TV); proceedings; progress, advancement [n5-sg]
Yonyulo of the election
unyulo election [n6-sg]
amalungu members [n-3pl]
Contrast: -**lungu** a European, knot, joint, a little bit
ePalamente parliament {Eng}
anyulwe they be selected
njani how
nja how, such, it is so [adv-found in compound form]
Contrast: -**nja** a dog
inkqubo yethu our progress
isekelwe that it be supported
kuludwe in a row [loc+n-6sg]
dwe a chain of mountains, a row of things [n-6sg]
lwamaqela of the companies
iqela company, group; line, file of men; number of people; [ext] gang [n3-sg; pl: **amaqela**]
Contrast: -**qela** a plough furrow, scratched line
njengoko like that, and
bekwenziwe it was done
luka of
nomgaqosiseko of/in the Constitution
inguqu change, turn-around; return; rally [n5-sg]
guqu verb root from which is derived: a rally, return, turn, repentance, changed, altered [v-tr]
kumgaqosiseko in the Constitution
wakuba if it is to be [verb-to be-temporal form]
wokugqibela to end
wamkelwe it be received
zenziwe be done [= z-enz-iw-e]
veza produce, make appear, show, bring forth [v-tr]
izimvo opinions [n6-pl]
ephepheni on paper, in writing, to the newspaper
phepha a light thing, a paper, newspaper [n-3sg]
Contrast: blow away, flutter [v-tr&intr]
kwaye and also
unike you give
iimbono views, outlooks, visions, sights, prospects [n5-pl]
iziphakamiso motions, submissions
umlawuli ruler, governor [n1-sg]
omkhulu large, major, superior, chief [adj-n1-sg]
indlu house, hut, den, dwelling – in this context Parliament
yowiso of 'make fall-law' place where law is made.
-**wa** fall, drop; cross over [v-intr, derived from: a club, snare, stumbling block]
sincede help us
sibumbe that we form [= si-bumb-e]
-**bumb**- mould, form, shape, a corporation [v-tr]
ikamva in future, the hereafter [n-5sg]
Cf: **kamva** afterwards, after [adv-time]
sonke we all [pro-enum-1pl]

Iinkcukacha Zemfundo

«1»

Imfundo iguqukile eMzantsi Afrika kunyaka ka 1997. ICurriculum 2005 nemfundo esekelwe kwiziphumo iye yaqaliswa kanti kufakwe imali eninzi kwiMfundo Noqeqesho Lwabantu Abadala. Kule nyanga uTyhila Ufunde ukuphathele izinto eziya kukwenza uziqhele yaye uzazi ezi nguqu.

«2»

Ukuphathwa kwezikolo

Leading Together

Incwadana yeeKomiti Eziphethe Izikolo

«3»

ISouth African Schools Act ka-1996 ithi izikolo kufuneka zikhethe iikomiti eziza kuzilawula. Abazali, abafundi noluntu ngokubanzi ngoku banenxaxheba enkulu ekuphathweni kwezikolo yaye banegunya lokwenza izigqibo ngemicimbi yemali neyolawulo.

«4»

Kungenxa yoko kuye kwaveliswa incwadana ethi Leading Together. Le ncwadana iluncedo kumalungu eekomiti zezikolo noluntu ngokubanzi. Le ncwadana ichaza okuthethwa ngokuphatha nokuthi amalungu angayenza isebenze kakuhle njani ikomiti yabo.

«5»

Le ncwadana ithetha ngezi zinto zilandelayo:

- Imisebenzi nezikhundla zekomiti elawula izikolo;
- indlela yokuyila inkqubo yolawulo;
- ukuphatha isikolo.

«6»

Kukho nemibuzo ngezinto ofanele uzenze xa ikomiti elawula isikolo ingasebenzi kakuhle. Incwadana ethi Leading Together iluncedo yaye isisikhokelo somsebenzi wekomiti elawula isikolo. Xa ufuna ukuyiodola le ncwadana, bhalela kule dilesi: The Catholic Institute of Education, P.O. Box 2083, Southdale, 2135.

Vocabulary

iinkcukacha details [n5-pl = iin-kcukach-a]
inkcukacha detail, particular [n5-sg]
zemfundo [= za-im-fund-o] educational
«1»
iguqukile it has changed
-**guquk**- turn around, back ~ over; convert, change one's mind, repent [v-intr]
kunyaka in the year [n1a-sg-time = ku-(u)nyaka]
ICurriculum {Eng}
nemfundo [= na-im-fund-o] (and) education
esekelwe supported by, based on
sekela support
kwiziphumo by the results, outcomes
iye it did , it was, became
yaqaliswa it started
ya- he, she, it VERBed [n5-sg-S3b]
-**qalisw-** be begun, get started [v-pass]
kufakwe ku fakwe put into [past]
faka put in, on, among; insert
kwiMfundo [= kw(a)-i-m-fund-o] from Education
noqeqesho and Training
uqeqesho training [n6-sg]
-**qeqesh**- break in, train (draft animal); discipline (child); educate s.o. [v-tr]
Lwabantu lu abantu of the people
Abadala parents, adult (here refers to Adult Education)
nyanga month
uTyhila (name)
Ufunde (surname) (lit: he learned)
ukuphathele she introduces you to
-**phathel**- carry for; bring to; [fig] introduce [v-ben]
eziya that will
kukwenza to make
uziqhele you get familiar [refl]
-**qhel-** be familiar with, get accustomed to, acquainted with
uzazi you know them [v-pro-2pl+n5-pl-obj]
nguqu [n5-sg-red]
inguqu change, turn-around; return; rally [n5-sg]
«2»
Ukuphathwa the management
phatha manage
kwezikolo of the schools
incwadana booklet, pamphlet [n5-sg-dim]
yeeKomiti of the committee
yee- of the
Komiti committee {Eng}
Eziphethe that are in charge of
«3»
ISouth African Schools Act (name of Act of Parliament)
ithi i thi (it) states/is as follows
zikhethe that they choose [v-sub]
eziza kuzilawula which are going to govern themselves
-**lawul**- govern, rule
abafundi students, pupils [n1-pl; Sg: **umfundi**]
Cf: **abafundi** they don't learn
noluntu and society ~ the community [= na-ulu-ntu]
banenxaxheba enkulu they have a big role (to play) [= ba-na-i-nxaxheba]
-**nenxaxheba** have a share/role in s.t.; show interest in s.t.; take part in (game, contest) [v-poss-cmp]
inxaxheba right hind-quarter of meat; chief's portion, share; [ext] interest in (an issue); participation [n5-sg]

ekuphathweni in managing or administering
banegunya they have authority or right [= ba-na-i-gunya]
lokwenza of making ~ doing
izigqibo decisions, conclusions, outcomes
ngemicimbi yemali about financial matters
umcimbi matter, subject (under discussion); affair, transaction [n2-sg]
yemali of money [n5-sg-poss-n2-pl]
neyolawulo and of control, management ~ administration
«4»
kungenxa ku ngenxa on account of
Cf: **ngenxa yoko** therefore [conj-expr]
yoko ya+oko of that [indefinite sense]
kuye comes [C8SC+ya(e)]
kwaveliswa kwa veliswa was produced
velisa produce
ethi which is called; [atr] named, called
ncwadana booklet [n5-sg-red; See: incwadana above]
iluncedo helpful
-**luncedo** helpful [n6-sg-atr]
uncedo help [n6-sg]
kumalungu to members [n3-pl-loc]
ilungu/amalungu member/s
ichaza it explains
okuthethwa oku thethwa what is being discussed (?)
ngokuphatha by the management
nokuthi and how
angayenza a nga yenza they can do, make
isebenze it works, that it may work (i.e., with above, 'they can make it work')
yabo their (own); theirs [pro-3pl-poss-n5-sg]
«5»
ithetha it discusses
ngezi about these [deic-1-n5-pl-relat]
zilandelayo which are the following
nezikhundla and situations, positions
isikhundla situation, position
elawula which governs, administers; [atr] administrative [v-rel]
e lawula administrative
ikomiti elawula isikolo board of education, governing body
yokuyila of planning, designing
-yila mark out, plan, design
inkqubo program
«6»
nemibuzo na imibuzo and questions
umbuzo/imibuzo question/s
ngezinto about things [= nga-izin-to]
ofanele o fanele suitable, right, proper
uzenze you should do them
ingasebenzi i nga sebenzi (that) it may work
isisikhokelo its guidance
somsebenzi of work
wekomiti of the committee
ukuyiodola to order it
-odola order [v-tr] {Eng}
bhalela write to
Southdale (name of town)

Ubonelelo Ngerhafu '95

«1»

Guest: Molo, ndifuna intwana-ntwana ze Kreshi. Wenzantoni Lindiwe?

«2»

Lindiwe: Ndizalisa uxwebhu lwam lwerhafu.

«3»

Guest: Kwowu, kufuneka ndiluzalise nam, kodwa ndiyoyika ukohlwaywa kuba ndingazange ndiluthumele uxwebhu lwam lwerhafu ngaphambili.

«4»

Lindiwe: Ngoba kutheni? Urhulumente uyazifuna iirhafu zethu ukuze azalisekise imfuno zabantu.

«5»

Guest: Ndiyazi, kodwa zeziphi iirhafu ekufuneka ndizihlawule? Ndiyoyika kananjalo ukuba ndizakuhlawuliswa inzala kwimali ekunokuthi kanti ndiyayibamba, okanye ndohlwaywe ngokungayihlawuli irhafu kwilixa elidlulileyo. Molo, Jabu liqhuba njani ushishino lweTaxi?

«6»

Jabu: Kakuhle, enkosi. Ndikuvile oko ukutshoyo. Andizange ndibhalisele irhafu ngaphambili, nangona bendifanele ukuba ndenze njalo.

«7»

Lindiwe: Ngethamsanqa, urhulumente wenza ubonelelo ngokwerhafu. Wonke umntu ongazange abhalisele irhafu ngomhla we 26 April, nobefanele ukuba wenze njalo, nabo bonke umkhomishinali angakhange akwazi ukubahlawulisa irhafu kuba engakhange abafumane, banokuthi ngoku bahlawule irhafu ngaphandle kokoyika isohlwayo.

«8»

Guest: Zavakala mnandi ezo ndaba. Singazifumanaphi iinkcukakca ezingaphezulu?

«9»

Lindiwe: Funa incwadana yobonelelo ngerhafu ukuze ubenakho ukufaka isicelo. Ukuba ufuna iinkcukakca ezingaphezulu unokutsalela imfono-mfono esimahla kule nombolo 0800-11-39-30. Uza kuncedwa ngolwimi olukhethwe nguwe.

«10»

Jabu: Sinexesha elingakanani?

«11»

Lindiwe: Kufuneka ufake isicelo sobonelelo ngokwerhafu phambi komhla we 31 Oktober.

«12»

Jabu: Ziindaba ezimnandi ezi. Ndiza kutsala umnxeba ngoku!

Vocabulary

ubonelelo provision; advantage; concession [n6-sg]
  -bonelel- provide for or against s.t.; take advantage of [v-intens]
ngerhafu (ngerafu) about taxes
  irhafu tax; the hut-tax [n5-sg; Alt sp: **irafu**]
«1»
Molo good morning! (greeting)
intwana-ntwana small things
  intwana a little, a small thing [in+to+(w)+ana]
ze of [c5-agr+a>e]
Kreshi creche {Eng} – daycare place for children
Wenzantoni What are you doing?
Lindiwe (personal name)
«2»
Ndizalisa I'm filling
uxwebhu discourse, long discussion, treatment; [ext] document; form (to be filled in) [n6-sg]
lwam my [pro-1sg-poss-n6-sg]
«3»
kwowu Oh! [astonishment]
ndiyoyika I'm afraid
ukohlwaywa to be punished
  -ohlway- reprove, punish, find fault, rebuke, repent [v-tr]
ndingazange I never
  -zange never VERBed [preverb used with pres sub]
ndiluthumele sent it
«4»
ngoba why? [qw-adv]
uyazifuna he/she wants them
azalisekise that it may cause fulfillment
imfuno needs
«5»
Ndiyazi I understand, I know
zeziphi which of
ndizihlawule I should pay
  hlawula expiate, pay
kananjalo in that way
  nja such, the like, so, how, thus, of that kind [used only in compound form]
inzala progeny; interest
  zala progeny, bear, generate, to be born
kwimali on the money
ekunokuthi which is ours (lit: which we have earned)
ndiyayibamba I am keeping
ndohlwaywe and I will be punished
  ndo- I will VERB [contracted or short positive future pro prefix]
kwilixa at the time
elidlulileyo that has passed
  -dlul- pass by, pass, pass through, go past; excel, the giraffe
Jabu (personal name)
liqhuba how is progress?
ushishino trade, act of doing business [n6-sg]

Cf: **ishishini** workshop, factory; trade, business; handicraft [n3-sg]
lweTaxi of the taxi
itaxi taxi [n5-sg] {Eng}
«6»
enkosi thank you
ndikuvile I heard
ukutshoyo that which you said
andizange I never
ndibhalisele (I) registered
-bhalisel- lit: make write to
bendifanele ukuba ndenze njalo I probably should have done that (so)
bendi- I was/have been VERBing [contracted near/recent past continuous prefix]
-fanele be fit, right for; suit, become s.o.; be one's duty, ought, should
-fanela ukuba probably
ndenze I did, I have done
«7»
Ngethamsanqa by good fortune
thamsanqa a lucky event, a benefit, good fortune, bestow
ngokwerhafu about tax
ngokwe (ngokwa- + i-) about
wonke umntu everybody
ongazange who never did
abhalisele (they) register
ngomhla on the day
nabo with it, and it, there it is, (here) with them, and they
umkhomishinali the commissioner {Eng}
angakhange he never
engakhange abafumane never being able to find them
abafumane he not finding them
banokuthi they can say
bahlawule they should pay
isohlwayo punishment [n4-sg]
«8»
zavakala be clear, be heard [= za-v-akal-a]
-vakal- perceptible, sensible, intelligible, sound; distinctly
ezo ndaba that (lit: those) news
ezo those (not far, just mentioned) [deic-2-n6-pl]
ndaba news; information [n6-pl-red]
singazifumanaphi where can we get
ezingaphezulu that are above
«9»
yobonelelo of the concession [n6-sg-poss-n5-sg]
ubenakho that you be there
ukufaka to put in
isicelo request, application [n4-sg]
unokutsalela you can call
tsala drag, pull, draw, haul, attract, cable, rope, a thong, cable
imfono-mfono phone {Eng}
esimahla which is free
-simahla free, gratis, for nothing
nombolo number {Afr, Eng}
0800-11-39-30 phone number
uza kuncedwa you will be helped
kuncedwa to be helped [red-inf]
ngolwimi in the language
ulwimi language; the tongue; a lie
olukhethwe that is chosen
nguwe by you
«10»
sinexesha we have time
elingakanani? how much?
ngaka so much, so great, how much, how great
-nani question suffix
«11»
sobonelelo of the concession [n6-sg-poss-n4-sg]
phambi kwa in front of; before [prep-cmp]
«12»
ndiza kutsala I will pull
tsala umnxeba phone [v-cmp] (lit: pull the cord)
umnxeba vine sp., cord; [ext] phone [n2-sg]

Bekuyimini Ebalulekileyo Kugraca Xa Umandela Ebesecaleni Kwakhe

«1»

UNelson Mandela kutshanje ubesecaleni kwakhe njengeqabane likaGraca Machel xa ebefumana isidanga sokuhlonitshwa eEssex University eUnited Kingdom ngomsebenzi wakhe wokuba ngummeli wamalungelo abantwana ehlabathini.

«2»

Isibini sokuqala esithandwayo eAfrika siye samkelwa sisihlwele ebesinemincili ekufikeni kwaso ngehelikopta eEssex University kufutshane naseColchester.

«3»

Kodwa kulo lonke olu tyelelo, iNkokeli yaseMzantsi Afrika enama-79 eminyaka ibingafuni ukuba kubalasele yona. "Kaloku oku akunanto yakwenza nam, kufuna uNksk. Machel," utshilo.

«4»

"Le yimini yakhe. Uyingqonyela."

«5»

Belinemincili iqabane lakhe elinama-51 eminyaka nelingumhlolokazi kaSamora Machel owayenguMongameli waseMozambique nowasweleka kuntlitheko lwenqwelo-moya ngo-1986.

«6»

Kuba ubomi bakhe wabubeka esichengeni ekubhukuqweni korhulumente wamaPhuthukezi waza wangumphathiswa wemfundo kwiMozambique ekhululekileyo apho wenza iinzame zokuphelisa ukungakwazi ukubhala nokufunda, uGraca ubekufanele ukuwongwa.

«7»

Isidanga sehonours usinikwe ngenxa yomsebenzi awenza ngokuphanda ngemfazwe neziphumo zayo kubantwana. UMachel ukhethwe yiUN njengengcali kulo mba yaza iYunivesithi yase Essex yamcela ukuba avelise izifundo ezibini ngalo mba.

«8»

"Eli wonga andilithabathi ngokuba lelam kuphela. Ndimele izigidi zabantwana abaye babona imfazwe," utshilo uNksk. Machel xa ebephuma kweli theko. ethwesw' isidanga.

Vocabulary

bekuyimini it was a day [= be-ku-yi-mini]
beku it was/has been VERBing [group 10 locative noun contracted near/recent past continuous prefix]
kuGraca to Graca (personal name)
uMandela Nelson Mandela
ebesecaleni he was at the side [recent past participial locative]
ebe- he/she was
kwakhe his/her (place), its (domain) [pro-3sg-poss-n10-loc]
«1»
uNelson (male personal name)
kutshanje recently [adv]
ubesecaleni he was at the side
ube- he was VERBing; she has been VERBing [group 1, 1a singular contracted near/recent past continuous prefix]
njengeqabane as her companion
likaGraca of Graca
lika- of [personal possessive prefix / marker for n3-sg]
Machel person's last name
ebefumana she was getting
isidanga necklace of beads; [ext] degree (academic) [n4-sg]
sokuhlonitshwa for respect, for honoring
soku for
eEssex University at Essex University {Eng}
eUnited Kingdom {Eng}
ngomsebenzi for the work
ngom for the [ng(a) +(u)m > ngom]
wokuba of being [poss + Verb]
ngummeli be a representative
ummeli representative [C2-noun]
wamalungelo of the rights
wama- [combo form indicating that n3 pl (**ama**-) is possessed by a n1-sg (**wa**-)]
«2»
isibini two; second; pair; the couple [n4-sg-num]
sokuqala of the first
soku- of the
esithandwayo adored
eAfrika in Africa
siye they did, were [C4-pl+aux]
samkelwa was welcomed
sisihlwele by a crowd
isihlwele crowd, retinue, company, band, a number of people [n4-sg]
ebesineminciIi that was rejoicing
imincili rejoicing, gladness, bursts of joy, merriment [n2-pl]
ekufikeni at the arrival
kwaso their [n4-sg-poss-n8-vn, refers to the couple's arrival]
ngehelikopta by helicopter {Eng}
ihelikopta helicopter {Eng}
kufutshane very near
naseColchester to Colchester (town)
«3»
kulo to, from, in, with him, her, it [n6-sg-pro-loc]
lonke all, entire, the whole of [pro-enum-n6-sg]
tyelelo visit [n6-sg-red]
utyelelo visit [n6-sg]
tyelela/tyelelela pay a visit to, visit (tell news to) [v-tr]
yaseMzantsi Afrika of South Africa
yase of [poss+loc]
enama-79 that has 79
enama that has [C5-sg.agr+na+(a)ma]
eminyaka of years [C2-pl.rel]
ibingafuni he did not want [v-recent past – he was not wanting]
ibi- he was/she has been VERBing [group 5 singular

contracted near/recent past continuous prefix]
kubalasele give attention to [C15(Inf)-verb (red)]
-**balasel**- give attention to
yona himself [n5-sg-abs-pro]
kaloku of course
akunanto it has nothing
akuna it has not [neg-indef SC+na]
yakwenza to do with
kufuna it needs, concerns
uNksk. [abr] Mrs.
See: **inkosikazi** lady
utshilo so he said
«4»
yimini it is a/the day
uyingqonyela she is the champion, the one who has achieved [see Lexicon for additional information]
«5»
belineminciIi who were rejoicing
elinama-51 aged 51
nelingumhlolokazi and who is a widow
nelingu- and who is
umhlolokazi widow [n1-sg-fem-kin]
Samora Machel (former president of Mozambique)
owayenguMongameli who was the ruler
owaye ngu who was the...
umongameli superintendent, chairman, overseer, ruler, supervisor, manager
waseMozambique of Mozambique
wase- poss + locative
nowasweleka and who died
na +a >o+(u)wa and who [conn +relative form]
-**swelek**- die [v-intr]
kuntlitheko in a crash [loc+N]
intlitheko crash [C5-sg +N]
lwenqwelo-moya of an airplane
inqwelo wagon, vehicle [n5-sg]
moya air [N2-red]
ngo-1986 in 1986
«6»
bakhe her/s
wabubeka she put it
-**bek**- put [v-tr]
esichengeni in danger
isichenge one in the front of the battle, one exposed to danger [N4-sg]
ekubhukuqweni in the overturn
-**bhukuq**- upset, turn out food, deceive, overturn, capsize, cheat [v-tr]
korhulumente of the government
wamaPhuthukezi of the Portuguese
amaPhuthukezi Portuguese {Eng}
waza wangumphathiswa and she became minister
umphathiswa minister, administrator [n1-sg]
wemfundo of education
kwiMozambique in Mozambique
ekhululekileyo that is free
khululeka free [v-atrib]
iinzame efforts [n5-pl]
zokuphelisa of ending
ukungakwazi ignorance, inability
nokufunda and to read
ubekufanele she deserved, was deserving of
ukuwongwa to be taken care of
See: **abongikazi**, -**ong**- in R3
«7»
sehonours of honors {Eng}
usinikwe she was given it
yomsebenzi of the work
awenza which she did [ind-rel]
ngokuphanda by examining
phanda dig up, examining into, scratch up [v-tr]
ngemfazwe about the civil war
neziphumo and the results
iziphumo results [C4-pl +N]
kubantwana to the children
ukhethwe she was selected
yiUN by the UN {Eng}

njengengcali as an expert
ingcali expert, specialist [n5-sg]
mba issue, problem [n2-sg-red]
umba narrow ridge, dangerous pass; [fig] problem, case, issue [n2-sg]
yaza therefore, it came about that [aux-past]
iYunivesithi the university {Eng}
yamcela it requested her
avelise she produce
velisa produce [v-caus]
ezibini two
«8»
iwonga degree, status, qualification; grace, dignity [n3-sg]
andilithabathi I don't take it
-thabatha take [v-tr]
ngokuba because (lit: as)
lelam it is mine
ndimele I stood for
-mel- stand for [v-tr]
izigidi million, a very large number, thousands [C4-pl]
abaye who [1-pl+aux]
babona they saw (witnessed)
uNksk. abbrev. for **Nkosikazi** Mrs.
ebephuma as she came out
kweli from this [deic-1-n3-sg-loc]
theko festivity, event, party, function, special occasion [n3-sg-red]
ethwesw' being crowned with
thwesa crown with, put on the head, initiate, supply with, instruct [v-tr]

Uyazi ukuthi...

Uyazi ukuthi kukho iimbiza ezisebenzisa ngokukhawuleza njengeSitofu ubone iziphumo ngentsuku ezintathu.

1. Umahlab' ekufeni wembiza ibhotile:

Eli yeza linyanga izintso nomqolo, ukutshisa komchamo, umoya notyhefu esiswini, intloko nesiyezi, ukuxinana kwesifuba, izinyawo ezitshisayo nenkantsi nomkhondo, ukutyhafa komzimba, isiluma, isitshisa nokungathandi ukutya nokunye negazi elimdaka namaqhakuva.

2. Imbiza yeDrop ibhotile:

Linyanga yonke iindidi yedrop entsha nendala, ligutyula yonk' into emdaka esinyeni nasezintsweni nomqolo. Inyanga nezilonda zedrop kunye nebeleko njalo njalo.

3. Imbiza yentonga ibhotile:

Iyeza lamadoda livula imithambo exinene ikwenza ube mtsha nivane kakuhle nomhlobo wakho wenene ihamba nepilisi.

4. Owentwala zehagu nomgqwaliso ibhotile:

Libulala intwala zehagu ngaphakathi nangaphandle izikhuphe namaqanda azo enza ukuba zife zivuke aphele tu. Liphelisa namaqhakuva ebusweni.

5. Owokhohlokhohlo ibhotile:

Linyanga isifuba, Asthma, ukuxinana kwesifuba, umsi osuka esinyeni, usuke uxinanisa isifuba ukhohlele isithukuthezi.

6. Imbiza yentloko engapheli ibhotile:

Yentloko enentamo ebuhlungu namahlaba, ukuphelelwa bubuthongo kunye ne-High Blood Pressure.

7. Imbiza yedliso ibhotile:

Eli yeza linyanga idliso notyhefu nomoya omdaka esiswini. Le mbiza iyabolisa litsho liqhekeke liphume ngezantsi ulibone ngamehlo.

Xa zizonke iimbiza ziyi-50 yi-R40 nganye nengulo zabantwana. Thumela i-R20.00 Deposit eshiyekileyo uzoyibhatala kwakufika iyeza kuwe.

Zonke zifunyanwa kwa:

N.H. Agencies
P.O. Box 48273, Qualbert 4078 Durban. Tel: (031) 3091627

Reading 25

Vocabulary

Uyazi do you know
ukuthi that [conj]
iimbiza pots [n5-pl]
 imbiza pot (of earthenware or iron) [n5-sg]
 Contrast: -**biza** call, summon
ezisebenzisa which work
njengeSitofu like an injection
isitofu injection [n4-sg] {Afr stof}
Contrast: **isitovu** stove {Afr, Eng}
ubone you should see [v-pres-sub]
ngentsuku in days
 iintsuku days
ezintathu that are three
1.
Umahlab'ekufeni the stabber-of-pain/sickness (metaphorical for 'cure-all')
Umahlab part of compound noun
 hlaba stab, prick [v-tr]
 ekufeni of dying/sickness
ibhotile bottle [n5-sg] {Eng, Afr}
linyanga it cures
izintso kidneys [n5-pl]
nomqolo and the spine
 umqolo spine, backbone, back between the shoulders [n2-sg]
 iqolo backbone of an animal [n3-sg]
ukutshisa to burn
 -**tsh**- to burn [v-tr]
 Contrast: -**tsha** recent, young, new
komchamo of urine
 chamo urine [n2-sg]
notyhefu and poison
 ityhefu poison [n5-sg]
esiswini in the stomach
 isisu stomach [n4-sg]
nesiyezi and dizziness
 isiyezi dizziness, giddiness, being stunned; state of mental confusion; blackout [n4-sg]
ukuxinana congestion
 xinana crowd, press, throng, congest [v-intr]
kwesifuba of the chest [n4-sg-poss-n8-vn]
 isifuba chest [n4-sg]
izinyawo feet
nenkantsi numb, benumbed [v-poss] (lit: having numbness)
 inkantsi numbness, cramps [n5-sg]
nomkhondo a track (in this context, something left on the track to harm you)
 umkhondo footprint, track, trace, trail; lead, clue; class, row [n2-sg]
ukutyhafa weakness [n8-vn]
komzimba of the body [n2-sg-poss-n8-vn]
isiluma pain [n4-sg]
isitshisa heartburn [n4-sg]
nokungathandi not to like
nokunye together with [conj]
negazi with blood
 igazi blood [n3-sg]
elimdaka dirty
namaqhakuva and pimples
2.
yeDrop of the drop (sexually transmitted disease) {Eng drop (discharge due to STD)}
yonke all, every; the whole (of) [pro-enum-n5-sg]
nendala and old
ligutyula it sweeps out [v-tr]
esinyeni in the bladder
 isinyi the bladder [n4-sg]
nasezintsweni and in the kidneys [= na-s-e-(i)zin-tso/w-eni]
 intso kidney [n5-sg]
nezilonda and sores [n4-pl-conj]
 isilonda ulcer, sore [n4-sg]
 Contrast: -**londa** preserve, protect
zedrop of the drop
nebeleko and the uterus

ibeleko uterus [n5-sg]
3.
yentonga of the stick
intonga rod, stick, weapon [n5-sg; Contrast: -**tonga** a chief's witch doctor]
lamadoda for men [n3-pl-poss]
livula it opens
imithambo veins and arteries [n2-pl]
umthambo vein, artery [n2-sg] Contrast: -**thamba** soften, lubricate; drill; slope
exinene that are crowded
-**xin**- dense, be crowded [XED:184]
Contrast: -**xina** oppressed, distressed; coin
ikwenza it makes you
ube that you become
Contrast: -**ba** deceive, steal
nivane you understand each other
nomhlobo wakho with your mate
wakho your [pro-2sg-poss-n1-sg]
wenene truly
ihamba it goes (here – it is accompanied by...)
nepilisi with a pill [n5-sg-comit]
ipilisi pill (medicine) [n5-sg; pl: **iipilisi**] {Eng}
4.
owentwala that of a louse; for lice
intwala louse [n5-sg]
zehagu of the pig
ihagu domestic pig [n5-sg]
nomgqwaliso one with discolored, pimply skin
libulala it kills
ngaphakathi inside
nangaphandle and on the outside; and also outside
phandle outside, out, without [n9-loc-adv]
izikhuphe it takes them out
namaqanda and the eggs
qanda an egg [n3-sg]
azo their [n5-pl-poss-n3-pl] agreeing with **iintwala** and **amaqanda**
zife they should die
zivuke and they wake up/rise
-**vuk**- rise, wake [v-intr]
aphele and they come to an end
tu be quiet, still; be none [ideophone]
liphelisa it terminates
namaqhakuva and pimples
iqhakuva pimple, pock, pustule [n3-sg]
ebusweni on the face
ubuso face [n6-sg]
5.
Owokhohlokhohlo that of coughing
ukhohlokhohlo: a cough, coughing (derived from **khohla** embarrass, be in difficulty [v-tr])
isifuba chest, thorax; breast, bosom [n4-sg]
Asthma asthma {Eng}
umsi smoke; vapor, steam [n2-sg]
osuka which originates
usuke it (smoke) just VERBs
-**suke** merely VERB; just VERBed; VERBed thereupon, immediately [preverb followed by S3b + past subjunctive]
uxinanisa (it) crowds together, gathers
isithukuthezi dreariness
6.
engapheli that does not end
enentamo with the neck
intamo the neck [n3-sg]
ebuhlungu that is painful
namahlaba and pains in the lungs
ihlaba pneumonia, pains in the lungs
ukuphelelwa bubuthongo insomnia, sleeplessness [n8-vn-cmp]
ukuphelelwa lack (of), being bereft of [n8-vn]
bubuthongo by sleep [n7-sg-agent]

ubuthongo sleep [n7-abs]
ne-High blood pressure and high blood pressure {Eng}
7.
yedliso of poisoning
idliso bewitching matter causing illness, poison [n3-sg]
-dlis- poison s.o.; give or administer poison to [v-tr]
iyabolisa it decomposes
litsho do thus
liqhekeke it breaks
-qhekek- split (in two), crack, break (up, into pieces), fracture, rupture [v-st]
liphume and it gets out [pres sub]
ngezantsi below, underneath
ulibone you should see it
ngamehlo with eyes
zizonke they are all
R40 forty rands (South African currency)
nganye each one, apiece [adv]
nengulo and the illness
ukugula groan, moan, be ill [v-intr]
iR20.00 twenty rand (South African currency)
eshiyekileyo balance, what is left
uzoyibhatala you will pay
-bhatal- pay, make a payment [v-tr]
kwakufika upon arrival [temporal mood]
kwaku- when it VERBs/VERBed [group 10 locative/impersonal noun temporal construction]
zifunyanwa they are found
N.H. Agencies (company name)
Qualbert (subdivision of Durban)
Durban (capital city of Natal)

Agxothiwe 'Amasela' Egusha

«1»

Inkuntsela yexhwele nomakhenikha weemoto nomabonakude bagxothiswe okomshologu kwilali yaseQuzini emva kokutyholwa ngabahlali ngokuba ngamatutu empahla emfutshane.

«2»

Ngokwengxelo esiyifumene ezi ntsapho zimbini zakwaGoniwe nakwaNqabisile luthe lwagxothwa ngabahlali emva kokuba kufunyenwe luxhele iigusha okungezona ezabo.

«3»

Abahlali abebewotha ubomvu bangqishe kwakuko besithi abanakuze bahlale namatutu. Kulowo mbhodamo ezi ntsapho zidilizelwe imizi yazo kwakhutshelwa iimpahla ngaphandle.

«4»

Ngethuba sityelele apho sifumanise imizi kububutyobo nje ezi ntsapho ziqokelela iintsalela ezishiyekile ukutya kuthe saa.

«5»

Kudliwanondlebe noMnu. Mthumele Goniwe nozidla ngokunyanga umhlaza uthe bonakalelwe gqitha akukho nenye impahla yabo engaphukanga. Utyhole ngokuba abahlali aba bazithathele impahla eninzi kwanokutya imbala okucacayo ukuba zizilambi.

«6»

Xa simngcambazisa ngezi gusha okuthiwa bazibile uMnu. Goniwe uthe yena wabona iigusha zingungqikana waqonda ukuba noko lide eli xesha akukho kwamntu ufunisayo makazinqumle kunye nomhlobo wakhe uMnu. Goodman Nqabisile.

«7»

"Uthe wakuvela umnikazi wezi gusha sathethathethana naye ndambhatala ngeebhokhwe ezine kodwa abahlali abafuna nokuva," utshilo uMnu. Goniwe. Ngaphandle kokuba uzakubafaka emagqwetheni ngolonakalo abamenzele wona.

«8»

Amapolisa akwaQhaza eZeleni nawo angqinile ngokugxothwa kwezi ntsapho zimbini kule lali yaseQuzini kufutshane naseHorseshoe Motel. USajini Zola Metuse uthe ezi ntsapho zigxothwe elalini yazo ngabahlali emva kokuba kufumaneke inyama yegusha ezibiweyo. Uthe ezi ntsapho basazigcine ebharaksi yamapolisa de zifumane enye indawo. Ngethuba besihambele phaya sifike kumise itraka enkulu yamapolisa nalapho ezi ntsapho bezibile zimanzi zilayisha impahla yazo kuyo.

Vocabulary

agxothiwe they were driven away/expelled
-gxoth- drive away, expel [v-intr]
amasela thieves [n3-pl; sg: **isela**]
egusha of sheep [n5-sg-poss-n3-pl]
«1»
inkuntsela the master
yexhwele of apprentice witch doctor
nomakhenikha and mechanic
umakenikha mechanic [n1a-sg]
weemoto of cars
iimoto cars [n5-pl]
nomabonakude and televisions
amabonakude televisions
bagxothiswe they were expelled
-gxothiswe expelled
okomshologu like a nightmare, evil spirit
umshologu phantom, ghost, spirit that sends misfortune (related to witchcraft); nightmare, bad dream
kwilali in the village
yaseQuzini of Quzini
kokutyholwa being accused [= kwa-uku-tyhol-w-a]
tyholwa blamed, accused [v-pass]
-tyhol- accuse, blame, denounce; calumniate [v-tr]
ngabahlali by the residents
abahlali residents [n1-pl]
ngamatutu they are cattle-rustlers
itutu cattle-rustler, robber, thief [n3-sg]
empahla e + mpahla of clothes [c3-pl.poss+n5-pl]
mpahla goods, furniture, tools, movable property of all kinds, livestock
emfutshane that is very short [C5.agr-atr]
«2»
ngokwengxelo according to a report
ngokwe according to
ingxelo report [N5-sg]
esiyifumene which we received
fumene received [v-perf]
ntsapho families [n-red]
zakwaGoniwe of Goniwe
Goniwe place name
nakwaNqabisile and of Nqabisile
luthe they (said) did [v-aux]
lwagxothwa they were expelled
kufunyenwe it was found
luxhele they have slaughtered
okungezona that were not the very ones
okung(a) that were not
ezona the very ones [abs. pron]
ezabo of theirs
«3»
abebewotha who were heating up
abebe who were
otha heat up, consume, warm oneself, spend, bask, burn [v-tr]
ubomvu redness [N7-abstr]
bangqishe they stamped on the ground
-ngqish- stamp on the ground [v-intr]
kwakuko (which was) there
besithi they saying [C1-pl-v-part]
abanakuze they will never
kuze never
namatutu with cattle-rustlers [n3-pl-comit]

amatutu thieves [n3-pl]
itutu (ama pl.) cattle-rustler, robber, thief [n3-sg]
kulowo in that
mbhodamo turmoil, confusion [n2-sg-red]
umbhodamo confusion, a struggling crowd [n-2sg]
zidilizelwe they were demolished to their disadvantage
-dilizelwe torn down
-diliz- demolish, tear down, pull down [v-tr]
kwakhutshelwa it was thrown out
kutshwa draw, bring , throw, get beyond [v-pass]
iimpahla clothes, goods, one's belongings, stock, livestock [N5-pl]
«4»
ngethuba on the occasion
sityelele we visited [v-perf]
-tyelel- visit, pay a visit to s.o. (tell news to) [v-tr]
sifumanise we found that
kububutyobo it was crushed to bits/a mess
kubu it was
-tyob- trample, crush to bits [v-intr]
ziqokelela they were gathering
qokelela gather, urge repeatedly, accumulate, collect [v-tr]
iintsalela the residue, remainder, rest [N5-pl]
ezishiyekile that remained
-shiyek- remain, be left [v-intr]
ukutya food [n8-vn]
kuthe saa it's all over the place (figure of speech)
saa all over [ideophone]
«5»
Kudliwanondlebe at the interview
udliwano-ndlebe interview [N7-comp] (lit: eat the ear!)
noMnu. with Mr.
Mtumele (male personal name)
Goniwe (Xhosa family name)
nozidla and who is proud of himself
-zidl- boast, be proud of oneself, vain, conceited [v-intr]
ngokunyanga for curing
umhlaza ulcer, a raw sore, cancer [n3-sg]
bonakalelwe they suffered a loss, were left destitute
gqitha a lot, also, surpass, exceed – here emphasizes destitution [ideophone]
nenye even one
engaphukanga that is not broken
aphuka break down, break [v-tr]
utyhole he denounced/blamed, accused
-tyhol- accuse, denounce [v-tr]
bazithathele they took for themselves
thathele took, picked up [v-tr]
thatha take [v-tr]
kwanokutya imbala and even the food, every last scrap
imbala only one, just one; [atr] one, single [n5-sg]
Contrast: **imbala** burn mark (on the shin) [n5-sg]
okucacayo what is clear
-cac- be clear, become obvious, plainly seen or heard, distinct [v-st]
zizilambi they become sufferers of starvation [n4-pl-pred]
isilambi someone suffering from starvation
See: **abalambele** in R16
«6»
simngcambazisa we make him hobble along
-ngcambazis- make hobble along [v-caus]
okuthiwa that is said
bazibile they have stolen
iba steal [v-tr]
wabona he saw [past sub]

zingungqikana they were wandering aimlessly [v-intr-recip]
waqonda he realized
-qond- understand, comprehend, grasp, realize; trust, be sure about; know, be acquainted with; be understanding or open-minded [v-tr]
noko although, notwithstanding [conj, followed by relative construction]
lide it is long
kwamntu anybody
ufunisayo who is searching
makazinqumle he should split/share them
-nquml- cut (off), split; divide; cross (a mountain) [v-tr]
Goodman Nqabisile (personal name)
Goodman given name {Eng}
Nqabisile Xhosa last name
«7»
uthe wakuvela when he finally appeared [temporal form]
uthe (in this context **uthe** is auxiliary to **wakuvela**)
wakuvela he showed up, appeared
-vel- show, appear, come into sight; come from [v-intr]
umnikazi owner [n1-sg-fem]
Cf: **umnini** owner [n1-sg]
wezi of these [deic-1-n5-pl-poss-n1-sg]
sathethathethana we chattered [past sub]
sa we [S3b]
thethathetha gabble, chatter [v-intr]
naye with him
ndambhatala I paid him
-bhatal- pay [v-ditr]
ngeebhokhwe with goats [n5-pl-instr]
ibhokhwe goat [n5-sg] {Afr bok}
ezine that are four
ne four [adj-num]
abafuna they did not want
nokuva to even hear
uzakubafaka he will put them in
emagqwetheni to the lawyers [n3-pl-loc = e-(a)ma-gqweth(a)-eni]
igqwetha (ama pl.) attorneys, lawyers [N3-sg]
ngolonakalo about the damage
ulonakalo damage, injury, harm [N6-sg]
abamenzele they caused him
wona it [pro-abs. C2sg] (see **ngomonakalo** above)
«8»
amapolisa police
akwaQhaza those of Qhaza
Qhaza place name (Xhosa)
eZeleni in Zeleni
Zeleni name of town (Xhosa)
angqinile they confirmed/agreed
ngqina bear witness to, testify [v-tr]
ngokugxothwa about the driving away
kwezi of these [deic-1-n6-pl-poss-n8-vn]
lali village [n5-sg-red]
yaseQuzini of Quzini (place)
Quzini name of the village
naseHorseshoe Motel and at the Horseshoe Motel {Eng}
USajini Sergeant
Zola Metuse Zola Metuse (name)
elalini from the village [n5-sg-loc]
kufumaneke it was discovered
-fumaneke discovered [v-intr-neut]
inyama yegusha mutton, lamb [n5-sg-poss-n5-sg] (lit: meat of sheep)
yegusha of sheep
ezibiweyo that were stolen
basazigcine they are still being kept
ebharaski in the barracks
bharaski barrack {Eng}
yamapolisa of the police
de until

zifumane they find
indawo place [n5-sg]
besihambele we were visiting
-**hambel**- visit [v-tr]
phaya that place (far), yonder [deic-3-n9-loc]
sifike we arrived
kumise (it) was standing
itraka truck [n5-sg] {Eng}
nalapho and there [conj+dem]
bezibile they were sweating
-**bil**- sweat, boil, ferment [v-intr]
zimanzi they being wet
zilayisha they being loaded
-**layish**- load [v-tr] {Eng}
kuyo in it [n5-sg-pro-loc]

Emapoliseni Zivuliwe Iingcango – Hewana

«1»

"Amasango esitishi samaPolisa eTamarha avuliwe ukwenzela ukuba wonke ubani eze ngaphambili azokuzuza uncedo lwamapolisa," utshilo UMphathi Stishi, UMnu S. Hewana kwintlanganiso ebibanjelwe kwisikolo iNonibe, eTamarha kutsha nje.

«2»

UMnu. Hewana oku ukuthethe ngethuba ephendula imibuzo yabemi beelali ezahlukeneyo kule ngingqi.

«3»

Uthe umntu xa ethetha nepolisa makalibuze igama lalo, ukuba umntu akoneliseki yinkcazelo ayifumana emapoliseni, makacele adityaniswe noSekela Mphathi okanye UMphathi buqu.

«4»

Uye wacela intsebenziswano phakathi koluntu namapolisa.

«5»

Abantu bakwaNonibe baye bacela ukuba iveni yamapolisa isoloko ijikeleza ingakumbi ngexesha lasebusuku.

«6»

UKapteni Hewana uvumile wacela nomntu ekufuneka amapolisa abhalise kuye, ukuqinisekisa ukuba zonke izinto zihamba ngendlela eyiyo okanye ngokwezicelo zabantu.

«7»

Abahlali bakwaNonibe baye benza ongazenzisiyo umbulelo, kuMphathi sikhululo ngendima ayindlalileyo, nangokuthi azihluphe okanye azidine azokuzazisa ebantwini bakule ngingqi.

«8»

Uhambise wathi, abantu mabayeke ukudla ngendebe endala izinto zitshintshile ngoku, makusetyenziswane.

«9»

Ukanti imibuzo ebibuzwa ngabahlali ibandakanya; ukungabikho kwamanzi neediphu zeenkomo, ze abantu badiphe kwiindawo abahlala kuzo.

«10»

Udlwengulo lwabantwana, nokubiwa kwemfuyo kule ngingqi, kuthiwa amapolisa ayoyiswa ngulo mba.

«11»

UKapteni Hewana uwuvuyele lo mba okanye le nkcazelo esithi yena ngokunokwakhe akayivumi into yokuba amapolisa aseTamarha ayoyiswa kukuphanda lamatyala. Uye wacacisa into yokuba la matyala ayavulwa apha esikhululweni samapolisa aze agqithiselwe kubantu abawaphandayo.

«12»

Kudlwengulo lwabantwana uthe iSebe lakwa Child protection Unit eMonti, lilo elijongene nalo mba.

«13»

Ukanti ukubiwa kwemfuyo kuphandwa liSebe elijongene nalo mba eFort Jackson ngaseMonti.

«14»

Oka Hewana wongeze ngelithi, isaxhomekeke kubahlali ukuba bafuna uncedo, "Thina singamapolisa aseTamarha singumlomo wabantu kwizikhalazo zabo sizise kwabasemagunyeni bazazi ezi zikhalazo, ukuba usana olungakhaliyo lufela embelekweni," utshilo.

Vocabulary

emapoliseni at the Police Station [n3-pl-loc = e-(a)ma-polis(i)-eni]
zivuliwe they are open
iingcango doors [n5-pl]
Hewana (name)
«1»
amasango gates [n3-pl]
isango gate, gateway; loop [n2-sg]
esitishi of the station
eTamarha in Tamarha
Tamarha (place name)
avuliwe they are open
ukwenzela to enable
-**enzel**- enable [v-tr-appl]
wonke ubani anyone whatsoever
ubani anyone, whoever; [neg] no one [pro-indef-n1a-sg]
azokuzuza (and) will get, obtain
azoku [n1-sg aux-inf + future tense combo]
-**zo**- [future prefix contracted]
-**zuz**- obtain, acquire, earn, gain, benefit [v-tr]
uncedo help, aid, assistance [n6]
lwamapolisa of the police
lwa [n6-sg poss combo]
umpathi bearer; master; manager, director, ruler; (government) minister [n1-sg]
stishi station
uMnu Mr. [n1a-sg-abr; full form: **uMnumzana**]
kwintlanganiso at the meeting
ebibanjelwe which was held
ebi which was
banjelwe held [v pass]
kwisikolo at the school
iNonibe Nonibe (name of the school)
«2»
ukuthethe he said it
-**ku**- it [n8-vn-obj]
ephendula he answering

imibuzo questions [n3 pl]
umbuzo question [n3-sg]
yabemi of the residents
abemi residents [N 1 pl]
beelali of the wards or villages
bee of [combo ba + ii]
ezahlukeneyo which are separate
ez- that are [rel red]
ngingqi area, region [n5-sg-red]
«3»
ethetha he speaks
nepolisa with the police
makalibuze he must ask it [v-hort]
lalo his, her, its; of him, her, it [n3-sg-poss-n3-sg]
akoneliseki he is not satisfied
ak- he is not [SC neg + ka (red)]
-**onelisek**- satisfy, have annulled [v-neut]
yinkcazelo by the explanation
ayifumana which he receives
makacele he should request [v-hort]
adityaniswe that he meet with...
dityaniswe (to) meet with
-**dibanis**- put together, arrange a meeting
noSekela Mphathi with the Assistant Manager
-**sekel**- support, assist [v-tr]
buqu himself, herself, yourself
«4»
Uye wacela He then asked, He next asked
intsebenziswano cooperation, working together [n5-sg = in-ts/sebenz-is-w-an-o]
CHANGE of **s** to **ts** (fricative in n6 sg becomes affricate in pl)
«5»
bakwaNonibe those of Nonibe
bakwa those (people) of
Nonibe proper name of the area
baye they go on to (ask) ...
iveni van [n5-sg] {Eng}
isoloko it always
ijikeleza it goes around
-**jikelez**- go around [V-tr/intr]

ingakumbi especially, particularly [adv]
lasebusuku (of being) at night
lase [poss + loc +]
«6»
ukapteni captain [n1a-sg] {Eng, Afr}
uvumile he agreed
nomntu someone, anyone
abhalise he/she should write to
ukuqinisekisa to make sure
zonke all, everything [pro-enum-n5-pl]
zihamba they go
ngendlela in a way
eyiyo as it should (lit: that is it)
ngokwezicelo by the requests
«7»
baye benza (and then) they had made [compound remote past]
benza they made
ongazenzisiyo not pretending
kuMphathi-sikhululo to the station Manager
ngendima by the role
ayindlalileyo he/she played
nangokuthi and by saying
azihluphe he did not consider himself inconvienced
azidine he never tired himself
azokuzazisa by coming to make himself known
bakule of this
«8»
uhambise he moved on
wathi he said
mabayeke they should leave
ukudla to eat, consume [v inf]
ngendebe with a cup
indebe ladle, cup, half of a split calabash; [ext] chalice [n5-sg]
endala old [n5-sg-adj]
zitshintshile they have changed
-**tshintsh**- change, exchange, give s.t. as a substitute; replace; change (money) [v-tr] {Eng change}
makusetyenziswane let's cooperate

«9»
ukanti nevertheless [conj]
ebibuzwa that were asked [see **-buza**]
ngabahlali by residents [n1-pl-agent]
ibandakanya it joins together into
-bandakany- unite, bring into connection, join together into [v-tr]
ukungabikho the absence, shortage [v inf neg]
kwamanzi of water
neediphu and dipping tanks {Eng}
zeenkomo of/for cattle
ze so, just [v aux]
badiphe they dip {Eng}
kwiindawo at the places
abahlala they live
kuzo to/at them (thus: **abahlali kuzo** where they live)
«10»
udlwengulo rape [n6-sg]
lwabantwana of children
nokubiwa and the being stolen
-biw- be stolen [v pass]
kwemfuyo of livestock
kuthiwa it is said
ayoyiswa they are afraid
-oyis- to fear, make afraid [v-caus]
ngulo this is
«11»
uwuvuyele he was rejoicing
nkcazelo explanation
esithi he saying [v part]
ngokunokwakhe personally [adv]
akayivumi he does not agree
yokuba that
aseTamarha who are in Tamarha
kukuphanda to investigate
lamatyala these crimes
ityala crime, guilt, debt, offense [n3-sg]
wacacisa he clarified
-cacis- clarify [v-tr caus]
matyala crimes, cases [n3-pl-red]
ayavulwa they are opened
apha here [deic adv 1 n9 loc]
esikhululweni (e-(i)sikhululo/w-eni) in the jail, at the police station
agqithiselwe they are passed on
abawaphandayo who are investigating
-phand- investigate
«12»
Kudlwengulo in the rape
eMonti in East London (city in E. Cape in South Africa)
iMonti East London [n5-sg-pn]
lilo it is it (**iSebe**)
elijongene that is looking
«13»
kuphandwa it is being investigated
eFort Jackson in Fort Jackson
ngase- nearby, near, close to, in the vicinity of [loc-cmp-prf]
«14»
Oka of the (Hewana) family
wongeze he added [past sub]
-ongez- put or bring more, add [v-tr]
ngelithi by saying it
isaxhomekeke it still depends upon
-xhomekek- depend upon; be dependent on s.o. (for support, help, etc.) [v-st]
-xhomek- hang on, be hung up [v-tr]
kubahlali to residents
singamapolisa we are the police
singumlomo we are the mouth
umlomo mouth [n2-sg]
wabantu of the people
kwizikhalazo in the cause of complaints
isikhalazo a cause of complaint [n4-sg]
zabo their [pro-3pl-poss-n4-pl]
sizise we bring them
kwabasemagunyeni to those in power or authority
bazazi they know them (referring to complaints)

zikhalazo complaints
usana baby, infant [n6-sg]
olungakhaliyo that does not cry
-khal- scream, complain, sound, cry out, wail, give voice, ring [v-intr]
lufela he/she dies
embelekweni on the mother's back [loc +n2sg]

Amabali Amafutshane
Ukuhamba Ngeenyawo Usuka Ematatiele

«1»

Kunzima ukufumana imisebenzi kule mihla kodwa iimeko zokusebenza zona ziphuculiwe kunento ebeziyiyo ngaphambili. Njengoko sisaqhubeka nokukuchazela ngezomsebenzi, kule nyanga sikuphathele ibali likaThandekile Memela. Usibalisela indlela unina owaya kufuna ngayo umsebenzi kwiminyaka emininzi eyadlulayo. Usibalisela ngeemeko zokusebenza ezifama.

«2»

Ndazalelwa eMatatiele. Umama wayengayigcini imihla ngoko andiqinisekanga nokuba ndineminyaka emingaphi. Emva kokusweleka kukatata, umama wacinga ngokuba sifudukele eThekwini ngenxa yokunqongophala kwemisebenzi eMatatiele. Ngelo xesha wayenabantwana abalishumi, wayeneentombi ezilithoba nenkwenkwe enye.

«3»

Umama wenza amalungiselelo okuba siye eThekwini. Zazinqongophele izithuthi ngaloo minyaka, nkqu namapolisa ayehamba ngamahashe. Thina ke kwakungekho nto sinokukhwela kuyo, ngoko sahamba ngeenyawo.

«4»

Sasingazi ukuba kukude kangakanani eThekwini. Saluqala uhambo kwakusasa nomama. Sahamba umgama omde, umntu ethwele iimpahla ezimbalwa. Sasinyuka iintaba neenduli sinqumla amahlathi. Sahamba sahamba de sadinwa. ...

«5»

Emva kokuhamba iintsuku ezintathu nobusuku bazo, saphelelwa kukutya. Wayengazi umama ukuba uza kuthini, kuba sasingekafiki eThekwini. Wabona abantu endleleni waza wabuza indlela eya eThekwini. Bambonisa ifama yomlungu ekwasekukho umhlolokazi wakhe kuphela apho. Ngemini yesine sihamba safika kuloo fama, waza umama wangena endlwini. Watsho ukuba ufuna umsebenzi, waza wamamkela umnini wefama ukuba asebenze apho.

«6»

Sonke sahlala kuloo fama, umama esebenza apho. Wayenobubele umlungu waloo fama. Wayenefama yengqolowa neyobisi yaye wayesinika ubisi. Umama wayesamkela i-R3,00 ngenyanga. EMatatiele wayenokwamkela i-R1,50 ngenyanga ngoko wayenelisekile ngumvuzo wakhe. Umama wasithengela izinto ezintle namalaphu okusithungela iilokhwe.

«7»

Emva konyaka esebenza apho, wagqiba ekubeni siqhubeke nohambo lokuya eThekwini. Wayeve ukuba unokwamkela imali ethe kratya kwezinye iifama. Wavalelisa kuloo mlimi saza saqhubeka nohambo lwethu.

Vocabulary

amabali stories [n3-pl]
ibali story [n3-sg] [n3-sg]
amafutshane short [adj]
ukuhamba uku hamba to travel
ngeenyawo on foot [= nga-ii-nyawo] (lit: by means of the feet)
iinyawo feet [n6-pl]
unyawo foot [n6-sg]
usuka she started off
eMatatiele from Matatiele
Matatiele place name
«1»
kunzima it is hard, difficult
zokusebenza of employment
zona they [group 5 plural absolutive pronoun]
ziphuculiwe have been improved
phucul improve, benefit; civilize, modernize [v-tr]
kunento compared to [= kuna-in-] to (lit: than the thing)
ebeziyiyo the way they were [= ebe zi yiyo]
yiyo he, she, it is ...; it is he, she, it [group 5 singular copulative/predicative]
njengoko as, whereas; accordingly [conj]
sisaqhubeka we are still continuing
-**qhubek**- happen, go on, continue, be in progress; advance, progress [v-atr]
nokukuchazela explaining to you, telling you [= na uku ku chazela]
chazela unravel, straighten s.t. out for s.o; [ext] explain s.t. to s.o. [v-ben]
ngezomsebenzi about work [= ngezo msebenzi]
sikuphathele we have brought you
-**phathele** brought
likaThandekile of Thandekile
Thandekile Memela (name)
usibalisela she is telling us
-**balisel**- tell to [v+ext]
-**balis**- tell, utter, express with words [v-caus]
unina (his/her) mother; their mother [n1a-sg-kin]
owaya who went [verbal relative]
ngayo for it/by means of it/through it
kwiminyaka in years
eyadlulayo past [= e ya dlul ayo]
ngeemeko about conditions
ezifama on (of the) farms
ifama farm [n5-sg] {Eng}
«2»
Ndazalelwa I was born
-**zalelw**- be born [v ben]
wayengayigcini she had not kept them
waye- he, she, it had VERBed [group 1, 1a singular contracted remote past compound tense]
andiqinisekanga I am not sure
-**qinisek**- be sure [v-intr]
emingaphi how many [qw-adj-n2-pl]

-ngaphi how many? [qw-adj-root]
emva kokusweleka after the death
emva koku- after [loc-n10+dem]
sweleka die
kukatata that of my father
wacinga she thought
sifudukele we moved to
-fudukele move to [v appl]
-fuduk- move [v-tr]
eThekwini to Durban
yokunqongophala of scarcity
-nqongophala be scarce [v-intr]
ngelo at that [deic-2-n3-sg-time]
elo that [deic-2-n3-sg]
wayenabantwana she had had children
abalishumi ten
wayeneentombi she had had girls
iintombi girls [n5-pl]
ezilithoba nine
nenkwenkwe and a boy
inkwenkwe boy, youngster [n5-sg]
«3»
amalungiselelo arrangements, preparations
okuba so that [conj]
zazinqongophele they were scarce
zazi- there were [v-aux. past]
-nqongophele scarce [atr]
izithuthi cars, bus, trucks, etc. (means of transportation other than by horse)
ngaloo in those (times) [deic-2-n2-pl-time]
loo those (not far, just mentioned) [deic-2-n2-pl]
nkqu even
namapolisa and police
ayehamba they had traveled
aye- they had VERBed [group 3 plural contracted remote past compound tense]
ngamahashe on horses
amahashe horses [n3-pl; sg: **ihashe**]
kwakungekho there was nothing
kwaku- there had VERBed [group 10 locative/impersonal noun contracted remote past compound tense]
sinokukhwela we can ride
-khwel- ride
sahamba we traveled, we walked [past sub]
«4»
sasingazi we had not known
sasi- we had VERBed [contracted remote past compound tense]
kukude how far
kangakanani how great, how much, how far [enum]
rw: **ngakanani**
saluqala we started it
uhambo journey [n6-sg]
kwakusasa in the morning
umgama distance [n2-sg]
omde long
ethwele carrying
ezimbalwa few, a small quantity [adj]
sasinyuka we had climbed
iintaba mountains [n5-pl]
neenduli and hills
induli hill [n5-sg]
sinqumla we crossing
amahlathi forests [n3-pl]
sahamba sahamba we walked and walked
sadinwa we got tired
«5»
kokuhamba walking
iintsuku days [n6-pl]
nobusuku and nights
bazo its, those [n6-pl-poss-n7-sg] agreeing with **iintsuku** and **ubusuku**
saphelelwa we ran out
-phelelw- be gone, get used up, exhausted; be bereft of [v-ben-pass]
kukutya of food
wayengazi she did not know

ukuba uza kuthini what she would do
kuthini to do what?
sasingekafiki we had not yet arrived
endleleni on the road
waza and, and she went [v-aux]
wabuza she asked
eya going
bambonisa they showed her
yomlungu of a white man
ekwasekukho of which there was
ngemini on (the) day
yesine four(th)
safika we arrived
kuloo to, at, in, from that [deic-2-n5-sg-loc]
fama farm [n5-sg-red] {Eng}
wangena she entered
 -ngen- enter, go in [v-tr]
endlwini into the house [e-(i)ndlu/w-ini]
watsho she said
wamamkela s/he accepted her
umnini the owner [n1-sg]
wefama of farm
asebenze she would work
«6»
sahlala we lived/stayed
esebenza working
wayenobubele she had had kindness
 ububele kindnesss [n7-sg.abstr]
Wayenefama she had a farm [= wa-ye-na-i-fama]
yengqolowa (of) wheat
neyobisi and also milk
 neyo- and also
 ubisi milk [n6-sg-mass]
wayesinika she had given it to
wayesamkela she had earned
i-R3,00 three rand (South African currency)
ngenyanga monthly
wayenokwamkela she could have earned
 -nokw- (**-noku-**) can, could VERB; be able or willing to VERB
i-R1,50 1.50 rand (South African currency)
wayenelisekile she was satisfied
ngumvuzo wage, salary, earning
 umvuzo reward; wage, payment, salary [n2-sg; pl: **imivuzo**]
wasithengela bought us
ezintle beautiful, nice
namalaphu fabric, cloth
okusithungela to sew for us
 -thung- sew [v-tr]
iilokhwe dresses [n5-pl]
«7»
konyaka a year
wagqiba she concluded
siqhubeke we continued
nohambo (with our) journey
lokuya of going
Wayeve she heard
unokwamkela she can earn
ethe which was
kratya more, extra [ideophone]
kwezinye in other
iifama farms
Wavalelisa took leave of
saza then
saqhubeka we continued

Imisebenzi

«1»

Njengomntu ongumthengisi, nguwe ekufuneka uyenze ithengwe. Kufuneka uxhulumane nabantu. Kufuneka wazi yaye uqonde abantu abohlukeneyo kanti nabo kufuneka bakwazi.

«2»

"Usebenza nabantu abohlukeneyo xa kuveliswa imveliso. Ngokomzekelo kukho abantu abajongene nokuthunyelwa kwemveliso kwiindawo ngeendawo, abantu abayithengisayo, abathengi, ekufuneka usoloko uxhulumene nabo. Ngulowo ke owona msebenzi wakho umkhulu."

«3»

Ngubani owufaneleyo lo msebenzi?

«4»

Zininzi izinto ezifunekayo ukuze ukulungele ukusebenza kwezentengiso.

«5»

"Kufuneka ube ngumntu okuthandayo ukuhlala nabantu. Kufuneka ukwazi okufunayo yaye uzame ukukufumana. Kufuneka ube lichule lokuthetha ukuze iimbono zakho zamkelwe ngabantu yaye kufuneka ukwazi ukucenga ukuze ubenze abantu bayibone ifanele ukuthengwa imveliso yakho."

«6»

Uvutho-ndaba

«7»

UMbulelo ukholelwa ekubeni uvutho-ndaba lwezentengiso kukubona imveliso yakho ithengwa okwamagwinya ashushu.

«8»

"Xa ubona abantu beyithenga imveliso yakho, oko kubonisa ukuba uyaphumelela umsebenzi wakho. Oko kuyakhuthaza. Usukile ekucengeni abantu ngoku ubabona beyithenga imveliso obubaxelela ngayo. Uba neqhayiya ngokuba negalelo ekwenzeni loo mveliso ithandwe ngabantu."

«9»

Imiqathango yokusebenza

«10»

Ufumana umvuzo oncumisayo kwezentengiso yaye maninzi

amathuba owafumanayo kulo msebenzi.

«11»

"Uninzi lwabantu abanezidanga kulo msebenzi baqala ngokuba ziiMarketing Assistants besamkela umvuzo we-R4 000 ngenyanga. Kulo msebenzi uncedisa iMarketing Manager neBrand Manager kwimisebenzi abafuna ukuba iqosheliswe. Ngale ndlela uyafunda ngale misebenzi."

«12»

Inyathelo lesibini kukuba usebenze ngeemveliso nokuba ube nemveliso eziphethwe nguwe. Uya kubizwa ngokuthi uyiBrand Manager yaye uya kuba phantsi kweMarketing Manager. Esona sikhundla siphezulu unokufikelela kuso sesokuba yiMarketing Director.

«13»

Ngumsebenzi omhle. UMbulelo uthi ezentengiso ngowona msebenzi mhle onokuwukhetha ngoku.

«14»

"Uninzi lwabantu kweli ngabantsundu. Abantu abantsundu ngabona bathenga kakhulu. Xa inkampani izimisele ukuthengisela abantu abantsundu imveliso yayo, kufuneka iqeshe abantu abantsundu.

«15»

Ezentengiso zixhomekeke ebantwini ababaqondayo abathengi. Maninzi gqitha amathuba kwezentengiso."

«16»

Iinkcukacha

«17»

Ukuze usebenze kwezentengiso, kufuneka uqhube kakuhle esikolweni kwezi zifundo zilandelayo:

«18»

IsiNgesi: Kwezentengiso uza kuqhagamshelana nabantu ngoko kufuneka ube lichule lokuthetha. Oko kufuna ulubethe kamnandi ulwimi lwesiNgesi.

«19»

IMaths: kufuneka uzazi iindleko zokuveliswa kwemveliso nokumiswa kwamaxabiso.

Although the first element in **kufuneka** is technically homographic with the second person singular pronoun (-**ku**-), and therefore could mean 'you must,' it always is in an IMPERSONAL CONSTRUCTION, and is therefore the n10 locative prefix. (Do note, however, that the 2Pers-sg form is an object form found nearest the verb root after subject concords and tense markers, so confusion should not arise.) Throughout this article, this construction reads 'it is necessary that you + present subjunctive.'

Vocabulary

«1»
njengomntu as a person
ongumthengisi who is selling
ongum- who is [rel prefix C1sg]
ekufuneka that it is necessary that you
eku- which [rel-prefix C10]
uyenze you should make
ithengwe it be bought
uxhulumane that you contact
-**xhuluman**- contact
nabantu with people
wazi that you know
uqonde that you understand
-**qond**- understand
abohlukeneyo who are going to be different (from one another)
abo- who are
-**hlukene**- different from one another [v-recip]
bakwazi that they should know you
«2»
usebenza you work
kuveliswa (here) marketing
-**velisw**- bring out, yield, bring forward, show
imveliso product
ngokomzekelo for example
abajongene who are responsible
-**jongene**- looking; responsible
nokuthunyelwa with being sent
kwemveliso product
kwiindawo to places
abayithengisayo who are selling it
-**thengisayo** selling
abathengi buyers
usoloko you always
soloko always VERB [v-aux]
uxhulumene you should contact
-**xhuluman**- contact
Ngulowo It is that which
owona the most, that very [pro-emph]
umkhulu big, large [cop-adj-n2-sg]
um- [cop-n2-sg]
«3»
ngubani who is it?
owufaneleyo who is suitable
owu- [rel+n2-sg.agr]
«4»
zininzi there are many
ezifunekayo which are needed
ukulungele you are ready
kwezentengiso in sales
intengiso sale; sales, marketing (as an occupation) [n5-sg-vn]
«5»
ngumntu be someone, be a person
okuthandayo who likes
ukuhlala to stay, sit, be among
okufunayo what you want
uzame you should try
ukukufumana to find ~ get it
lichule be an expert
ichule skilled trapper ~ hunter; [ext] skillful person, expert [n3-sg]
lokuthetha of ~ for speaking
zamkelwe that they be accepted
ukucenga to persuade
-**ceng**- plead, beg; persuade
ubenze you should make them

bayibone they should see ~ understand
ukuthengwa to be bought
«6»
uvutho-ndaba climax, outcome
vutha be hot, burn [v-tr]
«7»
UMbulelo (Xhosa male personal name)
ukholelwa he believes
-kholelw- believe [v-tr]
lwezentengiso about sales
kukubona to see it
ithengwa it be bought
okwamagwinya ashushu like hot cakes
amagwinya fat cakes
ashushu hot
«8»
beyithenga they buying it
kubonisa it shows
uyaphumelela you are succeeding
-phumelel- come into view, be prominent or conspicuous; speed; [ext] succeed, surpass; prosper; [fig] utter, disclose [v-intens]
kuyakhuthaza it is encouraging
-khuthaz- encourage [v-tr]
usukile you have moved
ekucengeni from begging
ubabona you see them
obubaxelela (who) you were telling
obu- [rel-n7] Note: This agreement seems suspect as there is no n7 around to qualify.
neqhayiya having pride
iqhayiya pride; [atr] proud, boasting [n3-sg]
negalelo having a contribution
igalelo contribution [n5-sg]
ekwenzeni in making
ithandwe it is liked
«9»
imiqathango guidelines
yokusebenza of working
«10»
oncumisayo makes you smile; satisfying, pleasing
-ncum- smile [v-intr]
maninzi there are many
amathuba opportunities
owafumanayo of you getting
«11»
abanezidanga who have degrees [= aba-na-izi-danga]
izidanga degrees [n5-pl]
baqala they begin
ziiMarketing Assistants they are Marketing Assistants {Eng}
besamkela they earning [part]
we-R4000 of 4,000 rand (South African currency)
uncedisa you help(ing)
iMarketing Manager {Eng}
neBrand Manager and Brand Manager {Eng}
abafuna they want
iqosheliswe wrapped up
-qoshelis- gather up, wrap up [v-tr.caus]
ndlela means, way, road [n5-sg red]
uyafunda you are learning
«12»
ube nemveliso you have produced
eziphethwe which are managed
nguwe by you
uya kubizwa you will be called
kubizwa to be called [v-inf-red]
-bizw- be called [v-pass]
ngokuthi as, like (lit: by saying) [conj]
uyiBrand Manager you are Brand Manager
kweMarketing Manager the Marketing Manager {Eng}
esona the real one, that very one; the most [n4-sg emphatic pro]
sikhundla position [n4-sg red]
siphezulu the highest
unokufikelela you can reach
sesokuba is to become
yiMarketing Director {Eng}
«13»
ngumsebenzi it is a job
omhle nice [atr-n2-sg]

ngowona it (is) the most
onokuwukhetha which you can choose
«14»
ngabantsundu they are black
-**ntsundu**- brown (color); black (race) [atr-root]
ngabona they are those
bathenga who buy
inkampani company {Eng}
izimisele it is serious
zimisele sincere, serious [v-refl-perf-atr]
ukuthengisela to sell to
iqeshe that it hires
«15»
zixhomekeke they depend on
-**xhomekek**- depend upon; be dependent on s.o. (for support, help, etc.) [v-st]
ababaqondayo who understand them
gqitha pass, surpass (in this context, however, **gqitha** is emphasizing the number of opportunities)
«17»
uqhube that you should pass
zifundo subjects [5-pl]
zilandelayo which are the following
«18»
kuqhagamshelana be in touch, be in contact, interact
lokuthetha of communicating
kufuna need (here, 'it is necessary')
ulubethe you speak it
-**beth**- hit, beat (Note: idiomatic use)
kamnandi nicely, sweetly, pleasantly; (here) fluently [adv]
ulwimi tongue; language [n6-sg]
lwesiNgesi of/in English
«19»
IMaths Math(ematics) {Eng}
uzazi you know it
iindleko expenses
zokuveliswa of growing
nokumiswa and the setting up [n8-vn-conj]
-**misw**- set up, make stand [v-caus-pass]
kwamaxabiso of prices [n3-pl-poss-n8-vn]
amaxabiso prices [n3 pl]

Phulaphula limbono Zelizwe

«1»

I-AIDS eluntwini lwakowethu

Eli phulo lenkqubela yoluntu liliphathelwe ukwenza ilizwe elinempilo: BP, Old Mutual, Aids Helpline, European Union

Le ncwadana ifumene inkxaso KwaBP

Uqala nini ukugula?

Inokukugulisa emva kweminyaka emininzi intsholongwane yeHIV. Xa sele ugula oko kubonisa ukuba uneAIDS.

«2»

Iimpawu zokuqala zokuba neAIDS

Unokuba nolunye lwezi mpawu xa uqala ukuba neAIDS...

- ukuhla komzimba
- ukudumba emqaleni, emva kwendlebe, emakhwapheni nasemiphakathweni.
- izilonda emilebeni ezingapholiyo
- irhashalala – irhashalala emhlophe emlonyeni okanye kumalungu angasese
- iimpawu zokuba neTB – ukukhohlela, ukubila nokuhla komzimba
- izilonda ezibuhlungu nerhashalala
- umfixane nokubila ebusuku
- izilonda ezingapholiyo kumalungu angasese
- utyatyambo olungapheliyo

«3»

Iimpawu zamva zeAIDS

Unokuba nazo ezinye zezi mpawu xa sele ikuphethe kakhulu iAIDS ...

- iTB
- inyumoniya
- irhashalala ebuhlungu
- ubuhlungu bezandla neenyawo
- ukuba buthathaka nokudinwa
- amabala aluhlaza kulusu lwakho
- ukuhla ngamandla komzimba

• intloko ebuhlungu, isifo sokuwa, isiyezi, ukulibala, nokungakwazi ukuzikisa ingqondo.

«4»

English	Xhosa
groin	umphakatho
weight loss	ukuhla komzimba
sweating	ukubila
fits	ukuwa
blackouts	isiyezi
loss of memory	ukulibala
concentrating	ukuzikisa ingqondo
tip	incam
semen	imbewu yesidoda
expiry date	imini yokuphelelwa

AIDS RELATED WORDLIST. The original gives English followed by Zulu, Xhosa, Sotho, and Afrikaans.

«5»

Indlela yokuthintela iAIDS

Iindibano zesondo ezikhuselekileyo

Indibano yesondo ikhuselekile xa indoda ifaka ikhondom.

Kubalulekile ukuyisebenzisa kakuhle ikhondom.

«6»

Kufuneka uyisebenzise ngolu hlobo

1. Sebenzisa ikhondom qho xa unendibano yesondo.

2. Faka ikhondom kwilungu lakho eliqinileyo ngaphambi kokuba ulifake kwiqabane lakho. Yicinezele incam yekhondom ukuze kuphume wonke umoya osenokuba ukuyo.

3. Yifake ikhondom iligqume lonke ilungu lobudoda. Ngoku ukulungele ukuba nendibano yesondo neqabane lakho.

4. Likhuphe ilungu lobudoda emva kwendibano yesondo. Yibambe ikhondom xa ulikhupha kungenjalo iya kushiyeka phakathi. Kufuneka ulikhuphe lingekathambi ilungu lobudoda.

5. Ngoku yikhuphe kakuhle ikhondom kwilungu lobudoda.

Ungavumeli kubekho imbewu yobudoda evuzayo kwikhondom.

6. Yisonge ngephepha ikhondom esetyenzisiweyo. Yilahle kumgqomo wezibi okanye kwindlu yangasese okanye naphi na apho bangenakufikela abantwana.

«7»

Khumbula!

• Jonga umhla ezifanele zisetyenziswe ngawo iikhondom – kuba ezindala ziyingozi.

• Abanye abantu basebenzisa isithambiso kunye nekhondom ukuze indibano yesondo ibe lula. Ungasebenzisi nayiphi na ivaselina kuba inokuyonakalisa ikhondom – fumana izithambiso ezikhuselekileyo.

Vocabulary

phulaphula listen (to), hearken; attend; obey [v-tr]
iimbono views, outlooks, visions, sights, prospects [n5-pl]
imbono view, point of view [n5-sg]
Cf: **umbono** sight, vision; perspective, point of view; view, scene; prospect; phenomenon [n2-sg; pl: **imibono**]
zelizwe of the country
«1»
I-AIDS AIDS {Eng}
eluntwini in the community [= e-(u)luntu/w-ini]
lwakowethu of ours
lwaka > **o** + **wethu** our [n6]
iphulo expedition, foray, prolonged hunting trip, excursion; [ext] article, (written) treatise; information, notice; project, program [n3-sg]
lenkqubela of the development [= la-in-kq/qub-el-a]
inkqubela progress, development [n5-sg]
-qhubel- drive (animal, vehicle) for/to; make steady progress on [v-ben]
yoluntu of the community; of society
liliphathelwe is being brought, carried on
elinempilo eli na impilo which is healthy (lit: has health)
impilo health [n5-sg]
BP acronym for British Petroleum [n5-sg-red] {Eng}
ncwadana pamphlet, booklet [n5-sg-dim-red]
ifumene it is (made) available
-fumene gotten, be available, made possible
KwaBP from BP (British Petroleum) {Eng}
uqala you start
ukugula to become sick [v-intr]
inokukugulisa it can make you sick
-gulis- sicken, make s.o. ill [v-caus]
kweminyaka kwa + iminyaka [for] NUM years
intsholongwane germ, microbe, bacillus, virus; disease [n5-sg]
yeHIV of HIV
ugula sick, infected [v part]
uneAIDS you have AIDS
«2»
iimpawu marks, signs, indications, symptoms [n6-pl]
CHANGE of **ph** to **p** after nasal

iim- [group 6 (Bantu class 10) plural noun prefix]
uphawu brand (on animal), distinguishing mark; notch; sign, indication, symptom [n6-sg]
unokuba even if you
nolunye have some
ukuhla loss, losing [v inf] (lit: to come down)
ukudumba swelling [v inf]
emqaleni of the throat [=e+(u)mqal(a) =(i)ni]
kwendlebe [emva] kwa indlebe behind the ears
emakhwapheni in the armpits [= e-(a)ma-khwaph(a)-eni]
ikhwapha armpit [n3-sg; pl: **amakhwapha**]
nasemiphakathweni and inside of the hands
imiphakathi inside, palm of hand [n2 pl]
izilonda sores, ulcers [n4-pl; Sg: **isilonda**]
emilebeni emi imilebe ni on the lips
imilebe lips [n2 pl]
ezingapholiyo which do not heal [a-izi-nga-phol-i-yo]
-**phol**- cool; abate, subside; heal [v-st]
irhashalala rash; [ext] chickenpox [n5-sg]
emhlophe white [atr-n5]
emlonyeni [e-(u)mlomo+y-eni] in/on the mouth
kumalungu angasese on the genitals
angasese secretly, not visible [= a-nga-sese]
ukukhohlela to have difficulty in breathing; coughing [n8-vn]
-**khohlel**- have difficulty in breathing; cough [v-ben]
ukubila sweat, sweating
nokuhla and losing
ezibuhlungu painful [n5-pl-atr = ezi-bu-hlungu]
Cf: **intlungu** pain [n5-sg = in-tl/hlungu]
nerhashalala and a rash
umfixane stuffiness of the nose [n6-sg]
-**mfixi** be stuffed up with a cold, have catarrh [ideophone]
nokubila na ukubila and sweating
utyatyambo throbbing [n6-sg]
olungapheliyo olu ngapheliyo which does not stop
«3»
zamva of later; [atr] subsequent, more advanced
umva back (anatomical/away from the front); reverse side; [ext] whatever is behind in space or time [n2-sg]
nazo ezinye zezi mpawu (if you) have some of these signs
nazo and/with these
ezinye ezi nye some
ikuphethe it has taken control of you
inyumoniya pneumonia [n5-sg] {Eng}
bezandla ba izandla of/on the hands
neenyawo and feet
buthathaka become weak
-**thathak**- weakness, feebleness, inefficiency
nokudinwa and being tired
amabala colors, markings [n3 pl]
ibala color, marking [n3-sg]
aluhlaza alu hlaza green, blue [atr color]
kulusu on the skin [n6-sg-loc]
ulusu skin (of human or small animal) [n6-sg]
ngamandla strongly, vigorously [adv]
intloko ebuhlungu headache [n5-sg-cmp]
isifo sickness, disease [n4-sg]
sokuwa of fits [= sa-uku-wa] (lit: to fall)
isiyezi blackout [n4-sg]
ukulibala to forget [inf]

nokungakwazi and not having the ability to/not knowing [= na-uku-nga-kw-azi]
ukuzikisa ingqondo to concentrate [v-inf-cmp]
  -zikis- use to the best advantage, cut deep, plough, make quite plain
ingqondo mind, intellect; understanding, reason; mental capacity, intelligence [n5-sg]
«4»
incam tip [n5-sg]
imbewu seed, semen
yesidoda of a man; [atr] male [n4-sg-poss-n5-sg = ya-isi-doda]
  isidoda men (collectively) [n4-sg]
expiry expiration {Eng}
imini yokuphelelwa expiration date, shelf date
yokuphelelwa of being expired; [atr] expiration
«5»
yokuthintela ya ukuthintela to prevent
  thintela to prevent, avoid [v-tr]
iAIDS AIDS
iindibano zesondo sexual intercourse, sex acts [pl]
iindibano gatherings [n5-pl]
zesondo of sex
  isondo lower edge of a garment, selvadge, lappet; corner of a blanket; [idiom] sex, sexual intercourse [n3-sg]
ezikhuselekileyo e zi khuseleka iyo which are protected
  -khuselek- be protected [v-intr]
ikhuselekile it is protected [v-perf]
ifaka he puts on
ikhondom condom [n5-sg]
«6»
ukuyisebenzisa to use it
ngolu by means of this, with this
hlobo type, sort, particular [n6-sg-red]
qho do VERB always, continually, persistently, frequently; keep on VERBing [ideophone]
unendibano yesondo [u na indibano ya isondo] you have sexual relations
kwilungu on the member/body part
eliqinileyo which is hard [= eli-qin-ile-yo]
  qina to be hard
ulifake you put it [= u li fake], here, penetrate
kwiqabane on partner
yicinezele press it! [object imperative]
  -cinezel- press (down), squeeze; oppress, afflict [v-tr]
yekhondom of the condom
kuphume it may come out [subj]
  ku- it [n10-impers]
  -phum- go ~ come out, exit; come from; rise (celestial body) [v-intr]
osenokuba which may still be [= o+sa +i-/ unokuba]
ukuyo which is in it
yifake put it [v imper +obj]
iligqume ili gqume so that it covers it
  -gqum- cover; smother; conceal, hide [v-tr]
lonke all, the whole of [pro-enum-n3-sg]
lobudoda of a male; [atr] male, masculine
ukulungele you are ready
neqabane with a partner
likhuphe li khuphe take it out
kwendibano kwa indibano [after] sex
yibambe hold it!
kungenjalo ku nge njalo in such a way
kushiyeka be left, remain
ulikhuphe that you take it out
lingekathambi it should not yet be soft

ungavumeli u nga vumeli you must not allow
kubekho ku be [from ba] kho that it be present/exist
evuzayo which leaks ~ oozes [= e-vuz-a-yo]
-**vuz**- leak, ooze [v-intr]
yisonge wrap it up
-**song**- roll up, wrap (up), fold; turn back, prevent, dissuade [v-tr]
ngephepha with/in paper [= nga-i-phepha]
iphepha paper [n3-sg; pl: **amaphepha**] {Eng}
esetyenzisiweyo which is used [= e-sebenz/ty-is-iw-e-yo]
yilahle throw it away!
-**lahl**- discard, throw away [v-tr]
kumgqomo into the garbage can
umgqomo bin, barrel, tub, drum; [ext] garbage can, trash bin [n2-sg]
wezibi wa izibi [of] waste disposal (named after cartoon character of anti-litter campaign)
kwindlu from the house [= ku-indlu]
yangasese out of sight, far away from; euphemism for toilet [atr-n5-sg]
-**ngasese** out of sight, secretly [adv-atr]
-**ses**- do s.t. underhand, out of sight; do through another; perform s.t. secretly [v-tr]
-**sese** done underhand; [atr] underhanded; out of sight; secret [v-perf]
naphi na anywhere; everywhere [adv-loc; alt sp: **naphina**]
bangenakufikela they cannot reach it [= ba nge na kufikela]
-**fikela** reach, gain access to, come upon [v-tr]

«7»

ezifanele ezi fanele which is right
zisetyenziswe they should be used
ngawo by it
ezindala which are old, old ones
ziyingozi zi yi ngozi they are dangerous
basebenzisa they use
isithambiso softening; lubrication, lubricant [n4-sg]
-**thambis**- soften, make supple, pliant; oil, lubricate, anoint; [ext] subdue, tame [v-caus]
nekhondom with a condom
ungasebenzisi you should not use
nayiphina any-, whatever, whichever [pro-indef-n5-sg]
yiphi which
inokuyonakalisa it may damage it
-onakalis- damage [v-tr]
izithambiso lubricants [n4-pl]

Izwi elivela kumhleli omkhulu

Fikani Niphila, Ningabanjelwa Ukuqhuba Niselile Ngamapolisa

«1»

Lixesha leeholide zeKrismesi kwakhona yaye kusweleka abantu abaninzi ngalo kwiingozi zendlela. Uninzi lwethu luza kuba lubonisa indlela oluzibalekisa ngayo iimoto nokuthi luyophula njani imithetho yendlela ebalulekileyo. Oku kwenzeka minyaka yonke.

«2»

Abaninzi baza kusinda kwingalo yomthetho. Abanye baza kubanjwa baze babe ngumzekelo kwabanye wokuba akulunganga ukungawuthobeli umthetho. Sifuna ukulumkisa abafundi bethu abangabaqhubi bezithuthi ngephulo lamvanje likarhulumente ekuthiwa yi-"Arrive Alive" (Fika Uphila). Eli phulo lokhuseleko ezindleleni liza kuqhutywa kwiindawo ezithile kwaye alibalumkisi, lingenayo nenceba kwabophula umthetho! Akukho mntu uza kusinda kulo – nokuba uhamba ngomnyobo onjani okanye ukwisikhundla esiphezulu kangakanani! Ezona zaphuli-mthetho zifunwa ngamandla ngabantu abaqhuba beselile - kwaye loo mntu isenokuba nguwe, utata wakho, umyeni, umfazi, umzala, unyana, intombi okanye isithandwa sakho!

«3»

Njengoko kulixesha lamatheko eKrismesi asezi-ofisini nawokuvala kweenkampani ezininzi, lumka! Emva kokuzityel' izinto zakho kwelo theko liseofisini, lisehotele okanye kwisirhoxo osithandayo, ungayilibali indlela egodukayo okanye ikharavan enezibane eziluhlaza ezilanyazayo ecaleni kwendlela. Amabhinqa namadoda akuyo enza umsebenzi wawo! Ungaziqhathi ngokuthi uza kuwanyoba! Xa ufunyaniswe ukuba ugqithisile kumyinge osemthethweni, uyavalelwa, uhlawuliswe imali enkulu ukuze ukhululwe ngebheyili, kanti unako nokuphulukana nelayisensi yakho yokuqhuba. Abanye bethu ke bazisebenzisa mihla le iilayisensi zabo. Ngoko kubhetele ukuyilondoloza, kunokugxwal' emswaneni!

«4»

Xa niphulaphula yaye nilumkile, niya kuyeka ukuba namatshamba xa "senitye izinto zenu." Xa usazi ukuba uza kusela kube kuza kufuneka uqhube, cela umntu ongaselanga akuqhubele, kungenjalo uya kusikhumbula esi silumkiso xa sele ufakwe iintsimbi zamabanjwa yaye uvalelwa kwesimnyama isisele! Unendlebe nje unetyala...

«5»

Liphelile ixesha lokushumayela. Sis' Barbara, uphi uBarman? De kube ngunyaka ozayo, nibe nexesh' elimnandi!

Ngu Daizer Mqhaba (Umhleli Omkhulu)

Vocabulary

izwi word [n3-sg]
elivela which appears
kumhleli omkhulu to / from the editor-in-chief
fikani arrive [v-pro-2pl-imp]
niphila you living
  ni- you [S2]
  -**phil**- be alive [v-intr]
ningabanjelwa you not being arrested for
  Note: negative passive suffix is -**a** NOT -**i**
ukuqhuba driving [n8-vn]
niselile you having drunk
ngamapolisa by the police
«1»
lixesha it is time
leeholide of holiday
  lee of [poss + C5 pl]
  holide holiday {Eng}
zeKrismesi of Christmas
kusweleka ku are (lit: there...)
  sweleka dying
ngalo then (refers to **ixesha** time)
kwiingozi in danger
  kwii in [loc C5 pl]
  ngozi accident, danger
zendlela of the road
luza will [v aux]
lubonisa showing
oluzibalekisa [rel], who will 'push' (their cars)
  olu who [rel C6sg]
  -**balekisa** make run or flee; spur on, race [v caus]
luyophula they will break them
«2»
kusinda escape [n8-vn]
kwingalo from the arm [loc-n5]
baze they thereby [S2 aux]
babe they become [3Pers pl aux]
ngumzeleko is an example
kwabanye to others
wokuba that, so that
akulunganga it is not ok
sifuna we want
ukulumkisa to warn
abangabaqhubi drivers
bezithuthi of automobiles
ngephulo about the campaign
lamvanje of lately
likarhulumente of government
ekuthiwa that is called
yi-"Arrive Alive" (Fika Uphila) (campaign name)
lokhuseleko of protection
liza it will [n3-sg aux]
kuqhutywa be promoted, driven
ezithile certain [n5-sg-atr]
alibalumkisi does not warn them
lingenayo it does not have
nenceba with mercy
kwabophula for those who break
uza that will
uhamba you travel
ngomnyobo in a model, with a design
onjani kind, whatever kind
ukwisikhundla you are in a position
esiphezulu which is high, up (i.e., high social standing)

ezona the real ones, those very ones; the most [group 4 plural emphatic pronoun]
zifunwa are wanted
abaqhuba who are driving
beselile having drunk
isenokuba it can be
umfazi wife [n1-sg]
umzala cousin [n1-sg kin]
unyana son [n1a-sg kin masc]
isithandwa lover [n4-sg]
sakho yours, your [pro 2sg poss n4 sg]
«3»
kulixesha it is time
lamatheko for/of the festivities
amatheko festivities [n3-pl]
eKrismesi of Christmas
asezi-ofisini of/for offices
nawokuvala and for closing
kweenkampani of companies
kokuzityel' of eating at them [= kwa-uku-zi-ty-el(-a)]
-tyel- eat at (place); eat from (dish); eat for (a reason); [ext] misappropriate, help oneself to s.t. belonging to another [v-ben]
kwelo to, at, in, from that [deic-2-n2-sg-loc]
liseofisini in the office
lisehotele at a hotel
kwisirhoxo in a sheeben, a secret (favorite) place
osithandayo which you love
ungayilibali do not forget
egodukayo going home
ikharavan caravan {Eng}
enezibane with lights
eziluhlaza that are green or blue
ezilanyazayo that are flashing
ecaleni on the side [loc-n3-sg]
Amabhinqa females [n3-pl]
namadoda and men
akuyo who are on/in it
wawo their [n3-pl-poss-n2-sg]
ungaziqhathi don't cheat yourself
qhata take advantage of, get the better of, cheat [v-tr]
kuwanyoba bribe (lit: make them rejoice)
ufunyaniswe you are found
ugqithisile you have passed
kumyinge to/over the limit
osemthethweni within the law
uyavalelwa you are arrested
uhlawuliswe you have to pay
ukhululwe you be released
ngebheyili on bail {Eng}
unako you can
nokuphulukana lose [v-tr]
nelayisensi license {Eng}
yokuqhuba for driving
bazisebenzisa they use [v-tr]
iilayisensi licenses [n5-pl] {Eng}
kubhetele it is better [cop atr-loan]
ukuyilondoloza to take care of it
-yi- [n5-sg-obj] refers here to an individual's license
-londoloz- take care of, preserve, protect, keep under one's care [v-tr]
kunokugxwala rather than cry out loud
-gxwala emswaneni cry one's heart out, wail, mourn [vp-idiom]
emswaneni at the stomach of a sheep (lit) [n2-sg-loc]
umswane chyme, stomach contents of a slaughtered animal; [ext] nonsense, rubbish [n2-sg]
«4»
niphulaphula you listen
nilumkile (that you may) be wise, cautious, prudent
niya kuyeka you will leave, abandon
namatshamba having a great feast
amatshamba great feast; great rejoicing [n3-pl]
senitye izinto zenu you have eaten your fill/to excess
usazi you know [v part]
kusela going to drink
kube and also [v aux]

kuza kufuneka there will be a need to/for
uqhube (for) you to drive [v subj]
ongaselanga who did not drink
akuqhubele drive for you
kungenjalo otherwise [conj]
kusikhumbula to remember (this)
silumkiso warning [n4-sg-red]
xa sele whenever, at such time that [conj-expr followed by participial construction] (lit: when already)
ufakwe that you be put in...
iintsimbi irons; [ext] handcuffs [n5-pl]
intsimbi iron, steel; iron bar/implement; bell, gong; [ext] o'clock [n5-sg]
zamabanjwa of prisoners
ibanjwa prisoner [sg]
amabanjwa prisoners [pl]
uvalelwa being locked,
kwesimnyama in a dark, black
isisele cell, pit; traditional grain pit
unendlebe you have an ear (i.e., you can hear)
unetyala you have a fault (i.e., you are guilty)
«5»
liphelile it has ended [v-intr stative]
lokushumayela to preach [v-tr/intr]
Sis' Barbara Sister Barbara
uBarman Barman
ngunyaka ozayo next year
nibe nexesh' elimnandi you have a good time
elimnandi good, pleasant, nice [adj-n3-sg]

Uluvo Lomhleli

«1»

IKhomishoni yeNyaniso iza kuvelisa onke amanyundululu!

«2»

Ukusekwa kweKhomishoni yeNyaniso nguRhulumente woBumbano kule veki iphelayo, yinto ebonisa ukuba uMongameli woMzantsi Afrika, uGqirha Nelson Mandela uvuthwe tu kubunkokeli bakhe beli lizwe.

«3»

Xa amaBhulu ayebamba uGqirha Mandela nabanye bomzabalazo we-ANC ooMnu. Walter Sisulu, Govan Mbeki, Raymond Mhlaba namanye amafanankosi omzabalazo wokukhulula abaNtsundu ababecinezelwe ngamahamba-nandlela angabaMhlophe phantsi kwemithetho yeqaqa elinukayo lomthetho wocalulo iApartheid abaMhlophe beli lizwe abazange babuze elangeni, ingakumbi uJohn Vorster no-Verwoerd iinjengele nabaseki be-Apartheid.

«4»

Babecinga ukuba la maxhwangusha aya kufa engazange alikhulule eli kunye nabacinezelwa ababebotshiwe izandla neenyawo yimithetho yamaBhulu ekhusela ibala nenzala ka-Van Riebeeck owayenguyise weembacu zaseYurophu ezabanga umhlaba wama-Afrika zakufika kweli ngemfakadolo yompu, kuhluthwa umhlaba kwiinkosi zomthonyama nakwizinxiba-mxhaka zakwaPhalo, kwasiKhukhuni, kwaCetywayo nakwaLobengula nakwaMzilikazi.

«5»

Le Khomishoni iza kubhentsisa onke amanyala enziwa ngolunya zizixhiphothi zezigebenga ezabulala amatsha-ntliziyo ase-Afrika anje ngoo-Steve Biko, Looksmart Solwandle Ngudle, Matthews Goniwe, Fort Calata, Sparrow Mhonto, Griffiths Mxenge, Victoria Mxenge, Bathandwa Ndondo, Atwell Maqekeza, Joe Gqabi, Hector Peterson nentlaninge yamagorha namagorhakazi akowethu.

«6»

Uphando lwale Khomishoni imalungu alishumi elinesixhenxe ilucwambu lwezifundiswa zomthetho kweli, inikwe umyalezo nguMongameli ukuba ingakhe ishiye nalinye ilitye nesuntswana lwesicwibi senyaniso singavunjululwanga kuxelelwe uluntu ngamanyundululu enziwa ngexesha kwakugquba i-apartheid kweloMzantsi Afrika.

«7»

Kamnandi uMongameli Mandela utyumbe ixhwangusha lase-Afrika negqala lomzabalazo elachasa i-apartheid lathetha kwavokotheka likhala lonke ilizwe ngexesha iinkokeli zeli, kukho noMongameli Mandela, zisejele zigwetywe ubomi esiqithini saseRobben Island. Lowo nguBhishophu wamaTshetshi uBawo oHloniphekileyo u-Desmond Mpilo Tutu, otyunjelwe ukuba abe nguSihlalo wale Khomishoni ye-Nyaniso (Truth Commission).

«8»

Kungoku nje abenza amanyundululu baya nkwantya, iingwatyu zijinga emanqineni nasemadolweni, kuba kaloku uHili uza kuphuma ngenkani ezingcongolweni, abonwe, athethe la manyala akhe okuhlupha uluntu.

«9»

Kunamhlanje nje, simothulela umnqwazi uMadiba ngokuseka le Khomishoni. Aza kuvela amanyala awayenziwa kubulawa abantwana baseAfrika ngenxa yokuzama ukubacutha, kwaye benqandwa ukuba bangakhe bakhulule ilizwe lakowabo elathathwa ngamaBhulu ngompu koobaw'omkhulu.

«10»

Sithi huntshu, tshotsho ubekho mfo kaMandela kaDalindyebo kaNgangelizwe!

Vocabulary

uluvo views
lomhleli of the editor
  lom of [combo form indicating that n1-sg is possessed by n6-sg] (Note: **uluvo** should command the possessive '**lwom**...' but many speakers drop the **-w-** these days such that the form is gradually weakening)
«1»
ikhomishoni commission [n5-sg] {Eng}
yeNyaniso of the truth
iza kuvelisa it will bring out
iza it will [v aux fut]
kuvelisa to bring out
amanyundululu atrocities [n3 pl]
  -nyundululu from **nyundula** [v-tr] (probably Zulu)
«2»
ukusekwa the establishment of [v8 inf]
kweKhomishoni of the commision [n5-sg-poss-n8-vn]
nguRhulumente by the government [cop n2 sg]
woBumbano National
  -bumban- form, shape, mould [v recip]
iphelayo which is ending, last
ebonisa that shows [rel v-tr]
uMongameli manager, overseer, ruler; supervisor, superintendent; chairman, president [n1-sg]

woMzantsi Afrika of South Africa
uGqirha Nelson Mandela Dr. Nelson Mandela
uvuthwe tu he is quietly enthusiastic
-**vuthiwe** in full red paint, mature, robust, thoroughly ripe, red hot, well-cooked, thoroughly healthy [v pass]
kubunkokeli in leadership
ubunkokeli leadership [n7-abs]
beli of this [deic-1-n3-sg-poss-n7-sg]
lizwe country [n3-sg-red]
«3»
amaBhulu the Afrikaners [n3 pl borr]
ayebamba they had arrested
aye- they had VERBed [group 3 plural contracted remote past compound tense]
bomzabalazo of the struggle [n2-sg-poss-n1-pl]
umzabalazo effort, attempt, endeavor; struggle for political liberation [n2-sg]
we-ANC of the African National Congress
ooMnu. gentlemen; Misters
numzana a gentleman [n1]
Walter Sisulu (name)
Govan Mbeki (name)
Raymond Mhlaba (name)
namanye and others
amafanankosi a bodyguard, guardians [n3 pl]
omzabalazo of the struggle [n2-sg-poss-n3-pl]
wokukhulula of setting free
-**khulul**- loosen, untie, set free
abaNtsundu black people
ababecinezelwe who were oppressed
ngamahamba-nandlela by those who go on the way, i.e., fellow travelers
nandlela with the way [conn n5sg]
angabaMhlophe who are white [cop n1 pl]
kwemithetho the laws
yeqaqa strong-smelling black beetle with striped back [XED:134]
elinukayo that smells
nuka smell [v-intr]
lomthetho this law
wocalulo of making a distinction, discriminate
calula make distinction between, distinguish [v-tr]
iApartheid Apartheid [n5-sg] {Afr}
abaMhlophe the Whites
beli of this [deic-1-n3-sg-poss-n1-pl]
Contrast: **beli** agreeing with n7-sg above
abazange babuze they never questioned
abazange they never (see **zange**)
babuze (they) questioned
elaṇgeni in the sun (lit: out in the open)
ilanga sun [3]
ingakumbi especially, particularly; mainly, mostly, chiefly [adv]
uJohn Vorster no-Verwoerd (names)
iinjengele the generals [n5 pl]
injengele brave man, hero; general [n5]
nabaseki and establishers
abaseki establishers [n1 pl]
be-Apartheid of Apartheid [n5-sg-poss-n1-pl]
«4»
babecinga they had thought [v-remote-past]
babe- they had VERBed [contracted remote past compound tense]
maxhwangusha experts, alt. ruffians [n3-pl-red]
See **ixhwangusha** below
aya kufa they will die

aya they will [C3 pl aux fut]
kufa to die [v-inf-red]
engazange they never having
alikhulule released, set free
nabacinezelwa and those who are oppressed
ababebotshiwe who were tied
-**botshw-** be tied, bound, saddled, yoked, harnessed [v-pass]
yimithetho it is the laws
yamaBhulu of the (white) Afrikaners
ekhusela which protect [n2-pl-rel]
ibala color, hue; marking; spot [n3-sg]
nenzala and the increase (i.e., future generations)
Van Riebeeck (name)
owayenguyise who was the father
uyise father, his, her, their [n1a]
weembacu of the destitute wanderers
iimbacu destitute wanderers
zaseYurophu of Europe {Afr Europa}
ezabanga who claimed
wama-Afrika of the Africans
zakufika upon their arrival [v temp] [Note: temporal mood]
-**a-ku**- when SUBJECT VERBs/VERBed [positive temporal verb construction]
ngemfakadolo with a breech-loading rifle
imfakadolo breechloading rifle [n5-sg]
yompu of a gun (i.e., type of gun)
kuhluthwa it was taken by force [v-pass]
kwiinkosi from the chiefs
zomthonyama traditional [n2 compound] (lit: of ancient kraals)
nakwizinxiba-mxhaka from the one wearing the ivory armband, a councillor of rank [n4 pl compound]
-**nxib**- wear, get dressed [v-tr/intr]
mxhaka ivory armband (badge of Royal Xhosa rank)
zakwaPhalo of Phalo's place (place in the Xhosa chieftainship of Phalo)
kwasiKhukhuni (place of Khukhuni in the Pedi region)
kwaCetywayo (place of Cetwayo in the Zulu region)
nakwaLobengula Lobengula (place name)
nakwaMzilikazi. (place of Mzilikazi in Shona region of the former Rhodesia, now Zimbabwe)

«5»

khomishoni commission [n5-sg-red]
kubhentsisa to expose
-**bhents**- sit in an exposed condition [v-intr]
amanyala shameless conduct, indecency, vulgarity, unwonted [v 3pl/non-count]
enziwa which were done
(zero) [n3-pl-rel] assimilated to initial vowel of **enza**
ngolunya with malice
ulunya ill-will, malice [n6-abs]
zizixhiphothi zezigebenga by the robust, bearded murderers (a reference to the stereotypical Afrikaner official) [n4-pl agent]
isixhiphothi heavily-bearded man; well-built, robust [n4 pl]
isigebenga murderer and robber; bandit, highwayman; giant, ogre [n4]
ezabulala that/who killed
amatsha-ntliziyo the young at heart, fervent young men and women
-**tsha** young [adj]
ase-Afrika of Africa
Steve Biko (name)
Looksmart Solwandle Ngudle (name)
Matthews Goniwe (name)
Fort Calata (name)
Sparrow Mhonto (name)

Griffiths Mxenge (name)
Victoria Mxenge (name)
Bathandwa Ndondo (name)
Atwell Maqekeza (name)
Joe Gqabi (name)
Hector Peterson (name)
nentlaninge and an abundance
  intlaninge abundance, plenty; a great number [n5-sg]
yamagorha of heroes
  igorha brave, valiant man; hero [n3]
namagorhakazi and brave women
  igorhakazi brave woman
akowethu of ours, of our nation [= a-k-o-wethu]
«6»
uphando investigation [n6]
  -**phand**- scratch up, dig up, examine into [v-tr]
lwale of this
imalungu members of which [n3 pl cop n5 sg]
  i- which [n5-sg-cop] (lit: they are)
  amalungu members [n3-pl]
alishumi that are ten
elinesixhenxe that has seven
  isixhenxe seven
ilucwambu it is the cream [n6-sg-pred-n5-sg]
  ucwambu cream [n6-sg]
lwezifundiswa of the educated
zomthetho of the law
inikwe it was given
umyalezo order, instruction, command [n2-sg]
nguMongameli by the ruler
ingakhe it should not
ishiye it should leave
nalinye a single one
ilitye stone, rock [n3-sg]
nesuntswana even a tiny piece
lwesicwibi of the smallest seed (Zulu) therefore grain (of truth)
senyaniso of the truth [poss-n5]
singavunjululwanga it has not been turned up
  -**vumbulul**- turn up, grub up (out of the ground) [v-tr ext]
kuxelelwe will be told [v neut pass]
ngamanyundululu about the atrocities
kwakugquba when there was raising dust
  -**gqub**- raise dust (esp. in a kraal) [v-tr]
kweloMzantsi Afrika of South Africa
«7»
utyumbe he picked out [3pers sg v-tr past]
  tyumba carry off, appropriate, pick out, raid [v-tr]
ixhwangusha expert, man of high intelligence or deep experience; high-ranking person; [fig] swindler, con-man [n3-sg]
lase-Afrika of Africa
negqala and an observer
  igqala observer, observant old man [n3-sg]
  -**gqal**- observe, look at attentively; notice; aim at [v-tr]
lomzabalazo the struggle [n2-sg-poss-n3-sg]
elachasa those who oppose
  -**chas**- oppose, be against [v-tr]
lathetha it talked
kwavokotheka with eloquent, lengthy argument
  -**vokothek**- be persuaded by lengthy argument [XED:178]
likhala it complaining (in fact, he, the appointee)
  khala give voice, ring, complain, cry out, wail, scream [XED:66]
noMongameli with the ruler
zisejele they were in jail
  jele jail {Eng} [n5]
zigwetywe they were condemned
  -**gwetyw**- ward off, condemn, decide, turn the horns defly to either side [XED:52] (lit: they are sentenced)

esiqithini on an island
Robben Island {Eng}
nguBhishophu is the bishop
wamaTshetshi collective Church (name of church group, e.g., Evangelists)
oHloniphekileyo who is well-respected
u-Desmond Mpilo Tutu (name)
otyunjelwe who were carried off
-tyumb- pick out and carry off; raid (cattle), appropriate [v-tr]
nguSihlalo be the chair person
isihlalo chair [n4]
wale of this [deic-1-n5-sg-poss-n1-sg]
«8»
kungoku it is now
abenza those who did
nkwantya tremble with fear; be terrified [v-intr]
iingwatyu loose trousers; low-hanging udders [n5-pl]
ingwatyu anything wide and flapping (e.g., loose trousers); lean cow with pendulous or flapping udder [n5-sg]
zijinga them swinging
jinga swing, wave in the air, hang, dangle [v-intr]
emanqineni on paws, on all fours; [ext] on one's feet [n3-pl-loc = e-(a)ma-nqin(a)-eni]
inqina hoof, paw, knuckle (animal), hock; hoof-mark, footprint [n3-sg; pl: **amanqina**]
nasemadolweni and on the knees [= na-s-e-(a)ma-dolo/w-eni]
idolo knee [n3-sg]
uHili fabled river-dwarf supposed to carry off children [n1a-sg]
kuphuma to come out [v-inf-red]
ngenkani with stubbornness
inkani stubbornness [n5-sg]
ezingcongolweni from the reeds
ingcongolo reed [n5-sg]
abonwe be seen
athethe he speaks
manyala shameless acts
akhe his [n1-sg-poss-n3-pl]
okuhlupha of inconveniencing
«9»
kunamhlanje it is today
simothulela we take off (our hats) for him
thulela relieve, take down for [v-tr ext]
umnqwazi headdress; [ext] hat, cap, bonnet [n2-sg]
uMadiba (clan name for Nelson Mandela)
ngokuseka for establishing
aza they will [v aux fut]
kuvela to appear [v-inf-red]
awayenziwa which were done
kubulawa murdering
-bulaw- be killed, get murdered [v-pass]
yokuzama of trying
ukubacutha to minimize
-cuth- narrow, contract, compress, reduce in size; minimize; bring to a point [v-tr]
benqandwa they were prevented
nqanda prevent [v-tr]
bangakhe they should just [3 pl prog subj]
bakhulule they free
lakowabo of theirs
lako of [poss n3-sg n1-pl]
elathathwa that was taken
ngamaBhulu by the Afrikaners
ngompu by the gun
koobaw'omkhulu from our grandfathers
oobawo our fathers [n1a-pl-kin]
«10»
huntshu victory! [intj]
tshotsho serves you or him right (in sense of being his just due) [intj]
ubekho you are here
umfo guy, fellow [n1-sg] {colloq}
kaMandela of Mandela
kaDalindyebo (praise name)
kaNgangelizwe (praise name)

Ngaba uTakalani uza kuba yinjuze yeeOlimpiki?

«0»

Inkoliso yamagqiyazana kule mihla ikhetha ukuba yimilonjikazi okanye ukungenela ukhuphiswano loonobuhle. UTakalani Rachel "Musquito" Nthulani yena uzimisele ekuqakaduleni kwimidlalo yee Olimpiki.

«1»

UTakalani ominyaka eli-17 ubeyimbaleki ebalaseleyo ukususela esafunda amabanga aphantsi.

«2»

"Ndaqala ndiselula ukubaleka ndaza ndabangela ukuxokozela ngeziphumo zam zokubaleka ndisafunda kwisikolo samabanga aphantsi. Kodwa kube ngo-1995 apho ndiqalise ukuzimisela ngokupheleleyo ekubalekeni ndikhuthazwa ngabazali bam, iititshala nabahlobo.

«3»

"EVaal Triangle ndagqwesa kwiEmfuleni 15 km ngemizuzu nje eyi-59 -- ndishiya iimbaleki eziphambili ezinjengoLydia Mofula noSarah Jane. Olo gqatso lwandivulela iingcango."

«4»

UTakalani obalasele ekubalekeni kwi-800m nakwi-1 500m, usimele ngempumelelo isikolo sakhe kugqatso lweUsasa obeluseKapa obeluquka namanye amaphondo eli. Wophula irekhodi xa washiya ezinye iimbaleki kwi-800m waza kwi-1 500m waphuma kwindawo yesithathu.

«5»

Waphumelela nakwi-3 000 m kwiSouth African Championships eSecunda apho wabaleka wamisa irekhodi entsha yemizuzu esi-8 nemizuzwana engama-30. Apho wayekhuphisana neyona mbaleki yaziwayo, uRene Kalmer.

«6»

"Ndandimele uMzantsi Afrika kwiWorld Cross Country eIthali apho ndaphuma kwindawo yama-62. Ndandibaleka nekhulu leembaleki zodumo zamazwe ngamazwe ehlabathi. Ndafunda lukhulu kolo gqatso. Uyazi, ngoku xa ndibaleka kweli ndisebenzisa ubuchule endabuzuza apho."

«7»

Uphinde wasezindabeni xa emva kokuba ezuze imbasa yebronze kwiSA Championships. Kodwa usibonise isiphiwo sakhe sokwenene xa ezuze imbasa yesilivere kwi-5 000m yabasetyhini kwiRegional Championships eThekwini. Ixesha alibalekayo yimizuzu eli-18 nemizuzwana engama-20. Amanye amazwe aseAfrika ali-11 aye anenxaxheba kolo gqatso. Uphume tanci kwi-1 500m ayibaleke ngemizuzu emi-4 nemizuzwana engama-48.

«8»

Iqabane abaleka nalo limazise kumqeqeshi walo, uGeorge Sebiloane weVosloorus Athletic Club.

«9»

Nangona singanazo izinto zokuziqeqesha ezisemgangathweni, ebuncinaneni zingama-40 iimbaleki eziziqeqesha kwibala elivulekileyo eZone 7 eMailula eVoslorus. Mna ndisoloko ndinenkolo yokuba xa unesiphiwo akukho nto enokuba ngumqobo phambi kwakho. Kodwa ndisoloko ndithandazela ukuba sifumane inkxaso-mali ukuze kuncedakale iimbaleki ezisakhasayo," utshilo obefudula eyimbaleki waza wangumqeqeshi.

«10»

"Ndicinga ukuba xa sineendawo zokuziqeqesha ezifana nezezinye iimbaleki esibaleka nazo elugqatsweni ndinokufika kusukelo lwam. Abanye abantu sele benabaxhasi kanti mna kufuneka ndibaleke kugqatso olumbalwa ukuze ndifumane izihlangu ezitsha zokuziqeqesha okanye ezokubaleka kugqatso," utshilo uTakalani.

«11»

"Ndinentlaninge yeembasa neendebe. Akukho nto iza kundinqanda ndingawufezi umnqweno wam wokumela eli kwi-Olimpiki zango 2004. Ndinethemba lokuba ndiya kuphumelela kuzo."

Vocabulary

ngaba can be; is it possible that; probably, to be supposed
uTakalani (proper name) {Tsonga}
yinjuze she is a champion
  injuze champion [n5-sg; pl: iinjuze]
yeeOlimpiki of the Olympics
«0»
inkoliso most, greater part, majority
yamagqiyazana of young women
  igqiyazana young single woman [n3-sg-dim]
ikhetha he/she chooses
yimilonjikazi they are singers [v-pred]

yimi- they are ... [group 2 plural copulative/predicative prefix construction]
imilonjikazi singers
Cf: **umlonji** cape canary [n2-sg]
Cf: **umlomo** mouth [n2-sg]
ukungenela to enter (into)
ukhuphiswano contest [n6-sg]
loonobuhle of a beauty queen
unobuhle beauty queen
Rachel (proper name)
Musquito (nickname)
Nthulani (family name) {Tsonga}
uzimisele she is serious
ekuqakaduleni in galloping
-**qakadul**- gallop, frolic, frisk, gambol, skip about (like calves or children) [v-intr]
kwimidlalo in the games
«1»
ominyaka who is years old [rel-atr]
eli-17 of 17
ubeyimbaleki she has been a runner
mbaleki runner
ebalaseleyo eminent, excellent
ukususela u kususela from that time
esafunda she was still studying
«2»
ndaqala I began [past-sub]
ndiselula I was already easily
ukubaleka to run
ndaza and then I
ndabangela I caused
-**bangel**- cause for, bring upon, give to [v-ben]
ukuxokozela to make a loud, confused noise or din; sensation
ngeziphumo with successes
zokubaleka of running
ndisafunda I am still studying
samabanga of grades
ngo-1995 in 1995
ndiqalise I started
-**qalis**- start anew, make a beginning; make s.o. begin s.t.
ukuzimisela to establish myself
ngokupheleleyo now completely [adv]
-**pheleleyo**- completely
ekubalekeni in running
ndikhuthazwa I having been encouraged [part]
ngabazali by parents
bam mine [pro-1sg-poss-n1-pl]
iititshala teachers [n5-pl]
«3»
EVaal in Vaal (place name)
Vaal Triangle (name of athletic competition taking place in Vaal Triangle, the industrial area of South Africa)
ndagqwesa I won [past sub]
-**gqwes**- win (in any contest), come out the best [v-intr]
kwiEmfuleni (name of competition)
Emfuleni at the river (refers to R. Vaal)
15km 15 kilometers
ngemizuzu by minutes [n2-pl-instr]
eyi-59 which are 59
ndishiya I passed, left behind (Cf: -**gqitha** pass)
-**shiy**- leave behind
iimbaleki runners
eziphambili who/that are in (ahead) front
ezinjengoLydia Mofula such as Lydia Mofula
Lydia Mofula (name)
noSarah Jane and Sarah Jane
olo that (not far, just mentioned) [deic-2-n6-sg]
gqatso race [n6-sg-red]
lwandivulela it [n6] opened for me
-**vulel**- open for [v-ben]
«4»
obalasele who is talented
-**balasele** eminent, talented, important
ekubalekeni in the race
kwi-800m in (the) 800m

nakwi-1,500m and in the 1,500m
usimele she represented
-simel- represent, stand for
ngempumelelo with success, successfuly [adv]
impumelelo success [n5]
sakhe his, her, its [pro-3sg-n4-sg]
kugqatso in (the) race
lweUsasa of/at Usasa
Usasa (name of athletic association)
obeluseKapa which was in Cape Town
iKapa Cape Town
obeluquka which included
-quk- include, take together, comprise
amaphondo provinces, regions [n3-pl]
Wophula he/she broke
wo absolute pronoun with suffix **-na** deleted [Pahl:551]
aphula break [v-tr]
irekhodi record
washiya she left behind, abandoned
kwi-800m in (the) 800m
kwi-1,500m in the 1,500m
waphuma she came out
kwindawo in a place
yesithathu third (lit: of three)
isithathu three
«5»
waphumelela he/she won
nakwi-3,000m and in (the) 3,000m
kwiSouth African Championships in the South African Championships
eSecunda in Secunda
Secunda (place name)
wabaleka she ran
wamisa she set
yemizuzu of minutes
esi-8 (which are) 8
nemizuzwana and seconds [n2-pl-conj]
umzuzwana little while; second (unit of time) [n2-sg-dim]
engama-30 (which are) 30
wayekhuphisana she had surpassed
-khuphis- crowd out, remove, dispossess [v-tr]
neyona and herself
yaziwayo who is (well) known
uRene Kalmer (proper name)
«6»
ndandimele I had represented
ndandi- I had [contracted remote past compound tense]
-mel- represent, stand for
uMzantsi Afrika South Africa
kwiWorld Cross Country in the World Cross Country {Eng}
eIthali in Italy
ndaphuma I came out
yama-62 62nd (lit: of 62)
ndandibaleka I had run [v-remote-past]
nekhulu with a hundred
leembaleki (of) runners
zodumo of fame, famous
udumo fame [6 abstr]
zamazwe ngamazwe of all kinds of countries, many countries (idiomatic phrase)
zamazwe of countries
ngamazwe by countries
ndafunda and I learned [past sub]
lukhulu a great deal [n6-agr adj] (agrees with **ugqatso**)
kolo to, at, in, from that [deic-2-n6-sg-loc]
olo that [deic-2-n6-sg]
ndibaleka I run
kweli in this (country) [**lizwe** understood]
ndisebenzisa I use
ubuchule skill [n7 abstr]
endabuzuza which I got
«7»
uphinde she again
-phind- to VERB again [aux]
wasezindabeni she was still in the news [= wa sa izin dab eni;

from **udaba** (pl: **iindaba**; locative **ezindaba**)]
See: -**sa**- still in R4d
ndisathandana
ezuze she got
imbasa medal [n5-sg]
yebronze of bronze
kwiSA Championships in the South African Championships
usibonise she showed it
isiphiwo gift [n4-sg]
sokwenene of the truth; [atr] very real
yesilivere of silver [atr] {Eng}
kwi-5000m in the 5000m
yabasetyhini women's [= ya ba se i-tyhini]
ityhini female, girl, woman [n3-sg; no plural]
kwiRegional in the Regional Championships {Eng}
alibalekayo in which she ran it [= a li balek a-yo]
yimizuzu they are minutes [pred]
eli-18 which are 18
nemizuzwana and in seconds
ali-11 that are 11
anenxaxheba they participate in, they have a part of
inxaxheba part, share [n5-sg]
uphume she came out
tanci first
kwi-1,500m in (the) 1,500m
ayibaleke she ran it
ngemizuzu by/in minutes
emi-4 4 [+plural marker]
nemizuzwana and in seconds
engama-48 which are 48
«8»
abaleka who is running
limazise he/she introduced her/him
kumqeqeshi to the trainer
umqeqeshi trainer [n1-sg]
walo of him/her [n1-sg-poss-n1-sg]
UGeorge Sebiloane (name)
weVosloorus of Vosloorus
iVosloorus place name
«9»
singanazo we not having them
zokuziqeqesha of self-training
ezisemgangathweni at a level or standard
umgangatho floor (mud floor); level; standard, quality [n2-sg]
ebuncinaneni which is small
ncinane small (very small), little, slight, tiny; young [adj-root-dim]
zingama-40 they are 40
eziziqeqesha who are training themselves
kwibala in a vacant lot
ibala yard, vacant lot, open space (near a house or other structure), lawn; glade (near a forest) [n3-sg]
elivulekileyo which is open
-**vulek**- open, be open, standing
eZone 7 in Zone 7
eMailula in Mailula (township)
eVoslorus in Voslorus
mna I; myself; as for me
ndisoloko I always
ndinenkolo I have faith
inkolo belief, faith, creed, religion [n5]
unesiphiwo you have a gift
isiphiwo gift, natural ability or talent
enokuba which can be, that can become
ngumqobo it is an obstacle
umqobo s.t. long and thick; obstacle, hindrance
ndithandazela I pray for
-**thandazel**- pray, intercede for [v-tr ext]
sifumane that we may find
inkxaso-mali financial support, stipend, scholarship
kuncedakale it is helped
-**ncedakal**- be helped, assisted
ezisakhasayo that are still developing
-**khas**- creep crawl, go on hands and knees (progress slowly)

obefudula eyimbaleki who used to be a runner
fudula used to VERB; formerly VERBed
eyimbaleki who is a runner
waza wangumqeqeshi and now she has become a trainer
wangumqeqeshi she is a trainer
umqeqeshi trainer [n1-sg]
«10»
sineendawo we have places
ezifana na- which are like/similar to
nezezinye with those of others
nezezi- with those of
zezinye others (plural)
esibaleka where we run [rel]
nazo with them [n5-pl-comit]
elugqatsweni in a race
ndinokufika ndi noku fika I can reach/arrive at
kusukelo at/to a goal
sukelo goal; pursuit
benabaxhasi they have supporters
-**xhas**- support
umxhasi supporter [n1-sg]
ndibaleke that I run
kugqatso in the race
olumbalwa which are few
izihlangu shoes [n4-pl]
ezitsha which are new
ezokubaleka for running
«11»
ndinentlaninge I have plenty
intlaninge abundance, plenty; a great number [n5-sg]
yeembasa of medals
neendebe and trophies
iindebe cups; trophies [n5-pl]
kundinqanda to prevent me
nqanda prevent [v-tr]
ndingawufezi I do not accomplish it [see full example for this entry in Lexicon]
-**fez**- accomplish [v-tr]
umnqweno desire [n2-sg]
wokumela of representing
kwi-Olimpiki in the Olympics
zango of
ndinethemba I have hope
ithemba hope [n3-sg]

Ikamva Ngeenkwenkwezi

«1»

Aries (March 21–April 21)

Lixesha elihle eli lokuba uvuthulule iingcinga zakho ngenjongo zokuqalisa ukuqhubela phambili iphulo elinengeniso. Uya kuvuya ngumothuko wokufumanisa ubuchopho obuthweleyo apha kuwe. Qalisa ngoku.
ITHAMSANQA: Umbala Orenji; Inani 2 & 8; Unobumba K & V.

«2»

Taurus (April 21–May 21)

Thabatha amanyathelo angqongqo okuzigcina uphile qete. Chitha ixesha ngokuzilolonga utye kamnandi. Landela imikhuba emihle wakhe ingqondo, uluvo nobume bomzimba wakho.
ITHAMSANQA: Umbala Luhlaza; Inani 3 & 9; Unobumba L & W.

«3»

Gemini (May 21–June 22)

Eli ithuba lifuna intsebenziswano ukufikelela kwindawo ebalulekileyo, hlanganisa ingqondo nolwazi lwezihlobo zakho osebenzisana nazo ngengqondo nangeminqweno. Uhlanganyelwano ngezimvo aluwi phantsi.
ITHAMSANQA: Umbala Blowu; Inani 1 & 4; Unobumba M & X.

«4»

Cancer (June 22–July 23)

Lixesha elihle eli lokuqalisa okanye ukuqhubela phambili iphulo lentlanganisela. Uthethwano lunga qhubela phambili ngelithuba kusekho umoya wovisiswano. Funa amalungelo athile.
ITHAMSANQA: Umbala Bomvu; Inani 2 & 5; Unobumba N &Y.

«5»

Leo (July 23–Aug 24)

Zimisele ukugcina inkqubela yekamva lakho ikhuselekile. Impilo yakho ixhomekeke okokuba ube ngumntu ozimeleyo; kufuneka ke usebenzele elo nqanam ngokulandela iinzame ezizizo.
ITHAMSANQA: Umbala Luthuli; Inani 3 & 6; Unobumba O & Z.

«6»

Virgo (Aug 24–Sept 23)

Ukuba unesiphiwo soshishino, nali ixesha lokusibonakalisa esidlangalaleni. Lixesha eli lokuqalisa iminqweno emitsha. Uya kuba uyazinceda ukuba usebenzisa umtsalane wakho. Kufuneka

uzuze intlonipho kwicandelo lezoshishino.
ITHAMSANQA: Umbala Ntsundu; Inani 4 & 7; Unobumba A & P.

«7»

Libra (Sept 23–Oct 23)

Ingcebiso evela kumhlobo wenene nosisilumko ingakubuyisela ekhondweni. Ukuzimisela nentsebenziswano yindibanisela elungileyo, ngoko dibana nabanye umvuzo oya kuwuzuza uya kuphinda-phindana.
ITHAMSANQA: Umbala Mfusa; Inani 5 & 8; Unobumba B & Q.

«8»

Scorpio (Oct 23–Nov 23)

Uqinisekile kwaye uthembekile ngoku; ungakwazi phandle ukuvelisa okungamahlebo oxhotyiswe ngawo, nobugcisa obuphezulu onabo. Lixesha kanye lokwakha ubuhlobo eli.
ITHAMSANQA: Umbala Mfusa; Inani 6 & 9; Unobumba C & R.

«9»

Sagittarius (Nov 23–Dec 22)

Ukusebenzisa isiqu sakho sisitshixo senkqubela yakho ngokweli hlabathi, ngoko ziqhubele phambili ngokuqinisekileyo uzuze iziphumo. Zimisele ngokupheleleyo unyanzelise ukuphumeza intlahla yakho.
ITHAMSANQA: Umbala Tyheli; Inani 1 & 7; Unobumba D & S.

«10»

Capricorn (Dec 22–Jan 21)

Lixesha lokuqiniseka ukuba usebenza ngokwenene kwiindlela ezinembuyekezo. Njengokuba ngeli thuba imali imomoza. Ubutyebi obuthe chatha buya nqweneleka.
ITHAMSANQA: Umbala Mthubi; Inani 2 & 8; Unobumba E & T.

«11»

Aquarius (Jan 21–Feb 20)

Unoqwalaselo uphaphamile ngoku, uyakwazi nokuthetha kanjalo, ngoko khulula ingqondo yakho izungeze kakhulu ngokukhululekileyo ibheka phambili.
ITHAMSANQA: Umbala Mhlophe; Inani 3 & 9; Unobumba F & U.

«12»

Pisces (Feb 20–March 21)

Uthando lwentsapho yakho luya bonakaliswa ngoku; nanje ngokuba unobubele nemeko yoxolo, ubudlelwane bakho apha

phakathi kwekhaya buza kuthi chatha ngoku. Impembelelo zakho ziya kunceda izizalwana zakho ukuba zihambe kakuhle apha ebomini.
ITHAMSANQA: Umbala Mnyama; Inani 1 & 4; Unobumba G & V.

The author of this article frequently does not join subject concords and tense markers to the verb root, thus causing possible confusion—see last line of "Capricorn," for example, where the normal convention would be **buyanqweneleka** 'will be desirable.'

Vocabulary

ngeenkwenkwezi by/through the stars
inkwenkwezi star [n5-sg]
«1»
elihle which is good, fine, right
uvuthulule you should shake off
-**vuthulul**- shake off, shake out of, shake off from [v-tr]
zokuqalisa of starting anew
ukuqhubela phambili to progress, drive forward
elinengeniso which will be an introduction to
isingeniso introduction
kuvuya to be glad
-**vuy**- rise in boiling; [ext] rejoice, be glad, joyful ~ delighted
ngumothuko by the shock
umothuko shock [n2-sg]
-**othuk**- be shocked, startled [v-st]
wokufumanisa of making or helping to find
ubuchopho brain [n7-sg]
obuthweleyo which is carried
-**thwele** bore a burden; carried; abducted [v-perf]
-**thwal**- bear (a burden, fruit); carry; abduct, elope with [v-tr]
ithamsanqa luck [n3-sg]
orenji orange {Eng}
inani number, numeral [n3-sg]
2 (isibini)
8 (isibhozo)
unobumba letter (of the alphabet)
«2»
thabatha amanyathelo take steps
amanyathelo steps [n3-pl]
angqongqo hard, severe [atr]
okuzigcina of taking care of oneself
uphile qete that you be bursting with good health [subj]
qete perfectly, completely [ideophone]
chitha ixesha spend time
-**chith**- spend; spill, scatter; waste; destroy [v-tr]
ngokuzilolonga by looking after yourself
-**lolong**- look at the various parts of s.t.; observe in detail/carefully; look out for, look after s.o. [v-tr]
utye that you eat [v-sub]
imikhuba habits [n2-pl]
umkhuba custom, practice; habit [n2-sg]
emihle which are well; beautiful; clear; thorough, complete [atr]
wakhe that you may build
nobume and the condition [n7-sg-conj]
bomzimba of the body

luhlaza green; blue [for 'blue' in contrast to 'green,' see -**blowu** in «3» below]
3 (isithathu)
9 (ithoba)
«3»
lifuna (it) wants/needs
intsebenziswano cooperation, working together [n5-sg = in-ts/sebenz-is-w-an-o]
ukufikelela to arrive at, reach
hlanganisa combine [v-imp]
-hlanganis- combine, bring together, assemble, join; meet, encounter; parry, ward off (spears with a shield) [v-caus]
nolwazi and/with knowledge
ulwazi knowledge [n6-sg]
lwezihlobo of friends
osebenzisana that you work together
ngengqondo through means of/with mind, intellect; understanding, reason; mental capacity, intelligence
nangeminqweno and through desires
uhlanganyelwano the bringing together [n6-sg]
-hlanganyel- attack, gang up on, join together against s.o., assail on all sides (when two or more attack one in a fight); [fig] tempt [v-tr]
ngezimvo through, by means of opinions, ideas, feelings
aluwi it [n6-sg] will not fall/succumb
wa fall
blowu blue [atr-root] {Eng}
1 (**isinye**)
4 (**isine**)
«4»
lokuqalisa of starting anew
lentlanganisela of meeting people
uthethwano communication [n6]
lungaqhubela will progress [n6+pot-aux+qhub+el+a]
ngelithuba by means of this opportunity
li (the) [group 3 singular reduced demonstrative]
kusekho it is still/already being/existing/there
wovisisiswano (of) agreement, harmony
imvisisiswano harmony [n5-sg]
amalungelo advantages, benefits; rights, privileges
athile certain [n3-pl-rel]
bomvu red; reddish brown [atr-root]
5 (isihlanu)
«5»
ukugcina to take care of; to preserve [v-inf]
inkqubela progress (noun)
yekamva of the future
impilo health; life; means [n5-sg]
ixhomekeke it should depend on [subjunctive]
ozimeleyo who is independent [v-refl-perf-rel-atr = o-zi-m-el-e-yo]
-zimeleyo having stood on one's own, independent, self-governing, free (from control)
usebenzele that you work for [subjunctive]
elo that (not far, just mentioned)
nqanam a section of a post; the capital of a pillar [XED:107] metaphorical – objective, goal
ngokulandela by following
ezizizo which are those (ones)
luthuli dust-colored
6 (**isithandathu**)
«6»
unesiphiwo you have a gift
soshishino for business [n6-sg-poss-n4-sg]
nali here it is
lokusibonakalisa it reveals it, it shows it (**isiphiwo**)
esidlangalaleni in public; publicly [n4-sg-loc]
isidlangalala open area, arena, amphitheater [n4-sg]

iminqweno desires [n2-pl]
emitsha which are new
uyazinceda u ya zi nceda you are helping yourself
umtsalane attraction, attractiveness [n2-sg]
uzuze that you acquire
intlonipho respect, showing reverence, avoiding [n5-sg-vn]
kwicandelo in the sector
icandelo sector, branch [n3-sg]
lezoshishino of business
ntsundu brown
7 (isixhenxe)
«7»
ingcebiso suggestion, advice
evela it [ingcebiso] comes from
kumhlobo from a friend
nosisilumko and/with/has wiseness
isilumko wise, cautious, prudent person [n4-sg]
ingakubuyisela it can return you to
ekhondweni to finality
Note: **umkhondweni** 'on track' would have provided a better fit
ikhondo last of a thing [n3-sg]
ukuzimisela being serious
nentsebenziswano and working together
yindibanisela is a combination
indibaniso combination [n5-sg]
elungileyo which is suitable
dibana meet together [v-recip]
nabanye with others
oya [it] is going
kuwuzuza to get you [inf+obj]
kuphinda-phindana multiply [v-redupl]
mfusa very dark; dark brown; [ext] purple, violet [atr-root]
«8»
uqinisekile you are confident
uthembekile you are trustworthy
ungakwazi you can know
ukuvelisa bring out ~ forth, produce, yield; put up (proposal), propose, suggest
okungamahlebo without slanderers [n8-agr+neg+n3-pl]
oxhotyiswe being armed
-xhotyw- be armed [pass of –**xhob**- arm oneself]
ngawo nga wo with, through, by means of them (slanderers)
nobugcisa with skill
ubugcisa skill, proficiency, expertise [n7-sg abs]
obuphezulu which is up, above
onabo and they; and as for them; and he, she, it; and as for him, her, it; there (not far, just mentioned) is
lokwakha to build
ubuhlobo friendship, intimacy
«9»
isiqu self, personality, individuality [n4-sg]
sisitshixo it is the key
isitshixo key; lock, bolt [n4-sg]
senkqubela of progress
ngokweli by/at the
hlabathi the world as a whole [n3-sg]
ziqhubele move yourself ahead
ngokuqinisekileyo for certain [adv]
unyanzelise force yourself
-nyanzel- press, squeeze, crumple up; [ext] force, compel, constrain [v-tr]
ukuphumeza to bring out or over
intlahla bloom [n5-sg]
tyheli yellow [atr-root] {Afr geel}
Syn: -**lubhelu** [atr-root]
«10»
lokuqiniseka to be sure, ensure
ngokwenene actually [adv]
kwiindlela in the ways
ezinembuyekezo which have large returns
imomoza it increases
-momoz- increase, grow; bush out luxuriously [v-intr]
ubutyebi wealth [n7-sg abs]

obuthe being [lit: say, used as aux before ideophone]
chatha pour out sparingly, carefully [ideophone]
buya(-)**nqweneleka** it would be desirable
mthubi pale yellow color
«11»
unoqwalaselo you are perceptive
uqwalaselo close observation, careful consideration [n6-sg]
uphaphamile you are vigilant
uyakwazi you are able, you know
nokuthetha and speaking, here, how to speak
kanjalo likewise, in such a way
khulula loosen, untie, unharness; undress, unfasten one's clothing; release, set free; save, deliver [v-tr IMP]
izungeze surround [v-tr]
ngokukhululekileyo extremely, completely [adv]
ibheka it looks towards
-**bhek**- look towards, turn towards, go towards
mhlophe white
«12»
lwentsapho of family
luya bonakaliswa it can be seen
nanje and [conj]
njengokuba whereas, as; considering that {legal}
unobubele you are kind
nemeko and the quality
imeko quality, attribute; mood, condition; state, circumstance [n5-sg]
yoxolo of peace
uxolo peace; pardon [n6-sg]
ubudlelwane friendship, fraternity, comradeship {Zulu} [formed from pass. of -**dlelan**-]
kwekhaya (inside) the house
kuthi say, do; here [v-aux]
impembelelo stirring up, instigation; encouragement; influence upon others [n5-sg]
kunceda to help, aid, assist
izizalwana kinfolk [n4-pl]
isizalwane [usual spelling] kin, family group or connection [n4]
zihambe they should go [v-sub]

Banikwa Inkxaso Abagogekileyo Kwiziko Labo

«1»

Kwintlalo yoluntu efanelekileyo bathatyathwa njengenxalenye yoluntu banikwe namalungelo abo. Endaweni yoko, abantu abanemizimba ephilileyo basuke babasizele, bangabahoyi, bangabaniki inkathalo, maxa wambi babanikele umva abantwana nabantu abakhulu abagogekileyo. Akunjalo eLetaba After-Care Centre.

«2»

IDutch Reformed Church yaseka iLetaba After-Care Centre ngo-1969 ngenjongo yokugcina abantu abangenamakhaya abagogekileyo. Ngoku emva kweminyaka engama-30, eli ziko sele linabantu abangaphezu kwama-70 abasukela kwabaneminyaka eli-16 ukuya kwengama-63. Ngoku liziko elingekho phantsi korhulumente (NGO) elizuza inkxaso-mali yenyanga kurhulumente.

«3»

Le ndawo ikumgama ongama-20km ngaphandle kwaseTzaneen kwiPhondo lomNtla, apho kukho abantu abaphuma kwiindawo ezikude lee njengaseKapa befumana ukutya, indawo yokuhlala bazuze noqeqesho kwimisebenzi enokubangenisela imali.

«4»

Phezu kokuba eli ziko lifumana inkxaso-mali kurhulumente, umnxulumanisi walo uReginah Hlomela kusafuneka alizamele imali yokuthenga ukutya, eyokucocwa kwalo neyokuhlawulwa imivuzo yabantu abaphangela kulo.

«5»

Izinto ezenziwe ngezandla ezifana neeminyazi neembiza zokuhombisa ziyathengiswa, oosomashishini basekuhlaleni bayacelwa ukuba benze igalelo kwenziwe neenkqubo zokuqokelela imali eluntwini. Ezi nzame azanelanga ekukhawuleleni iindleko zokugcina eli ziko liqhuba nasekulandiseni kuba kwangoku selinengxaki yokungabikho kwendawo eyaneleyo.

«6»

Iholo yalo ikwasetyenziswa njengendawo yokwenza izinto zobugcisa. Izakhiwo ezibini zisetyenziswa njengezakhiwo zokuhlala amadoda nabasetyhini kwaye kwigumbi ngalinye kukho malunga neebhedi ezi-4 ukuya kwezingama-20. Iibhedi ezikhoyo nezisasetyenziswayo, uninzi lwazo zenziwe ngeentsimbi noomatrasi abacekethekileyo neengutyana ezindala. Iilokari zenkcenkce zisetyenziselwa ukugcina impahla.

«7»

Inkampani yemigodi yasePhalaborwa isandul' ukwenza isipho seebhedi ezintsha ezingama-24 nempahla yokulala neewardrobhu kodwa ayinguye wonke ubani ozuzileyo kwezi zipho. Kubusika obudlulileyo, abantu abathathu babanesifo senyumoniya ngenxa yokungenwa yingqele.

«8»

Izixhobo zokuhlamba zibandakanya iindawo zokuhlamba zikawonke-wonke kunye namagumbi angasese avulekileyo kwihostele nganye.

«9»

Amalungu eLetaba After-Care Centre abhaliswe kwiNorthern Training Trust, apho bafundiswa ubugcisa abanobusebenzisa kweli ziko. Intlawulo yokufunda yenziwa leli ziko. Kwaqaliswa iphulo lokwenza izitena kodwa lanqunyaniswa ngenxa yokophuka komashini akwabikho mali yokuba ulungiswe kwakhona.

«10»

Abazali noluntu lwasekuhlaleni luyakhuthazwa ukuba luzibandakanye kwimisebenzi yeli ziko. Abantu abathathu basebenza ngaphandle kwentlawulo ukuze bancedise kunqongophalo lwabasebenzi.

«11»

"Uluntu lwalapha ngathi alulazi eli ziko," utshilo uReginah. "Abazidubi nokuza kukhangela ukuba kuqhubeka ntoni na apha. Abanye abahlali balapha bothuka xa bebona abantu abagogekileyo okokuqala kwesinye isiganeko sokunyusa ingxowa-mali."

«12»

Ukunqaba kwemali kubangele ubunzima ekwenzeni izincwangciso zexesha elizayo kweli ziko. Ngokwenjongo yalo kwasekusekweni kwalo yokulondoloza abantu abagogekileyo, lisuke labayindawo apho kuthatyathwa abantu eluntwini bagcinwe, batyiswe banikwe noqeqesho ixeshana elifutshane ukuze emva koko babuyiselwe eluntwini. UReginah uchaze ukuba, "Ngonyaka ka-2000 sifuna ukubona iLetaba After-Care Centre iliziko lokuqeqesha bonke abantu abagogekileyo kweli Phondo lomNtla.

«13»

"Kufuneka sibe neziko elitsha, apho kunokugcinwa abantu abagogekileyo abamalunga nama-250 abanikwa uqeqesho kuphela. Ekukhutshweni kwabo apho, baze baqalise amaphulo angawabo okanye bafumane ingqesho kwiindawo zamashishini."

«14»

Umyalezo ovela kwiLetaba After-Care Centre ngowokuba abantu abagogekileyo banokunikwa amagunya abo ngokuqeqeshwa, oku kubanika ithuba lokuba babe negalelo kwezoqoqosho kweli lizwe.

«15»

Kukho imibutho emininzi ekwingxaki efanayo neyeLetaba After-Care Centre. Ukucela uncedo koosomashishini nakuluntu akwaneli. Umhlali ngamnye kufuneka athwale uxanduva lokunika inkxaso abantwakwabo abagogekileyo eluntwini. Ukwenza igalelo kwiziko elifana neLetaba After-Care Centre sisiqalo esilungileyo. Ukwenziwa kwempumelelo eyiyo kunye nokuzimela, kungenziwa ngenkxaso yoosomashishini norhulumente, ngokunjalo noluntu.

Vocabulary

banikwa they are given
abagogekileyo those who are handicapped or disabled
 -gog- obstruct, prevent, disable [v-tr] {Zulu}
 Cf: Xhosa **-gog-** hesitate, be undecided; be silent; duck; do s.t. in the dark [v-intr]
 Cf: **gogo** walk with difficulty (as hobbled horse) [ideophone]
 Cf: **isigogo** person with stiff limbs (i.e., cannot stretch them out, due to the cold, infirmity, etc.); [atr] hobbled; embarrassed, at a loss, unable to speak [n4-sg]
kwiziko for (their) household (i.e., the Center)
 iziko hearth, fireplace; chief's kraal; [ext] special-purpose center; [pl] households [n3-sg]
labo their [pro-3pl-poss-n3-sg]
«1»
kwintlalo in the way (that people) live
 intlalo manner of living [n5-sg]
efanelekileyo which is proper, ideal
bathatyathwa they are taken
njengenxalenye as a single unit
 inxalenye unified body [n5-sg]
namalungelo with rights
abo of them; their (own); theirs [n1-pl-poss-n3-pl]
endaweni in place
abanemizimba who have bodies
ephilileyo that is healthy
basuke they on the other hand
 -suk- VERB on the contrary, on the other hand [v-aux followed by S3a + present subjunctive]
babasizele that they pity them
 -sizel- sympathize with, pity, help in [v-tr]
bangabahoyi be unconcerned about
bangabaniki they do not give them
akunjalo it is not like that

eLetaba After-Care Centre at the Letaba After-Care Center {Eng}
«2»
iDutch Reformed Church {Eng} [n5-sg-cmp]
yaseka it established
ngo-1969 in 1969
yokugcina for taking care of
abangenamakhaya the homeless (those who do not have homes)
linabantu it has people
abangaphezu who are over
 -phezu kwa- above; over [n9-loc-red]
kwama-70 70
abasukela who start from
kwabaneminyaka who have years
eli-16 from 16
kwengama-63 up to 63 in age
liziko it is a center
elingekho which is absent, is not...
NGO Non-Governmental Organization [abr]
elizuza which obtains
kurhulumente to or from the government [n1a-sg-loc]
«3»
ikumgama it is at a distance
ongama-20km that is 20 kilometers
kwaseTzaneen from Tzaneen
kwiPhondo in the province [n3-sg-loc]
 Contrast: **uphondo** horn
lomNtla of the North [poss n5]
apho there, that place
kukho there are
abaphuma who come from
ezikude that are far
lee very far off [adv-loc]
njengaseKapa such as from Cape Town [adv+loc]
befumana they getting
yokuhlala for living
bazuze they obtain
enokubangenisela that might bring in
«4»
lifumana it found
umnxulumanisi the correlator
 inxulumana correlation [n5-sg]
uReginah (personal name) {Eng}
Hlomela (family name)
kusafuneka it is still necessary
alizamele that he, she struggle for [v-sub]
yokuthenga for purchasing
eyokucocwa to be cleansed
 -coc- purify, cleanse [v-tr]
kwalo its, of it (the Center)
neyokuhlawula and for paying
abaphangela who work at
 -phangel- work for or at; out-run, run before; speak before one's turn; arrive before [v-ben]
kulo to, from, in, with him, her; in, at it [n3-sg-pro-loc, i.e., **iziko** n3]
«5»
ezenziwe that are done
ngezandla by hand
neeminyazi like rush baskets
 umnyazi rush basket [n2-sg]
neembiza like pots
zokuhombisa for adorning
 -hombis- deck out, adorn another [v-tr]
ziyathengiswa they are sold
oosomashishini business owners [n1a-pl]
 usomashishini businessman, entrepreneur, manufacturer (one who is engaged in, owns, or operates a business or factory) [n1a-sg]
basekuhlaleni who are nearby
bayacelwa they are requested
benze that they make
kwenziwe to make, to be used
neenkqubo and/with procedures
zokuqokelela of/for collecting
nzame efforts, attempts [n5-pl-red]
azanelanga they are not enough
ekukhawuleleni to cut short

-**khawul**- cut short, give up, break off, reach to, stop, conceive [v-tr]
nasekulandiseni and in expanding it
-**andis**- enlarge, multiply, expand [v-tr]
kwangoku even now [adv]
selinengxaki it has difficulty
yokungabikho there is no
eyaneleyo that is enough
«6»
iholo hall [n5-sg] {Eng}
ikwasetyenziswa its being used
njengendawo like a place
yokwenza for making
zobugcisa of skill
izakhiwo buildings [n4-pl]
isakhiwo building, erection, structure [n4-sg; rw: -**akh**-]
zisetyenziswa they are used
njengezakhiwo as buildings
zokuhlala for residing
nabasetyhini and women
Cf: **ityhini** female, girl, woman [n3-sg; no plural]
kwigumbi in the room
ngalinye each one [adv-enum]
malunga nebhedi ezi-4 about 4 beds
kwezingama-20 to the number or quantity of 20
ezikhoyo that are there [rel-deic]
nezisasetyenziswayo and the ones already being utilized
lwazo of them [n5-pl-poss-n6-sg] agreeing with iibhedi and uninzi
ngeentsimbi using iron, out of steel [n5-pl-instr]
noomatrasi with mattresses [conj-n1a-pl] {Eng}
Usually: **imatrasi** mattress [n5]
abacekethekileyo which are thin
-**cekethek**- fragile, wear away, become thin, transparent [v neut]
neengutyana and small blankets
see **ingubo** blanket [n5-sg]
iilokari lockers [n5-pl] {Eng}
zenkcenkce of zinc, tin, corrugated sheeting
zisetyenziselwa they are used for
«7»
inkampani company {Eng}
yemigodi of the mines
umgodi mine, mining shaft [n2-sg]
yasePhalaborwa (town in the Northern Province)
isandul' it recently, has just
isipho gift [n4-sg]
ezintsha that are new [adj-n5-pl]
ezingama-24 age 24
yokulala for sleeping
neewardrobhu wardrobe {Eng}
ayinguye it is not everyone
wonke every; all, the whole (of) [pro-enum-n1-sg]
ubani anyone, whoever; [neg] no one [pro-indef-n1a-sg]
ozuzileyo who acquired, who were recipients (of)
kwezi of these [poss n4-agr]
kubusika in the winter
ubusika winter [n7-sg]
obudlulileyo the past
abathathu three [adj-n7]
babanesifo they had the illness
senyumoniya of pneumonia {Eng}
yokungenwa of being entered [rw: –**ngen**–]
yingqele cold
«8»
izixhobo utensils, accouterments; weapons [n4-pl; sg: **isixhobo**]
zokuhlamba for washing
-**hlamb**- wash [v-tr]
zibandakanya they unite
zikawonke-wonke belonging to everybody
namagumbi with rooms [n3-pl]
avulekileyo that are opened
kwihostele in the hostel {Eng}
«9»
abhaliswe they are registered

kwiNorthern Training Trust at the Northern Training Trust {Eng}
bafundiswa they are taught
abanobusebenzisa that they can use
intlawulo payment, remuneration [n5-sg]
CHANGE of **hl** to **tl**
yokufunda for learning
kwaqaliswa it was/has been started
izitena bricks [n4-pl]
isitena brick [n4-sg] {Afr steen}
lanqunyaniswa it was ended
yokophuka of the breaking
komashini of the machine
Cf: **umatshini** machine [n1a-sg] {Eng}
akwabikho there was no presence of
ulungiswe be repaired
«10»
lwasekuhlaleni of the nearby residency [loc]
luyakhuthazwa is encouraged
luzibandakanye they unite
kwentlawulo of payment
bancedise they help with
kunqongophalo in the shortage
lwabasebenzi of the workers
«11»
lwalapha of this area [deic-1-n9-loc-poss-n5-pl]
alulazi it does not know
abazidubi they don't bother themselves [v-intr neg]
nokuza to come [rw: -**iza**]
kukhangela to look
kuqhubeka what is progressing
bothuka they are startled
bebona they obtaining [v-part]
kwesinye at another [loc-enum]
isiganeko demonstration, proof; important point; well know event [n4-sg]
sokunyusa of raising
«12»
ukunqaba scarcity [n8-vn]
-**nqab**- become fixed, imbedded, stuck fast; [perf] be secure, immobile, safe; be scarce; be dear, expensive; difficult, impossible [v-inch]
kwemali of money
kubangele cause for
ubunzima difficulty, hardship [n7-sg]
izincwangciso plans; budgets; activities [n5-pl]
-**cwangcis**- arrange in line [v-tr caus]
zexesha of time
elizayo that is coming; future [rw: -**iza**]
ngokwenjongo with the purpose
kwasekusekweni from the establishment
yokulondoloza for taking care of [n8-vn-poss]
-**londoloz**- take care of, preserve, protect, keep under one's care [v-tr]
lisuke it started to
labayindawo it became a place
kuthatyathwa they take and hold
bagcinwe they are taken care of
batyiswe they are fed
-**tyisa** feed, make eat; chew the cud [v-caus]
ixeshana little time [n3-sg-dim]
babuyiselwe be returned
uchaze she explained
ngonyaka by the year
ka-2000 of 2000
iliziko it is a center
lokuqeqesha for training
«13»
neziko and a center
elitsha that is new
kunokugcinwa for being taken care of
abamalunga who are members
nama-250 250 people
abanikwa who are given
ekukhutshweni at (their) graduation
baqalise they begin

angawabo that are theirs
bafumane they receive
ingqesho hire, license [n5-sg]
zamashishini of businesses [n3-pl-poss-n5-pl]
«14»
ovela come from [rel v-tr]
ngowokuba is that of [cop]
banokunikwa they can be given
amagunya the rights
ngokuqeqeshwa through training [adv]
kubanika it gives them
negalelo having a contribution
kwezoqoqosho in the economy
«15»
imibutho organizations [n2-pl]
ekwingxaki having problems [lit: which are in a problem]
efanayo similar [rw: **-fan-**]
neyeLetaba After-Care Centre of the Letaba After-Care Center
ukucela to request; asking, requesting [v inf]
koosomashishini from the business owners
nakuluntu and from people
akwaneli not enough
umhlali resident [n1-sg]
ngamnye per individual
athwale he/she should bear a burden
uxanduva responsibility, duty; burden, trouble, difficulty [n6-sg]
lokunika for giving to
abantwakwabo relatives, family members [n1-pl-cmp]
elifana similar [rel]
sisiqalo it is the beginning
esilungileyo that is good
kwempumelelo of success
nokuzimela and to stand on one's own
kungenziwa it can be done
ngenkxaso with the support
yoosomashishini of the business owners [poss n1a pl]
ngokunjalo accordingly [adv]

Amadoda Adlwengula Amanye

«0»

Nangona umthetho waseMzantsi–Afrika ukuchaza ukudlwengula njengo "...kuzithathela isondo kobhinqileyo ngokungekho mthethweni," nawo amadoda ayadlwengulwa, nanjengoko uPrimrose Williams efumanisile.

«1»

Yayikokokuqala egwetyelwa entolongweni uVuma (ekungelo gama lakhe lokwenene). Wayenoloyiko. Kanene la mabali ebedla ngokuwava angobomi basentolongweni? Wazithandazela ngaphakathi ecela ukhuseleko. Nangoku sele eziminxe ngomthandazo enye yezinto awayezixhalabele yayiza kwenzeka kanye ngobo busuku bakhe bokuqala.

«2»

Isihelegu esisamngcumngcuthekisa nangoku saqala akusiwa esiseleni sakhe. Wathi engena nje bambona elicham abo afika sele bengaphambili–nababeliqela eliyi–28 kanti yena "wayeyinkwenkwana yesikolo," ngokwentetho yasentolongweni.

«3»

UVuma uzibambe ngeenkophe iinyembezi kwaye ayithandabuzeki intlungu elizwini lakhe, xa echaza indlela ababetshintshisana ngayo bemdlwengula awayehlala nabo.

«4»

Ngokutsho kwengcali ngezesondo kubuhlungu mpela ukudlwengulwa uyindoda. "Ngaphandle kwentuthumbo yengqondo, umzimba uqaqamba kakhulu nanjengoko amadoda engadalelwanga kungenwa ngokwesondo," ichazile.

«5»

"Ndaziva ndinomsindo, uloyiko kunye nokuzonyanya ngakumbi njengokuba kwakungekho ndlela ndandingabanqandayo ngayo," utsho uVuma. "Ndimbuna ngokwendalo kwaye ndandijongene noomakad'enetha. Ndandisazi ukuba kuphandle ngam nanjengoko ndingemntu ulwa kuyaphi. Ndandiqhokrekile naluloyiko.

«6»

"Babungaphezu kwamandla am ubuhlungu. Ndandisithi ziyakupheza ezo zirhalarhume ndisakopha kodwa ucing'ukuba zayeka? Zaqhubeka zihleka zisithi kakade inkonyana iyasothuka isisinga. Uyazi yintoni, baba nalo nkqu igila lokundiqinisekisa ukuba kuyakuba mnandi xa sendiqhelile!"

«7»

UVuma uthi oku kwaba sisonka semihla ngemihla. Bamoyikisa ngokubuyisa izitya xa enokubaxela kwabasemagunyeni. Kodwa isikhuni sabuya nomkhwezeli. Uvavanyo lwegazi olwenziwa ngabasemagunyeni lwaveza ukuba unentsholongwane yeAids, uchazile.

«8»

Nangona kungathandabuzeki ukuba ngabafazi namantombazana abadlwengulwa rhoqo, NAWO amadoda ayadlwengulwa. Ngokutsho kweLife Line, "Ukudlwengulwa kwamadoda kuxhaphake ubukhulu becala entolongweni. Kungezo ntolongo kuphela nakumaziko ekungekho bantu babhinqileyo kuwo.

«9»

"La maziko abandakanya izinala zamakhwenkwe, iinkampi zamajoni, iindawo zamasoka, amatheko azinyaswa ngamadoda odwa kunye neenkampu. Kuvakala ukuba ukulalana kwamadoda okanye ukufakwa ilungu lobudoda emlonyeni yenye kwezenziwa nalulutsha lwasemaphandleni.

«10»

"Ukudlwengulwa kwamakhwenkwe kwenzeka kakhulu emakhayeni kusenziwa ngumzali, utatomkhulu, umkhuluwa, umzala, umalume/ubawokazi okanye sisalamane. Namakhwenkwana afulathela amakhaya asesichengeni.

«11»

"Kukwakho neendawo okanye iimeko eziyingozi kakhulu kwimilisela nemithinjana," balumkisile abeLife Line. Ezi ndawo zibandakanya iinight club, ukucela ukukhweliswa ezimotweni, ukuhamba wedwa kwampenge–mpenge nakwizindlu zangasese zikawonkewonke."

«12»

Uninzi lwamadoda angamaxhoba odlwengulo ngokutsho kweLife Line, "awakuthatheli manyathelo kuba engalindelanga kusizelwa kuyaphi ngabantu kwanabasemagunyeni. Ngenxa yokuba indoda ithathwa njengomntu owomeleleyo onokuzikhusela indoda inganelishwa lokungathathelwa ngqalelo xa izokuchaza ngokudlwengulwa kwayo. Uninzi lwabantu kubandakanywa oonompilo, alwazi ukuba namadoda anokugonyamelwa ngokwesondo.

«13»

"Kwaye ngenxa yokuba 'kunesondo' phakathi ukudlwengula akuyo nto amadoda aziva ekhululekile ukuthetha ngayo. Abantu balubona udlwengulo lwendoda njengehlazo. Ukuxhalabela ukwayanyaniswa nokuba uhambisana namany'amadoda kakade kusesinye sezizathu eziphambili zokungawuzisi ngaphambili lo mba."

«14»

Enye ewenza abe mathidala amadoda, esikufumene kwabezomthetho, kukuba ngokomthetho weli ngamanenekazi kuphela anokudlwengulwa. Ngokwalo mthetho libhinqa KUPHELA elinokudlwengulwa YINDODA. Lilonke ke indoda ayinakufunyaniswa inetyala ngokudlwengula enye kodwa ingathwaliswa ityala lokundlandlathekisa ngokwesondo okanye lokwenza isenzo esibi phantsi komthetho ojongene nokophula umthetho kwezesondo.

«15»

Umzekelo, abeChild Protection Unit baphatha amatyala angaphezu kwama–8992 okudlwengulwa kwababhinqileyo abangaphantsi kwe–18 leminyaka ngo–1995. Kodwa angama–600 abandakanya amakhwenkwe angaphantsi kwe–18 athatyathwa njengawokulalana kwamadoda.

«16»

Eneneni yintoni enokubangela ukuba indoda idlwengule enye? Kwaye, yindoda enjani esesichengeni sokudlwengulwa?

«17»

Ugqirha Irma Labuschagne, oyiForensic Criminologist, uchaza athi: "Umaphuli mthetho ukhuthazwa kokungaphezu kweenkanuko zomzimba. Ubukhulu becala amadoda adlwengula amanye (ngaphakathi nangaphandle kwentolongo) ukukhuphela umsindo, ukuzikhululula kumakhamandela oburhalarhume okanye ukubonakalisa amandla okanye ukulicaphukela ixhoba.

«18»

"Akubi sisenzo sokuba ayayikhanuka loo ndoda–umntu ufumanisa, umzekelo, iqela lamadoda azonwabisa ngokungcungcuthekisa 'oobhuti–sisi' (ukundlandlathekiswa kwamakhanukanodwa). Akwenziwa ziinkanuko zesondo oku nto nje kukonyanya okanye ukukhuphela umsindo.

«19»

"Entolongweni indoda idlwengulwa ngenxa yezizizathu ezininzi, esingabalula kuzo, xa igwetyelwe ukuphatha kakubi umntwana okanye imdlwengule 'ukumbeka endaweni emfaneleyo' kwaye amaninzi alalelwa 'ukuyazisa indlela ekuba yiyo.' Ndikwave ukuba kuyinto exhaphakileyo phakathi kwamabhantinti ukwamkela" lawo matsha ngokuwadlwengula.

«20»

"Entolongweni, amanye amadoda angaziphatha okwamakhanukanodwa kuba efuna ukwanelisa iinkanuko zesondo. Athi esakuphuma apho aphindele emabhinqeni. Ewe, umntu uyakoyikisela ukunwenwa kweAIDS entolongweni.

«21»

"Amadoda akwadlwengulwa nangamanye nangaphandle kwasentolongweni. Akho njengombophi–manxeba omphefumlo, endizame ukuwanceda ehlelwe sesi sihelegu–nasemlonyeni. Kwaye NAYIPHI na indoda ingaba lixhoba–kodwa amakhanukanodwa aba ngawona achaphazelekayo."

«22»

Kuthiwa endodeni, ukudlwengulwa kuba sisiqalo somzabalazo omde nonzima. Amaxhoba aye azonyanye atyiwe zizazela neentsizi. Uluntu luyakwamkela ukuba umntu obhinqileyo unokoyiswa lula kodwa yona indoda–eyiyo phofu inokuzikhusela. Lilonke, ixhoba eliyindoda lizibona kwaye libonwa lingento yanto.

«23»

UGqirha Labuschagne uyayingqina le kwaye uyalumkisa ukuba nawo amadoda angamaxhoba ayalufuna uncedo khonukuze amelane neziphumo zokudlwengulwa. "Kuninzi okunokubangelwa koku okunokuhlala ithuba elide okanye elincinane. Kungakodlula okwabantu ababhinqileyo. Amadoda azifumana engento emva koko–aphelelwa lithemba nokholo eluntwini, azibone ezi zinto ezimdaka kwaye atyiwe zizazela.

«24»

"Indoda elixhoba iyakuba nelo nxeba unaphakade ukuba ayifumani nkxaso yangcali. Amadoda kufuneka ancedwe ngokuchazelwa ngokubanzi ukuba akulohlazo ukufuna uncedo. Lifikile ixesha lokuba uluntu lukuqonde ukuba yingxaki enkulu le negxobha nobamadoda ubomi. IRape Crisis Service elawulwa yiLife Line inako ukuwaxhasa amadoda angamaxhoba.

«25»

Ngokuchaseneyo nokukholelwa ngabaninzi, iindaba ezimnandi ngokutsho kukaGqirha Labuschagne zezokuba "abubambeki ubungqina bokuba inkwenkwana edlwengulweyo ikhanuke amanye amadoda ayikho loo nto.

«26»

"Into endiyifumanisileyo yeyokuba amaxhoba ayadideka sisini sawo–ade abe nengxaki nokwambatha nomntu obhinqileyo ethubeni–kodwa oku akuthethi kuba aphela engamakhanukanodwa kwaphela," uqwelile.

Vocabulary

«0»
adlwengula who rape [v-rel]
-dlwengul- treat with violence; rape, ravish, violate [v-tr]
waseMzantsi-Afrika of (those) in South Africa [= wa-s-e-(u)m-zantsi-Afrika]
ukuchaza it explains it
ukudlwengula to rape; raping
njengo as, such as, like [conj]
kuzithathela to take for oneself
kobhinqileyo to a woman [= k(u)-o-bhinq-ile-yo]
-bhinq- tie s.o. around the waist; gird one's loins; fasten a belt on, buckle up; [fig] get ready [v-tr]
ngokungekho presently not
mthethweni in the law; lawful
ayadlwengulwa they get raped
nanjengoko even as
uPrimrose Williams (name)
efumanisile she/he find out
«1»
yayikokokuqala it had been the first time
yayi- he, she, it had VERBed [group 5 singular contracted remote past compound tense]
-kokoku- [contraction of deic koko + koku-]
egwetyelwa he being sentenced [v-part-pres-pass = e-gweb/ty-el-w-a]
-gweb- ward off; decide, settle; judge, sentence, convict, condemn {legal} [v-tr]
entolongweni to/in prison
uVuma (male personal name)
ekungelo not his/her [neg cop dem]
lokwenene for real
wayenoloyiko he/she had fear
mabali stories
ebedla he/she used [aux]
ngokuwava to hear them
angobomi about life
basentolongweni of those in prison
wazithandazela he prayed for himself
ecela he asking
ukhuseleko protection, state of being protected [n6-sg]
eziminxe holding himself tight
-minx- press, squeeze, interlock, hold tight, pinch, choke
ngomthandazo with a prayer
awayezixhalabele about which he was frightened
xhalaba to be startled, alarmed, made anxious [v-intr]
yayiza it was going to happen

ngobo on that (date), during that (time) [deic-2-n7-sg-time]
busuku night [n7-sg-red]
bokuqala of the first time
«2»
isihelegu disaster, catastrophe [n4-sg]
esisamngcumngcuthekisa impervious [rel formed from compound extended verb]
-ngcungcutha impervious, be impenetrable [v-intr]
nangoku even now
saqala it started
akusiwa when he was brought
-sa carry, bring, convey [v-tr]
esiseleni prison cell [n4-sg-loc borrowed]
engena he, she entering [part]
bambona they saw him
elicham as an easy prey
icham easy prey [n3-sg]
afika he arrived
bengaphambili who were ahead, before
nababeliqela and who were a gang [see **lwamaqela** in R21]
eliyi-28 which is 28
wayeyinkwenkwana he was a little boy
ngokwentetho by declaration, law
yasentolongweni of those in prison
«3»
uzibambe he held (them)
ngeenkophe with eyelashes
ukhophe eyelash [n6-sg; pl: **iinkophe**]
iinyembezi tears [n5-pl]
nyembezi a tear [n5-sg]
ayithandabuzeki it's not doubtful
-thandabuz- be doubtful, doubt, hesitate [v-intr]
elizwini in his voice
echaza he explains, explaining
ababetshintshisana they were exchanging
bemdlwengula they were raping him
awayehlala with whom he was staying
«4»
ngokutsho by declaring so, what was said
kwengcali of an expert
ngezesondo of sexuality
kubuhlungu it is painful
mpela entirely [adv]
uyindoda being a man
kwentuthumbo of inflammation
-thuthumb- inflammation, throbbing [v-tr]
yengqondo of the mind
uqaqamba it throbs
-qaqamb- be bright, white, pure; shine, glisten; throb, smart, tingle [v-intr]
engadalelwanga they are not created
kungenwa to be penetrated
ngokwesondo sexually
ichazile it explained
«5»
ndaziva I felt within myself
ndinomsindo I had an outburst of anger
umsindo anger, rage [n2-sg]
uloyiko fear [n6-sg]
nokuzonyanya as to dread myself
-nyany- dread, fear [v-tr]
ndandingabanqandayo whereby I could stop them
-nqand- hinder, stop, warn [v-tr]
ndimbuna I'm docile
buna docile, mellow, tame [atr]
ngokwendalo by nature
ndandijongene I had faced
noomakad'enetha with those long rained upon [cmp-n; idiom 'very experienced people']
-neth- get wet, rain, be caught in rain [XED:98]
ndandisazi I had already known
kuphandle ngam outside, apart from anything about me
ngam about me

ndingemntu I am not a person
ulwa who fights
ndandiqhokrekile I had become paralyzed [rw: -**qhokrek-**]
«6»
babungaphezu kwamandla am ubuhlungu the pain was beyond my endurance
babungaphezu it was beyond
babu- it had VERBed [group 7 singular contracted remote past compound tense]
kwamandla of the strength [n3-pl-poss-n10-loc]
am mine [pro-1sg-poss-n3-pl]
ndandisithi I had thought [v-remote-past]
ziyakupheza they will stop
-**phez**- leave off, stop, desist [v-intr]
zirhalarhume violent men [n4-pl-red]
isiralarume violent man, fierce person [n4 -sg]
-**ralarum**- rage, be violent [v-intr]
ndisakopha whilst I bled
zayeka they (should) leave
zaqhubeka they continued
zihleka they laughing
kakade no doubt, of course [intj]
Cf: **kakade** long ago [adv-time]
inkonyana a young sucking calf, foal [n5-sg]
iyasothuka it fears
isisinga tether for calves and lambs [n4-sg]
nkqu emphatic point (of information)
igila collide with, knock against, throw down [v-tr]
Cf: **igila** gizzard of a fowl [n3]
lokundiqinisekisa to reassure me
kuyakuba it will be [v fut]
sendiqhelile (when) I'm already accustomed
-**qhel**- acquainted with, familiar with, be accustomed to, habituate [v-tr]
«7»
sisonka the bread
isonka bread [n3-sg]
semihla ngemihla day by day
bamoyikisa they scared him
ngokubuyisa izitya by returning (idiom 'taking revenge')
izitya plates [n4 pl]
enokubaxela he can report them
kwabasemagunyeni to those in power
igunya power, authority [n6-sg]
isikhuni lighted firebrand; [idiom] what goes around, comes around
sabuya it returned
-**buy**- return, come back [v-intr]
nomkhwezeli with the fire maker
khweza go up, make up a fire [v-tr]
uvavanyo test, examination [n6-sg]
-**vavany**- test, try (out), examine, inspect, investigate; prove (a weapon) [v-tr]
lwegazi of the blood [n3-sg-poss-n6-sg]
olwenziwa that was done
ngabasemagunyeni by those in power
lwaveza it showed
unentsholongwane he has a virus [v-poss+n5-sg-obj]
yeAids of Aids {Eng}
uchazile he explained
«8»
kungathandabuzeki it is not doubtful, there is no doubt
ngabafazi it is women
namantombazana and girls
abadlwengulwa who get raped
rhoqo do often, always, continually [preverb; alt sp: **roqo**]
kweLife Line of Life Line {Eng}
kwamadoda of men

kuxhaphake it is plentiful
ubukhulu greatness, largeness, bigness; size; amount; dignity [n7-sg-abs]
becala of the side
  icala side, edge; facet, aspect [n3-sg]
kungezo it's not only
nakumaziko and in households
babhinqileyo who are women [= ba-bhinq-ile-yo]
kuwo to, from, in, with them
«9»
abandakanya they unite into, get together in/at
izinala seminary, boys' hostel
zamakhwenkwe of boys
iinkampi camps {Afr}
zamajoni of soldiers
  ijoni soldier [n3-sg]
zamasoka of the bachelors
  isoka a bachelor, an unmarried man; a wooer, a suitor; a monk [n3-sg]
azinyaswa which are frequented [= a-zimas/ny-w-a]
  -**zimas**- support, fix firmly, establish, confirm; frequent, support by one's presence or company [v-tr]
odwa only they; they alone [pro-quan-n3-pl]
neenkampu and camps
kuvakala it's perceptible
ukulalana the sleeping together
ukufakwa to be put in
yenye of another
kwezenziwa of the doing
nalulutsha by young people
lwasemaphandleni of the outside (Cf: inside, i.e., in jail)
«10»
kwamakhwenkwe of boys [n3-pl-poss-n8-vn]
emakhayeni in homes [n3-pl-loc = e-(a)ma-khay(a)-eni]
kusenziwa it's done
ngumzali by a parent
utatomkhulu grandfather
umkhuluwa an elder brother
  khuluwa eldest brother, an elder [n1a-sg]
umalume uncle [n1a-sg]
ubawokazi paternal uncle [n1a-sg]
sisalamane sibling [n3-sg]
namakhwenkwana and the little boys
afulathela who run away
  -**fulathel**- turn the back on, forsake, desert [v-tr]
asesichengeni who are in danger
  isichenge one who is exposed to danger [n4-sg]
«11»
kukwakho there are also
eziyingozi which are in danger
kwimilisela for the young men
  -**lisel**- transplant into, graft on to, make grow for [v-tr]
nemithinjana thinjana young men and maidens [n2-pl]
balumkisile they warned
abeLife Line those of Life Line {Eng}
iinight club night clubs [n5-pl] {Eng}
ukukhweliswa to be given a lift
ezimotweni in motor vehicles {Eng}
wedwa you alone; thou only [pro-quan-2sg]
kwampenge-mpenge airy place, sparsely peopled place
  mpengempenge half-clad person; open, airy place
nakwizindlu zangasese zikawonkewonke and in public toilets
  indlu zangasese toilet
zangasese secret
  -**sese** done underhand; [atr] underhanded; out of sight; secret [v-perf]
zikawonkewonke for everybody
«12»
angamaxhoba they can be prey
  ixhoba booty, spoil; victim, (easy) prey [n3-sg]

odlwengulo of rape
awakuthatheli they have not taken
manyathelo steps [n3-pl-red]
engalindelanga not waiting
-lind- wait, wait for [v-tr]
kusizelwa to sympathize
siza sympathize with, pity, help in [v-tr]
kwanabasemagunyeni and those in authority
igunya authority [n3-sg]
ngenxa yokuba therefore [conj-expr]
ithathwa he is taken
owomeleleyo who is strong, healthy
onokuzikhusela who can protect themselves
inganelishwa he can have the misfortune
ilishwa mishap, piece of ill luck, a misfortune, disaster, great loss [n3-sg]
lokungathathelwa ngqalelo not to be taken heed of
izokuchaza he will report it
kwayo his, her, its; of him, her, it [n5-sg-poss-n8-vn]
oonompilo health workers [n1a pl]
alwazi do not know
anokugonyamelwa they can be treated with violence
-gonyamel- treat with violence, act as a lion [v-tr]
«13»
akuyo it is not [neg cop c5]
aziva they do not feel
ekhululekile (feel) free
balubona they see it
njengehlazo as a disgrace
ihlaza a disgraceful need, a disgrace [n3-sg]
ukuxhalabela the great fright
xhalabela be in great distress, get a great fright [v-intr]
ukwayanyaniswa to be associated with
kusesinye it's one
sezizathu of the reasons
zokungawuzisi of not bringing
zisa bring [v-tr]
«14»
ewenza that makes
mathidala hesitation
amathidala misgivings, hesitation, indecision [n3 pl]
esikufumene what we found
kwabezomthetho by those of the law
ngokomthetho by the law
ngamanenekazi it is ladies
anokudlwengulwa who can be raped
ngokwalo by this
libhinqa it is a woman [pred]
ibhinqa woman [n3-sg; pl: **amabhinqa**]
elinokudlwengulwa who can be raped
lilonke in all
ayinakufunyaniswa he cannot be found
inetyala guilty, having a fault
ityala guilt [n3-sg]
ngokudlwengula for raping
ingathwaliswa he can be made to carry
lokundlandlathekisa of scaring
ndlandlantheka run off in fright, be scared [v-intr]
esibi ugly [adj]
phantsi kwa- below, under (down, towards the ground)
komthetho of the law [n2-sg-poss-n10-loc]
ojongene which is looked at
nokophula and breaking [= na-uku-aphul-a]
«15»
abeChild Protection Unit those at the Child Protection Unit {Eng}
baphatha they handled
angaphezu that are above
kwama-8992 8,992 cases
kwababhinqileyo of women

kwe-18 18
leminyaka of years
ngo-1995 in 1995
angama-600 600 (cases)
angaphantsi under (the age of)
athatyathwa who were taken
njengawokulalana like sleeping together
«16»
eneneni in reality
enokubangela which causes
enjani what kind [Interr]
esesichengeni exposed to danger
«17»
Irma Labuschagne (name)
oyiForensic Criminologist who is a Forensic Criminologist {Eng}
uchaza he explains
athi and he said
umaphuli the breakers
ukhuthazwa he is encouraged
kweenkanuko of desires
inkanuko appetite, lust, desire, longing [n5-sg]
-**khanuk**- long for, desire greatly, lust after [v-tr]
zomzimba of the body [n2-sg-poss-n5-pl]
ukukhuphela to release
ukuzikhulula to loosen, free themselves
kumakhamandela from the chains
ikhamandela fetter, chain [n3-sg]
oburhalarhume of rage [n7-sg-poss-n3-pl]
uburhalarhume rage, wrath [n7-sg-abs]
ukubonakalisa to show
ukulicaphukela to be annoyed at
caphukela be offended, annoyed at, feel sick at [v-tr]
«18»
akubi it does not become [v pred neg]
sisenzo it is an act
ayayikhanuka they desire it
ufumanisa he finds
fumanisa make or help find [v-casus]
azonwabisa who make themselves happy
-**onwabis**- delight, cheer up, make s.o. happy; please s.o., gratify [v-caus]
ngokungcungcuthekisa by making thin, causing to lose weight
-ngcungcuthek- get wasted, be thin, emaciated [v-st-atr]
oobhuti-sisi brother-sister {gay speech}
bhuti brother {Dutch boetie} [n1a-sg-kin]
sisi sister {Eng}
kwamakhanukanodwa for those who desire men
nodwa alone [enum]
akwenziwa it is not done
ziinkanuko by lust, out of desires
zesondo of sex
kukonyanya to be discontented
«19»
yezizizathu there are reasons
esingabalula which we could choose
igwetyelwe being acquitted [= i-gweb/ty-el-w-e]
Cf: **ugwetyelo** & **ukugwetyelwa** justification, acquittal [n6-sg]
ukumbeka to place him
emfaneleyo proper
alalelwa they are ambushed
lalela ambush, lie in wait for, lie in reserve [v-tr]
ukuyazisa to make known
ekuba become, becoming
Ndikwave I heard them
kuyinto it's a thing
exhaphakileyo common [rel]
kwamabhantinti of the prisoners
ukwamkela to receive [v inf]
lawo those (just menetioned)
matsha new ones

ngokuwadlwengula by raping them
«20»
angaziphatha they can behave
okwamakhanukanodwa of those who desire men
ukwanelisa to satisfy [v-tr]
Athi when they [v temp]
esakuphuma they come out
aphindele they returned to [c6-v-appl]
emabhinqeni to living with women [n3-pl-loc = e-(a)ma-bhinq(a)-eni]
uyakoyikisela fear, be extremely fearful of
ukunwenwa to be spread
nwenweza blaze, spread, like fire in grass [v-tr]
kweAIDS of Aids {Eng}
«21»
nangamanye by others
kwasentolongweni of prisons
akho they are here; they are present [v-exis-n3-pl]
njengombophi-manxeba as a fastener of wounds
-boph- bind, tie, fasten, harness, saddle, yoke, inspan [v-tr]
inxeba wound [n3-sg]
omphefumlo of the breath; of the soul [rel-atr]
-phefuml- respire, breathe, take a breath; rest [v-intr]
endizame which I strived
ukuwanceda to help them
ehlelwe experienced [rel]
sihelegu-nasemlonyeni trauma, 'kick-in-the-teeth'
isihelegu disaster, catastrophe [n4-sg]
nasemlonyeni and in the mouth [= na-s-e-(u)m-lom/ny-(o)-eni]
nayiphi na indoda any man
amakhanukanodwa those who prefer men, gays
ngawona it's them
wona them, they [pro n3 pl echo]
achaphazelekayo bespattered, dropped upon
-chaphazel- drop s.t. on s.o., besprinkle, besmatter [v-ditr]
«22»
somzabalazo of a struggle [n2-sg-poss-n4-sg]
umzabalazo struggle, effort, endeavor, attempt [n2-sg]
nonzima and heavy
amaxhoba victims [n3-pl]
azonyanye they fear for themselves [v-refl]
atyiwe who are eaten
zizazela by conscience
neentsizi and grief
iintsizi sorrow, affliction, grief [n5 pl]
luyakwamkela they receive
obhinqileyo female, woman [v-rel used as n = o-bhinq-ile-yo]
phofu then, in that case
libonwa it be seen
lingento not nothing
yanto of nothing
«23»
uyayingqina she renders, testifies
-qin- render, melt; roast, examine by torture [v-tr]
uyalumkisa she warns
ayalufuna they want it
khonukuze so that
amelane stand together with, cope with
kuninzi a lot
okunokubangelwa which can be achieved
koku to, toward this
okunokuhlala which can stay with (them)
elide long
elincinane small
kungakodlula it can pass
-dlul- pass by, go beyond, surpass, excel, pass through, pass over [v-tr]
okwabantu for people
azifumana they find themselves
aphelelwa they are bereft of

-phelelw- be gone, get used up, exhausted; be bereft of [v-ben-pass]
Cf: **ukuphelelelwa** complete exhaustion [n8-vn]
lithemba it is hope
nokholo and faith
ukholo trust, faith, belief, confidence [n6-sg abstr]
azibone and they see these
ezimdaka dirty
«24»
iyakuba he will have [c5-fut-have]
nelo (have) that [na-ilo]
nxeba wound
unaphakade for endless time
phakade time immemorial, endless time, eternity, eternal, innumerable [n-loc-time]
ayifumani he does not find
nkxaso support [n5-sg red]
yangcali of an expert
ancedwe they should be helped
ngokuchazelwa by being explained to
ngokubanzi at large
akulohlazo it is not a disgrace
ihlazo a disgraceful deed, a disgrace [n3-sg]
ukufuna to want [v inf]
lukuqonde to understand it
yingxaki it is a problem
negxobha and affect
nobamadoda that of men (their lives)
elawulwa that is administered
yiLife Line by Life Line {Eng}
inako can be
«25»
ngokuchaseneyo by opposing
nokukholelwa and to believe in
kukaGqirha Labuschagne of Doctor Labuschagne
zezokuba they will be for [v fut pred]
zezo- of things of [see MI:261]
abubambeki it doesn't grasp
ubungqina evidence, testimony [n7-sg]
ayikho there is none; it does not exist, it is not available [v-exis-neg-n5-sg]
«26»
endiyifumanisileyo which I found it out
yeyokuba is that [cop+comp]
ayadideka they are agitated
-didek- be alarmed, agitated, apprehensive [v-st]
sisini a gap between their teeth, shortcomings [cop n4-sg]
sawo of theirs
ade and then [v-aux]
nokwambatha to put on some covering
-ambath- dress oneself, put on some covering; go under the protection of; allude to; follow hard after [v-tr]
ethubeni on the occasion
akuthethi it does not mean
aphela they stop
engamakhanukanodwa being those who prefer other men
uqwelile she finished, she rounded off
-qwel- finish, round off; confiscate entirely, empty completely, ruin, destroy [v-tr]

Ibhodi Entsha Yeelwimi: Singazuza Sonke

«1»

UMgaqo-Siseko omtsha waseMzantsi Afrika udale amathuba okuvuleleka kwemibutho emininzi yokujongana, ukuphunyezwa nokuhlonitshwa kwamalungelo abantu. IPANSALB ngomnye wale mibutho. UNoxolo Mgudlwa ucacisa ngale bhodi yeelwimi nendlela olungafikelela ngayo uluntu olukumgangatho wentlalo esezantsi.

«2»

IPANSALB YIBHODI EZIMELEYO neyasekwa ePalamente nethi inike ingxelo kwindlu yowisomthetho. Oku kuthetha ukuba le bhodi ayilawulwa ngurhulumente okanye nguye nawuphina umphathiswa. Yasekwa khona ukuze ibe limehlo kurhulumente. IPANSALB ijongene nokuphuculwa, ukulungelelaniswa kwakunye nokukhuselwa kweelwimi zonke zalapha eMzantsi Afrika njengoko kubekiwe kwicandelo 3 loMgaqo Siseko.

«3»

Ezona lwimi sigxininisa kuzo apha zezo zityunjwe njengezisemthethweni kuMgaqo Siseko omtsha ezizezi zilandelayo:

«4»

IsiBhulu, isiNgesi, isiNdebele, Sesotho sa Leboa, Sesotho, siSwati. Xitsonga, Setswana, Tshivenda, isiXhosa nesiZulu. Naxa kunjalo nezinye iilwimi ezithethwa ngabantu balapha eMzantsi Afrika ezingakhankanywanga apha nazo siyazikhuthaza.

«5»

I-Palamente yaye yayila iDraft Bill yePANSALB. Abantu ngabantu kwanemibutho ngemibutho ejongene neelwimi yaye yathatha inxaxheba ngokuthi yenze iziphakamiso inika izimvo zayo ngale Draft Bill. Emva koko kwaye kwapasiswa iBill esemthethweni nto leyo eyenziwa ngokujonga izimvo zabantu abathi baziphakamisa kwiDraft Bill. Ezi zilandelayo yaba ziziphakamiso ezenziwa yiNLP yaye zisafuna ukuqwalaselwa naxa iphumile iBill esemthethweni.

«6»

INLP nayo, njengeminye imibutho esebenza ngeelwimi yathi yaphefumla ukuphuma komthetho oqulunqwayo (Draft Bill) yibhodi le. Imiba eyathi yaqwalaselwa yiNLP yile ikhankanywe apha ngezantsi.

«7»

INLP iyayixhasa kakhulu iPANSALB kwigalelo ezakuthi ilenze ngokuthi yenze uphando, kodwa okubalulekileyo kukuba oku kuza kuqhutywa njani na yile bhodi. Zimbini izinto esifuna ukuba ziqapheleke kwaye zicaciswe yile bhodi kolu xwebhu lwayo. Into yokuqala, yindlela uluntu oluyakuthi luyazi okanye lufikelele ngayo kule bhodi.

«8»

Okwesibini, kuya kuzalisekiswa njani ukuphuculwa nokuhlonitshwa kweelwimi ingakumbi ezabaNtsundu nebezikade zijongelwe phantsi ixesha elide?

«9»

LUNGAFIKELELA NJANI ULUNTU KULE BHODI?

«10»

Kwixesha elingaphambili iibhodi ebezikhona bezingaziwa ngabantu abakumgangatho osezantsi. Bekungekho ndlela abangathi abantu bafikelele ngayo kuzo. Bekungafunwa nxaxheba yabantu nje ngaphandle kwezifundiswa eziziprofesa zaseziyunivesithi. Ezi bhodi bezivele zikhuphe amagama zingakhange zenze phando lokuba abantu ezantsi bathini ngaloo magama okanye ngawaphi na amagama asetyenziswa luluntu. Kubalulekile ke ukuba oku kungaphindi kwenzeke.

«11»

Ngohlobo olubhalwe ngalo olu xwebhu kucacile ukuba abantu abayakuthi babenolwazi okanye bayisebenzise le bhodi ngabo bakumgangatho ophezulu nabanolwazi ngoMgaqo-Siseko. Asiqondi nokuba iititshala zona uqobo ziyayazi le bhodi okanye ziyakuba nako ukufikelela kuyo.

«12»

Kuphando olwenziwe nguAthalie Crawford kwizibhedlele zalapha eKapa, enye yezinto ezathi zaqapheleka kukuba abantu abangazange bakhalaze malunga nengxaki yeelwimi ezisetyenziswa ezibhedlele ngabantu abakumgangatho wentlalo osezantsi. Aba bantu uninzi lwabo ingabasuka emaphandleni. Nangona kunjalo, kwakucacile nje mhlophe ukuba abavani noogqirha kwanoonesi ngenxa yokungalandeli ulwimi abaluthethayo. Ingaba oku kusixelela ntoni ngeemfuno zabantu ngokubhekisele kwiilwimi?

«13»

Iindawo ezininzi ezisetyenziswa ngabantu abadala nabakumgangatho wentlalo osezantsi ezifana nebhanki, izibhedlele, iivenkile, iiofisi zikandabazabantu zisenabantu abangathethi iilwimi ezithethwa ngabantu abazisebenzisayo, nto leyo eyenza kube nzima kubantu abasebenzisa la maziko. Kula maziko siwakhankanye apha ngentla, zininzi iinkonzo ezithi zingabikho kwindawo zabantu abakumgangatho wentlalo osezantsi.

«14»

Umzekelo, phaya eNyanga kwiofisi zikandabazabantu awukwazi ukuya kufota i-International pasport, kufuneka ude uye edolophini ukuze ufumane inkonzo enjalo nto leyo eyenza kube nzima kubantu abasebenzisa la maziko. Mihla le kufumaniseka ukuba ngenxa yokuphazamiseka konxibelelwano ezibhedlele, ezibhankini njalo njalo kuye kubekho iingxaki zokungavisisani nto leyo ebangela ukuba umsebenzi ungahambi ngendlela eyiyo okanye kusebenziseke imali eninzi.

«15»

Umzekelo woku, uyakufumanisa ukuba abantu baquqa esibhedlele kuba besithi ugqirha khange abancede okanye bamana ukubatshintsha, kumaxesha amaninzi oku kubangelwa kukungalandeli imiyalelo kagqirha kakuhle okanye ukungamchazeli kakuhle ugqirha ingxaki yakhe aze ke naye amnyange ngohlobo olungangqamenanga nesigulo eso.

«16»

Yiyo ke le nto kuya kufuneka ukuba ibhodi izame ukwenza ngako konke okusemandleni ayo ukuba aba bantu bancedakale ngokuthi inike imibutho efana neNLP neminye, igunya lokwenza uphando oluya kuthi lwazise indlela emakulungiswe ngako oku. Luninzi uphando olufuneka lwenziwe khona ukuze kuqinisekiswe ukuba amalungelo eelwimi zabantu ayaphunyezwa. Kubalulekile ke ukuba le bhodi isebenzisane ngamandla nemibutho yabantu yona ithi isebenzisane ngqo nemfuno zabantu. Oku kunganako ukuqinisekisa ukuba inkonzo ezininzi ziba luncedo yaye uluntu luyakwazi ukuzisebenzisa ngendlela efanelekileyo.

«17»

Ndifuna ukuphinda ndiyigxininise into yokuba le bhodi iyakufana nebezikhona ngaphambili ukuba abantu abakumgangatho osezantsi abafikeleleli kuyo, yaye nomgangatho wezi lwimi awusayi kuphucuka konke konke. Ngoko ke kufuneka le bhodi iqinisekisile ukuba iyawavula amathuba okuba abantu bakwazi ukuyisebenzisa nokufikelela kuyo. Kubalulekile ukuba ibe yiyo ethatha uxanduva lokubonelela abantu ngeenkonzo eziluncedo hayi ukuba abantu bade baye kuzifunela. Kufuneka ibhodi isoloko ingaphambili kunabantu ekuphuculeni indlela yokuphila kwabo, iye ebantwini, izazi izinto ezifunwa ngabantu ngalo lonke ixesha. Oku kuya kuqinisekisa ukuba yonke into eyenzayo inenkxaso yabantu bonke yaye iqhutywa ngabantu bonke.

«18»

UKUPHUCULWA KWEELWIMI

«19»

Kubalulekile ukuba ibhodi iyicacise kakuhle indlela eziya kuthi ziphuculwe ngayo ezi lwimi kwanenxaxheba eyakuthi ithathwe yile bhodi ekuphuculeni ezi lwimi. Okunye okungacacanga apha kolu xwebhu kukuba ithetha ukuthini le bhodi xa ithetha ngokuphuculwa kweelwimi. Ixesha elide, abantu abathetha ezi lwimi bebengenayo indlela okanye bengakwazi ukuthatha inxaxheba ekuphuculeni isigama sezi lwimi. Yiyo ke le nto ibangele ukuba ezi lwimi zibe namhlanje zikumgangatho ophantsi ngohlobo lokuba azinakusetyenziselwa izinto ezifana nokufundisa ngazo iMaths, iScience, iHistory njalo njalo.

«20»

Inye kuphela into eyakuthi iphucule umgangatho wezi lwimi, kukuba zisetyenziswe, kwakhiwe amagama aze nalawo asetyenziswa ngabantu nathe akananzwa zibhodi ezidlulileyo anikwe ingqalelo kubonwe ukuba ngawaphi na anokusetyenziswa. Khona ukuze kuphumelele oku, kuya kufuneka ukuba ibhodi isebenzisane nemibutho ejongene nokwakhiwa kwesigama sezi lwimi khona ukuze incedise ngokubonelela ngendlela eyakuthi isetyenziswe ekusasazweni kwemisebenzi efana nale. Oku kuya kwenza ukuba abantu balwazi ulwimi lwabo yaye ibe lolo baluthethayo.

«21»

Enye into ekufuneka le bhodi iyilumkele ukuba ingaphindi yenzeke yinto yokuba kwakhiwe amagama angaziwayo ngabantu aze lawo asetyenziswa ngabantu angananzwa.

«22»

Ngako oko kuya kufuneka le nkqubo ibe iqhutywa ngabantu bonke khona ukuze yamkeleke.

«23»

IZIMVO ZABANTU ABABEKHO

«24»

Eyona nto yayibalulekile eyaqaphelekayo kukuba njengoko senditshilo abantu abaninzi abamele ukuba bathathe inxaxheba ekuqulunqweni kwale bhodi abafana nootitshala, abazali nabantwana bezikolo babengekho ukuza kumamela okanye ukunika ezabo imbono ngale bhodi.

«25»

Kwaye kwacaca ke nakubantu abakhoyo ukuba uluntu oluninzi ngakumbi olukumgangatho osezantsi alunalwazi lungako ngobukho bale bhodi nendlela abangathi bayisebenzise ngayo nabangayisebenzisela yona.

«26»

Enye into abathi bayiphawula abantu yindima eyakuthi ithathwe yimibutho yabafazi neminye yasekuhlaleni ukuba nolwazi nokusebenzisa le bhodi. Abantu bathi nabo bagxininisa into yokuba kufuneka kuqinisekiswe ukuba le bhodi ayiphindi iqhube ngohlobo ebezikade ziqhuba ngalo iibhodi ebezikhona ngaphambili khona ukuze urhwaphilizo luphele.

«27»

UNoxolo Mgudlwa usebenza kwi-National Language Project eKapa. Ungumphathi wenkqubo yeDemocratic Language Policy nombhali kaSincokola ngesiXhosa: Beginners' Conversational Xhosa.

Vocabulary

ibhodi board [n5-sg]
yeelwimi of languages [n6-pl-poss-n5-sg = ya-ii-lwimi]
singazuza we can benefit
«1»
isiseko basis, foundation [n4-sg]
omtsha new [adj-n2-sg]
udale it created [v-n2-sg-past]
okuvuleleka which cause to open
-vulelek- cause to open for
kwemibutho of organizations
yokujongana for looking at (together, one another)
ukuphunyezwa to cause the promotion of
nokuhlonitshwa and to be respected
kwamalungelo for the rights
iPANSALB Pan South African Language Board Bill [n5-sg-abr] {Eng}
ngomnye it is one
wale wa le of those
mibutho organizations [n2-pl-red]
UNoxolo (name) Noxolo
Mgudlwa (name) Mgudlwa
ucacisa she explains

ngale about this [deic-1-n5-sg-relat]
nendlela and [is the] way
olungafikelela in which it will be accessible
olukumgangatho wentlalo esezantsi those who have a low(er) standard of living
wentlalo of living, of life
intlalo abode; stay; state, condition; life, lifestyle, manner of living [n5-sg]
esezantsi which is lower
«2»
yibhodi It is a board [n5-sg-pred]
ezimeleyo which is independent
neyasekwa that was established
nethi and that says
inike it issued
ingxelo report [n5-sg poly]
yowisomthetho of administering laws
ayilawulwa it is not controlled
nguye by him, her, it
nawuphina anyone, whoever [pro-indef-n1-sg]
ibe limehlo be the eyes
ijongene is faced with [v-recip-perf; rw: -**jonga**]
nokuphuculwa with the improvement
-**phucul**- improve, benefit; civilize, modernize [v-tr]
ukulungelelaniswa to make equal or parallel to each other
-**lungelelanis**- arrange in order, adapt to each other, make equal or parallel to each other [v-tr]
kwakunye and even [conj]
nokukhuselwa [= na-uku-khus-el-w-a] and to be protected
kweelwimi of the languages (of) [n6-pl-domain = kwa-ii-lwimi]
eMzantsi Afrika in South Africa [pn-loc]
kubekiwe it is put, set out
«3»
sigxininisa we refer to emphatically [v-tr]
zityunjwe they were selected
-**tyumb**- select, appropriate, pick out and carry off; raid (cattle) [v-tr]
njengezisemthethweni like the ones in the law
ezizezi are those which
zilandelayo which are the following
«4»
isiNdebele Ndebele
Sesotho sa Leboa Northern Sotho
Leboa (area name)
Sesotho Sotho
siSwati Swazi
Xitsonga Tsonga
Setswana Tswana
Tshivenda Venda
nesiZulu and Zulu
naxa and whenever
ezithethwa that are spoken
ezingakhankanywanga that were not referred to
-**khankany**- mention, refer to [v-tr]
nazo and them, and those
siyazikhuthaza we encourage (them)
«5»
yaye yayila it had designed; it did draft [past subjunctive]
iDraft Bill Draft Bill {Eng}
yePANSALB of/for PANSALB
abantu ngabantu many different people
kwanemibutho ngemibutho and also many different organizations
ejongene that are responsible (for)
yathatha they took
yenze making, doing
inika it gives
kwaye kwapasiswa there had also been passed
kwaye it ~ there had VERBed; it did VERB [class 10 locative ~ impersonal remote past auxiliary verb]

kwapasiswa they were passed
esemthethweni into law
ngokujonga by looking at
baziphakamisa they raise them
yaba were/became
ziziphakamiso concerns/motions
zizi- they were [n4-pl-pred]
ezenziwa which were made
yiNLP by the NLP
zisafuna they still need
ukuqwalaselwa to be addressed ~ viewed [v-pass-inf]
iphumile it came out
«6»
nayo and it [n2 pl conj]
njengeminye like the others
ngeelwimi with/in languages
yathi it said [v-aux]
yaphefumla it breathed out
oqulunqwayo that is smoothed
-qulunq- tidy, smooth, comb [v-tr]
imiba issues, problems [n2-pl; sg: **umba**]
eyathi that said, it was said [v-aux]
yaqwalaselwa they were addressed
yile these are [deic-n2-pl-pred]
ikhankanywe they are referred to [v-pass]
«7»
iyayixhasa it is supporting it
kwigalelo in a contribution
ezakuthi which will [v-aux rel]
ilenze it (the Board) may do it
okubalulekileyo what is important
esifuna which we want
ziqapheleke they should get noticed [v-atr-sub]
-qaphelek- get noticed, be paid attention (to); be obvious, get cleared up [v-atr] {Zulu; see entry in Lexicon}
zicaciswe they have been explained
kolu for this
yindlela it is the way
oluyakuthi those who (**uluntu**) would say [v-aux]
luyazi to know it [v-tr]
lufikelele attain [v-tr]
«8»
Okwesibini secondly
kuzalisekiswa will fulfilment be caused (complement to **kuya**)
ukuphuculwa to be improved
ezabaNtsundu of the black people
nebezikade and those of long ago
zijongelwe which/who were looked on as
«9»
lungafikelela it can be reached
«10»
kwixesha in time [n3-sg-loc]
elingaphambili that is ahead
ebezikhona that were there
bezingaziwa they were not known, without being known
abakumgangatho who are at a level [rw: **umgangatho**]
osezantsi which is low
bekungekho there has been no, there was no
abangathi who can say; here, by which
bekungafunwa it was not considered necessary
kwezifundiswa for the educated
eziziprofesa who are professors {Eng}
zaseziyunivesithi of the university {Eng}
bezivele they would always appear to
zikhuphe they released, issued
zingakhange without having [v-aux past emph]
zenze made [v-tr past]
phando investigation [n6-sg]
bathini what are they saying?
ngaloo about these [deic-2-n3-pl-relat]
magama words [n3-pl-red; see **amagama** ABOVE]

ngawaphi which ones? [cop n3pl interrog]
asetyenziswa they are used
luluntu by the community [n6-sg-agent]
kungaphindi it does not again [v aux neg n8 vn]
«11»
ngohlobo of the manner; in a way
olubhalwe it is written
kucacile it is obvious
-cacile obvious, plain, distinct [v-perf-atr]
abayakuthi who do VERB; who would VERB [v fact]
babenolwazi have an idea or knowledge [v aux+n6sg]
bayisebenzise they used it
ophezulu above
nabanolwazi and who have knowledge
ngoMgaqo-Siseko about the Constitution
asiqondi we are not sure
uqobo actually [adv]
ziyayazi they know it
ziyakuba they will be [v aux]
nako and it; and as for it
«12»
kuphando in the investigation
olwenziwe which has been made
nguAthalie Crawford by Athalie Crawford [pass agent]
kwizibhedlele in the hospitals
zalapha of this place (here)
eKapa in Cape Town
ezathi that were (lit: which say)
zaqapheleka that were obvious
abangazange they never [v aux]
bakhalaze they complain [v-tr]
ingabasuka they may originate from
emaphandleni in rural areas
nangona kunjalo be that as it may
kwakucacile it was obvious
abavani they don't hear each other
noogqirha with doctors
kwanoonesi and even nurses
oonesi nurses [n1-pl]
yokungalandeli of not following
abaluthethayo what they are saying
kusixelela it tells us
ngeemfuno about the needs
ngokubhekisele concerning
«13»
iindawo places, localities [n5-pl; sg: **indawo**]
ezisetyenziswa which are used
ezifana na such as (lit: which resemble)
nebhanki and banks {Eng}
iivenkile shops {Afr winkel} [n5-pl]
iiofisi offices [n5-pl]
zikandabazabantu of the affairs of the people; [atr] governmental
zisenabantu they have people (i.e., are staffed by)
abangathethi who do not speak
abazisebenzisayo who use them
abasebenzisa who utilize
kula in these [deic-1-n3-pl-loc]
siwakhankanye we mentioned
iinkonzo services [n5-pl; rw: **-khonz-**]
zingabikho they are not present
«14»
eNyanga (name of place)
kwiofisi in the office {Eng}
awukwazi you don't know
kufota to photograph
pasport passport {Eng}
kufuneka it is necessary; must, should
ude even or until [v aux]
edolophini in/to town
idolophu town {Afr dorp}
ufumane you get
enjalo which is like that
leyo that
kufumaniseka it is found, discovered
yokuphazamiseka to be disturbed
konxibelelwano to be connected together

nxibelela be connected together [v-tr applic]
ezibhankini in banks
zokungavisisani of not understanding [= za-uku-nga-vis-is-an-i]
ebangela which causes for (them)
umsebenzi worker, laborer [n1-sg]
ungahambi it not going [v-n2-sg-S2-neg-pres-part]
kusebenziseke it will be used up, here, wasted
«15»
woku of this [deic-1-n8-vn-poss-n2-sg]
baquqa they go often
abancede they help
bamana they just [v aux]
ukubatshintsha to change them
kumaxesha on many occasions, many times
kubangelwa it is caused by
kukungalandeli not following
kagqirha of the doctor
ukungamchazeli not to explain to him [v-inf-neg]
amnyange he/she may be cured
olungangqamenanga which is/was not in relation [rel neg]
nesigulo to the sickness
eso that [deic-2-n4-sg]
«16»
ngako about it
konke all [enum pro n8]
okusemandleni that is in its strength
ayo his, her, its [poss prn]
bancedakale that they be assisted
efana that is similar
neminye and others
oluya that yonder
lwazise it informs
emakulungiswe that repairs should be...
luninzi there is plentiful
olufuneka that needs
lwenziwe to be done
kuqinisekiswe be convinced
eelwimi of languages
ayaphunyezwa be taken out, brought to the fore
ngqo go straight ahead; keep on, work steadily at; do right away; [adv] exactly [ideophone]
nemfuno with the wants
kunganako can have
ziba they are, they become
luyakwazi it does know (how)
ukuzisebenzisa to use them
«17»
ndifuna ukuphinda ndiyigxininise I want to again emphasize
ukuphinda again [v-aux]
ndiyigxininise I should emphasize
iyakufana it will be the same as
nebezikhona as those which were there
ngaphambili before
abafikeleleli they are not reached out to
nomgangatho and the level
awusayi it won't be
kuphucuka improve [v inf red]
iyawavula it opens (them)
nokufikelela and to reach
ethatha that takes
lokubonelela of enlightening
ngeenkonzo with the services
eziluncedo that are helpful
bade they even [v aux]
kuzifunela to want them
ingaphambili should be in front
kunabantu than/of the people
ekuphuculeni in the improving of
yokuphila of living [= ya-uku-phil-a]
izazi it should know (them)
ezifunwa that are wanted
kuqinisekisa will guarantee ~ justify
eyenzayo which is done
inenkxaso it has the support
iqhutywa it is directed, it is controlled by

«19»
iyicacise (that) it explains
kwanenxaxheba [= kwa-na-i-nxaxheba] (and) which part
eyakuthi that will really
ithathwe be taken
okunye there is another (thing)
okungacacanga not clear
ithetha ukuthini what does it mean? [dummy verb]
ngokuphuculwa by being improved
abathetha they say
bebengenayo they did not have it
bengakwazi they did not know how
ukuthatha to take
sezi of the
zikumgangatho they are of a standard
azinakusetyenziselwa they won't be utilized for
nokufundisa for teaching
ngazo about those
iScience Science {Eng}
iHistory History {Eng}
«20»
inye there is one
iphucule it might improve
kwakhiwe built, constructed [v-pass-past = ku-akh-iw-e]
nalawo and those
nathe should be [v aux]
akananzwa not liked or preferred
-nanz- like, approve of, be pleased with; care for, pay attention to; look at with recognition; admire; [neg] dislike, not care for, care little for [v-tr]
zibhodi by the board
ingqalelo commencement
kubonwe it is seen
anokusetyenziswa that will be utilized
nokwakhiwa with the building of
kwesigama of the vocabulary
incedise it assists
ekusasazweni in scattering about
balwazi who know it
lolo that [deic-2-n6-sg-pred]
baluthethayo of which they speak; they who speak it [v-rel]
«21»
iyilumkele (it) should be careful about
ingaphindi it does not again
yenzeke it might happen
angaziwayo not known
angananzwa are not liked, are not taken into consideration
«22»
yamkeleke be received
«23»
ababekho who were there
«24»
yayibalulekile it had been important
eyaqaphelekayo that it be cleared up
senditshilo I have already said
abamele who are standing for
ekuqulunqweni in tidying
kwale of this [deic 1 n5 sg poss n8 vn]
abafana are those such as/who resemble
nootitshala with teachers
bezikolo of the schools
babengekho should be there (included)
kumamela to listen to [v inf red]
«25»
kwaye kwacaca it had become clear
nakubantu to the people
abakhoyo who are here
oluninzi many
alunalwazi does not have knowledge
lungako about it
ngobukho of the presence or existence
«26»
bayiphawula they noted it
yindima it is something obvious (lit: it is the land of a day's ploughing)

yimibutho by organizations
yabafazi of women
yasekuhlaleni of those who are lying down, i.e., marginalized minorities
ebezikade which was of the past
urhwaphilizo cheating
-**rhwaphiliz**- cheat [v-tr]; be greedy, gluttonous; be selfish; be fraudulent [v-intr]
luphele it may end
«27»
ungumphathi she is the chairperson
wenkqubo of the advancement
nombhali and author
umbhali author, writer [n2-sg]
kaSincokola (book name) (lit: we converse)

Translations

Reading 1
Amandla Meats

Meat Market
Meat For Everybody
We sell premium meat
All our prices are low
Our meat is always in demand
And there are weekend specials
Market Square, King William's Town

Reading 2
On The Idle Wandering Of Youth

In the animal kingdom, the young are not allowed to wander around at night or during the day because they might get hurt. Human parents who do not care about their children are worse than animal parents. They let their children roam around at night, stealing and getting into trouble.

Reading 3
Respect Teachers

The time has come when we should respect our parents as well as our teachers. I think that teachers are essential to society. Without teachers, could you say that there would be doctors, lawyers, nurses, translators, or anyone else necessary for the nation's progress?
by S.M., from Reitz

Reading 4
ISO, Part A

I am looking for a young woman age 20. I am 22 years old. I do not smoke and do not drink. I go to church. I was arrested in June. I request that you send me a picture.
Mncedisi Nethi, Stutterheim Prison P/Bag X 5, Stutterheim 4930

ISO, Part B

Edward Matyana, age 27, would like to be in correspondence with unattached women between the ages of 18 and 35. He likes playing soccer, tennis, listening to music, reading, writing, and going to church. Please write to him in Xhosa, Afrikaans, or English, and don't forget to enclose a photo. His address is: Correctional Services, Private Bag X2, Patensie, 6335.

ISO, Part C

I am a 26–year–old girl. I am looking for a partner who is tired of worldly things. As for me, I do not drink or smoke, but it is okay if he smokes so long as he doesn't drink. I like watching sports on television and listening to gospel music. Anyone who is interested should include his picture in the first letter. I will also do the same. Those from Port Elizabeth should not bother; they have made a fool of me often enough.
Doris Roberts, P. O. Box 2352, Port Elizabeth

ISO, Part D

I am looking for a female companion between the ages of 38 and 42 who would be willing to become my wife. She need not be pretty, but she must work hard at becoming a housewife. We should meet, go out together, grow together, and rely on each other with the love of God. I am a perfect husband, but women say that I still fall in love the old-fashioned way.[1] Whereas they say they want a person with money. I want someone who has a sincere love of the truth and strong convictions, with love coming from the heart and the soul.
Bongane Mashilwane, P. O. Box 391, Warrenton 8530

Reading 5
Thank You

The Mabhele family of Masele extends a thank you to all who came to mourn with them when they were under the dark cloud of the loss of the father of their home, J. D. Mabhele, especially to fellow church members (Bible Holders) Mrs. Mnamata, Magingxa, Xayiya, Sonjani, Gwayi, and Tokoyi. They are lifelong friends. Submitted by Lottie Mabhele, Bible Holder, and her family at Masele.

---

[1] This is typical of the clash which occurs between rural and urban cultures - the writer's views are that he would love his wife in the traditional way, and would expect her to reciprocate. Marrying for money is not traditional!

Reading 6

Usage Of Medicines

• Study the directions carefully: you should take it (or administer it) according to the directions.

• Take medicine appropriate for yourself: don't give it to others and don't take others' medicine.

• When warned about taking it, you should not drive or operate machinery. When you use a particular medicine, follow the instructions. Not following them can put you in danger.

• If you are pregnant, ask your doctor before you take any other medicine that he has not prescribed for you.

• Lock up medicines.

Reading 7

Do You Want To Become Rich?

Study to be a witch doctor's assistant by correspondence. Our lessons are so easy that you can follow them even if you do not have much education. Our lessons are written in Xhosa, Sotho, English, and Zulu. In life there is no job that will make you as rich as being a witch doctor's assistant.

When you have become a witch doctor or a witch doctor's assistant we can help you get a certificate to be a member of the union of witch doctors and witch doctors' assistants. To get a complete explanation with lessons you must first send R80.00 by registered mail to this address:

A.H. C.C., P. O. Box 254, Butterworth 4960

Reading 8

Spicy Lamb Sishebo

30 ml oil

500 g lamb chops or knuckles

2 onions, diced

2 tomatoes, diced

3 carrots, peeled, cut into circles

2 potatoes, cut up

250 ml chopped green beans

60 ml Jikelele Sishebo Mix with Rajah

250 ml water

Heat up the oil, cook the meat until it becomes golden brown.
Add onion, cook until tender.
Add tomatoes, carrots, potatoes, and green beans.
Add water to the Jikelele Sishebo Mix.
Simmer on the stove on low heat for 45 minutes to an hour or until the meat becomes tender.
Serve with rice, cornmeal mush, or porridge.

Reading 9

Children Being Forced To Raise Funds

I am bothered by the way elementary schools are forcing children to work at fundraising for them. Our children are being sent out on the streets and to people's homes to ask for money. Don't they realize the risks they are exposing our children to? Rapists and child abusers are all over the place nowadays—it's just like throwing a sheep to the lions! This means that our children should not trust anybody they do not know! Principals and teachers should work together with us—our children are important, so let's protect them! Let's try other means of raising money for schools.
By L.S., Zimbabwe

Reading 10

There Should Be Compulsory Education

There is no compulsory education in South Africa. This situation exists despite the fact that it is an accepted practice not to exclude a child from school if that child has no school fees. Although this is a step in the right direction, why does the government only support lower education and never higher education where school fees are even much higher per term? It is a known fact that people in rural areas do not have the money to pay for higher education. Most of them do not work; others still earn low wages even now. In addition, our government is afraid to guarantee us job security and create new employment opportunities.
T.J.Z., Elandsfontein

Reading 11

Protect The Innocent!

The lives of some individuals are not respected in our country. People kill for no reason at all. Crime rates are rising because criminals know that they won't be punished for their deeds. They do anything, no matter what. Prisons are attractive and admired because they are just like their homes. As I see it, South Africa must have stricter laws, just like other nations. Murderers, rapists, and other criminals must be severely punished so they will fear the consequences of their actions in the future. I am talking about this because there is nothing I feel more strongly about than people who break the law, even if they are our nation's children. We love them, but we detest their behavior.

by O.F., in Kwaeng

Reading 12

Rice Grown In The U.S. Gives You Strength

In order for a man to have muscles which, in turn, make him strong, he needs natural organic food, such as the high-quality rice grown in the U.S. That is because rice grown in the U.S. contains certain special ingredients which contain a mixture of carbohydrates. This means that when you eat rice grown in the U.S. you'll find that it makes you feel truly satisfied without giving you that bloated feeling. You'll find that you have more than enough strength to defend yourself, to face a long day at work, or to play sports.

In addition, rice grown in the U.S. contains Vitamin B, Protein, Calcium, and Iron.

So whenever you buy rice, ask for the brands which have quality rice grown only in the U.S.

The leading brands of rice contain rice grown only in the U.S.

Yes!!! I'm asking that you send me your small book of favorite recipes.

Rice helps your children to always be bright and cheerful.

Reading 13
God Bless Africa

«1»
God Bless Africa
May her horn rise up
Hear Thou our prayers
And bless us.
«2»
Descend Oh Spirit
Descend Oh Holy Spirit.
«3»
Bless our chiefs
May they remember their Creator
May they fear Him and revere Him
And bless them.
«4»
Bless the men of the nation
Bless also the youth
That they may carry the land with patience
And bless them.
«5»
Bless the wives
And also all young women
Lift up all young girls
And bless them.
«6»
Bless the ministers
Of all the churches of this land
Fill them with Thy Spirit
And bless them.
«7»
Bless agriculture and livestock
Banish all famine and diseases
Fill the land with good health
And bless it.
«8»
Bless our efforts
Of union and self-improvement

Of education and mutual understanding
And bless them.
«9»
God Bless Africa
Blot out all its wickedness
And its transgressions and sins
And bless it.

First stanza of the official South African English version:
Sounds the call to come together,
And united we shall stand,
Let us live and strive for freedom,
In South Africa our land.

Reading 14

Friends

Friends are very important in your youth.

Friends can tempt you to do things which are not yet suitable for you. They can make you dislike yourself. At such times it is important to decide whether or not to keep those friends. What makes a friend a suitable friend? Let's take a little look:

...they will support you in good times and bad times. They will be with you when you're happy. They will not forget you when you are sad, nor will they make fun of you.

...they will listen to whatever you say. Sometimes they may disagree with what you say, but that will not change the fact that they care about you.

...they will forgive you. Sometimes you may disagree with your friends. Other times they may be jealous of you or they may disagree with you. Learn to reconcile and agree with people who are peaceful.

...they are people you can speak with about your ideas. Learn to be open with your students. Share your opinions and your emotions with them.

And as for them, give them the opportunity to do the same in return.

Reading 15

Nompumelelo

A healer from Mozambique

P. O. Box 12922

Jacobs 4026

Phone (031) 420313

Do you have a problem with your home?

Do you have children? Is your house falling apart (no erection)?[2]

Does money leave from your hands before you can even see what you've done with it?

Do you need help? If that's the case, see Nompumelelo, a healer from Nampuza in Mozambique. She can cure you in many different ways.

Once you have called the number above or written to the address above you will receive all the help you need.

Reading 16

A School For African Leaders

The majority of African leaders need to study the example set by the South African leader, Nelson Mandela. He is an important person who is concerned about and loves his people. He is respected by all of Africa as well as by his own nation. I urge father Mandela to establish a school for training the leaders of Africa. We have a blending of political minds who can teach such topics as respect for the law, the constitution and how to use it, free elections, and the due process for knowing how to use authority properly. The low standards of political conduct in the majority of African countries, caused by dictators who hunger for position, are perceived as the normal leadership style for an African country. A democratically-elected leader must learn under father Nelson Mandela, and then be evaluated by examination. For many years military leaders had to study Gerry Rawlings of Ghana. These two leaders have the interests of the people at heart. I would be grateful if father Mandela would be able to open such a school before he leaves politics.

By A.M., in Keemanshoop, in Namibia

---

[2] The author of the advertisement, Nompumelelo, obviously feels that her euphemism for penile dysfunction needs clarification!

Reading 17

Let's Look Up To Madiba [3]

«1»

Editor, it makes me feel bad that people who claim to be educated are doing one thing and saying another.

«2»

It seems like yesterday that these educated people sat down while we were prancing around, saying we were not educated because "they respect the Afrikaners."

«3»

Today, when it is acceptable to make demands for what we want, they want to obstruct us. If I may say so, what is being done by hospital nurses is uncivilized: they purposely abandon sick people to die when they are supposed to want to make them healthy.

«4»

This bad thing will disqualify us in the eyes of those countries that sought to support our efforts to civilize this wilderness land we're in.

«5»

The words spoken by nurses make me sick; let's all sincerely respect father Madiba [Mandela], and not just invoke his name.

«6»

We should think about the time he spent sitting on the island.[4] We should be a little patient; we should look up to Madiba [Mandela] and his group; perhaps things will work out.

«7»

If I may be allowed to say so, don't be impetuous, black people of our land.

Fuzile Mxoli, Western Holdings, D24, Welkom

Reading 18

Vandals Burn Schoolbooks

«1»

The Nonceba High School in Zwelitsha, near Qonce, finds itself in big trouble with students' parents because, after being open for just one year, its books have already been burned by unknown vandals.

---

[3] "Madiba" is the tribal name for Nelson Mandela.

[4] The phrase "to sit" is a South African euphemism for time spent in prison.

«2»
This occurred in one of the rooms filled with books which were donated by the regional government, carried out without a single sound or any other clue noticed by owners of homes near the school.
«3»
At the investigation, which was conducted in the school principal's office, Mrs. S. M. Mtika said that the loss sustained by the school had reached an estimated 50,000 Rand.
«4»
She said the main problem is that the Board of Education announced that they would not be releasing any new books this year. Mrs. Mtika also said that they had decided to quickly convene a meeting for parents.
«5»
This source also conferred with Superintendent Clive Nkopo of the Zwelitzsha police station, which confirmed that major damage occurred even though the amount and extent of the damage will not be known until the ongoing police investigation is complete.
«6»
He said that they want anyone with information to come forward and be assured that the information released will remain confidential.

Reading 19

Thandi Solves Your Problems

P. O. Box 190, King Williams Town 5600
«1»
Thandi: I am a 22-year-old man. My problem is that while I was still at school I fell in love with a 24-year-old girl who hid from me the fact that she was married and had a daughter.
«2»
As time went by, this girl became pregnant with my child. It was at that same time, though, that she told me she was married, and we were forced to separate. After my son was born, they (she and the baby) separated from her husband.
«3»
This girl returned to me, telling me that she could not live without me. What's bothering me, however, is that her husband took my child because he doesn't know that it isn't his.

—Bothered in East London.

«4»

What is this girl's conscience telling her? To begin with, she fell in love with you, then went back to her husband again, pregnant with a child that wasn't his.

«5»

Separated again from her husband, she returned to you without the child. Either you or she must tell her husband that the child is not his.

«6»

Expect that there will be a lot of problems, because you will eventually be forced to prove that the child isn't his.

Reading 20

People Know Their Leaders[5]

«1»

To the Editor:

I say I should support the transformation of the people known as traditional leaders (chiefs).

«2»

No, my brothers and sisters, if you do not know your chiefs by now, you will never know them. An elected leader is chosen by the people, which allows the people to know what their leader stands for. On the other hand, a chief is a traditional leader of the people; if there were no people, there would be no chiefs.

«3»

Many chiefs have bloated stomachs that were nurtured by Apartheid; people were trapped by the Boers (the Apartheid government) because of their chiefs.

«4»

Many chiefs did not want to abandon Apartheid because they had become "baas boys."[6] When you think about it, dear reader, what

[5] The writer distinguishes between elected and traditional leaders — "chief" refers to traditional leadership as the term "inkosi" originally meant "one of royal blood."

was happening that all these puppet governments were ruled by chiefs?
«5»
Look in KwaZulu, Venda, Bophuthantswana, Transkei, Ciskei, and Ndebele. They were ruled by chiefs who ate well and lived extravagantly because of Apartheid.
«6»
We were not surprised to see that they refused to take part in the elections—they were showing unity with the Boers—but because people knew their chiefs[7] they cast off those chains of the past.
«7»
Even now they are preaching that sermon. Why do the chiefs want their rights while they continue to exploit the people? What have they done for the nation all these years when leaders were in jail or in exile? Down with Westerners.
Paulos Tshathu,
P. O. Box 324 Isiphingo 4110

Reading 21
Explain To Us In Your Own Words The State Of Things Which Are About To Happen
«1»
There is still time for you to have a voice in the making of the Constitution. We would like to hear from you about these important amendments.
Volkstaat/the self-determination of the people
«2»
Is it necessary that the Constitution pay close attention to the self-determination of the people of one particular traditional culture?
«3»
If you think that the Constitution should consider this, should there be an external state, for example, a "volkstaat"? Or is there a more satisfactory solution?

---

[6] "baas" comes via Afrikaans from the Dutch word for master or employer, and has the same origin as "boss" in American English. The term "baas boy" usually meant the appointed African leader of a work team, particularly in the mines, but later became a derogatory term for an African person who is perceived to side with his white overseers.
[7] I.e., were wise to their ways.

«4»
What kind of society is it that needs to be bound together by tradition in order to establish their position?
«5»
Why is it necessary that the people support a program of self-determination? Deadline 4 June 1995
«6»
The progress of the elections.
«7»
How should the members of Parliament be selected?
«8»
Is it necessary that the progress of the elections be supported by a row[8] of political parties as was the case in the elections of 1994, or should it be linked with the Constitution? Deadline: 19 June 1995
«9»
Changes to the Constitution
«10»
In order for the Constitution to be accepted, what changes should be made? Deadline: 20 June 1995
«11»
Present your opinions in this paper. You may also present your views or motions to the Speaker, The House of Assembly, P. O. Box 15, Cape Town 8000, or send it by fax (021) 24 1160/1. Help us shape a future for all of us.

Reading 22
Issues In Education

«1»
Education in South Africa has changed since 1997. "Curriculum 2005" and outcome-based education have been introduced, generously funded by Adult Education and Training. This month Tyhila Ufunde introduces you to information which will acquaint you with these changes.

[8] The Xhosa word "uludwe" used by the writer means a "row or line of things." It reflects the large number of political parties which were allowed to stand for South Africa's first democratic elections in 1994.

«2»
Being Led By The Schools
A Handbook for School Governing Bodies
«3»
The South African Schools Act of 1996 states that schools need to select boards to govern them. Parents, students, and the general public now have the important responsibility of leading the schools with the authority to make decisions regarding finances and administration.
«4»
For this reason, a pamphlet entitled "Leading Together" was produced. This pamphlet is helpful for school board members and the general public. The pamphlet explains what should be discussed by leaders and reported by members so that their committees may function properly.
«5»
The pamphlet talks about the following matters:
• School board tasks and positions
• How to plan an administrative program
• School leadership
«6»
There are questions about the appropriate things to be done so that the School Board can work effectively. The pamphlet entitled "Leading Together" is helpful in guiding the work of the school board leadership. If you want to order the pamphlet, write to this address: The Catholic Institute of Education, P. O. Box 2083, Southdale, 2135.

Reading 23
Tax Concessions '95

«1»
Guest: Good morning, I want a few little things for the crèche. What are you doing, Lindiwe?
«2»
Lindiwe: I am filling out my tax forms.
«3»
Guest: Oh! I need to fill out mine, but I am afraid I will be punished because I have never sent in my tax forms before.

«4»
Lindiwe: And why is that? The government wants our taxes to fulfill the needs of the people.
«5»
Guest: I know that, I just don't know which taxes I should pay. I am afraid that they will make me pay interest on the money that I earn or punish me for not having paid taxes in the past.
Hello, Jabu, how is the taxi business doing?
«6»
Jabu: Fine, thank you. I overheard what you said. I've never registered for taxes before either, even though I should have done so.
«7»
Lindiwe: Luckily, the government is being accommodating about taxes. Everyone who never registered to pay taxes before 26 April and was supposed to have done so, as well as anyone who the commissioner could never find and force to pay taxes, has been told that he or she can pay taxes without fear of punishment.
«8»
Guest: That's good news. Where can we get more details?
«9»
Lindiwe: Find the booklet of tax advice so that you can put in a request. If you want more details, you can call this phone number: 0800-11-3930. You will be helped in the language of your choice.
«10»
Jabu: How much time do we have?
«11»
Lindiwe: You need to submit a request for tax advice before 31 October.
«12»
Jabu: That's good news. I will make a phone call now!

Reading 24

An Important Day For Graca With Mandela At Her Side

«1»
Nelson Mandela was at the side of his companion, Graca Machel, when she was awarded an honorary degree at Essex University for her work in worldwide children's rights.

«2»

The most loved couple in Africa were welcomed by a large crowd when they arrived by helicopter at Essex University near Colchester.

«3»

But throughout this entire visit, the 79-year-old president of South Africa did not want to take center stage. "This has nothing to do with me. This is for Mrs. Machel," he said.

«4»

This is her day. She is the person of the moment."

«5»

His 51-year-old companion was filled with excitement. She is the widow of Samora Machel, the former president of Mozambique who died in an airplane crash in 1986.

«6»

Once the constant danger she was exposed to during the overthrow of the Portuguese government came to an end, she became the Minister of Education in a free Mozambique, where she made great efforts to end illiteracy. Graca certainly deserves to be honored.

«7»

This honorary degree is conferred in recognition of her work in examining the civil war and its effect on children. Recognized as an expert in these affairs by the UN, Mrs. Machel was invited to produce two studies on the subject by Essex University.

«8»

"I don't accept this degree in my own name alone. I represent the millions of children who have seen war," said Mrs. Machel upon leaving the ceremony, regaled with her degree.

Reading 25[9]

Did You Know That...?

There are remedies that work as fast as an injection, allowing you to see results in three days.

1. Remedy for dispelling all illnesses, per bottle[10]: This medicine cures kidney problems, back pain, burning urine, air and poison in the stomach, headache and dizziness, chest congestion, burning feet, cramps and problems caused by somebody leaving a bad charm in your path, fatigue, ulcers, heartburn, loss of appetite, "dirty"[11] blood, and pimples.

2. A remedy for drop,[12] per bottle: Cures every kind of drop, new and old, cleanses everything dirty in the fallopian tubes, in the kidneys, and in the back. It cures genital sores, uterus inflammation, etc.

---

[9] This advertisement is for a Durban-based company, and thus comes from a predominantly Zulu-speaking area. Consequently, some of the words reflect Zulu spelling rather than Xhosa, and must be considered dialectal differences rather than mistakes. The differences are similar to the 'tomayto/tomahto' debate, and with about as much linguistic significance. Professor S. C. Satyo, in private conversation, said that the Zulus are perceived as being better traditional healers than their Xhosa counterparts, so a little bit of Zulu interference is probably good for business.
I have generally translated the term "imbiza/iimbiza" as "remedy"—it is a metaphorical extension from the original meaning of 'cooking pot' and indicates that the remedy in question has been prepared by traditional means in such a pot and will be required to be taken in fairly large quantities, normally a 750ml bottle ('bhotile'). Idliso is a kind of poison associated with witchcraft. It makes you sick for a long period of time; in most cases, medical doctors cannot cure it and cannot even diagnose the illness. It can be in the form of animal hair, etc., and remains in your system longer than chemical poison. In some cases when it has been diagnosed, it can be expelled. According to some stories about Idliso, a man coughed up a live spider and a ball of hair was found in a woman.

[10] Most traditional remedies are herbal infusions, and thus are dispensed in substantial quantities, hence the term "per bottle" after most entries.

[11] Many cultures seem to have practioners of the concept of improving health through purification, even if it is as simple as flushing the kidneys with a dose of Epsom salts. The Xhosa culture is no exception and it is this concept which is referenced here.

[12] "Drop" is a euphemism for sexually transmitted diseases.

3. Stick[13] remedy, per bottle: This medicine for men opens congested veins, makes you young again, and allows you to get along better with your mate, supplied with a pill as well.
4. For swine lice and facial discoloration, per bottle: It kills this species of lice internally and externally, killing them and their hatching eggs, making them completely disappear. Also cures acne.
5. For coughing, per bottle: Cures chest complaints, asthma, chest congestion, smoke coming from the kidneys. Allowing your chest to become congested will lead to chronic coughing.
6. Remedy for persistent headache, per bottle: For headache and stabbing pains in the neck, as well as for high blood pressure.
7. Remedy for poisons, per bottle: This medicine cures various poisons and bad air in the stomach. This remedy causes the impurities to break up and be passed in the feces, as you will see with your own eyes.
Altogether there are 50 remedies at R40 each as well as those for children's ailments. Send R20.00 as a deposit and pay the balance when you receive the medicine.
All are found at
N.H. Agencies
P. O. Box 48273, Qualbert 4079 Durban Tel: (031) 390 1627

Reading 26
Sheep Thieves Expelled
«1»
A master witch doctor and a car-and-television mechanic were expelled like bad spirits from the village of Quzini after residents accused them of being cattle rustlers and petty thieves.
«2»
The two families, the Goniwe and the Nqabisile, were reportedly expelled after it was discovered that they had been slaughtering other people's sheep.
«3»
Angry residents vehemently said that they will never live with thieves. In the resulting turmoil the two families had their homes torn down and their possessions thrown into the streets.

[13] "Stick" is a euphemism for the penis.

«4»
By the time we arrived, we found that the homes were a mess and the families were collecting scraps of their food from all over the place.
«5»
In a discussion with Mr. Mtumele Goniwe, who claims to be able to cure cancer, he said there was a lot of damage, even to the point that everything they own was broken. He accused the residents of taking their clothing and even their food as a way to starve them.
«6»
When we touched on the subject of the sheep they are supposed to have stolen, Mr. Goniwe said he saw some sheep roaming around and decided that since no one had looked for them in a long time he should slaughter them with his friend, Mr. Goodman Nqabisile.
«7»
"We talked with the owner of the sheep when he arrived and I paid him four goats, but the residents weren't willing to listen," said Mr. Goniwe. On top of that, he will take the matter to the lawyers about the damage they (the residents) did.
«8»
The Qhaza Police in Zeleni also testified about the expulsion of these two families from the village of Quzini next to the Horseshoe Motel. Sergeant Zola Metuse said the families were expelled from their village by the residents after they found the meat of the stolen sheep. He said that the families are being kept in the police barracks until they find another place. By the time we visited there we found a large police truck parked in front, and the families were hurrying to load all their possessions onto it.

Reading 27

At The Police Station, The Doors Are Open – Hewana

«1»
"The doors of the police station at Tamaraha are open to ensure that the general public has access to police assistance." So said the manager of the station, Mr. S. Hewana, at a recent meeting held at the Nonibe school in Tamaraha.

«2»

Mr. Hewana said this during a question-and-answer session with residents of the various villages of the region.

«3»

He said, "Anybody who speaks to a police officer should get the officer's name, and if they're not satisfied by the explanation received from the officer they should request to meet with the assistant manager or the manager himself."

«4»

He requested cooperation between the community and the police.

«5»

The residents of Nonibe asked that a police van circulate the district, especially at night.

«6»

Captain Hewana agreed, asking that anybody needing the services of the police should write to him to make sure that things are going the way they should, that is to say, according to the wishes of the people.

«7»

The residents of Nonibe also expressed their heartfelt gratitude to the manager of the station for the role he played and for selflessly and tirelessly making himself known to the people of this region.

«8»

He (Capt. Hewana) moved on to say that people should not eat out of an old dish[14]: "things have changed now, so let's cooperate," he added.

«9»

Nevertheless the questions that the residents were united in asking concerned:

• the absence of water and dipping tanks for cows so that people can dip close to where they live; and

«10»

• the rape of children and the stealing of livestock in the region, it being said that the police are afraid to face up to these issues.

[14] I.e., should keep up with the times

«11»

Captain Hewana was glad that this issue had been raised and this explanation suggested, saying that he personally does not agree that the police in Tamaraha are scared to investigate these crimes. He went on to clarify that such cases are opened here at the police station and are then passed on to the investigators.

«12»

In the event that a child is raped, he said that the Child Protection Unit in East London is the department that deals with such cases.

«13»

On the other hand, cases of livestock theft are investigated by a department at Fort Jackson near East London that specializes in these cases.

«14»

Hewana added by saying that it is still the residents' responsibility to say that they need help. "As for us, we are the police officers of Tamaraha; we are the mouthpiece for the people's complaints as we take them to those in authority so that they know of them—the baby that does not cry dies on its mother's back," he said.

Reading 28

Short Stories

Travelling On Foot From Matatiele

«1»

It is hard to find jobs these days, but employment opportunities are improved from what they were before. As we are continuing to report on employment,[15] this month we bring you the story of Thandekile Memela. She tells us how her mother went to find work many years ago. She also tells about working conditions on farms.

«2»

I was born in Matatiele. My mother kept no record of days so I am not sure how old I am. After the death of my father, mother thought about moving to Durban because of the scarcity of work in Matatiele. At that time she had ten children: nine girls and one boy.

---

[15] The text mentions continuing to talk about employment because this selection is part of a series of reports.

«3»
Mother made arrangements to go to Durban. There were few cars in those days, and even the police traveled on horseback. We had nothing to ride on, so we traveled on foot.
«4»
We did not know how far it was to Durban. We started our journey in the morning with mother. We traveled a great distance, each person carrying a little luggage. We went up mountains and hills and crossed forests. We walked and walked until we were tired...
«5»
After walking three days and nights, we ran out of food. Mother did not know what to do, because we had not yet reached Durban. She saw people on the road and asked the way to Durban. They showed her a white-owned farm occupied only by a widow. On the fourth day of walking, we arrived at the farm, and mother entered the house. She said that she wanted work, and the owner of the farm agreed that she could work there.
«6»
All of us stayed on that farm, mother working there. The owner of that farm was a kind white person. She farmed wheat and dairy and she gave us milk. Mother earned R3.00 a month. In Matatile she would have been earning R1.50 a month, so she was satisfied with her salary. Mother was able to buy us nice things and material to make us dresses.
«7»
After a year of working there, she concluded that we should continue on our journey to Durban. She heard that she could earn more money on other farms. She bid goodbye to that farmer and we continued on our journey.

Reading 29
Jobs
«1»
As a business person you need to be able to sell. You need to communicate with people. You need to understand people who are different and they need to understand you too.

«2»

You work with different people when displaying a product. For example, there are people who overlook the shipping of produce to various places, people who sell it, and people who buy it, all of whom you need to communicate with regularly. That is your biggest job.

«3»

Who is suitable for this job?

«4»

There are many qualities needed in order to work in sales.

«5»

"You need to be a person who likes to be with people. You need to know what you want and try to get it. You need to be an expert communicator so that your views can be accepted by people and you need to know how to convince people into believing that they should buy your product."

«6»

Successful outcome

«7»

Mbulelo believes that the successful outcome of good sales technique is seeing your product bought like hotcakes.

«8»

"Seeing people buy your product shows that you are succeeding in your work. This encourages you. You have moved from begging people to buy from you to seeing them buy the product you were telling them about. You become proud to have helped make that product so popular."

«9»

Guidelines for working

«10»

You get a satisfying reward in sales, and there are many opportunities available in this field.

«11»

"The majority of people who have degrees in this field start out as marketing assistants earning salaries of R4,000 a month. In this job you help a marketing manager, or a brand manager, with the jobs they need some support in. This way you learn on the job."

«12»
The second step is to work with a product and have products over which you are the exclusive manager. You will be called a brand manager and you will report to the marketing manager. The highest position you can reach is to become a marketing director.
«13»
It's a nice job, Mbulelo says about sales, being one of the most pleasant you can choose nowadays.
«14»
"The majority of people in South Africa are black. Black people must be seen as big buyers. If a company is serious about selling their products to black people, it's necessary to hire people who are black (as salesmen).
«15»
"Sales depend on people who understand the buyers. There are many opportunities in sales."
«16»
Details
«17»
In order to work in sales it is necessary for you to do well in school in the following subjects:
«18»
English: In marketing you will interact with people, so it's necessary that you become an expert speaker. This means you will need to speak English fluently.
«19»
Mathematics: It's necessary to know how to calculate expenses for marketing the product and how to set up prices.

Reading 30

Listen Carefully To The Perceptions Of The Nation

This community service to motivate people to build a healthy nation is sponsored by: BP[16]; Old Mutual; AIDS Helpline; European Union
AIDS In Our Community
This pamphlet was made possible by a grant from BP.
When do you start getting sick?

[16] "BP" stands for British Petroleum.

It can make you sick many years after being infected with HIV. When you have become sick, that shows that you have AIDS.

Early signs that you have AIDS

You will have some of these symptoms when you start to develop AIDS:

- weight loss
- swelling of the throat, behind the ears, in the armpits, and on the palms.
- open sores on the lips
- rash—white rash on the mouth or the genitals
- signs that you have TB—difficulty in breathing (coughing); sweating and weight loss
- painful sores and rash
- stuffiness and night sweating
- open sores on the genitals
- continuous throbbing

ADVANCED SYMPTOMS OF AIDS

If you have some of these symptoms, then AIDS has really taken hold of you:

- TB
- pneumonia
- painful rash
- sores on the hands and feet
- frequent fatigue
- blue and green lesions on your skin
- significant weight loss
- headache, fits, blackouts, memory loss, inability to concentrate

MEANS OF PREVENTING AIDS:

PROTECTED SEXUAL ENCOUNTERS

The sex act is protected when a man uses a condom

It is important to use a condom properly.

It is necessary to use it in this way:

1 - Use a condom whenever you have intercourse

2 - Put the condom on your erect penis before you penetrate your mate. Press the tip of the condom so that all remaining air is released.

3 - Place the condom so that it covers the entire penis. Now you are ready to have intercourse with your mate.

4 - Remove the male genital organ following intercourse. Hold the condom in such a way that when you take it out, it will stay in place. It is necessary to remove it before the penis has become limp.
5 - Now carefully take the condom off the penis. You must not allow semen to leak out of the condom.
6 - Wrap the used condom in paper. Throw it away in the toxic waste bin or in the toilet or wherever children cannot reach it.
Remember!
Look at the expiration date by which the condoms should have been used because old ones are dangerous.
Some people use lubrication along with the condom so that the sex act is easier. You cannot put Vaseline on it because it may destroy the condom—get a proper protective lubricant.

Reading 31

A Word From Our Editor

Arrive Alive! Don't Get Arrested For Drunk Driving!

«1»

It's Christmastime again, which means that many people will die in car accidents. Many of us will display our reckless driving by breaking important traffic laws. This happens every year.

«2»

Many will escape the arm of the law. Others will be arrested and become an example to others that it is not acceptable to disregard the law. We want to advise our readers who drive cars about the recent government campaign called "Arrive Alive." This road safety campaign, which will be enforced in random places without warning, will show no mercy on those who break the law! No one will escape from it, regardless of the car you drive or the social position you occupy. The lawbreakers who are most strongly targeted are those who drink and drive—this can be you, your father, husband, wife, cousin, son, your daughter, or your lover.

«3»

As it is the time for Christmas office parties for many companies closing over the period, beware! After drinking at an office party, in a hotel, or in your favorite shebeen[17] you might lose your way home and encounter a caravan with flashing blue lights next to the road.

---

[17] A "shebeen" is an illegal liquor establishment (shack).

The men and women inside it are doing their job! Don't fool yourself by thinking you will be able to bribe them; when you are found having exceeded the legal limit, you will not only be arrested and required to pay a huge bail bond, but you can also lose your license to drive. Some of us use our licenses daily. So it's better to take care of them rather than to "bellow at the offal." [18]

«4»

If you listen and are prudent, you will not indulge in a great feast where you "eat your stuff."[19] When you know that you are going to drink and you will have to drive afterwards, ask someone who does not drink to drive for you, otherwise you will only remember this warning when you have prisoners' handcuffs on and are locked in a dark cell. You have ears, you are guilty...

«5»

The time to preach has ended. Sister Barbara, where is the bartender? Until next year then, have a good time.

By Daizer Mqhaba

Senior Editor

Reading 32

The Editor's Views

«1»

The Truth Commission will reveal all corruption.

«2»

The creation of the Truth Commission by the national government last week shows that the president of South Africa, Dr. Nelson Mandela, is deeply motivated in his leadership of this country.

«3»

When the Afrikaners arrested Dr. Mandela and other members of the resistance movement of the African National Congress (ANC)—including Mr. Walter Sisulu, Govan Mbeki, Raymond Mhlaba, and other guardians of the struggle to free black people from the oppression of white fellow-travelers[20] under the putrid[21]

[18] The phrase "bellow at the offal" means "flog a dead horse; rant and rave over something that you cannot change."

[19] The phrase "eat your stuff" means "drink too much."

[20] This refers to the perception (probably correct) that most whites were happy to enjoy the fruits of Apartheid, whether they supported the Afrikaner government or not.

laws of the discriminatory policy called Apartheid—white South Africans never raised any questions, especially not of John Vorster and Verwoerd, the generals and creators of Apartheid.

«4»

They thought that these ruffians would die without liberating this country and its oppressed people whose hands and legs were tied by the laws of Afrikaners protecting the purity of color and the progeny of Van Riebeeck, the father of destitute European wanderers who claimed the soil of Africa when they arrived in this country armed and forcibly took the land from the kings of the black people and from the high-ranking councilors of Phalo, siKhukhuni, and Cetywayo, as well as Lobengula and Mzilikazi.[22]

«5»

This commission will expose the shameless conduct maliciously carried out by the heavy-bearded bandits[23] who killed African patriots such as Steve Biko, Looksmart Solwandle Ngudle, Matthews Goniwe, Fort Calata, Sparrow Mhonto, Griffiths Mxenge, Victoria Mxenge, Bathandwa Ndondo, Atwell Maqekeza, Joe Gqabi, Hector Peterson, and many more of the valiant men and women of our nation.[24]

«6»

The commission's investigative team has seventeen members, comprising the top legal experts of this country, and was given a message by the President not to leave any stone unturned, not even a small piece of undisclosed truth so that the nation may learn of the atrocities carried out when Apartheid was in force in South Africa.

«7»

Fortunately, President Mandela selected a highly experienced African expert known for his stubborn opposition to Apartheid who talked persuasively to people in lengthy arguments, crying all over the land at a time when the (African) leaders of this country,

---

[21] Literally, "skunk-smelling."

[22] These are the black kings/chiefs from whom the whites took the land when they came to South Africa.

[23] The phrase "heavy-bearded bandits" is an allusion to the stereotypical Dutch settler of the seventeenth century, perpetuated in the appearance of more extreme thinkers today.

[24] These are people who dedicated their lives to the struggle.

including President Mandela, were in jail, sentenced for life on Robben Island. It is Bishop of the Anglican Church, His Grace Desmond Mpilo Tutu, who is nominated to be the chairman of the Truth Commission.

«8»

And now, those who perpetrated those deeds are trembling with fear, their wide trousers flapping around their knees and ankles because the dwarf is relentlessly coming out from the reeds;[25] they will be exposed and forced to talk about their shameless conduct in persecuting the people.

«9»

Today, we take off our hats to Madiba[26] for establishing this commission. The shameful acts that were done to the children of Africa will be exposed: they were killed in an attempt to reduce their numbers, they were prevented from liberating their country, and they were conquered by the Afrikaners with the power of their forefathers' guns.

«10»

We wish you victory as you claim your birthright as the son of Mandela, of Dalindyebo of Ngangelizwe.

Reading 33

Is Takalani Going To Be An Olympic Star?

«0»

The majority of young girls these days choose to become singers or to enter beauty pageants. Takalani Rachel "Mosquito" Nthulani is serious about running in the Olympic Games.

«1»

Seventeen-year-old Takalani has been an excellent runner since primary school.

«2»

"I had only been running for a little while when I caused a bit of a sensation with my running successes in primary school. But it was in 1995 when I really started to establish myself as a runner after being encouraged by my parents, teachers, and friends.

[25] This refers to the myth of the river dwarf supposed to carry off children.

[26] The tribal name for Mandela (see note 1).

«3»
"I won at Vaal Triangle in the Emfuleni 15 km with a time of only 59 minutes—I passed in front of runners such as Lydia Mofula and Sarah Jane. That race opened doors for me."
«4»
Takalani, this exceptional runner, successfully represented her school in the 800 m and 1,500 m Usasa race and at Cape Town, which included other (schools) in the region. She broke the record when she beat several runners in the 800 m and finished third place in the 1,500 m.
«5»
She won in the 3,000 m at the South African Championships in Secunda, running to set a new record of 8 minutes and 30 seconds. In that race she overtook the well known runner, Rene Kalmer.
«6»
"I represented South Africa in the World Cross Country in Italy where I finished in 62nd place. I ran with 100 famous runners from various countries of the world. I learned a lot in that race. You know, when I run now I really use the skills I learned there."
«7»
She was once again in the news after she won the bronze medal at the South African championships. But she showed her rare gift when she won the silver medal in the 5,000 m for women in the Regional Championships in Durban. Her time was 18 minutes and 20 seconds. Eleven African nations participated in that race. She came in first in the 1,500 m with a time of 4 minutes and 48 seconds.
«8»
A friend running in (the race) introduced her to her trainer, George Sebiloane, of the Vosloorus Athletic Club.
«9»
"Although we do not have any standard training equipment, a few of the 40 runners are training at the open-air sports ground in Zone 7 in Mailula, Voslorus. As for me, I always believe that whenever you have a natural ability, there is nothing to stand in your way. But I always pray that we will find the financial support to help runners who are still in the development stage," explained the former runner turned trainer.

«10»
"I think that whenever we have training facilities comparable to those of our competitors, I can reach my goal. Some people have already been supporters, but I need to run in a few races in order to get new shoes for training or running at competitions," explained Takalani.
«11»
"I have a lot of trophies and cups. There is nothing to prevent me from fulfilling my wish of representing this country at the 2004 Olympics. I am hopeful that I will be successful there."

Reading 34
Your Future Told By The Stars

«1»
Aries March 21–April 21
This is a good time to throw out your old ideas and start afresh with renewed vigor on life's journey. You are going to be pleasantly surprised at the strength of purpose you discover within yourself. Begin now.
LUCKY ELEMENTS: the color orange, the numbers 2 & 8, the letters K & V.
«2»
Taurus
April 21–May 21
Take firm steps to take care of yourself and stay in perfectly good health. Spend time making sure that you eat well. Maintain good habits so that you may build your mind, your opinions, and the general condition of your body.
LUCKY ELEMENTS: the color green, the numbers 3 & 9, the letters L & W.
«3»
Gemini
May 21–June 22
This period requires that you work together to arrive at an important destination, bringing together the thoughts and knowledge of friends who work with you by sharing their ideas and their aspirations. Collective opinions do not fail.

LUCKY ELEMENTS: the color blue, the numbers 1 & 4, the letters M & X.

«4»

Cancer

June 22–July 23

It's a good time to start or to continue forward on a confrontational journey. Communication can improve while there is an air of understanding. Search for certain rights and privileges.

LUCKY ELEMENTS: the color red, the numbers 2 & 5, the letters N & Y.

«5»

Leo

July 23–Aug 24

Be serious about ensuring that your future is protected. Your life depends on your being an independent person. So it's necessary to work toward that objective by chasing useful goals.

LUCKY ELEMENTS: the color gray (dust), the numbers 3 & 6, the letters O & Z.

«6»

Virgo

Aug 24–Sep 23

If you have a gift for business, this is the time to reveal it in public. It is time to renew your hopes. You will help yourself if you make use of your attractiveness. You need to acquire the respect of the business sector.

LUCKY ELEMENTS: the color brown, the numbers 4 & 7, the letters A & P.

«7»

Libra

Sept 23–Oct 23

Advice coming from a close, wise friend can get you back on track. Establishing yourself and working together is a good combination, so meet with others and your future reward will multiply over and over again.

LUCKY ELEMENTS: the color violet, the numbers 5 & 8, the letters B & Q.

«8»
Scorpio
Oct 23–Nov 23
You are confident and reliable now. You know how to make proposals openly and, above all, skillfully without revealing your secret arsenal. Now is the perfect time to build a friendship.
LUCKY ELEMENTS: the color dark brown, the numbers 6 & 9, the letters C & R.
«9»
Sagittarius
Nov 23–Dec 22
Using your personality as a key to your progress in this world, move ahead confidently so that you get results. Be totally committed, forcing yourself to develop your fortune.
LUCKY ELEMENTS: the color yellow, the numbers 1 & 7, the letters D & S.
«10»
Capricorn
Dec 22–Jan 21
It's time to be sure that you are working in ways that produce substantial rewards. That's because during this time your money will multiply greatly. Increased wealth is most desirable.
LUCKY ELEMENTS: the color orange, the numbers 2 & 8, the letters E & T.
«11»
Aquarius
Jan 21–Feb 20
You are observant and vigilant now, you know how to speak in a certain way, so unharness your mind and explore it freely so that it can move forward.
LUCKY ELEMENTS: the color white, the numbers 3 & 9, the letters F & U.
«12»
Pisces
Feb 20–Mar 21
Your love of your family is apparent now, and because you are kind and of a peaceful disposition, your fellowship inside the home will

be increased greatly now. Your influence is going to help your relatives do well in life.
LUCKY ELEMENTS: the color black, the numbers 1 & 4, the letters G & V.

Reading 35
Handicapped Are Given A Subsidy For Their Center

«1»
In an ideal world, everyone receives equal treatment and enjoys equal rights. In place of this ideal, however, able-bodied people, despite their pity for the disabled, are unconcerned about, don't give extended care to, and even neglect many disabled children and adults. It's not like that at the Letaba After-Care Center.
«2»
The Dutch Reformed Church established the Letaba After-Care Center in 1969 to care for homeless disabled people. Now, after 30 years, this center has more than 70 people between the ages of 16 and 63. This non-governmental center (NGO) now obtains a monthly subsidy from the government.
«3»
This place, 20 kilometers outside of Tzaneen in the Northern Province, is home to people who come from places as far away as Cape Town; it provides food, a place to live, and hiring and training for potentially lucrative jobs.
«4»
Although this center receives a subsidy from the government, the coordinator, Regina Hlomela, still finds it necessary to try to obtain additional funds for purchasing food, for cleaning, and for paying the wages of the people who work there.
«5»
Handicrafts such as ornamental rush basket pots are sold to nearby business owners who are requested to join in collecting money from the community. These efforts, however, are not enough to reduce the expenses of keeping this center operating or expanding because it already faces the difficulty of lack of space.
«6»
The hall is used as a place for making handicrafts. Two other buildings are used as housing for men and women; in each individual

room there are between four and twenty beds. The majority of the beds are made of steel with thin mattresses and old blankets (small blankets). Lockers made of zinc (or tin) are used for individuals' property and clothes.

«7»

The Phalaborwa mining company has just made a gift of 24 new beds, bedclothes, and some wardrobes[27] but not everyone was able to receive these gifts. Last winter three people suffered pneumonia because of the cold.

«8»

Washing facilities are combined with the toilets that stand open in each hostel.

«9»

The staff of the Letaba After-Care Center are registered at the Northern Training Trust where they are taught skills they can use in the center. The payment for this training is provided by the center. A project to make bricks was started, but it ended when the machine broke and there wasn't enough money to repair it.

«10»

Parents and neighbors are encouraged to join in the work of the center. Three people work as volunteers to help relieve the shortage of workers.

«11»

The larger community in this area probably does not know the center exists, said Regina. They do not bother even to come and look at what is going on here. Other residents were surprised when they saw disabled people for the first time at another demonstration for raising pocket-money.

«12»

The scarcity of money makes budgeting for the future of the center difficult. Since the beginning, its purpose has been to look after disabled people by providing them a place where they can be sheltered, fed, and given enough training to return again to society. Regina explained that, "By the year 2000, they want to see the Letaba After-Care Center become a center for training all the disabled people of the Northern Province.

[27] Self-standing cupboards for hanging clothes.

«13»
"It is necessary to have a new center where we can keep 250 disabled people who would be given training only. Upon graduating from there they will be able to start projects of their own or find employment in places of business."
«14»
The message coming from the Letaba After-Care Center is that if disabled people are empowered through training, they will have the opportunity to join in the national economy.
«15»
There are many organizations with problems similar to the Letaba After-Care Center. Asking for help from business owners and society is not enough. All residents should help bear the burden of subsidizing society's disabled family members. Joining in the work at centers similar to the Letaba After-Care Center is a good start. Making it a success and allowing it to stand on its own requires the contributions of business owners, the government, and the community.

Reading 36
Men Who Rape Men

«0»
Although South African law describes rape as "unlawful sexual intercourse with a woman," there are who men get raped, as Primrose Williams found out.
«1»
Vuma (whose real name we haven't used) was in jail for the first time. He was very scared when he thought of those dreadful stories which he always used to hear about life in jails. He prayed silently within himself asking for protection. Despite praying hard, one of the things that happened to him was more frightening than he ever imagined, and it happened on his first night in jail.
«2»
This horrible event, which has deeply affected Vuma's life, started as soon as he was locked up in the jail cell. His cellmates, all of whom were members of the "28s",[28] regarded him as an easy target

[28] The "28s" are one of many prison gangs.

because he was still a youngster according to the "laws" of the prison.
«3»
Vuma tried to hold back his tears, but there was no doubt about the pain in his voice when he described how his cellmates took turns raping him.
«4»
According to one sex therapist, rape is the most painful thing that can ever happen to men. "Besides the psychological trauma, the body experiences great physical pain because men are not created to be penetrated sexually," this expert explained.
«5»
"I got very angry, I shook with fear, and I became overcome by grief because there was nothing I could do to stop what they were doing to me," Vuma said. "I am docile by nature, but I was confronted by these experienced gangsters. I knew that apart from anything else I am not the kind of guy who knows how to fight. I shriveled up with fear.
«6»
"The pain was unbearable. I thought that maybe these violent people would stop when they saw I was bleeding, but did they ever let me be? They continued and laughed a lot; they said a calf is startled by the first sight of the tether. In fact, they made an emphatic point of informing me that I would enjoy it next time when I got used to it!"
«7»
Vuma said this became a nightly event. They threatened that they would inflict a painful revenge upon him if he reported this matter to the authorities. But the firebrand returns with the lamplighter[29]: the prison authorities took his blood for testing and it was found to be HIV positive, he explained to us.
«8»
Although it is usually women and girls who get raped, even men do. According to the people at Life Line, "It is now almost commonplace for men to be raped in jail. In addition to it happening there, they also get raped whenever they live in places of residence where there are no women."

[29] This is similar to the English phrase, "what goes around, comes around."

«9»
The abuse of boys is found in several kinds of residential situations, such as military barracks, bachelor quarters, situations where only males are gathered, and camps. It is said that for males to sleep together, or to put the male organ in another's mouth, is commonplace amongst the youth of the surrounding areas.
«10»
"The sexual abuse of boys usually occurs in homes and is often carried out by fathers, grandfathers, elder brothers, cousins, uncles, or other relatives of the family. Young boys who run away from home also run into this danger.
«11»
"Then again, there are places or situations which are dangerous for young men and women," Life Line explains. "These include going to nightclubs, asking for lifts in strangers' cars, walking alone in places where there are not many people, and even using public toilets, just to mention a few," they concluded.
«12»
According to Life Line, "Many men who get raped do not take any preventative steps because they do not expect to receive sympathy from anybody, not even from the authorities. Due to the fact that men are considered to be strong and able to protect themselves, men can suffer the misfortune of not being taken seriously if they report the problem of having been raped. Many people engaged in health work do not realize that men can be subjected to sexual violence.
«13»
"Men do not like to talk freely about such 'sexual' matters. Most people regard a man's being raped as a disgrace for that man. Men avoid reporting being raped because they think that they will be considered homosexual."
«14»
Another reason that makes men hesitant, it was suggested by officials, is that, according to the law, only women can be raped. Rape is a crime committed by a MAN against a WOMAN. A man does not get charged with having raped another man, even though he can be charged with felonies such as unnatural acts, i.e., sodomy or sexual injury, under the Sexual Offences Act.

«15»
By way of example, in 1995 the Child Protection Unit handled more than 8,992 cases involving the rape of women under the age of 18. However, only about 600 cases concerning boys under 18 involved in sleeping with men were processed.
«16»
In reality, what causes a man to rape another? Also, what kind of man is exposed to the danger of being raped?
«17»
Dr. Irma Labuschagne, who is a forensic criminologist, explained it thus: "The evildoers are not driven by lust alone. Men inflict sexual pain upon other men (in jail or on the outside) because they want to alleviate their own pain or show their superiority."
«18»
It's not a conscious act that they find themselves attracted to men. For example, a number of men refuse to be frightened off by gay people.[30] It is not done out of lust, but as a means of expressing discontent or anger.
«19»
In prison, men get raped for a number of reasons: for instance, when a person who has been sentenced for indecent assault or rape of a child, he is raped "to put him in the same position"; similarly, others are ambushed to "show them how it is." I have heard from some of them that it is a common thing to "initiate" new prisoners by raping them.
«20»
"Some men lead a gay lifestyle because they want to satisfy their sexual urges. These men, even upon their release from jail, return to living with women. Indeed, a person should fear that AIDS may increase a great deal in jails.
«21»
"There are men who have been raped by others outside of jail. They are people with wounded spirits. I have tried to help men who have been abused in this way. ANY MAN AT ALL can be prey to this, but gay men are those most likely to be affected."

---

[30] A more literal way of saying "refuse to be frightened off by gay people" would be "are content to be unperturbed by the 'brother-sister' scene."

«22»
It is said of men that being raped is the beginning of a long and heavy struggle. Victims fear for themselves and are consumed by feelings of guilt and sorrow. "People believe that a woman may show fear easily, but men—'true' men—are supposed to be able to protect themselves. That is why a male victim sees himself as less than whole."
«23»
Dr. Labuschagne testifies to this and warns that men who have undergone this tragedy really need help to be able to handle the consequences of their rape. "Much can be done to determine whether the trauma will consume a large or small portion of their lives. Their suffering is more than that which a woman feels. Men feel like dirt after this. Their faith in human nature is lost, they see these things as dirty, and they are consumed by their consciences.
«24»
"Unless this kind of man seeks professional support, he will never forget this incident for the rest of his life. It is necessary for men to be helped by explaining broadly that it is no disgrace to ask for help. The time has now come for people to understand that these are genuine problems which can negatively affect peoples' lives." The Rape Crisis Service administered by Life Line is there to support men who are victims.
«25»
Contrary to popular belief, the good news from Dr. Labuschange is that there is no evidence "that those who have been used like a woman will become attracted to other men—there's just no truth in it."
«26»
"The thing that I have found is that victims will be apprehensive about their shortcomings. At some point they have problems in being able to have sex with women as adults, but this does not mean they are gay," he concluded.

Reading 37
The New Language Board
All of Us Can Benefit

«1»

The new South African constitution has paved the way for establishing a number of organizations to examine, promote, and respect the rights of all citizens. "PANSALB" is one of these organizations. Noxolo Mgudlwa sheds some light about the purpose and aims of this language organization and its accessibility to previously disadvantaged communities.

«2»

"PANSALB" is an independent organization established by parliament that reports to the House of Representatives. This means that it is not directly ruled by the government or any one particular cabinet minister. This organization was established to be the eyes of the government and has the responsibility of improving and preserving South Africa's languages, as set out in section three of the new constitution.

«3»

Those languages which are emphasized are South Africa's official languages, as identified below:

«4»

Afrikaans, English, Ndebele, Northern Sotho, Sotho, Swazi, Tsonga, Tswana, Venda, Xhosa, and Zulu, together with any other languages which are not mentioned here and which are in need of promotion.

«5»

The PANSALB draft bill was passed by parliament. Many different individuals and organizations involved in languages took part by raising issues and expressing opinions on the proposed draft bill. The eventual passing of the bill into law could thus be said to have been influenced by these groups and organizations. That which follows is an outline of the issues raised by the NLP[31] and which still need to be addressed even though the bill has been passed by parliament.

«6»

The NLP, along with other language and cultural organizations, spoke out about the passing of the amended bill to establish the

[31] NLP is the acronym for the National Language Project.

board. Issues which have been examined by the NLP are referred to in the following paragraphs:
«7»
The NLP strongly supports the concept of the PANSALB for its potential contribution in carrying out investigations, but it is important to know how this will be handled. There are two aspects we want the board to watch for and to discuss in connection with their report. The first thing is to know how the public will be informed about or have access to the board.
«8»
The second is how it will achieve the improvement of and respect for languages, particularly African languages and languages which have historically been disregarded.
«9»
HOW WILL COMMUNITIES BE ABLE TO REACH PANSALB?
«10»
In the past, existing organizations were unknown to the members of disadvantaged communities. There was no way for these people to contact these organizations. It was not considered necessary to interest anyone other than educated people who were university professors. The organizations reached conclusions without ever investigating whether the words in question were actually used by the communities under consideration. It is therefore of utmost importance that this not happen again.
«11»
It is clear from how this document is written that the people who would know about and make use of this board are from the upper classes and are familiar with the present South African constitution. We do not believe that teachers themselves are really familiar with this board and would be able to utilize its facilities.
«12»
According to Athalie Crawford's research on the hospitals of the Cape, one of the things that became obvious was that people who never complained about problems of language usage in hospitals were from the lower classes. Many of those people came from rural areas. Be that as it may, it was quite clear that they did not communicate well with either doctors or nurses because of an

inability to understand the language they were using. What does this tell us about the language needs of the people?

«13»

Many public places that are used by the elderly and the lower classes, namely banks, hospitals, shops, government offices, etc., are still staffed by people who are not familiar with the languages spoken by the majority of people who utilize these facilities, making it difficult for the people to use them. Of these facilities mentioned above, many do not offer full services to people of low socioeconomic status.

«14»

For example, the government offices at Nyanga do not issue international passports, forcing one to travel to the city to receive this service, which is another way that the situation is made difficult for those people to use the facilities. Every day it is found that due to mistakes connected with hospitals, banks, and so on, there will be communication problems which will lead to improperly completed work or wasted money.

«15»

For example, you will find that people end up making frequent trips to the hospitals because they say the doctor never helps them, or else they often change doctors; many times this happens when people do not properly follow doctor's instructions or when they inaccurately explain the nature of the trouble to the doctor such that the treatment he offers is unrelated to the sickness of the patient.

«16»

Thus, it is necessary for the board to try to do everything in its power to help these people by giving organizations such as NLP and others the authority to investigate ways to resolve these problems. Many investigations need to be carried out to ensure that the language rights of the people are brought to the fore. It is important that the board work together closely with those peoples' organizations that work directly with the people and their needs. Thus, there can be assurance that many of the services will be more helpful and that the community will have the knowledge to utilize these services in the most effective way.

«17»

I want to emphasize again that the board will merely resemble its predecessors if it does not reach out to disadvantaged and suppressed people and uplift the standard of the various languages. Thus, it is necessary for the board to ensure that it opens opportunities for people to learn how to use and approach it. It is important that it takes the initiative to enlighten people about its helpful services and not leave it to the people to create a desire for such services. It is necessary for the board to be seen as leading the people by advising them how to improve their standard of living, going among the people, and finding out their wants all the time. This will ensure that all its actions have the support of the people and are driven by the people themselves.

«18»

THE UPLIFTING OF LANGUAGES.

«19»

It is important that the board (PANSALB) thoroughly explains the ways the languages will be promoted and the role that this organization will play in such a promotion. There is one thing which has not been clarified in this lengthy document, and that is what the board means when it talks about "uplifting languages." In the past, people who speak these (indigenous) languages never had the opportunity to, nor the knowledge of how to, have a share in the vocabulary-building process of these languages. This has resulted in the marginalization of these languages today; consequently, they have not been included as languages of instruction in subjects such as Mathematics, Science, History, etc.

«20»

One final thing that will promote the foundations of these languages, if they are used, will be to compile vocabularies of words used by the people, and not those words perceived by previous boards, which will begin to show how these vocabularies may be effectively used.

If that objective is to be met, it will be necessary for the board to work together with the communities in studying and building these vocabularies of the various languages so that it works to the maximum advantage in promoting the acceptability of its tasks in this regard. This will come about if those people with knowledge of their language allow themselves a voice.

«21»
The board should be careful not to continue introducing words which are unknown to the people and bringing into use words they do not understand.
«22»
Therefore, it requires the input of all concerned parties to make this project successful.
«23»
THE OPINIONS OF THE PEOPLE
«24»
Another thing which is important to clear up is that, as I have said before, many different people who take up a share of the participation on the board, like young people and teachers, parents and schoolchildren, were not there (in the early stages) to hear about or to give their views on the formation of such a board.
«25»
It became clear to the people who were there, especially those people in the lower classes, that they were not made aware of the existence of the board (PANSALB) and how they could make use of and benefit by such an organization.
«26»
Another aspect which was noted by those in authority is the role of women's organizations and other groups which should be informed of and make use of the board. Assurance should be given that corruption will come to an end because this board's aims are not replicas of its predecessors' failures.
«27»
Noxolo Mgudlwa works for the National Language Project in the Cape region. She is the chairperson of the Democratic Language Policy. She is also the author of "Sincokola ngesiXhosa" ("Beginner's Conversational Xhosa".)

Lexicon

#[1] *change* loss (elision) of -A before another A • *babanye 'of individuals' [= ba-(a)-ba-nye], ngabantu 'by people' [= ng(a)-aba-ntu]* CGB:119; 120, PCX:192, R11

#[2] *change* zero (loss of noun group article after E- locative prefix) R2=5, R4c, R6, R9=3

#[3] *change* zero (loss of -A or -E before suffix -ENI) PCX:68, R9, R11

#[4] *change* zero (loss of final vowel of a prefix before vowel-initial root) • *zizangqa 'they are circles' [= ziz(i)-angqa]* R8

#[5] *change* loss of -I before another vowel • *Ndazi 'I know' [= nd(i)-azi]; ndonwaba 'I am happy' [= nd(i)-onwab-a]; naakha 'you built' [= n(i)-a-akha]* CGB:119, PCX:192

#[6] *change* loss of N before H, L, M, N, NY, R • *inyama 'meat' (= in-nyama)* E&S:51

#[7] *n1a-pl-red-prf* [group 1a plural reduced noun prefix] • *aba NoBible 'these Bible holders'* Loss of prefix oo- R5

-[8] *n1a-sg-voc-prf* oh!, hey! [group 1 singular vocative noun prefix] • *bawo 'father!', mama 'mother!'* Agr: u- AXG:28, E&S:32

-[9] *n3-pl-them* [group 3 plural zero thematic consonant prefix] ☞ See: onke R1=2

#[10] *n5-sg-red-prf* [group 5 singular reduced noun prefix] • *ngale bhodi 'through this board', ingxowa-mali 'funds' [= ingxowa-(i)mali]* Loss of prefix i- R9=2, R37=20

A

a-[1] *emph-prf* [emphatic formative before noun groups starting with a] ☞ See: abona, awona TD, R3

-**a**[2] *n-suf* [noun-forming suffix] • *impela 'end', igqwetha 'lawyer', umhlaba 'earth'* R1, R3=2, R4c

a-[3] *n1-sg-S3a* (and) he, she VERBs [group 1, 1a singular present subjunctive verb subject (S3a) agreement prefix] CGB:167, R4c=2, R4d, R9, R10, R14

a-[4] *n1-sg-S4* he can VERB; she may VERB [group 1, 1a singular potential / conditional verb subject (S4) agreement prefix] • *UFani angayipheka inyama 'Fani can cook the meat'* E&S:45, PCX:165f, SXWU:149, R4c

a-[5] *n1-sg-ind-rel1* whom, which [group 1, 1a singular indirect relative 1 agreement prefix] E&S:35, SXWU:165, R6, R9, R33

a-[6] *n1-sg-ind-rel2* whom, which [group 1, 1a singular indirect relative 2 agreement prefix] E&S:35

a-[7] *n3-pl-poss* of [group 3 plural possessive agreement prefix] Agr: ama- AM-94:163, E&S:22, SXWU:35f, XED:xv; 1, R1, R4b, R14, R16

a-[8] *n3-pl-S1* they [group 3 plural subject (S1) agreement prefix] Agr: ama- CGB:117; 158, E&S:17f, PCX:51, SXWU:28, XED:1, R2, R12

a-[9] *n3-pl-S3a* (and) they VERB [group 3 plural present subjunctive verb subject (S3a) agreement prefix] CGB:167, R2, R8

a-[10] *n3-pl-S3b-pos* (and) they VERBed [group 3 plural past subjunctive positive verb subject (S3b) agreement prefix] (CGB:189), E&S:42, MI:247, SXWU:141

a-[11] *n3-pl-rel1* they who / those which [group 3 plural direct relative 1 attributive agreement prefix positive or negative construction] CGB:174, E&S:23; 28; 34, MI:153; 248, SXWU:155, XED:xv, R1, R4b, R9, R10, R12=2, R14, R36.0

a-[12] *n3-pl-rel2* they who / those which [group 3 plural direct relative 2 construction, attributive agreement prefix used predicatively] E&S:34, MI:153; 248, PCX:151, R1

a-[13] *n3-pl-ind-rel1* whom, which [group 3 plural indirect relative 1 agreement prefix] E&S:35

a-[14] *n3-pl-ind-rel2* whom, which [group 3 plural indirect relative 2 agreement prefix] E&S:35

a-[15] *poss-pro-prf* [possessive pronoun formative before noun groups starting with a] ☞ See: abam SXWU:84

a-[16] *pro-3sg-S3a* (and) he, she VERBs [S3a present subjunctive subject pronoun] CGB:167

a-[17] *v-prf-neg-pres* not [negative present verb prefix] • *Andifuni 'I don't want'* ☞ See also: aka-, aku-, awu-, ayi- CGB:124, E&S:18, PCX:36f, XED:1, R2

-a[18] *v-pres-short* VERBs, is VERBing [short indicative present tense verb construction] • *Irayisi ikunika amandla 'Rice gives you strength'* Structure: S1-#-Δ-a; used when an object and/or an adverb follow the verb CGB:122f, E&S:18, PCX:27, R1=3, R2=4, R3, R4a=3, R4c, R4d=4, R5, R6, R9=6, R12=3

-a[19] *v-suf-pres-long* [long present tense verb suffix, used in conjunction with -ya-] Structure: S1-ya-Δ-a ☞ See: -ya- -a CGB:122f, E&S:17, PCX:30, R11=3

-a[20] *v-suf* VERBing [present tense participial construction] R1, R2=3, R3, R4b, R4d, R6, R7, R9, R12=2, R33, R36

-a[21] *v-suf-pos-past-sub* did VERB, had VERBED [remote past / past subjunctive positive verb suffix] • *Ndabanjwa ngoJuni 'I was arrested in June'; bandiphoxa 'they have made a fool of me'* ☞ Neg: S3b Δ-anga CGB:189, R4a, R4c

-a[22] *v-suf-imp-sg* do VERB! [positive imperative singular verb suffix] • *Qhotsa inyama 'Fry the meat!'* Structure: #-Δ-a ☞ -a is also found as a general suffix for the Indicactive mood present tense, and the Infinitive mood. PCX:22, R6, R7=2, R8=6, R11, R12

-a[23] *v-inf-pos-suf* to VERB; VERBing [positive infinitive / gerund verb suffix] ☞ See: uku-Δ-a CGB:121, PCX:20, R4b=4, R4c=3, R5, R6, R7=2, R10=2

-a[24] *v-suf* can / may VERB [present tense positive potential / conditional construction] R4c, R7

a- -a *v-suf-neg-pres-pass* is not VERBed [negative present tense passive verb construction] • *Imfundo ayinyanzelwa ngumthetho eMzantsi-Afrika 'Education is not compulsory in South Africa'* Structure: a-SNEG-Δ-w-a (note -a and not -i negative suffix) CGB:188, R10=2

a- -i *v-suf-neg-pres* do(es) not VERB [negative present tense active verb construction] • *Andiseli 'I don't drink'* Structure: a-SNEG-Δ-i [if an OBJ follows, it loses its initial vowel]; Note: the negative subject pronoun undergoes several changes; this negates both the long and short present tense constructions ☞ See: aka-, aku-, awu-, ayi- AM-94:120, AXG:103, CGB:124; 127, E&S:18, PCX:36f, R2, R4c=2

a- ka- -i *v-neg-punc* not yet [negative punctual aspect verb construction in independent clause] • *Andikafundi 'I haven't studied yet'* Structure: a-SNEG-ka-Δ-i CGB:127, PCX:83f

a- -sa- -i *v-neg-prog* no longer, not anymore [negative progressive aspect verb construction] • *Inja ayisabaleki 'The dog is not running anymore'* Structure: a-SNEG-sa-Δ-i CGB:127

-a-ku- *v-temp-pos-prf* when SUBJECT VERBs / VERBed [positive temporal verb construction] • *Zakufika kweli 'Upon their arrival here...'; Akufika umqhubi ekhaya 'When the driver* *arrived home...'* Structure: THEM-a-Δ-a (if a subject is stated, it follows the verb) E&S:42, PCX:91f, R32

-a-ku-nga- *v-temp-neg-prf* when SUBJECT does not VERB / did not VERB [negative temporal verb construction] • *Akungafiki 'When he didn't arrive...'* Structure: THEM-a-nga-Δ-i (if a subject is stated, it follows the verb) E&S:42, PCX:91f

aa *change* loss (elision) of -A before AA- • *baakha 'they built' [= b(a)-a-akha]* PCX:192

aAfrika *n3-pl-poss-n5-sg* of Africa • *yaseMzantsi aAfrika 'of South of Africa'* poss formative for n3-pl (amazantsi) + Afrika (proper noun) ☞ Cf: UMzantsi-Afrika 'South Africa' R16

ab-[1] *n1-pl-red-prf* [reduced form of group 1 (Bantu class 2) plural noun prefix before vowel-inital root] • *abakhi 'builders', abenzi 'doers', abongikazi 'nurses'* ☞ Sg: um-; See: aba- AXG:17, PCX:52, R3

ab-[2] *neg-pres-n1-pl-prf* they do not VERB [group 1 plural negative present subject prefix before vowel-initial verb] • *abazi 'they do not know'* ☞ See: a- ba- -i R9

aba-[1] *n1-pl-prf* [group 1 (Bantu class 2) plural noun prefix] • *abantu 'people'* Consists of article a- + classifier ba- ☞ Sg: um- AXG:17, E&S:17, PCX:51f;23f, RD-96:372, SXWU:15, XED:1, R2, R3, R9=5, R11, R14=4

aba-[2] *n1-pl-adj* [group 1, 1a plural adjective agreement prefix] CGB:172; 174, E&S:28, MI:248, XED:xv, R3, R6, R11, R37

aba-[3] *n1-pl-rel1* they who [group 1, 1a plural direct relative 1 attributive agreement prefix positive or negative construction] CGB:174, E&S:23; 28; 34, MI:153; 248, SXWU:155, XED:xv; 1, R2=2, R3, R5, R9, R11=2

aba-[4] *pro-3pl-dir-rel1* they who [direct relative 1] without antecedent MI:248, XED:xvi, R4c

aba-[5] *n1-pl-ind-rel1* whom, which [group 1, 1a plural indirect relative 1 agreement prefix] E&S:35

aba-[6] *neg-pres-n1-pl-prf* they do not VERB [group 1 plural negative present subject prefix] ☞ See: a- ba- -i AM-94:163, CGB:124; 127, E&S:18, MI:247, PCX:40, SXWU:28, R9

aba-[7] *n1-pl-S3b-neg* (and) they did not VERB [group 1, 1a plural past subjunctive negative verb subject (S3b) agreement prefix] E&S:42, SXWU:141

aba-[8] *n7-S3b-neg* (and) it did not VERB [group 7 singular past subjunctive negative verb subject (S3b) agreement prefix] E&S:42, SXWU:141

aba[9] *deic-1-n1-pl* these; those (known or recently referred to) Agr: aba- ☞ Sole form (no alternate) CGB:163, E&S:26, MI:159, PCX:24, SXWU:157, XED:xvi; 1, R5, R20.1, R26.5, R36.21, R37.12.16

-aba[10] *v-tr* distribute, divide, share ☞ Pass: -abiwa EXD:167, RD-96:375, XED:1

aba- -i *n1-pl-doer* -ers, -ors [plural doer noun circumfix] • *ababulali 'murderers', abazali 'parents'* ☞ Red: ab-, as in abongikazi 'nurses' R2, R3=2, R11

abaa *deic-3-n1-pl* those (far, yonder) Agr: aba- ☞ Alt: abaya CGB:163, E&S:26, MI:160, SXWU:157, XED:xvi

ababa- *n1-pl-adj-neg-pred* they are not ADJ [group 1, 1a plural negative adjective agreement prefix used predicatively] • *ababade 'they are not tall'* E&S:28

ababaphatha *v-pres-rel* who handle them R9

ababaqondayo *v-rel-pres-n1-pl-rel-n1-pl-obj* who understand them R29.15

ababebotshiwe *v-rel-pass* who were tied R32.4

ababecinezelwe *v-rel-pass* who were oppressed R32.3

ababekho *v-rel-n1-pl* who were there R37.23

ababetshintshisana *v-rel-aux-redupl-recip* they were exchanging R36.3

ababhinqileyo *v-rel-perf* women, females [atr] relative verb construction used as noun EXD:731, R36.23

ababhulu *n1-pl* white people (particularly Afrikaners) from R17

ababulali *n1-pl* killers, murderers ☞ Sg: umbulali R11

abacekethekileyo *v-perf-rel* which are thin -cekethek- to become thin, transparent R35.6

abadala *adj-n1-pl* old, aged; adult • *iMfundo noQeqesho Lwabantu Abadala, 'Adult Education and Training'* R22.1, R37.13

abadlwengulwa *v-pass* who get raped R36.8

abafana *n1-pl* young men ☞ Sg: umfana E&S:56, PCX:23, R37.24

abafazi *n1-pl* women; married women, wives ☞ Sg: umfazi CGB:102, E&S:17; 56, PCX:23

abafikeleleli *v-intens* they are not reached out to • *abantu abafikeleleli kuyo 'the people are not reached out to by it'* R37.17

abafumane *v-part* they find participial portion of a negative construct R23.7

abafuna[1] *v-pres-n1-pl* who want, who need R29.11

abafuna[2] *v-neg-pres* they did not want R26.7

abafundi *n1-pl* students, pupils; readers (of a publication) ☞ Sg: umfundi AXG:17, E&S:56, SXWU:15, R22.3, R31.2

abafunekayo *v-rel-atr* who are needed R3

abagogekileyo *v-perf-rel* those who are handicapped or disabled R35=9

abaguquli *n1-pl* translators R3

abahlala *v-rel-intr* (where) they live R27.9

abahlali *n1-pl* residents ☞ Sg: umhlali R26.3.5.7, R27.7, R35.11

abahlobo *n1-pl* friends ☞ Sg: umhlobo Also cf: ihlobo 'summer', uhlobo 'sort, kind' E&S:56, SXWU:15, R14=3

abajongene *v-recip-perf* who are responsible for R29.2

abakho *v-exis-neg-n1-pl* there are none; they are not present / available E&S:29

abakhoyo *rel-n1pl-kho* who are here R37.25

abakhulu *n1-pl-adj* big; old R35.1

abakuhleki *v-tr-neg* they don't laugh at you R14

abakumgangatho *rel-n1pl* who are at a level R37.10.12.13.17

abakuthanda *v-rel* they like you • *...indlela abakuthanda 'the way in which they like you'* aba- is rel.prefix for class1-pl , -ku- is object concord R14

abalambele *v-ben-past* they were hungry for R16

abaleka *v-rel-intr* who is running R33.8

abalimi *n1-pl* farmers ☞ Sg: umlimi E&S:22;56

abalishumi *num* ten R28.2

abaluthethayo *v-rel-pres* what they are saying [lit: that which they are speaking] R37.12

abamalunga *n1-pl-cop-n3-pl* who are members R35.13

abamele *v-perf-rel* who are standing for R37.24

abamenzele *v-tr-ben* they caused him R26.7

abamhlophe *n1-pl* the Whites R32.3

abamsulwa *n1-pl-rel* those who are innocent ☞ Sg: umsulwa; rw: sula R11

abanakuze *v-aux-neg-fut* they will never R26.3

abanakwabo *n1-pl-kin* their brothers (used by women only) ☞ Sg: umnakwabo PCX:116

abanakwenu *n1-pl-kin* your brothers (used by women only) ☞ Sg: umnakwenu PCX:116

abanakwethu *n1-pl-kin* my brothers; our brothers (used by women only) ☞ Sg: umnakwethu PCX:116

abanayo *v-part-n1-pl-SNEG-poss* they not having R10

abancede *v-perf-rel* they help R37.15

abandakanya *v-tr-recip* they unite into, get together in / at R36.9.15

abanemizimba *v-poss-rel-n1-pl-n2-pl-obj* who have bodies R35.1

abanezidanga *v-n1-pl-assoc.cop-n4-pl* who have degrees R29.11

abangabahoyi *v-neg-pres-part* who are not concerned about them R2

abangabaqhubi *rel-cop-n1-pl* those who are drivers R31.2

abangaphantsi *rel-cop-loc* they are down, below, beneath R36.15

abangaphezu *n1-pl-cop-loc* who are over, above R35.2

abangathethi *v-pres-neg-rel* who do not speak R37.13

abangathi *v-pot-rel* who can say; about whom it can be said R37.10.25

abangazange *v-aux-rel* they never R37.12

abangeba- *n1-pl-adj-neg* [group 1, 1a plural negative adjective agreement prefix] • *abangebade 'not tall'* E&S:28

abangenamakhaya *v-poss-rel-n1-pl-neg-n3-pl-obj* the homeless (those who do not have homes) R35.2

abanikwa *v-rel-pass* who are given R35.13

abaninzi *adj-n1-pl* many, plenty XED:104, R31.1.2, R37.24

abanobusebenzisa *n1-pl-pot-v-tr-caus* that they can use R35.9

abantakwethu *n1-pl-kin* our brothers (said by sisters); cousins (where parents are brothers) ☞ Sg: umntakwethu E&S:56, R11x

abantsundu *n1-pl* black people R29.14=3, R32.3

abantu *n1-pl* people; persons • *Into eyenziwa ngabantu. 'A thing which is done by people' ('something people do')* ☞ Sg: umntu CGB:102, PCX:23f, RD-96:375;372, SXWU:15, XED:112, R1, R3, R9, R10, R11=3, R14, R16, R17.3, R20=5, R27=3, R28.5, R29=10, R30.7, R31.1, R33.10, R35=11, R36.13, R37=16

abantwakwabo *n1-pl-cmp* to relatives, family members R35.15

abantwana *n1-pl* children ☞ Sg: umntwana CGB:102, E&S:31, PCX:23, SXWU:15, XED:112, R2=3, R9=5, R12, R24.1, R30.6, R32.9, R35.1

abanye *adj-num-n1-pl* others EXD:425, R3, R6, R10, R30.7, R31.2.3, R33.10, R35.11

abaphangela *v-ben-n1-pl-rel* who work at R35.4

abaphathi *n1-pl* rulers; managers ☞ Sg: umpathi E&S:56, R16

abapheki *n1-pl* cooks ☞ Sg: umpheki CGB:182, E&S:56, SXWU:15

abaphuma *v-rel-intr-n1-pl* who come from R35.3

abaqhuba *v-rel-tr* who are driving R31.2

abaqhubi *n1-pl* drivers ☞ Sg: umqhubi CGB:182, XED:139

abasebenzisa *v-pres-rel* who utilize R37.13.14

abaseBhayi *n5-sg-pn-geog-rel* those who are from Port Elizabeth R4c

abasukela *v-rel-n1-pl* who start from R35.2

abathathu *n1-pl-num-adj* three R35.7.10

abathe *v-aux-perf-rel* who did R5

abathengi *n1-pl* buyers R29.2.15

abathetha *v-pres-rel* they say R37.19

abathi *v-pres-rel* who said • *Abantu abathi bafundile... 'People who call themselves educated.'* R17.1, R37.5.26

abaThwa *n1-pl* San (Xhosa name for the ethnic group) CGB:8

abatshakazi *n1-pl* bridal couple ☞ Sg: umtshakazi (q.v.) AXG:18

abavani *v-pres-neg* they don't hear each other R37.12

abawaphandayo *v-rel* who are investigating R27.11

abaxolisayo *v-caus-rel-n1-pl* who are peaceful Note: -yo relative suffix when no adjunct present R14

abaya *deic-3-n1-pl* those (far, yonder) Agr: aba- ☞ Alt: abaa CGB:163, E&S:26, MI:160, PCX:86, SXWU:157

abayabulayo *v-rel-n1-pl* they who wander R2

abayakuthi *v-fut-rel* who do VERB; who would VERB [fact] R37.11

abaye *rel-pron* who R24.8

abayeni *n1-pl* bridegroom's party; male relatives (by marriage); [ext] associates, boon companions ☞ Sg: umyeni AXG:18, E&S:56, XED:188

abayi *v-aux-neg* they will not • *abayi kukulibala, 'they will not forget you...'* verb 'to come' as aux. forming future tense (near), followed by main verb in infinitive. Object concord 2-pers-sg is present R14

abayithengisayo *v-caus-rel-n1-pl-n5-sg-obj* who are selling it R29.2

abazali *n1-pl* parents no gender distinction implied ☞ Sg: umzali AM-94:108, E&S:56, XED:190, R2, R3, R22.3, R35.10, R37.24

abazange *v-aux-past* they never R32.3

abazi *v-neg-pres* they do not know R9

abazidubi *v-neg-refl-n1-pl* they don't bother themselves R35.11

abazisebenzisayo *v-rel-n1-pl-rel+n5-pl-obj* who use them (languages) R37.13

abe-[1] *n1-pl-ir-prf* [group 1 (Bantu class 2) irregular plural noun prefix before latent i-roots and some consonant stems with u in the first syllable] • *abeLungu 'Whites', abemi 'residents', abeSuthu 'Sotho people'* ☞ Sg: um-; See: aba- AXG:17, PCX:52, SXWU:15

abe[2] *preverb-recent-pro-n3-pl* they were VERBing [group 3 plural recent past compound tense preverb] Structure: abe e-Δ (participial construction) AXG:91f, E&S:37f, PCX:183

abe[3] *preverb-past-n3-pl* they had VERBed; they did VERB [group 3 plural remote past compound tense preverb] Structure: abe e-Δ (participial verb form) ☞ Alt: aye E&S:39, GDX3:714, PCX:186

abe-[4] *v-n3-pl-recent-past* they were / have been VERBing [group 3 plural contracted near / recent past continuous prefix] ☞ Alt: ebe- AXG:91f, E&S:37f, PCX:183

ab e[5] *v-pred-sub* that he, she become R14

ab e[6] *v-aux* that he, she be R32.7, R36.14.26

abebewotha *v-rel-n1-pl* who were heating up • *Abahlali abebewotha 'The residents who were getting steamed up...'* R26.3

abeChild Protection Unit *loan* those of the Child Protection Unit R36.15

abefundisi *n1-pl* preachers aba+ fundisi (from old Bantu funda 'to learn') ab(a)>(e) by assimilation of foll high vowel R13.6

-abela *v-ditr* allocate s.t. to s.o., divide (up), distribute s.t. among, share out, apportion to EXD:167, RD-96:375, XED:1

abeLife Line *loan* those of Life Line R36.11

abeLungu *n1-pl-ir* White people ☞ Sg: umLungu AXG:17, CGB:102, PCX:52, SXWU:15, XED:85

abembi *n1-pl-ir* diggers, excavators, miners PCX:52

abemi *n1-pl-ir* inhabitants, occupants, residents ☞ Sg: ummi; rw: -ma (latent: -ima) AXG:17, PCX:52, XED:86

abeNguni *n1-pl-ir* Nguni Bantu (people) ☞ Sg: umNguni PCX:52

abenza *v-rel-tr* those who did R32.8

abeSuthu *n1-pl-ir* Sotho people ☞ Sg: umSuthu AXG:17, PCX:52, SXWU:15

abeTshwana *n1-pl-ir* Tswana people ☞ Sg: umTshwana SXWU:15

abevi *n1-pl* examiners ☞ Sg: umvi AXG:17

abhalise *v-sub* he, she should write to R27.6

abhalisele *v-pass* not been written for, did not register (i.e., brought into the tax system) • *ongazange abhalisele irhafu 'who has never been written up for tax'* R23.7

abhaliswe *v-caus-pass* they are registered R35.9

-abo[1] *n1-pl-poss-root* their (own); theirs ☞ See: babo, labo, lwabo, sabo, zabo CGB:183, XED:1

abo[2] *n1-pl-poss-n3-pl* of them; their (own); theirs E&S:22, GDX3:691, R35.1.14

abo[3] *n3-pl-poss-abs-n1pl* for them, their • *bambona elicham abo 'they saw them as easy prey'* R36.2

ab o[4] *n7-poss-n3-pl* its; of it GDX3:691

abo[5] *deic-2-n1-pl* those (not far, just mentioned) Agr: aba- CGB:163, E&S:26, MI:159, PCX:86, SXWU:157, XED:xvi; 1, R14

abohlukeneyo *v-rel-short-fut* who will be different (from one another) R29.1.2

abona *n1-pl-pro-emph* the real ones, those very ones; the most [group 1, 1a plural emphatic pronoun] • *abona bantwana 'the very children'; abona nyana 'the real sons'* E&S:23, PCX:164, R3

abongikazi *n1-pl-fem* nurses ☞ Sg: umongikazi E&S:56, R3

abonwe *v-pass-perf* be seen R32.8

abophula *v-rel-pres* those who break it R11

abu- *neg-pres-n7-sg-prf* it does not VERB [group 7 singular negative present subject prefix] Note - this prefix belongs to the neuter/abstract class 7 (cl.14 meinhof) therefore he, she as an interpretation is inappropriate. ☞ See: a- -i AM-94:163, E&S:18, MI:247, SXWU:28, R11

abubambeki *v-neg* it does not grasp R36.25

abubu- *n7-adj-neg-pred* it is not ADJ [group 7 singular negative adjective agreement prefix used predicatively] • *abubude 'it is not long'* E&S:28, PCX:158

abuhlonitshwa *v-neg-pass-pres-n7-sg* it is not respected The change of -ph- to -tsh- is the result of palatalization caused by the velar labial in the passive -wa R11

abukho *v-exis-neg-n7* there is none; it does not exist, it is not available E&S:29

achaphazelekayo *v-ben-rel* bespattered R36.21

act *n5-sg-red* act R22.3

address *n5-sg-red* address R7

ade *v-aux* and then R36.26

adityaniswe *v-caus-pass-sub* he, she, it should be met • *makacele adityaniswe noSekela 'let him ask to be met by Sekela'* R27.3

adlwengula *v-rel-pres* who rape R36.0.17

afake *v-pres-sub* he should enclose R4c

afika *v-intr* he arrived R36.02

African *loan* African R22.3, R33.5

Afrika *pn5-root-loc* Africa RD-96:53, R10, R11, R16, R22, R24, R32=2, R33, R36, R37=3

After-Care Centre *loan* After-Care Center loan word R35=7

afulathela *v-rel-n3-pl* they who run away R36.10

agencies *loan* agencies (Company name) R25

agqithiselwe *v-caus-ben-pass* they are passed on R27.11

agxothiwe *v-pass-perf* they were driven away / expelled XED54, R26.0

-ahlukana *v-recip* separate, part, go in different ways, be severed from; lose one another EXD:571, XED:1, R19x

-ahlukene *v-recip-perf* different, separate DNZ:69, R15x

AIDS *n5-sg-red* AIDS loanword ☞ See: iAIDS R30=5, R36

aka-[1] *neg-pres-n1-sg-prf* he, she does not VERB [group 1 singular negative present subject prefix] • *Umntu akaboni nja 'The man does not see the dog'* ☞ See: a- -i AM-94:163, CGB:124, E&S:18, MI:247, PCX:40, SXWU:28

aka-[2] *n1-sg-S3b-neg* (and) he, she did not VERB [group 1, 1a singular past subjunctive negative verb subject (S3b) agreement prefix] E&S:42, SXWU:141

aka-[3] *neg-pres-n3-pl-prf* they do not VERB [group 3 plural negative present subject prefix] ☞ See: a- -i AM-94:163, CGB:124, E&S:18, MI:247, SXWU:28

aka-[4] *n3-pl-S3b-neg* (and) they did not VERB [group 3 plural past subjunctive negative verb subject (S3b) agreement prefix] ☞ Note: awa- in some grammars (e.g., SXWU:141). This seems to be an alternative form. E&S:42

akakho[1] *v-exis-neg-n1-sg* there is no one; he, she is not present E&S:29

akakho[2] *v-exis-neg-n3-pl* there are none; they are not present / available E&S:29

-akal- *v-atr-suf* -able, -ible; become VERB [attributive, stative, subjective, neuter verb suffix] • *bonakala 'be visible, seem,' enzakala 'be done to, get hurt,' ncedakala* ☞ Perf: -akele; See also: -ek- AXG:115f, E&S:44, PCX:93, XED:xv, R2, R26, R30, R37

akam- *n1-sg-adj-neg-pred* he, she, it is not ADJ [group 1, 1a singular negative adjective agreement prefix used predicatively] • *akamde 'he is not tall'* E&S:28, PCX:157

akama- *n3-pl-adj-neg-pred* they are not ADJ [group 3 plural negative adjective agreement prefix used predicatively] • *akamade 'they are not long'* E&S:28, PCX:157

akamntu *pro-neg* nobody, no one; [idiom] he is inhuman, she is wicked [lit: he, she is not a person] AXG:158, RD-96:375, XED:112

akananzwa *v-pass-neg* it is not approved of, not perceived of R37.20

akayivumi *v-neg* he does not agree R27.11

-akha *v-tr* build; form, construct CGB:125f, PCX:20ff, RD-96:375, SXWU:31, R37.20.21

akhe *n1-sg-poss-n3-pl* his, her, its E&S:22, GDX3:691, R32.8

akho[1] *pro-2sg-poss-n3-pl* your, yours; your own [singular] E&S:22, GDX3:691, RD-96:375

akho[2] *v-exis-n3-pl* they are here; they are present E&S:29, ITX:17, R36.21

akhuthalele *v-sub-pres* she should be hard-working R4d

ak o[1] *n8-vn-poss-n3-pl* its, of it GDX3:691

ak o[2] *n10-loc-poss-n3-pl* its, of it GDX3:691

akoneliseki *v-ben-caus-neg* he is not satisfied, have annulled • *akoneliseki yinkcazelo 'satisfied with the explanation (i.e., that the problem is not annulled by the explanation)* R27.3

akowethu *n3-pl-poss-loc-pron* of ours R32.5

aku-[1] *n1-sg-temp* when he, she, it VERBs / VERBed [group 1, 1a singular temporal verb construction] • *Akusiwa 'When he was brought'* E&S:42, PCX:91f, R36.0

aku-[2] *n3-pl-temp* when they VERB / VERBed [group 3 plural temporal verb construction] • *Akufika 'When they arrive...'* E&S:42, PCX:91

aku-[3] *neg-pres-n8-vn-prf* it does not VERB [group 8 verbal noun negative present subject prefix] ☞ See: a- -i AM-94:163, CGB:137, E&S:18, MI:247, SXWU:28

aku-[4] *neg-pres-n10-loc-prf* there is no VERBing [group 10 locative noun / impersonal verb negative present subject prefix] ☞ See: a- -i R2, R7

aku-[5] *neg-pres-pro-2sg-prf* you not VERB [second person singular negative subject prefix] • *Akuvuki 'Aren't you getting up?'; nokuba akufundanga 'even if you have not studied'* ☞ See also: -wu-; See: a- -i AM-94:120, CGB:124, E&S:18, MI:247, PCX:36f, SXWU:29, R7, R15x

akubi *v-pred-neg* it does not become R36.18

akufundanga *v-neg-perf* you have not studied R7

akukho[1] *v-exis-neg-n8-vn* there is no VERBing; there are none E&S:29

akukho[2] *v-exis-neg-n10-impers* there is not; there are none E&S:29, PCX:150, R7, R18.4, R26.5.6, R31.2, R33=2

akukho[3] *v-exis-neg-pro-2sg* you (thou) are not here / present E&S:29

akuku-[1] *n8-vn-adj-neg-pred* it is not ADJ [group 8 verbal noun negative adjective agreement prefix used predicatively] • *akukude 'it is not long'* E&S:28, PCX:158

akuku-[2] *n10-loc-adj-neg-pred* it is not ADJ there [group 9 and 10 locative noun / impersonal negative adjective agreement prefix used predicatively] • *akukude 'it is not long there'* E&S:28, PCX:158

akulohlazo *neg-cop-n3-sg* it is not a disgrace R36.24

akulunganga *v-intr-neg* it is not ok R31.2

akunakuguqula *v-temp-2-sg-v* they do not turn away from you R14

akunanto *cop-neg-n5-sg* it has nothing R24.3

akunjalo *cop-neg-deic* it is not like that R35.1

akuqhubele *v-sub* (may) drive for you R31.4

akusiwa *v-temp-pass* when he was brought R36.02

akuthethi *v-neg-pres* it does not mean R36.26

akuvumeleki *v-atr-neg-pres* it is not allowed R2

akuyo[1] *rel-loc* who are on / in it R31.3

akuyo[2] *neg-cop-n5-sg* it is not R36.13

akwa-[1] *n8-vn-S3b-neg* (and) it did not VERB [group 8 verbal noun past negative subjunctive verb subject (S3b) agreement prefix] E&S:42, SXWU:141

akwa-[2] *n10-loc-S3b-neg* (and) it did not VERB [group 10 locative noun / impersonal verb past negative subjunctive verb subject (S3b) agreement prefix] • *akwabikho mali 'and there was never money...'* R35.9

akwabikho *v-cop-loc-neg* there was no presence of R35.9

akwadlwengulwa *v-rel-pass* (there are men) who have been raped • *Amadoda akwadlwengulwa nangamanye 'men who have been raped by others'* R36.21

akwaneli *cop-neg-v-tr* not enough R35.15

akwaQhaza *n3-pl-poss-pn* those of Qhaza R26.8

akwazi *v-vowel-neg* he, she does not know R23.7

akwenziwa *v-neg-pass* it is not known R36.18

ala-[1] *n3-sg-S3b-neg* (and) he, she, it did not VERB [group 3 singular past subjunctive negative verb subject (S3b) agreement prefix] E&S:42, SXWU:141

ala[2] *deic-1-n3-pl-poss* of these • *amathole ala mahobe 'the young of these doves'* PCX:140

-ala[3] *v-tr* refuse EXD:517, SXWU:31

-alal- *v-suf* do VERB completely, thoroughly, efficiently, well [perfective / intensive verb suffix] ☞ Alt: -elel- E&S:44

alalelwa *v-pass* they are ambushed R36.19

ali-[1] *rel-prefix* these • *amanye amazwe aseAfrika ali-11 aye anenxaxheba kolo gqatso 'several of these 11 African countries participated in that race'* R33.7

ali-[2] *neg-pres-n3-sg-prf* he, she, it does not VERB [group 3 singular negative present subject prefix] ☞ See: a- -i AM-94:163, E&S:18, MI:247, SXWU:28

alibalekayo *v-rel* in which she ran (it) R33.7

alibalumkisi *v-tr-neg* does not warn R31.2

alikho *v-exis-neg-n3-sg* there is none; it does not exist, it is not available E&S:29

alikhulule *v-part-perf* released, set free participial part of compound tense R32.4

alili- *n3-sg-adj-neg-pred* he, she, it is not ADJ [group 3 singular negative adjective agreement prefix used predicatively] • *alilide 'it is not long'* E&S:28, PCX:157

alishumi *rel-cop-num* that are ten R32.6

alive *loan* alive ☞ See: Arrive Alive R31.2

alizamele *v-tr-ben-sub* that he, she struggle for • *kusafuneka alizamele imali 'it was still necesary for her to struggle for money'* R35.4

al o[1] *n3-sg-poss-n3-pl* his, her, its; of him, her, it GDX3:691

al o[2] *n6-sg-poss-n3-pl* his, her, its; of him, her, it GDX3:691

alu- *neg-pres-n6-sg-prf* he, she, it does not VERB [group 6 singular negative present subject prefix] ☞ See: a- -i AM-94:163, E&S:18, MI:247, SXWU:28, R10, R34.3

aluhlaza *-atr-color* green, blue R30.3

alukho *v-exis-neg-n6-sg* there is none; it does not exist, it is not available E&S:29

alulazi *n6-sg-v-tr-neg* it does not know R35.11

alulu- *n6-sg-adj-neg-pred* it is not ADJ [group 6 singular negative adjective agreement prefix used predicatively] • *alulude 'it is not long'* E&S:28, PCX:158

alunalwazi *v-neg-rel* who does not have knowledge R37.25

alusebenzi *v-neg-pres-n6-sg* does not work R10

aluwi *v-intr-neg* it [n6-sg] will not fall/succumb neg a- + lu (n6-sg) + w + neg -i R34.3

alwa- *n6-sg-S3b-neg* (and) he, she, it did not VERB [group 6 singular past subjunctive negative verb subject (S3b) agreement prefix] E&S:42, SXWU:141

alwazi *v-neg-n6-sg* do not know R36.12

am *pro-1sg-poss-n3-pl* of me; my, mine; my own • *amehlo am 'my eyes'* AM-94:151, CGB:181, E&S:22, GDX3:691, PCX:60; 72, SXWU:36, R36.06

ama-[1] *n3-pl-prf* [group 3 (Bantu class 6) plural noun prefix] • *amatswele 'onions'; amandla 'strength' [mass noun]* Consists of article a- + classifier ma- ☞ Sg: ili- / i- AXG:19; 20, CGB:104, E&S:17, PCX:51ff, RD-96:372, SXWU:17, XED:2, R1, R2, R3, R4a, R4b=2, R4d=2, R6, R8, R9=2, R10=2, R11, R12, R36=20

ama-[2] *n3-pl-adj* [group 3 plural adjective agreement prefix] CGB:174, E&S:28, MI:248, XED:xv, R11, R12

ama-45 emizuzu *n2-pl-poss-n3-pl* for 45 minutes [lit: 45 of minutes] R8

amaAfrika *n3-pl* African (people) ☞ Sg: umAfrika EXD:11

amabala *n3-pl* colors, hues; spots, markings ☞ Sg: ibala AM-94:107, EXD:368, XED:6, R30.3

amabali *n-3-pl* stories R28

amabanga *n3-pl* grades (school levels); standards ☞ Sg: ibanga EXD:253, R9x, R10, R33.1

amaBhaca *n3-pl* Bhaca, Baca (people, ethnic group within the greater Xhosa community) ☞ Sg: umBhaca; Alt sp: amaBaca AXG:20, CGB:111

amabhenya *n3-pl* evasions, subterfuges, artifices Usually plural only CGB:112, EXD:636, XED:11

amabhinqa *n3-pl* women ☞ Sg: ibhinqa; Loc: emabhinqeni R31.3, R36x

amaBhulu *n3-pl* Afrikaners ☞ Sg: iBhulu EXD:11, R17.2, R32.3

amabini *num-n3-pl* two NDK-91:621, TD, R8x

amacala *n3-pl* sides; aspects • *Yifunde macala onke 'Study every aspect of it!'* ☞ Sg: icala EXD:31

amachithi *n3-pl* troublemakers, those who cause discord CGB:112

amaculo *n3-pl* songs, hymns ☞ Sg: iculo E&S:56

amadladla *n3-pl* vagabonds CGB:112

amadlozi *n3-pl-mass* semen; blood relatives, people of the same descent group; [atr] seminal EXD:569, XED:31

amadoda *n3-pl* men ama +doda Class6(Bantu) /n3-pl Singular form in Class9 (n5-sg). ☞ Sg: indoda ubudoda [n7-sg] 'manhood' CGB:116, E&S:57, SXWU:17;19, R13.4, R35.6, R36=15

amadolo *n3-pl* knees ☞ Sg: idolo SXWU:17, XED:32, R32x

amafanankosi *n3-pl* bodyguards EXD:62, R32.3

amafu *n3-pl* clouds ☞ Sg: ilifu; Loc: emafini AXG:19, CGB:104, E&S:56; 17, PCX:68

amafutha *n3-pl-mass* fat, oil, grease No singular AM-94:22, AXG:20, E&S:57, SXWU:17

amafutshane *n3-pl-adj* short (attribute) • *Amabali Amafutshane 'News Briefs'* R28.0

amagama *n3-pl* words; names; brands (commerical products) ☞ Sg: igama AM-94:24, E&S:56, R12=2, R37=4

amaGcaleka *n3-pl* Gcaleka (people, ethnic group within the greater Xhosa community) ☞ See: Gcaleka CGB:111

amagqirha *n3-pl* medicine men, traditional doctors, witch doctors ☞ Sg: igqirha E&S:56, SXWU:17, R7x

amagqiyazana *n3-pl-dim* young single women Naledi, R4b, R33x

amagqwetha *n3-pl* lawyers ☞ Sg: igqwetha EXD:334, R3

amagumbi *n3-pl* rooms ☞ Sg: igumbi E&S:56, R18x, R35

amagunya *n3-pl* the rights ☞ igunya 'right' R35.14

amahashe *n3-pl* horses ☞ Sg: ihashe AXG:19, E&S:56; 17, R28x

amahlathi *n3-pl* forests R28

amakhanukanodwa *n3-pl-cmp* gays, people with homosexual preferences ☞ Cf: -khanuka R36.21

amakhaya *n3-pl* homes; residences E&S:56, PCX:53, R9x, R35.2, R36.10

amakhosazana *n3-pl* young ladies ☞ Sg: inkosazana SXWU:19

amakhosi *n3-pl* chiefs ☞ Sg: inkosi SXWU:19, R20=6

amakhosikazi *n3-pl-fem-ir* chief's wives; wives; ladies, women ama [n3-pl] + -khosi 'chief' + -kazi feminine suffix; note -kh- is underlying phonemic form - becomes k' (ejective) after nasal in n5-sg ☞ Sg: inkosikazi [n5] CGB:111, E&S:57, SXWU:19, XED:74, R13.5

amakhulu amahlanu *num-n3-pl-cmp* five hundred (500) [lit: five hundreds] R8

amakhwapha *n3-pl* armpits ☞ Sg: ikhwapha XED:78, R30

amakhwenkwe *n3-pl-ir* boys, youngsters ☞ Sg: inkwenkwe [n5] AM-94:164, E&S:57, EXD:67, SXWU:17; 19, XED:79, R36.15

amaKroza *n3-pl-pn-geog* Orion (constellation) [lit: stars in rows] Plural only AXG:218, CGB:111, EXD:424

amalandalahla *n3-pl* nowhere; Utopia CGB:112

amaLawu *n3-pl* Khoikhoi (Lawu people, Xhosa nickname for the ethnic group) ☞ Sg: iLawu; See also: amaQheya CGB:8

amalengelenge *n3-pl* firmament CGB:112

amalinga *n4-pl* attempts [n3-pl] prefix + verb-derived linga from ukulinga, 'to try'. EXD:35, R13.8

amalongwe *n3-pl* caked cow dung ☞ Cf: ubulongwe EXD:179, XED:83

amalungelo *n3-pl* advantages, benefits; rights, privileges ☞ Sg: ilungelo XED:84, R20.7, R34.4, R37.16

amalungiselelo *n3-pl* provisions ☞ Sg: ulungiselelo EXD:489, R28.3

amalungu *n3-pl* members R21.7, R22.4, R32.6, R35.9

amalwimi *n3-pl-ir* tongues ☞ Sg: ulwimi; Contrast: iilwimi 'languages' AM-94:101

amamPondo *n3-pl* Pondo, Mpondo (people, ethnic group within the greater Xhosa community) ☞ Loc: emamPondweni; See: Mpondo AXG:20, CGB:109; 111, XED:129

amandla *n3-pl-mass* strength, energy, power; force; biceps No singular ☞ Cf: isandla AM-94:22, AXG:20, E&S:57, EXD:263, RD-96:375, SXWU:17, XED:97, R1x, R12, R36.17

Amandla Meats *name* Amandla Meats (meat market in King William's Town) R1

amanenekazi *n3-pl* ladies see amakhosikazi - same use of feminine sufix -kazi R13.5, R36.14

amanga *n3-pl-mass* lies No singular AXG:20, CGB:112

amaninzi *adj-n3-pl* many XED:104, R20.3.4, R36.19, R37.15

amankazana *n3-pl-ir* young married women; females (generic) ☞ Sg: inkazana CGB:111, XED:66; 70

amankonyana *n3-pl-ir* young foals, suckling calves ☞ Sg: inkonyana CGB:111, XED:74

amantloko *n3-pl* upper parts ☞ Cf: intloko CGB:112

amantombazana *n3-pl-ir-dim* little girls (young, single) ☞ Sg: intombazana [n5] CGB:105; 111, E&S:57, EXD:246, XED:162

amantshontsho *n3-pl* pups, cubs, chicks, fledglings, the young (of animals) XED:112, R2

amanxeba *n3-pl* wounds ☞ Sg: inxeba R36x

amanya *n3-pl* wrinkles (in clothing) Plural only CGB:111, EXD:735

amanyala *n3-pl-mass* indecency, vulgarity, shameless conduct, filth No singular AXG:20, XED:115, R32.5.9

amanyange *n3-pl* old people CGB:112

amanyathelo *n3-pl* steps ☞ Sg: inyathelo EXD:623, R34.2, R36.12

amanye *n3-pl* others R33.7, R36=4

amanyundululu *n3-pl* the atrocities prob. Zulu rather than Xhosa from -nyundula - to cause enmity R32.1.8

amanzi *n3-pl-mass* water; [atr] wet, damp, moist No singular ☞ Loc: emanzini AM-94:22, AXG:20, CGB:111; 139, E&S:57; 58, PCX:68, RD-96:375, SXWU:17, R8x=2

amaphandle *n3-pl* outer parts CGB:112

amaphondo *n3-pl* provinces, regions ☞ Sg: iphondo R33.4

amaphulo *n3-pl* expeditions; business R35.13

amapolisa *n3-pl* policemen CGB:104; 140, R18.5, R26.8, R27.6.10.11

amaqanda *n3-pl* eggs ☞ Sg: iqanda CGB:104, E&S:31

amaqela *n3-pl* a number of people ☞ Sg: iqela (q.v.) XED:136, R21

amaQheya *n3-pl* Khoikhoi (Qheya, Xhosa name for the ethnic group) ☞ See also: amaLawu CGB:8

amaRharhabe *n3-pl* Rharhabe (ethnic group within the greater Xhosa community) ☞ See: Rharhabe CGB:2; 4

amarhe *n3-pl* rumors, reports • *Kukho amarhe okuba ... 'It is rumored that'* ☞ Alt sp: amare EXD:546, XED:144

amarhewu *n3-pl-mass* corn beer No singular E&S:57

amasango *n3-pl* gates, gateways ☞ Sg: isango R27.1

amasela *n3-pl* thieves ☞ Sg: isela E&S:57, XED:159, R26

amasele *n3-pl* frogs ☞ Sg: isele CGB:104, RD-96:372

amashumi *n3-pl-num* tens ☞ Sg: ishumi TD, R4ax, R4bx, R8x

amashumi amabini *num-n3-pl-cmp* twenty (20) [lit: two tens] NDK-91:621, TD, R4ax, R4bx

amashumi amahlanu *num-n3-pl-cmp* fifty (50) [lit: five tens] NDK-91:623

amashumi amathathu *num-n3-pl-cmp* thirty (30) [lit: three tens] NDK-91:622, R8x

amashwa *n3-pl* misfortunes ☞ Sg: ilishwa E&S:56, PCX:50; 52

amasi *n3-pl-mass* sour milk, fermented milk No singular AM-94:22, AXG:20, CGB:111

amasimi *n3-pl* gardens, fields, cultivated lands ☞ Sg: intsimi [n5] E&S:57, XED:152

amasini *n3-pl* gums ☞ No singular CGB:111, KED:392, XED:152

amathandabuzo *n3-pl-cmp* doubts CGB:112, XED:157

amathatha *n3-pl* nostrils ☞ Sg: ithatha CGB:111, EXD:408

amathe *n3-pl-mass* saliva, spittle No singular AXG:20, CGB:111, EXD:611, SXWU:17

amatheko *n3-pl* events, occasions ☞ Sg: itheko R36.9

amathuba *n3-pl* opportunities, chances ☞ Sg: ithuba R10, R29.10.15, R37.1.17

amathumbu *n3-pl* intestines, entrails, viscera; bowels ☞ Syn: izibilini; Loc: emathunjini EXD:66;191;312, PCX:69, XED:169

amatsha-ntliziyo *n3-pl-comp* young at heart R32.5

amaTshawe *n3-pl* Tshawe (people, original royal clan of the Xhosa community) CGB:3

amatswele *n3-pl* onions ☞ Sg: itswele EXD:419, R8

amatutu *n3-pl* cattle-rustlers, thieves, robbers R26x=2

amatyala *n3-pl* offenses R36.15

amava *n3-pl* impressions; convictions; [col] experience ☞ Sg: iliva; Contrast: ameva XED:175, R4d

amaxabiso *n3-pl* prices ☞ Sg: ixabiso R1

amaxesha *n3-pl* times, instances R14

amaxhoba *n3-pl* victims; spoils (of war) ☞ Sg: ixhoba EXD:706, XED:184f, R36.22.26

amaXhosa *n3-pl-ir* Xhosa (people) ☞ Sg: umXhosa; Loc: emaXhoseni AM-94:22, AXG:17, CGB:105; 109; 111, E&S:56, SXWU:17

amaxhwele *n3-pl* herbalists, medicine men ☞ Sg: ixhwele R7x

amayana *n3-pl* disdain CGB:112

amayeza *n3-pl* medicines ☞ Sg: iyeza R6

amaziko *n3-pl* hearths; households ☞ Sg: iziko XED:191, R37.13=2.14

amazinyo *n3-pl* teeth ☞ Sg: izinyo; Alt: amenyo AXG:20

amazolo *n3-pl-irreg* night air, night dew, frost ☞ See: izolo 'yesterday' AXG:20, XED:192

amazulu[1] *n3-pl* skies ☞ Sg: izulu E&S:57

amaZulu[2] *n3-pl-ir* Zulu (people) ☞ Sg: umZulu AM-94:22, AXG:17, CGB:109; 111, XED:193

amazwana *n3-pl-dim* a few words AXG:37

amazwe *n3-pl* countries ☞ Sg: ilizwe CGB:104, E&S:56, PCX:23; 52, R11, R16, R33.7

amazwi *n3-pl* words • *amazwi akhe, 'his/her words'* ☞ Sg: ilizwi AXG:37, E&S:56, XED:193, R17.5, R21

-ambatha *v-tr* dress oneself, put on some covering; go under the protection of; allude to; follow hard after R36.26

ame- *n3-pl-ir-prf* [group 3 (Bantu class 6) irregular plural noun prefix before latent i-roots] • *amehlo 'eyes', ameva 'thorns'* ☞ Sg: um-; See: aba- AXG:19

amehlo *n3-pl-ir* eyes ☞ Sg: iliso; Loc: emehlweni AXG:19, CGB:105, PCX:53; 68, SXWU:17

amelane *v-recip* stand for R36.23

amendu *n3-pl-mass* speed, pace; endurance No singular AXG:20, EXD:609, XED:36

amenyo *n3-pl* teeth {archaic} ☞ See: amazinyo AXG:20

ameva *n3-pl-ir* thorns ☞ Sg: iliva; Contrast: amava CGB:105; 111, PCX:53, SXWU:17, XED:175; 63, R4dx

-amkela *v-tr* receive, accept; adopt; welcome; agree EXD:13, RD-96:375, XED:3, R10, R14, R24, R28.6, R29, R36.19

-amkelekileyo *v-atr-perf-rel* acceptable RD-96:375

amnyange *v-sub* so that he, she may be cured R37.15

-an- *v-suf-recip* each other, one another [reciprocal or mutual verb suffix] • *-sebenzisana 'cooperate, work together'* AXG:113f, E&S:44, R4a, R4d=5, R5, R7, R9, R12, R14, R37.14.16.20

-ana *n-suf-dim* little, small; somewhat [diminutive noun suffix] • *abantwana 'children'; intwana 'small item'* CGB:175, E&S:33, MI:262, R2=3, R9, R10, R12, R22=7, R33=3

ancedwe *v-pass-pres-sub* they should be helped R36.24

-anda *v-inch* become larger, extend, expand, increase XED:3, R11

andi *neg-pres-pro-1sg-prf* I am not VERBing, I do not VERB [first person singular negative present subject prefix] • *Anditshayi kwaye andiseli 'I don't smoke and I don't drink'* ☞ See: a- -i AM-94:120, CGB:124; 127, E&S:18, MI:247, PCX:39f, SXWU:29, R4a=2, R4c=2

andikho *v-exis-neg-pro-1sg* I am not here / present E&S:29

andilithabathi *v-tr-neg* I don't take it R24.8

andiqinisekanga *v-intr-caus-atr-neg* I am not sure R28.2

-andisa *v-tr* enlarge, expand, extend, magnify, multiply RD-96:375, XED:3

andiseli *v-neg-pres* I don't drink R4a, R4c

anditshayi *v-neg-pres* I don't smoke R4a, R4c

andizange *v-aux-neg-past* I never R23.6

-ane *suf-dim* very little, smallish; somewhat [diminutive suffix] • *-futshane 'very short' [= fuph(i)/tsh-ane], -ncinane 'very small' [= ncin(ci)-ane]* R10

-anela[1] *v-intr* be enough (for); suffice, be sufficient XED:3, R4c, R12x

-anela[2] *v-aux* just, only, merely VERB • *Wanela nje ukuvuka wahamba 'He just woke up and left'* Structure: takes infinitive complement E&S:47, XED:3

-aneleyo *v-rel-atr* enough, sufficient EXD:190

-anelisa *v-caus* suffice, satisfy, gratify, make enough XED:3, R12x

-aneliseka *v-caus-atr* be satisfying, gratifying, sufficient, enough R12

aneminyaka *v-poss-rel* who have NUM years R4b

anenxaxheba *v-poss-cmp* they took part in • *Amanye amazwe aseAfrika anenxaxheba kolo gqatso. 'Several African countries took part in that race.'* R33.7

anerayisi *v-poss-rel* which have rice R12

-anga[1] *v-suf-neg-past-recent* did not VERB, have not VERBed [negative perfect verb suffix] Structure: a-SNEG-Δ-anga; Note: This negates both the short (-e) and long (-ile) positive constructions

☞ Pos: S1-Δ-ile or S1-Δ-e AXG:103f, CGB:153, R6, R7, R20

-anga[2] *v-suf-neg-past-sub* did not VERB, had not VERBED [remote past / past subjunctive negative verb suffix] ☞ Pos: S3b Δ-a CGB:189

angabamhlophe *cop-n1-pl* who are white R32.3

angakhange *v-aux-neg-past* he never R23.7

angakunikanga *v-ind-rel-neg-perf* which he did not give you R6

angama *n3-pl-pred-num-n3-pl-expr* a quantity of, a number of; about NUM • *angama-600 'about 600'* R36.15

angamaxhoba *v-pot* they can be prey R36.12.23.24

angamaziyo *v-neg-rel-pres+pro-obj* whom he does not know R9

angananzwa *v-pres-pass* are not liked or favored; are not taken into consideration R37.21

angaphantsi *v-cop-n3pl* who were or are under • *amakhwenkwe angaphantsi kwe-18 'boys under the age of 18'* R36.15

angaphezu *cop-loc* that are above R36.15

angaseli *v-neg-sub* and he does not drink denoting sequence R4c

angasese *adv-n3-pl-atr* out of sight; secretly KED:382, R30.2=2, R35.8

angatshaya *v-pot* he may smoke R4c

angawabo *rel-cop-deic* that are theirs R35.13

angayenza *v-tr-pot* they [amalungu] can make R22.4

angayixhasi *v-neg-n5-sg-obj* not supporting it R10

angaziphatha *v-pot-refl* they can behave R36.20

angaziwayo *v-rel-neg-pot-pass* not known, unknown R37.21

angema- *n3-pl-adj-neg* [group 3 plural negative adjective agreement prefix] • *angemade 'not tall'* E&S:28

angobomi *n7-sg-abs* about life R36.01

angqinile *v-tr-perf* they confirmed / agreed / testified R26.8

angqongqo *atr* hard, severe R34.2

ani-[1] *neg-pres-pro-2pl-prf* you (all) are not VERBing; you do not VERB [second person plural negative present subject prefix] ☞ See: a- -i AM-94:120; 163, E&S:18, MI:247, PCX:40, SXWU:29

-ani[2] *v-suf-imp-pl* do VERB! [positive imperative plural verb suffix] comprises two morphemes, the regular termination -a and the suffix -ni ☞ See: -ni PCX:22f, R3, R11

anikho *v-exis-neg-pro-2pl* you (all) are not here / present E&S:29

anikwe *v-past-pass* it be taken R37.20

anisokuze *v-aux-neg* you won't R20.2

aniwazi *v-tr-neg* you don't know R20.2

anje *atr-n3-pl* such as R14, R32.5

anokudlwengulwa *v-rel-abil-pass* who can be raped R36.14

anokugonyamelwa *v-abil-pass* they can be treated with violence [lit: like lions would treat them] R36.12

anokusetyenziswa *v-rel-abil* that can be utilized R37.20

anokwenzakala *v-atr* they could get hurt R2

anqunqwe *v-pass-pres-sub* they should be chopped R8

-anyana *n-suf-dim* tiny, very small [diminutive noun suffix] • *injanyana 'very small dog',* *intwanyana 'tiny thing', izilwanyana 'insects'* AXG:36, CGB:175, E&S:33, MI:262, R2=3

anyulwe *v-pass* they be selected R21.7

Apartheid *loan* Apartheid R32.3.6.7

apha *deic-1-n9-loc-adv* this place, here ☞ Cf: apho 'there', phaya 'yonder' AM-94:109, AXG:144; 213, CGB:178, E&S:59, MI:256, PCX:29; 86, RD-96:375, R27.11, R34.1.12=2, R35.11, R37=5

apha nalapho *deic-expr* here and there AM-94:109

aphambili *atr-n3-pl* ahead of, before; foremost R12

aphantsi *atr-n3-pl* lower, which are low • *amabanga aphantsi 'lower grades (in school)'; amaxabiso aphantsi 'low prices'* R1, R9, R10, R33.1.2

aphela *v-intr* they stop R36.26

aphele *v-intr-sub* and they come to an end R25.4

aphelelwa *v-ben-pass* they are bereft of R36.23

aphi *qw-loc-adv-n3-pl* where are? ☞ See: -phi E&S:31

aphindele *v-ben-perf* he returned to R36.20

apho *deic-2-n9-loc-adv* there, that place (not far, just mentioned) ☞ Cf: apha 'here', phaya 'yonder' AM-94:109, AXG:144; 213, CGB:178, E&S:59, MI:256, PCX:86, R10, R19.2, R24.6, R26.4, R28=4, R30.6, R33=5, R35=5, R36.20

apho sukuba *deic-2-n9-loc-adv-rel* wherever • *Apho sukuba usiya khona 'wherever you go'* AXG:173

-aphula *v-tr* break; break down EXD:68, XED:4, R11=4, R31.1.2, R33.4, R36.14.17

April *n-time-loan* April R23.7, 34.1.2

Aquarius *loan* Aquarius R34.11

aqulethe *v-st-perf* they contain; they have R12

Aries *loan* Aries R34.1

Arrive Alive *loan* Arrive Alive (safe-driving slogan) R31.2

asa- *n4-sg-S3b-neg* (and) he, she, it did not VERB [group 4 singular past subjunctive negative verb subject (S3b) agreement prefix] E&S:42, SXWU:141

aseAfrika *n5-sg* African, of (those) in Africa R16=3, R33.7

asebenze *v-intr-sub* she would work R28.5

aseke *v-tr-sub* that he establish R16

-asekhohlo *n6-sg-atr* left (direction, hand, etc.) ☞ Opp: -asekunene EXD:339

-asekunene *n10-loc-atr* right (direction, hand, etc.) ☞ Opp: -asekhohlo EXD:537

asenzele *v-tr-past* they did R20.7

asesichengeni *cop-loc* who are in danger isichenge 'one who is exposed to danger' R36.10

aseTamarha *pn-rel-loc* who are in Tamarha R27.11.14

asetyenziswa *v-rel-pres-pass* which are used R37.10.20.21

asezi *rel-n5-pl* belonging to, of the • *kulixesha lamatheko eKrismesi asezi-ofisini 'it is the time for those office Christmas parties'* R31.3

ashushu *atr* warm; hot R29.7

asi-[1] *neg-pred* it is not [negative copulative or predicative] Structure: asi- + PRED ☞ Alt: ayi- CGB:135, E&S:21, PCX:96f, R19

asi-[2] *neg-pres-n4-sg-prf* he, she, it does not VERB [group 4 singular negative present subject prefix] ☞ See: a- -i AM-94:163, E&S:18, MI:247, SXWU:28

asi-[3] *neg-pres-pro-1pl-prf* we are not VERBing; we do not VERB [first person plural negative present subject prefix] ☞ See: a- -i AM-94:120, CGB:124, E&S:18, MI:247, PCX:39, SXWU:29, R37.11

asibubo *n7-neg-pred* it is not it [negative copulative or predicative] E&S:21, PCX:98

asikho[1] *v-exis-neg-n4-sg* there is none; it does not exist, it is not available E&S:29

asikho[2] *v-exis-neg-pro-1pl* we are not here / present E&S:29

asikuko[1] *n8-vn-neg-pred* it is not it [negative copulative or predicative] E&S:21, PCX:98

asikuko[2] *n10-loc-neg-pred* it is not (the place, domain) [negative copulative or predicative] PCX:98

asililo *n3-sg-neg-pred* it is not he, she, it [negative copulative or predicative] E&S:21, PCX:98

asiloli- *n3-sg-neg-pred-prf* it is not [group 3 singular negative copulative or predicative prefix construction] • *asilolizwe 'it is not a country'* PCX:96

asilulo *n6-sg-neg-pred* it is not he, she, it [negative copulative or predicative] E&S:21, PCX:98

asimangalanga *v-pro-1pl-neg-perf* we were not surprised R20.6

asindim *pro-1sg-neg-pred* it is not I [negative copulative or predicative] E&S:21, PCX:97

asingaba *deic-1-n1-pl-neg-pred* it is not these PCX:99

asingabo *n1-pl-neg-pred* it is not they [negative copulative or predicative] E&S:21, PCX:97

asingawo *n3-pl-neg-pred* it is not they [negative copulative or predicative] E&S:21, PCX:98

asingo- *n1a-sg-neg-pred-prf* he, she, it is not [group 1a singular negative copulative or predicative prefix construction] PCX:96, R19.3.5.6

asingoba- *n1-pl-pred-neg-prf* they are not [group 1 plural negative copulative or predicative prefix construction] • *asingobantwana 'they are not children'* PCX:96

asingom-[1] *n1-sg-neg-pred-prf* he, she, it is not [group 1 singular negative copulative or predicative prefix construction] • *asingomtwana 'he is not a child'* PCX:96

asingom-[2] *n2-sg-neg-pred-prf* it is not [group 2 singular negative copulative or predicative prefix construction] • *asingomthi 'it is not a tree'* PCX:96

asingomntwana *n1-sg-neg-pred* it is not a child • *asingomntwana wakhe 'it is not his child'* PCX:96, R19

asingoo- *n1a-pl-neg-pred-prf* they are not [group 1a plural negative copulative or predicative prefix construction] • *asingoonyana 'they are not sons'* PCX:96

asingowakhe *n1a-sg-neg-pred* it is not his R19.3.5

asingulo[1] *deic-1-n1-sg-neg-pred* it is not this one PCX:99

asingulo[2] *deic-1-n2-sg-neg-pred* it is not this one PCX:99

asinguwe *pro-2sg-neg-pred* it is not you [singular negative copulative or predicative] E&S:21, PCX:97

asinguwo *n2-sg-neg-pred* it is not he, she, it [negative copulative or predicative] E&S:21, PCX:97

asinguye *n1-sg-neg-pred* it is not he, she, it [negative copulative or predicative] E&S:21, PCX:97

asinini *pro-2pl-neg-pred* it is not you [plural negative copulative or predicative] E&S:21, PCX:97

asiqondi *v-neg-pro-1pl* we are not sure R37.11

asisi- *n4-sg-adj-neg-pred* he, she, it is not ADJ [group 4 singular negative adjective agreement prefix used predicatively] • *asiside 'it is not long'* E&S:28, PCX:157

asisiso *n4-sg-neg-pred* it is not he, she, it [negative copulative or predicative] E&S:21, PCX:98

asisithi *pro-1pl-neg-pred* it is not we [negative copulative or predicative] E&S:21, PCX:97

asiyile *deic-1-n2-pl-neg-pred* it is not these PCX:99

asiyiyo[1] *n2-pl-neg-pred* it is not they [negative copulative or predicative] E&S:21, PCX:97

asiyiyo[2] *n5-sg-neg-pred* it is not he, she, it [negative copulative or predicative] E&S:21, PCX:98

asiyomi- *n2-pl-neg-pred-prf* they are not [group 2 plural negative copulative or predicative prefix construction] • *asiyomithi 'they are not sons'* PCX:96

asizizo[1] *n4-pl-neg-pred* it is not they [negative copulative or predicative] E&S:21, PCX:98

asizizo[2] *n5-pl-neg-pred* it is not they [negative copulative or predicative] E&S:21, PCX:98

as o *n4-sg-poss-n3-pl* his, her, its; of him, her, it GDX3:691

asokuze *v-neg-aux-fut* who is not going (as part of compound) R20.2

assistants *loan* assistants R29.11

asthma *loan* asthma loanword ☞ Syn: iphika R25.5

athatyathwa *v-pass* who were taken R36.15

athembele *v-pres-sub* he should trust in R9

athethe *v-tr-part* he speaks R32.8

athethwa *v-rel-pass* which were spoken R17.5

athi *v-past-sub* he said R36.17.20

athile *rel* certain R34.4

athletic *loan* athletic R33.8

athwale *v-tr-sub* bear a burden R35.15

Atwell *-pn* Atwell (personal name) No grammar R32.5

atyiwe *v-pass* who are eaten R36.22.23

avelise *v-tr-sub* she produce R24.7

avulekileyo *v-rel-perf* that is opened R35.8

avuliwe *v-pass-perf* they are open R27.1

awa-[1] *n2-sg-S3b-neg* (and) he, she, it did not VERB [group 2 singular past subjunctive negative verb subject (S3b) agreement prefix] E&S:42, SXWU:141

awa-[2] *n3-pl-S3b-neg* (and) they did not VERB [group 3 plural past subjunctive negative verb subject (S3b) agreement prefix] ☞ E&S:42 say AKA-, but all other books examined use awa- here. SXWU:141

awaba- *combo* of • *okanye usele awabanye 'nor should you take (the medicine) of others'* combo form showing that n1 pl (aba-) is possessed by n3 pl (ama-) R6

awabanye *n1-pl-poss* that of others R6

awakuthatheli *v-neg* they have not taken R36.12

awayehlala *v-ind-rel* with whom he was staying R36.3

awayenziwa *v-rel-pass* which were done R32.9

awayezixhalabele *v-rel* about which he was frightened R36.1

awemfundo *n5-sg* education awa=imfundo > awemfundo. This form is emphatic possessive where the possessive for the class (n3-pl) is not elided with the following vowel but becomes awa- R13.8

awenza *v-rel-tr* which she did R24.7

awimanyano *n3-pl-poss-emph-n6-sg* of union emphatic form awa + imanyano R13.8

awo[1] *n2-sg-poss-n3-pl* its, of it GDX3:691

awo[2] *n3-pl-poss* their, of them • *Kutheni amakhosi xa efuna amalungelo awo esebenzisa uluntu? 'Why is it that when chiefs want their rights they use people?'* GDX3:691, XED:4, R20.7

awona *n3-pl-pro-emph* the real ones, those very ones; the most [group 3 plural emphatic pronoun] • *awona mahashe 'the very horses'* E&S:23, PCX:165

awu-[1] *neg-pres-n2-sg-prf* he, she, it does not VERB [group 2 singular negative present subject prefix] ☞ See: a- -i AM-94:163, CGB:124, E&S:18, MI:247, SXWU:28

awu[2] *intj* oh! PCX:29

awukho *v-exis-neg-n2-sg* there is none; it is not present / available E&S:29

awukwazi *v-pres-neg* you don't know R37.14

awum- *n2-sg-adj-neg-pred* he, she, it is not ADJ [group 2 singular negative adjective agreement prefix used predicatively] • *awumde 'it is not long'* E&S:28, PCX:157

awusayi *v-aux-prog-neg* it won't be R37.17

awutholi *v-pres-neg* you do not get ☞ See Xhosa: akufumani R15

aya-[1] *n2-pl-S3b-neg* (and) they did not VERB [group 2 plural past subjunctive negative verb subject (S3b) agreement prefix] E&S:42, SXWU:141

aya-[2] *n5-sg-S3b-neg* (and) he, she, it did not VERB [group 5 singular past subjunctive negative verb subject (S3b) agreement prefix] E&S:42, SXWU:141

aya[3] *v-aux-fut* they will R32.4

ayabule *v-sub-pres* that they should roam R2

ayadideka *v-st* they are agitated R36.26

ayadlwengulwa *v-pass* they get raped R36.0.8

ayalufuna *v-tr* they want it R36.23

ayandigulisa *v-pres-prog* they make me sick R17.5

ayaphunyezwa *v-pass* be taken out, brought to the fore R37.16

ayavulwa *v-pass* they are opened R27.11

ayayikhanuka *v-tr* they desire it R36.18

aye-[1] *n3-pl-remote-past* they had VERBed [group 3 plural contracted remote past compound tense] • *nkqu namapolisa ayehamba ngamahashe 'and even the police had gone on horseback (in those days)'* AXG:93f, E&S:39, PCX:186, R20=2, R28, R32

aye[2] *preverb-past-n3-pl* they had VERBed; they did VERB [group 3 plural remote past compound tense preverb] Structure: aye e-Δ (participial verb form) ☞ Alt: abe AXG:93f, E&S:39, GDX3:714, R36.22

aye[3] *v-aux-past-n3-pl* they did VERB; they had VERBed • *Amanye amazwe aseAfrika aye anenxaxheba kolo gqatso 'Several African countries had participated in that race'* R33.7

ayebamba *v-remote-past* they had arrested • *Xa amaBhulu ayebamba uGqirha Mandela 'When the Afrikaners had arrested Dr. Mandela'* R32.3

ayehamba *v-remote-past* they had traveled; they used to travel R28.3

ayeke *v-pres-sub* he might leave R16

ayengafuni *v-remote-past-neg* they had not wanted R20.4

ayetsho *v-remote-past* who said R20.3

ayezii *n5-pl* being • *ayezii-baas boy 'that they become baas boys' (similar to 'Uncle Tom')* R20.4

ayi-[1] *neg-pres-n2-pl-prf* they do not VERB [group 2 plural negative present subject prefix] ☞ See: a- -i AM-94:163, CGB:124, E&S:18, MI:247, SXWU:28

ayi-[2] *neg-pres-n5-sg-prf* he, she, it does not VERB [group 5 singular negative present subject prefix] ☞ See: a- -i AM-94:163, CGB:127, E&S:18, MI:247, SXWU:28, R10, R19, R36.24

ayi-[3] *neg-pred* it is not [negative predicative prefix] Structure: ayi- + PRED ☞ Alt: asi- E&S:21

ayibaleke *v-tr-perf* she ran it R33.7

ayifumana *v-rel* which he receives R27.3

ayifumani *v-tr-neg* he does not find R36.24

ayikho[1] *v-exis-neg-n2-pl* there are none; they are not present / available E&S:29

ayikho[2] *v-exis-neg-n5-sg* there is none; it does not exist, it is not available E&S:29, R36.25

ayilawulwa *n5-sg-VERB-pass* it is not controlled R37.2

ayimi- *n2-pl-adj-neg-pred* they are not ADJ [group 2 plural negative adjective agreement prefix used predicatively] • *ayimide 'they are not long'* E&S:28, PCX:157

ayiN- *n5-sg-adj-neg-pred* he, she, it is not ADJ [group 5 singular negative adjective agreement prefix used predicatively] • *ayinde 'it is not long'* E&S:28, PCX:158

ayinakufunyaniswa *v-neg-pass-caus* he cannot be found R36.14

ayinakwenza *v-tr-neg* she cannot do R19.3

ayindlalileyo *v-rel-tr-perf* which he, she played R27.7

ayinguye *cop+pro-abs* it is not everyone R35.7

ayinyanzelwa *v-n5-sg-SNEG-neg-pres-pass* it is not forced R10

ayiphindi *v-aux-neg* does not return, does not do again, repeat R37.26

ayiphucukanga *v-intr-neg* it is not civilized R17.3

ayithandabuzeki *v-atr-neg-pres* it is not doubtful R36.3

ayivuki *v-intr-neg* does not get up • *indoda ayivuki? 'does the man not wake up?'* R15

ayo[1] *n2-pl-poss-n3-pl* their; of them GDX3:691

ayo[2] *n5-sg-poss-n3-pl* his, her, its; of him, her, it • *ibhodi izame ukwenza ngako konke okusemandleni ayo* GDX3:691, R37.16

ayoyiswa *v-caus-pass* they are made to be afraid R27.10.11

az- *neg-pres-n4-pl-prf* they do not VERB [group 4 plural negative present subject prefix before vowel-initial verb] ☞ See: azi- R11

aza-[1] *n4-pl-S3b-neg* (and) they did not VERB [group 4 plural past subjunctive negative verb subject (S3b) agreement prefix] E&S:42, SXWU:141

aza-[2] *n5-pl-S3b-neg* (and) they did not VERB [group 5 plural past subjunctive negative verb subject (S3b) agreement prefix] E&S:42, SXWU:141

aza[3] *v-aux-fut* they will R32.9

azalisekise *v-atr-caus-sub* so that it may cause fulfilment • *azalisekise imfuno zabantu 'so that (the Government) may fulfil the needs of the people'* R23.4

-azana *n-suf-dim* [feminine diminutive noun suffix] • *intombazana 'young girl' [= in-t/thomb-azana]* AXG:36, E&S:33, MI:262, R4b, R4c

azanelanga *n5-pl-v-tr-neg* they are not enough R35.5

aze *v-aux / conj* so that Derived from -za 'come' R10, R27.11, R37.15.20.21

-azel- *v-suf* do VERB persistently, do repeatedly [persistive verb suffix] ☞ Alt: -ezel- E&S:44

azi-[1] *neg-pres-n4-pl-prf* they do not VERB [group 4 plural negative present subject prefix] ☞ See: a- -i AM-94:163, E&S:18, MI:247, SXWU:28

azi-[2] *neg-pres-n5-pl-prf* they do not VERB [group 5 plural negative present subject prefix] ☞ See: a- -i AM-94:163, E&S:18, MI:247, SXWU:28

azi-[3] *neg-pres-n6-pl-prf* they do not VERB [group 6 plural negative present subject prefix] ☞ See: a- -i MI:247

-azi[4] *v-tr-ir* know, know how to, be versed in; understand; be aware of; be acquainted with; be conscious of; [fig] be guilty of retains k(u) >kw as root begins with vowel. Also retains -i as terminating vowel AM-94:106, CGB:123, E&S:45, PCX:21, RD-96:375, SXWU:31, XED:4, xvi, R9, R10, R11, R20, R29=5

azibone *v-tr* and they see R36.23

azidine *v-refl* tire oneself R27.7

azifumana *v-refl* they find themselves R36.23

azihluphe *v-refl* he did not consider himself inconvienced R27.7

azikho[1] *v-exis-neg-n4-pl* there are none; they are not present / available E&S:29

azikho[2] *v-exis-neg-n5-pl* there are none; they are not present / available E&S:29

aziN- *n5-pl-adj-neg-pred* they are not ADJ [group 5 plural negative adjective agreement prefix used predicatively] • *azinde 'they are not long'* E&S:28, PCX:158

azinakusetyenziselwa *caus-ben-pass-change-ty* they won't be utilized for R37.19

azinyaswa *v-pass* which are frequented KM, R36.9

-azisa *v-caus* inform, make known, notify; announce, proclaim, give notice; acquaint, introduce, cause s.o. to know; advertise EXD:483, RD-96:375, XED:5, R18

azisikelele *v-tr-sub* let him bless them Subjunctive form, denoting 'let him (God) bless them (in this case the chiefs iinkosi [n5-pl] [subj-prefix + obj-agr + verb + subj-suffix] R13.3

aziva *v-tr-neg* they do not feel R36.13

-aziwayo *v-rel-atr* famous, popular, well-known RD-96:375

azizi- *n4-pl-adj-neg-pred* they are not ADJ [group 4 plural negative adjective agreement prefix used predicatively] • *azizide 'they are not long'* E&S:28, PCX:158

az o[1] *n4-pl-poss-n3-pl* their; of them GDX3:691, XED:5

az o[2] *n5-pl-poss-n3-pl* their; of them GDX3:691, XED:5, R25.4

azohlwaywa *v-pass-vowel-neg-n4-pl-SNEG* they will not be punished The full form is azizi kohlwaywa - the class prefix and the future auxiliary -za are elided and reduced to az(o) + ohlwayw- +a R11

azokuzazisa *v-fut-refl-caus* by coming to make himself known R27.7

azokuzuza *v-tr* will get, will obtain • *eze ngaphambili azokuzuza '(those) who come will get'* R27.1

azonwabisa *v-refl* who make themselves happy R36.18

azonyanye *v-refl* they fear for themselves R36.22

B

b[1] *change* change of BH to B • *imbalelwano 'correspondence' [= im-bhal-el-w-an-o]* R7

b-[2] *n1-pl-them* [group 1 plural thematic consonant prefix] ☞ See: bonke R1, R5

-b-[3] *n1-pl-obj-prf* them [group 1 plural short object form before vowel initial verb] ☞ Alt: -ba- E&S:18

b-[4] *n7-them* [group 7 singular thematic consonant prefix] ☞ See: bu-, bonke XED:16

-b-[5] *n7-obj-prf* him, her, it [group 7 singular short object form before vowel initial verb] ☞ Alt: -bu- E&S:18

b-[6] *pro-3pl-S1* they [short form before vowel initial root] • *bazi 'they know' = b(a)-azi* CGB:119

ba-[1] *n1-pl-red-prf* [group 1 plural reduced noun prefix] • *aba bantu* Loss of article a- from aba- R3, R36.8, R37.12.16

ba-[2] *n1-pl-poss* of [group 1, 1a plural possessive agreement prefix] Agr: aba-, oo- AM-94:163, E&S:22, SXWU:35f, XED:5, xv, R2=2, R11

-ba-[3] *n1-pl-obj* them [group 1, 1a plural object agreement prefix] Agr: ba-, oo- E&S:18, PCX:51, SXWU:44, XED:5, R2, R8, R9=3, R11=2

ba-[4] *n1-pl-adj-pred* they are ADJ [group 1, 1a plural adjective agreement prefix used predicatively] E&S:28, MI:248, PCX:117f, R2

ba-[5] *n1-pl-enum-prf* [group 1, 1a plural enumerative agreement prefix] ☞ See: bambi, baphi E&S:27, PCX:110f

ba-[6] *n1-pl-voc-prf* oh!, hey! [group 1 plural vocative noun prefix] • *bantwana 'children!'* Agr: aba- AXG:28, E&S:32

ba-[7] *n1-pl-S1* they [group 1, 1a plural subject (S1) agreement prefix] Agr: aba-, oo- CGB:117; 158, E&S:17f, PCX:51;24, SXWU:28, XED:5, R2, R4d=3, R5, R9=6, R11, R14

ba-[8] *n1-pl-S3a* (and) they VERB [group 1, 1a plural present subjunctive verb subject (S3a) agreement prefix] CGB:167, R2, R4c=2, R12

ba-[9] *n1-pl-S3b-pos* (and) they VERBed [group 1, 1a plural past subjunctive positive verb subject (S3b) agreement prefix] CGB:189, E&S:42, MI:247, SXWU:141, R4c, R5

ba-[10] *n1-pl-S4* they can VERB; then may VERB [group 1, 1a plural potential / conditional verb subject (S4) agreement prefix] PCX:165f, SXWU:149

ba-[11] *n1-pl-rel2* they who [group 1, 1a plural direct relative 2 construction, attributive agreement prefix used predicatively] E&S:34, MI:153; 248, PCX:151, R3, R10

ba-[12] *n1-pl-ind-rel2* whom, which [group 1, 1a plural indirect relative 2 agreement prefix] E&S:35

ba-[13] *n7-poss* of [group 7 singular possessive agreement prefix] Agr: ubu- AM-94:163, E&S:22, SXWU:35f, XED:5, xv

ba-[14] *n7-S3b-pos* (and) it VERBed [group 7 singular past subjunctive positive verb subject (S3b) agreement prefix] (CGB:189), E&S:42, MI:247, SXWU:141

-ba-[15] *pro-3pl-obj-prf* them no direct antecedent XED:5

ba-[16] *pro-3pl-S1* they • *basasebenza 'they are still working'* Structure: when there is no direct antecedent CGB:115, RD-96:375;373, SXWU:28, XED:5, xviRS-451

ba-[17] *pro-3pl-S3a* (and) they VERB [S3a present subjunctive subject pronoun] CGB:167

ba-[18] *pro-3pl-S3b-pos* (and) they VERBed [S3b past subjunctive positive subject pronoun] no direct antecedent CGB:189, E&S:42, MI:247, SXWU:141

-ba[19] *v-tr* steal; cheat, deceive, get the better of latent vowel verb ☞ Cf: iba E&S:51, RD-96:375, SXWU:32, XED:5, R2

-ba[20] *v-aux* think, assume, presume • *Ndiba nguye 'I think it's him'; Be ndiba lihashe 'I thought it was a horse'* special application of the predicative verb -ba AXG:126

-ba[21] *v-pred* be; become Structure: used in all moods and tenses except the present indicative (where copulative forms occur) AXG:125f, RD-96:375, XED:5, R2, R3=3, R4d

-ba-[22] *preverb* be VERBing [progressive preverb] • *Siya kuba sihlamba 'We shall be washing'; Ndingaba ndicinga 'I may be thinking'* Structure: frozen form of the predicative verb -ba, used in combination with non-past tenses to indicate a progressive or ongoing action AXG:125

-ba-[23] *preverb* be VERBing [perfective preverb] • *Niya kuba nifikile 'You will have arrived'; Angaba uhambile / ehambile 'He may have gone'; Akuba efikile 'When he had arrived'* Structure: frozen form of the predicative verb -ba, used in combination with past tenses to indicate a perfective or completed action AXG:125

-ba[24] *preverb-wish* if only [expressing an urgent wish] • *Akwaba wawukho 'If only you were present!'; Ayaba intloko yam ibingamanzi 'If only my head were waters!'* frozen negative past subjunctive form of the predicative verb -ba AXG:125

baas *loan* master, overlord R20

baas boy *n5-sg-red* Uncle Tom, White Man's lackey, fink (collaborator during the Apartheid era) ☞ See: baas + boy R20.4

baba *v-aux* they had R36.6

babachanaba *v-tr-pres* they are exposing them R9

babafundi *-n1-pl-poss-n1-pl* of students R18.1

babalulekile *v-atr-perf-n1-pl* they are important R9, R14

babalulekileyo *v-perf-rel2-n1-pl* who are important R3

babanesifo *n1-pl-assoc.cop-n4-sg* they had the illness R35.7

babangela *v-ben* they give in to R2

babanikele *n1-pl-v-tr-perf* they give them R35.1

babanye *adj-n1-pl-poss* of some R11

babasizele *n1-pl-v-tr-ben-perf* they pity them R35.1

babe[1] *preverb-recent-pro-n1-pl* they were VERBing [group 1, 1a plural recent past compound tense preverb] Structure: babe be-Δ (participial construction) AXG:91f, E&S:37f, PCX:183

babe-[2] *n1-pl-remote-past* they had VERBed [group 1, 1a plural contracted remote past compound tense prefix] Structure: babe-Δ (participial verb construction) AXG:93f, E&S:39, PCX:186, R32

babe[3] *preverb-past-n1-pl* they had VERBed; they did VERB [group 1, 1a plural remote past compound tense preverb] Structure: babe be-Δ (participial verb form) ☞ Alt: baye E&S:39, GDX3:714, PCX:186

babe[4] *preverb-past-n7* it had VERBed; it did VERB [group 7 singular remote past compound tense preverb] Structure: babe bu-Δ (participial verb form) ☞ Alt: baye E&S:39, GDX3:714, PCX:186

babe[5] *v-pred-sub* they become • *babe ngumzekelo 'they become an example'* R31.2

babe[6] *v-aux* they have VERBed R35.14

babecinga *v-remote-past* they had thought R32.4

babengekho *n2-pl-Verb-neg-part* not being there, were not there (included) R37.24

babenolwazi *v-aux-conj-n6-sg* have an idea or the knowledge R37.11

babhinqileyo *v-rel-atr* who are women • *bantu babhinqileyo 'people who are women; females'* from bhinqa 'tie around the waist' [lit: those who are tied around the waist] R36.8

babi *n1-pl-adj-pred* they are bad R2

babi kunezilwanyana *adj-expr* they are worse than animal parents R2

babizwa *v-tr-pass* they are called R20.1

babo[1] *n1-pl-poss-n1-pl* of them; their (own); theirs CGB:183, E&S:22, GDX3:691, XED:5, R2=2

babo[2] *n1-pl-poss-n7* of them; their (own); theirs E&S:22, GDX3:691, XED:5

babo[3] *n7-poss-n1-pl* its; of it GDX3:691

babo[4] *n7-poss-n7* its; of it GDX3:691

babona *v-tr* they saw (witnessed) R24.8

babu- *n7-remote-past* it had VERBed [group 7 singular contracted remote past compound tense] AXG:93f, E&S:39, PCX:186, R36

babulala *v-tr-n1-pl-S1* they kill R11

babungaphezu *v-remote-past-n7* it was beyond R36.6

babuyiselwe *n1-pl-v-caus-ben-pass-perf* be returned R35.12

babuze *v-tr-perf* they questioned R32.3

bacela *v-tr* they ask R27.5

bade *v-aux* they even from -de 'long' R37.17

badiphe *v-tr-sub* they dip R27.9

bafikelele *v-intens* they reached R18.4, R37.10

bafumane *n1-pl-v-tr-perf* they receive R35.13

bafuna *v-pres* they want R4d, R17.3, R18.6, R27.14

bafunde *v-tr-sub* they should study R16

bafundile *v-perf* they are learned (EXD:337), R17.1

bafundiswa *n1-pl-v-caus-pass* they are taught R35.9

bag *n5-sg-red* postal bag ☞ See: private bag R4b

bagcinwe *n1-pl-vpass-perf* they are taken care of R35.12

bagxininisa *v-tr-caus* they are concerned about R37.26

bagxothiswe *v-caus-pass* they were expelled R26.1

bahlale[1] *v-pres-sub* they live R26.3

bahlale[2] *v-aux-pres-sub* that they always VERB R12

bahlawule *v-sub* that they should pay • *banokuthi ngoku bahlawule irhafu 'they have an opportunity to pay tax now'* R23.7

bahlobo *n1-pl-red* friends • *abo bahlobo 'those friends'. Bahlobo! 'Friends!'* pre-prefix is elided when following a demonstrative, or a negative verb, or in Vocative. ☞ See: abahlobo R14

baka[1] *n1-pl-poss-prf* of [personal possessive prefix / marker for noun group 1 plural] Agr: aba- E&S:23f, PCX:109, SXWU:37

baka[2] *n1a-pl-poss-prf* of [personal possessive prefix / marker for noun group 1a plural] Agr: oo- E&S:23f, PCX:109

bakhalaze *v-intr-perf* they worried • *abangazange bakhalaze 'they never worried...'* participial following aux. in negative form R37.12

bakhe[1] *n1-sg-poss-n1-pl* his, her, its CGB:182, E&S:22, GDX3:691, XED:6

bakhe[2] *n1-sg-poss-n7* his, her, its • *ubunkokeli bakhe 'his leadership'* E&S:22, GDX3:691, XED:6, R24, R32, R36

bakho[1] *pro-2sg-poss-n1-pl* your, yours; your own [singular] • *abahlobo bakho 'your friends'* CGB:182, E&S:22, GDX3:691, PCX:60, XED:6, R12, R14=2

bakho[2] *pro-2sg-poss-n7* your E&S:22, GDX3:691, XED:6, R14, R34

bakho[3] *v-exis-n1-pl* they are here; they are present ☞ See: -kho E&S:29, ITX:17, RD-96:375

bakhulule *v-tr-part* they free follows auxiliary -khe, thus is participial R32

bako[1] *n8-vn-poss-n1-pl* its, of it GDX3:691

bako[2] *n8-vn-poss-n7* its, of it GDX3:691

bako[3] *n10-loc-poss-n1-pl* its, of it GDX3:691

bako[4] *n10-loc-poss-n7* its, of it GDX3:691

baku-[1] *n1-pl-temp* when they VERB / VERBed [group 1, 1a plural temporal verb construction] • *Bakufika 'When they arrive...'* E&S:42, PCX:91f

baku-[2] *n7-temp* when it VERBs / VERBed [group 7 singular temporal verb construction] • *Bakufika 'When it arrives...'* E&S:42

bakule *n1-pl-poss1-pl-loc-dem* of this R27

bakumgangatho *n1-pl-comp* they who are trampled on, underprivileged R37.11

bakwanonibe *n1-pl-poss-loc-n-prop* those of Nonibe R27.5.7

bakwazi *v-tr* they know R29, R37

-bala *v-tr* count; calculate, reckon; narrate, relate RD-96:375, XED:6

balapha[1] *deic-1-n9-loc-poss-n1-pl* of this place (here) • *abantu balapha 'the people of this place'* PCX:140, R35, R37.4

balapha[2] *deic-1-n9-loc-poss-n7-sg* of this place (here) • *nobutyebi balapha emhlabeni 'and the wealth of this earth...'* CD2

bale *n7-sg-poss-n5-sg-deic* of the • *ngobukho bale bhodi 'about the existence of the board'* R37.25

-baleka *v-intr* run; flee, run away; fly away PCX:20f; 92, XED:7, R33

-balisa *v-caus* tell, utter, express with words EXD:653, R28=2

balo[1] *n1-pl* its, of it Prn-c7+poss-stem-c6 R21

balo[2] *n3-sg-poss-n1-pl* his, her, its; of him, her, it GDX3:691

balo[3] *n3-sg-poss-n7* his, her, its; of him, her, it GDX3:691

balo[4] *n6-sg-poss-n1-pl* its; of it GDX3:691

balo[5] *n6-sg-poss-n7* its; of it GDX3:691

balubona *v-tr* they see it -lu- C6 OC R36

-balula *v-tr* pick (out), choose, select; distinguish, specificy; make an exception of XED:7, R3x, R9x

baluleka *v-atr* get selected; become good; be distinguished, notable, important CGB:155, RD-96:376, XED:7, R3, R9, R14, R37

balulekile *v-atr-perf* important RD-96:376, R3, R9, R14=2, R16, R21, R24, R30, R31, R34.3, R37.7.10

-balulekileyo *v-atr-perf-rel* important, distinguished MI:154, RD-96:376, R3, R37.7

balumkisile *v-tr-caus-perf* they warned R36

baluthethayo *v-rel-n1-pl-n6-sg-obj* of which they speak R37

balwazi *v-tr* who know it R37.20

bam[1] *pro-1sg-poss-n1-pl* of me; my, mine; my own • *abahlobo bam 'my friends', oonyana bam 'my sons'* AM-94:151, CGB:181, E&S:22, GDX3:691, PCX:60; 72, SXWU:36, R33

bam[2] *pro-1sg-poss-n7* of me; my, mine; my own • *ubuso bam 'my face'* AM-94:151, CGB:181, E&S:22, GDX3:691, PCX:60; 72, SXWU:36

bamana *v-aux* they just R37

-bamba *v-tr* hold, grasp; seize, catch; keep, retain, hold for; arrest, apprehend, take prisoner; [ext] regard as XED:7, R4ax, R30

bambi *enum-pro-n1-pl* others, some others (of a different kind) Structure: RED noun form + ENUM / ENUM + FULL noun form ☞ See: -mbi E&S:27, PCX:110

bambona *v-tr-perf* they saw him R36

bambonisa *v-tr-caus* they showed her R28

bamoyikisa *v-tr-caus* they scared him R36

banayo *v-poss-rel* which they have R18

bancedakale *v-atr-sub* that they be assisted R37.16

bancede *v-pres-sub* they should please R4c

bancedise *n1-pl-v-tr-caus-perf* they help with R35

-banda *v-st* be cold to the touch (of inanimates) ☞ Contrast: -godola 'be ~ feel cold (of animate beings)' AM-94:112, CGB:143, XED:7

-bandakanya *v-tr* unite, bring into connection, join together into R27.9, R35.8.10, R36.9.11.15

bandiphoxa *v-past-sub* they have made a fool of me R4c

banegunya *v-poss* they have the authority / right R22

-baneka *v-tr* light up, enlighten; flash AXG:117, XED:8

banenxaxheba enkulu *v-poss-cmp* they have a big role (to play) R22

-banga[1] *v-tr* cause, occasion, bring on, produce EXD:87, XED:8, R2x, R9x, R10x

-banga[2] *v-tr* allege, claim; demand RD-96:376, XED:8, R9x, R33x

bangabahoyi *v-tr-neg* they being unconcerned about R35

bangabaniki *n1-pl-v-tr-neg* they do not give them R35

bangabantakwethu *n1-pl-cop* they are our brothers Full form copulative. ba-prefix+cop n1pl+ n1pl prefix+noun root +baka (n1a pl poss)+kwethu' R11

bangakhe *v-sub* they should just R32

bangazihluphi *v-neg-sub-pres* they should not waste their time R4c

-bangela[1] *v-ben* cause for; bring upon; allow, give in to XED:8, R2, R37.14

-bangela[2] *v-ben* claim s.t. for s.o. XED:8, R2, R37.14

bangenakufikela *v-neg-pot-ben* they cannot reach R30.6

bangqishe *v-n1-pl* they stamped on the ground R26.3

bani *qw-n1-pl* who? [subject]; whom? [object]; what sort of? • *Bantu bani? 'What kind of people?'* CGB:129f, E&S:33, PCX:28; 118, XED:8

banike *v-n1-pl-pres-sub* they should give R14

banikwa *n1-pl-v-pass* they are given R35

banikwe *n1-pl-v-pass-past* they are given R35=2

-banjwa *v-pass* be arrested ☞ rw: -bamba XED:7, R4a

banokukuhenda *v-n1-pl-S1-abil-pro-2sg-obj* they can tempt you R14

banokukwenza *v-abil+pro-2sg-obj* they are able to make you R14

banokunikwa *v-abil-pass* they can be given R35

banokuthi *v-abil* they can say • *banokuthi ngoku bahlawule irhafu ngaphandle kokoyika isohlwayo 'They now say they can pay tax without fear of penalty'* R23.7

banta *n1-pl* children ☞ Sg: umnta; Red: bantwana R11

bantu *n1-pl-red* people ☞ See: abantu PCX:24, R1, R3, R36.8, R37.12.16

bantwana *n1-pl-red* children R15

-banzi *atr-root* wide, broad E&S:30, EXD:725, RD-96:376, R16, R22, R36

baphatha *v-tr-past* they handled R36

baphathwe *v-tr-pass* they are ruled R20

baphe *v-obj-imp* serve them! R8

baphi[1] *qw-n1-pl* which (ones)? E&S:27, GDX3:703, PCX:111

baphi[2] *qw-loc-adv-n1-pl* where are? ☞ See: -phi AXG:141, E&S:31, PCX:111

baqala *v-tr* they begin R29

baqalise *v-sub* they begin R35

baquqa *v-intr* go often XED141, R37

Barbara *loan* Barbara R31

basamkela *v-prog-n1-pl* they still receive R10

basazigcine *v-tr-prog* they are still being kept R26.8

baseAfrika *n1-pl-poss-loc-pred* those of Africa R32

basebenza *n1-pl-v-intr* they work R35

basebenzisa *v-caus* they use R30

basekuhlaleni *rel-loc-n1-pl* who are nearby ba + se + kuhlala +(e)ni R35

basentolongweni *loc-n5-sg* of those in prison R36

basetyenziswa *v-caus-pass-n1-pl* they are used R9

basezilalini *n1-pl-rel-n5-pl-loc* those who are in rural areas R10

baso[1] *n4-sg-poss-n1-pl* his, her, its; of him, her, it GDX3:691

baso[2] *n4-sg-poss-n7* his, her, its; of him, her, it GDX3:691

basuke *v-aux* they on the other hand VERB R35.1

Bathandwa Ndondo *-pn* Bathandwa Ndondo (name) R32

bathathe *v-tr-sub* that they take R37.24

bathatyathwa *v-pass* they are taken R35

bathenga *v-tr* they buy R29

bathi *v-pres* they say R4d=2, R37

bathini *v-qw* what are they saying? R37.10

bathunywa *v-pass-pres* they are sent R9

batyiswe *n1-pl-v-pass* they are fed R35.12

bawaqhawula *v-tr* they cut short R20

bawo[1] *n2-sg-poss-n1-pl* its; of it GDX3:691

bawo[2] *n2-sg-poss-n7-sg* its; of it GDX3:691

bawo[3] *n3-pl-poss-n1-pl* their; of them GDX3:691

bawo[4] *n3-pl-poss-n7-sg* their; of them GDX3:691

baxelele *v-sub-n1-pl* they should tell R14

baxhaphakile *v-st-perf* they are all over the place R9

baya[1] *v-aux-fut-n1-pl* they will R14=4

baya[2] *v-aux* they are R32

baya kuba *v-n1-pl-fut* they will be R14

baya kukuphulaphula *v-n1-pl-fut-pro-2sg-obj* they will listen to you R14

baya kukuxhasa *v-n1-pl-fut-pro-2sg-obj* they will support you R14

baya kukuxolela *v-n1-pl-fut* they will forgive you R14

bayabule *v-pres-sub* that they should roam R2

bayacelwa *-n1-pl-v-pass* they are requested R35

bayayazi *v-tr* they know R20

bayazazi *v-pres-1/1a-pl* they know them (Class 5pl) SC+Pres+C5pl+Verb+i R20=2

baye[1] *preverb-past-n1-pl* they had VERBed; they did VERB [group 1, 1a plural remote past compound tense preverb] Structure: baye be-Δ (participial verb form) ☞ Alt: babe AXG:93f, E&S:39, GDX3:714, R27.7

baye[2] *v-aux* they should VERB; they would VERB Used as auxiliary in compound tenses R19.2, R27.5, R37.17

baye[3] *preverb-past-n7* it had VERBed; it did VERB [group 7 singular remote past compound tense preverb] Structure: baye bu-Δ (participial verb form) ☞ Alt: babe AXG:93f, E&S:39, GDX3:714

bayibone *v-tr* they should see it R29

bayiphawula *v-tr* they marked it, noted it • *phawula = brand, mark* XED:125, R37

bayisebenzise *v-caus* they used it R37.11.25

bayiyo *v-rel-cop* which they are n1-pl+ cop-n5+rel.term-n5 R17.1

bayo[1] *n2-pl-poss-n1-pl* their, of them GDX3:691, XED:9

bayo[2] *n2-pl-poss-n7-sg* their, of them GDX3:691, XED:9

bayo[3] *n5-sg-poss-n1-pl* its, of it GDX3:691, XED:9

bayo[4] *n5-sg-poss-n7-sg* its, of it [n7-abstr + possessor in n5-sg (Africa) GDX3:691, XED:9, R13

bayongqiba *v-short-fut* they will beg for it R9

baza[1] *v-aux-past-sub* they came (to do s.t.) ☞ Usually: beza; See: -za [venitive aux] R5

baza[2] *v-fut-aux* they will R31=2

baza kulilisana *v-fut* they came to share in the mourning R5

bazazi *v-tr* they know R27

baze *-C1-pl-+aux* they thereby, so that they R31, R35

bazibile *v-tr-perf* they have stolen R26

baziphakamisa *n1-pl-S1-n-5-pl-obj-v-caus* they raise them (opinions) R37

baziphethe *v-refl-past* they have behaved R11

bazisebenzisa *v-tr* they use R31

bazithathele *v-refl-perf* they took for themselves R26

bazo[1] *n4-pl-poss-n1-pl* their; of them GDX3:691

bazo[2] *n4-pl-poss-n7-sg* their; of them GDX3:691

bazo[3] *n5-pl-poss-n1-pl* their; of them GDX3:691

bazo[4] *n5-pl-poss-n7-sg* their; of them GDX3:691

bazo[5] *n6-pl-poss-n7-sg* their; of them • *Emva kokuhamba iintsuku ezinthathu nobusuku bazo* R28

bazuze *n1-pl-v-tr* they obtain R35.3

be-[1] *n1-pl-S2* they [group 1, 1a plural participial subject (S2) agreement prefix] • *Irayisi inceda abantwana bakho bahlale bekrelekrele bedlamkile 'Rice helps your children stay intelligent (and) lively'* Structure: with n1-pl antecedent stated AXG:89; 91, CGB:191, R2=2, R5, R12=2

be-[2] *pro-3pl-S2* they VERBing [s2 participial subject] • *ngebekho oogqirha, amagqwetha, abongikazi 'would there be doctors, lawyers, nurses?'* either no antecedent stated or referring to plural nouns of varied classes AXG:91, CGB:191, R3

be[3] *v-pred-past-part* was being [past participial of predicative verb 'to be'] • *beku - 'it was' actually contraction of kube ku... in compound tense.* ☞ See: ba R5, R24

-be[4] *preverb* was VERBing, have been VERBing [recent past preverb] Structure: S1-be S2-Δ , i.e., followed by participial verb form (frozen perfect tense form of predicative verb -ba) AXG:90f, E&S:37f, PCX:181, R24, R36, R37.10

-be[5] *preverb* had VERBed; did VERB [remote past compound tense preverb] • *Sabe sifuneka 'We were sought'; Ndabe ndidiniwe 'I was tired'* Structure: S3b-be S2-Δ (followed by participial verb form); frozen remote past form of predicative verb -ba ☞ Alt: -ye AXG:125, E&S:39, GDX3:714, PCX:185f

-be[6] *preverb-conj* and • *Uya zazi zonke izimvu zakhe, zibe nazo zimazi yena 'He knows all his sheep, and they know him'* frozen present subjunctive form of the predicative verb -ba AXG:125

-be[7] *v-pred-pres-sub* that [S3a] be; that it (should) become ☞ See: -ba; -be na- R3, R4d, R8, R11, R12=2x, R14

-be na- *v-poss-pres-sub* that [S3a] might have • *ukuze isizwe sibe nenkqubela 'that the nation would have progress'* ☞ See: ba + na R3, R4d, R12=2

beans *n5-sg-red* beans R8=2

beApartheid *n5-sg-poss* of Apartheid R32

bebe[1] *v-n1-pl-recent-past* they were being [group 1 plural recent past participial predicative] E&S:48, R5

bebe-[2] *v-n1-pl-recent-past* they were / have been VERBing [group 1, 1a plural contracted near / recent past continuous prefix] AXG:91f, E&S:37f, MI:247, PCX:183

bebengenayo *v-rel-poss-neg* that they did not have it R37.19

bebona *n1-pl-S2-v-part* they obtaining • *xa bebona 'when they obtain'* R35.11

bebu- *v-n7-sg-recent-past* it was / it has been VERBing [group 7 singular contracted near / recent past continuous prefix] AXG:91f, E&S:37, MI:247, PCX:183

becala *n3-sg-poss* of the side R36=2

bedlamkile *v-st-n1-pl-S2* being lively R12

beelali *n5-pl-poss* of the wards or villages R27

befumana *n1-pl-S2-v-part* they getting R35.3

Beginners *loan* beginners R37

-behle *preverb* VERB in good time • *Sibehle safika 'We arrived in good time'* Structure: takes S3b + past subjunctive complement E&S:47

behlonipha *v-n1-pl-S2-part-pres* they respecting note Class1-pl form of subject concord be- for participial form. R17.2

-beka *v-tr* put on top, set in honor CGB:143, R24

bekho *verb-cop* There was R3, R30, R37.14.23

bekrelekrele *v-st-n1-pl-S2* they being bright, smart, intelligent R12

beku-[1] *v-n8-vn-recent-past* it was / has been VERBing [group 8 verbal noun contracted near / recent past continuous prefix] AXG:91f, E&S:37, MI:247, PCX:183

beku-[2] *v-n10-loc-recent-past* it was / has been VERBing [group 10 locative / impersonal noun contracted near / recent past continuous prefix] • *bekuyimini 'It was the day...'* E&S:37, PCX:183, R24

bekungafunwa *v-pass-past-neg* it was not considered necessary R37

bekungekho *v-exis-neg* there has been no; there was no R37.10

bekuyimini *n5-sg-recent-n10-loc-past-pred* it was a day R24

bekwenziwe *v-pass* it was done R21

beli-[1] *combo* of • *abantu belizwe 'people of the country'* indicates that n3 sg (ili-) is possessed by a n1 pl (ba-) ☞ See: ba- + ili- CGB:181

beli[2] *deic-1-n3-sg-poss-n1-pl* of this • *abaMhlophe beli lizwe 'the Whites of this country'* R32

beli[3] *deic-1-n3-sg-poss-n7* of this • *kubunkokeli bakhe beli lizwe 'in his leadership of this country'* R32

beli-[4] *v-n3-sg-recent-past* he was / she has been VERBing [group 3 singular contracted near / recent past continuous prefix] AXG:91f, E&S:37f, MI:247, PCX:183, R24.5

belidlana indlebe *v + n5-sg-obj* they conferred R18

belinemincili *v-poss-recent-n3-sg+n2-pl-obj* who was rejoicing [lit: who was with rejoicing] beli- [recent past (agrees with 'iqabane')] + na- + imincili R24.5

belizwe *n3-sg-poss* of the country CGB:181

belu- *v-n6-sg-recent-past* he was / she has been VERBing [group 6 singular contracted near / recent past continuous prefix] AXG:91f, E&S:37, MI:247, PCX:183

bemdlwengula *v-tr-past* they were raping him R36

bemikhosi *n1-pl-poss-n2-pl* military R16

bemvaba *n5-sg-poss-n1-pl* of a missionary society [ba + imvaba[R13

benabaxhasi *v-poss-n1-pl* they have supporters R33.10

bendi- *v-pro-1sg-recent-past* I was / have been VERBing [contracted near / recent past continuous prefix] AXG:91f, E&S:37f, MI:247, PCX:183, R23.6

bendifanele *v-ben-perf-oblig-pro-1sg* I should have (done so) R23

bengafuni *n1-pl-pot-neg-VERB* they could not want/find, they not finding R20

bengakwazi *v-tr-past-neg* they did not know (how) R37

benganakwazi *v-tr-pot-neg* they cannot know R18

bengaphambili *v-aux-cop-loc* who were ahead, before R36.2

bengekho *v-exis-neg-part* they being absent Derived from absolute pronoun khona 'there' R20.2

beni- *v-pro-2pl-recent-past* you (all) were / have been VERBing [contracted near / recent past continuous prefix] AXG:91f, E&S:37f, MI:247, PCX:183

benqandwa *v-pass* they were prevented R32

benu[1] *pro-2pl-poss-n1-pl* of you; your, yours; your own [plural] • *abahlobo benu 'your friends'* CGB:182, E&S:22, GDX3:691, PCX:60

benu[2] *pro-2pl-poss-n7* of you; your, yours; your own [plural] E&S:22, GDX3:691

benza *v-tr-part* they do R27

benze *v-sub* that they make v subj R35

besamkela *v-part-pres* they still earning R29

beselile *v-perf-part* having drunk R31

besenza *v-tr-past* they are doing, R20

besi[1] *deicl-n4-sg-poss-n1-pl* of this • *abafundi besi sikolo 'the students of this school'* R18

besi[2] *deicl-n4-sg-poss-n7-sg* of this • *uboya besi silo 'the fur of this animal'* PCX:140

besi-[3] *v-n4-sg-recent-past* he was / she has been VERBing [group 4 singular contracted near / recent past continuous prefix] AXG:91f, E&S:37, MI:247, PCX:183

besi-[4] *v-pro-1pl-recent-past* we were / have been VERBing [contracted near / recent past continuous prefix] AXG:91f, E&S:37f, MI:247, PCX:183

besiba *v-part* they stealing R2

besifa *v-part-pres* they being sick note Class1-pl form of subject concord be- for participial form. R17.3

besihambele *v-tr-ben* we were visiting R26

besithanda *v-tr-past* we liked R21

besithi *v-part-past* we said, we saying note Class1-pl form of subject concord be- for participial form. R17.2, R26, R37

-betha[1] *v-tr* hit, beat, strike; assault; punish; reach EXD:277, XED:11, R15x

-betha[2] *v-aux* make s.o. VERB; cause to VERB XED:11

bethela *v-ben* beat s.t. for s.o.; nail down to XED:12

bethu[1] *pro-1pl-poss-n1-pl* of us; our, ours; our own [plural] • *abantwana bethu 'our children'; abafundi bethu 'our readers'; abanye bethu 'some of us'* CGB:182, E&S:22, GDX3:691, PCX:60, R9=3, R31=2

bethu[2] *pro-1pl-poss-n7* of us; our, ours; our own [plural] E&S:22, GDX3:691

-bethwa *v-pass-st* be moved, affected, overpowered by (sleep, love, sorrow, fear, any strong emotion) XED:11

beyithenga *v-part-pres* they buying it R29=2

bezandla *n4-pl-poss-n7* of the hands • *ubuhlungu bezandla neenyawo 'painful hands and feet'* R30

bezi[1] *deic-1-n4-pl-poss* of these PCX:140

bezi-[2] *v-n4-pl-recent-past* they were / have been VERBing [group 4 plural contracted near / recent past continuous prefix] AXG:91f, E&S:37, MI:247, PCX:183

bezi-[3] *v-n5-pl-recent-past* they were / have been VERBing [group 5 plural contracted near / recent past continuous prefix] AXG:91f, E&S:37, MI:247, PCX:183

bezi-[4] *v-n6-pl-recent-past* they were / have been VERBing [group 6 plural contracted near / recent past continuous prefix] AXG:91f, MI:247

bezibile *v-refl-past* they were sweating R26

bezifaka *v-refl* they get themselves involved R2

bezihleli *v-intr-past* they lay themselves (down) • *izifundiswa bezihleli phantsi 'the learners lay themselves down'* R17.2

bezikolo *n1-pl-poss-n4-pl* of the schools R37

bezingaziwa *n1pl-neg.part-verb-pass* without being known R37

bezithuthi *n1-pl-poss-n4-pl* of vehicles/automobiles R31

bezivele *v-intr-past* they would always appear to R37

Bhaca *clan* Bhaca, Baca (clan or ethnic group within the greater Xhosa community) ☞ See: umBhaca, amaBhaca AXG:20, CGB:1, MI:273

-bhala *v-tr* mark, make a mark; write ☞ Cf: -lesa 'read' CGB:114, PCX:26, XED:6, R4b, R7x, R24

-bhalela *v-ben* write to / for s.o. AM-94:115, XED:6, R4b=2, R22

-bhalelana *v-recip* correspond (with), write to one another EXD:126, XED:6, R7x

bhaxa *ideophone* fall on; squelch in mud E&S:59

-bheka *v-tr* look towards, turn towards, go towards XED:10, R34.11

-bhetele *atr-root* better E&S:30

-bhinqa *v-tr* tie s.o. around the waist; gird one's loins; fasten a belt on, buckle up; [fig] get ready XED:13, R36=8

bhodi *n5-sg-red* board ☞ See: ibhodi R37=20

bhota *intj-sg* greetings! ☞ Pl: bhotani PCX:29f

bhotani *intj-pl* greetings! [to a group] ☞ Sg: bhota PCX:33; 54

-bhubha *v-intr* die (of a human) ☞ Syn: -sweleka; Contrast: -fa CGB:143

-bi *adj-root* bad, evil; ugly ☞ Opp: -hle AM-94:193f, AXG:63, CGB:171f, E&S:30, PCX:120, RD-96:376, R2, R9, R30

Biko *pn* Biko (family name) ☞ See: Steve Biko R32

-bila *v-intr* sweat, perspire EXD:643, R26x, R30x=2

Bill *loan* Bill R37=4

-bini *adj-root* two AM-94:76, AXG:64, CGB:171, E&S:30, PCX:29; 120, R8x, R16, R37.7

-biza *v-tr* call, summon; name; ask for, demand (payment) PCX:196, XED:14, R12

blood *loan* blood loanword ☞ See: high blood pressure R25

-blowu *atr-root* blue AM-94:107, CGB:172, NDK-91:31, Uys:4, R34

-bo[1] *n1-pl-root* they; their (own); theirs [group 1 plural pronoun / possessive root] ☞ See: #abo, babo, kwabo, labo, lwabo, sabo, wabo, yabo, zabo CGB:183, E&S:22, SXWU:36, R2=2

bo-[2] *n1a-pl-voc-prf* oh!, hey! [group 1a plural vocative noun prefix] • *bosisi 'sisters!', botata 'fathers!'* Agr: oo- ☞ Alt: boo- AXG:18; 28, E&S:32, PCX:52, SXWU:14

-bo[3] *n7-pro-root* it; its [group 7 singular pronoun root] E&S:22

-bo-[4] *preverb* should not VERB, will have to VERB [emphatic future subjunctive] • *abohamba 'he should walk'* Structure: Pos: -bo-(ku)-Δ-a. Contracted form of -be ku- ☞ Neg: -nga-bo-(ku)-Δ-a E&S:42, SG-1.

bo-[5] *v-n1-pl-short-fut* they will VERB [contracted / short positive future group 1, 1a plural noun prefix] E&S:20, R19, R29

bo-[6] *v-n7-sg-short-fut* it will VERB [contracted / short positive future group 7 singular noun prefix] E&S:20

bobaa *deic-3-n7-sg-pred* that (far, yonder) is E&S:26

bobo *deic-2-n7-sg-pred* that (not far, just mentioned) is E&S:26

bobu *deic-1-n7-sg-pred* this is E&S:26

bodwa[1] *pro-quan-n1-pl* only they; they alone Agr: aba-, bona E&S:27, PCX:62

bodwa[2] *pro-quan-n7-sg* it alone; only it Agr: ubu-, bona E&S:27, PCX:62

bohlukana *v-short-fut* and they would separate R19.2

bokuba *n7-sg-poss-n8-vn* of being; [conj] that, so that • *ubungqina bokuba inkwenkwana edlwengulweyo 'evidence that boys who have been raped'* ☞ See: ukuba R19.6, R36.25

bokuqala *v7-sg-poss-vn* of the first time R36

-bolile *v-perf-atr* rotten E&S:30

Bomvana *clan* Bomvana (clan or ethnic group within the greater Xhosa community) CGB:1, MI:273

-bomvu *atr-root* red; reddish brown AM-94:107, CGB:172f, E&S:30, EXD:514, NDK-91:248, RD-96:376;113, UEX:14, Uys:4, R34

bomzabalazo *n2-sg-poss-n1-pl* of the struggle R32.3

bomzimba *n2-sg-poss-n7* of the body R34

bona[1] *pro-n1-pl-echo* they [group 1, 1a plural echo / absolutive pronoun] AM-94:92; 163, CGB:158, E&S:21, PCX:57, R3, R11, R17.3=2

bona[2] *pro-3pl-abs* they; themselves; them, as for them without antecedent AM-94:92; 163, CGB:158, RD-96:376

bona[3] *pro-n7-sg-echo* it [group 7 singular echo / absolutive pronoun] AM-94:163, CGB:158, E&S:21, PCX:57

-bona[4] *v-tr* see, behold; perceive; find PCX:23; 73, RD-96:376, XED:15, R4cx, R11, R30x

-bonakala *v-atr* be seen; be visible; seem, appear; be intelligible ☞ Perf: bonakele AXG:116, PCX:93, RD-96:376, XED:15, R16x

-bonakalayo *v-rel-atr* visible, conspicuous RD-96:376

-bonakalela *v-atr-ben* be transparent, be visible, be seen to be; suffer a loss, be left destitute XED:15, R16, R26.5

bonakalelwe *v-atr-ben-pass* they suffered a loss, were destitute R26.5

-bonakalisa *v-atr-caus* show, reveal, make visible XED:15, R19, R34.6.12, R36.17

-bonakaliswa *v-atr-caus-pass* can be seen R34.12

-bonana *v-recip* see one another • *...bonana no-Nompumelelo. 'See Nompumelelo'* R15

-bonana na- *v-recip-cmp* visit, see, consult with R15

-bonelela *v-intens* provide for, make provision against s.t.; take advantage of EXD:489, KED:41, XED:15, R23.0, R37x

-bonga *v-tr* praise, celebrate, eulogize, extol s.o. (in poetry) MI:277, XED:15

Bongane *pn* Bongane (personal name) R4d

-bongoza *v-tr* beseech, implore, entreat, coax XED:15, R16

-bonisa *v-caus* show, exhibit, illustrate; make s.o. see s.t. AXG:111, ITX:66, RD-96:376

bonk' *n7-adj-quant* all b(a)- + -onke [Class14 (Bantu) n7-abstr agreement + onke 'all' R13

bonke[1] *pro-enum-n1-pl* all; every • *bonke abantu 'all the people; everybody'* Agr: aba-, bona AM-94:163, CGB:176, E&S:27, PCX:62f;24, XED:15, R1, R5, R20, R23, R35, R37=3

bonke[2] *pro-enum-n7* all; the whole (of); every Agr: ubu-, bona AM-94:163, E&S:27, PCX:62

bonomgogwana *n1a-sg-poss-n1a-pl* puppet • *bonke oorhulumente bonomgogwana 'all those puppet governments'* ba-u-no-(u)m-gog-w-ana adjective formed from attributive compound noun, prefix truncated because of bonke preceding noun R20

Bophuthatswana *pn* (province in South Africa) R20

bothuka *v-n1-pl* they are startled, they get shocked R35.11

Box *n5-sg-red* box loanword ☞ See: PO Box; ibhokisi R4c, R4d, R7, R15, R20, R21, R22, R25

boy *loan* boy R20

BP *n5-pn-red* British Petroleum (acronym) R30.1

bu-[1] *n7-red-prf* [group 7 singular reduced noun prefix] Loss of article u- from ubu- SXWU:20

-bu-[2] *n7-obj* [group 7 singular object agreement prefix] Agr: ubu-, u- E&S:18, PCX:51, SXWU:44, R24

bu-[3] *n7-adj-pred* it is ADJ [group 7 singular adjective agreement prefix used predicatively] E&S:28, MI:248, PCX:118f

bu-[4] *n7-enum-prf* [group 7 singular enumerative agreement prefix] ☞ See: bumbi, buphi E&S:27, PCX:110f

bu-[5] *n7-S1* he, she, it [group 7 singular subject (S1) agreement prefix] Agr: ubu- CGB:117; 158, E&S:17f, PCX:51, SXWU:28, R33x

bu-[6] *n7-S2* he, she, it [group 7 singular participial subject (S2) agreement prefix] AXG:91, CGB:191

bu-[7] *n7-S3a* (and) it VERBs [group 7 singular present subjunctive verb subject (S3a) agreement prefix] (CGB:167)

bu-[8] *n7-rel2* that which [group 7 singular direct relative 2 construction, attributive agreement prefix used predicatively] E&S:34, MI:153; 248, PCX:151

bu-[9] *n7-sg-ind-rel2* which [group 7 singular indirect relative 2 agreement prefix] E&S:35

bube *preverb-recent-pro-n7-sg* it was VERBing [group 7 singular recent past compound tense preverb] Structure: bube bu-Δ (participial construction) AXG:91f, E&S:37, PCX:183

bubo *n7-pred* it is; it is it [group 7 singular copulative or predicative] E&S:21, PCX:98

bubu-[1] *n7-pred-prf* it is [group 7 singular copulative or predicative prefix construction] • *bubuso 'it is a face'* CGB:135, E&S:21; 25, PCX:96, XED:xvi

bubu-[2] *n7-agent-prf* by (done by, produced by) it [marker of group 7 singular agent of passive verb] E&S:25;43

bubuthongo *n7-abs-agent* by sleep R25

bugxwayiba *n7-sg-red* (in) this country overgrown with bush preceded by a locative demonstrative R17.4

-buhlungu *atr-root* painful, sore; poisonous AM-94:107f, CGB:172, E&S:30, XED:61, R25, R30=4

buka[1] *n7-poss-prf* of [personal possessive prefix / marker for noun group 7 singular] Agr: ubu- E&S:23f, PCX:109

-buka[2] *v-tr* admire, like, look at (with pleasure, admiration); prize; take care of; conserve, be sparing with; browse (through a book), watch (TV), see (a movie) CGB:144, XED:17, R1x, R4cx, R11x

-bukeka *v-atr* be admired, liked; [perf] admirable, exquisite, comely XED:17, R1, R11

-bukela *v-ben* watch (TV, etc. for one's own enjoyment) • *Ndithanda ukubukela ezemidlalo kumabonakude 'I like to watch sports on television.'* R4c

-bukhali *atr-root* sharp CGB:172

bukho *v-exis-n7* it is here / present E&S:29, ITX:17

-bula *v-intr* confess, admit (to incest, immorality, immoral feelings) XED:17, R5x

-bulala *v-tr* kill, murder; hurt; destroy ☞ Perf: -bulele; Pass: -bulawa EXD:327, PCX:89, XED:17; 36, R11=2, R32x

-bulawa *v-pass* be killed; get murdered ☞ rw: -bulala XED:17, R32.9

-bulela *v-ben* admit an obligation to; be grateful, give thanks to / for XED:17, R5x

Bulelani *n1a-sg-pn-masc* Bulelani (male personal name) [lit: be thankful] SXWU:11

-bumba *v-tr* mould, form, shape; incorporate • *Sincede ekubeni sibumbe ikamva lethu sonke. 'Help us to shape the future for all of us.'* ☞ Cf: unobumba 'letter (of the alphabet)' XED:18, R21, R34x=12

bumbi *enum-pro-n7* other, some other, different Structure: RED noun form + ENUM / ENUM + FULL noun form ☞ See: -mbi E&S:27, PCX:110

buni *qw-n7* what kind?, of what sort? ☞ See: -ni PCX:118

buphi[1] *qw-n7* which (one)? E&S:27, GDX3:703, PCX:111

buphi[2] *qw-loc-adv-n7* where is? ☞ See: -phi E&S:31, PCX:111

buqu *ideophone* himself, herself, yourself R27

busuku *n7-sg-red* night ☞ See: ubusuku R36

-butha *v-intr* gather, congregate, come together, collect; lie down together (as cattle); [v-tr] collect, gather, bring together XED:19

buthathaka *n7-abs-red* weakness, feebleness, softness, inefficiency ☞ See: ubuthathaka R30

-buthelana *v-ben-recip* gather together, congregate NDK-91:383

-buthuntu *atr-root* blunt CGB:172

Butterworth *n5-sg-pn-loc* Butterworth (coastal town) ☞ See: iGcuwa R7

buya[1] *v-aux-pres-n7-sg* it is R34.10

-buya[2] *v-intr* return, come / go back; revert XED:19

-buya[3] *v-aux* re-, do VERB again • *Ndobuya ndithembe 'I'll hope again'* Structure: followed by S3a + present subjunctive E&S:42; 47, XED:19

-buyela *v-ben* return to / for PCX:92, XED:19

-buza *v-tr* ask, question, enquire, interrogate; examine, investigate CGB:143, XED:19, R6, R34

C

-caca *v-st* be clear, become obvious; plainly seen or heard, distinct CGB:155, R26.5, R37.11.12.19.25

-cacile *v-perf-atr* obvious, clear, plain, distinct RD-96:377, R37.11.12

-cacisa *v-tr* explain, clarify; account (for); illuminate RD-96:377, R37.1.7.19

-cacisa ngeenkcukacha *v-cmp* explain s.t. in detail ☞ Cf: inkcukacha EXD:155

Calata *pn* Calata (family name) ☞ See: Fort Calata R32

calcium *n5-sg* calcium R12

-calula *v* discriminate EXD:162, R20, R32

calulo *n6-sg-comp-redupl* Apartheid [latter half of compound] ☞ See: lucalu-calulo 'apartheid' R20.3

Cancer *loan* cancer R34

Cape Town *n5-sg-pn-geog* Cape Town ☞ See: iKapa (eKapa) R21

Capricorn *loan* Capricorn R34

carbohydrate *n5-pl* carbohydrates • *ngumxube weecarbohydrate 'it is a mixture of carbohydrates'* R12

care *loan* care ☞ See: After-Care Centre R35=7

Catholic Institute of Education *loan* Catholic Institute of Education R22

-ceba *v-tr* advise, counsel; devise, scheme, conspire against XED:21

-cebisa *v-caus* advise, give advice to XED:22

-cela *v-tr* ask for s.t., request, beg CGB:143, XED:22, R4a, R12, R31

centre *loan* center ☞ See: After-Care Centre R35=7

championships *loan* championships R33=3

-chanaba *v-tr* expose (s.o. to great heat, public view) XED:21, R9

-chaphazela *v-ditr* drop s.t. on s.o., besprinkle, besmatter XED:21, R36.21

-chasa *v-tr* oppose, be against XED:21

chatha *ideophone* pour out carefully, sparingly, let out in drops XED:21, R34=2

-chaza *v-tr* comb; straighten out, unravel; make incisions in the skin, scarify; [ext] explain; report s.t. EXD:107, XED:21, R7, R36.0.3.4.7.12.17.24, R37.15

-chazela *v-ben* unravel, straighten s.t. out for s.o; [ext] explain s.t. to s.o. XED:21, R7x, R37.15

child *loan* child ☞ See: Child Protection Unit R27

Child Protection Unit *loan* Child Protection Unit R27, R36

-chitha *v-tr* spend; spill, scatter; waste; destroy XED:23, R34.2

-chitha ixesha *v-cmp* spend time [lit: scatter time] R34.2

chops *n5-sg-red* chops ☞ See: yelamb chops R8

-chuba *v-tr* peel, pick (grains off a corn cob), pick out (kernel of a nut); [fig] select the best (of s.t.); [ext] train, civilize KED:65, XED:25, R8x

church *loan* church ☞ See: Dutch Reformed Church R35.2

-cima *v-tr-imp* put out (fire), turn off (light), extinguish In reading 13, imperative form = verb root. ☞ Pass: -cinywa PCX:34, XED:23, R13

-cinezela *v-tr* press down, squeeze; oppress, afflict XED:23, R30x

-cinga *v-intr* think, imagine, suppose; intend to (do) XED:23, R3, R14x

-cinywa *v-pass* be extinguished ☞ rw: -cima PCX:103

Ciskei *pn-geog* Ciskei (Xhosa region settled by the descendants of Rharhabe) ☞ See: emaXhoseni; Phalo, Rharhabe CGB:4, R20

Clive *loan* Clive (personal name) R18

club *loan* club R33, R36

commission *loan* commission ☞ See: Truth Commission R32

Conversational *loan* conversational R37

correctional services *loan* correctional services R4b

-coselela *v-tr* attend to closely, take interest in XED:24, R6

country *loan* country R33

Crawford *pn* Crawford R37

criminologist *loan* criminologist R36

crisis *loan* crisis R36

cross *loan* cross R33

-cula *v-intr* sing PCX:89, XED:25, R4bx, R4cx

cwaka *ideophone* be silent, calm, still E&S:59

D

-da[1] *v-intr* be long, take a while ☞ Perf: de; Neg: danga XED:26

-da[2] *v-aux* eventually, finally, at last VERB • *Yada yafika imoto 'Eventually the car arrived'* Structure: followed by S3b + past subjunctive construction ☞ See: de E&S:47, SXWU:140, XED:26

-dada *v-intr* swim (of animal or bird), float ☞ Contrast: -qubha (human) CGB:143, EXD:644

Daizer Mqhaba *pn* Daizer Mqhaba (Editor-in-chief of *Bona* magazine) R31

-dala[1] *adj-root* old, aged, adult; senior; eldest; stale AXG:63, CGB:171, E&S:30, PCX:118ff, RD-96:378, XED:27, R4dx, R30, R37.13

-dala[2] *v-tr* create, make s.t. new; cause, originate; ordain CGB:189, EXD:87, RD-96:378, XED:27, R13x, R37.1

Damaqua *clan* Damaqua (Khoi ethnic group which became part of the greater Xhosa community) CGB:9

-dana *adj-dim* tallish, a bit tall, a little long ☞ See: -de + -ana AXG:37, XED:28

-danyana *adj-dim* tallish, a bit tall; longish, somewhat long ☞ See: -de + -anyana AXG:37, XED:28

-dazana *adj-dim* not very tall, somewhat long ☞ See: -de + -azana AXG:37

-de[1] *adj-root* long; tall, high AXG:37; 63, CGB:171; 179, E&S:30, PCX:120, XED:28, R12

-de[2] *preverb* until, as far as VERB • *Phumla de afike 'Rest until he arrives'* Structure: takes S3a + present subjunctive; derived from aux verb, now fossilised as de ☞ See: -da E&S:47, XED:28, R8=2, R26, R28, R31

-de[3] *preverb* eventually, finally, at last VERB • *Bade bavuma 'They eventually agreed'* Structure: followed by S3b + past subjunctive ☞ See: -da E&S:47

deadline *loan* deadline R21=3

dela *v-tr* despise, have contempt for XED:28

deposit *loan* deposit R25

dibana *v-recip* meet together R34.7

-dikidiki *atr-root* lukewarm, tepid CGB:172, E&S:30

dilesi *n5-sg-red* address • *ubhale kuleyo dilesi engentla. 'Write to the box number above.'* ☞ See: idilesi R15, R22

-dina *v-tr* tire, fatigue ☞ Pass: -dinwa XED:29, R4cx

-diniwe *v-perf-atr* tired E&S:30

-dinwa *v-pass* be tired, get tired, become fatigued ☞ Perf: -diniwe CGB:155f, XED:29, R4c, R30

director *loan* director R29

dl *change* change of L to DL • *indledlana 'small path' [= in-dlel(a)-ana]; khudlwana 'fairly large' [= khulu-ana]* XED:31

-dla[1] *v-tr* eat, consume; [ext] cost; fine; [fig] cheat, defraud AXG:107, XED:30

-dla[2] *v-aux* usually VERB, used to VERB • *Kanene la mabali ebedla ngokuwava angobomi basentolongweni? Were these stories he used to hear about prison life true?* Structure: followed by ngoku- (adverbial + infinitive) construction E&S:47, R36

dlabhu *ideophone* tear, pierce, wound E&S:59

-dlala *v-tr* play AM-94:155, R4b, R4cx, R12x

-dlamka *v-st* be merry, lively, frolicsome, in good spirits XED:30, R12

-dlana indlebe na *vp-idiom* confer XID:27, R18

-dlelana *v-ben-recip* eat together; have fellowship; [fig] be friends, have friendly relations XED:30

-dlisa[1] *v-caus* feed (animal), make eat; pasture, herd (livestock) XED:30, R25x

-dlisa[2] *v-tr* poison s.o.; give or administer poison to EXD:466, XED:30, R25x

-dlwengula *v-tr* treat with violence; rape, ravish, violate XED:31f, R9x, R11x, R36=27

Draft *loan* draft R37=2

drop *n5-sg-red* drop R25

-duduma *v-intr* thunder; rumble (as a stampede or a crowd in motion) AM-94:112, AXG:218, EXD:664, XED:33

-dulu *atr-root* expensive ☞ Opp: -tshiphu AM-94:107, E&S:30

-dumbile *v-perf-atr* swollen E&S:30

dungu *ideophone* scatter, disperse, fly off E&S:59

Durban *pn-geog* Durban ☞ See: iTheku (eThekwini) R25

-dwa *pro-quan-root* only, alone ☞ See: -odwa CGB:176, E&S:27, PCX:62

dy *change* change of TY to DY • *indyebo 'wealth' [= in-dy/tyeb-o], iindywala 'beer-parties' [= iin-dy/(u)tywala]* PCX:195

dyumpu *ideophone* plop, plunge into water E&S:59

E

e[1] *change* change (coalescence) of -A + I- to E • *eminyaka 'of years' [= a-imi-nyaka], neminyaka 'have years' [= na-imi-nyaka]* CGB:120, PCX:192, R4a=2, R4b, R6

e[2] *change* loss (elision) of -A before E- • *benza 'they make' [= b(a)-enza]* PCX:192

e-[3] *loc-prf* in, at, to [locative prefix] • *ebusuku 'at night' [= e-(u)bu-suku], eKapa 'in Cape Town' [= e-(i)Kapa]* Structure: replaces initial vowel (article) of noun group prefix; on non-personal and non-locative nouns, the suffixes -eni or -ini are used (q.v.) ☞ Contrast: kwa- [domain locative], ku [person locative] CGB:138, E&S:32, PCX:29ff;68ff, SXWU:101, R2=5, R3, R4b, R4c, R6, R7, R9=5, R10=5, R12=7, R14, R16=2, R24, R27, R30, R36.00

e-[4] *emph-prf* [emphatic formative before noun groups starting with i] ☞ See: elona, esona, eyona, ezona TD

e-[5] *n1-sg-S2* he, she [group 1, 1a singular participial subject (S2) agreement prefix] AXG:89; 91, CGB:191, R4b, R10=2

e-[6] *n2-pl-dir-rel1* those which [group 2 plural direct relative 1 attributive agreement prefix positive or negative construction] CGB:174, E&S:23; 28; 34, MI:153; 248, SXWU:155, XED:xv, R4a=2, R4b, R4c, R4d, R10, R12

e-[7] *n2-pl-ind-rel1* which [group 2 plural indirect relative 1 agreement prefix] E&S:35

e-[8] *n3-pl-S2* they [group 3 plural participial subject (S2) agreement prefix] ☞ Rep: ama- AXG:89; 91, CGB:191, R10

e-[9] *n5-sg-dir-rel1* he, she who / that which [group 5 singular direct relative 1 attributive agreement prefix positive or negative construction] CGB:174, E&S:23; 28; 34, MI:153; 248, SXWU:155, XED:xv, R4b, R7, R9, R10=2, R12=8, R14, R19, R22=2, R28, R30, R37.14

e-[10] *n5-sg-ind-rel1* whom, which [group 5 singular indirect relative 1 agreement prefix] E&S:35

e-[11] *poss-pro-prf* [possessive pronoun formative before noun groups starting with i] ☞ See: eyam SXWU:84, R4c

e-[12] *pro-3sg-S2* he, she VERBing [S2 participial subject] • *esafunda = he/she was still studying* no antecedent stated AXG:91, CGB:191

-e[13] *n-suf* [noun-forming suffix] • *indlebe 'ear', iqabane 'intimate friend', umxube 'mixture'* R4a, R4c, R4d, R12

-e[14] *v-suf-perf* VERBed [short indicative perfect / recent past tense suffix] Structure: is used instead of -ile if an object is expressed ☞ See also: -we [passive past] CGB:152f, R6, R12=2

-e[15] *v-suf-perf* VERBed [perfect / recent past tense benefactive verb suffix] • *kwanele 'it is enough'* ☞ See: -ele TD, R4c

-e[16] *v-suf-perf-part* (who) VERBed [short participial perfect / recent past relative tense suffix] AXG:172, R4d=2, R12

-e[17] *v-sub-pres-suf* that / should VERB [present subjunctive verb suffix] Structure: S3a Δ-e CGB:167f, R2=2, R3=2, R4a, R4b=3, R4c=2, R4d=5, R6=4, R8=9, R9=4, R10, R11, R12=2, R14=3, R16

-e[18] *v-obj-imp-suf* VERB it! [positive object-oriented imperative singular verb suffix] • *Imiyalelo yifunde ngocoselelo 'Read the instructions carefully'; Mbuze 'Ask him!'; Ndincede 'Help me!'* Structure: OBJ-Δ-e AXG:99, R6=4, R8=2

eAfrika *n5-sg-pn-geog-loc* in Africa R24

east *pn-geog* east R2

ebalaseleyo *adj* eminent (EXD:187), R33

ebalulekileyo *v-perf-rel* important R21.1, R24.0, R31.1, R34.3

ebangela *v-ben* which causes for (them) R37.14

ebantwini *loc-n1-pl* on people R27, R29, R37.17

eBarkly East *n5-sg-pn-geog-loc* in / from East Barkley R2

ebe-[1] *v-n1-sg-recent-past* he VERBED [group 1, 1a singular contracted near / recent past continuous prefix] Structure: ebe-Δ (participial verb form) ☞ Alt: ube- AXG:91f, E&S:37, MI:247, PCX:183

ebe-[2] *v-n3-pl-recent-past* they were / have been VERBing [group 3 plural contracted near / recent past continuous prefix] Structure: ebe-Δ (participial verb form) ☞ Alt: abe- E&S:37, MI:247, PCX:183, R24

ebedla *v-past-part* he, she used R36

ebefumana *v-tr-part* she was getting R24

ebekufanele *v-ben-perf-oblig* she ought R24

ebephuma *v-part* as she came out R24

ebesecaleni *v-aux-loc-n3-sg* he was at the side • *...UMandela ebesecaleni kwakhe... 'Mandela at her side...'* R24

ebesinemincili *v-rel-aux-n2-pl* that was rejoicing R24.2

ebezikade *v-rel-aux-adv-adj* which was of the past R37.26

ebezikhona *v-rel-aux-loc* which were there R37.10.26

ebeziyiyo *v-rel-aux-cop-deic* the way they were R28

ebharaksi *loc-n5-sg* to/from/at the barracks R26

ebibanjelwe *v-rel-pass* which was held R27

ebibuzwa *v-rel-tr-pass* that were asked R27

ebomini *n7-abs-loc* in life ☞ See: ubomi R7, R34

ebonisa *v-rel* which shows R32

ebuhlungu *n5-sg-atr* painful R25, R30=2

ebuncinaneni *rel-adj-root-dim* which is small R33

ebusuku *n7-time* at night, by night, during the night AM-94:63, AXG:143, CGB:139, E&S:59, PCX:29f; 70, SXWU:102, XED:155, R2=2, R30

ebusweni *n7-sg-loc* on the face CGB:139, PCX:68, R25

ebutsheni *n7-abs-loc* in youth R14

ecaleni kwa *loc-n3-sg* next to, by one's side; at, by, on the side of • *ecaleni kwendlela 'on the side of the road'* ☞ See: icala AM-94:108, EXD:586, XED:20, R31

ecela *v-tr-part* he asking R36

echaza *v-part* he explains R36

edlwengulweyo *v-pass-rel* raped R36

edolophini *loc-n5-sg* in town, to town CGB:129; 139, EXXE:29, R37.14

Education *loan* education ☞ See: Catholic Institute of Education R22

e e[1] *change* change (coalescence) of -A + II- to EE • *neekati 'and cats' = na-ii-kati* CGB:120, PCX:192, R9

e e[2] *change* loss (elision) of -A before EE- • *beenza 'they made' [= b(a)-e-enza]* PCX:192

eekomiti *loc-n5-pl* of the committee R22

eElandsfontein *pn-geog-loc* Elandsfontein (town) R10

eelwimi *n3-pl-poss-n6-sg* of languages R37.16

eEssex University *n5-sg-cmp-pn-geog-loc* at Essex University R24=2

efana *v-rel-recip* that is similar R37=2

efanayo *v-rel* similar e+fan+a+yo R35.15

efanelekileyo *v-atr-perf-rel* which is proper, correct R35, R37

eFort Jackson *pn-geog-loc* in Fort Jackson R27

efumanisile *v-part-caus-perf* she/he find out R36

efuna *v-tr-part* want R20, R36

efunwa *v-pass* needed R10

egodukayo *v-rel-intr* going home R31

egusha *n5-sg-poss-n3-pl* of sheep • *amasela egusha 'sheep thieves'* R26

egwetyelwa *v-part-pass* he being sentenced ☞ See: -gweba R36.1

ehlabathi *loc-n3-sg* in the world R33

ehlabathini *loc-n3-sg* in soil; [ext] around the world R12, R24

ehlelwe *v-part-pass* experienced R36

ehlotyeni *loc-n3-sg* in the summer, during summer ☞ See: ihlobo AM-94:73, CGB:138; 142, PCX:69; 70; 196, XED:60

eIthali *pn-loc* in Italy R33.6

ejongene *v-recip-perf* face, stare at one another, be involved with. • *Abantu ngabantu kwanemibutho ngemibutho ejongene neelwimi 'people from various organizations involved with language'* The reciprocal can be used to indicate activity of a person in pursuit of something, as in UMama ufunana nesibonisi sakhe 'Mother goes about looking for her spectacles.' R37.05.20

-ek- *v-atr-suf* -able, -ible; be / become VERB [attributive, stative, subjective, or neuter verb suffix] • *tyhil-ek-a 'be disclosed, get revealed'* ☞ See also: -akal- AXG:114f, E&S:44, PCX:93, XED:36, R1, R2, R3=2, R9, R10, R11, R12, R14, R36.21

eKapa *n5-sg-pn-geog-loc* in, to, from Cape Town AM-94:62f, CGB:138, PCX:31; 69, SXWU:101, R37=2

eKeetmanshoop *pn-geog-loc* in Keetmanshoop R16

ekhatywayo *v-rel-n5-sg-pass-part* which is being kicked R4b

ekhaya *loc-n3-sg* at home AM-94:62f, CGB:139, PCX:70

ekhohlo *loc-n6-sg* to the left, on the left ☞ Opp: ekunene AXG:144, E&S:27; 32, PCX:70, XED:72

ekhohlo kuka *prep-cmp* to the left of s.o.; on the left side of s.o. used with nouns of group 1a E&S:32

ekhondweni *loc-n3-sg* at last • *ingakubuyisela ekhondweni. 'It can get you back on track'* emkhondweni means 'on track', which suggests a better translation to the example R34

ekhululekile *v-st-atr-perf* feel free R36

ekhululekileyo *v-perf-rel* that is free R24

ekhusela *v-rel-n2-pl* which protect R32.4

eKrismesi *pn-loc* at Christmas, Christmastime R31

ekuba *v-part-aux* become R36

ekubalekeni *n8-vn-loc* in the running R33=2

ekubeni *conj* seeing that, in that, inasmuch as, whereas Structure: followed by the participial AXG:151, E&S:41, XED:175, XS-92:165f, R18, R21, R28, R29

ekubhukuqweni *rel-loc-n7-sg* in the overturn R24

ekucengeni *loc-v-inf* from begging R29

ekufeni *loc-v-inf* of dying, in dying, while dying, in death R25

ekufikeni *loc-v-inf-red* at the arrival R24

ekufuneka[1] *v-st-atr* it is necessary that R23, R27, R29=2, R37

ekufuneka[2] *v-rel-atr* who need to, which is necessary R23, R27, R29=2, R37

ekufutshane *loc-adv-atr* near XED:41, R18.2

ekuhambeni *loc-v-inf* in (the) going R19.2

ekukhawuleleni *-loc-vn* to cut short XED:69, R35

ekukhutshweni *loc-vn* take out R35

ekunene *n10-loc-adv* to the right; on the right AXG:144, E&S:27; 32, PCX:70, SXWU:102, XED:98

ekunene kuka *prep-cmp* to the right of s.o. E&S:32

ekungathiwa *v-rel-pot-pass* that can be said R21.4

ekungekho *v-rel-neg-loc* which are absent R36.8

ekungelo *v-rel* not his, not her R36.1

ekunokuthi *rel-loc-pro-1pl* which is ours R23.5

ekunyuseni *n8-vn-loc* in raising R9

ekuphathweni *loc-v-inf* in managing or administering R22

ekuphuculeni *loc-v-inf* in the improving of R37.17.19=2

ekuqakaduleni *loc.* in galloping, about frolicking GDX3-5-6x, R33

ekuqulunqweni *loc-v-inf* in tidying R37

ekusasazweni *loc-v-inf* in scattering about, distributing sasaza = scatter about, strew, give bountifully XED:148, R37

ekuseni *n8-vn-loc* at dawn PCX:68

ekuthini[1] *adv-loc* in such a place XED:160

ekuthini[2] *conj* so, to the end that XED:160

ekuthiwa *v-rel-pass* which is called R31

ekuzameni *loc* in an effort to, in trying R17.4

eKwaeng *pn-geog-loc* from Kwaeng R11

ekwasekukho *v-rel-past-loc* of which there was R28

ekwenzeni *n8-vn-loc* in making R29, R35

ekwenziweni *loc-v-inf-pass* in the making R21

ekwindla *n10-time-loc* in the autumn ☞ See: ukwindla AM-94:73, CGB:138, PCX:70, XED:62

ekwingxaki *n2-pl-rel-loc-n5-sg* which are in a problem; having problems R35.15

-el- *v-suf-ben* do VERB for / to s.o. [benefactive / directive / applied verb suffix] • *khusela 'protect' [= khusa 'keep off / out']* indicates either purpose or direction, i.e., that the action is carried out for, on behalf of, directed towards, or done to the detriment of s.o. or s.t. AXG:109f, E&S:44, PCX:92, R2=2, R3=2, R4a, R4b=2, R4c, R4d=4, R5, R6=6, R7=6, R8=3, R9=2, R11, R12, R14=2, R16

-el- ni *qw-expr* why?, what for? Structure: S1-Δ-el-a ni? (consists of benefactive verb suffix and interrogative ni) E&S:44

elaa *deic-3-n3-sg* that (far, yonder) Agr: ili- ☞ Alt: eliya CGB:163, E&S:26, MI:160, SXWU:157, XED:xvi

elachasa *v-rel-tr* those who oppose R32

elalini *loc-n5-sg* from the village = e- (i) lali +ni R26

elangeni *loc-n3-sg* in the sun, in the open (opposing to secretively) R32

-elapha *v-tr* cure, treat (medically) • *Yelapha ngezindlela eziningi ezahlukene 'She cures by means of many different methods'* ☞ See Xhosa: -nyanga DNZ:58, EZZE:184, R15x

elathathwa *v-rel-pass* which was taken R32

elawula *v-rel* which governs, administers; [atr] administrative R22=3

elawulwa *v-rel-pass* that is administered R36.24

-ele[1] *v-suf-perf* VERBed [perfect / recent past tense benefactive verb suffix] • *kwanele 'it is enough'* Structure: used on verbs with -el- suffix TD, R4c

-ele[2] *v-suf-perf* VERBed [perfect / recent past tense suffix] • *bulele 'killed'* Structure: used on verbs ending with -ala XED:36

ele[3] *adv-loc* beyond, out of sight ☞ Syn: ese AXG:200, PCX:70, XED:36

ele kwa- *prep-expr* beyond, on the other side of; out of sight of XED:36

-elel-[1] *v-suf-cmp* do VERB to, for, on behalf of [double benefactive verb compound suffix] • *-lungiselela 'make s.t. right for s.o.'* R6

-elel-[2] *v-suf* do VERB completely, thoroughly, efficiently, well [perfective / intensive verb suffix] • *-omelela 'harden, dry out', -phumelela 'succeed'* ☞ Alt: -alal- E&S:44, R6x, R12

eLetaba After-Care Centre *n5-sg-cmp-pn-loc* at the Letaba After-Care Center R35=2

eli-[1] *n3-sg-adj* [group 3 singular adjective agreement prefix] AXG:15, CGB:174, E&S:28, MI:248, XED:xv, R10

eli-[2] *n3-sg-rel1* he, she who / that which [group 3 singular direct relative 1 attributive agreement prefix positive or negative construction] AXG:15, CGB:174, E&S:23; 28; 34, MI:153; 248, SXWU:155, XED:xv, R4a, R4c, R4d, R5, R6=2, R30

eli-[3] *n3-sg-ind-rel1* whom, which [group 3 singular indirect relative 1 agreement prefix] E&S:35

eli[4] *deic-1-n3-sg* this • *izolo eli 'just recently' [lit: this yesterday]; more often a straight demonstrative eli ziko 'this fireplace'* Agr: ili- ☞ Sole form (no alternate) AXG:15, CGB:163, E&S:26, MI:159, PCX:25; 86, SXWU:157, XED:xvi,

R10, R17.2, R18, R24, R25=2, R26, R30, R31, R32, R33=4, R34=5, R35=5

eli[5] *deic-1-n3-sg-poss* of this • *amathole eli hobe 'the young of this dove'* PCX:140

elicham *rel-cop-n3-sg* as an easy prey n3 sg as cop R36

elide *n3-sg-atr* long R36, R37=2

elidiniweyo *v-pass-perf-rel* who has been made tired (by) R4c

elidlulileyo *v-rel-st* that has passed R23.5

elifana *rel-n3-sg-v-recip* similar relative formed from verb 'ukufana' R35

elifutshane *adj-n3-sg* very short R10, R35.12

elihle *rel-atr* which is good, fine, right R34=2

elijongene *v-rel-tr* that is looking R27=2

elilungiselelwe *v-rel* which is right for R6

elimdaka *atr* dirty R25

elimnandi *adj-n3-sg* good, marvelous • *nibe nexesh' elimnandi 'have a good time!'* R31

elimnyama *n3-sg-atr* which is dark R5

elinama *rel-prefix* aged R24

elincinane *rel-cop-adj* small R36

elineminyaka *v-poss-rel* who has NUM years R4a

elinempilo *v-poss-rel* which is healthy [lit: which has health] R30

elinengeniso *rel-n5-sg* which is an introduction • *see isingeniso* R34

elinesixhenxe *num* that has seven R32

elingakanani *rel-interr* how much? R23

elingaphambili *v-rel-loc* which lies ahead R37

elingekho *v-exis-neg-rel1* which is absent R35

elingeli- *n3-sg-adj-neg* [group 3 singular negative adjective agreement prefix] • *elingelide 'not tall'* E&S:28

elinokudlwengulwa *v-rel-abil-pass* who can be raped R36.14

elinukayo *v-rel* which smells R32.3

eliqinileyo *v-perf-rel-n3-sg* which is hard R30

elithile *atr-n3-sg* a particular R6

elitsha *adj* that is new R35.13

elivela *v-rel-intr* which appears R31.0

elivulekileyo *v-rel-perf* which is open R33.9

elixhoba *n5-sg-cop-rel-n3-sg* which is prey • *Indoda elixhoba ' a man who is prey to...'* R36.24

eliya[1] *deic-3-n3-sg* that (far, yonder) Agr: ili- ☞ Alt: elaa AXG:15, CGB:163, E&S:26, MI:160, PCX:86, SXWU:157, R10x

eliya[2] *v-dir-rel1* which goes R10

eliyi *cop3-sg* it is • *eliyi-28 'it is 28'* R36

eliyindoda *cop3-sg-n5-sg* who is male R36

eliza kuba *v-pred-fut-rel* who will become R4d

elizaliswe *v-rel-pass-past* which were full R18

elizayo *v-rel* that is coming; which will come, [atr] future • *zexesha elizayo 'of the future' [lit: of the time which will come]* R35.12

elizuza *v-rel-tr* which obtains, that is receiving R35.2

elizweni *loc-n3-sg* in the country; on the land ☞ See: ilizwe PCX:68, R11

elizwini *loc-n3-sg* in his voice R36

elo[1] *deic-2-n3-sg* that (not far, just mentioned) Agr: ili- AXG:15,

CGB:163, E&S:26, PCX:86, SXWU:157, XED:xvi, R34

el o[2] *deic-2-n3-sg-poss* of that one (not far) DFG

elona *n3-sg-pro-emph* the real one, that very one; the most [group 3 singular emphatic pronoun] • *elona hashe lithandwa kakhulu 'the horse that is loved the most'* E&S:23, EXD:391, PCX:164

elu- *loc-n6-sg-prf* in, at, to [noun group 6 singular locative prefix] CGB:142

elubhacweni *loc-n6-sg* in exile from ukubhaca 'to wander about destitute' R20

elugqatsweni *loc-n6-sg* in the race R20, R33

elungileyo *v-perf-rel* which is R34

eluntwini *loc-n6-sg* in the community ☞ rw: uluntu R30, R35=4, R36

elusatsheni *loc-n6-sg* in the family ☞ See: usapho CGB:142, PCX:69, XED:148

elwandle *loc-n6-sg* at sea; in the sea ☞ See: ulwandle AM-94:63, CGB:139, PCX:70

em- *n5-sg-adj* [group 5 singular adjective agreement prefixX] XED:xv

emabhinqeni *loc-n3-pl* to women R36.20

emagqwetheni *loc-n3-pl* to the lawyers R26.7

eMailula *pn-geog-loc* in Mailula R33

emakhayeni *loc-n3-pl* in homes R36.10

emakhwapheni *loc-n3-pl* in the armpits R30

emakulungiswe *v-pass-n5-sg-pres-sub* that repairs should be... R37.16

emanqineni *loc-n3-pl* on paws, on all fours; [ext] on one's feet R32.8

emanzini *loc-n3-pl* in the water ☞ See: amanzi CGB:139, PCX:68

emaphandleni *loc-n3-pl* in rural areas R37.12

emapoliseni *loc-n3-pl* at the police (station) R27.0.3=2

eMatatiele *pn-geog-loc* in Matatiele R28=4

emathunjini *loc-n3-pl* in the bowels ☞ See: amathumbu PCX:69, XED:169

emaXhoseni *pn-geog* Ciskei (formerly known as Kaffirland) [lit: among the Xhosas] XED:194

embelekweni *loc-n2-sg* on the mother's back R27

emdaka *atr* that is dirty R25

emehlweni *loc-n3-pl* in the eyes ☞ See: amehlo PCX:68

eMelika *n5-sg-pn-geog-loc* in, to, from America AM-94:63, R12=7

emfaneleyo *v-rel-ben* proper R36.19

emfundo *loc-n5-sg* in education R10

emfutshane *C5-atr* that is very short R26.1

emhlophe *atr* white R30

emi-[1] *combo* of • *unama-27 eminyaka 'he has 27 of years'* indicates that n2 pl (imi-) is possessed by a n3 pl (a-) ☞ See: a- + imi- R4b, R8

emi-[2] *n2-pl-adj* [group 2 plural adjective agreement prefix] CGB:174, E&S:28, MI:248, XED:xv, R28, R37.1

em i[3] *cop* which are [NUM] • *ngemizuzu emi-4 'in 4 minutes'* R33

emihle *n2-pl-adj* which are well; beautiful; clear; thorough, complete R34

emilebeni *loc-n2-pl* on the lips R30

emingaphi *qw-adj-n2-pl* how many? • *iminyaka emingaphi 'how many years?'* R28

emini *n5-sg-time-loc* by day, during the day, in the daytime; at noon AM-94:63, AXG:143, CGB:139f, E&S:59, MI:231, PCX:31f; 70, SXWU:102, R2

emininzi *adj-n2-pl* many R28, R30, R35, R37.1

eminyaka *n2-pl-poss* of years; [atr] years old ☞ See: a- + iminyaka R4b, R16, R24=2

emisebenzi *loc-n2-pl* in jobs R10

emitsha *rel-atr* which are new R34

emizuzu *n2-pl-poss-n3-pl* of minutes R8

emlanjeni *loc-n2-sg* in the river ☞ Contrast: ngasemlanjeni 'near the river' CGB:142, PCX:69, SXWU:102

emlonyeni *loc-n2-sg* in / on the mouth ☞ See: umlomo CGB:142, PCX:69; 196, R30.2, R36.9

emntwini *loc-n1-sg* to a person ☞ See: umntu CGB:139, PCX:68

eMonti *n5-sg-pn-geog-loc* at, in, to, from East London ☞ See: iMonti AM-94:63, CGB:138, MI:246, SXWU:101, XED:194, R19, R27

empahla *n3-pl-poss-n5-sg* of clothes/goods R26

emqaleni *loc-n2-sg* in the throat [e- + umqala + -ini] R30

emsebenzini *loc-n2-sg* at work; to work AM-94:62, R12

emswaneni *loc-n2-sg* in nonsense ☞ See: umswane R31

emthonjeni *loc-n2-sg* in a spring; at the spring ☞ See: umthombo PCX:69

emva[1] *adv-loc* behind, after, at the back, in the rear [locative] • *emva kwendlebe 'behind the ear'* ☞ Opp: phambili 'in front'; See: umva AM-94:108, AXG:200, CGB:178, XED:176, R30.2

emva[2] *adv-time* after, next [temporal] • *emva kwimini 'in the afternoon'* ☞ See: emva koko; umva AM-94:112, CGB:178, EXD:12, XED:176, R19.2, R26.1.2.8, R28.2.5.7, R30.1.6, R31.3, R33.7, R35.2

emva koko *conj-expr* after that; thereafter, thereupon ☞ See: umva E&S:26; 27, EXD:659, MI:257, R35.12, R36.23, R37.5

emva kokuzityel *prep-loc-v-inf-red* after eating at them R31.3

emva kwa-[1] *prep-expr* after [temporal] • *emva kokutyholwa 'after being accused'; emva kwendibano yesondo 'after sex'* CGB:140, E&S:27; 32, XED:176, R26, R30, R31, R35

emva kwa-[2] *prep-expr* behind, at the back of [locative] CGB:140, E&S:27;32

emva kwemini *time-expr* in the afternoon E&S:59

emyenini *loc-n1-sg-term* to the husband R19.4

eMzantsi-Afrika *n2-sg-cmp-pn-geog-loc* in South Africa ☞ See: uMzantsi-Afrika AM-94:63, SXWU:101, R10, R22, R37.2.4

eN- *n5-sg-adj* [group 5 singular adjective agreement prefix] CGB:174, E&S:28, MI:248, XED:xv, R10, R37.0

enama *rel-prefix* that has R24

eNamibia *pn-geog-loc* in Namibia R16

-enda *v-intr* wed, go to get married (of a woman) XED:36

endabuzuza *v-rel-tr-past* which I got, that I obtained R33.6

endala *atr* old R27

endaweni *loc-n5-sg* instead of [lit: in place] ☞ See: indawo PCX:68, XED:28, R35, R36

endi-[1] *pro-1sg-dir-rel1* I who [direct relative 1] MI:248, XED:xvi

endi-[2] *pro-1sg-ind-rel1* I who [different subject]; me whom [indirect relative 1] E&S:35, R11, R36=2

endibona *v-pres-ind-rel1* I who see; as I see (it) • *Ngokwendlela mna endibona 'In the way I see it'* R11

endikhathazayo *v-rel-pres-dir-rel1* that which bothers me R19

endiyifumanisileyo *v-perf-ind-rel1* which I found it out R36.26

endizame *v-perf-ind-rel1* which I strived R36.21

endle *adv-loc-n5-sg* in the veld; out in the open, outside; away from home; [atr] wild AXG:200, CGB:139-141, PCX:70, XED:31

endleleni *loc-n5-sg* on the way, on the road ☞ See: indlela PCX:68, R28

endlwini *loc-n5-sg* into the house; at home; [atr] in place • *umama wangena endlwini 'my mother went into the house'* CGB:139f, E&S:58, SXWU:102, XED:31, R28

endodeni *loc-n5-sg* of men • *Kuthiwa endodeni 'It is said about men'* R36

-ene *v-recip-suf-perf* VERBed [perfect / recent past tense reciprocal verb suffix] Structure: used on verbs with -an- suffix XED:36

eneminyaka engama *v-poss-rel-n2-pl-pred-num-n3-pl-expr* who is NUM years old [lit: who has NUM of years] R4c, R19.1

eneneni *loc-n3-sg* in reality R36

enentamo *rel-conj-n5-sg* with the neck R25

enetha *v-intr-part* rain • *Used in compound idiom oomakad'enetha 'those who have had many rains,' i.e., 'those with long experience'; cf: English 'I've seen more winters than you've had hot dinners!'* R36.5

enezibane *v-poss-n4-pl-obj* with lights R31

engadalelwanga *v-rel-ben-pass-neg* they are not created R36.4

engakhange *v-rel-aux-neg* it never VERBed R23.7

engalindelanga *v-part-ben-neg* not waiting R36

engama *n2-pl-pred-num-n3-pl-expr* which are NUM • *-neminyaka engama-NUM 'NUM years old'* ☞ See also: -nama-NUM eminyaka R4a=2, R4c, R19.1=2, R33.5.7, R35.2

engamakhanukanodwa *rel-cop-n3-pl* they being gay R36

engapheli *v-rel-neg* that does not end R25.6

engaphukanga *v-rel-neg-perf* that is not broken R26.5

engathanda *v-pot-pres-part* he would like R4b

engayazi *v-rel-tr-neg* that he does not know R19.3

engazange *v-aux-neg* they never having R32

engemi- *n2-pl-adj-neg* [group 2 plural negative adjective agreement prefix] • *engemide 'not tall'* E&S:28

engeN- *n5-sg-adj-neg* [group 5 singular negative adjective agreement prefix] • *engende 'not tall'* E&S:28

engena *v-part* he, she entering • *Wathi engena 'when he entered'* R36.2

engenayo *v-rel-neg* he who does not have R10

engenhla *adv-loc* above ☞ See Xhosa: entla EZZE:189, R15=2

engento *rel-neg-n5-sg* as nothing • *amadoda azifumana engento 'men find themselves as nothing'* R36

engozini *loc-n5-sg* in danger R6

engqongqo *atr* hard, severe R11

eni-[1] *pro-2pl-dir-rel1* you (all) who [direct relative 1] MI:248, XED:xvi

eni-[2] *pro-2pl-ind-rel1* you (all) whom [indirect relative 1] E&S:35

-eni[3] *loc-suf* at, in, to [locative suffix after non-high vowels] • *ekuseni 'at dawn' [= e-(u)kus(a)-eni]; elizweni 'in the country' [=*

e-(i)lizw(e)-eni]; endaweni 'in a place' [= e-(i)ndaw(o)-eni]; esikolweni 'in school' [= e-(i)sikolo-eni] Structure: used in conjunction with e- prefix on nouns that end in -a, -e, or -o, usually replacing those final vowels ☞ Alt: -ini (which is the deep structure form) CGB:139, PCX:68ff, SXWU:101f, XED:36, R2, R4b, R9=3, R11, R14, R24, R27

enini *qw-loc* to what (kind)? R9

eninzi *adj-n5-sg* lots of, much, many • *imali eninzi 'lots of money'* R10, R22, R26, R37.14

enjalo *rel-n5-sg-deic* which is like that R37

enjani *rel-interr* what kind R36

enjengokuhlonipha *rel-adv-v-inf* which are such as respect R16

enkonzweni *loc-n5-sg* to church service XED:74, R4b

enkosi *intj* thank you R23

enkulu *adj-n5-sg* big, large R18, R22, R26, R31, R36

enokuba *v-rel-pred-abil* which can be, that can become R33.9

enokubangela *v-rel-abil-ben* which can cause R36.16

enokubangenisela *v-rel-abil-caus-ben* that might bring in R35.3

enokubaxela *v-abil* he can report them R36.7

entanyeni *loc-n5-sg* on the neck PCX:69; 196

entla *loc-n2-sg* higher up, above; in the north ☞ Opp: ezantsi CGB:141, E&S:27; 32, EXD:407, PCX:70, SXWU:102, XED:111

entolongweni *loc-n5-sg* in a jail, in prison • *from Afr. tronk, 'jail'* R36=5

entsha *adj-n5-sg* new, modern = e- + N- + -tsha ☞ See: -tsha KED:421, R25, R33, R37.0

enu *pro-2pl-poss-n3-pl* of you; your, yours; your own [plural] E&S:22, GDX3:691

eny'indlela *n5-sg-cmp* another way R9

eNyanga *pn-geog-loc* in, at, from Nyanga AM-94:63, R37

enye[1] *num-adj* one, the same R21, R26, R28, R36=4, R37=3

enye[2] *atr-n5-sg* other, another (of the same kind) • *eny'indlela 'another way'* R9

enyulwe *v-pass-short-past* elected R16

-enza *v-tr* do, make; perform; execute; cause ☞ Perf: enzile; Pass: -enziw- AM-94:106, EXD:87, PCX:20, RD-96:378, SXWU:31, XED:36, R2x, R4c, R5, R8, R9x, R10x, R11=2, R14, R22, R25, R31

-enzakala *v-atr* be done to; get hurt, be injured XED:36, R2

-enzeka *v-atr* happen, occur; get done; be possible RD-96:103; 378, XED:36, R10

enzima *atr* pregnant [lit: heavy (with child)] R19

-enziwa[1] *v-pass* be made; be done R9, R32=3

enziwa[2] *v-pass-rel-n3-pl* which were done R32=2

ePalamente *loc-n5-sg* in Parliament R21, R37.2

ephakamileyo *v-perf-rel* which are higher, advanced R10, R18

ephakathi *n2-pl-rel* which are between R4b

ephakemeyo *n5-sg-rel* which is raised Note: the short form of the perfective is not common in Xhosa - ephakamileyo would have been more likely. The form used is Zulu but it cannot be assumed that it is a borrowing on just one occurrence - it is thus considered to be interference; that is, the writer is either a second-language Xhosa speaker or has many Zulu friends! R10

ephantsi *atr-n2-pl* lower R10

ephatshini *loc-n3-sg* in / from the heart ☞ See: iphaphu XED:125

epheleleyo *v-perf-rel* which is complete R7

ephendula *v-part* he answering 3pers sg+ participial R27

ephepheni *loc-n5-sg* on paper, in writing, to the paper (newspaper) • *Veza izimvo zakho ephepheni...'Send your opinions to the newspaper'* R21

ephilileyo *v-rel-st* that is healthy R35.1

eReitz *n5-sg-pn-geog-loc* from Reitz R3

eRhawutini *pn-geog-loc* in Johannesburg (city) ☞ See: iRhawuti MI:246, PCX:69, XED:194

esaa *deic-3-n4-sg* that (far, yonder) Agr: isi- ☞ Alt: esiya CGB:163, E&S:26, MI:160, SXWU:157, XED:xvi

esafunda *v-tr-prog* she was still studying R33

esakuphuma *v-part-fut* they come out R36

esasiyifuna *rel-prog-v-tr* the thing we still want R17.3

ese *adv-loc* beyond, out of sight ☞ Syn: ele PCX:70

esebenza *v-part* working R28=2, R37.6

esebenzisa *v-tr-part* they use R20

eSecunda *pn-loc* in Secunda R33

esekelwe *v-rel-pass-perf* which has been supported verb in passive with relative concord R22

esemthethweni *loc-n2-sg* into law R37.5=2

esesichengeni *rel-cop-n4-sg-loc* exposed to danger R36

esesiqithini *rel-loc-n4-sg* while still on the island R17.6

esetyenzisiweyo *v-caus-pass* which is used R30

esezantsi *v-rel-loc* which is low R37.1

eshiyekileyo *v-perf-rel* balance, what is left R25

eshumayela *3-sg-v-part* preaches Participial form R20

esi-[1] *n4-sg-adj* [group 4 singular adjective agreement prefix] CGB:174, E&S:28, MI:248, XED:xv

esi-[2] *n4-sg-rel1* he, she who / that which [group 4 singular direct relative 1 attributive agreement prefix positive or negative construction] CGB:174, E&S:23; 28; 34, MI:153; 248, SXWU:155, XED:xv, R8, R12

esi-[3] *n4-sg-ind-rel1* whom, which [group 4 singular indirect relative 1 agreement prefix] E&S:35

esi[4] *deic-1-n4-sg* this • *esi sitya 'this dish'* Agr: isi- ☞ Sole form (no alternate) CGB:163, E&S:26, MI:159, PCX:25; 86, SXWU:157, XED:xvi, R31, R33, R37

esi-[5] *pro-1pl-dir-rel1* we who [direct relative 1] MI:248, XED:xvi

esi-[6] *pro-1pl-ind-rel1* us whom [indirect relative 1] E&S:35

esibaleka *rel* where we run R33

esibhedlele *loc-n4-sg* at, in, to, from the hospital CGB:138, R37

esibi *adj* ugly, bad R36

esichengeni *rel-loc* in danger R24

esidlangalaleni *loc-n4-sg* out in the open, in public; publicly ☞ See: isidlangalala EXD:491, R34

esifuna *v-rel-tr-pro-1pl-rel* which we want R37.7

esikhululweni *loc-n4-sg* in the jail R27

esikolweni *loc-n4-sg* in, at, to school CGB:139, PCX:68, R10, R29

esikubushushu *n4-sg-rel-n7-loc* which is at a temperature R8

esikufumene *v-perf* what we found R36

esilungileyo *v-rel-perf* that is good R35.15

esimahla *atr-rel-n5-sg* which is free, gratis, for nothing R23

esingabalula *rel-1pl-pot-v-tr* choose R36

esingathi *v-pot-part-n5-sg-dir-rel1* which can be said; so to speak R12

esingesi- *n4-sg-adj-neg* [group 4 singular negative adjective agreement prefix] • *esingeside 'not tall'* E&S:28

esinje *adv* such [a] R16

esinyeni *n4-sg* in the bladder R25=2

esiphezulu *rel-loc* higher R31

esiqithini *loc-n4-sg* on an island R32

esisamngcumngcuthekisa *rel-n4-sg* impervious R36

esiseleni *rel-n4-sg-loc* prison cell R36

esiswini *loc-n4-sg* in the stomach ☞ See: isisu R25.1.7

esithandwayo *v-rel-pass* adored R24

esithi *v-part* he saying R27

esitishi *loc-n-4-sg-loan* of the station R27

esitya *v-part* they eating R20

esiya *deic-3-n4-sg* that (far, yonder) Agr: isi- ☞ Alt: esaa CGB:163, E&S:26, MI:160, PCX:86, SXWU:157

esiyifumene *v-perf* which we received R26

esizwe *loc-n4-sg* of the nation R13

eso *deic-2-n4-sg* that (not far, just mentioned) Agr: isi- CGB:163, E&S:26, MI:159, PCX:86, SXWU:157, XED:xvi, R37.15

esona *n4-sg-pro-emph* the real one, that very one; the most [group 4 singular emphatic pronoun] • *esona silo 'the very animal'* E&S:23, PCX:165, R29

esondliwa *v-rel-pass* that is fed R20.3

esukela *v-ben-rel* which are starting from R4d

eTamarha *pn-geog-loc* in Tamarha R27=2

ethatha *v-rel-tr* that takes, taking • *yiyo ethatha 'it is that (one) that takes'* R37.17

ethe *v-rel* which was R28

eThekwini *n5-sg-pn-geog-loc* in Durban ☞ See: iTheku MI:246, XED:194, R28=6, R33

ethetha *v-part* he speaks • *xa ethetha 'when speaking...'* participial form following xa R27

ethi *v-n5-sg-rel* which is called; [atr] named, called R22=2

-ethu[1] *pro-1pl-poss-root* of us; our, ours; our own [plural possessive root] Red: -a-ithu ☞ See: #ethu, bethu, kwethu, lethu, lwethu, sethu, wethu, yethu, zethu CGB:182, R1=2

ethu[2] *pro-1pl-poss-n3-pl* of us; our, ours; our own [plural] E&S:22, GDX3:691, R1, R13

ethubeni *rel-n3-sg-loc* on the occasion R36

ethwele *v-rel-perf* carrying ☞ See: -thwala R28

ethwesw' *v-pass* being crowned with R24

etyalwe *v-rel-pass* planted, which was planted R12=7

eUnited Kingdom *n5-sg-cmp-pn-geog-loc* United Kingdom R24

eVaal Triangle *pn-loc* in the Vaal Triangle R33

evela *v-rel-ben* that comes from R34.7

eVoslorus *pn-geog-loc* in Voslorus R33

evuzayo *v-rel-pres* which leaks, that oozes R30

ewe *intj* yes ☞ Opp: hayi AM-94:85, E&S:59, PCX:26, R12, R36

ewenza *v-rel-tr* that makes R36.14

exhaphakileyo *v-perf-rel* common • *kuyinto exhaphakileyo 'it is a thing which is common'* R36

exhasa *v-pres-part* it supporting R10

exinene *v-recip-perf* that are crowded R25

eya *v-rel* going [lit: which was going] R28

eyadlulayo *v-rel* which have passed R28

eyakuthi *v-rel-intr* that it is said R37=4

eyandifihlelayo *v-rel* who (from) me was someone who hid R19.1

eyaneleyo *v-rel-ben* that is enough R35.5

eyaqaphelekayo *v-atr-rel* that it be cleared up ☞ See: -qapheleka R37.24

eyathi *rel-aux* it was said here as aux., giving emphasis to following verb, yaqalaselwa, 'they were addressed' R37

eyaziwa *v-pass-rel* which is known R10

eyenza *v* it makes; it acts • *yintoni eyenza? 'What is it that makes...?'* relative a- + latent i of (i)yenza gives eyenza, ' ...that makes' R14, R37=2

eyenzayo *v-rel* which is done R37

eyenzeke *v-rel-atr* that happened R18

eyenziwa *v-rel-n5-sg-pass-iw* which is being done R17.1.3, R37.5

eyi *rel-prefix* which are R33

eyimbaleki *rel-n5-pl* who is a runner R33

eyiyo *rel-deic-n5-sg* as it should [lit: that is it] R27.6, R35.15, R36.22, R37.14

eyokucocwa *v-rel-pass* to be cleansed R35.4

eyona[1] *n2-pl-pro-emph* the real ones, those very ones; the most [group 2 plural emphatic pronoun] • *eyona mithi 'the real trees'* E&S:23, EXD:391, PCX:164

eyona[2] *n5-sg-pro-emph* the real one, that very one; the most [group 5 singular emphatic pronoun] • *eyona nja 'the very dog'* E&S:23, EXD:391, PCX:165, R18, R37.24

ez- *n4-pl-rel1* they who / those which [group 4 plural direct relative 1 attributive agreement prefix positive or negative construction before a vowel verb] R12

ezaa[1] *deic-3-n4-pl* those (far, yonder) Agr: izi- ☞ Alt: eziya CGB:163, E&S:26, MI:160, SXWU:157, XED:xvi

ezaa[2] *deic-3-n5-pl* those (far, yonder) Agr: iziN- ☞ Alt: eziya CGB:163, E&S:26, MI:160, SXWU:157, XED:xvi

ezaa[3] *deic-3-n6-pl* those (far, yonder) Agr: izi- ☞ Alt: eziya CGB:163, XED:xvi

ezabanga *v-rel-tr* who claimed R32.4

ezabaNtsundu *n5-pl-poss-emph-n1-sg* of the black people R37

ezabo *rel-n5pl-n1pl* of theirs R26, R37

ezabulala *v-rel-tr* who killed R32.5

ezahlukene *v-perf-rel* which are different DNZ:69x, R15

ezahlukeneyo *v-rel-recip-perf* which are separate R27.2

ezakuthi *v-aux-rel-fut* which will VERB R37.7

ezandleni *loc-n4-pl* in / from the hands R15

ezantsi *loc-n3-sg* beneath, below; in the south ☞ Opp: entla; See: izantsi CGB:141, E&S:27; 32, PCX:70, XED:190, R37.10

ezantsi kwa *prep-expr* beneath, underneath, below ☞ Opp: entla; See: izantsi E&S:32

ezathi *rel-aux* that were [lit: which say] R37

eze *v-sub* he, she should come • *wonke ubani eze 'whoever comes'* R18.6, R27

-ezel- *v-suf* do VERB persistently, do repeatedly [persistive verb suffix] ☞ Alt: -azel- E&S:44

eZeleni *pn-loc* in Zeleni R26

ezelwe *v-rel-pass* it had been born R19.2

ezemidlalo *n2-pl-poss* sports ones, sporting events (i.e., programs) • *Ndithanda ukubukela ezemidlalo kumabonakude 'I like to watch sports shows on television'* R4c, R12x

ezentengiso *loc-poss-n5-sg* in sales, in trade R29=2

ezenziwa *v-rel-pass* which were made R37.5

ezenziwe *v-rel-pass* that are done R35.5

ezi-[1] *n4-pl-adj* [group 4 plural adjective agreement prefix] CGB:174, E&S:28, MI:248, XED:xv, R11x=2

ezi-[2] *n4-pl-rel1* they who / those which [group 4 plural direct relative 1 attributive agreement prefix positive or negative construction] CGB:174, E&S:23; 28; 34, MI:153; 248, SXWU:155, XED:xv

ezi-[3] *n4-pl-ind-rel1* whom, which [group 4 plural indirect relative 1 agreement prefix] E&S:35

ezi-[4] *n5-pl-rel1* they who / those which [group 5 plural direct relative 1 attributive agreement prefix positive or negative construction] CGB:174, E&S:23; 28; 34, MI:153; 248, SXWU:155, XED:xv, R30

ezi-[5] *n5-pl-ind-rel1* whom, which [group 5 plural indirect relative 1 agreement prefix] E&S:35

ezi-[6] *n6-pl-rel1* they who / those which [group 6 plural direct relative 1 attributive agreement prefix positive or negative construction] CGB:174, MI:248, XED:xv

ezi-[7] *n6-pl-ind-rel1* which [group 6 plural indirect relative 1 agreement prefix] • *umfazi ezintsana zilambile ufikile 'the mother whose children are hungry has arrived'* SG1:68-77

ezi[8] *deic-1-n4-pl* these Agr: izi- ☞ Sole form (no alternate) CGB:163, E&S:26, MI:159, PCX:25; 86, SXWU:157, XED:xvi, R37

ezi[9] *deic-1-n5-pl* these Agr: izi- ☞ Sole form (no alternate) CGB:163, E&S:26, MI:159, PCX:86, SXWU:157, XED:xvi, R16, R22, R23, R26=6, R27, R35=2, R36=2, R37=6

ezi[10] *deic-1-n6-pl* these Agr: izi- ☞ Sole form (no alternate) CGB:163, XED:xvi

ezibhankini *loc-n5-pl* in or at banks R37.14

ezibhedlele *loc-n4-pl* in hospitals R17.3, R37=2

ezibini *n4-pl-num* two R24, R35

ezibiweyo *v-rel-pass* that were stolen R26.8

ezibuhlungu *atr* painful R30

ezidlulileyo *v-perf-rel* previous, past, that which has passed by • *zibhodi ezidlulileyo 'they are the previous boards'* R37

ezifama *rel-n-3-sg-loan* on farm(s) R28

ezifana *rel-n5-pl-VERB* which are like, that resemble R33, R35, R37=2

ezifanele *v-ben-perf-oblig* which are suitable, right, appropriate R30

ezifunekayo *v-rel-atr* needed, required R29

ezifunwa *v-rel-pass* that are wanted R37.17

ezikhoyo *rel-loc* that are there R35

ezikhuselekileyo *v-rel-perf* which are protected R30.5.7

ezikude *rel-cop-adj* that are far R35

ezilanyazayo *v-rel* that are flashing R31

ezilithoba *rel-cop-num* nine, which is nine R28

eziluhlaza *atr-color* that are green; which is blue (e.g., a police trap) R31

eziluncedo *n6-sg-atr* they are helpful R37

ezim- *n5-pl-adj* [group 5 plural adjective agreement prefix] • *iitumato ezimbini 'two tomatoes'* SXWU:58, XED:xv, R8x

eZimbabwe *n5-sg-pn-geog-loc* in Zimbabwe R9

ezimbalwa *rel-adj* few R28

ezimbi *adj5-pl* which are bad R16

ezimdaka *rel-atr* dirty R36.23

ezimeleyo *v-rel-refl-perf* which is independent, that stands on its own R37.2

eziminxe *v-part-refl* holding oneself tight rw: -minx- 'hold tight' R36.1

ezimnandi *atr* nice, pleasant • *iindaba ezimnandi 'the good news...'* R23, R36

ezimotweni *loc-n5pl* motor vehicles R36

eziN-[1] *n5-pl-adj* [group 5 plural adjective agreement prefix] CGB:174, E&S:28, MI:248, SXWU:58, XED:xv

ezin-[2] *n6-pl-adj* [group 6 plural adjective agreement prefix] CGB:174, MI:248, XED:xv, R25

ezindala *adj-n5-pl* old ones R30, R35

ezindleleni *loc-n5-pl* in roads R31

ezine *rel-enum* that are four R26

ezinembuyekezo *rel-n5-sg-comp* which have (large) returns R34

ezinenjongo *rel-conj-n5-sg* which have the purpose R17.4

ezingafaniyo *v-rel-atr* which are not like or similar to R17.1

ezingakhankanywanga *v-rel-pass-perf* that were not referred to R37.4

ezingama *n5-pl-pred-num-n3-pl-expr* which are NUM • *(iibhedi) ezingama-24 '(beds) which are 24 in number'* R35.6

ezingaphezulu *rel-loc* that are above R23=2

ezingapholiyo *v-neg-rel* which do not heal R30=2

ezingaziwayo *v-rel-neg* unknown [lit: which they not they are known] R18.1

ezingcongolweni *loc-n5-pl* from the reeds R32

ezingeN- *n5-pl-adj-neg* [group 5 plural negative adjective agreement prefix] • *ezingende 'not tall'* E&S:28

ezingezi- *n4-pl-adj-neg* [group 4 plural negative adjective agreement prefix] • *ezingezide 'not tall'* E&S:28

eziningi *adj-n5-pl* many ☞ See Xhosa: ezininzi DNZ:58, R15

ezininzi *adj-n5-pl* many • *kweenkampani ezininzi 'of many companies'* R31, R36, R37.13.16

ezinjengoLydia *pn-adv* such as Lydia R33

ezinkathazweni *loc-n5-pl* in troubles R2

ezinokufundisa *v-rel-abil* which they can teach R16

ezintathu *num-adj-n6-pl* three • *iintsuku ezintathu 'three days'* ☞ See: -thathu R25, R28

ezintle *adj* beautiful, nice R28

ezintsatsheni *loc-n6-pl* in families ☞ See: iintsapho (usapho) PCX:69

ezintsha *adj-n5-pl* which are new R35

ezinye *num-adj* some R30, R33

eziphambili *n4-pl-rel-loc* leading, formost, in front • *sezizathu eziphambili 'there are formost reasons'* R33, R36

eziphaya *rel-loc* that are over there R20

eziphethe *v-rel-past* that are in charge of R22.2

eziphethwe *v-rel-pass-short-past* which are managed by R29.12

ezisakhasayo *v-rel-prog* that are still developing R33.9

ezisebenzisa *v-rel-caus* which work; that are useful for R25.0

ezisemgangathweni *rel-loc-n5-sg* at a standard/level R33.9

ezisetyenziswa *v-rel-caus-pass* which are used R37=2

ezisezakwenzeka *v-rel-prog-atr* that are still to happen R21

ezishiyekile *v-st-atr* that remained R26

ezisisipho *cop-n4-pl* which are gifts R18.2

ezithethwa *v-rel-pass* which are spoken R37=2

ezithi *rel-aux* which are said (to be) • *iinkonzo ezithi zingabikho 'services supposedly available'* R37

ezithile *adj* certain • *kwiindawo ezithile 'in certain places'* R31

ezitratweni *loc-n4-pl* on the streets R9

ezitsha *adj-n4-pl* which are new R33

ezitshisayo *v-caus-rel* burning R25

eziya[1] *deic-3-n4-pl* those (far, yonder) Agr: izi- ☞ Alt: ezaa CGB:163, E&S:26, MI:160, PCX:86, SXWU:157

eziya[2] *deic-3-n5-pl* those (far, yonder) Agr: iziN- ☞ Alt: ezaa CGB:163, E&S:26, MI:160, PCX:86, SXWU:157

eziya[3] *deic-3-n6-pl* those (far, yonder) Agr: izi- ☞ Alt: ezaa CGB:163

eziya[4] *v-rel-n5pl-aux* which will come (be) • *iindlela eziya kuthi ziphuculwe '...ways in which they (languages) will be promoted'* R22, R37

eziyingozi *rel-cop-n5-sg* in danger R36

eziza kuzilawula *v-rel-refl* which are going to govern themselves R22

ezizezi *rel-deic-1-n4-pl* are those which • *ezizezi zilandelayo 'those which follow'* R37

eziziprofesa *rel-n4-pl* who are professors R37

eziziqeqesha *v-n5-pl-rel-refl* who are training themselves R33

ezizizo *deic-rel* which are those e+zi+zi+zo R34

ezo[1] *deic-2-n4-pl* those (not far, just mentioned) Agr: izi- CGB:163, E&S:26, PCX:86, SXWU:157, XED:xvi, R36

ezo[2] *deic-2-n5-pl* those (not far, just mentioned) Agr: iziN- CGB:163, E&S:26, PCX:86, SXWU:157, XED:xvi

ezo[3] *deic-2-n6-pl* those (not far, just mentioned) Agr: izi- CGB:163, XED:xvi, R23

ezokubaleka *v-rel* for running; that are for running R33.10

ezomeleleyo *v-rel-st-perf* which are strong R12

ezona[1] *n4-pl-pro-emph* the real ones, those very ones; the most [group 4 plural emphatic pronoun] • *ezona zilo 'the real animals'* E&S:23, EXD:391, PCX:165, R31

ezona[2] *n5-pl-pro-emph* the real ones, those very ones; the most [group 5 plural emphatic pronoun] • *ezona zinja 'the very dogs'* E&S:23, EXD:391, PCX:165

ezona[3] *n6-pl-pro-emph* the real ones, those very ones; the most [group 6 plural emphatic pronoun] EXD:391, R37.3

ezone *loc-n-loan* in zone R33

ezuze *v-tr-sub* she got R33.7=2

F

-fa *v-st* die (of / like an animal), be dying; be sick, get ill; be broken (of a thing) ☞ Contrast: -sweleka ~ -bhubha AXG:107, CGB:125; 143; 155, XED:37, R25

-faka *v-tr* put in, on, among, into; insert, enclose CGB:143, XED:37, R2x, R4b, R4c, R6, R30

fama *n5-sg-red* farm ☞ See: ifama R28=3

-fana *v-aux* VERB in vain; VERB casually, aimlessly, carelessly • *Ufana athethe 'He talks carelessly'* Structure: followed by S3a + present subjunctive ☞ See also: -fumana, -fane E&S:47, XED:37

-fana na *vp* resemble, be like, appear similar to • *kufana nje nokuphosa igusha kwiingonyama 'it's just like throwing sheep to the lions'* CGB:150, EXD:347, RD-96:378, XED:37, R9, R11

-fanela *v-ben* become like, be similar to ☞ See also: -fanele XED:37

-fanele *v-ben-perf* be fit, right for; suit, become s.o.; be one's duty, ought, should, be dseserving of ☞ See also: -fanela XED:37, R23, R24

fax *n5-sg-red* fax ☞ See: ifaksi R21

-fihla *v-tr* hide AXG:116

-fihlakala *v-atr* be hidden ☞ See also: -fihleka AXG:116

-fihleka *v-atr* get hidden ☞ See also: -fihlakala AXG:116

-fika *v-intr* arrive; reach (destination) CGB:42; 189, RD-96:379, XED:38, R3, R24, R31, R37x

fikani *v-imp-pl* you (all) arrive! R31.0

-fikela *v-ben* reach to; come upon; reach up to, gain access to; succeed XED:38, R30

-fikelela *v-intens* attain, reach RD-96:379, R18.3.4, R29.12, R34.3, R37.1.7.9.10.11.17

Fort Calata *pn* Fort Calata (black freedom fighter) R32

-fota *v-tr* photograph, take a picture of s.o. EXD:453, RD-96:379, R4ax, R4bx, R37.14

-fuda *v-aux* used to VERB; formerly VERBed • *Fuda ecula 'He used to sing'* Structure: followed by S2 + participial verb construction ☞ Alt: -fudula E&S:47

-fuduka *v-intr* resettle, migrate, move to a new home CGB:42, XED:40, R28x

-fudula *v-aux* used to VERB; formerly VERBed • *Ufudula ecula 'He used to sing'* Structure: followed by S2 + participial verb construction ☞ Alt: -fuda AXG:88, E&S:47

-fudumala *v-st* be warm ☞ Caus: -fudumeza AXG:112

-fudumeza *v-caus* warm up, heat ☞ rw: -fudumala AXG:112

-fukama *v-intr* brood, sit on, lie in; digest (prey, of a snake) XED:40, R17.6

-fumana[1] *v-tr* come upon, reach (to); find; get, obtain; attain to; overtake ☞ Pass: -funyanwa

EXD:243, PCX:103, XED:40, R7+x, R12+x, R15, R24, R30

-fumana[2] *v-aux* VERB in vain; VERB casually, aimlessly, carelessly Structure: followed by S3a + present subjunctive ☞ See also: -fana, -fane E&S:47, XED:40

-fumane *v-aux* just VERBed • *Sifumane sabiza 'We just called'* Structure: followed by S3b + past subjunctive E&S:47

-fumanisa *v-caus* make s.o. get s.t.; help s.o. to find XED:40, R7, R12, R37.15

-fumanywa *v-pass* be found ☞ rw: -fumana PCX:103

-funa *v-tr* need; want, wish, desire; seek, search, look for EXD:400, RD-96:379, XED:40, R3x, R4a, R4c, R4d=3, R7x, R9x, R10, R12x, R23, R34

-funa uku- *v-aux* want to VERB, like VERBing • *Ndifuna ukuhamba 'I want to go'; Ihashe lifuna ukuphala 'The horse wants to gallop'* Structure: followed by uku- (infinitive construction) when the subject of both clauses is the same PCX:20ff; 165, R7, R12

-funa ukuba *v-aux* want to VERB, like VERBing • *Ndifuna ukuba uhambe 'I want you to go'; Ndifuna ukuba ihashe liphale 'I want the horse to gallop'* Structure: followed by ukuba + S3a (subjunctive construction) when the subject of both clauses is different PCX:165

-funda *v-tr* learn (to do); study; read AM-94:155, PCX:26, XED:40, R4b, R6, R7x=5, R10x, R14=2, R16=5, R24, R33=3

fundela *v-ben* learn for / at; study for / about PCX:92, XED:40, R7

fundile *v-perf* learned EXD:337, R17

-fundisa *v-caus* teach, instruct [lit: cause to learn] AM-94:155, XED:40, R16=2

-fundiseka *v-atr-caus* be teachable PCX:93

-funeka[1] *v-atr* be sought, wanted, desirable, necessary AXG:115, PCX:93, XED:40, R3, R9, R11=2, R16=2, R22, R29=11, R30=2, R37=7

Funeka[2] *n1a-sg-red-pn-fem* Funeka (female personal name) [lit: wanted] SXWU:11

-funwa *v-pass* be needed R10

-fuphi *adj-root* short, squat ☞ Dim: futshane; Cf: -kufuphi AXG:37; 63, CGB:171, E&S:30, PCX:120, XED:41, R10x

-fusa *v-tr* blacken; smoke s.t. XED:41

futhi *adv-time* often, continually ☞ Alt: kafuthi AXG:142, CGB:178, EXD:416

-futshane *adj-root* short, very short ☞ rw: -fuphi AXG:37; 63, CGB:171, E&S:30, PCX:120, XED:41, R10, R18.2, R24.2, R26.1.8, R28.0, R35.12

Fuzile *-pn-name* Fuzile (personal name) R17.7

G

g *abr* gram ☞ See: igraam R8

-gala *v-tr* pour XED:42, R8x

-galela *v-ben* pour out; mix in; join with; throw stones at; attack EXD:473, XED:42, R8=3, R37.7

gama *n3-sg-red* name R36

Gcaleka *clan* Gcaleka (the Great House of Gcaleka - ethnic group within the greater Xhosa community who originally lived east of the Great Kei River (Transkei), descendants of Phalo) ☞ See: Phalo, Rharhabe CGB:2; 4, MI:274

-gcina *v-tr* keep, take care of, preserve; defend, protect EXD:324, XED:44, R14, R26.8, R34.2, R35.5.12.13

-gcoba *v-intr* rejoice, be glad, merry, joyful XED:44

Gemini *loan* Gemini R34

-godola *v-st* be, get, feel cold (of animate beings) ☞ Contrast: -banda 'be cold to the touch (of things)' AM-94:112, CGB:143

-goduka *v-intr* go home ☞ Caus: -godusa AXG:112, CGB:42

-godusa *v-tr* send s.o. home ☞ rw: -goduka AXG:112

-goga[1] *v-intr* hesitate, be undecided; be silent; duck; do s.t. in the dark KED:122, XED:46, R35.0x

-goga[2] *v-tr* obstruct, prevent, disable EZZE:253, R35.0

-gogeka *v-atr* be handicapped, crippled, disabled EZZE:253, R35

gogo *ideophone* walk with difficulty (like a hobbled horse) KED:122, R35x

Gonaqua *clan* Gonaqua (Khoi ethnic group which became part of the greater Xhosa community) CGB:9

Goniwe *pn* Goniwe (family name) ☞ See: Matthews Goniwe R26=3, R32

-gonya *v-intr* act with great force XED:47, R9x

Goodman *loan* Goodman R26

Govan Mbeki *pn* Govan Mbeki R32

Gqabi *pn* Gqabi (family name) ☞ See: Joe Gqabi R32

-gqala *v-tr* observe, look at attentively; notice; aim at XED:47, R32x

gqatso *n6-sg-red* race ☞ See: ugqatso R33=3

gqi[1] *intj* look!, behold!, lo! KED:127, XED:48, R4bx

gqi[2] *ideophone* happen suddenly XED:48, R4bx

-gqiba *v-tr* finish, end, complete; end by saying; resolve ☞ Pass: -gqitywa CGB:143, EXD:215, PCX:103, XED:48, R14x

-gqitha[1] *v-tr* pass (by), go past; surpass, exceed, excel; be in great numbers; [ext] trespass, transgress EXD:440; 641, XED:48, R12, R27, R29, R31

gqitha[2] *ideophone* a lot, also, very much so R26.5

-gqithisa *v-caus* make pass; pass s.t. on; surpass XED:48, R12, R27, R31

-gqithisela *v-caus-ben* pass s.t. on to s.o., send s.t. to s.o. XED:48, R27

-gqitya *v-pass* be finished, get completed ☞ rw: -gqiba PCX:103

-gqobhoza *v-tr* pierce, penetrate, perforate, open; smash, burst / break through; seize (as bird of prey) ☞ Pass: -gqojozwa PCX:103, XED:48

-gqojozwa *v-pass* be pierced, penetrated ☞ rw: -gqobhoka PCX:103

-gquma *v-tr* cover; smother; conceal, hide XED:49, R30

-gqwesa *v-intr* win (in any contest), come out the best XED:50, R33x

-gqwetha *v-tr* turn upside down; distort, misrepresent, pervert XED:50, R3x

green beans *n5-sg-red-cmp* green beans R8

Griffiths Mxenge *pn* Griffiths Mxenge R32

-guga *v-st* get old; become weary, wear out CGB:155

-gula *v-intr* be sick SXWU:18, XED:51, R30x

-gulisa *v-caus* sicken, make s.o. ill XED:51, R30

-guquka *v-intr* turn around, back, over; convert, change one's mind, repent EXD:90, R22

-guqula *v-tr* turn s.t. back; change, convert, revolutionize; translate; say in reply EXD:533, XED:51, R3x, R14

gusha *n5-pl-red* sheep, sheep (pl) ☞ See: iigusha R26=2

Gwayi *pn* Gwayi (name) R5

-gweba *v-tr* ward off; decide, settle; judge, sentence, convict, condemn {legal} ☞ Pass: -gwetywa XED:52, R32.7, R36.1.19

-gxobha *v-tr* muddle, stir up mud; disturb water (so as to make it murky) ☞ Pass: -gxojwa PCX:103; 200, XED:54

-gxojwa *v-pass* be muddled ☞ rw: -gxobha PCX:103

-gxotha *v-tr* expel, drive off / away, put to flight; defeat KED:144, PCX:134, XED:54, R10, R13, R26

-gxwala emswaneni *vp-idiom* cry one's heart out, wail, mourn GDX3:238, R31

H

-hamba *v-intr* go, walk, move, travel; go (away, from, on), depart, leave; proceed, advance; flow (water); [fig] behave ☞ Pass: -hanjwa; Contrast: -ya 'go (to)' AXG:17, CGB:42; 114; 144, PCX:20, RD-96:380;373, SXWU:20, XED:55, R4a, R4dx

hambayo *v-rel-atr* mobile, moving NDK-91:435, RD-96:380

-hambela *v-ben* journey towards, travel to ☞ Perf: -hambele CGB:153

-hambisa *v-caus* cause to go, walk; make s.o. move (on); forward; deliver; dispatch, send off; advance, promote; circulate; proceed with (a speech) KED:146, NDK-91:435, RD-96:380, XED:55, R4dx

-hambisana *v-caus-recip* move forward together, make mutual progress R4d

hayi *intj-neg* no, how! ☞ Opp: ewe E&S:59, PCX:36f, XED:55, R14, R20, R37

Hector Peterson *pn-loan* Hector Peterson R32

-henda *v-tr* tempt s.o. to evil XED:55, R14

Hewana *pn* Hewana (name) R27=6

high blood pressure *loan* high blood pressure R25

-hla[1] *v-intr* go down, descend, come down, dismount; befall, happen latent vowel verb ☞ Cf: ihla CGB:125, E&S:51, SXWU:32, XED:56

-hla[2] *v-aux* VERB soon, quickly, in good time • *Uya kuhla abuye 'He will soon return'* Structure: followed by S3a + present subjunctive ☞ See also: -hle E&S:42; 47, XED:56

hlabathi *n3-sg-red* the world (as a whole) ☞ See: ihlabathi KED:150, R34

-hlafuna *v-tr* chew EXD:93

-hlala[1] *v-intr* sit, get seated; live, reside, dwell; stay, be still; be awake; be well, healthy EXD:351, PCX:34, XED:57, R1x, R37.1

-hlala[2] *v-aux* always VERB; keep on VERBing; do VERB continually, constantly • *Babehlala bezama 'They kept on trying'* Structure: followed by S2 + participial construction E&S:47, XED:57, R1, R12

-hlamba *v-tr* wash, launder ☞ Pass: -hlanjwa AM-94:73, PCX:20ff, R35

-hlanganisa *v-caus* combine, bring together, assemble, join, meld, weld; meet, encounter; parry, ward off (spears with a shield) XED:58, R34

-hlanganyela *v-tr* attack, gang up on, join together against s.o., assail on all sides (when two or more attack one in a fight); [fig] tempt, assail by temptations EXD:34, KED:155, XED:58, R34.3x

-hlanjwa *v-pass* be washed ☞ rw: -hlamba PCX:103

-hlanu *adj-root* five (5) AM-94:76, AXG:64, CGB:171, E&S:30, PCX:120

hlasi *ideophone* grab, snatch, snap up E&S:59

-hlawula *v-tr* pay, settle; expiate XED:58, R10x, R23

-hle[1] *adj-root* beautiful, pretty, elegant; good, fine, nice, pleasing AM-94:193, AXG:63, CGB:171; 179, E&S:30, PCX:120, RD-96:109, XED:59, R4d, R11x, R28x

-hle[2] *v-aux-perf* VERBed quickly, in good time Structure: followed by S3a + present subjunctive ☞ See: -hla E&S:47

hleze *conj* lest, so that ... not Structure: followed by present subjunctive AXG:95, E&S:42

hlobo *n6-sg-red* kind, sort, particular KED:159, XED:60, R30

Hlomela *pn* (family name) R35.4

-hlona *v-st* be shy, bashful, timid ☞ See: -hlonela, -hlonipha XED:60, R3x=2

-hlonela *v-tr* respect, fear, revere, reverence, show deference to EXD:532, XED:60, R3

-hlonipha *v-tr* respect, pay / show respect to; revere; observe name or word taboo XED:60, R3, R11x, R16, R24

hloniphani *v-tr-imp-pl* you (all) respect! R3

-hlonitshwa *v-pass* be respected ☞ rw: -hlonipha R11

Hlubi *clan* Hlubi (clan or ethnic group within the greater Xhosa community) CGB:1f, MI:273

-hluma *v-intr* sprout, grow, shoot (up); thrive, flourish XED:61

-hlungisa *v-caus* hurt, cause pain XED:61

-hlupha *v-tr* inconvenience; cause anxiety; waste s.o.'s time KED:163, R4cx

-hlutha[1] *v-inch* become sated, satisfied; [perf] have enough, be full (after eating) hlútha (high tone) ☞ Perf: hluthi (prob. because of high vowel u preceding) AXG:13, XED:61, R12

-hlutha[2] *v-tr* take s.t. from s.o. by force, plunder, rob; deprive s.o. of s.t. hlùtha (low tone) AXG:13, XED:61, R32

-hluza *v-tr* strain, filter, sift XED:61

-hlwa *v-pass* fall (of night), get late, become evening XED:61

-hobe *atr-root* grey, gray RD-96:85; 380

Hoengiqua *clan* Hoengiqua (Khoi ethnic group which became part of the greater Xhosa community) CGB:9

-hoya *v-tr* mind, be concerned about; attend to; obey XED:62, R2

huntshu *intj* victory! XED:62, R32

I

i[1] *change* addition of vowel I to break up a consonant cluster • *ukusetyenziwa 'usage' [= uku-/ty-sebenz+i-w-a]* R6

i-[2] *n2-pl-S1* they [group 2 plural subject (S1) agreement prefix] Agr: imi- CGB:117; 158, E&S:17f, PCX:51, SXWU:28, XED:62

i-[3] *n2-pl-S2* they [group 2 plural participial subject (S2) agreement prefix] AXG:89; 91, CGB:191

i-[4] *n2-pl-S3a* (and) they VERB [group 2 plural present subjunctive verb subject (S3a) agreement prefix] (CGB:167), R8=3

i -[5] *n2-pl-rel2* those which [group 2 plural direct relative 2 construction, attributive agreement prefix used predicatively] E&S:34, MI:153; 248, PCX:151

i -[6] *n2-pl-ind-rel2* which [group 2 plural indirect relative 2 agreement prefix] E&S:35

i -[7] *n3-sg-prf* [group 3 (Bantu class 5) singular noun prefix on roots of two or more syllables] • *iqabane 'partner', ixabiso 'worth', ixesha 'time'* ☞ Pl: ama-; Alt: ili- AXG:19, CGB:104, E&S:17, PCX:53, RD-96:372, SXWU:17, XED:62, R4a, R4d, R5, R7, R9x, R10

i -[8] *n5-sg-prf* [group 5 (Bantu class 9) singular noun prefix] • *ibhokhwe 'goat'* ☞ Alt: in-, im-, iN-; Pl: ii- CGB:105f, E&S:17, PCX:54, RD-96:372, SXWU:19, XED:62, R1=4, R4b=5, R4c=3, R4d, R8, R12=12, R30, R37.0

i -[9] *n5-sg-S1* he, she, it [group 5 singular subject (S1) agreement prefix] • *inika 'it gives'* Agr: i-, iN- CGB:117; 158, E&S:17f, PCX:51, SXWU:28, XED:62, R1, R4b, R12=3, R21=2, R25, R37=2

i -[10] *n5-sg-S2* he, she, it [group 5 singular participial subject (S2) agreement prefix] AXG:91, CGB:191, R1, R12

i -[11] *n5-sg-S3a* (and) he, she, it VERBs [group 5 singular present subjunctive verb subject (S3a) agreement prefix] When used as hortative OC form, is accusative case (CGB:167), R8, R10, R12=2, R30

i -[12] *n5-sg-S4* he, she, it can VERB; it may VERB [group 5 singular potential / conditional verb subject (S4) agreement prefix] • *Imvula ingana ngomso 'It may rain tomorrow'* E&S:45

i -[13] *n5-sg-rel2* he, she who / that which [group 5 singular direct relative 2 construction, attributive agreement prefix used predicatively] E&S:34, MI:153; 248, PCX:151

i -[14] *n5-sg-ind-rel2* whom, which [group 5 singular indirect relative 2 agreement prefix] E&S:35

- i[15] *n-suf* [noun-forming suffix] • *umsebenzi 'work'* ☞ See also: um--i [agent noun circumfix] SG3:199

- i[16] *v-suf-neg-pres* do(es) not VERB [negative present tense verb suffix] Structure: a-SNEG-VB-i [if OBJ follows, it loses its article (initial vowel)] ☞ See also: -nga--i, uku-nga--i AM-94:120, CGB:124, E&S:18, PCX:36f, XED:62, R2=2, R4a=2, R4c=2, R9, R10, R14

- i[17] *v-sub-pres-neg* (that / should) not VERB [negative present subjunctive verb suffix] • *bangazihluphi 'they should not waste their time'* ☞ See: S3a-nga-Δ-i CGB:168, R4c=2, R6, R10, R14

- i[18] *v-inf-neg-suf* not to VERB; not VERBing [negative infinitive / gerund verb suffix] • *ukungawuthobeli 'not obeying it'* ☞ See: uku-nga-Δ-i CGB:121, R6=2

- i[19] *v-irreg-perf-suf* -ed [irregular perfect tense suffix] • *uhluthi 'you get full'* XED:61, R12

i-meat market *n5-sg* meat market R1

i-R *n5-sg-abr* [NUM] rand (units of South African currency) R28=2

iAfrika *pn5-sg* Africa R13=2, R16

iAIDS *n5-sg* AIDS R30=2, R36x

iApartheid *n5-sg* Apartheid R32=3

iapile *n3-sg* apple ☞ Pl: amaapile SXWU:17

-iba *v-tr* steal latent vowel verb ☞ See: -ba E&S:51, SXWU:32, XED:5; 62

ibala[1] *n3-sg* color, hue; marking; spot ☞ Pl: amabala EXD:107, KED:20, XED:6, R32

ibala[2] *n3-sg* clearing, vacant lot, bare or open space (near a house or other structure), lawn, yard, courtyard; (forest) glade ☞ Pl: amabala KED:20, XED:6, R33.9x

ibali *n3-sg* story R28

ibandakanya *v-tr* it joins together into R27.9

ibane *n3-sg* torch, firebrand XED:8

ibanga *n3-sg* interval, space; grade (in school); step, pace; ground, reason ☞ Pl: amabanga EXD:253, XED:8, R9x, R10x, R21, R33x

ibangele *v-tr-past* has resulted in R37

ibangelwe *v-pass-short-past* have been caused R16

ibawa *n3-sg* miser, niggardly or greedy person ☞ Pl: amabawa CGB:111, XED:9

ibe[1] *preverb-recent-pro-n2-pl* they were VERBing [group 2 plural recent past compound tense preverb] Structure: ibe i-Δ (participial construction) AXG:91f, E&S:37f, PCX:183

ibe[2] *v-pred-pres-sub-n2-pl* they should be; that they be; that they might become R8

ibe[3] *preverb-recent-pro-n5-sg* he, she, it was VERBing [group 5 singular recent past compound tense preverb] Structure: ibe i-Δ (participial construction) AXG:91f, E&S:37, PCX:183

ibe[4] *v-aux-n5-sg* it was, would have, should have Class 5-sg + past form -be R19.2, R20, R30, R37=4

ibe[5] *v-pred-pres-sub-n5-sg* it should be; that he be; that it might become E&S:49, R8x, R12x=2

ibe na- *v-poss-pres-sub-n5-sg* he, she, it should have • *indoda ibe nezihlunu ezomeleleyo 'so that a man might have strong muscles'* E&S:49, R8, R12=2

ibekwiliphi *rel-pron* be where, which • *ibekwiliphi ibanga? 'for which reason?'* R21

ibele *n3-sg* breast, udder ☞ Pl: amabele CGB:111, SXWU:17, XED:10

ibeleko *n5-sg* womb, uterus ☞ Pl: iibeleko R25.2

ibhadi *n3-sg* springbuck, springbok ☞ Pl: amabhadi E&S:56, EXD:614, SXWU:17

ibhanti *n3-sg* belt ☞ Pl: amabhanti AM-94:72, EXD:52

ibhasi *n5-sg* bus ☞ Pl: iibhasi E&S:58, PCX:34; 54, RD-96:63

ibhatyi *n5-sg* jacket ☞ Pl: iibhatyi AM-94:72, E&S:58

iBhayi *n5-sg-pn-geog* Port Elizabeth; Algoa Bay ☞ Loc: eBhayi AM-94:63, CGB:40; 138, MI:246, XED:194, R4c

ibheka *v-tr* it looks towards R34.11

ibhinqa *n3-sg* woman ☞ Pl: amabhinqa KED:511, XED:13, R36x

ibhinqawa *n3-sg* girdle; belt XED:13

iBhobhofolo *pn-geog* Beaufort West (town) distortion of Eng. place name ☞ Loc: eBhobhofolo MI:246

ibhodi *n5-sg* board; blackboard; council • *IBhodi entsha yeelwimi. 'the new language board'* NDK-91:374, RD-96:380, R37=5

iBhofolo *pn-geog* Fort Beaufort (town) ☞ Loc: eBhofolo CGB:41, MI:246, XED:194

ibhokhwe *n5-sg* goat ☞ Pl: iibhokhwe CGB:113, E&S:58, EXD:250, PCX:54, RD-96:380;372, XED:14, R26.7

ibhokisi *n5-sg* box MI:273, PCX:54

ibhola[1] *n5-sg* auger, gimlet, borer XED:14

ibhola[2] *n5-sg* ball ☞ Pl: iibhola E&S:58, R4b

ibhola ekhatywayo *n5-sg-cmp* soccer EXD:602, R4b

ibhotile *n5-sg* bottle EXD:65, R25=7

iBhulu *n3-sg* Afrikaner ☞ Pl: amaBhulu AXG:20, EXD:11, R32x

ibhulukhwe *n5-sg* pants, pair of trousers ☞ Pl: iibhulukhwe AM-94:72, E&S:58

ibi-[1] *v-n2-pl-recent-past* they were / have been VERBing [group 2 plural contracted near / recent past continuous prefix] AXG:91f, E&S:37f, MI:247, PCX:183

ibi-[2] *v-n5-sg-recent-past* he was / she has been VERBing [group 5 singular contracted near / recent past continuous prefix] AXG:91f, E&S:37, MI:247, PCX:183, R24

iBill *n5-sg* bill R37=2

ibingafuni *v-recent-past* he did not want R24

ibukeka *v-st-atr* it being admired or prized R1

ibunzi *n3-sg* forehead ☞ Pl: amabunzi; Loc: ebunzi CGB:138, EXD:227, PCX:70

ibutho *n3-sg* collection (of similar items); assembly, gathering, organization; [ext] squadron NDK-91:383, XED:19, R37x

ibuyele *v-intr-past* she returned R19.3

iCacadu *pn-geog* Lady Frere (town) ☞ Loc: eCacadu MI:246, XED:194

icala *n3-sg* side, edge; facet, aspect ☞ Pl: amacala CGB:111, EXD:31, XED:20, R36x

icandelo *n3-sg* sector, branch ☞ Pl: amacandelo EXD:566, R34, R37

icawa[1] *n5-sg* religious service, church (worship) • *Ndihamba icawa 'I go to church'* AM-94:73, XED:21, R4a

iCawa[2] *n5-sg-time* Sunday ☞ Alt: iCawe (EXD:639), AM-94:73, CGB:46, MI:232, PCX:47, XED:21, R4ax

iCawa[3] *pn-geog* Port Alfred (town) Place names with clicks normally indicate original Khoi or San names. ☞ Loc: eCawa MI:246, XED:194

icephe *n3-sg* spoon; chip (used for eating) ☞ Pl: amacephe CGB:111, E&S:56; 31, RD-96:381;122, XED:22

icertificate *n4-sg* certificate ☞ See: isatifiketi R7

ichaza *v-pres* it explains R22

ichazile *v-tr-perf* it explained R36

ichule *n3-sg* skilled trapper, hunter; [ext] skillful person, expert EXD:200, XED:25, R29=2

ichutywe *v-pass-pres-sub* they should be peeled R8

icici *n3-sg* earring ☞ Pl: amacici CGB:111

iciko *n3-sg* eloquent speaker, fluent person ☞ Pl: amaciko CGB:111, XED:23

icimi *n3-sg* darkness XED:23

iculo *n3-sg* song, hymn ☞ Pl: amaculo CGB:111, E&S:56

iCumakala *pn-geog* Stutterheim (town) ☞ Loc: eCumakala MI:246, XED:194

icurriculum *n5-sg* curriculum, in this context Curriculum 2005 - a new curriculum to be in place by 2005 R22

idada *n3-sg* duck; [ext] swimmer ☞ Pl: amadada AXG:19, E&S:56, EXD:177

iDaliwe *pn-geog* Cathcart (town) ☞ Loc: kuDaliwe; Syn: iKathikati; Cf: udaliwe CGB:40, XED:194

idike[1] *n3-sg* deep pool (in a river); lake; natural dam, vlei CGB:39, PCX:69, XED:29

iDike[2] *pn-geog* Alice, Lovedale (town) ☞ Loc: eDikeni CGB:39, MI:246, PCX:69, XED:194

idilesi *n5-sg* address EXD:8, R4b

idilesi yeposi *n5-sg-poss-n5-sg* postal address TD

idlelo *n3-sg* pasture ☞ Pl: amadlelo E&S:56

idliso *n3-sg* poison (associated with witchcraft; can be in the form of animal hair, etc.; remains in one's system longer that chemical poison) ☞ Cf: ityhefu NTM, XED:30, R25

idlwengule *v-tr* he rapes R36

idlwengulwa *v-pass* (a man) is raped R36

idobo *n3-sg* dobbo grass (long coarse grass sp.); [ext] jungle ☞ Loc: edotyeni PCX:69, XED:32

idolo *n3-sg* knee (human); hock (animal) ☞ Pl: amadolo EXD:277; 328, RD-96:15, SXWU:17, XED:32, R32x

idolophana *n5-sg-dim* village, small town MI:262

idolophu *n5-sg* town, village; city ☞ Pl: iidolophu; Syn: isixeko CGB:42; 139, E&S:58, EXD:97, MI:262, R37.14x

iDraft Bill *n5-sg-cmp* Draft Bill R37.5

idrop *n5-sg* drop R25

iduna *n3-sg* bull, male animal • *ithol'iduna 'bull calf'* used with animal names of group 3 ☞ Contrast: induna [n5] AXG:35, XED:34

iDutch Reformed Church *n5-sg-cmp* Dutch Reformed Church R35.2

iDutywa *pn-geog* Idutywa ☞ Loc: eDutywa PCX:69

ifaka *v-tr* he puts on R30

ifaksi *n5-sg* fax TD

ifama *n5-sg* farm ☞ Pl: iifama; Loc: efama AM-94:62f, EXD:208, R28

ifanankosi *n3-sg* bodyguard EXD:62, R32

ifanele *v-perf* it is proper, suitable, right, fitting; ought, should R16, R29

ifani *n5-sg* family name, surname ☞ Pl: iifani AM-94:164, E&S:58

ifestile *n5-sg* window E&S:58, PCX:54, SXWU:19

ifikelele *v-intens-perf* it reached R18.3

ifoli *n3-sg* python ☞ Pl: amafoli CGB:111

ifolokhwe *n5-sg* fork ☞ Pl: iifolokhwe E&S:58

ifoni *n5-sg* phone, telephone ☞ Pl: iifoni E&S:58

ifoto *n5-sg* photograph, picture EXD:453, R4a, R4b, R4c

ifumene *v-perf* it is (made) available R30

ifuna *v-pres* he wants R12

ifunde *v-tr-sub* that he (the leader) study R16

igaba *n3-sg* hoe ☞ Pl: amagaba E&S:56

igadi *n5-sg* garden ☞ Pl: iigadi E&S:58

igalelo *n5-sg* joining (with s.o. in a battle or an action); contribution R29.8, R35.5.14.15, R37.7

igama *n3-sg* name; kind, sort; letter (of the alphabet); brand (product); word {ling} • *Ungubani igama lakho? 'What is your name?'* ☞ Pl: amagama AM-94:24, E&S:56, RD-96:372, SXWU:17, XED:42, R9x, R12x=2, R17.5, R27, R37x

igaraji *n5-sg* garage ☞ Pl: iigaraji; Loc: egaraji AM-94:63, E&S:58

igazi *n3-sg* blood ☞ Pl: amagazi (types of blood) CGB:111, E&S:56, XED:43, R25x, R36x

igcisa *n3-sg* skillful person ☞ Pl: amagcisa CGB:111

iGcuwa *pn-geog* Butterworth (coastal town) Click in name sugests perh. original Khoi place name. ☞ Loc: eGcuwa MI:246, XED:194

igila[1] *n3-sg* gizzard (of a fowl) ☞ Pl: amagila XED:45

igila[2] *v-tr* collide with, knock against, throw down R36.6

igoli[1] *n5-sg* gold (metal, color) ☞ Alt: igolide PCX:69

iGoli[2] *pn-geog* Johannesburg (city) ☞ Loc: eGoli; Alt: iRhawuti - IGoli is usu. considered Zulu, whereas iRhawuti (from Afr, Dutch goud) is Xhosa AM-94:62f, CGB:40; 138, MI:246, PCX:69

igolide *n5-sg* gold (metal, color) ☞ Alt: igoli CGB:40, EXD:251, XED:46

igorha *n3-sg* hero, valiant man, brave person ☞ Pl: amagorha; Alt sp: igora CGB:111, EXD:274, XED:47, R32x

igosipile *n5-sg* gospel R4c

igqala *n3-sg* observer; observant old man ☞ Pl: amagqala XED:47, R32x

igqirha *n3-sg* doctor (traditional), medicine man, witch doctor ☞ Pl: amagqirha E&S:56, RD-96:382, SXWU:17, XED:48, R7x

igqiyane *n3-sg-dim* young single woman ☞ Alt: igqiyazana; Rep: intombazana KED:513, R4bx

igqiyazana *n3-sg-dim* young single woman ☞ Alt: igqiyane, iqiyana; Pl: amagqiyazana; Rep: intombazana Naledi, R4b, R33x

igqiza *n3-sg* small group, small number (of people) XED:48, R17x

igqwetha *n3-sg* distorter; lawyer, attorney, advocate ☞ Pl: amagqwetha EXD:334, XED:50, R3x

igqwirha *n3-sg* sorcerer, wizard, magician; one guilty of unnatural crimes ☞ Syn: umthakathi; Alt sp: igqwira EXD:605, MI:273, XED:50

igraam *n5-sg* gram R8x

igubu *n3-sg* drum {music} ☞ Pl: amagubu; Loc: egubini AXG:37, EXD:177, PCX:69

igumbi *n3-sg* room ☞ Pl: amagumbi E&S:56, R18x, R35x

igunya *n3-sg* authority, right (given to s.o.) ☞ Pl: amagunya EXD:36, RD-96:382, R16, R37.16

iguqukile *v-n5-sg-perf* it has changed R22

igusha *n5-sg* sheep (merino sheep); sheepskin coat ☞ Pl: iigusha E&S:58, MI:273, RD-96:382, XED:52, R9, R26=6

igutyana *n3-sg-dim* little drum, toy drum {music} AXG:37

igwala *n3-sg* coward ☞ Pl: amagwala CGB:111, E&S:56

igwetyelwe *v-pass* being acquitted ☞ See: -gweba R36.19

igxobho *n3-sg* marsh ☞ Pl: amagxobho; Loc: egxojeni; Alt: umgxobhozo PCX:69; 200

ihagu *n5-sg* pig ☞ Pl: iihagu E&S:58, R25x=2

ihamba *v-intr* it goes R25

ihambo yokuqala *n5-sg-cmp* maiden voyage NDK-91:435

ihashe *n3-sg* horse ☞ Pl: amahashe; Loc: ehasheni AXG:19, CGB:139, E&S:56; 58

ihempe *n5-sg* shirt ☞ Pl: iihempe AM-94:72, CGB:113, E&S:58

iHistory *n5-sg* History R37.19

-ihla *v-intr* go down, descend latent vowel verb ☞ See: -hla RD-96:382, SXWU:32, XED:62, R9x

ihlaba[1] *n3-sg* pain in one's side or lungs; [ext] pneumonia ☞ Pl: amahlaba CGB:111, XED:56

ihlaba[2] *n3-sg* small aloe sp.; thistle ☞ Pl: amahlaba XED:56

ihlabathi *n3-sg* soil, sand; [ext] the world (as a whole) ☞ Pl: amahlabathi CGB:42, KED:150, XED:56, R12x, R24x, R33x, R34x

ihlala *v-aux-n5-sg* it is always VERB R1

ihlanganiswe *v-tr-pass-sub* that it be joined together . subjunctive form R21

ihlathi *n3-sg* forest ☞ Pl: amahlathi; Loc: ehlathini EXD:227, PCX:68

ihlobo *n3-sg-time* summer [lit: friendly, genial season] ☞ Pl: amahlobo; Loc: ehlotyeni AXG:217, CGB:46, E&S:56, EXD:638, KED:159, PCX:69; 196, XED:60

ihlwempu *n3-sg* poor (person), pauper ☞ Pl: amahlwempu; Loc: ehlwentshini CGB:107; 142, EXD:443; 469, XED:62

ihobe *n3-sg* pigeon, dove; Cape turtle dove ☞ Pl: amahobe E&S:56, KED:164, NDK-91:446, PCX:140, XED:62

iholide *n5-sg* holiday ☞ Pl: iiholide E&S:58

iholo *n5-sg-loan* hall R35.6

ihostele *n5-sg* hostel ☞ Pl: iihostele; Loc: ehostele CGB:138, EXD:282

ihotele *n5-sg* hotel ☞ Pl: iihotele; Loc: ehotele CGB:138, EXD:282

ii- *n5-pl-prf* [group 5 (Bantu class 10) plural noun prefix on roots beginning with a nasal sound and on loanwords] • *iinyosi 'bees', iitapile 'potatoes'* ☞ Alt: iin-, iim- ~ iziN-; Sg: i- CGB:106, E&S:17, PCX:54; 28, RD-96:372, SXWU:19, R8=5

iibhedi *n5-pl* beds R35

iibhodi *n5-pl* boards ☞ Sg: ibhodi R37=2

iibhokhwe *n5-pl* goats ☞ Sg: ibhokhwe E&S:58, PCX:54, RD-96:372, R26.7

iifama *n5-pl* farms ☞ Sg: ifama R28

iigusha *n5-pl* sheep, sheeps, herds of sheep ☞ Sg: igusha E&S:58, PCX:54, R26=2

iihagu *n5-pl* pigs CGB:182, E&S:58

iikhondom *n5-pl* condoms ☞ Sg: ikhondom R30

iiknuckles *n5-pl* knuckles R8

iikomiti *n5-pl* committees, boards ☞ Sg: ikomiti R22

iilayisensi *n5-pl* licenses R31

iilokari *n5-pl* lockers R35

iilokhwe *n5-pl* dresses ☞ Sg: ilokhwe CGB:113, E&S:58, R28

iilwimi *n6-pl* languages ☞ Sg: ulwimi CGB:107, PCX:55, R37.4.13

iim- *n5-pl-prf* [group 5 (Bantu class 10) plural noun prefix on polysyllabic roots beginning with a labial] • *iimfene 'baboons'* ☞ Alt: ii-, iin- ~ iziN-; Sg: im- CGB:106, PCX:53, RD-96:372, XED:62, R30

iimbaleki *n5-pl* runners CGB:113, R33=5

iimbiza *n5-pl* pots; [ext] medicinal preparation (made in such a pot, and sold, consumed in 750ml quantity) ☞ Sg: imbiza PCX:53, R25=2

iimbono *n5-pl* views, outlooks, visions, sights, prospects ☞ Sg: imbono R21, R29, R30

iimeko *n5-pl* qualities; circumstances ☞ Sg: imeko R16, R28, R36

iimfene *n5-pl* baboons ☞ Sg: imfene CGB:113, E&S:57, PCX:53, RD-96:372

iimfudo *n6-pl* tortoises ☞ Sg: ufudo CGB:107, PCX:55, RD-96:372

iimini *n5-pl* days ☞ Sg: imini CGB:176, E&S:57, PCX:54

iimoto *n5-pl* cars, automobiles ☞ Sg: imoto E&S:58; 17, R31

iimpahla *n5-pl* goods ☞ Sg: impahla AM-94:108, E&S:57, R26, R28

iimpawu *n6-pl* marks, signs, indications, symptoms ☞ Sg: uphawu EXD:587; 646, R30=3

iimvisiswano *n5-pl* agreements; harmonies EXD:13; 266

iin-[1] *n5-pl-prf* [group 5 (Bantu class 10) plural noun prefix on polysyllabic roots] • *iintaka 'birds'* ☞ Alt: izi(n)- ~ iim-; Sg: in- CGB:106, E&S:17, PCX:53, RD-96:372, SXWU:19, XED:62, R11

iiN-[2] *n6-pl-prf* [group 6 (Bantu class 10) plural noun prefix on polysyllabic roots] • *iimfudo 'tortoises', iindidi 'categories', iingcango 'doors'* Structure: realized as iim-, iin-, iing- depending on the following consonant ☞ Alt: izim-; Sg: u- CGB:107, PCX:53, RD-96:372, SXWU:20, XED:62, R30=3

iincwadi *n5-pl* books; letters ☞ Sg: incwadi E&S:57, PCX:54, SXWU:19, R18.0.1

iindaba *n6-pl* news, tidings; information; intelligence ☞ Sg: udaba (q.v.) AXG:37, EXD:403, XED:27, R18.6, R23.8.12, R33x, R36

iindatyana *n6-pl-dim* a little news; some information ☞ See: iindaba AXG:37

iindawo *n5-pl* places, localities ☞ Sg: indawo E&S:57, R27x, R35, R36.11, R37.13

iindibano *n5-pl* gatherings, meetings R30

iindidi *n6-pl* sorts, kinds, types ☞ Sg: udidi R25.2

iindleko *n5-pl* expenses ☞ Sg: indleko EXD:200, R29, R35

iindlela *n5-pl* ways; roads ☞ Sg: indlela E&S:57, PCX:53

iindywala *n7-pl* beers, brews, strong drinks; [ext] beer-parties ☞ Sg: utywala (q.v) EXD:50, PCX:195

iingcango *n6-pl* doors ☞ Sg: ucango CGB:107, E&S:58, PCX:55; 69, RD-96:372, R27, R33

iingcinga *n5-pl* thoughts, ideas ☞ Sg: ingcinga R14x, R34

iingonyama *n5-pl* lions ☞ Sg: ingonyama CGB:113, E&S:57, EXD:349, R9x

iingwatyu *n5-pl* loose trousers; low-hanging udders ☞ Sg: ingwatyu R32.8

iingxaki *n5-pl* difficulties; problems; troubles ☞ Sg: ingxaki R19.0, R37.14

iinight club *n5-pl* night clubs R36

iinjengele *n5-pl* generals ☞ Sg: injengele R32.3

iinkampi *n5-pl-loan* camps R36

iinkanuko *n5-pl* strong desires R36.17.18

iinkcukacha *n5-pl* particulars, details • *-cacisa ngeenkcukacha 'explain s.t. in detail'* ☞ Sg: inkcukacha EXD:155; 439, NDK-91:515, R22.0, R29.16

iinkcukakca *n5-pl* details, particulars ☞ Sg: inkcukakca; See: inkcukacha R23.8.9

iinkokeli *n5-pl* leaders ☞ Sg: inkokeli E&S:57, R16=3, R20=3, R32

iinkomo *n5-pl* cows, oxen, cattle ☞ Sg: inkomo CGB:176, E&S:57, PCX:53; 69, R27x

iinkonzo *n5-pl* services R37

iinkosi *n5-pl* chiefs; rulers ☞ Sg: inkosi E&S:57, R13

iinkqubo *n5-pl* programs; procedures ☞ Sg: inkqubo EXD:483; 484, R4cx

iinkuni *n6-pl* logs; firewood ☞ Sg: ukhuni XED:77

iinkwenkwezi *n5-pl* stars AXG:218, EXD:619, R34x

iintaba *n5-pl* mountains R28

iintaka *n5-pl* birds ☞ Sg: intaka E&S:17; 57, RD-96:372, SXWU:19

iintlanti *n7-pl* corrals ☞ Sg: ubuhlanti (q.v.) CGB:107

iintlobo *n6-pl* sorts, types ☞ Sg: uhlobo XED:60

iintolongo *n5-pl* prisons, jails R11

iintombi *n5-pl* girls, daughters ☞ Sg: intombi (q.v.); Loc: ezintombini CGB:142, E&S:57, PCX:53f

iintsalela *n5-pl* the residue, remainder, rest R26

iintsana *n6-pl* babies, infants ☞ Sg: usana AM-94:100, E&S:58, PCX:55; 69, XED:148

iintsapho *n6-pl* families; children ☞ Sg: usapho AM-94:100, AXG:37, CGB:107, E&S:58, PCX:69, SXWU:20, XED:148

iintsatshana *n6-pl-dim* little ones XED:148

iintsiba *n6-pl* feathers; pens ☞ Sg: usiba AM-94:100, E&S:58, XED:151

iintsimbi *n5-pl* irons; [ext] handcuffs R31

iintsini *n6-pl* gums; [ext] grinning, laughter ☞ Sg: usini EXD:260, KED:392, XED:152

iintsuku *n6-pl-time* days (24-hour periods) ☞ Sg: usuku AM-94:100, AXG:37, E&S:58, EXD:144, MI:231, SXWU:20, XED:155, R28

iintsukwana *n6-pl-time-dim* a few days AXG:37

iintuli *n6-pl* dust storm ☞ See: uthuli 'dust' PCX:55, XED:168

iintuthu *n6-pl* ashes ☞ Sg: uthuthu CGB:114, PCX:54

iintywala *n7-pl* beers, strong drinks; [ext] beer-parties ☞ Alt: iindywala; Sg: utywala (q.v) CGB:107

iinyawo *n6-pl* feet ☞ Sg: unyawo; Loc: ezinyaweni CGB:107, E&S:58, PCX:55; 69, SXWU:20, R28x=2, R30x

iinyembezi *n5-pl* tears R36

iinzame *n5-pl* efforts, attempts ☞ Sg: inzame R24.6, R34.5, R35.5

iiofisi *n5-pl* offices R37

iirhafu *n5-pl* taxes ☞ Sg: irhafu R23.4.5

iisigalethi *n5-pl* cigarettes ☞ Sg: isigalethi ITX:66

iitapile *n5-pl* potatoes ☞ Sg: itapile E&S:31; 58, R8=2

iititshala *n5-pl* teachers ☞ Sg: ititshala E&S:58, R9, R33.2, R37.11

iitumato *n5-pl* tomatoes R8=2

iivenkile *n5-pl* shops ☞ Sg: ivenkile E&S:58, R37.13

iJamani *n3-sg* German (person) ☞ Pl: amaJamani SXWU:17

ijelo *n3-sg* tube, pipe, spout, gutter; barrel (of gun); telescope; [fig] source (of information); channel (TV, radio) • *amajelo athembekileyo 'reliable sources'; amajelo eendaba 'news channels'* ☞ Pl: amajelo MI:262, XED:64, R18x=2

ijezi *n5-sg* sweater, pullover, jersey, light jacket AM-94:72, EXD:319

iJikelele Sishebo Mix *n5-sg-cmp* Jikelele Flavoring Mix (brand name) R8

ijikeleza *v-tr* it goes around R27

ijongene *v-recip-perf* it is faced (with) -jongana na 'be faced with' R37.2

ikamva *n3-sg* future, the hereafter nominal formed from adverbial form kamva, 'in future'. C.f. ikakhulu, in same sense, may even be copulative prefix. ☞ See: umva KM, NDK-91:493, RD-96:83, R21, R34

iKapa *n5-sg-pn-geog* Cape Town ☞ Loc: eKapa AM-94:62f, CGB:41; 138, MI:246, PCX:29; 69, SXWU:101, XED:194, R37x=2

iKathikati *pn-geog* Cathcart (town) ☞ Syn: iDaliwe CGB:40

ikati *n5-sg* cat ☞ Pl: iikati CGB:142, E&S:58

ikawusi *n5-sg* sock, stocking ☞ Pl: iikawusi AM-94:72, E&S:58

iketile *n5-sg* kettle ☞ Pl: iiketile E&S:58

ikeyiki *n5-sg* cake ☞ Pl: iikeyiki E&S:58

ikhalipha *n3-sg* brave person, bold man; [atr] energetic, active ☞ Pl: amakhalipha CGB:111, XED:67

ikhankanywe *v-pass* they are referred to from -khankany- to mention, refer to R37.6

ikhanuke *v-tr-sub* being attracted to, having a desire for R36

ikhaphetshu *n3-sg* cabbage ☞ Pl: amakhaphetshu CGB:104, SXWU:17

ikharavan *n5-sg* van, caravan (MPV) R31

ikhaya *n3-sg* home, (one's own) residence, domicile, abode • *ikhaya lam. 'my house'.* ☞ Pl: amakhaya; Loc: ekhaya; Cf: umzi CGB:139, E&S:56, EXD:279, MI:259, PCX:53; 70, XED:70, R4dx, R5x, R9x, R15x, R35.2, R36.10

ikhemesti *n5-sg* pharmacy, drug store, chemist ☞ Loc: ekhemesti AM-94:63, EXD:93

ikhetha *v-tr* he, she chooses R33.0

ikhethwa *v-tr-pass* he, she, it is chosen R20.2

iKhimbali *pn-geog* Kimberley (diamond town) ☞ Loc: eKhimbali AM-94:63

ikhiwane *n3-sg* fig (fruit) ☞ Pl: amakhiwane; See: umkhiwane (tree) CGB:111

ikho[1] *v-exis-n2-pl* they are here / present E&S:29, ITX:17

ikho[2] *v-exis-n5-sg* it is here; he, she is present E&S:29, ITX:17

ikholeji *n5-sg* college EXD:106

ikhomishoni *n5-sg* commission R32

ikhona *loc-pro* it is there R21

ikhondo *n3-sg* last of a thing XED:73, R34x

ikhondom *n5-sg* condom ☞ Pl: iikhondom R30=9

ikhowa *n3-sg* large edible mushroom sp. ☞ Cf: inkowane [n5-dim] AXG:37, XED:74

ikhuba *n3-sg* hoe ☞ Pl: amakhuba CGB:111

ikhuselekile *v-atr-perf* it is protected R30.5, R34.5

ikhwalithi *n5-sg* quality R12x=2

ikhwapha *n3-sg* armpit ☞ Pl: amakhwapha XED:78, R30x

ikofu *n5-sg* coffee E&S:58, SXWU:19

ikomiti *n5-sg* committee, board ☞ Pl: iikomiti R22=2

ikomityi *n5-sg* cup ☞ Pl: iikomityi CGB:113, E&S:58, SXWU:19

ikumgama *n5-sg-loc-n2-sg* it is at a distance R35.3

ikunika *v-pres* it gives you R12

ikuphethe *v-n5-sg-pro-2sg-obj-past* it has taken control of you R30

ikwasetyenziswa *n5-sg-cop-v-caus-pass* its being used R35

ikwenza *v-mod* it makes you R25

ilali[1] *n3-sg* meek, gentle person ☞ Pl: amalali XED:80

ilali[2] *n5-sg* location, settlement; village, ward; rural area ☞ Pl: izilali XED:80, R10, R26x, R27x

ilanga[1] *n3-sg* sun ☞ Pl: amalanga AM-94:108, AXG:19; 218, CGB:42; 173, E&S:56

iLanga[2] *pn-geog* Langa (suburb of Cape Town named after a great chief) ☞ Loc: kwaLanga AM-94:64, CGB:40; 140

iLawu *n3-sg* Khoikhoi, Hottentot (person, Xhosa nickname for the ethnic group) ☞ Pl: amaLawu AXG:20

-ile *v-suf-perf* has VERBed [long perfect or recent past tense suffix; denotes current relevance on stative verbs] • *Lifikile ixesha 'The time has arrived ...', usebenzile 'he, she worked'* Structure: is not used if an object is expressed CGB:152;155f, PCX:73f, RD-96:373, XED:62, R3=2, R4c, R9=2, R10, R11, R12=2, R14

ilekese *n5-sg* candy, sweet ☞ Pl: iilekese E&S:58, EXD:81; 644

ilenze *n5-sg-obj-n3-sg-v-subj* (the Board) may do it subjunctive form R37

ileta *n5-sg* letter R4c

iLetaba After-Care Centre *n5-sg-cmp-pn-loan* the Letaba After-Care Center R35=2

ili- *n3-sg-prf* [group 3 (Bantu class 5) singular noun prefix on monosyllabic roots] • *ilitye 'stone'* Consists of article i- + classifier li- ☞ Pl: ama-; Alt: i- AXG:19, CGB:104, E&S:17, PCX:51f;23f, RD-96:372, SXWU:17, XED:62, R5

ilifu *n3-sg* cloud ☞ Pl: amafu; Loc: elifini AM-94:24, AXG:19, CGB:104; 139, E&S:56; 17, R5x

iligqume *v-pres-sub* so that it covers it R30

iligxa *n3-sg* shoulder ☞ Pl: amagxa AXG:19, CGB:111, SXWU:17

ilihlo *n3-sg* eye ☞ Pl: amehlo PCX:53

ilinga *n3-sg* try, attempt EXD:35, PCX:26

ilintla *n3-sg* back part of a hut; the master place XED:111

ilinyathelo *n3-sg-pred* it is a step R10

ilishwa *n3-sg* misfortune ☞ Pl: amashwa E&S:56, PCX:50; 52

iliso *n3-sg* eye ☞ Pl: amehlo AM-94:87, AXG:19, CGB:105, PCX:53, SXWU:17, XED:63; 153

ilisu *n3-sg* laterals, obliques (muscles on the side of the body) XED:154

ilitere *n5-sg* liter (metric liquid measure) EXD:351, R8x

ilitye *n3-sg* stone, rock, pebble; tombstone; gem, jewel [in compounds] ☞ Pl: amatye; Loc: elityeni AXG:19; 36, CGB:104, E&S:56; 22, PCX:23, RD-96:383f;372, XED:172, R32

ilityekazi *n3-sg-aug* boulder, large stone, huge rock AXG:36

iliva *n3-sg* thorn; [ext] impression, s.t. felt; conviction ☞ Pl: amava 'impressions' vs. ameva 'thorns'; Cf: iva, -va CGB:105, PCX:53, SXWU:17, XED:175; 63, R4d

iliwa *n3-sg* cliff, precipice; rock ☞ Pl: amawa AXG:19, CGB:111, E&S:56, PCX:23

ilixa *n3-sg* time (point in time); hour; chance ☞ Alt: ixa GDX3:556, XED:181, XS-92:183

iliziko *n3-sg-cop-pred* it is a home or center R35.12

ilizo *n3-sg* present, contribution, donation ☞ Pl: amalizo AM-94:164, XED:83

ilizwe *n3-sg* land, region, country; [ext] a great deal; a large number; very often ☞ Pl: amazwe; Loc: elizweni AXG:19, CGB:42; 104, E&S:56, MI:262, PCX:23; 69, SXWU:17, XED:193, R11, R13=2, R30+x, R32=2

ilizwi *n3-sg* sound; word, voice, speech, language ☞ Pl: amazwi; Loc: elizwini AXG:19, E&S:56, PCX:68, SXWU:17, XED:193, R17x, R21x

ilokhwe *n5-sg* dress ☞ Pl: iilokhwe AM-94:72, CGB:113, E&S:58, R28x

ilucwambu *n6-sg-pred-n5-sg* it is the cream R32

iluncedo *n6-sg-atr* it is helpful R22=2

ilungelo *n3-sg* advantage, benefit; right, privilege ☞ Pl: amalungelo EXD:535, XED:84, R37x

ilungile *v-perf* it is ok R17.3

ilungu *n3-sg* joint (of body); node (of plant), knot; member (of a group); [fig] genitals ☞ Pl: amalungu EXD:242, R7x, R30=3, R36

im- *n5-sg-prf* [group 5 (Bantu class 9) singular noun prefix] • *impela 'ending'* iN > im before bilabial root ☞ See: iN-; Pl: iim- CGB:105f, PCX:27f;53, RD-96:372, SXWU:19, XED:62, R1, R7, R10=3

-ima *v-st* stand; stop; live, dwell latent vowel verb ☞ See: -ma XED:62

imalana *n5-sg-dim* small sum, a little money, petty cash MI:262

imali *n5-sg* money, coin, cash, currency; price, value ☞ Pl: iimali CGB:106, E&S:58; 31, NDK-91:486, PCX:34, RD-96:384, XED:86, R4dx, R9=2+2x, R10=3, R15, R22, R28, R31, R34, R35=3, R37.14

imali iphelela ezandleni *idiom* money disappears in your hands, money burns a hole in your pocket R15

imalungu *n3-pl-rel2-n5-sg* members of which R32

imaphu *n5-sg* map CGB:144

imarketing *n5-sg* marketing R29

iMaths *n5-sg* Mathematics R29.19, R37.19

imazi *n5-sg* cow, mare; [atr] female (animal) • *imazi yenkomo 'cow'; imazi yehashe 'mare (female horse)'* ☞ Pl: iimazi; Opp: inkunzi AXG:35, CGB:128, E&S:57

-imba *v-tr* dig (up), excavate latent vowel verb ☞ See: -mba; Pass: -mbiwa CGB:125, E&S:51, PCX:21, SXWU:32, XED:87

imbabala *n5-sg* bushbuck ☞ Pl: iimbabala CGB:106, XED:5

imbala[1] *n5-sg* only one, just one; [atr] one, single ☞ Cf: -mbalwa KED:19, XED:6, R26.5

imbala[2] *n5-sg* burn mark, spot, blotch (e.g., on the shins of old people who have sat near a fire all their lives) ☞ Cf: umbala 'shin' KED:20, XED:6, R26.5x

imbaleki *n5-sg* runner CGB:113, R33x=5

imbalelwano *n5-sg* correspondence (XED:6), EXD:126, R7x

imbali[1] *n5-sg* story, tale, account, narrative imbàli (low tone) ☞ rw: -bala AXG:13, XED:6

imbali[2] *n5-sg* good writer, expert in writing imbáli (high tone) ☞ rw: -bhala AXG:13, CGB:113, XED:6

imbalo *n5-sg* art of writing XED:6

imbangi[1] *n5-sg* cause, reason; source, origin; author, producer XED:8

imbangi[2] *n5-sg* claim, matter in dispute XED:8

imbasa *n5-sg* medal, trophy EXD:375;681, R33.7=2.11

imbeko *n5-sg* respect, honor ☞ Pl: iimbeko CGB:106

imbewu *n5-sg* seed ☞ Pl: iimbewu; Cf: -mba EXD:567;243, XED:12, R30=2

imbewu yesidoda *n5-sg-cmp* semen R30=2

imbi *v-pred* it is bad R17.4

imbiza *n5-sg* pot (of earthenware or iron) ☞ Pl: iimbiza [see note attached] PCX:53, XED:14, R25=4

imbizo *n5-sg* meeting to which people are called, men's official assembly PCX:196, XED:14

imbongi *n5-sg* poet, bard, eulogizer, person who writes or sings praise poems XED:15

imbono *n5-sg* view; point of view ☞ Pl: iimbono R30x, R37.24

imbutho *n5-sg* assembly, gathering (of people); [ext] company; [fig] resort ☞ Alt:

umbutho [n2-sg] NDK-91:383, XED:19

imdlwengule *v-tr-past* has raped him (a child) R36

imeko *n5-sg* quality, attribute; mood, condition; state, circumstance ☞ Pl: iimeko; rw: -ma EXXE:56, RD-96:384, XED:86, R34.12

imela *n5-sg* knife ☞ Pl: iimela E&S:57

iMelika *n5-sg-pn-geog* America ☞ Loc: eMelika AM-94:63, R12x=7

imendo *n2-pl* highways, roads ☞ Sg: umendo AXG:19, PCX:52, XED:36

imesa *n5-sg* knife ☞ Pl: iimesa EXXE:56

imfakadolo *n5-sg* with a breechloading rifle XED:37, R32.4

imfama *n5-sg* blind (person) ☞ Pl: iimfama CGB:107, EXD:59, XED:89

imfanelo *n5-sg* duty, what is fitting; one's just deserts ☞ Pl: iimfanelo EXD:179, XED:37

imfazwe *n5-sg* war [lit: death of the land] EXXE:56, RD-96:384, R24

imfe *n5-sg* sweet-reed ☞ Pl: izimfe PCX:53

imfene *n5-sg* baboon ☞ Pl: iimfene CGB:113, E&S:57, PCX:53, RD-96:384;372

imfesane *n5-sg* umbilical cord; [fig] compassion XED:38

imfono-mfono *n-loan* phone ☞ Alt sp: imfonomfono R23

imfula *n5-sg* watercourse, brook, stream; [ext] valley ☞ Pl: iimfula; Alt: umfula [n2] XED:40

imfundo *n5-sg* education, learning ☞ Pl: iimfundo AM-94:155, CGB:113, RD-96:384, R10 = 3, R22

imfuneko *n5-sg* need, necessity; requisite, condition, requirement ☞ Pl: iimfuneko EXD:525, RD-96:384, XED:40

imfuno *n5-sg* desire, need, requirement Derived from -funa 'to want.' Although not in some dictionaries, it follows normal word formation rules and is thus understandable. R23, R37.12

imhlophe *n5-sg* white ox ☞ Cf: -mhlophe XED:60; 89

imi- *n2-pl-prf* [group 2 (Bantu class 4) plural noun prefix] • *iminqathe 'carrots,' imizuzu 'minutes'* Consists of article i- + classifier mi- ☞ Sg: um- AXG:18f, CGB:104, E&S:17, PCX:51f;27, RD-96:372, SXWU:16, R4a=2, R4b=2, R4c, R6=2, R8=2, R10

imiba *n2-pl* issues, problems ☞ Sg: umba R37.6

imibutho *n2-pl* assemblies, gatherings; organizations, societies ☞ Sg: umbutho R35, R37=2

imibuzo *n2-pl* questions E&S:56, PCX:52, R27=2

imicimbi *n2-pl* matters; subjects (of discussion) • *ngemicimbi 'about matters'* TD

imidaka *n2-pl* common people; black people ☞ Sg: umdaka 'very dark person' XED:27

imidlalo *n2-pl* games; sports ☞ Sg: umdlalo E&S:56, R4cx, R12x

imifuno *n2-pl* edible plants; vegetables ☞ Sg: umfuno E&S:31; 56

imigaqo-ntetho *n2-pl-cmp* grammar {ling} MI:262

imihla *n2-pl-time* days, dates, points in time CGB:110, E&S:56, MI:231, PCX:27, XED:56, R9x, R28

imihla ngemihla *time-expr* day by day, day after day MI:231, XED:56

imikhuba *n2-pl* customs, practices; habits ☞ Sg: umkhuba R34.2

imilebe *n2-pl* lips ☞ Sg: umlebe EXD:350, R30x

imililo *n2-pl* fires ☞ Sg: umlilo E&S:22; 56

iminciIi *n2-pl* joyousness No singular AXG:18, R24

imini *n5-sg-time* day, daytime ☞ Pl: iimini; Loc: emini AM-94:63, CGB:139; 176, E&S:57, EXD:144, MI:231, PCX:29; 54, RD-96:384, R2x, R24, R30

imini yokuphelelwa *n5-sg-cmp* expiration date R30

iminqathe *n2-pl* carrots ☞ Sg: umnqathe R8=2

iminqweno *n2-pl* desires ☞ Sg: umnqweno R34

iminyaka *n2-pl-time* years ☞ Sg: umnyaka CGB:110, E&S:56, EXD:737, XED:115, R4ax, R4bx=2, R28x

iminyaka ngeminyaka *n2-pl-expr-time* year by year; year after year EXD:737, XED:115

iminyanya *n2-pl* fathers, forefathers, ancestral spirits EXD:209, XED:116

iminzunzu *n2-pl* pangs No singular AXG:18

imiqathango *n2-pl* guidelines R29

imisebenzi *n2-pl* jobs, works, efforts; functions ☞ Sg: umsebenzi R10x, R22, R28, R29

imisila *n2-pl* tail ☞ Sg: umsila PCX:140

imithambo *n2-pl* veins and arteries R25

imithetho *n2-pl* laws, rules, regulations ☞ Sg: umthetho R11, R31.1, R32.4

imithi *n2-pl* trees ☞ Sg: umthi CGB:110, E&S:56; 17, PCX:50; 52, RD-96:372

imivuzo *n2-pl* wages ☞ Sg: umvuzo R10, R35

imiyalelo *n2-pl* directions, instructions R6+x, R37

imizi *n2-pl* homes; homesteads CGB:104, E&S:56, R11, R18.2, R26=2

imizuzu *n2-pl* minutes ☞ Sg: umzuzu R8x, R33x=4

imizuzwana *n2-pl-dim* seconds ☞ Sg: umzuzwana R33x=3

imo *n5-sg* abode; state, status; habit, form Derived from -ma 'stand, stop, stand beside each other' ☞ rw: -ma XED:86, R21

imomoza *v-intr-n5-sg-S1* it increases • *imali imomoza 'money will grow astonishingly'* R34.10

iMonti *n5-sg-pn-geog* East London ☞ Loc: eMonti AM-94:63, CGB:40; 138, MI:246, SXWU:101, XED:194, R19x, R27x=2

imoto *n5-sg* car, automobile ☞ Pl: iimoto; Loc: emotweni AM-94:42, CGB:139, E&S:58; 17, RD-96:384

impahla *n5-sg* stock; [pl] goods, clothes, any owned thing ☞ Pl: iimpahla E&S:57, XED:122, R26=3, R35

impela *n5-sg* end, ending; [adv] entirely, completely, thoroughly ☞ Alt: impelo XED:126, R1

impela-veki *n5-sg-cmp* weekend ☞ Pl: iimpela-veki E&S:57, R1

impelo *n5-sg* end, ending, termination; the end ☞ Pl: iimpelo XED:126, R1x

impembelelo *n5-sg* stirring up, instigation; encouragement; influence upon others XED:126, R34.12

impempe *n5-sg* whistle (tubular wind instrument) ☞ Pl: iimpempe CGB:106, EXD:724, MI:259

impendulo *n5-sg* answer, reply ☞ Pl: iimpendulo; rw: phendula 'answer'; Cf: umbuzo 'question' PCX:26; 28, XED:126

impi *n5-sg* regiment, detachment; army, force; foe, adversary; colony of ants on the march ☞ Pl: izimpi E&S:57, PCX:53, XED:127

impilo *n5-sg* health; life; means ☞ rw: -phila EXD:270, ITX:2, XED:128, R34

iMpofu *pn-geog* Seymour (town) CGB:39, XED:194

impuku *n5-sg* mouse ☞ Pl: iimpuku E&S:57, PCX:53, SXWU:19

impumalanga *n5-sg* east ☞ Loc: empumalanga CGB:138, EXD:181, PCX:70, SXWU:102

impumlo *n5-sg* nose EXD:408

imvaba *n5-sg* skin milksack; [ext] source of supply; [fig] missionary society XED:176, R13x

imveliso *n5-sg* produce XED:177, R29=6

imvisiswano *n5-sg* agreement, harmony ☞ Pl: iimvisiswano EXD:13; 266

imvu *n5-sg* fat-tailed sheep ☞ Pl: izimvu; Syn: igusha AXG:35, E&S:57, MI:273, PCX:53, XED:178

imvubu *n5-sg* hippopotamus ☞ Pl: iimvubu CGB:113, EXD:276, PCX:53, XED:178

imvukazi *n5-sg-fem* ewe, female sheep AXG:35

imvula *n5-sg* rain [lit: that which opens the ground for plowing] ☞ Pl: iimvula; Cf: -na [v] AM-94:113, AXG:218, E&S:57, SXWU:19, XED:178

imvumi *n5-sg* singer (a good singer) ☞ Pl: iimvumi CGB:106, XED:178

in-[1] *n5-sg-prf* [group 5 (Bantu class 9) singular noun prefix] • *intaka 'bird'* Consists of article i- + classifier n- ☞ Alt: i- ~ im-; Pl: iin- CGB:105, E&S:17, PCX:51; 53, RD-96:372, SXWU:19, XED:62, R3, R4c, R7, R37.1

iN-[2] *n5-sg-prf* [group 5 (Bantu class 9) singular noun prefix] • *impela 'ending', inja 'dog'* Consists of article i- + classifier N- ☞ Alt: in- ~ im-; Pl: iziN- CGB:106, E&S:17, PCX:51; 53, RD-96:372, SXWU:19, R9=2

iN-[3] *n5-sg-adj-pred* he, she, it is ADJ [group 5 singular adjective agreement prefix used predicatively] E&S:28, MI:248, PCX:117f, R17

inako *v-aux* it can be R36.24

inamba *n5-sg* python PCX:54

inani *n3-sg* number, numeral ☞ Pl: amanani EXD:410, R34=12

incam *n3-sg* end, point, tip; apex; [fig] highest; best RD-96:385, XED:93, R30=2

incasa *n5-sg* taste EXD:651, PCX:140

inceda *v-n5-sg-pres* it helps R12

incedise *v-tr* it assists R37

iNciba *n3-sg-pn-geog* Great Kei River ☞ Loc: eNciba CGB:111, XED:194

incoko *n5-sg* chat, conversation, talk; joker, jester, storyteller ☞ Pl: iincoko E&S:57, PCX:29; 37, RD-96:385, XED:95

incopho *n5-sg* peak, pinnacle ☞ Loc: encotsheni PCX:69, XED:95

incwadana *n5-sg-dim* booklet, pamphlet [lit: small book] RD-96:385, R12, R22=3, R23

incwadi *n5-sg* book; letter ☞ Pl: iincwadi; Loc: encwadini AM-94:187, CGB:139, E&S:57, PCX:29; 54, RD-96:385, R12x, R18x=2

indawo *n5-sg* place, locality, position, site; residence, abode; topic, subject, matter; [ext] s.t. wrong; [neg] nothing ☞ Pl: iindawo; Loc: endaweni CGB:42, E&S:57, PCX:68, RD-96:385, XED:28, R26, R35, R37.13

indebe *n5-sg* ladle, cup, half of a split calabash; [ext] chalice; trophy KED:253, R27.8, R33.11

indibano *n5-sg* intermixture, medley; meeting, gathering ☞ Pl: iindibano RD-96:385, XED:29, R30=2

indindi *n5-sg* smooth, round thing; [ext] problem, enigma ☞ Pl: iindindi EXD:483, XED:97, R25x

indiphatha *v-n5-sg-S1-pro-1sg-obj* it feels to me, it seems to me R17.1

indixelela *v-tr* (and) told me R19.3

indlala *n5-sg* hunger, famine, drought; dearth, scarcity RD-96:385, XED:30, R13.7

indle *n5-sg* veld, open field Usually used in locative ☞ See: endle (ezindle) CGB:139, XED:31; 97, R3

indlebe *n5-sg* ear ☞ Pl: iindlebe EXD:180, R18

indledlana *n5-sg-dim* narrow path; small road AXG:37, XED:31

indlela *n5-sg* path, road, street, thoroughfare; direction, route; drive; way, method, system, mode, means; way of life, lifestyle ☞ Pl: iindlela; Loc: endleleni AXG:37, CGB:42; 113, E&S:57, NDK-91:404;337, PCX:53; 68, RD-96:385, SXWU:19, XED:31, R9, R11+x, R14, R21, R22, R28=2, R30, R31=2, R36=2, R37=4

indlela yale nto *expr* how this goes XED:31

indlovu *n5-sg* elephant ☞ Pl: iindlovu; Loc: endlovini CGB:113; 175, E&S:57, PCX:68, RD-96:385, SXWU:19, XED:31;97

indlovukazi *n5-sg-aug* huge elephant CGB:175

indlu *n5-sg* house, home, hut, dwelling; appropriate place for doing s.t.; den, nest, hive, web, lair; household, family ☞ Pl: izindlu; Loc: endlwini CGB:113; 175, E&S:57; 58, PCX:53, RD-96:385, SXWU:19, XED:31, R21, R28x

indlukazi *n5-sg-aug* mansion, very large house CGB:175

indlwana *n5-sg-dim* cottage, small house; booth; cage AXG:36, RD-96:385, XED:31

indlwane *n5-sg-dim* nest; cage, snare-trap RD-96:385, XED:31

indoda *n5-sg* man, male; husband ☞ Pl: amadoda E&S:57, RD-96:385, SXWU:17; 19, XED:32, R12, R30.5, R36=8

indodakazi *n5-sg-fem-kin* sister-in-law (of a woman, husband's sister) • *indodakazi* ☞ Pl: amadodakazi AXG:216, EXD:590

indudumo *n5-sg* thunder ☞ Pl: iindudumo; Alt: ududumo [n6] EXD:664, XED:33

induku *n5-sg* club, knobbed stick, knobkerrie; [euphemism] penis R15

induli *n5-sg* hill, kopje ☞ Pl: iinduli; Cf: isiduli 'anthill' CGB:42; 175, EXD:276

indulikazi *n5-sg-aug* mound, very large hill CGB:175

induna[1] *n5-sg* bull, male animal • *ingwe induna 'male tiger'* used with animal names of group 5 ☞ Contrast: iduna [n3] AXG:35, XED:34

induna[2] *n5-sg* man of rank; chief councilor; officer, military leader XED:34

indwe *n5-sg* blue crane ☞ Pl: izindwe E&S:36; 57

indyebo *n5-sg* wealth ☞ Pl: iindyebo EXD:717, PCX:195

inene[1] *n3-sg* nobleman, gentleman; upright reliable person; right-hand man, principal councilor of a chief XED:98

inene[2] *n5-sg* truth, reality; [atr] real, true; [adv] truly, indeed ☞ Pl: iinene PCX:54; 203, XED:98, R12x

inenekazi *n3-sg-fem* lady ☞ Pl: amanenekazi RD-96:385, XED:98, R13.5, R36.14

inenkxaso *v-poss-n5-sg+n5-sg-obj* it has the support • *yonke into eyenzayo inenkxaso yabantu bonke 'everything it does has everybody's support'* R37.17

inetyala *v-poss-n5-sg+n3-sg-obj* having a fault; [atr] guilty R36.14

ingaba *conj* maybe, perhaps, it seems, suppose [lit: it may be] • *ingaba ufuna uncedo? 'it seems you need help'* Often used to introduce a question MI:257, R15=2, R19.4, R21=6, R36, R37

ingabasuka *v-pot* they may originate from • *ingabasuka emaphandleni 'they may come from rural areas' [lit: from outsides]* R37.12

ingakanani *qw-n5-sg* how big? • *Indlu yakho ingakanani? 'How big is your house?'* CGB:129f

ingakhe *n5-sg-neg* it should not R32.6

ingakubuyisela *v-pot-caus-ben* [it] can return you to R34

ingakumbi *adv* especially, particularly; mainly, mostly, chiefly EXD:194;391;439, R27, R32, R37.8

ingalo *n5-sg* arm; forearm; [ext] peninsula ☞ Pl: iingalo E&S:57, RD-96:385

inganelishwa *v-pot-pass* he can have the misfortune ☞ ilishwa 'bad luck' R36

ingaphambili *v-aux-loc* should be in front, be ahead • *ingaphambili kunabantu ' it should be ahead of the people...'* R37

ingaphindi *v-aux-neg-n5-sg* it does not again R37.21

ingasebenzi *v-sub* (that) it may work R22

ingathwaliswa *v-pot-pass* he can be made to carry R36

ingca *n5-sg* grass ☞ Syn: utyani CGB:173, E&S:57, MI:273, PCX:89, RD-96:386, UEX:14, XED:93

ingcali *n5-sg* expert, specialist ☞ Pl: iingcali EXD:200, R36.04

ingcambu *n5-sg* root (of plant) ☞ Pl: iingcambu; Loc: engcanjini EXD:541, PCX:69

ingcebiso *n5-sg* suggestion R34

ingcinezelo *n5-sg* pressure; oppression RD-96:386, XED:23

ingcinga *n5-sg* thought, idea; bud ☞ Pl: iingcinga E&S:57, RD-96:386, XED:23, R14x

iNgcobo *pn-geog* Engcobo (town) ☞ Loc: eNgcobo PCX:69

ingcwangu *n5-sg* outrage; quickness of temper; viciousness, cruelty; [atr] savage, vicious, fierce, cruel (person or animal) ☞ Pl: iingcwangu EXD:427, KED:252, XED:96

iNgesi *n3-sg* English (person), Englishman ☞ Pl: amaNgesi AXG:20, SXWU:17

iNgilani *pn-geog* England ☞ Loc: eNgilani AM-94:63

ingoma *n5-sg* verse (of poetry), song, music ☞ Pl: iingoma EXD:605, PCX:89

ingomso *n3-sg-time* tomorrow, the morrow ☞ rw: -sa XED:147

ingonyama *n5-sg* lion ☞ Pl: iingonyama CGB:113, E&S:57, EXD:349, PCX:89, XED:47, R9x

ingozi *n5-sg* danger, peril, risk; accident, misfortune; injury ☞ Pl: iingozi EXD:143, KED:125; 264, NDK-91:70; 510, RD-96:386, XED:47, R6x

ingqalelo *n5-sg* start, beginning, commencement XED:133, R37

ingqele *n5-sg* frost; cold; cold (illness) AM-94:112, XED:48

ingqesho *n5-sg* hire, license XED:136, R35

ingqiba *n3-sg* beggar, mendicant ☞ Pl: amangqiba XED:108

ingqibo *n5-sg* end, completion, finish, finale XED:48

ingqina *n3-sg* witness, eyewitness; attester; godparent EXXE:60, RD-96:386, XED:108

ingqithiselo *n5-sg* excellence ☞ Pl: ingqithiselo XED:48

ingqondo *n5-sg* mind, intellect; understanding, reason; sense, mental capacity, intelligence E&S:57, SXWU:19, XED:138, R30=2, R34.2.3.11, R36.4

ingqonyela *n5-sg* principal, the "person of the moment"; {archaic} champion (one who excels or achieves his or her ambitions) • *apho wafika waba yinqonyela 'it turned out that he was the man of the moment'* ☞ See Sinxo, G.B. UNomsa, Chap. 12, p61 in 1980 reprint GBS, GDX2, NOM, R24.4

ingubo *n5-sg* blanket; garment ☞ Pl: iingubo; Loc: engubeni E&S:57, EXXE:60, PCX:68; 196

inguqu *n5-sg* change, turnaround; return; rally ☞ Pl: iinguqu XED:51, R21=2, R22

inguquko *n5-sg* change (of mind, in conduct), turnaround; return; rally ☞ Pl: iinguquko EXD:90

ingwatyu *n5-sg* anything wide and flapping (e.g., loose trousers); lean cow with pendulous or flapping udder KED:139, R32.8x

ingwe *n5-sg* leopard; [ext] tiger ☞ Pl: izingwe/ iingwe AXG:35, CGB:113, KED:140, SXWU:19

ingxaki *n5-sg* difficulty, hindrance; bar, obstruction, obstacle; problem, quandary, trouble ☞ Pl: iingxaki EXXE:60, RD-96:386, XED:182, R18.4, R19.1, R37.15

ingxangxasi *n5-sg* waterfall, cascade ☞ Pl: iingxangxasi CGB:42, EXD:715, KED:268, RD-96:386, SXWU:19

ingxelo *n5-sg* report, statement, declaration, what is told; account; result ☞ Pl: iingxelo CGB:113, E&S:57, EXD:524, EXXE:60, RD-96:386, XED:184, R37

ingxolo *n5-sg* noise, uproar; rattle; brawling ☞ Pl: iingxolo CGB:113, EXXE:60, RD-96:386, XED:103

ingxowa *n5-sg* bag, sack, case RD-96:386, R9=2, R35.11

ingxowa-mali *n5-sg-cmp* money bag; fund (for a special purpose) EXD:236, R9=2, R35.11

ingxoxo *n5-sg* conversation, discussion; argument; conference ☞ Pl: iingxoxo E&S:57, EXXE:60, RD-96:386, XED:186

-ini *loc-suf* at, in, on, to [locative suffix after high vowels] • *emthini 'in a tree' [= e-(u)mth(i)-ini]; emanzini 'in the water' [= e-(a)manz(i)-ini]; ezulwini 'in heaven' [= e-(i)zulu-ini]; emafini 'in the clouds' [= e-(a)maf(u)-ini]* Structure: used in conjunction with e- prefix on nouns that end in -i or -u, usually replacing those final vowels ☞ Alt: -eni CGB:139, PCX:68ff, SXWU:101f, XED:62, R6, R7, R9, R10, R12=2

inika *v-tr* it gives R37

inike *v-tr-past* it gave R37=2

inikwe *v-pass-perf* it was given R32

inja *n5-sg* dog; [fig] person of the basest character, person in the meanest circumstances ☞ Pl: izinja; Loc: enjeni AXG:35, CGB:106; 139, E&S:57, PCX:50; 53, RD-96:386;372, SXWU:19, XED:104

injakazi *n5-sg-fem* bitch (female dog) AXG:35, CGB:128, MI:262, RD-96:386, XED:104

injana *n5-sg-dim* puppy (baby dog); little dog (small dog breed) MI:262, RD-96:386, XED:104

injanyana *n5-sg-dim* very small dog CGB:175

injengele *n5-sg* brave man, hero; general ☞ Pl: iinjengele EXD:242, XED:104, R32.3

injinga *n5-sg* professor (of some subject or in a specialized field), one versed in a subject EXXE:61, XED:64

injingalwazi *n5-sg* professor RD-96:386

injongo *n5-sg* aim, object, purpose, goal; meaning ☞ Pl: iinjongo EXD:494, EXXE:61, RD-96:386, XED:65, R35x

injuze *n5-sg* athlete, runner, fighter; [ext] champion EXD:90, XED:65, R33x

inkabi *n5-sg-atr* gelding (any spayed, castrated, or neutered animal) • *inkabi yehagu 'neutered pig', inkabi yenkuku 'capon'* AXG:36, CGB:128

inkampani *n5-sg* company ☞ Pl: iinkampani R29, R31x, R35

inkani *n5-sg* stubbornness EXD:632, R32.8

inkantsi *n5-sg* cramp, numbness XED:68, R25x

inkathalo *n5-sg* interest, concern, care (for s.o.), attention (to s.t.); anxiety ☞ See: -khathala EXD:83, XED:69, R16, R35.1

inkathazo *n5-sg* trouble, worry, annoyance (given) ☞ Pl: iinkathazo E&S:57, XED:69, R2x, R19

inkazana *n5-sg-dim* young married woman (still staying at her father's place) ☞ Pl: amankazana [n3]; Cf: umka [n1] AXG:37, XED:66; 70

inkcaza *n5-sg* comb ☞ Pl: iinkcaza EXD:107, XED:21

inkcazelo *n5-sg* explanation ☞ Pl: iinkcazelo XED:21, R7, R27.11

inkcazo *n5-sg* explanation, declaration, official report EXD:147; 200

inkcukacha *n5-sg* detail, particular ☞ Pl: iinkcukacha; Alt: inkcukakca EXD:155; 439, NDK-91:76, R22.0, R29.16

inkinga *n5-sg* difficulty, problem; perplexity; source of astonishment or surprise XED:71, R15x

inkokeli *n5-sg* leader ☞ Pl: iinkokeli; Alt: umkhokeli E&S:57, EXD:336], RD-96:386, XED:72, R16=4, R20=2, R24

inkoliso *n5-sg* most, greater part, majority XED:72, R16, R33

inkolo *n5-sg* belief, faith, creed, religion ☞ rw: -khol- RD-96:386, XED:72

inkomo *n5-sg* cow, ox, one head of cattle ☞ Pl: iinkomo; Loc: enkomeni AXG:37, CGB:128; 173, E&S:57, PCX:53; 68; 196

inkonyana *n5-sg-dim-ir* young foal, suckling calf; [ext] extensor muscle of the arm; [atr] muscular ☞ Pl: amankonyana AXG:37, XED:74, R36

inkonzo *n5-sg* service; religious or church service XED:74, R4bx, R37=2

inkosazana *n5-sg* young lady ☞ Pl: amakhosazana SXWU:19

inkosi *n5-sg* chief, chieftain, master, lord; ruler; sir {address} ☞ Pl: iinkosi; amakhosi [n3] CGB:113; 128, E&S:57, EXD:93, SXWU:19, XED:74, R13x, R20

inkosikazi *n5-sg-fem-ir* chieftainess, chief's wife; lady; madam! {address} ☞ Pl: amakhosikazi [n3] AXG:35, CGB:128, E&S:33; 57, EXD:725, MI:262, SXWU:19, XED:74

inkowane *n5-sg-dim* toadstool; small edible mushroom sp. ☞ Cf: ikhowa [n3] AXG:37, XED:74

inkqubela *n5-sg* progress EXD:485, R3x, R30x, R34

inkqubo *n5-sg* procedure; program (radio, TV); proceedings; progress, advancement ☞ Pl: iinkqubo EXD:483; 484, RD-96:387, XED:139, R16, R21=2, R22

inkqubo yomthetho *n5-sg-expr* due process (an established course for judicial proceedings or other governmental activities designed to safeguard the legal rights of the individual) AH:569, R16

inkuku *n5-sg* domestic fowl, chicken, rooster • *Inkuku isikwe umlomo 'The blabbermouth has been silenced' [idiom; lit: the fowl has had its beak cut]* ☞ Pl: iinkuku (EXD:93), AXG:35, E&S:57, XED:75

inkululeko *n5-sg* deliverance, being set free XED:76

inkuntsela *n5-sg* master (e.g., apprentice master), senior R26.1

inkunzi *n5-sg* bull; [atr] male (animal); [ext] capital (financial) • *inkunzi yenkomo 'bull (male bovine)'* ☞ Pl: iinkunzi; Opp: imazi AXG:35, CGB:128, E&S:57, MI:262

inkwenkwana *n5-sg-dim* little boy R36

inkwenkwe *n5-sg-ir* boy, youngster ☞ Pl: amakhwenkwe [n3] E&S:57, EXD:67, SXWU:17; 19, XED:79, R28x, R36x

inkwenkwezi *n5-sg* star EXD:619, R34x

inkxaso *n5-sg* support, maintenance; subsidy ☞ rw: -xhas- NDK-91:515, RD-96:387, SXWU:19, R21.5, R30.1, R33.9, R35.0.2.4.15, R36.24, R37.17

inkxaso-mali *n5-sg-cmp* stipend, scholarship R33

INLP *abr* INLP R37=2

inokukugulisa *v-abil-caus* it can make you sick R30

inokuyonakalisa *v-abil-atr-caus* it may damage it R30.7

inokuzikhusela *v-abil-refl* they are able to protect themselves R36.22

inombolo *n5-sg* number TD

inomntwana *v-poss-n1-sg-obj* has a child R19.1

iNonceba *n5-pn* name of a school R18.1

iNonibe *pn* Nonibe (school) R27

inqenera *n3-sg* lazy person XED:108

inqina *n3-sg* hoof, paw, knuckle, foot (animal), hock; hoof-mark, footprint ☞ Pl: amanqina; Cf: idolo EXD:329, XED:108, R32

inqununu *n5-sg* principal (of a school) ☞ Pl: iinqununu; Syn: utitshala omkhulu EXD:481, JPD:122, RD-96:387, R9x

iNqweba *pn-geog* Kirkwood; Jansenville (town); Sunday River CGB:39, XED:194

inqwelo *n5-sg* wagon; vehicle ☞ Pl: iinqwelo CGB:113, PCX:54, XED:110, R24x

inqwelo-moya *n5-sg-cmp* airplane [lit: wagon of the wind] AM-94:60, R24x

Institute *loan* Institute ☞ See: Catholic Institute of Education R22

intaba *n5-sg* mountain ☞ Pl: iintaba; Loc: entabeni CGB:139f, EXD:392, SXWU:102

intaka *n5-sg* bird ☞ Pl: iintaka; Loc: entakeni AXG:36, CGB:139, E&S:17; 57, RD-96:387;372

intamo *n5-sg* neck ☞ Pl: iintamo; Loc: entanyeni EXD:400, PCX:69; 196, XED:157

intando *n5-sg* will, desire; love, affection; aphrodisiac, love potion ☞ Pl: iintando; rw: -thand- CGB:113, XED:157

intanyana *n5-sg-dim* small neck XED:157

intelekelelo *n5-sg* estimate EXD:195, NDK-91:99, R18

intenetya[1] *n5-sg* rock hare AXG:36, XED:159, R4bx

intenetya[2] *n5-sg* tennis EXD:54;655, RD-96:387;127, R4b

intengiso *n5-sg-vn* sale; sales, marketing (as an occupation) ☞ See: -thengisa R29=8

International *loan* International R37.14

intethi *n5-sg* orator, fine speaker ☞ Pl: iintethi; rw: -theth- XED:159

intetho *n5-sg* speech; declaration ☞ Pl: iintetho; rw: -theth- EXD:609, SXWU:19, XED:159

intla *n5-sg* upper side, the higher part of a hill or valley; [ext] north XED:111

intlaba *n5-sg* red aloe flower ☞ Pl: iintlaba; See: umhlaba XED:56

intlahla *n5-sg* bloom, blossom • *ukuphumeza intlahla yakho 'blossom out, bring out the best in you'* R34#9

intlakohlaza *n5-sg* spring, springtime, springtide [lit: head of green] ☞ Pl: iintlakohlaza; Loc: entlakohlaza; Alt sp: intlak'ohlaza AM-94:73, AXG:217, CGB:46; 138, E&S:57, EXD:614, PCX:70

intlalo *n5-sg* abode; stay; state, condition, lifestyle, manner of living ☞ rw: -hlala XED:57, R37.1.12.13=2

intlanganiso *n5-sg* assembly, meeting, congregation of people KED:414, XED:58, R18.4

intlango *n5-sg* desert; wilderness ☞ Pl: iintlango; Loc: entlango CGB:42, PCX:70

intlaninge *n5-sg* abundance, plenty; a great number KED:414; 291, R16x, R32x, R33x

intlanzi *n5-sg* fish ☞ Pl: iintlanzi E&S:57, EXD:217

intlawulo *n5-sg* payment, remuneration XED:58, R35

intliziyo *n5-sg* heart (human organ, also in a moral sense); [ext] mind, disposition, feeling; conscience ☞ Pl: iintliziyo; Cf: iphaphu (animal heart) E&S:57, EXD:270, RD-96:13, XED:111, R4dx

intloko *n5-sg* head; chief person; main point ☞ Pl: iintloko; Loc: entloko AM-94:63; 87, CGB:113; 138, E&S:57, PCX:50; 70, RD-96:87, SXWU:19, XED:161, R25, R30

intloko ebuhlungu *n5-sg-cmp* headache R30

intlonipho *n5-sg-vn* respect, showing reverence, avoiding ☞ rw: -hlonipha XED:60, R34.6

intlumo *n5-sg* sprouting, growth XED:61

intlungu *n5-sg* pain, suffering XED:61, R30x, R36

intluzo *n5-sg* strainer, filter, sieve; strainings, siftings XED:61

into *n5-sg* thing, item, article, object; element, substance; phenomenon; subject matter • *yintoni le? 'What is this (thing)?'* ☞ Pl: izinto CGB:106;113, E&S:17; 57, PCX:53, RD-96:387, XED:161, R4c, R10x, R15, R17.1.3, R19, R25.2, R27.11=2, R36.26, R37=7

intobeko *n5-sg* humility ☞ Syn: ukuthobeka AM-94:164

intolongo *n5-sg* prison, jail XED:162, R4ax, R11x, R36x

intombazana *n5-sg-ir-dim* girl (young, single), little girl ☞ Pl: amantombazana [n3]; See: intombi AXG:36, CGB:105, E&S:57, EXD:246, KED:513, MI:262, XED:162, R4c, R19.1.2.3.4

intombi *n5-sg* girl (young); maiden, virgin; daughter; niece (brother's daughter) ☞ Pl: iintombi; rw: -thomb- AXG:35;215f, CGB:113, E&S:57, EXD:144; 246; 404, MI:262, PCX:53, SXWU:19, XED:162, R4cx, R28x, R31

intonga *n5-sg* rod, stick; weapon R25.3

intsebenziswano *n5-sg* cooperation, working together R27, R34

intsebenzo *n5-sg* use, utility; operation, work, business; reward, wage (that for which one works) XED:149

intseli *n5-sg* drinker ☞ Pl: iintseli; rw: -sela EXD:175, XED:149

intselo *n5-sg* drink; draught ☞ Alt: isiselo [n4-sg], uselo [n6-sg] XED:149

intsholongwane *n5-sg* germ, microbe, bacillus, virus; disease perh. diminutive form, hence -ane ending ☞ Pl: iintsholongwane EXD:243, R30.1, R36.7

iNtshona-Koloni *n5-sg-cmp-pn-geog* Western Cape (one of nine provinces in South Africa) • *eNtshona-Koloni 'in the Western Cape'; uRhulumente weNtshona Koloni 'the Western Cape Governement'* MI:246

intshonalanga *n5-sg* west ☞ Loc: entshonalanga CGB:138, EXD:720, PCX:70, SXWU:102

intshontsho *n3-sg* disgusting thing, s.t. ugly, fowl-smelling; pup, cub, chick, fledgling ☞ Pl: amantshontsho EXD:93, XED:112, R2x

intshukumo *n5-sg* shaking, movement; [ext] earthquake XED:150

intsimbi *n5-sg* iron, steel; iron bar / implement; bell, gong; [ext] o'clock GDX3:420, XED:167, R31x, R35x

intsimi *n5-sg* garden, field, cultivated land ☞ Pl: amasimi [n3] E&S:57, XED:152

intsintsi *n5-sg* seed of the Kafferboom (tree) ☞ Pl: iintsintsi XED:153

intso *n5-sg* kidney ☞ Pl: izintso EXD:326, RD-96:13, R25x

intsomi *n5-sg* tale, folktale, fable, legend ☞ Pl: iintsomi CGB:190, EXD:648

intsumpa *n5-sg* wart ☞ Pl: iintsumpa AXG:37, EXD:713

intsumpana *n5-sg-dim* small wart No sound change (mp remains and does not change to ntsh) AXG:37

intwala *n5-sg* louse • *owentwala 'having lice'* EXD:358, XED:170, R25+x

intwana *n5-sg-dim* trifle, small item, little thing, s.t. petty in+to+(w)+ana [N5+w+dim] AXG:36, CGB:175, E&S:33, MI:262, R23x

intwana-ntwana *n5-sg-dim-redup* small things R23

intwanyana *n5-sg-dim* trifle, very small item, tiny thing E&S:33

intyafo *n5-sg* weakness, feebleness, lack of energy E&S:51, XED:171f

intyatyambo *n5-sg* flower, blossom, bloom; [fig] shooting pain ☞ Pl: iintyatyambo CGB:173, E&S:57, XED:172

-inu *pro-2pl-poss-root* your, yours; your own [plural possessive root] ☞ See: #enu, benu, kwenu, lenu, lwenu, senu, wenu, yenu, zenu CGB:182, E&S:22, SXWU:36

inxaxheba *n5-sg* right hind-quarter of meat; chief's portion, share; [ext] interest in (an issue); participation ☞ Pl: iinxaxheba EXD:311; 438; 578, KED:298, XED:114, R22, R33x, R37.5.19.24

inxeba *n3-sg* wound ☞ Pl: amanxeba AXG:20, XED:114, R36

inxele *n3-sg* left-handed person ☞ Pl: amanxele AXG:20, XED:114

inxiwa *n3-sg* deserted homestead, a ruin, an old village site ☞ Pl: amanxiwa AXG:20, XED:114

iNxukhwebe *pn-geog* Healdtown original Khoi place name ☞ Alt sp: iNxukwebe; Loc: eNxukhwebe MI:246, XED:194

inyama *n5-sg* meat, fleshy; muscle ☞ Pl: iinyama E&S:57, SXWU:19, XED:116, R1=3, R8=2, R26

inyama yegusha *n5-sg-cmp* mutton, lamb R26.8

inyamakazi *n5-sg* antelope; venison; game ☞ Pl: iinyamakazi CGB:113, EXD:22, XED:116

inyanga[1] *n5-sg* diviner, tribal doctor, healer, herbalist ☞ See Xhosa: inyangi, umnyangi EZZE:620, R25=2

inyanga[2] *n5-sg* moon; month ☞ Pl: iinyanga AXG:218, CGB:42, E&S:57, EXD:389, MI:232, XED:116, R15=2

iNyanga[3] *pn-geog* Nyanga (town) Nearby iLanga sounds like Xhosa for 'sun' - iNyanga means 'moon' by extension. ☞ Loc: eNyanga AM-94:63, R37

inyangi *n5-sg* diviner, tribal doctor, healer, herbalist ☞ Alt: umnyangi XED:116, R25x

inyaniso *n5-sg* truth ☞ Pl: iinyaniso E&S:57, KED:303, PCX:37;54;204, XED:116, R4dx

iNyarha *pn-geog* Bedford (town) ☞ Loc: eNyarha; Alt sp: iNyara CGB:40, XED:194

inyathelo *n3-sg* step, footstep; step forward ☞ Pl: amanyathelo; Pred: ilinyathelo EXD:623, XED:117, R10, R29.12

inye *num* there is one RD-96:388;103, R37.20

inyhweba *n5-sg* bliss PCX:54

inyoka *n5-sg* snake, serpent ☞ Pl: iinyoka CGB:106; 173, E&S:57, XED:118

inyosi *n5-sg* bee ☞ Pl: iinyosi CGB:106, EXD:50, SXWU:19

inyumoniya *n5-sg* pneumonia R30

inzala *N-5Sg* progeny; interest R23

inzame *n5-sg* effort, try, attempt ☞ Pl: iinzame EXD:183, R24.6, R34.5, R35.5

iodolo *n5-sg* order (request to supply goods) • *Xa ufuna ukuyiodola le ncwadana....* EXD:423, NDK-91:203

iofisi *n5-sg* office (business office); magistrate's office or court XED:120, R37x

ioli *n5-sg* oil (e.g., cooking oil, vegetable oil) ☞ Alt: ioyile EXD:417, XED:120, R8x

ioyile *n5-sg* oil (e.g., cooking oil, vegetable oil) ☞ Alt: ioli R8+x

iPalamente *n5-sg* Parliament NDK-91:210, R37.5

iPANSALB *n5-sg-abr* Pan South African Language Board Bill R37=4

ipensile *n5-sg* pencil ☞ Pl: iipensile E&S:58

ipetroli *n5-sg* gas, gasoline, petrol E&S:58

-ipha *v-tr* pluck, pull (up / out) latent vowel verb ☞ See: -pha XED:63; 122

iphaphu *n3-sg* heart, liver, lungs (of an animal) ☞ Loc: ephatshini, ephaphini; Cf: intliziyo (human organ) EXD:270, KED:324, PCX:69, XED:124f, R4dbx

iphela *v-intr* all [of] (in this context) • *I-Afrika iphela 'all of Africa'* R16

iphelayo *v-rel-pres* which ended, hence 'last' • *iveki iphelayo ' last week'* R32

iphelela *v-pres* it is the last of; it ends in nothing R15

iphepha *n3-sg* paper ☞ Pl: amaphepha E&S:57, EXD:436, R30x

iphi[1] *qw-loc-adv-n2-pl* where are? ☞ See: -phi E&S:31

iphi[2] *qw-loc-adv-n5-sg* where is? ☞ See: -phi AXG:141, E&S:31

iphika *n3-sg* asthma ☞ Pl: amaphika CGB:111

iphimpi *n3-sg* cobra ☞ Pl: amaphimpi CGB:111

iphoba *n3-sg* skull ☞ Pl: amaphoba CGB:111

iphondo *n3-sg* large side branch; [ext] province, region, administrative division ☞ Pl: amaphondo EXD:489, XED:129, R18x

iphucule *v-tr-sub* it might improve R37.20

iphulo *n3-sg* expedition, foray, prolonged hunting trip, excursion; [ext] article, (written) treatise; information, notice; project, program, campaign ☞ Pl: amaphulo NDK-91:544, XED:131, R30.1, R31.2, R34.1.4, R35.9.13

iphumile *v-intr-perf* it came out R37

ipilisi *n5-sg* pill (medicine) ☞ Pl: iipilisi EXD:457, R25

ipinki *n5-sg* pink EXD:458, RD-96:107;389

iPitoli *pn-geog* Pretoria (city) ☞ Loc: ePitoli; Alt: iTswani AM-94:63, CGB:41; 138, MI:246

iplanga *n3-sg* plank, wood board ☞ Pl: amaplanga CGB:104

ipleyiti *n5-sg* plate ☞ Pl: iipleyiti E&S:58

ipolisa *n3-sg* policeman, policewoman, police officer ☞ Pl: amapolisa CGB:104, E&S:57, SXWU:17, R18.5, R27.1.11

iposi *n5-sg* postage; [atr] postal ☞ See: idilesi yeposi TD

iprojekthi *n5-sg* project TD

iqabane *n3-sg* intimate friend; companion, mate, partner, comrade ☞ Pl: amaqabane CGB:111, E&S:57, XED:133, R4ax, R4c, R4dx, R24, R30, R33

iqabanekazi *n3-sg-fem* female friend, partner, lady companion R4a, R4d

iqanda *n3-sg* egg; [ext] small soft ball (tennis ball); hour, o'clock; [fig] heir to the chieftainship; favorite, darling, apple of one's eye ☞ Pl: amaqanda AXG:19, CGB:104, E&S:57, GDX3:12, ITX:66, SXWU:17

iqaqa *n3-sg* striped civet cat; strong-smelling black beetle with striped back; skunk; [ext] anything (a person, something said, a deed) that is abhorrent, repulsive, repugnant, despised, regarded as unworthy of notice • *kwemithetho yeqaqa 'laws that stink'* EXD:592, GDX3:13, XED:134, R32.3

iqatha *n3-sg* ankle ☞ Pl: amaqatha EXD:21, RD-96:12

iqela *n3-sg* company, group; line, file of men; number of people; [ext] gang ☞ Pl: amaqela CGB:111, EXD:239, XED:136, R21, R36.2.18

iqeshe *v-tr-sub* that it hires R29.14

iqhenqa *n3-sg* leprosy No plural CGB:111

iqhina *n3-sg* necktie, neck cloth ☞ Pl: amaqhina AM-94:72, EXD:400

iqhiya *n5-sg* kerchief, head covering; handkerchief R4bx

iqhube *v-tr-sub* it drove, pressed on • *ayiphindi iqhube ngohlobo ebezikade 'it should not press on in the same way as before'* R37.26

iqhutywa *v-pass-ty-change* it is directed, it is controlled by R37.17.22

iqinisekisile *v-caus-atr* it is assured, it is guaranteed R37

iqokolo *n3-sg* Kei apple ☞ Pl: amaqokolo CGB:111

iqolo *n5-sg* ridge (on a hill) ☞ Pl: iiqolo CGB:42

iQonce *n3-sg-pn-geog* King William's Town; Qonce (the Buffalo River) ☞ Loc: eQonce CGB:111; 138, MI:246, XED:194, R18x

iQora *pn-geog* Alicedale (town); Bushmans River XED:194

iqosheliswe *v-pass-short-past* wrapped up R29

iqudu *n3-sg* koodoo ☞ Pl: amaqudu CGB:111

iqulethe *v-st-perf* it contains; it has R12=2

iquphele *n3-sg* knuckle (human) ☞ Pl: amaquphele EXD:329, RD-96:12

iradiyo *n5-sg* radio ☞ Syn: iwayilesi, unomathotholo AM-94:60, EXD:502

iramba *n3-sg* puff adder ☞ Pl: amaramba AXG:19, CGB:111

iramncwa *n3-sg* beast of prey ☞ Pl: amaramncwa CGB:111

irape *n5-sg* rape R36

irayisi *n5-sg* rice E&S:58, XED:144, R8, R12=9

irekhodi *n5-sg-loan* record R33=2

iresiphi *n5-sg* receipe ☞ Pl: iiresiphi R12

irhafu[1] *n5-sg* tax; the hut tax ☞ Pl: iirhafu XED:143, R23=6

iRhafu[2] *pn-geog* Graaff-Reinet (town) As regional center, the place to pay tax ☞ Loc: eRhafu MI:246, XED:194

irhanuga *n3-sg* migrant worker, rootless emigrant, "tramp" (person who has abandoned his traditional area to work on a farm or in the city); [atr] migrant; rootless, foreign ☞ Pl: amarhanuga E&S:57, GDX3:117, XED:143

irhashalala *n5-sg* rash; [ext] chickenpox EXD:506, RD-96:389;112, R30=3

iRhawuti *pn-geog* Johannesburg (city); the Rand Mines ☞ Loc: eRhawutini; Alt sp: iRawuti; Syn: iGoli CGB:40; 139, MI:246, PCX:69

iRhini *pn-geog* Grahamstown ☞ Alt sp: iRini; Loc: eRhini CGB:175, MI:246, XED:194

Irma *loan* Irma (personal name) R36

iron *n5-sg* iron • *ne iron 'and iron'* R12

is-[1] *n4-sg-prf* [group 4 (Bantu class 7) alternate singular noun prefix before a root beginning with a vowel] • *isenzo 'deed', isonka 'bread'* ☞ Alt: isi-; Plural: iz- CGB:105, PCX:53, RD-96:372, SXWU:18

-is-[2] *v-suf-caus* make VERB, cause to VERB [causative or transitive verb suffix] • *sebenzisa 'use, apply, cause to work', thethisa 'make s.o. speak'* AXG:111f, E&S:44, XED:63, R1=2, R4d=3, R5, R6=4, R7=2, R8, R9=2, R12=3, R16

-isa *v-tr* bring, carry, convey latent vowel verb ☞ See: -sa E&S:51, XED:63; 147

isakhiwo *n4-sg* building ☞ Pl: izakhiwo CGB:112, EXD:73

isalathiso *n4-sg* guidepost, mark, index; index finger, forefinger ☞ Pl: izalathiso EXD:300, XED:2

isandi *n4-sg* sound ☞ Pl: izandi PCX:53, SXWU:18

isandla *n4-sg* hand; [ext] agent, assistant, clerk; instrument, tool • *imali iphelela ezandleni. 'Money slips through your hands'.* ☞ Pl: izandla; Cf: amandla AM-94:23, E&S:57, EXD:263, SXWU:18, XED:3, R15x, R30, R32x

isandul' *v-aux* has just VERBed R35

isango *n3-sg* gate; gateway; loop ☞ Pl: amasango AXG:19; 20, XED:148, R27x

isangqa *n4-sg* circle; halo EXD:96, XED:3, R8x

isanuse *n4-sg* diviner, forecaster • *isanuse semozulu 'weather forecaster'* Derived from -nuka 'smell' ☞ Pl: izanuse MI:262, PCX:53, XED:4

isaphuli-mthetho *n4-sg-cmp* criminal, lawbreaker Noun formation rules put -i at the end of verbs to describe 'doers of,' or -o to describe the act itself, hence isaphulo-mthetho 'breach or violation of the law' ☞ Pl: izaphuli-mthetho EXD:134; 334, R11=2

isatifiketi *n4-sg* certificate EXD:89, R7x

isaxhomekeke *v-st* it still depends upon R27

isazela *n4-sg* consciousness, inward knowledge; conscience ☞ rw: azi EXD:118, XED:4, R19.4, R36.22.23

isazi *n4-sg* sage, wise man ☞ Pl: izazi CGB:112

isaziso *n4-sg* notice, announcement ☞ Pl: izaziso CGB:112, EXD:21;409

iScience *n5-sg* Science (as a subject in school) R37.19

isebe *n3-sg* branch, bough; tributary (of river); social group; department XED:149, R18, R27

isebenze *v-sub* (that) it works R22

isebenzisane *v-caus-recip* cooperating, working together R37.16=2.20)

isekelwe *v-pass* that it be supported R21

isela *n3-sg* thief ☞ Pl: amasela E&S:57, EXD:660, PCX:95, SXWU:17, XED:149

isele *n3-sg* frog, toad ☞ Pl: amasele CGB:104, RD-96:390;372, SXWU:17, XED:149

isenokuba *v-pred-abil* can be R31.2

isenzi *n4-sg* verb {ling} EXD:704, RD-96:390

isenzo *n4-sg* deed, act, performance ☞ Pl: izenzo CGB:112, EXD:48, PCX:53, XED:36, R11x, R36

isepha *n5-sg* soap ☞ Pl: iisepha. From Afrikaans 'seep' soap CGB:113, E&S:58, EXD:602

isetyenziswe *v-caus-pass-short-past-change-ty* it is used by R37

ishishini *n3-sg* workshop, factory; trade, business undertaking (other than farming); handicraft ☞ Pl: amashishini EXD:76; 675, GDX3:174, XED:150, R23x

ishiye *v-pres-sub* it should leave R32.6

ishumi *num-n3-sg* ten (10) ☞ Pl: amashumi AM-94:76, NDK-91:621, Uys:2

ishumi elinambini *num-cmp* twelve (12) NDK-91:621, Uys:2

ishumi elinantlanu *num-cmp* fifteen (15) NDK-91:621

ishumi elinanye *num-cmp* eleven (11) NDK-91:621, Uys:2

isi- *n4-sg-prf* [group 4 (Bantu class 7) singular noun prefix] • *isitya 'plate, dish'* Consists of article i- + classifier si- ☞ Alt: is-; Pl: izi- CGB:105, E&S:17, PCX:51; 53, RD-96:372, SXWU:18, XED:63, R4b=3, R14

isibadama *n4-sg* lethargic, torpid, stupid person ☞ Pl: izibadama CGB:112, XED:6

isibadubadu *n4-sg* wanderer, rover, vagabond; stray (animal); person in search of s.t. ☞ Pl: izibadubadu CGB:112, XED:6

isibala *n4-sg* expanse, flat area, open space; the greater pectoral muscle ☞ Pl: izibala KED:20, XED:6

isibane *n4-sg* light, lamp; candle ☞ Pl: izibane E&S:22; 57, PCX:34, XED:8

isibhakabhaka *n4-sg* sky, firmament ☞ Pl: izibhakabhaka CGB:42

isibhalo *n4-sg* inscription, writing (what is written) ☞ Pl: izibhalo XED:6

isibhedlele *n4-sg* hospital ☞ Pl: izibhedlele; Loc: esibhedlele AM-94:63, CGB:138, E&S:57, EXD:282, RD-96:390, R37

isibhozo *num-n4-sg* eight (8) AM-94:76, NDK-91:621, Uys:2, R34=3

IsiBhulu *n4-sg* Afrikaans (language) AM-94:23, CGB:112, E&S:57, R4b, R37

isibindi *n4-sg* liver (internal organ); [ext] courage; vigor ☞ Pl:

izibindi EXD:351, RD-96:13; 390, XED:13

isibini *n4-sg-num* second [ordinal]; two (2); pair; couple CGB:113, NDK-91:621, RD-96:390, SXWU:18, Uys:2, R24, R34=3

isibizo *n4-sg* noun {ling} EXD:409, RD-96:390

isibonakude *n4-sg* telescope ☞ Pl: izibonakude; Cf: umabonakude EXD:653, NDK-91:307; 379

isibongo *n4-sg* praise poem ☞ Pl: izibongo MI:277, XED:15

isibovubovu *n4-sg* blusterer, hooligan, rude or violent person ☞ Pl: izibovubovu CGB:112, XED:16

isibuliso *n4-sg* salutation, greeting ☞ Pl: izibuliso EXD:256, XED:17

isicaka *n4-sg* servant, man-servant ☞ Pl: izicaka AXG:35, CGB:182, EXD:572, RD-96:390, XED:20

isicakakazi *n4-sg-fem* maid, female servant ☞ Pl: izicakakazi AXG:35, EXD:362

isicelo *n4-sg* request, plea; application RD-96:390, R23=2

isidalwa *n4-sg* creature RD-96:390

isidanga *n4-sg* necklace of beads; [ext] degree (academic) EXD:149, XED:28, R24=3, R29x

isidenge *n4-sg* fool ☞ Pl: izidenge CGB:107, E&S:57, SXWU:18

isidima *n4-sg* worth, value; virtue, good character; dignity; weight; authority EXD:159, XED:29

isidlangalala *n4-sg* open area, arena, amphitheater ☞ Loc: esidlangalaleni 'in public' XED:30, R34x

isidlele *n4-sg* cheek ☞ Pl: izidlele CGB:113

isidlo *n4-sg* meal; feast; [ext] pasture RD-96:390, XED:30

isidlo sa kusasa *n4-sg-cmp* breakfast EXD:69, RD-96:390

isidlwengu *n4-sg* violent person, rapist, ravisher ☞ Pl: izidlwengu XED:31f, R9x, R11x

isidoda *n4-sg* men, males [collectively] XED:32, R30

isiduko *n4-sg* clan name ☞ Pl: iziduko AM-94:164, MI:275

isiduli *n4-sg* ant hill, termite mound ☞ Pl: iziduli; Cf: induli 'hill' CGB:42, EXD:276

isifazi *n4-sg* women (collective), womankind CGB:112, XED:38

isifo *n4-sg* disease, sickness, illness ☞ Pl: izifo; Loc: esifeni AM-94:23, E&S:57, PCX:68, RD-96:391, SXWU:18, R30

isifuba *n4-sg* chest, thorax; breast ☞ Pl: izifuba CGB:113, RD-96:391, R25=2

isifundo *n4-sg* lesson; lecture ☞ Pl: izifundo AM-94:23; 155, E&S:57, PCX:20; 53, RD-96:391, R7x=3

isigama *n4-sg* vocabulary AM-94:23, R37.19.20

isiganeko *n4-sg* demonstration, proof; well know event; important point XED:43, R35.11

isigcawu *n4-sg* spider ☞ Pl: izigcawu SXWU:18

isigogo *n4-sg* person with stiff limbs (i.e., cannot stretch them out, due to the cold, infirmity, etc.); [atr] hobbled; embarrassed, at a loss, unable to speak KED:122, R35.0x

isigqibo *n4-sg* decision ☞ Pl: izigqibo EXD:146, R14, R22x

isigqitho *n4-sg* trespass, transgression ☞ Pl: izigqitho XED:48, R13x

isigulana *n4-sg* patient, sick person ☞ Pl: izigulana SXWU:18

isigwebo *n4-sg* decision; sentence, judgment ☞ Pl: izigwebo XED:52

isihelegu *n4-sg* disaster, catastrophe R36.21

isiHindi *n4-sg* Hindi (language, culture, way of doing things) ☞ Pl: iziHindi SXWU:18

isihlaba *n4-sg* clump of aloes (place where aloe is abundant); thistle thicket ☞ Pl: izihlaba CGB:112, XED:56

isihlahla *n4-sg* wrist ☞ Pl: izihlahla CGB:113, EXD:735, RD-96:12

isihlalo *n4-sg* seat, chair, stool PCX:34, XED:57

isihlangu *n4-sg* shoe ☞ Pl: izihlangu AM-94:23; 72, CGB:183, E&S:57, SXWU:18

isihlanu *n4-sg-num* fifth [ordinal]; five (5) CGB:113, NDK-91:621, Uys:2, R34=2

isihlobo *n4-sg* friend, buddy; relative, blood relation • *isihlobo esibuhlungu 'bosom buddy'* ☞ Pl: izihlobo; Alt: umhlobo [n1-sg] KED:159, XED:60, R5

isihlomelo *n4-sg* addition, supplement; rider, amendment XED:60

isihlunu *n4-sg* muscle; flesh; lean (meat) ☞ Pl: izihlunu EXD:395, XED:61, R12x

isihlwele *n4-sg* crowd, retinue, company, band; a number of people XED:62, R24

isihoyo *n4-sg* care, concern; an object of concern XED:62

isiJamani *n4-sg* German (language) CGB:112, PCX:27

isiketi *n4-sg* skirt AM-94:72

isikhewu *n4-sg* gap, nick, notch; tooth (of a saw); pass (between mountains) ☞ Pl: izikhewu; Loc: esikhewini EXD:239, PCX:69, XED:71

isikhoba *n4-sg* yellowwood tree grove, cluster of yellowwoods ☞ Pl: izikhoba CGB:112

isikhokelo *n4-sg* lead EXD:336, R21, R22.6

isikhukukazi *n4-sg-fem* hen ☞ Cf: inkuku AXG:35, XED:75

isikhululo *n4-sg* release (from jail) EXD:520, KED:199, R18, R27

isikhundla *n4-sg* form, imprint left (by an animal lying down); lair; situation, position, place, stead ☞ Pl: izikhundla XED:77, R16, R22x

isikhuni *n-4-sg* a lighted firebrand • *isikhuni sabuya nomkhwezeli 'the torch returned with the firelighter' idiom - then came bad news.* R36

isiko *n3-sg* cut; custom, habit; fashion; (the practice of) circumcision AXG:20, XED:151

isikolo *n4-sg* school; mission station ☞ Pl: izikolo; Loc: esikolweni AM-94:23, CGB:113, E&S:57, MI:273, PCX:37; 68, RD-96:391, SXWU:18, XED:73, R9x=2, R10x=2, R16=3, R18, R22=3, R33

isikwe *v-pass-pres-sub* they should be cut (up) R8

isilambi *n4-sg* hungry person, someone suffering from starvation ☞ Pl: izilambi; Cf: -lamba R26.5

isilangazelelo *n4-sg* desire, longing ☞ Pl: izilangazelelo XED:81, R16

isiLimela *n4-sg-pn-geog* Pleiades (constellation) [lit: the plowing cluster] ☞ Pl: izinqanawa AXG:218, CGB:112, EXD:463

isilimo *n4-sg* crop XED:82, R13x

isilo *n4-sg* animal (wild, harmful), beast; bewitching matter ☞ Pl: izilo; Loc: esilweni; rw: -lwa AXG:36, E&S:17; 57, MI:262, PCX:23; 53; 68, XED:83

isilonda *n4-sg* sore, ulcer ☞ Pl: izilonda XED:83, R25x, R30x

isiluma *n4-sg* pain XED:84, R25

isilumko *n4-sg* wise, cautious, prudent person ☞ Pl: izilumko CGB:112, KED:221, R34.7

isilwanyana *n4-sg-dim* animal (small, noxious), vertebrate, insect [lit: little fighter] ☞ Pl: izilwanyana; rw: lwa- ~ lo- AXG:36, EXD:21; 704, MI:262, RD-96:392, XED:83, R2x=4

isimeko *n4-sg* condition, term, stipulation ☞ rw: -ma EXXE:56, XED:86

isimo *n4-sg* standing, rank, position; shape, form ☞ rw: -ma XED:86

isiNdebele *n4-sg* Ndebele (language) R37

isine *n4-sg-num* fourth [ordinal]; four (4) CGB:113, NDK-91:621, SXWU:18, Uys:2, R34=3

isinga *n4-sg* clump of thorn trees, cluster of mimosa thorn trees ☞ Pl: izinga CGB:112

isingeniso *n4-sg* introduction, preamble EXD:474, XED:100

isiNgesi *n4-sg* English (language) AM-94:23, CGB:112, E&S:57, PCX:27, RD-96:392, R4b, R7, R29, R37

isinqanawa *n4-sg* fleet ☞ Pl: izinqanawa CGB:112, EXD:220

isintu *n4-sg* mankind, humankind CGB:112

isinye *num-n4-sg* one (1) NDK-91:621, Uys:2, R34=3

isinyi *n4-sg* bladder ☞ Pl: izinyi EXD:57, KED:306, RD-96:13, XED:117

isiphakamiso *n4-sg* lift; [ext] motion (in meeting) ☞ Pl: iziphakamiso NDK-91:536, R37.5

isiphatho *n4-sg* handle (of utensil); treatment, handling, management; [ext] domestic economy, running a household ☞ Pl: iziphatho CGB:112+, EXD:264, XED:125

isiphiwo *n4-sg* natural ability or talent EXD:245, R33

isipho *n4-sg* gift ☞ Pl: izipho; rw: -pha AM-94:23f; 164, E&S:57, R35

isiphumo *n4-sg* utterance; pronunciation XED:131, R34x

isipili *n4-sg* mirror ☞ Pl: izipili SXWU:18

Isipingo *pn* Isipingo (city in South Africa) R20

isiPutukezi *n4-sg* Portuguese (language) CGB:112

isiqalo *n4-sg* beginning, start, commencement XED:133

isiqithi *n4-sg* island ☞ Pl: iziqithi CGB:42, R17.6x

isiqu *n4-sg* self, personality, individuality R34

isirhalarhume *n4-sg* violent man, fierce person XED:143, R36

-isis- *v-suf* do VERB well, thoroughly, persistently [intensive verb suffix] E&S:44

isisa *n4-sg* benevolence, liberality, kindness of heart, charity; [atr] charitable, benevolent MI:259, XED:147

isiseko *n4-sg* basis, foundation NDK-91:563, R37.1

isisele *n4-sg* pit, cell R31

isiselo *n4-sg* drink, beverage ☞ Alt: intselo [n5-sg], uselo [n6-sg] XED:149

isishebo *n4-sg* mixed meal, mixed grill ☞ See: iSpicy Lamb Sishebo, Jikelele Sishebo Mix R8

isisikhokelo *n4-sg-cop-n4-sg-cop-noun* it is guidance R22.6

isisinga *n4-sg* thong, tether for calves and lambs • *inkonyana iyasothuka isisinga 'young calves are shocked at (the first sight of) the thong'* R36.6

isisu *n4-sg* stomach, belly, abdomen; stomachache • *nesisu 'pregnant' [lit: having a stomach]* ☞ Pl: izisu; Loc: esiswini PCX:68, RD-96:13, XED:154, R25.1.7

isisulu *n4-sg* windfall, piece of good luck; easy prey, s.t. easily come by; [ext] bargain ☞ Pl: izisulu CGB:112, XED:155, R1

isiSuthu *n4-sg* Sotho (language) ☞ Loc: esiSuthwini AM-94:23, SXWU:102, R7, R37

isiSwazi *n4-sg* Swazi (language, culture, way of doing things) ☞ Pl: iziSwazi SXWU:18

isitalato *n4-sg* street ☞ Pl: izitalato; Alt: isitrato AM-94:23, CGB:113, MI:273

isitampu *n4-sg* stamp ☞ Pl: izitampu AM-94:23

isitena *n4-sg* brick ☞ Pl: izitena AM-94:23, E&S:57, EXD:69, XED:159, R35x

isithambiso *n4-sg* softening; anointing; lubrication, lubricant; [ext] taming ☞ Pl: izithambiso EXD:359, XED:157, R30

isithandathu *num-n4-sg* six (6) NDK-91:621, Uys:2, R34=2

isithandwa *n4-sg* loved one, darling, beloved ☞ Pl: izithandwa AM-94:155, R31

isithathu *n4-sg-num* third [ordinal]; three (3) CGB:113, NDK-91:621, SXWU:18, Uys:2, R34=3

isithende *n4-sg* heel ☞ Pl: izithende EXD:272, RD-96:12

isithethe *n4-sg* tradition, custom ☞ Pl: izithethe XED:159

isithethi *n4-sg* speaker, (public) orator ☞ Pl: izithethi AM-94:155, CGB:113, SXWU:18, XED:159

isithetho *n4-sg* speech, oration; order, command ☞ Pl: izithetho CGB:113, XED:159

isithoba *num-n4-sg* nine (9) NDK-91:621

isithuba *n4-sg* space, gap, interval; opening, vacancy NDK-91:580, RD-96:392f

isithubi *n4-sg* milk porridge ☞ Cf: -mthubi XED:168

isithukuthezi *n4-sg* dreariness Derived from -thukuthezela 'be anxious about' R25

isitofu *n4-sg* injection, inoculation meaning by extension of isitofu, 'lymph', or from Afr. 'stof' ('stuff') EXD:305, R25

isitovu *n4-sg* stove ☞ Pl: izitovu; Loc: esitovini CGB:113, EXD:305, SXWU:102, R8x, R25x

isitrato *n4-sg* street ☞ Pl: izitrato; Alt: isitalato E&S:57, R9x

isitshisa *n4-sg* heartburn R25.1

isitshixo *n4-sg* key; lock, bolt PCX:34, XED:166

isitulo *n4-sg* chair, stool ☞ Pl: izitulo; Loc: esitulweni AM-94:23, CGB:105; 139, E&S:57, SXWU:18

isitya *n4-sg* dish, plate, bowl, vessel; basin ☞ Pl: izitya; Loc: esityeni CGB:105; 112; 139, E&S:31; 57, PCX:23, RD-96:393;372, SXWU:18

isityalo *n4-sg* plant ☞ Pl: izityalo E&S:57, EXD:461, SXWU:18

isityebi *n4-sg* rich person ☞ Pl: izityebi SXWU:18

isixeko *n4-sg* city ☞ Pl: izixeko; Syn: idolophu CGB:42; 105, EXD:97

isixhenxe *num-n4-sg* seven (7) AM-94:76, NDK-91:621, Uys:2, R34=2

isixhobo *n4-sg* weapon ☞ Pl: izixhobo (q.v. with specialized meanings) E&S:57, EXD:717, R35x

isixholo *n4-sg* chisel ☞ Pl: izixholo CGB:112

isiXhosa *n4-sg* Xhosa (language, culture, way of doing things) AM-94:23, CGB:112, E&S:57, PCX:26f, SXWU:18, R4bx, R7x, R37

isiyezi *n4-sg* dizziness, giddiness, being stunned; state of mental confusion; blackout ☞ Pl: iziyezi XED:188, R25, R30=2

isizalo *n4-sg* womb XED:190

isizalwane *n4-sg* kin, family group or connection ☞ Pl:

izizalwane EXD:326, XED:190, R34.12

isizathu *n4-sg* reason, cause; proof ☞ Pl: izizathu EXD:510, XED:190, R11

isiZulu *n4-sg* Zulu (language) AM-94:23, CGB:112, PCX:27, XED:193, R7x, R37x

isizwe *n4-sg* nation; tribe ☞ Pl: izizwe E&S:57, PCX:23, R3, R20

island *n5-sg-red* island ☞ See: Robben Island R32

isohlwayo *n4-sg* punishment R23

isoka *n3-sg* bachelor, unmarried man; suitor, wooer; [ext] monk, celibate ☞ Pl: amasoka AXG:218, CGB:111, XED:153f

isoloko *atr-n5-sg* it always R27, R37.17

isondo *n3-sg* lower edge of a garment, selvage, lappet; corner of a blanket; [idiom] sex, sexual intercourse ☞ Pl: amasondo AXG:20, GDX3:221, KED:395, XED:154, R30=5, R36=8

isoni *n4-sg* wrongdoer, habitual sinner XED:121

isonka *n4-sg* bread; loaf; cornbread ☞ Pl: izonka; Loc: esonkeni AM-94:23, CGB:105, E&S:57; 58, RD-96:393;372, SXWU:18, XED:121

isono *n4-sg* sin ☞ Pl: izono PCX:53

isosala *n5-sg* saucer ☞ Pl: iisosala E&S:58

iSouth African Schools Act *n5-sg-cmp* The South African Schools Act (Act of Parliament) R22

iSpicy Lamb Sishebo *n5-sg-cmp* Spicy Lamb Mix (brand name) R8

iswekile *n5-sg* sugar E&S:58

itafile *n5-sg* table ☞ Pl: iitafile; Loc: etafileni CGB:106; 139, E&S:58, MI:273, PCX:54, SXWU:19

itakane *n3-sg* lamb ☞ Pl: amatakane E&S:57

itapile *n5-sg* potato (plant, foodstuff) ☞ Pl: iitapile E&S:58, XED:158, R8x

iTB *n5-sg-abr* TB R30

iteksi *n5-sg* taxi ☞ Pl: iiteksi E&S:58, R23x

itelevizhini *n5-sg* television ☞ Syn: umabonakude, iTV AM-94:60

ithala *n3-sg* exposed rock ☞ Pl: amathala CGB:111

ithambe *v-pres-sub* it (the meat) should become tender R8

ithambo *n3-sg* bone ☞ Pl: amathambo CGB:111

ithamsanqa *n3-sg* luck ☞ Pl: amathamsanqa EXD:359, R34=12

ithandwe *v-pass-short-past* it is liked R29

ithanga *n3-sg* pumpkin; cattle post; thigh This homonymic noun has three different meanings and which actually have different tonal patterns, which is not reflected by the orthography ☞ Pl: amathanga XED:157f

ithatha *n3-sg* nostril ☞ Pl: amathatha EXD:408

ithathwa *v-pass* he is taken R36

ithathwe *v-pass-short-past* (it) be taken R37.19.26

itheko *n3-sg* festivity, event, function, special occasion; specific place; position, office; subject (of public discussion) ☞ Pl: amatheko GDX3:283, XED:158, R24x, R31x

iTheku *n5-sg-pn-geog* Durban (city) ☞ Loc: eThekwini MI:246, XED:194, R28x=6, R33x

ithemba *n3-sg* hope, trust, expectation AM-94:164, XED:159, R33

ithengwa *v-pass* it is bought R29

ithengwe *v-pass-sub-pres* it should be bought R29

ithetha[1] *n3-sg* spokesperson, spokesman ☞ Pl: amathetha XED:159

ithetha[2] *v-pres* he, she says; it discusses R22, R37.19

ithetha[3] *v-pres* it means R37.19

ithi *v-pres/aux-n5-sg* is as follows -thi is widely used as an auxiliary giving sense of 'let's say...' R4b, R22, R37

ithoba *n3-sg-num* nine (9) AM-94:76, Uys:2, R34=3

ithokazi *n3-sg-fem* heifer, female young (of animal) ☞ Cf: ithole AXG:36, XED:162

ithole *n3-sg* yearling, large calf, young (of animal) AXG:36, XED:162

-ithu *pro-1pl-poss-root* of us; our, ours; our own [plural possessive root] ☞ Also: -ethu (= -a-ithu); See: #ethu, bethu, kwethu, lethu, lwethu, sethu, wethu, yethu, zethu CGB:182, E&S:22, SXWU:36, R1=2, R11

ithuba *n3-sg* moment; opportunity, occasion; turn, chance; [atr] interim ☞ Pl: amathuba E&S:57, NDK-91:580, RD-96:394, R10x, R14, R27, R34, R34x.10, R35, R36

ithuma *n3-sg* Cape gooseberry ☞ Pl: amathuma CGB:111

ithungula *n3-sg* Natal plum (fruit) ☞ Pl: amathungula; Cf: umthungula (tree) CGB:111, XED:169

iti *n5-sg* tea ☞ Pl: iiti E&S:58, EXD:651, PCX:54, SXWU:19

itikiti *n3-sg* ticket ☞ Pl: amatikiti PCX:53;34

iTinarha *pn-geog* Uitenhage (town); Zwartkops River ☞ Alt sp: iTinara; Loc: eTinarha CGB:41, MI:246, XED:194

itipoti *n5-sg* teapot ☞ Pl: iitipoti E&S:58

ititshala *n5-sg* teacher ☞ Pl: iititshala; Alt: utitshala [n1a] E&S:58, EXD:652, JPD:154, XED:161, R9

ititshalakazi *n5-sg-fem* teacher (female), school marm ☞ Pl: iititshalakazi E&S:58

itraka *n5-sg* truck R26

itshatile *v-st-perf* she is married, she was married ☞ See: -tshata R19.1

iTswani *pn-geog* Pretoria (city) ☞ Alt: iPitoli XED:194

itswele *n3-sg* onion ☞ Pl: amatswele EXD:419, R8

itutu *n3-sg* cattle-rustler, robber, thief ☞ Pl: amatutu XED:170, R26x

ityala *n3-sg* crime, guilt, fault, offense, debt ☞ Pl: amatyala R31.4, R36.14.15

ityhefu *n5-sg* poison EXD:466, GDX3:454f, R25

ityhini *n3-sg* female, girl, woman ☞ No plural GDX3:456, R33, R35x

ityuwa *n5-sg* salt E&S:58

-iva *v-tr* hear latent vowel verb ☞ See: -va E&S:51, SXWU:32, XED:63; 175, R4dx

ivaselina *n5-sg* Vaseline R30

iveki *n5-sg-time* week ☞ Pl: iiveki E&S:58, EXD:718, MI:231, PCX:37, R1x

iveni *n5-sg-loan* van R27

ivenkile *n5-sg* shop ☞ Pl: iivenkile; Loc: evenkileni E&S:58, SXWU:102, R37.13x

ivila *n3-sg* lazy person, sluggard ☞ Pl: amavila AXG:19, E&S:57, XED:177

ivili *n3-sg* wheel ☞ Pl: amavili E&S:57, XED:177

ivimba *n3-sg* miser AXG:19

-iw- *v-suf-pass* be VERBed [passive verb suffix on monosyllabic and vowel verbs] • *elidiniweyo 'who is tired of' [= eli-din-iw-e-yo], enziwa 'be made'* CGB:188, R4c, R9, R10, R26

iwayilesi *n5-sg* radio ☞ Syn: iradiyo, unomathotholo AM-94:60, EXD:502

iwayini *n5-sg* wine E&S:58

-iwe *v-suf-pass-past* was / were VERBed [long form passive past verb suffix] Structure: used when the verb is sentence final (i.e., when nothing follows the verb); Note: do not confuse with -iw- suffixed to monosyllabic verbs + -e short past ending CGB:187, XED:63, R4cx

iwonga *n3-sg* degree, status, qualification; grace, dignity XED:181, R24.8

iwu *intj* come on! XED:63

ixa *n3-sg* time (point in time); hour; chance ☞ Alt: ilixa GDX3:556

ixabiso *n3-sg* bar; limit; worth, value, price; importance ☞ Pl: amaxabiso XED:182, R1x

ixesha *n3-sg* time; period (of time); clock, watch, timepiece ☞ Pl: amaxesha E&S:57, EXXE:79, RD-96:394, SXWU:17, XED:184, R3, R10x, R14x, R21, R31.5, R33.7, R34.2.6, R36.24, R37.8.17.19

ixeshana *n3-sg-dim* moment, small amount of time ixesha + ana (diminutive suffix) R35

iXesi *pn-geog* Middledrift (town); Keiskama River ☞ Loc: eXesi MI:246, XED:194

ixhalanga *n3-sg* vulture ☞ Pl: amaxhalanga CGB:111

ixhama *n3-sg* hartebeest (red); [fig] outcast, outlaw ☞ Pl: amaxhama CGB:111, PCX:89, XED:182

ixhego *n3-sg* old man ☞ Pl: amaxhego E&S:57, SXWU:17, XED:183

ixhegokazi *n3-sg-fem* old woman ☞ Pl: amaxhegokazi AXG:36

ixhegwazana *n3-sg-dim-fem* little old woman ☞ Cf: ixhego, ixhegokazi AXG:36

ixhoba *n3-sg* booty, spoil; victim, (easy) prey ☞ Pl: amaxhoba EXD:706, XED:184f, R36.17.22

ixhomekeke *v-st-sub-pres* it should depend on R34

iXhora *pn-geog* Elliotdale (town) ☞ Loc: eXhora XED:194

ixhwangusha *n3-sg* expert, man of high intelligence or deep experience; high-ranking person; [fig] swindler, con-man; [ext] bully, ruffian ☞ Pl: amaxhwangusha GDX3:594, R32.4.7

ixhwele[1] *n3-sg* herbalist, medicine man (witch doctor who uses traditional medicines along with chants and dances for black or white magic) ☞ Pl: amaxhwele EXD:273, GDX3:594f, KED:476, SXWU:17, XED:187, R7

ixhwele[2] *n3-sg* ankle joint, foot and ankle, fetlock ☞ Pl: amaxhwele EXD:213, GDX3:595, KED:476, XED:187, R7x

ixina *n3-sg* brass ☞ Pl: amaxina CGB:111

ixolo *n3-sg* bark (tree); peel (fruit); scale (fish) ☞ Pl: amaxolo CGB:111

ixolongo *n3-sg* hollow reed; [ext] stethoscope ☞ Pl: amaxolongo EXD:623, MI:262

iXonxa *pn-geog* Glen Grey (town); White Kei River ☞ Loc: eXonxa XED:194

iya *v-aux-fut* it is going to R17.4

iya kushiyeka *v-fut* it will be left R30

iyabolisa *v-intr* it decomposes R25

iyakuba[1] *v-aux* it will be R18

iyakuba[2] *v-aux-fut* he will have R36

iyakufana *v-fut-recip* it will be the same as, will resemble R37

iyasothuka *v-tr-prog* it fears R36

iyawavula *v-tr* it opens (them) C5sg pres C3pl VERB R37

iyayixhasa *n5-sg-pres-n5-sg-v* it supports it R37.7

iye *v-aux* it was, became R22, R37

iyeza *n3-sg* medicine, (medicinal) herb; drug; cure, specific remedy ☞ Pl: amayeza E&S:57, EXD:273, XED:188, R6=3, R25=2

iyicacise *v-tr* it explains R37.19

iyilumkele *v-ben* it should be careful about R37

iyinkosi *cop-n5-sg* he is a chief R20

iyunivesithi *n5-sg* college, university ☞ Loc: eyunivesithi AM-94:63, EXD:694, R24

iyure *n5-sg* hour ☞ Pl: iiyure CGB:48, EXD:283, R8x

iz- *n4-pl-prf* [group 4 (Bantu class 8) alternate plural noun prefix before a root beginning with a vowel] • *izandla 'hands', izenzo 'deeds', izonka 'breads'* compare with izikolo, 'schools' [n4-plural] ☞ Sg: is-; See: izi- CGB:105, PCX:53, RD-96:372, SXWU:18, R11=2, R15

-iza[1] *v-intr* come latent vowel verb ☞ See: -za E&S:51, PCX:21f, RD-96:394, SXWU:32, XED:63;189

iza[2] *v-aux-fut* it will R32=2, R33

izakhiwo *n4-pl* buildings ☞ Sg: isakhiwo R35

iZalu *pn-geog* Palmerton (town) XED:194

izame *v-sub* that it try • *ukuba ibhodi izame ukwenza '...that the board trys to do...'* R37.16

izandla *n4-pl* hands ☞ Sg: isandla E&S:57, SXWU:18, R15x, R32

izantsi *n3-sg* lower part; lower course; foot ☞ Pl: amazantsi XED:190

izaphuli-mthetho *n4-pl-cmp* criminals, lawbreakers R11=2

izazi *v-tr* it should know (them) R37

ize *conj* so that, in order to ☞ Cf: -za XED:63

izembe *n3-sg* axe ☞ Pl: amazembe CGB:111

izenzo *n4-pl* deeds, acts ☞ Sg: isenzo PCX:53, R11x

izi- *n4-pl-prf* [group 4 (Bantu class 8) plural noun prefix] • *izitya 'plates, dishes'* Consists of article i- + classifier zi- ☞ Sg: isi- CGB:105, E&S:17, PCX:51; 53, RD-96:372, SXWU:18, XED:63, R1, R2=3, R7=2, R9=3

izibele *n4-pl* kindnesses, acts or feelings of affection CGB:107, EXD:10

iziBhalo *n4-pl* Scriptures XED:6

izibhedlele *n4-pl* hospitals ☞ Sg: isibhedlele E&S:57, R37

izibhidi *n4-pl* dregs, lees Plural only CGB:113, EXD:174, XED:12

izibilini *n4-pl* entrails, intestines, bowels; [fig] affections No singular ☞ Syn: amathumbu CGB:113, EXD:191, XED:13

izibongo *n4-pl* praise poems; [ext] poem describing the character and achievements of a chief ☞ Sg: isibongo MI:277, XED:15

izibuko *n3-sg* ford, crossing place; harbor ☞ Pl: amazibuko AXG:20, XED:191

izidanga *n4-pl* degrees (academic) R29x

izidlwengu *n4-pl* rapists ☞ Sg: isidlwengu R9, R11

izifundiswa *n4-pl* the educated, learned R17.2

izifundo *n4-pl* lessons ☞ Sg: isifundo E&S:57, PCX:53, R7=2, R24

izigidi *n4-pl* million, a very large number, thousands R24.8

izigqibo *n4-pl* decisions ☞ Sg: isigqibo R22

izihlangu *n4-pl* shoes ☞ Sg: isihlangu AM-94:72, CGB:182, E&S:31; 57, R33

izihlobo *n4-pl* friends, buddies R5x

izikhohlela *n4-pl* phlegm [col]; expectoration Usually plural only CGB:113, EXD:453, XED:72

izikhuphe *v-tr* it takes them out R25

iziko *n3-sg* hearth, fireplace; chief's kraal; [ext] depot, headquarters, special-purpose center; [pl] households • *iziko lovoto 'polling both'* ☞ Pl: amaziko; Loc: eziko CGB:139, MI:262, PCX:70, XED:191, R35, R37.13

izikolo *n4-pl* schools ☞ Sg: isikolo CGB:135, E&S:57, R9x=2, R22=3

izikrelemnqa *n4-pl* vandals compound noun - poss. ikrele ('spear') and umnqa ('one who appears suddenly') ☞ Sg: isikrelemnqa (q.v.) R18.0

izilo *n4-pl* animals (wild, harmful) ☞ Sg: isilo; rw: lwa E&S:17; 57, PCX:53

izilonda *n4-pl* sores, ulcers ☞ Sg: isilonda R25, R30=3

izilwanyana *n4-pl-dim* small animals [lit: little fighters] ☞ Sg: isilwanyana R2=3

izim- *n6-pl-prf* [group 6 (Bantu class 10) plural noun prefix] • *izimvo 'opinions'* Consists of article i- + classifier zim- CGB:107, PCX:53, RD-96:372, SXWU:20, XED:63

izimisele *v-refl-perf* it is serious R29

izimu *n3-sg* cannibal; ogre ☞ Pl: amazimu AXG:20, XED:192

izimvi *n6-pl* gray hairs ☞ Sg: uluvi KED:240, PCX:54, XED:91

izimvo *n6-pl* opinions, ideas, feelings • *Veza izimvo zakho! 'Voice your opinions!'* ☞ Sg: uluvo; Loc: ezimveni CGB:107, E&S:58, PCX:50; 54;68, RD-96:372, SXWU:20, R17.0, R21, R34x, R37.5

iziN- *n5-pl-prf* [group 5 (Bantu class 10) plural noun prefix on monosyllabic roots] • *izinja 'dogs', izindlu 'houses', izinto 'things'* Consists of article i- + classifier ziN- ☞ Sg: iN- CGB:106, E&S:17, PCX:51; 53, RD-96:372, SXWU:19, XED:63, R2

izinala *n4-pl* seminary, mission school from Eng. seminary sing form 'isinala' R36

izincwangciso *n5-pl* budgets, plans, activities ☞ Cf: -cwangcis- 'arrange in line' [XED:26] R35.12

izindlu *n5-pl* houses ☞ Sg: indlu E&S:57, PCX:53

izinja *n5-pl* dogs ☞ Sg: inja; Loc: ezinjeni CGB:107; 142, E&S:57, PCX:50; 53, RD-96:372, SXWU:19

izinti *n6-pl* sticks; [ext] weapons ☞ Sg: uluthi AM-94:101, E&S:58, PCX:54, SXWU:20

izintlu *n6-pl* rows (of things), lines; ranks (military) ☞ Sg: uluhlu CGB:114, E&S:58, PCX:54, XED:61

izinto *n5-pl* things, items uses full prefix as root (-tho) is monosyllabic ☞ Sg: into; Cf: ulutho 'nothing' CGB:107, E&S:17; 57, PCX:53; 28, R4c, R14, R17.1, R22, R27=2, R28, R29, R31=2, R33, R35=2, R37=3

izintso *n5-pl* kidneys ☞ Sg: intso EXD:326, R25

izintsu *n6-pl* skin (mass); skins ☞ Sg: ulusu (q.v.) CGB:107

izinyawo *n6-pl* feet Singular form unyawo (Class6) XED 117, R25

izinyo *n3-sg* tooth; [pl] teeth ☞ Pl: amazinyo; amenyo {archaic} AXG:20, CGB:111, E&S:57, EXD:671

iziphakamiso *n4-pl* motions (in meeting), submissions ☞ Sg: isiphakamiso R21, R37.5

izipho *n4-pl* gifts ☞ Sg: isipho AM-94:23f, E&S:57

iziphumo *n4-pl* sayings, utterances, results ☞ Sg: isiphumo R24, R25, R33x, R34

izisulu *n4-pl* bargains R1

iZitapile *pn-geog* Bensonvale (town) ☞ Cf: itapile 'potato' - perhaps grown locally XED:194

izitena *n4-pl* bricks ☞ Sg: isitena E&S:57, R35

izithambiso *n4-pl* lubricants ☞ Sg: isithambiso R30.7

izithuthi *n4-pl* cars, buses, trucks (means of transportation other than by horse) R28.3

izitrato *n4-pl* streets ☞ Sg: isitrato E&S:57, R9x

izitya *n4-pl* plates, dishs; basins; crockery ☞ Sg: isitya CGB:105, E&S:57, PCX:23f, RD-96:395;372, R36

iziveliso *n4-pl* produce [collective] XED:177

izixhobo *n4-pl* furnishings, utensils, accouterments; weapons ☞ Sg: isixhobo CGB:113, E&S:57, XED:185, R35.8

izizalwana *n4-pl* relatives, kin ☞ See: isizalwane R34.12

izizalwane *n4-pl* kin, kinfolk, family groups or connections ☞ Sg: isizalwane EXD:326, XED:190, R34.12

izizwe *n4-pl* nations; tribes ☞ Sg: isizwe E&S:57, PCX:23f

izokuchaza *v-tr-fut-n5-sg-S1+n8-vn-obj* he will report it R36.12

izolo *n3-sg-time* yesterday No direct plural ☞ Cf: amazolo 'night air, frost, dew' AXG:20; 143, E&S:57, EXD:737, MI:231, RD-96:395;373, XED:192, R17.2

izonka *n4-pl* breads (loaves, types of bread) ☞ Sg: isonka CGB:105, E&S:57, RD-96:372

izulu *n3-sg* sky; heaven; atmosphere; weather; [ext] lightning • *Liya duduma (izulu) 'It is thundering'; Liya baneka (izulu) 'It is lightning'* ☞ Pl: amazulu; Loc: ezulwini; Cf: phezulu AXG:19; 218, E&S:57, PCX:68, XED:193

izungeze *v-tr* surround R34.11

izwekazi *n3-sg* continent (EXD:121), MI:262, XED:193

izwi *n3-sg* word R31.0

J

j *change* change of BH to J • *-bhujelwa 'be bereaved' [= bhubh-/j-el-w-a]* CGB:142, MI:147, PCX:69; 103; 196

Jabu *n1a-sg-red-pn* Jabu (personal name) R23

Jacobs *pn-geog* Jacobs (town in Mozambique) R15

Jane *loan* Jane R33

jelo *n3-sg-red* pipe, tube; source (of information) ☞ See: ijelo R18=2

-jibilika *v-intr* go back on one's word, be unfaithful to a promise; tergiversate AXG:117, KED:170

jibilili *ideophone* change (of mind); be inconstant, unfaithful, a turncoat; break a promise AXG:117, KED:170

-jika *v-intr* turn around, rotate; change XED:64

-jikela *v-intr* go around (to) PCX:89; 92

-jikelele *atr* all around, universal; [adv] universally EXD:694, R8x

Joe Gqabi *-pn* Joe Gqabi R32

-jolisa *v-tr* aim at, level s.t. at XED:65

-jonga *v-tr* look (at fixedly), watch, stare; [intr] glare, look fierce CGB:144, XED:65, R12x, R14, R20, R30, R37.2

-jongana *v-recip* stare at each other, look fixedly at one another KED:173, XED:65, R12x

-jongana na- *v-cmp* face (the day, a problem, death) • *selejongene nokufa 'he has already stared death in the face'; ukujongana nosuku olude 'to face the entire day'* KED:173, XED:65, R12

June *loan* June R21=3

K

k[1] *change* change of KH to K • *inkokeli 'leader' [= in-khok-el-i], inkosi 'chief' [= in-khosi]* E&S:51, PCX:195, R2, R4b, R16=8, R20

k[2] *change* change (merger) of KU and KWA to K before O and U • *ngaphandle kootitshala 'without teachers' [= nga-pha-ndle kwa-ootitshala]* AXG:38, E&S:27, R3

k[3] *change* let him, her [noun group 1 singular form added to hortative construction] • *makacele 'he should request' [= ma+k-a-cel-e]* R10, R19, R27=2

k-[4] *n8-vn-them* [group 8 verbal noun thematic consonant prefix] ☞ See: ku-, konke XED:75

-k-[5] *n8-vn-obj* [group 8 verbal noun object agreement prefix before o-vowel initial verb] ☞ Alt: -ku- ~ -kw- E&S:18

-k-[6] *pro-2sg-obj-prf* you (thee) [short object form before o-vowel initial verb] ☞ Alt: -ku- ~ -kw- E&S:18

-k-[7] *v-suf* [verb forming suffix] • *-khewuka 'be nicked' [isikhewu 'nick'], -nyoluka 'be greedy' [nyolu-nyolu 'greedy']* AXG:116f

ka[1] *n1-sg-poss-prf* of [personal possessive prefix / marker for noun group 1 singular] Agr: um- E&S:23f, PCX:109, SXWU:36

ka[2] *n1a-sg-poss-prf* of [personal possessive prefix / marker for noun group 1a singular] • *ngomsa kaThixo 'with the love of God'* Agr: u- CGB:180, E&S:23f, PCX:109, R4d, R22=2, R32=2, R37.15

-ka-[3] *n1-sg-obj-infix* him, her • *makahambe 'let him go'* class 1 singular object infix only used in Hortative mood R10, R19

ka[4] *n2-sg-poss-prf* of [personal possessive prefix / marker for noun group 2 singular] Agr: um- E&S:23f, PCX:109

ka[5] *n2-pl-poss-prf* of [personal possessive prefix / marker for noun group 2 plural] Agr: imi- E&S:23f, PCX:109

ka[6] *n3-pl-poss-prf* of [personal possessive prefix / marker for noun group 3 plural] Agr: ama- E&S:23f, PCX:109

ka[7] *n5-sg-poss-n1a-sg* of [personal possessive prefix / marker for noun group 5 singular] Agr: i-, iN- E&S:23f, PCX:109

ka[8] *n5-sg-poss-prf* of [possessive formative for noun group 5 singular] • *Ngonyaka ka-2000 'by the year two thousand'* R35

ka-[9] *preverb* yet (not yet) [negative punctual preverb] • *Abakathethi 'They have not yet spoken'; lingekathambi 'it not yet being soft'* Negative only; Structure: a-SNEG-ka-Δ-i (in independent clause); S2-nge-ka-Δ-i (in participial clause) CGB:127, E&S:46, PCX:83f, R14, R28, R30

ka-[10] *adv-prf* -ly [adverb-forming prefix] • *kakhulu 'very', kaninzi 'often', kamnandi 'nicely'* ☞ See also: kaku- CGB:179, E&S:33, MI:256, R9, R11, R12, R17

kabani *qw-n1-pl-poss* whose? CGB:129f

kabanzi *adv* widely, broadly MI:256

kabini *adv-num* twice, two times MI:256

kabuhlungu *adv* painfully MI:256

kabukhali *adv* sharply MI:256

kaDalindyebo *n1-sg* Dalindyebo (praise name) R32

kade *adv-time* long ago; late AXG:142, CGB:178f, MI:256, XED:66;28

kafuthi *adv-time* often MI:256

kagqirha *n1a-sg-poss* of the doctor R37.15

kahlanu *adv-num* five times MI:256

kakade[1] *intj* of course, no doubt XED:66, R36=2

kakade[2] *adv-time* long ago AXG:142, CGB:178

kakhulu *adv* much, most, very, a lot, greatly AM-94:115, CGB:179, E&S:59, EXD:391, MI:256, R17.4, R29.14, R30, R34.11, R36.4.10.11, R37.7

kaku- *adv-prf* -ly [limited adverb-forming prefix] • *kakubi 'badly', kakuhle 'well'* ☞ See: ka- E&S:33, R9

kakubi *adv* badly, poorly, abusively E&S:33, EXD:40, MI:256, R9, R17.1, R36.19

kakuhle *adv* well, fine; beautifully; clearly; thoroughly, completely CGB:179, E&S:33; 59, MI:256, PCX:29, RD-96:395, R20, R22=2, R23, R25, R29, R30=2, R34, R37=3

Kalmer *n1a-sg-pn-loan* Kalmer (family name) ☞ Cf: uRene Kalmer R33.5

kaloku *conj-adv* of course Probably formed from adverbial ka- + loku (demonstrative) MI:257, R19, R24, R32

kaloku nje *adv-expr* right now, at once AXG:142

kalukhuni *adv-n6-sg* hard; harshly, strictly, severely [lit: wood-like] ☞ See: ukhuni 'firewood' R11

kalula *adv* easily, with ease MI:256

kalusizi *adv* sadly CGB:179, MI:256

kaMandela *n1a-sg-poss* of Mandela R32

kambe *adv* probably, to be sure, of course, no doubt AXG:214, XED:67

kambe ke *adv-expr* by the way, remember ☞ Cf: kanene 'by the way, remind me' MI:257

kamhlophe *adv* clearly, plainly, distinctly ☞ Cf: -mhlophe XED:89

kamnandi *adv* well, nicely, sweetly, pleasantly; (speak) fluently CGB:179, E&S:33; 59, MI:256, XED:67, R29.18, R32.7, R34.2

kamsinya *adv-time* soon ☞ Alt: msinya; kamsinyane AM-94:115, EXD:605, MI:256, XED:67

kamsinyane *adv-time* soon; quickly; early ☞ Alt: msinyane; kamsinya AXG:142, CGB:178, E&S:59, MI:256, XED:67

kamva *adv-time* after, afterwards ☞ See: umva AXG:143, CGB:178, XED:67, R21x, R34x

kananjalo *adv* so, in that way R12=2, R23

kancinane *adv* little by little, slowly, slightly CGB:179, MI:256

kane *adv-num* four times, fourfold MI:256, XED:68

kanene *adv* really, truly, indeed; by the way; remind me ☞ Cf: kambe ke 'by the way, remember' AXG:145, CGB:179, MI:257, PCX:37, XED:68; 98, R36

kangaka *adv* so much; so greatly CGB:179, XED:68

kangakanana *qw* how great?, how much? ☞ Alt: kangakanani (na) XED:68

kangakanani *qw* how great?, how much? ☞ Alt: kangakanani na E&S:33, XED:68; 99, R28, R31

kangako *adv* so much, so great; as much, as great (as) XED:68

kaNgangelizwe *n1a-sg-pn-poss* of Ngangelizwe (praise name) R32

kangangoko *adv* therefrom ☞ Cf: ngoko R12

kangaphi *qw-time* how often? AXG:142, CGB:129, E&S:33

kaninzi *adv* often, frequently, many times CGB:179, E&S:33, MI:256, XED:68; 104

kanjako *adv* besides, moreover, again ☞ Syn: ngaphezu koko XED:68

kanjalo *adv* again, also, likewise, in such a way CGB:178, XED:68, R34.11

kanti *conj* and yet, on the other hand; nevertheless, notwithstanding; whereas AXG:148, MI:257, PCX:80, XED:68, R10, R19.2, R20, R22, R23, R29, R31, R33, R36

kanye[1] *adv-num* once E&S:33, MI:256, R34

kanye[2] *adv* exactly, precisely R36

kanzima *adv* with difficulty CGB:179, MI:256

kanzulu *adv* deeply MI:256

kaSamora Machel *n1-sg* of Samora Machel ☞ See: Machel R24

kaSincokola *pn-poss* of Sincokola • *nombhali kaSincokola ngesiXhosa 'and author of "We Converse in Xhosa"'* possessive followed by book title R37.27

kasisa *adv* bountifully [lit: with benevolence] ☞ See: isisa XED:147

kathathu *adv-num* thrice, three times MI:256

kaThixo *n1a-sg-poss* of God R4d

-kazi[1] *n-suf-aug* largish, very big [augmentative noun suffix] • *indlukazi 'mansion, very large house'* AXG:36, CGB:175, E&S:33, MI:262, R3x

-kazi[2] *n-suf-fem* -ess, -ine, female- [feminine noun suffix] • *iqabanekazi 'female friend', ukumkanikazi 'queen'* AXG:35f, CGB:128, E&S:33, MI:262, R3, R4a, R4d

-kazi[3] *n-suf-kin* [kin suffix indicating sibling or affinal relationship] • *ubawokazi 'my father's brother', umakazi 'my mother's sister'* AXG:36, E&S:33, MI:262

kc *change* change of CH to KC • *inkcaza 'comb' [= in-kc/chaz-a]* E&S:51, PCX:195, R7

ke[1] *enclitic* then, now, so • *Hamba ke, 'Go then', ndeza ke, 'and so I came'* XED:70, R19, R20=2, R21, R28, R29, R31, R34, R36, R37=7

ke[2] *conj-adv* so, then; and so; but; well AXG:148, PCX:26, XED:70

ke kaloku *conj-expr* now [discourse marker, not temporal] • *Ke kaloku unyana wakhe omkhulu ebesentsimini 'Now his elder son was in the field'* AXG:148

-kha[1] *v-tr* scoop, draw (water), dip (up); pull (out), pick (fruit off a tree), pluck (flower) CGB:125, XED:65

kha-[2] *preverb* won't you just VERB [hortative preverb used with the second person] • *Khawulinde apha 'Just wait here!'* Structure: kha-S3a-Δ-e (followed by present subjunctive) ☞ Cf: khawu-, khani- CGB:169, E&S:42; 47, R4b, R9

-kha[3] *preverb / v-aux* do VERB sometimes, ever, a little, at all Structure: followed by S3a + present subjunctive ☞ Perf: -khe E&S:47, XED:65f, R3, R14, R32

-khaba *v-tr* kick s.o. / s.t.; [intr] shoot, sprout (plant) ☞ Pass: khatywa XED:66, R4b

-khala *v-intr* scream cry out, wail; complain; sound, give voice, ring XED:66, R32.7

-khanda *v-tr* hammer s.t. AXG:17

-khanga *preverb* not at all; never ☞ See: -khange E&S:47

-khange *preverb* not at all; did not VERB, never VERBed • *(Aka)khange abuze 'She didn't ask'; ugqirha khange abancede 'the doctor never helped them'* Structure: emphatic negative followed by S3a + present subjunctive E&S:47, R18, R23, R37

-khangela *v-tr* look (intensely at / for); search; study (a map); check, read (gauge) CGB:144, R17.6, R35.10

khani- *preverb-hort* won't you (all) [plural hortative preverb] • *Zinqununu neetitshala khanisebenzisane nathi 'Principals and teachers, won't you work together with us?'* ☞ See: -kha- + -ni CGB:169, R4b, R9

khanimbhalele *v-hort* won't you write to him R4b

khanisebenzisane *v-caus-recip-hort* won't you work together with R9

-khankanya *v-tr* mention; refer to s.t. XED:68, R37.4.6.13

-khanuka *v-tr* long for, desire greatly, lust after XED:68, R36.17.18.20.21.25.26

-khanya *v-intr* shine, give (off) light; be bright; be clear CGB:114, XED:68

-khanyisa *v-caus* light up; make shine, polish; turn on (light) PCX:34, XED:69

-khasa *v-intr* creep, crawl, go on hands and knees; [ext] move slowly KED:183, XED:69, R33x

-khathala *v-st* be interested (in), care for or about; get worn out; be troubled, vexed, anxious; [perf] exhausted, tired ☞ Perf: -khathele; Caus: -khathaza AXG:112, EXD:83, XED:69, R9, R35.1x

-khathaza *v-tr* bother, perturb, annoy, distress; hinder; trouble, pester, plague; wear s.o. out, fatigue ☞ rw: -khathala AXG:112, RD-96:395, XED:69, R2x, R9

-khathazwa *v-pass* be bothered, troubled, perturbed ☞ See: -khathala R9

-khatywa *v-pass* be kicked ☞ See: -khaba XED:66, R4b

khawu- *preverb* won't you [singular] ☞ See: -kha- + -u CGB:169, MI:277

khawutsho *qw-expr* would you ever say? R3

-khe[1] *n1-sg-root* he, she, it; his, her, its (own) [group 1, 1a singular pronoun / possessive root] ☞ See: akhe, bakhe, kwakhe, lakhe, lwakhe, sakhe, wakhe, yakhe, zakhe CGB:182, E&S:22, RD-96:395, SXWU:36

-khe[2] *preverb* VERBed ever, at all • *Wakhe wambona? 'Have you ever seen him?'; Imvula ikhe yana 'It rained a little'* Structure: followed by S3b + past subjunctive construction E&S:47, SXWU:140

khe[3] *v-pres-sub* should VERB sometimes; might VERB a little present subjunctive ☞ See: kha R17.6

khetha *v-tr* select, choose, pick out, be partial to XED:71, R20.2, R22.3, R23.9, R24.7, R29.13, R33.0

-kho[1] *n10-loc-root* it; its [group 10 locative pronoun root] E&S:22, R3x

-kho[2] *pro-2sg-poss-root* your, yours, thy; your own [singular possessive root] • *ngawakho amazwi, 'in your own words'* ☞ See: bakho, lakho, sakho, wakho, zakho CGB:182, E&S:22, SXWU:36, XED:71

-kho[3] *v-exis* exist, be present; am, is, are here; be there Note: a n10 locative root serving as an unchanging verb root, or locative copulative formative ☞ See: akho, bakho, bukho, ikho, kholo, -khoyo, kukho, likho, lukho, ndikho, sikho, ukho, zikho AXG:144, E&S:29, ITX:17, TD, XED:71, R3, R7, R11

-khohla *v-tr* embarrass, place s.o. in a difficult position; puzzle; escape one's memory XED:72, R30x

-khohlela *v-ben* have difficulty in breathing; cough XED:72, R30

-khoka *v-tr* draw out; lead out XED:72, R16x=7

-khokela *v-ben* go in front of; lead XED:72, R16=7, R21.5, R22.6

-khola *v-tr* satisfy, content; convince XED:72, R16x

-kholisa[1] *v-caus* satisfy, please, give satisfaction to s.o.; inspire confidence in s.o. XED:72, R16x

-kholisa[2] *v-aux* VERB thoroughly, efficiently, enough, much; do VERB mostly • *Ukholisa ngokudlula apha 'He often passes here'* Structure: -kholisa ngoku-Δ-a (i.e., with nga- + infinitive) E&S:47, XED:72

khomishoni *n5-sg-red* commission ☞ See: ikhomishoni R32=4

khona[1] *pro-n10-loc-echo* it (situation / domain), there (place) [group 10 locative echo / absolutive pronoun] E&S:22, PCX:57; 90, XED:73

khona[2] *v-exis* be present, be here; be there Related to: apho ☞ See also: kona AM-94:109, AXG:144, XED:73, R1, R21, R37=6

khonukuze *conj* so that R36

-khonza *v-intr* serve, do service Structure: used with locative XED:74, R4bx

-khudlwana *adj-dim* fairly large AXG:37

-khula *v-inch* grow (up), become big; increase XED:75f, R4dx, R6x

-khulela *v-ben* grow up in a certain place; grow up with / among s.o.; become large for; [ext] be too big / strong for s.o. KED:198, XED:76, R6x

-khulelwa *v-pass-ben* be full of, get filled with s.t.; be big with; [fig] be pregnant EXD:476f, KED:198, XED:76, R6

-khulisa *v-caus* cause to grow; raise, bring up; increase, magnify, make great; extol XED:76, R4dx

-khulisana *v-caus-recip* cause each other to grow, nurture one another R4d

-khulu *adj-root* big, large, great AM-94:115, AXG:37; 63, CGB:171f; 179, E&S:30, PCX:120

-khulula *v-tr* loosen, untie, unharness; undress, unfasten one's clothing; release, set free; save, deliver AM-94:73, XED:76, R34.11

-khululeka *v-atr* get loose; become free XED:76, R24, R36.13

-khumbula *v-tr* remember ☞ Caus: -khumbuza AXG:112, R13

-khumbuza *v-caus* remind ☞ rw: -khumbula AXG:112

-khupha *v-tr* take out, withdraw; send out; submit, release (report) ☞ Pass: -khutshwa PCX:34; 103, R5x, R25x

-khuphisa *v-tr* crowd out, remove, dispossess KED:203, R33

-khusa *v-tr* keep off / out (rain, wind, danger) XED:77, R9x, R11x

-khusela *v-ben* screen, shelter, protect • *masibakhusele 'let us protect them'* XED:77, R9, R10, R11, R18.6, R30.5.7, R31.2, R32.4, R36.1.12.22, R37.2

khuselani *v-imp-pl* you (all) protect! R11

-khuthala *v-st* be active, industrious, diligent ☞ Perf: khuthele XED:78, R4dx

-khuthalela *v-st-ben* be active for s.o.; be industrious, diligent, hard-working at s.t. R4d

-khuthaza *v-tr* activate, make active; animate, encourage, promote; rouse to action XED:78, R29.8, R33.2, R35.10, R36.17, R37.4

-khuthele *v-st-perf* was active; [atr] industrious, diligent, hard-working EXD:301, XED:78, R4dx

-khutshwa *v-pass* be taken out, get withdrawn; be submitted, be released ☞ rw: -khupha PCX:103, R5, R18.4

-khwaza *v-tr* shout EXD:583, PCX:89

-khwela *v-tr* board, get on; climb; ride PCX:34

King William's Town *pn-geog* King William's Town ☞ See: iQonce R1

Kingdom *pn-loan* Kingdom ☞ See: United Kingdom R24

km *abr* km, kilometers R33, R35

ko[1] *n1a-sg-poss-n5-sg* in it, of R21

-ko[2] *n8-vn-root* it; its [group 8 pronoun root] E&S:22

ko-[3] *v-n8-vn-short-fut* it will VERB [contracted / short positive future group 8 verbal noun prefix] E&S:20

ko[4] *n10-loc-poss-prf* of [personal possessive prefix / marker for locative noun group 10] • *phambi koWiso 'in front of Wiso', emva koWiso 'behind Wiso'* Agr: uku- PCX:109, R6

ko-[5] *v-n10-loc-short-fut* it (time, place, situation) will VERB [contracted / short positive future group 10 locative / impersonal noun prefix] [not found in any references]

kobaa[1] *deic-3-n7-sg-loc* to, at, in, from that (far, yonder) • *kobaa busi 'in that honey'* E&S:27

kobaa[2] *deic-3-n7-domain* in, at, on, to, from that (yonder domain) E&S:27

kobhinqileyo *v-perf-rel* to a woman R36.0

kobo[1] *deic-2-n7-loc* to, at, in, from that E&S:27

kobo[2] *deic-2-n7-domain* in, at, on, to, from that (domain) E&S:27

kobu[1] *deic-1-n7-loc* to, at, in, from this • *kobu bugxwayiba 'in this bushland'* E&S:27, R17.4

kobu[2] *deic-1-n7-domain* in, at, on, to, from this (domain) E&S:27

kodwa[1] *conj* but AXG:148, E&S:59, MI:257, PCX:31, R4c, R4d=2, R11, R12, R19.2, R20, R23=2, R24, R26, R28, R33=3, R35=2, R36=7, R37

kodwa[2] *pro-quan-n8-vn* it alone; only VERBing Agr: uku-, kona E&S:27, PCX:62

kodwa[3] *pro-quan-n10-loc* it alone; there is only Agr: uku-, khona PCX:62, R12

koko[1] *deic-2-n8-vn-pred* that (not far, just mentioned) is E&S:26, R37.5

koko[2] *deic-2-n8-vn-domain* in, at, on, to, from that (domain of VERBING) E&S:27

koko[3] *deic-2-n8-vn-loc* to, at, in, from that VERBing E&S:27

koko[4] *deic-2-n10-loc-pred* that (place not far, situation just mentioned) is; there R37.5

koko[5] *deic-2-n10-domain* in, at, on, to, from that (domain) • *ngaphezu koko 'in addition to that'* R10

koko[6] *deic-2-n10-loc-loc* to, at, in, from that (time, place, situation) R10, R23, R35, R36, R37

koko[7] *conj-deic* except, but that • *emva koko, after that. ngaphezu koko, more than that, moreover.* deictic expression indicating that place or time. Formed from dem. oko + loc. prefix ku XED:72, R10

kokoyika *v-inf* having to fear R23

koku[1] *deic-1-n8-vn-loc* at, to this ku + oku E&S:28, R36.23

koku[2] *deic-1-n8-vn-domain* in, at, on, to, from this (domain) E&S:27

koku[3] *deic-1-n8-vn-pred* this is E&S:26

koku[4] *deic-1-n10-loc-poss* of this (place, time, situation) • *phambi koku 'before this time'* PCX:140

kokuba *n8-vn-poss-n8-vn* of being; [conj] that, so that ☞ See: ukuba R16, R19.2, R26=3, R30, R33, R35

kokuhamba *loc-v-inf-red* walking R28

kokungaphezu *adv-neg-loc* not above everything, not exclusively • *Umaphuli mthetho ukhuthazwa kokungaphezu kweenkanuko zomzimba 'The perpetrators are not driven by bodily desire alone'* R36

kokusweleka *adv-v-inf* after the death R28

kokutyholwa *loc-v-inf-pass* being accused kwa (red = ko) after emva R26

kokwaa[1] *deic-3-n8-vn-pred* that (far, yonder) is E&S:26

kokwaa[2] *deic-3-n8-vn-loc* to, at, in, from that VERBing (far, yonder) • *kokwaa kucula 'in that singing'* E&S:27

kokwaa[3] *deic-3-n8-vn-domain* in, at, on, to, from that (yonder) VERBing E&S:27

kokwaa[4] *deic-3-n10-loc-loc* to, at, in, from that (far place, yonder time, situation) [not found in any references; cf: E&S:26]

kokwaa[5] *deic-3-n10-loc-domain* in, at, on, to, from that (yonder time, place, situation) [not found in any references; cf: E&S:26]

kokwenziwa *n8-vn-pass-adv* on account of being made R9

kolo[1] *deic-2-n6-sg-loc* to, at, in, from that • *Ndafunda lukhulu kolo gqatso 'I learned a lot in that race'* E&S:27, R33=2

kolo[2] *deic-2-n6-sg-domain* in, at, on, to, from that (domain) E&S:27

kolu[1] *deic-1-n6-sg-loc* at this, for this E&S:27, R37=2

kolu[2] *deic-1-n6-sg-domain* in, at, on, to, from this (domain) E&S:27

kolu[3] *deic-1-n6-sg-poss* of this • *ukutya kolu sana 'this baby's food'* PCX:140

koluntu *loc-n6-sg* to, by the people • *ukuzibalula koluntu 'self-determination of the people'* [kwa+uluntu] R21.1.2, R27.4

kolwaa[1] *deic-3-n6-sg-loc* to, at, in, from that (far, yonder) • *kolwaa luthi 'on that stick'* E&S:27

kolwaa[2] *deic-3-n6-sg-domain* in, at, on, to, from that (yonder domain) E&S:27

kom- *combo* of • *phantsi komthetho 'under the law'* indicates that n2 sg (um-) is possessed by a n10 loc (kwa-, reduced to k-) R36.14

komashini *loc-n6-sg* of the machine R35

komchamo *n2-sg* of urine ku+ (u)mchamo R25

komhla *n2-sg* (before) the day of R23

komntwana *loc-n1-sg* to the child R19

komthetho[1] *n2-sg-poss-n8-vn* of the law • *ukuphuma komthetho 'the passage of the law'* R37.06

komthetho[2] *n2-sg-poss-n10-loc* of the law • *phantsi komthetho 'under the law'* R36.14

komzimba *n2-sg-poss-n8-vn* of the body R25, R30=4

kona *pro-n8-vn-echo* it [group 8 verbal noun echo / absolutive pronoun] ☞ Contrast: khona AM-94:163, CGB:158, E&S:21, PCX:57, XED:73

konke[1] *pro-enum-n8-vn* all; the whole (of); every; [adv] at all Agr: uku-, kona AM-94:163, E&S:27, PCX:62;37, R37=3

konke[2] *pro-enum-n10-loc* all; the whole (of); every (place, time, situation) Agr: uku-, khona PCX:62

konxibelelwano *loc-n5-sg* to be connected together ☞ rw: -nxibelela 'be connected together' XED:114, R37.14

konyaka *loc-n2-sg* a year R28

koobawomkhulu *n1a-pl-cmp-kin-loc* from our grandfathers R32

koosomashishini *n1a-pl-loc* from the business owners R35.15

kootitshala *n1a-pl-loc* to / from teachers R3

korhulumente *n1a-sg-poss* of the government • *phantsi korhulumente 'under the government'* R24, R35

kq *change* change of QH to KQ • *inkqubo 'program; progress' [= in-kq/qhub-o]* Note that the -k- has no phonetic value - it merely denotes that the click is articulated with delayed breathy voice after the nasal. E&S:51, PCX:195, R3, R16, R22, R30, R37

-krakra *atr-root* bitter ☞ Cf: -mnandi 'sweet', -muncu 'sour' CGB:172, E&S:30

kratya *ideophone* more, extra R28

-krelekrele *v-st* shine, be bright; [ext] be smart, intelligent MI:198, RD-96:396, R12

kreshi *loan* daycare R23.1

-kroba *v-tr* peek, peep, look through (hole, window, doorway) CGB:144

-krwada *atr-root* raw, unripe, green (fruit); rude, uncouth E&S:30, EXD:255, RD-96:396

ku[1] *loc-prf-n1a* at, on, in, to, for, from, with, of, among [general locative prefix for noun group 1a, a named person, kin term, pronoun, or deictic] • *ku Mlawuli Omkhulu '(write) to the Chief Executive'* ☞ Contrast: e- [simple locative], kwa- [domain locative] AM-94:93, AXG:38, CGB:141, E&S:21; 32, SXWU:101, R1, R5, R9=2, R21

ku[2] *loc-prf* to, towards, of ☞ Alt: kw- AXG:38, E&S:32, Pahl:186, R2, R3, R4c, R4d=2, R5, R8x, R12x

ku-[3] *n8-vn-red-prf* [group 8 reduced verbal noun prefix] Loss of article u- from uku- SXWU:20, R9

-ku-[4] *n8-vn-obj* [group 8 verbal noun object agreement prefix] Agr: uku-, ukw-, uk- E&S:18, PCX:51, SXWU:44; R27

ku-[5] *n8-vn-adj-pred* it is ADJ [group 8 verbal noun adjective agreement prefix used predicatively] E&S:28, MI:248, PCX:118f, R24

ku-[6] *n8-vn-enum-prf* [group 8 verbal noun enumerative agreement prefix] ☞ See: kumbi, kuphi E&S:27, PCX:110f

ku-[7] *n8-vn-S1* it [group 8 verbal noun subject (S1) impersonal agreement prefix] Agr: uku- CGB:117; 158, E&S:17f, PCX:51, SXWU:28, R6, R9

ku-[8] *n8-vn-S2* he, she, it [group 8 verbal noun participial subject (S2) agreement prefix] AXG:91, CGB:191, R11

ku-[9] *n8-vn-S3a* (and) it VERBs [group 8 verbal noun present subjunctive verb subject (S3a) agreement prefix] (CGB:167)

ku-[10] *n8-vn-rel2* the VERBing which [group 8 verbal noun direct relative 2 construction, attributive agreement prefix used predicatively] E&S:34, MI:153; 248, PCX:152

ku-[11] *n8-vn-ind-rel2* which VERBing [group 8 verbal noun indirect relative 2 agreement prefix] E&S:35

ku-[12] *n10-loc-prf* [group 10 (Bantu class 17) locative noun prefix] • *kuTsolo 'the Tsolo place', kuQumbu 'the Qumbu place'* Consists only of classifier ku-; designates specific places ☞ Alt: uku- AXG:200, PCX:51; 56

-ku-[13] *n10-loc-obj* [group 10 locative noun object agreement prefix] Agr: uku-; also used for agreement with n9 (pha-) locative nouns PCX:51

ku-[14] *n10-loc-adj-pred* it is ADJ there [GROUP 10 locative NOUN / impersonal ADJECTIVE AGREEMENT PREFIX used predicatively] • *kude 'it is far'* E&S:28, PCX:119, R12

ku-[15] *n10-loc-enum-prf* [group 10 locative noun enumerative agreement prefix] ☞ See: kumbi, kuphi PCX:110

ku-[16] *n10-loc-S1* it [group 10 locative noun subject 1 agreement prefix] Agr: uku-; often marks impersonal constructions; also used for agreement with n9 (pha-) locative nouns PCX:51, R9, R12x

ku-[17] *n10-loc-S2* it [group 10 locative or impersonal noun participial subject (S2) agreement prefix] R10

ku-[18] *n10-loc-S4* it can VERB; it may VERB [group 10 impersonal potential / conditional verb subject (S4) agreement prefix] • *Kungaba uyafunda? 'Can it be you are studying?'* E&S:45 R24

ku-[19] *n10-loc-rel2* the (place, time, situation) which [group 10 locative noun direct relative 2 construction, attributive agreement prefix used predicatively] • *apho kufudumeleyo 'place that has warmed up'* PCX:152

ku-[20] *n10-loc-ind-rel2* which (time, place, situation) [group 10 locative / impersonal noun indirect relative 2 agreement prefix] [not found in any references; refer to PCX:152]

-ku-[21] *pro-2sg-obj-prf* you (thee) [object form] E&S:18, SXWU:44, R6=2, R7=2, R12, R14

ku-[22] *v-expr* it is; one VERBs; they VERB [impersonal verb marker] • *kuyabanda 'it is cold', kunjani? 'how is it?', kunjalo 'it is like that'* AM-94:112, CGB:137, R2=3, R4cx, R9=4, R10

-ku-[23] *v-inf-red-prf* [reduced form of infinitive prefix] ☞ Red: uku- CGB:165f, E&S:20, R4cx, R4d, R5=2, R12, R14

kuba[1] *n8-vn-red* being R6x

kuba[2] *v-red-inf* to be • *baya kuba 'they will be', eliza kuba 'who will become'* reduced infinitive in future construction R4d, R14

kuba[3] *conj* because, for, as [lit: it being] Structure: followed by the participial ☞ Alt: ngokuba AXG:151, E&S:41; 59, MI:257, PCX:34, R2, R10, R11, R12=2, R14, R17.2, R19=2, R20=2, R23=2, R24, R28, R29, R30=2, R31, R32, R33, R34, R35, R36=4, R37

kubafundi *loc-n1-pl* to students R14

kubahlali *loc-n1-pl* to residents R27

kubakho *loc-pro2-sg* is yours, rests with you R14

kubalasele *v-tr-inf-red* give attention to R24

kubalulekile *v-atr-perf* it is important BS, R14, R30, R37=4

kubandakanywa *v-tr-pass* are engaged in • *Uninzi lwabantu kubandakanywa oonompilo 'Many* *people are engaged in health work'* R36.12

kubangele *n8-v-perf* cause for R35

kubangelwa *v-ben-pass* it is caused by R37

kubanika *n8-v-tr* it gives them R35

kubanjwa *v-inf-red-pass* to be arrested R31

kubantu *loc-n1-pl* to people, for people R1, R27.11, R37.13.14

kubantwana *loc-n1-pl* to the children R24

kubaw' *loc-n1a-sg* from father R16

kube[1] *v-pred-n8-sg* it [indefinite] is • *kube nzima 'it (is) difficult'* R31=2, R33, R37=2

kube[2] *preverb-recent-pro-n8-vn* it was VERBing [group 8 verbal noun recent past compound tense preverb] Structure: kube ku-Δ (participial construction) AXG:91f, E&S:37, PCX:183

kube[3] *preverb-recent-pro-n10-loc* there was VERBing [group 10 locative noun / impersonal recent past compound tense preverb] Structure: kube ku-Δ (participial construction) E&S:37, PCX:183

kubekho *v-pred* there is; it exists, it is present R30, R37.14

kubekiwe *v-n10-impers-pass* it is set out • *kubekiwe kwicandelo 3 'it is set out in Section 3'* R37

kubhentsisa *v-inf-red* to expose R32

kubhetele *v-n8-impers-loan* it is better R31

kubizwa *v-pass* it is called R29

kubizwe *v-n10-impers-pass* it was called R18

kubo[1] *n1-pl-pro-loc* to, from, in, with them AM-94:93, E&S:21, PCX:90, R5

kubo[2] *n7-pro-loc* to, from, in, with him, her, it E&S:21

kubonisa *v-caus* it shows R29, R30

kubonwe *v-pass-short-past* it is seen R37

kububutyobo *cop-n-7-sg* it was crushed to bits / a mess R26

kubuhlungu *cop-atr* it is painful R36

kubulawa *v-pass* murder ☞ See: -bulala R32.9

kubunkokeli *loc-n7-sg-abs* in leadership R32

kubusika *n7-time-loc* in the winter R35

kucacile *v-n10-impers-perf* it is obvious or clear R37.11

-kudala[1] *atr-poss-root* old-fashioned; [adv] of old; long ago • *impahla yakudala 'old-fashioned clothing', ngolwathando lwakudala 'loving the old-fashioned way'* Structure: uses possessive agreement markers ☞ rw: -dala EXD:417, XED:75, R4d

kudala[2] *preverb* VERB for a long time; it is a while since, it has been a long time that • *Kudala ndingakuboni 'Long time no see!'; Kudala behlala apha eKapa 'They have been living here in Cape Town for a long time'* Structure: followed by participial construction SXWU:164

kude[1] *n10-loc / adv* far off, far away, from afar; [atr] distant, remote; long distance AXG:144; 200, CGB:178, RD-96:396, XED:75;28, R4cx

kude[2] *conj* until, till RD-96:396, XED:75

kude ku- *prep-cmp* far from [PRONOUN or DEICTIC] E&S:32

kude na- *prep-cmp* far from [PRONOUN or DEICTIC] • *kude naloo ndlu 'far from that house'* E&S:32

kudliwanondlebe *n-loc-cmp* at the interview [lit: eat the ear] R26.5

kudlwengulo *loc-n6-sg* in the rape R27

kufa *v-inf-red* to die R32

kufakwe *v-pass-short-past* put into [past] ku- = indefinite concord + verb in passive R22

kufana na *vp* it is the same as; it is just like R9

kufota *v-loan* photograph • *ukuya kufota i-International passport 'come to issue an International passport...'* verb borrowed from English, meaning extended to incluse issue of document. R37.14

kufumaneke *v-atr-perf* it was discovered R26

kufumaniseka *v-caus-atr* it is found, discovered R37

kufuna *v-inf-red* need R24, R28, R29

kufuneka[1] *v-aux-impers* must, need to, ought to, should [lit: it is necessary] • *kufuneka ukuqwalasele... 'it is necessary to examine...'* Structure: reduced infinitive, or neuter concord ku-, followed by present subjunctive CGB:168, XS-92:175, R9, R11, R16=2, R17.6, R21=6, R22.3, R23.3.11, R29=11, R30.6=2, R31.4, R33.10, R34.5.6, R35.13.15, R36.24, R37.16

kufuneka[2] *v-aux-impers* must, need to, ought to, should [lit: it is necessary] • *kufuneka le Bhodi iqinisekisile 'it is necessary for the Board to ensure...'; Kufuneka betyile phambi kokuba bahambe 'They must eat before they go'* Structure: followed by perfect participial (situative) XS-92:175, R37.17

kufuneka ukuba *v-aux-expr* it is necessary that Structure: followed by subjunctive CGB:168, R37.16.20

kufunyenwe *v-n10-impers-pass-perf* it was found R26

kufuphi *n10-loc;-adv* near, close, nearby; short distance • *IRhini ikufuphi kuneKomani ukusuka eKapa 'Grahamstown is nearer than Queenstown to Cape Town'* ☞ Alt: kufutshane AXG:144; 200, CGB:175; 178

kufuphi ku- *prep-cmp* close to, near [PRONOUN or DEICTIC] • *kufuphi kubo* E&S:32

kufuphi na- *prep-cmp* close to, near [PRONOUN or DEICTIC] • *kufuphi nabo 'near them'* E&S:32

kufutshane *adv-loc* near, close to ☞ Alt: kufuphi CGB:178, R24.2, R26.8

kuGerry *pn-loc* with Gerry R16

kugqatso *loc-n6-sg* to the race R33=3

kuGraca *pn-loc* with Graca (Machel) R24

kuhlawulwa *v-n10-impers-pass* it is paid R10

kuhle *adv* well, nicely; beautifully; steadily CGB:179, E&S:59, PCX:37

kuhluthwa *v-tr-pass* it was taken by force • *kuhluthwa umhlaba kwiinkosi 'the land was taken by force from the chiefs'* ku- is indefinite subject - note reverse word order in this case R32.4

kuka[1] *n8-vn-poss-prf* of [personal possessive prefix / marker for verbal noun group 8] Agr: uku- E&S:23f, PCX:109

kuka[2] *n10-loc-poss-prf* of [personal possessive prefix / marker for locative noun group 9 and 10] Agr: uku- E&S:32

kukagqirha *loc-n1a-sg* from the Doctor R36

kukatata *loc-poss-n1-sg* that of my father R28

kukhangela *v-inf-red* to look R35.11

kukho[1] *v-exis-n8-vn* it is here / present ☞ See: -kho E&S:29, ITX:17

kukho[2] *v-exis-n10-impers* there is, there are; it is present • *Kukho amanzi kolo dikeni. 'There is water in that dam.'* ☞ See: -kho AM-

94:112, CGB:163, E&S:29; 59, PCX:150, SXWU:58, R22, R25, R29, R32, R35=3

-kukhona *conj* the more • *Okukhona wabayalayo, kwaba kokukhona bakuvakalisa ngakumbi 'The more he charged them, the more they published it'* ☞ Alt: kungona AXG:148

kuko[1] *n8-vn-pro-loc* to, from, in, with it E&S:21

kuko[2] *n8-vn-pred* it is; it is it [group 8 verbal noun copulative or predicative] E&S:21, PCX:98

kuko[3] *n10-loc-pred* it is (the place, domain) [copulative or predicative] PCX:98

kukodwa *v-pred-n10-pro-quant* it is alone; all by itself R12

kukonyanya *v-inf-red* to be discontented R36.18

kuku-[1] *n8-vn-pred-prf* it is [group 8 verbal noun copulative or predicative prefix construction] • *kukutya 'it is food'* E&S:21; 25, PCX:96, XED:xvi

kuku-[2] *n8-vn-agent-prf* by (done by, produced by) it [marker of group 8 verbal noun agent of passive verb] E&S:25;43, R28.5

kuku-[3] *n10-loc-pred-prf* it is [group 10 locative noun copulative or predicative prefix construction] • *kukuTsolo 'it is (in) Tsolo'* PCX:96

kukuba[1] *conj* because Structure: followed by the participial R18.4, R19.3, R29.12, R37=5

kukuba[2] *v-aux-conj* it is because R36.14

kukubona *v-inf* is to see R29

kukude *loc-cop-atr* how far R28

kukulibala *v-inf-fut* they will not forget you part of future tense compound R14

kukungalandeli *v-inf-neg* not following R37.15

kukuphanda *v-inf-red* to investigate R27

kukuphulaphula *v-red-inf-pro-2sg-obj* to listen to you R14

kukutya *n8-sg-agent* of food • *saphelelwa kukutya 'we ran out of food'* R28.5

kukuxhasa *v-red-inf-pro-2sg-obj* to support you • *baya kukuxhasa 'they will support you'* R14

kukuxolela *v-red-inf-pro-2sg-obj* to forgive you R14

kukwakho *v-cop-loc* there are also R36

kukwenza *v-inf-red* to make part of future construct R22

kula *deic-1-n3-pl-loc* to, at, in, from these • *kula maziko 'in these households'* E&S:27, R37.13

kulaa[1] *deic-3-n1-sg-loc* to, at, in, from that (far, yonder) • *kulaa mlimi 'to that farmer'* E&S:27

kulaa[2] *deic-3-n2-sg-loc* to, at, in, from that (far, yonder) • *kulaa mzi 'to that home'* E&S:27

kulaa[3] *deic-3-n2-pl-loc* to, at, in, from those (far, yonder) • *kulaa mizi 'to those homes'* E&S:27

kulaa[4] *deic-3-n3-pl-loc* to, at, in, from those (far, yonder) • *kulaa mazwe 'to those countries'* E&S:27

kulaa[5] *deic-3-n5-sg-loc* to, at, in, from that (far, yonder) • *kulaa ndlu 'to that house'* E&S:27

kule[1] *deic-1-n2-pl-loc* at, on, to these • *kule mihla 'nowadays' [n2-pl-cmp-time; lit: in these days]* E&S:27, EXD:409, MI:231, R9, R28.1, R33.0

kule[2] *deic-1-n5-sg-loc* in, at, on, to this E&S:27, R7, R22.1.6, R23.9, R26.8, R27.2.10, R28.1, R32.2, R37.7.9

kuleyo *loc-deic-n5-sg* to that R15

kulilisana *v-red-inf* to make each other cry R5

kulixesha *n10-indef-pred-n3-sg* it is time R31.3

kulo[1] *n3-sg-pro-loc* to, from, in, with him, her; in, at it E&S:21, R35

kulo[2] *n6-sg-pro-loc* to, from, in, with him, her, it E&S:21, R24.3

kulo[3] *deic-1-n1-sg-loc* to, at, in, from this E&S:27

kulo[4] *deic-1-n2-sg-loc* to, at, in, from this • *kulo nyaka 'in this year'* E&S:27, R18.4, R24.7, R29=3, R31.2

kulo-[5] *loc-prf* at (the home of someone's parents) [locative prefix for a person's (parents') place of residence] • *Kufuneka siye kuloZolani 'We must go to Zolani's (parents') home'* CGB:141, PCX:71, SXWU:102

kuloko *conj* but that, only that, just [contrastive] • *Ingwe ifana nekati, kuloko yona inkulu 'The leopard is like a cat, it is just larger'* AXG:148, XED:76

kuloo[1] *deic-2-n1-sg-loc* to, at, in, from that • *kuloo mlimi 'to that farmer'* E&S:27, R28

kuloo[2] *deic-2-n2-sg-loc* to, at, in, from that • *kuloo mzi 'in that home'* E&S:27

kuloo[3] *deic-2-n2-pl-loc* to, at, in, from those • *kuloo mizi 'in those homes'* E&S:27

kuloo[4] *deic-2-n3-pl-loc* to, at, in, from those • *kuloo mazwe 'to those countries'* E&S:27

kuloo[5] *deic-2-n5-sg-loc* to, at, in, from that • *safika kuloo fama 'we arrived at that farm'* E&S:27, R28=2

kulowo *loc-deic* in that R26

kuludwe *loc+n-6sg* in a row loc+n-6sg R21

kulunga *v-red-inf* to be all right • *kuza kulunga 'it will be all right'* R17.6

kulungile *expr* ok, it's all right! E&S:59, PCX:37

kuluntu *loc-n6-sg* to society R3

kulusu *loc-n6-sg* on the skin R30

kum *pro-1sg-loc* to, from, in, with me AM-94:93, E&S:21, PCX:90, R19.3

kuma *loc-n3-pl* from, (reach) to • *ifikelele kuma R50 000 'It reached a value of R50 000'; iqabanekazi ... libe neminyaka esukela kuma-38 ukuya kuma-42 'a female companion who should be from 38 to 42 years old'* locative of n3 pl R4d=2, R18

kumabonakude *n1a-sg-loc* on television, on TV R4c

kuMadiba *n1a-sg-pn-loc* to Madiba (Nelson Mandela) R17.0.6

kumakhamandela *loc-n3-pl* from the chains R36

kumakhulu *loc-n3-pl* for many R16

kumalungu[1] *loc-n3-pl* to members R22

kumalungu[2] *loc-n3-pl* on the genitals R30=2

kumamela *v-inf-red* to listen to R37

kumaxesha *loc-n3-pl* on many occasions, many times R37

kumaziko *loc-n3-pl* of / for households R10

kumazwe *loc-n3-pl* in countries R16

kumbe *conj* or ☞ See Xhosa: okanye DNZ:176, EXXE:323, R15

kumbi[1] *enum-pro-n8-vn* other, some other (act), a different (course of action) Structure: RED noun form + ENUM / ENUM + FULL noun form ☞ See: -mbi E&S:27, PCX:110

kumbi[2] *enum-pro-n10-loc* some other (place), a different (location) Structure: RED noun form + ENUM / ENUM + FULL noun form ☞ See: -mbi PCX:110

kuMgaqo-Siseko *n2-sg-cmp-loc* in the Constitution R21, R37

kumgqomo *loc-n2-sg* into the garbage can R30

kumhleli *loc-n1-sg* to / from the editor R31.0

kumhlobo *loc-n1-sg* to a friend R34

kumise *v-sub* it was standing R26.8

kumphathi *loc-n1-sg* to the Manager R27.7

kumqeqeshi *loc-n1-sg* to the trainer R33

kumyinge *loc-n2-sg* to/over the limit R31.3

kuna- *prep-comp* than, in comparison with [comparative] Introducing the second (lesser) part of a comparison; that which is of higher degree is placed ahead or first ☞ Cf: kunezi- CGB:175, E&S:21, EXD:657, RD-96:127, TD, R2, R28

kunabantu *adv-n1-pl* than people; [ext] of the people • *ingaphambili kunabantu 'it should be ahead of the people'* R37.17

kunamhlanje *v-impers-adv-time* it is today R32

kunceda *v-inf-red* to help, aid, assist R34.12

kuncedakale *v-atr* it is helped R33.9

kuncedwa *v-inf-red* to be helped R23

kundinqanda *v-tr-pro-1sg-obj* to prevent me R33

kunene *adv* very, very much XED:98

kunento *n5-sg-comp* compared to [lit: than the thing] • *zona ziphuculiwe kunento ebeziyiyo ngaphambili 'things have improved compared to the way they were before'* R28

kunesondo *cop8-conn-n3-sg* it is of/about sex R36.13

kunezi- *combo* than • *babi kunezilwanyana 'they are worse than animals'* indicates that the comparative (kuna-) is linked to n4 pl (izi-) ☞ See: kuna- + izi- R2

kunezilwanyana *comp-expr* than animals R2

kungaba *n10-impers-pot* can it be?, is it possible? E&S:45

kungakodlula *v-pot-intr* it can pass R36

kunganako *v-poss-loc* it can have [lit: it can be with] R37

kungani *qw-expr* why?; why is it? ☞ Alt: kungani na, ngani na; Syn: kutheni E&S:33, EXD:723, KED:259, R10

kungaphindi *v-aux-neg* it does not again R37.10

kungathandabuzeki *v-atr* it is not doubtful R36

kungekho *v-exis-neg-part* there not being any E&S:49, R11

kungekuko *cop-pot-loc* it could be like this • *Ndithetha oku kungekuko... I say that it should be like this...* ku C8 (neuter) prefix + nge (potential-can) + ku (c8 neuter) +ko (there) R11

kungelo *prep-deic* at that R19.2

kungenjalo *conj* otherwise; in such a way (so that it is so) • *Kungenjalo aniyi kuphumelela 'Otherwise you will not succeed'* AXG:148, R30, R31

kungenwa *v-inf-pass* to be penetrated R36

kungenxa *prep-expr* on account of KED:263, R22

kungenziwa *n8-v-pot-pass* it can be done R35

kungezo *v-impers-neg* its not only R36

kungoko *conj* wherefore • *Kungoko ndithi 'Wherefore I say ...'* AXG:148

kungoku *v-n10-impers* it is now R32

-kungona *conj* the more ☞ See: kukhona AXG:148

kuni[1] *pro-2pl-loc* to, from, in, with you [plural] E&S:21, PCX:90

kuni[2] *qw-n8-vn* what kind?, of what sort? ☞ See: -ni PCX:118

kuninzi *n10-impers* there are a lot R36

kunjalo *v-expr* it is so, it is like that • *Xa kunjalo ubonane no-Nompumelelo. 'If it is so, then see Nompumelelo'.* AM-94:112, XED:104, R15, R37=2

kunjani *qw-expr* how is it? AM-94:112, SXWU:26

kunje *v-expr* it is like this AM-94:112

kunokugcinwa *n8-vn-pass* for being taken care of R35.13

kunokugxwal' *v-inf-red* rather than cry out loud R31.3

kunokukufak' *v-abil* it can put you R6

kunqongophalo *n8-n6-sg* in the shortage R35

kuntlitheko *loc-n5-sg* in a crash R24

kunyaka *n1a-sg-time* in the year R22

kunyanzelekile *v-st-perf* it is compulsory R19.6

kunye[1] *num-expr-impers* it is one XED:77;75;117

kunye[2] *n10-loc;-adv* together [lit: one distance] • *Sahamba kunye 'We walked together'* AXG:144; 200

kunye na- *conj-expr* and, as well as; together with • *basebenzisa isithambiso kunye nekhondom 'they use a lubricant with a condom'* CGB:150, R3x, R7, R14, R18, R19, R25=2, R26, R30, R32, R35=2, R36=2

kunyulo *loc-n6-sg* at the Election R21

kunzima *v-n10-impers-atr* it is difficult R28

kupha- *n9-loc-pred-prf* it is [group 9 locative noun copulative or predicative prefix construction] • *kuphakathi 'it is inside'* PCX:96

kuphandle *adv-loc* apart from R36

kuphando *loc-n6-sg* in the investigation R18.3, R37.12

kuphandwa *v-impers-pass* it is being investigated R27

kuphela *adv* only ☞ Syn: qha GDX3:26, XED:77, R10, R12, R24, R28, R35, R36=3, R37

kuphi[1] *qw-n8-vn* which (one)? E&S:27, GDX3:703, PCX:111

kuphi[2] *qw-n10-loc* which (time, place, situation)? GDX3:703

kuphi[3] *qw-loc-adv-n8-vn* where is? ☞ See: -phi E&S:31, PCX:111

kuphinda-phindana *v-redup-inf-red* multiply EXD:394, R34

kuphucuka *v-inf-red* to improve; to become civilized R37.17

kuphuma *v-inf-red* to come out R32

kuphume *v-pres-sub* it may come out R30

kuphumelela *v-inf* to succeed R33

kuphumelele *v-intens* that it should succeed • *Khona ukuze kuphumelele oku 'in order that it succeeds'* R37

kuqala *adv-time* first E&S:59

kuqhagamshelana *v-inf-ben-recip* to be in touch, to be in contact, to interact R29.18

kuqhubeka *v-st-atr* what is progressing R35.11

kuqhutywa *v-inf-red* to be driven R31, R37

kuqinisekisa *v-inf-red* will guarantee ~ justify R37

kuqinisekiseke *v-st-atr* be confirmed R21

kuqinisekiswe *v-pass-short-past* be convinced R37=2

kuQumbu *n10-loc* the Qumbu place [lit: a sudden drop] (GDX3:93), PCX:56

kurhulumente *loc-n1a-sg* to or from the government R35.2.4, R37.2

kusafuneka *v-intr-prog* it is still necessary R35

kusasa *adv-time* early; in the morning [lit: it still dawning] ☞ rw: sa AXG:143; 214, E&S:59, EXD:180, PCX:34, XED:77, R28x

kusebenziseke *v-caus* it will be used up; it will be wasted • *kusebenziseke imali eninzi 'much money will be wasted' [reversal]* R37.14

kusekho *cop-loc* it is (already) there R34

kusela *v-inf-red* to drink • *uza kusela 'you are going to drink'* R31

kuseloko *conj-rel* from the time that Structure: followed by relative construction E&S:36

kusenziwa *v-pass* it is done R36

kusesinye *n8-cop-num* it is one R36.13

kushiyeka *v-st-atr* to be left, remain XED:150, R30

kusikhumbula *v-inf* to remind us R31

kusinda *v-inf-red* escape R31=2

kusithiwa *v-pass-part* it is being said R10

kusixelela *v-ben-n10-impers+pro-1pl-obj* it tells us R37

kusizelwa *v-ben-pass* to sympathize R36

kuso *n4-sg-pro-loc* to, from, in, with him, her, it • *Esona sikhundla siphezulu unokufikelela kuso sesokuba yiMarketing Director 'As for those higher levels [Xhosa has used singular form here], you can reach them by becoming a Marketing Director'* E&S:21, R29.12

kusukelo *n-loc* to a goal, with an aim R33.10

kusweleka *v-inf-red* are dying R31

kuthatyathwa *v-pass* they take and hold R35

kuthe *v-aux-past* it was auxiliary before ideophone R26.4

kutheni *qw-adv* why? Structure: followed by S2 + participial; Note: only qw to come at the beginning of the sentence CGB:131, E&S:33; 59, EXD:724, SXWU:147, R20, R23

kuthetha *v-pres* it means, it is to say [indefinite] • *oku kuthetha 'this means, this is to say'* R9, R12, R37.2

kuthi[1] *pro-1pl-loc* to, from, in, with us E&S:21, GDX3:293, PCX:90, XED:160

kuthi[2] *v-aux-inf-red* say, do. Used as auxiliary for ideophones to allow conjugation R34, R37=2

kuthini *v-qw-inf-red* to do what? R28.5

kuthiwa *v-impers-pass* it is said that R27, R36

kutsala *v-inf-red* to pull R23

kutsha *adv-comp* recently part of compound with '-nje' ☞ see R24 R27

kutshanje *adv* recently R24

kuTsolo *n10-loc* the Tsolo place [lit: at the point] (GDX3:424), PCX:56

kuvakala *v-atr* it is perceptible R36.9

kuvakale *v-inf-red* to hear R18

kuvela *v-inf-red* to appear R32

kuvelisa *v-inf-red* to bring out R32

kuveliswa *v-caus-pass* bring out, yield, bring forward, show R29

kuvuya *v-inf-red* to be glad R34

kuwanyoba *v-inf-red* bribe R31

kuwe *pro-2sg-loc* to, from, in, with you AM-94:93, E&S:21, PCX:90, R19, R21, R25, R34

kuwo[1] *n2-sg-pro-loc* to, from, in, with him, her, it E&S:21, PCX:90

kuwo[2] *n3-pl-pro-loc* to, from, in, with them E&S:21, R36

kuwuzuza *v-inf-red+pro-obj* to get you R34.7

kuxelelwe *v-ben-pass* to be told R32

kuxhaphake *v-impers* it is plentiful R36

kuya *v-aux-fut-n10- impers* it will VERB R37=6

kuyakhuthaza *v-tr-prog* it is encouraging R29.8

kuyakuba *v-aux-fut* it will be R36

kuyaphi *loc-pro-n8* to any point; anywhere; [ext atr] at all ku (n8) + yaphi (n5) R7, R36=2

kuye[1] *n1-sg-pro-loc* to, from, in, with him, her AM-94:93, E&S:21, PCX:90, R27.6, R37.14

kuye[2] *v-aux* it comes • *Kungenxa yoko kuye kwaveliswa. ' Out of (on account of) this comes the production...'* R22.4

kuyeka *v-inf-red* to leave reduced part of future construct R31

kuyinto *n8-pred-n5-sg* it is a thing R36.19

kuyiwe *v-inf-red* to fall out • *bengafuni kuyiwe elugqatsweni 'they not wanting to fall out of the race...'* R20

kuyo[1] *n2-pl-pro-loc* to, from, in, with them E&S:21, PCX:90

kuyo[2] *n5-sg-pro-loc* to, from, in, with him, her, it AM-94:93, E&S:21, R26, R28, R30, R37=3

kuza *v-aux-fut-n10-impers* it will VERB, it is going to VERB • *kuza kufuneka uqhube 'it will be necessary for you to drive'* R17.6, R31.4, R37.7

kuzalisekiswa *v-inf-pass-red* will fulfilment be caused • *kuya kuzalisekiswa 'fulfilment will be achieved'* R37

kuzifunela *v-inf-red* to want them R37

kuzilawula *v-inf-red* to govern them R22

kuzithathela *v-refl-ben* to take for oneself R36.0

kuzo[1] *n4-pl-pro-loc* to, from, in, with them E&S:21

kuzo[2] *n5-pl-pro-loc* to, from, in, with them; to them [neuter items] E&S:21, R27, R33, R36, R37

kuzo[3] *n6-pl-pro-loc* to, from, in, with them • *Ezona lwimi sigxininisa kuzo ' we give emphasis to those languages'* R37.3

kw[1] *change* change (merger) of KU and KWA to KW before A or E E&S:27

kw-[2] *loc-prf* in, among [alternate form of the specific locative prefix KU before the vowels E and I] • *kwiingonyama 'to the lions', kwizilwanyana 'in the animal kingdom', kwisitovu 'on the stove'* ☞ Alt: ku AXG:38, E&S:32, R2, R4c, R5, R8=2, R9, R12, R16

kw-[3] *loc-prf* to, in, at, from [short form of the domain locative prefix before another vowel] ☞ See: kwa- R4c, R5, R16

-kw-[4] *n8-vn-obj* [group 8 verbal noun object agreement prefix before vowel initial verb (other than o)] ☞ Alt: -ku- E&S:18

kw-[5] *n10-loc-S1* [group 10 locative noun S1 subject agreement prefix before vowel initial verb (other than o)] Agr: uku- ☞ Alt: -ku- R10, R12

-kw-[6] *pro-2sg-obj-prf* you (thee) [short object form before vowel initial verb (other than o)] ☞ Alt: -ku- E&S:18

kw-[7] *v-expr* it is; one VERBs; they VERB [impersonal verb marker before vowel-initial verbs] R4c

kw-[8] *v-inf-prf* [shortened form of infinitive prefix used in future constructions on vowel-initial verbs, except those beginning with o-] ☞ See: ku-; Red: uku- R4c

kwa-[1] *loc-prf* to, in, at, from [locative prefix for the domain, residence, property, company, or office of s.o.] • *kwaFani 'at Fani's place'; kwaLanga 'in Langa'* used with personal names and nouns designating kin or human relationships; also with names of professions, businesses, companies, or stores ☞ Contrast: e- [simple locative], ku- [person locative] AM-94:64, AXG:38, CGB:140, E&S:32, PCX:71, SXWU:101, XED:78, R1x, R3x, R4bx, R5=4, R11=2, R14, R25, R37.2

kwa-[2] *n8-vn-poss* of [group 8 verbal noun possessive agreement prefix] • *ukumiswa kwamaxabiso 'the setting up of prices'; ukudlwengulwa kwababhinqileyo 'the raping of women'* Agr: uku- AM-94:163, E&S:22, SXWU:35f, XED:xv; 78, R6, R29, R36

kwa-[3] *n8-vn-S3b-pos* (and) it VERBed [group 8 verbal noun past positive subjunctive verb subject (S3b) agreement prefix] CGB:190, E&S:42, MI:247, SXWU:141

kwa-[4] *n10-loc-poss* of [group 10 locative noun possessive agreement prefix] Agr: uku- E&S:22;32(25.4)

kwa-[5] *n10-loc-S3b-pos* (and) it VERBed [group 10 locative noun / impersonal verb past positive subjunctive verb subject (S3b) agreement prefix] • *kwakuxa libantu-bahle 'it was early evening'* IN:3

-kwa-[6] *preverb* also [implying similarity or inclusion] • *Bakwafunda apha 'They are also studying here'* E&S:46

kwa-[7] *adv-prf* even [emphatic adverb] • *kwayena 'even he'* ☞ See also: kwa na- EXD:196, XED:78, R3, R4a

kwa-[8] *adv-prf* just • *kwangoku 'just now'* XED:78

kwa na- *adv* even, and even [emphatic prefix combination] • *kwanootitshala 'and even teachers'* ☞ See also: kwa-, na-, kwana-, kwane-, kwano-, kwanoo- EXD:196, XED:78, R3, R37.12

kwaba[1] *deic-1-n1-pl-loc* to, at, in, from these E&S:27

kwaba[2] *deic-1-n1-pl-domain* in, at, on, to, from these (domains) E&S:27

kwaba[3] *v-pred-past-sub* it became R36

kwabaa[1] *deic-3-n1-pl-loc* to, at, in, from those (far, yonder) • *kwabaa bantu 'to those people'* E&S:27

kwabaa[2] *deic-3-n1-pl-domain* in, at, on, to, from those (yonder domains) E&S:27

kwababhinqileyo *n1-pl-poss-n8-vn* of women • *ukudlwengulwa kwababhinqileyo 'the rape of women'* R36.15

kwabaneminyaka *rel-aux-assoc.cop-n2-pl* who have years R35

kwabanye *adj-num-n1-pl-loc* to others R31

kwabasemagunyeni *loc-n1-pl* to those in power R27, R36

kwabe[1] *preverb-past-n8-vn* it had VERBed; it did VERB [group 8 verbal noun remote past compound tense preverb] Structure: kwabe ku-Δ (participial verb form) ☞ Alt: kwaye E&S:39, GDX3:714, PCX:186

kwabe[2] *preverb-past-n10-loc* it / there had VERBed; it did VERB [group 10 locative noun / impersonal remote past compound tense preverb] Structure: kwabe ku-Δ (participial verb form) ☞ Alt: kwaye GDX3:714, PCX:186

kwabezomthetho *poss-n2-sg* those of the law R36

kwabo[1] *n1-pl-poss-n8-vn* of them; their (own); theirs E&S:22, GDX3:691, R35, R37.17

kwabo[2] *n1-pl-poss-n10-loc* of them; their (own place); (domain is) theirs E&S:22, GDX3:691

kwabo[3] *n7-poss-n8-vn* its; of it GDX3:691

kwabo[4] *n7-poss-n10-loc* its; of it GDX3:691

kwabo[5] *deic-2-n1-pl-loc* to, at, in, from those • *kwabo bantu 'from those people'* E&S:27

kwabo[6] *deic-2-n1-pl-domain* in, at, on, to, from those (domains) E&S:27

kwabophula *v-rel-loc* for those who break R31.2

kwaBP *pn-loc* from BP (British Petroleum) R30.1

kwacaca // **kwaye kwacaca** *v-remote-past* it had become clear R37.25

kwaCetywayo *pn-geog* Cetywayo (place in the Zulu region) R32

kwagqirha *n1a-sg-domain* at the doctor's office AM-94:64

kwakhe[1] *n1-sg-poss-n8-vn* his, her, its E&S:22, GDX3:691, R17.6

kwakhe[2] *n1-sg-poss-n10-loc* his / her (place), its (domain) E&S:22, GDX3:691, R24=2

kwakhiwe *v-pass-iw-past* built, constructed R37.20.21

kwakho[1] *pro-2sg-poss-n8-vn* your, yours; your own [singular] E&S:22, GDX3:691

kwakho[2] *pro-2sg-poss-n10-sg* of you; your (place); your own (domain) • *phambi kwakho 'ahead of you'* E&S:22, GDX3:691, R33

kwakhona *adv* again, in the same way CGB:179, MI:256, R18, R19=2, R31, R35

kwakhutshelwa *v-pass-past* it was thrown out R26

kwako[1] *n8-vn-poss-n8-vn* its, of it GDX3:691

kwako[2] *n8-vn-poss-n10-loc* its, of it GDX3:691

kwako[3] *n10-loc-poss-n8-vn* its, of it GDX3:691

kwako[4] *n10-loc-poss-n10-loc* its, of it GDX3:691

kwaku-[1] *n8-vn-remote-past* it had VERBed [group 8 verbal noun contracted remote past compound tense] AXG:93f, E&S:39, PCX:186

kwaku-[2] *n8-vn-temp* when it VERBs / VERBed [group 8 verbal noun temporal construction] • *Kwakufika 'When it arrives...'* E&S:42

kwaku-[3] *n10-loc-remote-past* there had VERBed [group 10 locative / impersonal noun contracted remote past compound tense] PCX:186, R28, R36

kwaku-[4] *n10-loc-temp* when it VERBs / VERBed [group 10 locative / impersonal noun temporal construction] • *Kwakufika 'When it (time, situation) arrives...'* R25, R32

kwakubanjwa *v-temp* when they were arrested R20

kwakucacile *v-st-past-n10-impers* it was obvious KM, R37.12

kwakufika *v-temp* upon arrival R25

kwakugqguba *v-temp* when there was raising dust R32

kwakuko *cop-loc-red* there was/were R26

kwakungekho *v-remote-past* there was nothing R28, R36

kwakunye *conj* and even KM, R37.2

kwakuphethe *loc-past-VERB* they were ruled • *kwakuphethe amakhosi 'they (Transkei, Ciskei etc.) were ruled by chiefs...'* R20

kwakusasa *adv-time* in the morning R28

kwakusenziwa *v-pass-part* what was causing R20

kwakutheni *qw-adv-past* why? [past tense] CGB:129

kwala *deic-1-n3-pl-domain* in, at, on, to, from these (domains) E&S:27

kwalaa[1] *deic-3-n1-sg-domain* in, at, on, to, from that (yonder domain) E&S:27

kwalaa[2] *deic-3-n2-sg-domain* in, at, on, to, from that (yonder domain) E&S:27

kwalaa[3] *deic-3-n2-pl-domain* in, at, on, to, from those (yonder domains) E&S:27

kwalaa[4] *deic-3-n3-pl-domain* in, at, on, to, from those (yonder domains) E&S:27

kwalaa[5] *deic-3-n5-sg-domain* in, at, on, to, from that (yonder domain) E&S:27

kwaLanga *pn-geog-loc* in, to, from Langa (suburb) ☞ See: iLanga AM-94:64, CGB:140, E&S:32

kwale[1] *deic-1-n2-pl-domain* in, at, on, to, from these (domains) E&S:27

kwale[2] *deic-1-n5-sg-poss-n8-vn* of this R37.24

kwale[3] *deic-1-n5-sg-domain* in, at, on, to, from this (domain) E&S:27

kwalo[1] *n3-sg-poss-n8-vn* his, her, its; of him, her, it • *eyokucocwa kwalo 'for the cleaning of it'* GDX3:691, R35.4.12

kwalo[2] *n3-sg-poss-n10-loc* his, her, its; of him, her, it GDX3:691

kwalo[3] *n6-sg-poss-n8-vn* its; of it GDX3:691

kwalo[4] *n6-sg-poss-n10-loc* its; of it GDX3:691

kwalo[5] *deic-1-n1-sg-poss* of this (person) DFG

kwalo[6] *deic-1-n1-sg-domain* in, at, on, to, from this (domain) E&S:27

kwalo[7] *deic-1-n2-sg-domain* in, at, on, to, from this (domain) E&S:27

kwaloo[1] *deic-2-n1-sg-domain* in, at, on, to, from that (domain) E&S:27

kwaloo[2] *deic-2-n2-sg-domain* in, at, on, to, from that (domain) E&S:27

kwaloo[3] *deic-2-n2-pl-domain* in, at, on, to, from those (domains) E&S:27

kwaloo[4] *deic-2-n3-pl-domain* in, at, on, to, from those (domains) E&S:27

kwaloo[5] *deic-2-n5-sg-domain* in, at, on, to, from that (domain) E&S:27

kwam[1] *pro-1sg-poss-n8-vn* of me; my, mine; my own • *ukutya kwam 'my food'* AM-94:151, E&S:22, GDX3:691, PCX:60; 72, SXWU:36

kwam[2] *pro-1sg-poss-n10-loc* my (place); of me, mine; my own (domain) • *phambi kwam 'in front of me', emva kwam 'behind me'* E&S:22, GDX3:691, PCX:60; 72, R19

kwama-[1] *combo* of • *ukusetyenziwa kwamayeza 'the usage of medicines'* indicates that n3 pl (ama-) is possessed by a n8 vn (kwa-) ☞ See: kwa- + ama- R6, R36=3

kwama-[2] *combo* of • *baphatha amatyala angaphezu kwama-8992 'they handled more than 8,992 cases'* indicates that n3 pl (ama-) is possessed by a n10 loc (kwa-) R36

kwama[3] *n8-vn-poss-n5-pl* of [NUM] • *kwama-70 'of 70 in number'* R35

kwamabhantinti *n-loc-poss-n3-pl* of the prisoners kwa following locative noun R36

kwamadoda *n3-pl-poss* of men • *ukudlwengulwa kwamadoda 'the rape of men'; ukulalana kwamadoda 'the sleeping together of men'* R36=3

kwamakhanukanodwa *prep-n3-pl* by gay people R36

kwamakhwenkwe *n3-pl-poss* of boys • *ukudlwengulwa kwamakhwenkwe 'the rape of boys'* R36

kwamalungelo *poss-n3-pl* of the rights; for the rights R37.1

kwamandla *n3-pl-poss* of the strength R36

kwamanzi *n8-vn-poss-n3-pl* of water R27

kwaMasele *pn-geog-loc* from Masele R5=2

kwamaxabiso *n3-pl-poss* of prices R29

kwamayeza *n3-pl-poss* of medicines R6

kwamntu *loc-n1-sg* anybody • *akukho kwamntu 'there is nobody'* R26.6

kwampenge-mpenge *loc-n5-sg-redup* in isolated places ☞ See: mpengempenge R36.11

kwanabasemagunyeni *conj-n1-pl-loc* and those in authority R36

kwaNdlovukazi *pn-geog-loc* at Lesseyton AXG:38, XED:194

kwanele *v-perf* it is enough R4c

kwaneliseka *v-caus-atr* it is satisfying, sufficient, enough R12

kwanemibutho *conj-n2-pl* as well as organizations R37

kwanenxaxheba *rel-n5-sg* which portion or part EXD:311, R37.19

kwangoko *adv-cmp* there and then EXD:659

kwangoku *adv* even now R35

kwanobunkokeli *adv-n7-abs* by leadership ☞ see other kwano- entries R16

kwanokukwazi *v-loc-abil* for being able to know how ☞ see other kwano- entries R16

kwanokutya *conj-n8-sg* and even the food, every last scrap R26.5

kwanomlisele *conj-n1-sg* and even the youth kwa- 'even' + -no- 'one who has characteristics of' + umlisele 'youth' R13

kwanoo- *combo* as well as • *noogqirha kwanoonesi 'and doctors as well as nurses'* indicates that emphatic adverb (kwa-) and conjunctive (na-) are linked to n1a pl (oo-), but note that na(o) imparts the meaning of 'one who has characteristics of, is skilled in, etc. ☞ See: kwa- + na- + oo-; Also written: kwa noo- R3, R37.12

kwanoonesi *conj-n1a-pl* and even nurses ☞ see other kwano- entries R37.12

kwanootitshala *conj-n1a-pl* and even teachers ☞ see other kwano- entries R3

kwanyanzeleka *v-ben-atr* it forced (us) [ku + a + nyanz- + el + ek- + a] R19.2

kwapasiswa // **kwaye kwapasiswa** *v-remote-past* there had been passed R37.5

kwaphela *adv* entirely, completely R36

kwaqaliswa *v-intr-past-pass* (a project) was started R35

kwasekusekweni *loc-v-pass* from the establishment R35

kwasentolongweni *loc-n5-sg* of prisons R36

kwaseTzaneen *pn-loc* from Tzaneen R35.3

kwasiKhukhuni *pn-geog* Khukhuni 's place (place in the Pedi region) R32

kwaso[1] *n4-sg-poss-n8-vn* their; of them GDX3:691, R24

kwaso[2] *n4-sg-poss-n10-loc* their; of them GDX3:691

kwaveliswa *v-caus-pass* was produced ku- (C8SC) neuter, or indefinite form + verb root + passive R22

kwaVenda *pn-geog* land of the Venda people R20

kwavokotheka *adv* with lengthy argument R32

kwawena *pro-2sg-domain* for yourself; as a person R14

kwawo[1] *n2-sg-poss-n8-vn* its; of it • *umgaqo-siseko nokusetyenziswa kwawo 'its useful constitution'* GDX3:691, XED:78, R16

kwawo[2] *n2-sg-poss-n10-loc* its; of it GDX3:691

kwawo[3] *n3-pl-poss-n8-vn* theirs; of them GDX3:691

kwawo[4] *n3-pl-poss-n10-loc* theirs; of them GDX3:691

kwaye[1] *preverb-past-n8-vn* it had VERBed; it did VERB [group 8 verbal noun remote past compound tense preverb] Structure: kwaye ku-Δ (participial verb form) ☞ Alt: kwabe AXG:93f, E&S:39; 49, GDX3:714, KED:206f

kwaye[2] *preverb-past-n10-loc* it / there had VERBed; it did VERB [group 10 locative noun / impersonal remote past compound tense preverb] Structure: kwaye ku-Δ (participial verb form) ☞ Alt: kwabe GDX3:714, R37.5.25

kwaye[3] *v-aux-conj* and even; and also; as well as [n8-prefix + aux -ya] Structure: links coordinate verb clauses together ☞ Alt: yaye Pahl-1983:102, R4a, R18.6, R19.1, R21.11, R31.2=2, R32.9, R34.8, R35.6, R36=9, R37.7

kwayo[1] *n2-pl-poss-n8-vn* their; of them GDX3:691

kwayo[2] *n2-pl-poss-n10-loc* their; of them GDX3:691

kwayo[3] *n5-sg-poss-n8-vn* his, her, its; of him, her, it • *indoda inganelishwa lokungathathelwa ngqalelo xa izokuchaza ngokudlwengulwa kwayo 'a man can have the misfortune of not being taken seriously if he will report his having been raped'* GDX3:691, R36.12

kwayo[4] *n5-sg-poss-n10-loc* his, her, its; of him, her, it GDX3:691

-kwazi uku- *v-neg-abil-cmp* cannot VERB, don't know how to VERB [implying lack of skill at doing] Structure: SNEG-kwazi uku-Δ-a E&S:45

kwazo[1] *n4-pl-poss-n8-vn* their; of them GDX3:691

kwazo[2] *n4-pl-poss-n10-loc* their; of them GDX3:691

kwazo[3] *n5-pl-poss-n8-vn* their; of them GDX3:691

kwazo[4] *n5-pl-poss-n10-loc* their; of them GDX3:691

kwaZulu *pn-geog* Natal; [loc] in Zululand (one of nine provinces in South Africa; former homeland) AM-94:64, MI:246, SXWU:101, R20.5

kwaZwelitsha *pn-loc* in Zwelitsha R18

kwe-[1] *loc-combo* of s.t. • *ephakathi kwe-18 nama-35 'who is between the ages of 18 and 35'* 'Pha-" words are usually followed by ku- ; in this case ku has combined with -a- and -i to denote the relationship to Class 3 ☞ See: kwa- + i- R4b

kwe[2] *n8-vn-poss-change* of R36=2

kweAIDS *loan* of, about AIDS R36

kwee- *combo* of • *kweelwimi 'of the language of'* indicates that the possessive (kwa-) is linked to n6 pl (ii-) ☞ See: kwa- + ii- R37.2

kweelwimi *n6-pl-poss* of the languages (of) R37.2.8.18.19

kweenkampani *loc-n5-pl* of (the) company R31

kweenkanuko *adv-n5-pl* of desires R36.17

kwekhaya *loc-poss-n3-sg* of the home • *phakathi kwekhaya 'inside the house'* R34.12

kwekhomishoni *n5-sg-poss-n8-vn* of the commission R32

kwelaa[1] *deic-3-n3-sg-loc* to, at, in, from that (far, yonder) • *kwelaa lizwe 'to that country'* E&S:27

kwelaa[2] *deic-3-n3-sg-domain* in, at, on, to, from that (yonder domain) E&S:27

kwelase *loc-deic* in, inside kwelaseMozambique 'in (that) Mozambique' R15

kweli[1] *deic-1-n3-sg-loc* to, at, in, from this; of, for this • *kweli lizwe 'in this country'; xa ebephuma kweli theko 'as she was coming out of this event'; kweli ziko 'at this* *establishment'* AXG:38, E&S:27, R24, R29, R32=2, R33, R35=4

kweli[2] *deic-1-n3-sg-domain* in, at, on, to, from this (domain) E&S:27

kweli[3] *deic-1-n3-sg-poss-n8-vn* of this VERBing • *Ngenxa yokungamkeleki kweli bala 'because this color is not acceptable'* GX

kweLife *n8-vn-poss-pn* of Life (Line) R36=2

kwelijikayo *adv-deic-n3-sg* of this turnaround • *Ndiseke kwelijikayo 'I am supportive of this turnaround'* R20

kwelinye *loc-enum* in one R18

kwelo[1] *deic-2-n3-sg-loc* to, at, in, from that E&S:27, R31

kwelo[2] *deic-2-n3-sg-domain* in, at, on, to, from that (domain) E&S:27

kwelomzantsi *loc-deic-n2-sg* of (the) South (Africa) R32

kwemali *n5-sg-poss-n8-vn* of money R35

kwemarketing *loc-n5-sg* in marketing R29

kwemfuyo *n5-sg* of livestock kwa = agent copulative following passive R27=2

kwemibutho *n2-pl-poss* of organizations R37.1

kweminyaka *n2-pl-poss* of years R30, R35

kwemisebenzi *n2-pl-poss* of jobs R28, R37.20

kwemithetho *n8-pn-poss-n2-pl* the laws R32

kwempumelelo *adv-n5-sg* of success R35

kwemveliso *loc-n5-sg* in produce R29=2

kwendawo *adv-n5-sg* of the place R35

kwendibano *n5-sg-poss* of a meeting • *emva kwendibano yesondo 'after sexual relations'* R30

kwendlebe *loc-n5-sg* behind the ears R30

kwendlela *n5-sg* of the road R31

kwengama *loc-prep-pred-num-n3-pl-expr* up to NUM in age • *kwengama-63 'up to the age of sixty three'* R35.2

kwengcali *n5-sg* of an expert R36.04

kwentlawulo *adv-n5-sg* of payment; wage R35

kwentolongo *n5-sg* in jail R36

kwentuthumbo *loc-poss-n5-sg* of inflammation Derived from -thuthumba 'throb' R36.4

kwenu[1] *pro-2pl-poss-n8-vn* of you; your, yours; your own [plural] E&S:22, GDX3:691

kwenu[2] *pro-2pl-poss-n10-loc* of you; your (place); your own (domain) E&S:22, GDX3:691

kwenza *vn8-inf* to do [short infinitive] R4c, R37

kwenzeka *v-atr-n10-impers* it happens R10, R31.1, R36.1.10

kwenzeke *v-atr-sub* it might happen R18.5, R37.10

kwenziwe *vn-pass* to make R35

kwesaa[1] *deic-3-n4-sg-loc* to, at, in, from that (far, yonder) • *kwesaa sikolo 'to that school'* E&S:27

kwesaa[2] *deic-3-n4-sg-domain* in, at, on, to, from that (yonder domain) E&S:27

kwesi[1] *deic-1-n4-sg-loc* to, at, in, from this • *kwesi sikolo 'in this school'* E&S:27, R18

kwesi[2] *deic-1-n4-sg-domain* in, at, on, to, from this (domain) E&S:27

kwesifuba *n4-sg-poss-n8-vn* of the chest • *ukuxinana kwesifuba 'congestion of the chest'* R25=2

kwesigama *n4-sg-poss-n8-vn* of the vocabulary • *ukwakhiwa kwesigama 'the construction of the vocabulary'* R37.20

kwesimnyama *n4-sg-atr-loc* kwesimnyama isisele 'in a dark cell' R31

kwesinye *loc-enum* at another R35

kweso[1] *deic-2-n4-sg-loc* to, at, in, from that E&S:27

kweso[2] *deic-2-n4-sg-domain* in, at, on, to, from that (domain) E&S:27

kwethu[1] *pro-1pl-poss-n8-vn* of us; our, ours; our own [plural] E&S:22, GDX3:691

kwethu[2] *pro-1pl-poss-n10-sg* of us; our (place); our own (domain) E&S:22, GDX3:691, R11

kwexesha *adv* of time R19.2

kwezaa[1] *deic-3-n4-pl-loc* to, at, in, from those (far, yonder) • *kwezaa zikolo 'to those schools'* E&S:27

kwezaa[2] *deic-3-n4-pl-domain* in, at, on, to, from those (yonder domains) E&S:27

kwezaa[3] *deic-3-n5-pl-loc* to, at, in, from those (far, yonder) • *kwezaa zindlu 'to those houses'* E&S:27

kwezaa[4] *deic-3-n5-pl-domain* in, at, on, to, from those (yonder domains) E&S:27

kwezaa[5] *deic-3-n6-pl-loc* to, at, in, from those (far, yonder) • *kwezaa ntsapho 'to those families'* see deic 3 n5 pl loc

kwezaa[6] *deic-3-n6-pl-domain* in, at, on, to, from those (yonder domains) see deic 3 n5 pl domain

kwezemidlalo *loc-poss-n2-pl* in sporting events R12

kwezentengiso *loc-poss-n5-sg* in sales, in marketing intengiso is singular, but English idiom says 'sales' as the name of the occupation. R29=5

kwezenziwa *n8-vn-poss* of the doing R36.9

kwezesondo *n8-vn-poss-n5-pl* of sexual acts (here, Sexual Offences) R36

kwezi[1] *deic-1-n4-pl-loc* to, at, in, from these; up to [NUM] • *kwezi zifundo 'in these subjects'; kwezingama-20 'about twenty'* E&S:27, R29, R35.7

kwezi[2] *deic-1-n4-pl-domain* in, at, on, to, from these (domains) E&S:27

kwezi[3] *deic-1-n4-pl-poss-n8-vn* of these • *ukukhula kwezityalo 'to grow this plant...'* GX

kwezi[4] *deic-1-n4-pl-poss-n10-loc* of these (times, places, situations) • *phakathi kwezi zizwe 'in these nations'* GX

kwezi[5] *deic-1-n5-pl-loc* to, at, in, from these E&S:27

kwezi[6] *deic-1-n5-pl-domain* in, at, on, to, from these (domains) E&S:27

kwezi[7] *deic-1-n5-pl-poss-n8-vn* of these • *ukujika kwezinto 'the turnaround of these things'* GX

kwezi[8] *deic-1-n5-pl-poss-n10-loc* of these (times, places, situations) • *phakathi kwezi ntetho 'in these two speeches'* GX

kwezi[9] *deic-1-n6-pl-loc* to, at, in, from these • *Maninzi amagama avela kwezi lwimi 'many words come from languages'* GX

kwezi[10] *deic-1-n6-pl-domain* in, at, on, to, from these (domains) • *kwezi lwimi 'of these tongues'* GX

kwezi[11] *deic-1-n6-pl-poss-n8-vn* of these • *ukugxothwa kwezi ntsapho zimbini 'the expelling of these two families'* R26.8

kwezi[12] *deic-1-n6-pl-poss-n10-loc* of these (times, places, situations) • *Phakathi kwezinye zezinto 'in one of these things'* GX

kwezifundiswa *n-loc-poss-n4-pl* for the educated (ones) kwa follows locative phrase 'ngaphandle' R37.10

kwezikolo *n8-vn-poss-n4-pl* of schools R22=2

kwezingama *loc-prep-n5-pl-pred-num-n3-pl-expr* up to NUM • *kwezingama-20 'up to 20 (beds)'* R35.6

kwezinye *loc-enum* in other R28

kwezo[1] *deic-2-n4-pl-loc* to, at, in, from those E&S:27

kwezo[2] *deic-2-n4-pl-domain* in, at, on, to, from those (domains) E&S:27

kwezo[3] *deic-2-n5-pl-loc* to, at, in, from those E&S:27

kwezo[4] *deic-2-n5-pl-domain* in, at, on, to, from those (domains) E&S:27

kwezo[5] *deic-2-n6-pl-loc* to, at, in, from those see deic 2 n5 pl loc

kwezo[6] *deic-2-n6-pl-domain* in, at, on, to, from those (domains) G.B. 1922:48, Sinxo

kwezoqoqosho *loc-n5-pl* in the economy R35.14

kwi- *combo* in (the) • *usebenza kwi-National Language Project eKapa 'she works in the National Language Project in Cape Town'* indicates that the specific locative prefix (ku-) is linked to a noun prefixed with the article i- ☞ See: ku- + i- R12, R33=6, R37.7.27

kwi-National Language Project *n5-sg-cmp-loc* in the National Language Project R37.27

kwibala *loc-n3-sg* in a vacant lot, open space, sports terrain R33.9

kwicandelo *loc-n3-sg* in the section R34, R37.2

kwiDraft Bill *n5-sg-cmp-loc* in the Draft Bill R37.5

kwiEmfuleni *pn-loc* in Emfuleni R33

kwigalelo *loc-n5-sg* in a contribution R37.7

kwigumbi *loc-n3-sg* in the room R35

kwihostele *loc-n5-sg* in the hostel R35

kwiilwimi *loc-n6-pl* in languages R37.12

kwiin- *combo* to, among • *kufana nje nokuphosa igusha kwiingonyama 'It's just like throwing sheep to the lions'* indicates that the specific locative (ku-) is joined to n5 pl (iin-) ☞ See: ku- + iin- R9

kwiindawo *loc-n5-pl* in (such) places [specific locative] R27, R29, R31, R35=2

kwiindlela *loc-n5-pl* in the ways R34

kwiingonyama *loc-n5-pl* to the lions R9

kwiingozi *loc-n5-pl* in dangers, accidents R31

kwiinkosi *loc-n5-pl* from chiefs R32

kwiipolitiki *loc-n5-pl* in politics R16=2

kwikhondom *loc-n5-sg* from the condom R30

kwilali *loc-n5-sg* in the village R26

kwileta *loc-n5-sg* in the letter R4c

kwiLetaba After-Care Centre *n5-sg-cmp-pn-loc* from the Letaba After-Care Center R35

kwilifu *loc-n3-sg* in the cloud R5

kwilixa *loc-n3-sg* at / in the time R23

kwilokishi *loc-n5-sg* located in R18

kwilungu *loc-n3-sg* on the genitals R30=2

kwimali *loc-n5-sg* on the money R23

kwimfundo *loc-n5-sg* by education R22

kwimidlalo *loc-n2-pl* in the games R33

kwimilisela *prep-n2-pl* for the youth, young men R36

kwiminyaka *loc-n2-pl* in years R28

kwimisebenzi *loc-n2-pl* in jobs R29, R35=2

kwimo *loc-n5-sg* the state Derived from -ma 'stand', i.e., kw(a)-imo R21.3

kwiMozambique *pn-loc* in Mozambique R24

kwindawo *loc-n5-sg* to the position R33=2, R34, R37.13

kwindlu *loc-n5-sg* from the house R30, R37.2

kwingalo *loc-n5-sg* from the arm R31

kwinkokeli *loc-n5-sg* from the leader R16

kwinkoliso *loc-n5-sg* in the majority R16

kwiNorthern Training Trust *loan* to the Northern Training Trust R35

kwinqununu *loc-n5-sg* to principal R18

kwintlalo *adv-n5-sg* in the way (that people) live R35

kwintlanganiso *loc-n5-sg* at the meeting R27

kwiofisi *loc-n5-sg* in the office R37.14

kwiphondo *adv-n3-sg* in the province R35

kwiqabane *loc-n3-sg* on a partner R30

kwirayisi *loc-n5-sg* among rice • *Amagama aphambili kwirayisi 'The brands foremost among rice'* R12

kwiRegional Championships *loc-n-loan* in the Regional Championships R33

kwisa *loc-n-loan* in the South African R33

kwisikolo *loc-n4-sg* at the school R27, R33

kwisirhoxo *loc-n4-sg* in a shebeen (a secret, favorite place) R31.3

kwisitovu *loc-n4-sg* on the stove R8

kwiSouth African Championships *loan* in the South African Championships R33

kwiWorld Cross Country *loc-loan* in the World Cross Country (race) R33

kwixesha *loc-n3-sg* in the time R37.10

kwiyure *loc-n5-sg* to an hour R8

kwizibhedlele *loc-n4-pl* in hospitals R37.12

kwizikhalazo *n8-vn-poss-n4-pl* in the cause of complaints, for (their) complaints R27

kwiziko *loc-n3-sg* for the household; in the center R35.0.15

kwizilangazelelo *loc-n4-pl* in the desires R16

kwizilwanyana *n4-pl-dim* in the animal kingdom [lit: among small animals] R2

kwiziphumo *loc-n4-pl* on the results, by the outcomes • *imfundo esekelwe kwiziphumo 'Outcome-based Education'* R22.1

kwizizwe *loc-n4-pl* in countries R17.4

kwowu *intj* Oh! [astonishment] R23

k x *change* change of XH to KX • *inkxaso 'maintenance' [= in-kx/xhas-o]* E&S:51, PCX:195

L

l[1] *change* [consonant added to the inflected forms of deictic n9 roots apha and apho] • *balapha* CGB:179, R37.2.4.12

l-[2] *n3-sg-them* [group 3 singular thematic consonant prefix] • *formed from class concord li-, the -i- of which is elided before other vowels* ☞ See: li-, lonke XED:82

-l-[3] *n3-sg-obj-prf* him, her, it [group 3 singular short object form before vowel initial verb] ☞ Alt: -li- E&S:18

l-[4] *n6-sg-them* [group 6 singular thematic consonant prefix] ☞ See: lu-, lonke XED:84

-l-[5] *n6-sg-obj-prf* him, her, it [group 6 singular short object form before o-vowel initial verb] ☞ Alt: -lu- ~ -lw- E&S:18

la-[1] *n3-sg-poss* of [group 3 singular possessive agreement prefix] Agr: ili-, i- AM-94:163, AXG:15, E&S:22, SXWU:35f, XED:xv, R3, R5x, R9x

la-[2] *n3-sg-S3b-pos* (and) he, she, it VERBed [group 3 singular past subjunctive positive verb subject (S3b) agreement prefix] CGB:190, E&S:42, MI:247, SXWU:141

la[3] *deic-1-n3-pl* these • *la mabali* Agr: ama- ☞ Sole form (no alternate) CGB:163, E&S:26, MI:159, PCX:86, SXWU:157, XED:xvi, R27, R32=2, R36=2, R37=2

laa[1] *deic-3-n1-sg* that (far, yonder) Agr: um- / u- ☞ Alt: lowa CGB:163, E&S:26, MI:160, SXWU:157, XED:xvi

laa[2] *deic-3-n2-sg* that (far, yonder) Agr: um- ☞ Alt: lowa CGB:163, E&S:26, MI:160, SXWU:157, XED:xvi

laa[3] *deic-3-n2-pl* those (far, yonder) Agr: imi- ☞ Alt: leya CGB:163, E&S:26, MI:160, SXWU:157, XED:xvi

laa[4] *deic-3-n3-pl* those (far, yonder) Agr: ama- ☞ Alt: lawa CGB:163, E&S:26, MI:160, SXWU:157, XED:xvi

laa[5] *deic-3-n5-sg* that (far, yonder) Agr: iN- ☞ Alt: leya CGB:163, E&S:26, MI:160, SXWU:157, XED:xvi

labayindawo *n3-sg-aux-past-cop-n5-sg* it became a place R35

labe *preverb-past-n3-sg* he, she, it had VERBed; he, she, it did VERB [group 3 singular remote past compound tense preverb] Structure: labe li-Δ (participial verb form) ☞ Alt: laye E&S:39, GDX3:714, PCX:186

labo[1] *n1-pl-poss-n3-sg* of them; their (own); theirs CGB:183, E&S:22, GDX3:691, R35

labo[2] *n7-poss-n3-sg* its; of it GDX3:691

Labuschagne *pn* Labuschagne R36=3

-lahla *v-tr* throw s.t. away; cast off; abandon, forsake; lay down; lose XED:80, R30

-lahlekile *v-perf-atr* lost; confused, bewildered E&S:30, XED:80

lakhe *n1-sg-poss-n3-sg* his, her, its CGB:182, E&S:22, GDX3:691, R17.5.6, R24, R36=2

lakho *pro-2sg-poss-n3-sg* your, yours; your own [singular] • *ikhaya lakho 'your home'* CGB:182, E&S:22, GDX3:691, R15, R30=3, R34

lako[1] *n8-vn-poss-n3-sg* its, of it GDX3:691

lako[2] *n10-loc-poss-n3-sg* its, of it GDX3:691

lakowabo *n3-sg-poss-pron-abs* of theirs R32

laku- *n3-sg-temp* when it VERBs / VERBed [group 3 singular temporal verb construction] • *Lakufika 'When it arrives...'* E&S:42

lakwa *n3-sg-poss-loc* of the R27

-lala *v-intr* lie down; go to sleep; rest; [v-tr] lie with s.o. PCX:29; 34, XED:80

lali-[1] *n3-sg-remote-past* he, she, it had VERBed [group 3 singular contracted remote past compound tense] AXG:93f, E&S:39, PCX:186

lali[2] *n5-sg-red* village • *kule lali 'in this village'* ☞ See: ilali R26

lalo[1] *n3-sg-poss-n3-sg* his, her, its; of him, her, it GDX3:691, R27

lalo[2] *n6-sg-poss-n3-sg* its; of it GDX3:691

lam *pro-1sg-poss-n3-sg* of me; my, mine; my own • *iliso lam 'my eye'* AM-94:151, CGB:181, E&S:22, GDX3:691, PCX:60; 72, SXWU:36

lamadoda *n3-pl-poss* of men R25, R36

lamagumbi *n3-pl-poss* of the rooms R18

lamatheko *n3-pl-poss* of the festivities R31

lamatyala *n3-pl+deic* these crimes R27.11=2

lamb *n5-sg-red* lamb R8

-lamba *v-st* get hungry; [perf] be hungry ☞ Perf: -lambile CGB:155f, XED:80f, R16, R26.5

-lambela *v-ben* hunger for XED:80, R16

-lambile *v-st-perf* hungry E&S:30

lamvanje *n3-sg-poss-adv-clitic* of lately R31

-landa *v-tr* follow (by scent), track, trace, pursue, follow up XED:81, R7x, R22x, R37x

-landela *v-ben* follow, go / come after, chase, pursue; be after, come next XED:81, R7, R22x, R34, R37x

Language *loan* Language R37=2

lanqunyaniswa *v-caus-pass* it was ended R35

lase-Afrika *n3-sg-poss-pn* of Africa R32.7

lasebusuku *n3-sg-poss-loc-n7-sg* of being at night R27

laso *n4-sg-poss-n3-sg* his, her, its; of him, her, it GDX3:691

lathetha *v-tr* it talked R32

lawa *deic-3-n3-pl* those (far, yonder) Agr: ama- ☞ Alt: laa CGB:163, E&S:26, MI:160, PCX:86, SXWU:157

lawo[1] *n2-sg-poss-n3-sg* its, of it GDX3:691

lawo[2] *n3-pl-poss* their; of them GDX3:691

lawo[3] *deic-2-n3-pl* those (not far, just mentioned) Agr: ama- ☞ Alt: loo CGB:163, E&S:26, MI:159, PCX:86, SXWU:157, R36, R37

-lawula *v-tr* order, direct; rule, govern, administer; reign over; [ext] bless or put a charm on s.o. in preparation for war XED:81, R22=3

laye *preverb-past-n3-sg* he, she, it had VERBed; he, she, it did VERB [group 3 singular remote past compound tense preverb] Structure: laye li-Δ (participial verb form) ☞ Alt: labe AXG:93f, E&S:39, GDX3:714

layo[1] *n2-pl-poss-n3-sg* their, theirs GDX3:691

layo[2] *n5-sg-poss-n3-sg* his, her, its; of him, her, it GDX3:691

lazisa *v-tr-caus-past* make known • *iSebe lazisa ukuba 'The Department made known that'* n3-sg + a +az + is + a ('Long' past formative a is present) R18

lazo[1] *n4-pl-poss-n3-sg* their; of them GDX3:691

lazo[2] *n5-pl-poss-n3-sg* their; of them GDX3:691

le[1] *deic-1-n2-pl* these • *le mini 'these days'* Agr: imi- ☞ Sole form (no alternate) CGB:163, E&S:26, MI:159, PCX:86, SXWU:157, XED:xvi, R9, R20

le[2] *deic-1-n5-sg* this, these; far away, much, far • *le nto 'this matter'* Agr: iN- ☞ Sole form (no alternate) CGB:163, E&S:26, MI:159, PCX:86, SXWU:157, XED:xvi; 81, R11, R17.3, R19.2.3, R22=4, R24, R25, R30, R31, R32=2, R35, R36=2, R37=15

le[3] *adv, atr* far (away), afar; much XED:81, R11x

Leading Together *loan* Leading Together R22=3

Leboa *pn-loc* Leboa R37

lee *adv-loc* very far off Usually used with -kude AXG:144, R35

leeholide *n3-sg-poss-n5-pl-loan* of (the) holiday R31

leembaleki *n3-sg-poss-n5-pl* of the runners R33

lelaa *deic-3-n3-sg-pred* that (far, yonder) is E&S:26

lelam *cop-pron-abs* it is mine R24

leli[1] *deic-1-n3-sg-pred* this is; it is this one E&S:26, PCX:99

leli[2] *deic-1-n3-sg-agent* by this E&S:26, R18=2, R35

lelo *deic-2-n3-sg-pred* that (not far, just mentioned) is E&S:26

lem- *combo* of • *ISebe leMfundo 'the Department of Education'* indicates that n5 sg (im-) is possessed by a n3 sg (la-) ☞ See: la- + im- R18

lemfundo *n3-sg-poss-n2-sg* of learning R18

leminyaka *adv-n2-pl* of years, of age R36

lenkqubela *n5-sg-poss-n3-sg* for the progress R30

lentlanganisela *poss-n5-sg* of meeting people R34

lenu *pro-2pl-poss-n3-sg* of you; your, yours; your own [plural] E&S:22, GDX3:691

Leo *loan* Leo R34

-lesa *v-tr* read ☞ Cf: -bhala 'write' PCX:26

lesibini *n3-sg-poss-num* second R29

lethu *pro-1pl-poss-n3-sg* of us; our, ours; our own [plural] CGB:182, E&S:22, GDX3:691, R11, R21

leya[1] *deic-3-n2-pl* those (far, yonder) Agr: imi- ☞ Alt: laa CGB:163, E&S:26, MI:160, PCX:86, SXWU:157

leya[2] *deic-3-n5-sg* that (far, yonder) Agr: iN- ☞ Alt: laa CGB:163, E&S:26, MI:160, PCX:86, SXWU:157

leyo[1] *deic-2-n2-pl* those (not far, just mentioned) Agr: imi- ☞ Alt: loo CGB:163, E&S:26, MI:159, PCX:86, SXWU:157

leyo[2] *deic-2-n5-sg* that (not far, just mentioned) Agr: iN- ☞ Alt: loo CGB:163, E&S:26, MI:159, PCX:86, SXWU:157, R37=4

lezoshishino *n6-sg* business R34.6

li-[1] *n3-sg-red-prf* [group 3 singular reduced noun prefix] • *zeli lizwe (things) of the nation* Loss of article i- from ili- R13.6, R32.2.3, R35.14

-li-[2] *n3-sg-obj* [group 3 singular object agreement prefix] Agr: ili-, i- E&S:18, PCX:51, SXWU:44, R6, R8, R15, R27, R30

li-[3] *n3-sg-pred-prf* he, she, it is [group 3 singular copulative or predicative prefix construction on polysyllabic roots] • *ligama 'it is a name'; lipolisa 'he is a policeman'* Agr: i- ☞ Contrast: lili- [on monosyllabic roots] CGB:136, E&S:21, PCX:96, SXWU:22f, R7=2, R10, R36

li-[4] *n3-sg-adj-pred* he, she, it is ADJ [group 3 singular adjective agreement prefix used predicatively] • *lisekhona, 'it is still there...', lisekhona ixesha, 'there is still time'* copulative E&S:28, MI:248, PCX:118f

li-[5] *n3-sg-enum-prf* [group 3 singular enumerative agreement prefix] ☞ See: limbi, liphi E&S:27, PCX:110f

li-[6] *n3-sg-S1* he, she, it [group 3 singular subject (S1) agreement prefix] Agr: ili-, i- CGB:117; 158, E&S:17f, PCX:51;24f, SXWU:28, R3, R25

li-[7] *n3-sg-S2* he, she, it [group 3 singular participial subject (S2) agreement prefix] AXG:89; 91, CGB:191

li-[8] *n3-sg-S3a* (and) he, she, it VERBs [group 3 singular present subjunctive verb subject (S3a) agreement prefix] (CGB:167), R4d, R8

li-[9] *n3-sg-rel2* he, she who / that which [group 3 singular direct relative 2 construction, attributive agreement prefix used predicatively] E&S:34, MI:153; 248, PCX:151

li-[10] *n3-sg-ind-rel2* whom, which [group 3 singular indirect relative 2 agreement prefix] E&S:35

libe[1] *preverb-recent-pro-n3-sg* he, she, it was VERBing [group 3 singular recent past compound tense preverb] Structure: libe li-Δ (participial construction) AXG:91f, E&S:37f, PCX:183

libe[2] *v-pred-sub-pres* he, she may be R4d

libhinqa *n3-sg-pred* it is a woman R36.14

libonwa *v-pass* it be seen R36

Libra *loan* Libra R34

libulala *v-tr* it kills R25

lichule *n3-sg-atr-ped* be an expert R29=2

lide *cop-adj* it is long R26

Life Line *loan* Life Line (crisis counseling phone service) R36=4

lifikile *v-intr-perf* it arrived; it has arrived R3, R36

lifumana *v-tr* it found R35

lifuna *v-tr* (it) wants/needs R34

ligutyula *v-tr* it sweeps out C3-sg+gutyula R25

lika *n3-sg-poss-prf* of [personal possessive prefix / marker for noun group 3 singular] Agr: ili- E&S:23f, PCX:109, R24.1, R28.1, R31.2

likaGraca *n3-sg-poss-n1a-sg* of Graca (Machel) R24.1

likarhulumente *n3-sg-poss-n1a-sg* of the government R31.2

likaThandekile *n3-sg-poss-n1a-sg* of Thandekile • *ibali likaThandekile 'the story of Thandekile'* R28.1

likhala *v-part* it complaining R32.7

likho *v-exis-n3-sg* it is here; he, she is present E&S:29, ITX:17

likhuphe *v-imp* take out R30

-lila *v-intr* cry, weep, shed tears; mourn; crow (of rooster); ring (of bell) EXD:137, XED:82, R5x

lili-[1] *n3-sg-pred-prf* he, she, it is [group 3 singular copulative or predicative prefix construction on monosyllabic roots] • *lilifu 'it is a cloud'; lilizwe 'it is a country'* Agr: ili- ☞ Contrast: li- [on polysyllabic roots] CGB:135, E&S:25, PCX:96, XED:xvi

lili-[2] *n3-sg-agent-prf* by (done by, produced by) him, her, it [marker of group 3 singular agent of passive verb] E&S:25;43

liliphathelwe *v-ben-pass-n3-sg* so that it be made R30.1

-lilisa *v-caus* make s.o. cry, cause to weep, crow (of rooster), ring (of bell) XED:82, R5x

-lilisana *v-caus-recip* make each other cry, cause one another to mourn R5

lilo *n3-sg-pred* he, she, it is; it is he, she, it [group 3 singular copulative or predicative] E&S:21, PCX:98, R27.12

lilonke *cop-enum* in all R36=2

lilungu *n3-sg-pred* be a member R7

limazise *v-tr-perf* he introduced her, she introduced him R33.8

limbi *enum-pro-n3-sg* other, some other, different Structure: RED noun form + ENUM / ENUM + FULL noun form ☞ See: -mbi E&S:27, PCX:110

limehlo *n3-sg-pred* be the eyes • *(l)ibe limehlo kurhulumente 'it should be the eyes of the government'* R37.2

limeko *cop-n3-pl* are the situations R16

linabantu *cop-n1-pl* it has people R35.2

-linda *v-tr* wait for, await; watch for; drive off, chase away AM-94:164, XED:82

-lindela *v-ben* wait expectantly for XED:82, R19

Lindi *n1a-sg-pn-masc/fem* Lindi (male / female personal name) [short form] ☞ Cf: Lindile [pn-m], Lindiwe [pn-f] AM-94:164

lindithumele *v-ben-sub* that she should send to me R4a

Lindiwe *n1a-sg-pn* Lindiwe (personal name) R23

-linga *v* try, attempt PCX:26

lingekathambi *v-neg* it should not yet be soft R30.4

lingenayo *v-poss-conj-neg* it does not have R31

lingento *cop-neg-n5-sg* not nothing R36

lini *qw-n3-sg* what kind?, of what sort? • *lizwe lini? 'what sort of country?'* ☞ See: -ni PCX:28; 118

linyanga *v-tr* it cures R25=4

liphelile *v-intr-perf* it has ended R31

liphelisa *v-tr-caus* it terminates R25

liphi[1] *qw-loc-adv-n3-sg* where is? ☞ See: -phi AXG:141, E&S:31, PCX:111

liphi[2] *qw-n3-sg* which (one)? E&S:27, EXD:722, GDX3:703, PCX:111, R6x

liphume *v-sub* and it gets out R25

liqhekeke *v-st* and it breaks R25

liqhotse *v-obj-imp* fry it! R8

liqhuba[1] *v-tr* it is progressing R23

liqhuba[2] *v-tr* it operates R35

lisebe *n3-sg-agent* by the department R27

lisehotele *loan* it is a hotel R31

lisekhona *cop-aux-prn-abs* it is there [c-3sg-s(a)-(i)kho-na] Copulative formed from absolute pronoun khona R21

liseofisini *loan* in (the) office R31

lisuke *v-aux* it started to VERB R35.12

lithambe *v-pres-sub* it (the onion) should become soft R8

lithemba *n3-sg-pred* it is hope R36

litsho *v-aux* it says, it does aux R25.7

livula *v-tr* it opens R25

lixesha *n3-sg-pred* it is time R31, R34=5

lixhoba *n3-sg-pred* he is a prey R36

liyamhlonipha *v-tr-pres* it respects him R16

liza *v-aux-fut* will R31

Lizeka *n1a-sg-pn-fem* Lizeka (female personal name) [lit: present] AM-94:164

lizibona *v-tr* it sees them R36

liziko *n3-sg-pred* it is a home; it serves as a center R35.2

Lizo *n1a-sg-pn-masc* Lizo (male personal name) [lit: present] AM-94:164, PCX:36

lizwe *n3-sg-red* country ☞ See: ilizwe E&S:26, PCX:25, R13, R32=2, R35

-lo[1] *n3-sg-root* he, she, it; his, her, its [group 3 singular pronoun root] AXG:14, E&S:22

lo-[2] *v-n3-sg-short-fut* he, she, it will VERB [contracted / short positive future group 3 singular noun prefix] E&S:20

-lo[3] *n6-sg-root* he, she, it; his, her, its [group 6 singular pronoun root] E&S:22

lo-[4] *v-n6-sg-short-fut* it will VERB [contracted / short positive future group 6 singular noun prefix] E&S:20

lo[5] *deic-1-n1-sg* this • *lo mntu 'this person'* Agr: um- ☞ Sole form (no alternate) CGB:163, E&S:26, MI:159, PCX:86, SXWU:157, XED:xvi, R19=3, R20, R21, R27, R36

lo[6] *deic-1-n2-sg* this Agr: um- ☞ Sole form (no alternate) CGB:163, E&S:26, MI:159, PCX:86, SXWU:157, XED:xvi, R6, R29

lobudoda *n7-abs-poss* of a man; [atr] male, masculine RD-96:98, R30=4, R36

lodwa[1] *pro-quan-n3-sg* it alone; only it Agr: i(li)-, lona E&S:27, PCX:62

lodwa[2] *pro-quan-n6-sg* it alone; only it Agr: u(lu)-, lona E&S:27, PCX:62

lokhuseleko *n3-sg-poss-n6-sg* of protection R31.2

loku- *combo* of VERBing • *ngegama lokuba zinyusa ingxowa-mali 'in the name of raising funds'; lixesha lokubuyela esikolweni 'it is the time for returning to school'* indicates that n8 vn (uku-) is possessed by n3 sg (la-) ☞ See: la- + uku- R3, R5, R9

lokuba *n8-vn-poss-n3-sg* of being; [conj] that, so that ☞ See: ukuba GDX3:475, R3, R9, R21, R33, R34, R35, R36, R37=2

lokubonelela *n8-vn-intens* of enlightening (the people) R37

lokundiqinisekisa *n8-vn-poss-n3-sg* to reassure me R36

lokundlandlathekisa *n8-vn-poss-n3-sg* of scaring R36

lokungathathelwa *n8-vn-poss-n3-sg* not to be taken heed of R36.12

lokunika *n8-vn-poss-n3-sg* for giving R35

lokuqalisa *n8-vn-poss-n3-sg* of starting anew R34=2

lokuqeqesha *n8-vn-poss-n3-sg* for training R35

lokuqiniseka *n8-vn-poss-n3-sg* to be sure, ensure R34

lokushiywa *n8-vn-poss-n3-sg* of being left by R5

lokushumayela *n8-vn-poss-n3-sg* of preaching R31

lokusibonakalisa *v-n8+n4-sg-obj* it reveals it, it shows it R34.6

lokuthetha *n8-vn-poss-n3-sg* of communicating R29=2

lokuya *n8-vn-poss-n3-sg* of going R28

lokwakha *n3-sg-poss-v-inf* to build • *lixesha lokwakha 'it is time to build'* R34.8

lokwenene *adv* for real, truly R36

lokwenza *n3-sg-poss-n8-vn* of doing R14, R22.3, R35.9, R36.14, R37.16

lolo *deic-2-n6-sg-pred* that (Dem 2 Pos) normally 'olo' in Xhosa, but Zulu influence may have caused 'lolo' E&S:26, R37.20

-lolonga *v-tr* look at the various parts of s.t.; observe in detail / carefully; look out for, look after s.o. KED:219, XED:83, R34x

lolu *deic-1-n6-sg-pred* this is E&S:26

lololuntu *n3-sg-poss-n6-sg* of the community probably a typographical error - loluntu is preferred R21.4

lolwaa *deic-3-n6-sg-pred* that (far, yonder) is E&S:26

lom- *combo* of • *ilungu lombutho 'member of the association'* indicates that n2 sg (um-) is possessed by a n3 sg (la-) ☞ See: la- + um- R7

lombutho *n2-sg-poss* of the society, association • *lilungu lombutho wamagqirha 'be a member of the witch doctors' association'* R7

loMgaqo *n3-sg-poss-n2-sg* of the constitution R37

lomhleli *n1-sg-poss* of the editor R32

lomntla *loc-n2-sg* of the north • *kwiPhondo lomNtla 'in the Northern Province'* R35=2

lomthetho *n2-sg* this law R32

lomzabalazo *n2-sg-poss-n3-sg* of the struggle R32.7

lona[1] *pro-n3-sg-echo* he, she, it [group 3 singular echo / absolutive pronoun] AM-94:93; 163, AXG:14, CGB:158, E&S:21, PCX:57, R6

lona[2] *pro-n6-sg-echo* he, she, it [group 6 singular echo / absolutive pronoun] AM-94:163, CGB:158, E&S:21, PCX:57

-londoloza *v-tr* take care of, preserve, protect, keep under one's care XED:83, R31x, R35x

lonke[1] *pro-enum-n3-sg* all; every; the whole (of) • *lonke ilizwe 'the whole country; every country'* Agr: i(li)-, lona AM-94:163, CGB:176, E&S:27, PCX:62f;24f, R30, R32, R37

lonke[2] *pro-enum-n6-sg* all; every; the whole (of) Agr: u(lu)-, lona AM-94:163, E&S:27, PCX:62, R24

loo[1] *deic-2-n1-sg* that (not far, just mentioned) • *loo mntu 'that person'* Agr: um- ☞ Alt: lowo CGB:163, E&S:26, MI:159, SXWU:157, XED:xvi, R31.2

loo[2] *deic-2-n2-sg* that (not far, just mentioned) Agr: um- ☞ Alt: lowo CGB:163, E&S:26, MI:159, SXWU:157, XED:xvi

loo[3] *deic-2-n2-pl* those (not far, just mentioned) Agr: imi- ☞ Alt: leyo MI:159, SXWU:157

loo[4] *deic-2-n3-pl* those (not far, just mentioned) Agr: ama- ☞ Alt: lawo CGB:163, E&S:26, MI:159, SXWU:157, XED:xvi, R20.6

loo[5] *deic-2-n5-sg* that (not far, just mentioned) Agr: iN- ☞ Alt: leyo CGB:163, E&S:26, MI:159, SXWU:157, XED:xvi, R29.8, R36.18.25

Looksmart *n1a-sg-pn* Looksmart Solwandle Ngudle (personal name) R32

loonobuhle *deict2-n1-sg-poss-atr* that one of beauty R33

Lottie *pn* Lottie (name) R5

lowa[1] *deic-3-n1-sg* that (far, yonder) Agr: um- / u- ☞ Alt: laa CGB:163, E&S:26, MI:160, PCX:86, SXWU:157

lowa[2] *deic-3-n2-sg* that (far, yonder) Agr: um- ☞ Alt: laa CGB:163, E&S:26, MI:160, PCX:86, SXWU:157

lowo[1] *deic-2-n1-sg* that (not far, just mentioned) • *Lowo nguBhishophu 'that one is a Bishop'* Agr: um- ☞ Alt: loo CGB:163, E&S:26, MI:159, PCX:86, SXWU:157, R19, R32

lowo[2] *deic-2-n2-sg* that (not far, just mentioned) Agr: um- ☞ Alt: loo CGB:163, E&S:26, MI:159, PCX:86, SXWU:157

lu-[1] *n6-sg-red-prf* [group 6 singular reduced noun prefix] Loss of article u- from ulu- SXWU:20

-lu-[2] *n6-sg-obj* [group 6 singular object agreement prefix] Agr: ulu-, u- E&S:18, PCX:51, SXWU:44, R13

lu-[3] *n6-sg-pred-prf* he, she, it is [group 6 singular copulative or predicative prefix construction on polysyllabic roots] • *lusana 'it is a baby'* PCX:96

lu-[4] *n6-sg-adj-pred* it is ADJ [group 6 singular adjective agreement prefix used predicatively] E&S:28, MI:248, PCX:118f

lu-[5] *n6-sg-enum-prf* [group 6 singular enumerative agreement prefix] ☞ See: lumbi, luphi E&S:27, PCX:110

lu-[6] *n6-sg-voc-prf* oh!, hey! [group 6 singular vocative noun prefix] • *lusana 'baby!'* Agr: u-, ulu- AXG:28, E&S:32, PCX:55

lu-[7] *n6-sg-S1* he, she, it [group 6 singular subject (S1) agreement prefix] Agr: ulu-, lu- CGB:117; 158, E&S:17f, PCX:51, SXWU:28, R11

lu-[8] *n6-sg-S2* he, she, it [group 6 singular participial subject (S2) agreement prefix] AXG:91, CGB:191

lu-[9] *n6-sg-S3a* (and) he, she, it VERBs [group 6 singular present subjunctive verb subject (S3a) agreement prefix] (CGB:167)

lu-[10] *n6-sg-rel2* that which [group 6 singular direct relative 2 construction, attributive agreement prefix used predicatively] E&S:34, MI:153; 248, PCX:151

lu-[11] *n6-sg-ind-rel2* which [group 6 singular indirect relative 2 agreement prefix] E&S:35

lube *preverb-recent-pro-n6-sg* he, she, it was VERBing [group 6 singular recent past compound tense preverb] Structure: lube lu-Δ (participial construction) AXG:91f, E&S:37, PCX:183

-lubhelu *atr-root* yellow ☞ Syn: -tyheli AM-94:107, CGB:172, E&S:30, EXD:737, NDK-91:344, Uys:4, XED:11

lubonisa *v-tr-part* showing part of compound tense R31

lucalu-calulo *n6-sg-comp* Apartheid R20.3

lufela *v-ben* he, she dies R27

lufikelele *n6-sg-v-intens* it should have access to R37.7

luhlangene *v-intr-recip-past* it met R21

-luhlaza *atr-root* green; blue; fresh, raw ☞ See: -blowu AM-94:107, CGB:172f, E&S:30, EXD:60; 255, NDK-91:128, RD-96:397;85, UEX:14, Uys:4, XED:59, R34

luhlobo *n6-sg-pred* it is a kind R21

luka *n6-sg-poss-prf* of [personal possessive prefix / marker for noun group 6 singular] Agr: ulu- E&S:23f, PCX:109, R21

lukho *v-exis-n6-sg* it is here, it is present E&S:29, ITX:17

lukhulu *cop-adj* a great deal R33

-lukhuni *atr-root* hard (as a rock); difficult, tough; enduring; strict; harsh, severe, stern, hard-hearted ☞ Cf: ukhuni CGB:172, EXD:265; 267, XED:77, R11

lukuqonde *v-tr-sub* understand R36

-lula *atr-root* light; easy ☞ Opp: -nzima; -lukhuni AM-94:107, CGB:172, E&S:30, R7, R30, R36

lulo *n6-sg-pred* he, she, it is; it is he, she, it [group 6 singular copulative or predicative] E&S:21, PCX:98

lulu-[1] *n6-sg-pred-prf* he, she, it is [group 6 singular copulative or predicative prefix construction on monosyllabic roots] • *luluvo 'it is an opinion'* CGB:135, E&S:21; 25, PCX:96, XED:xvi

lulu-[2] *n6-sg-agent-prf* by (done or produced by) him, her, it [marker of group 6 singular agent of passive verb] E&S:25; 43

luluntu *n6-sg-agent* by the community R37

lumbi *enum-pro-n6-sg* other, some other, different Structure: RED noun form + ENUM / ENUM + FULL noun form ☞ See: -mbi E&S:27, PCX:110

-lumka *v-st* be prudent, careful, wary; take care CGB:155, XED:84, R6x, R31

-lumkisa *v-caus* make s.o. prudent, careful, wise; instruct, teach a lesson to; warn; [fig] take advantage of, cheat XED:84, R6x

-luncedo *n6-sg-atr* helpful EXD:273, R22=2, R37

-lunga *v-st* be right, good, suitable, fitting, becoming, OK XED:84, R4c, R6x, R14x

lungafikelela *c6-sg-pot-v-intens* can be arrived at R37.9

lungako *adv-deic* about it R37

lungaqhubela *v-pot-n7-sg-S1* it can progress or move forward • *Uthethwano lungaqhubela phambili 'Communication can move forward'* R34.4

-lungela *v-ben* be right, suitable, good for; be better for; suit, become, fit; [pass] deserve XED:84, R14

-lungelelanisa *v-ben-recip-caus* arrange in order, adapt to each other, make equal or parallel to each other XED:85

-lungile *v-st-perf-atr* right, good, ready E&S:30, PCX:37, XED:84, R4c, R14, R34

-lungisa *v-caus* make right, good, suitable, ready; outfit, fit out; repair, mend; do the right thing; [ext] reward s.o. AM-94:73, XED:85, R6x

-lungiselela *v-diben* make s.t. right for s.o.; transact s.t. for another; provide s.t. for s.o., do service to XED:85, R6

luni *qw-n6-sg* what kind?, of what sort? ☞ See: -ni PCX:118, R21

luninzi *n6-sg* there is plentiful R37

-lunyikiswa *v-pass* be warned; get instructed R6

luphele *v-sub* it may end R37

luphi[1] *qw-loc-adv-n6-sg* where is? ☞ See: -phi E&S:31

luphi[2] *qw-n6-sg* which (one)? E&S:27, GDX3:703

-lusizi *atr-root* sad; sorry • *Andilusizi 'I am not sad'* AM-94:107, CGB:179, MI:153

luthe *v-aux* they said, did aux. verb with meaning of 'did' R26

-luthuli *atr-root* dusty (color), grayish ☞ See: uthuli R34

-luthuthu *atr-root* ash-gray CGB:172

luxhele *v-tr-n6-sg-S1* they have slaughtered lu- refers to usapho 'family' [n6], hence Eng 'they' R26.2

luya *v-aux-pres-n6-sg* it is R34.12

luyakhuthazwa *v-pass* it is encouraged R35.10

luyakwamkela *v-prog-ben* they receive R36

luyakwazi *v-tr* it knows how R37

luyazi *v-tr* to know it • *uluntu oluyakuthi luyazi 'society will come to know it'* R37

luyophula *v-short-fut* they will break them R31.1

luza *v-aux-fut* will c6-agr+fut R31

luzibandakanye *v-recip-tr* they unite R35.10

-lw- *n6-sg-obj-prf* him, her, it [group 6 singular short object form before vowel initial verb (other than o)] ☞ Alt: -lu- E&S:18

lwa-[1] *n6-sg-poss* of [group 6 singular possessive agreement prefix] Agr: ulu-, u- AM-94:163, E&S:22, SXWU:35f, XED:xv, R4d=3

lwa-[2] *n6-sg-S3b-pos* (and) he, she, it VERBed [group 6 singular past subjunctive positive verb subject (S3b) agreement prefix] (CGB:189), E&S:42, MI:247, SXWU:141

-lwa[3] *v-intr* fight, struggle ☞ Pass: -liwa AXG:107, XED:85, R2x

lwabantu *n1-pl-poss-n6-sg* of people R22.1, R29.11.14, R36.12

lwabantwana *n6-sg-poss-n1-pl* of children R27=2

lwabasebenzi *n6-sg-poss-n1-pl* of the workers R35

lwabe *preverb-past-n6-sg* it had VERBed; it did VERB [group 6 singular remote past compound tense preverb] Structure: lwabe lu-Δ (participial verb form) ☞ Alt: lwaye E&S:39, GDX3:714, PCX:186

lwabo[1] *n1-pl-poss-n6-sg* of them; their (own); theirs CGB:183, E&S:22, GDX3:691, R10, R37=2

lwabo[2] *n7-poss-n6-sg* its; of it GDX3:691

lwagxothwa *v-pass* they were expelled R26.2

lwakhe *n1-sg-poss-n6-sg* his, her, its E&S:22, GDX3:691

lwakho *pro-2sg-poss-n6-sg* your, yours; your own [singular] E&S:22, GDX3:691, R30

lwako[1] *n8-vn-poss-n6-sg* its, of it GDX3:691

lwako[2] *n10-loc-poss-n6-sg* its, of it GDX3:691

lwakowethu *n3-sg-poss-adv-pron* of ours R30

lwaku- *n6-sg-temp* when it VERBs / VERBed [group 6 singular temporal verb construction] • *Lwakufika 'When it arrives...'* E&S:42

lwakudala *atr-poss-n6-sg* old-fashioned R4d

lwalapha *deic-1-n9-loc-poss-n6-sg* of this place (here) • *Uluntu lwalapha 'the community of this area'* R35

lwale *n6-sg-poss-deic* of this R32

lwalo[1] *n3-sg-poss-n6-sg* his, her, its; of him, her, it GDX3:691

lwalo[2] *n6-sg-poss-n6-sg* its; of it GDX3:691

lwalu- *n6-sg-remote-past* it had VERBed [group 6 singular contracted remote past compound tense] AXG:93f, E&S:39, PCX:186

lwam *pro-1sg-poss-n6-sg* of me; my, mine; my own • *usana lwam 'my baby'* AM-94:151, CGB:181, E&S:22, GDX3:691, PCX:60; 72, SXWU:36, R23=2, R33

lwamadoda *n6-sg-poss-n3-pl* of men R36

lwamapolisa *n6-sg-poss-n3-pl* of the police R27

lwamaqela *n6-sg-poss-n3-pl* of the companies ☞ See: iqela R21

lwandile *v-inch-n6-sg-S1* it has increased R11

lwandivulela *v-tr-ben-past* it opened for me R33

lwasekuhlaleni *n6-sg-poss-loc* of the nearby residency R35

lwasemaphandleni *n6-sg-n3-pl-loc* of the outsides R36

lwaso *n4-sg-poss-n6-sg* his, her, its; of him, her, it GDX3:691

lwaveza *v-caus-past* it showed R36

lwawo[1] *n2-sg-poss-n6-sg* its; of it GDX3:691

lwawo[2] *n3-pl-poss* their, of them GDX3:691

lwaye *preverb-past-n6-sg* it had VERBed; it did VERB [group 6 singular remote past compound tense preverb] Structure: lwaye lu-Δ (participial verb form) ☞ Alt: lwabe AXG:93f, E&S:39, GDX3:714

lwayo[1] *n2-pl-poss-n6-sg* their; of them GDX3:691

lwayo[2] *n5-sg-poss-n6-sg* his, her, its; of him, her, it • *Nkosi sikelel' iAfrika, Maluphakanyis' uphondo lwayo 'Lord bless Africa, may its horn be exalted'* GDX3:691, R13, R37.7

lwazise *v-tr* it informs R37

lwazo[1] *n4-pl-poss-n6-sg* their; of them GDX3:691

lwazo[2] *n5-pl-poss-n6-sg* their; of them • *uninzi lwazo zenziwe ngeetsimbi 'the majority of them (iibhedi = beds) are made of steel'* GDX3:691, R35.6

lwe- *combo* of • *ozimisele ngothando lwenyaniso 'who is serious about love of the truth'* indicates that a n5 sg (i-) is possessed by a n6 sg (lwa-) ☞ See: lwa- + i- R4d=2

lwegazi *n3-sg-poss-n6-sg* of the blood R36

lwendoda *n6-sg-poss-n5-sg* of a man R36

lwenqwelo-moya *n5-sg-cmp-poss-n6-sg* of an airplane R24

lwentliziyo *n5-sg-poss* of the heart R4d

lwentsapho *n6-sg-poss-n6-pl* of family R34.12

lwenu *pro-2pl-poss-n6-sg* of you; your, yours; your own [plural] E&S:22, GDX3:691

lwenyaniso *n5-sg-poss* of the truth R4d

lwenziwe *v-pass-past* to be done R37

lwerhafu *n5-sg-poss* of tax R23=2

lwesicwibi *n6-sg-poss-n4-sg* of the smallest piece (isicwibi, a Zulu word for a small seed) R32

lwesiNgesi *n6-sg-poss-n4-sg* of English R29

lwetaxi *n5-sg-poss-n6-sg* of taxi R23

lwethu *pro-1pl-poss-n6-sg* of us; our, ours; our own [plural] • *uninzi lwethu 'many of us'* E&S:22, GDX3:691, R28, R31

lweUsasa *n6-sg-poss-pn* of Usasa (Association of S.A. Athletes) R33

lwezentengiso *loc-poss-n5-sg* about sales R29.7

lwezi *deic-1-n5-pl-poss* of these DFG, R30

lwezifundiswa *n6-sg-poss-n4-pl* of the educated R32

lwezihlobo *n6-sg-poss-n4-pl* of friends lwa+izihlobo >lwezi... R34

lwimi *n6-sg-red* language ☞ See: ulwimi R37=9

M

m[1] *abr* meters R33=7

m[2] *change* change of MB to M • *umona 'you see him' [= u-m-(b)ona]* PCX:194, R14

m[3] *change* change of N to M (before B, F, P, V) • *zimbini 'two' [= zin-bini]* E&S:51, PCX:195f

-m-[4] *atr-prf* [archaic attributive prefix] ☞ Cf: -m-daka 'dirty', -m-fusa 'purple', -m-hlophe 'white, clear', -m-nyama 'black, dark', -m-sulwa 'innocent' R11

m-[5] *n1-sg-red-prf* [group 1 singular reduced noun prefix] Loss of article u- from um- PCX:194

-m-[6] *n1-sg-obj* [group 1, 1a singular object agreement prefix] Agr: um-, o- E&S:18, PCX:51, SXWU:44, R4b, R6, R9

m-[7] *n1-sg-adj-pred* he, she, it is ADJ [group 1, 1a singular adjective agreement prefix used predicatively] E&S:28, MI:248, PCX:117f; 194, R4d

m-[8] *n1-sg-voc-prf* oh!, hey! [group 1 singular vocative noun prefix] • *mhleli 'editor!'* Agr: um- AXG:28, E&S:32, R17, R20

m-[9] *n2-sg-red-prf* [group 2 singular reduced noun prefix] Loss of article u- from um- PCX:194, R6, R11=3

m-[10] *n2-sg-adj-pred* he, she, it is ADJ [group 2 singular adjective agreement prefix used predicatively] E&S:28, MI:248, PCX:118f; 194

m[11] *pro-1sg-root* I; my, mine; my own [absolutive pronoun / short possessive root] Agr: mna ☞ See: am, bam, kwam, lam, lwam, sam, wam, yam, zam E&S:22, SXWU:36, R4c

-m-[12] *pro-3sg-obj-prf* him, her, it no direct antecedent PCX:194

ma-[1] *n3-pl-red-prf* [group 3 plural reduced noun prefix] • *ngaloo magama 'about these words'* Loss of article a- from ama- R20, R27, R32, R36, R37

ma-[2] *n3-pl-adj-pred* they are ADJ [group 3 plural adjective agreement prefix used predicatively] E&S:28, MI:248, PCX:117f

ma-[3] *n3-pl-voc-prf* oh!, hey! [group 3 plural vocative noun prefix] • *madoda 'men!'* Agr: ama- E&S:32

ma-[4] *preverb-hort* let VERB, may it be so [hortative preverb]; had better VERB [implicative preverb] • *Mawuphile! 'May you thrive!'* Structure: ma-S3a-Δ-e (followed by present subjunctive); the weak subject concords are strengthened: u- > wu-, a- > ka-, i- > yi- ☞ Cf: maka-, mandi-, masi-, maze- CGB:170, E&S:42; 47, PCX:90f, XED:86, R4c, R9=2, R10, R14, R27=2

-ma[5] *v-st* stand, be standing; stop; wait; live, inhabit, dwell, occupy latent vowel verb ☞ Perf: mi ~ mile; Sub: eme; Pass: miwa; Cf: ima CGB:125; 155, E&S:51, PCX:21, XED:86, R4dx

mabali *n3-pl-red* stories R36

mabayeke *v-imp-pl* they should leave R27

Mabhele *pn* Mabhele (family name) R5=3

Machel *pn* Machel (family name of former president of Mozambique) R24=4

magama *n3-pl-red* words • *ngaloo magama 'about these words'* ☞ See: amagama R37.10

Magingxa *pn* Magingxa (name) R5

maka- *preverb-hort* he must, she should, let him/her Structure: followed by present subjunctive ☞ See: ma- +k a- R10, R19, R27=2

makacele *v-hort* he, she should request R27

makalibuze *v-hort* he, she must ask it R27

makamxelele *v-hort* he, she must tell him R19

makangagxothwa *v-hort-pass* he, she should not be turned away R10

makazinqumle *v-hort* he should split them R26

makhe *preverb-+-aux* let's do VERB a little followed by present subjunctive ☞ See: ma- (hortative) + kha- [v-aux] R14, R17.6, R20

makube *v-hort* let there be R21

makusetyenziswane *v-hort-caus-pass* let's cooperate, let there be cooperation R27.8

mali *n5-sg-red* money ☞ See: inkxaso-mali, ingxowa-mali 'fund' R9=2, R33, R35=4

malunga *adv* towards; about, concerning, regarding, with regard to • *malunga nebhedi ezi-4 'about four beds'* XED:86, R21, R35, R37.12

malunga khona *adv-cmp* thereabouts ☞ Syn: ngakhona EXD:659

maluphakamis' *v-imp-caus* let it be exalted R13

-mamela *v-tr* listen CGB:114, XED:86, R4c

-mana[1] *v-recip* stand beside each other XED:86

-mana[2] *v-aux* always, constantly, persistently VERB; often VERB; keep on, continue VERBing • *bamana ukuhleka 'they are always laughing'* Structure: takes infinitive complement (uku-) E&S:47, XED:86

-mana[3] *v-aux* always, constantly, persistently VERB; often VERB; keep on, continue VERBing • *bamana behleka 'they are always laughing'* Structure: takes S2 + participial complement E&S:47, XED:86

manager *loan* manager R29=4

Mandela *n1a-sg-pn* Nelson Mandela R16=3, R24, R32=4

Mandla *n1a-sg-pn-masc* Mandla (male personal name) [lit: power] SXWU:11

manga *ideophone* marvel, be surprised, get startled E&S:59

mani *qw-n3-pl* what kind?, of what sort? • *mazwe mani? 'what sort of countries?'* ☞ See: -ni PCX:28; 118

maninzi *cop-adj* there are many R29=2

manxeba *n3-pl-red* wounds ☞ See: amanxeba (inxeba) R36

-manya *v-tr* unite, join XED:87

manyala *n3-pl-red* shameless acts R32

manyathelo *n3-pl-red* steps R36.12

-manzi *n3-pl-red-atr* wet, damp, moist ☞ See: amanzi AM-94:107, CGB:172, E&S:30, XED:87, R8x=2

Maqekeza *pn* Maqekeza (personal name) R32.5

market *loan* market R1

Masele *pn-geog* Masele (village in the Eastern Cape) TD, R5=2

Mashilwane *pn* Mashilwane (family name) R4d

masi- *preverb* let us, let's Structure: ma-si(S3a)-Δ-e CGB:170, R9=2, R17

masibakhusele *v-hort* let us protect them R9

masijonge *v-hort* let's look at / up to R17.0

masimhlonipheni *v-hort* let us respect him R17.5

masizame *v-hort* let us try R9

mathidala *n3-pl-red* hesitation R36

matsha *adj-red* new R36

Matthews Goniwe *pn* Matthews Goniwe R32

matyala *n3-pl-red* crimes R27.11

Matyana *pn* Matyana (family name) R4b

matyathanga *n3-pl-red-cmp* eaters of pumpkin compound noun from ukutya 'to eat,' and ithanga/amathanga 'pumpkin' R20

mawukuqwalasele *v-tr-imp* let it be carefully examined R21

maxa *conj* when XED:181, R14=2, R35

maxa wambi *adv-time* sometimes; [cmp] sometimes ... other times GDX3:556, XED:181, R14=2, R35

maxhwangusha *n3-pl-red* bullies, ruffians ☞ See: ixhwangusha R32.4

mayinyanzelwe *v-hort* let it be forced; it should be compulsory R10

maze- *preverb* may VERB [hortative, expressing a wish or hope] • *Maze uphile! 'May you thrive!'* Structure: maze S3a-Δ-e (followed by present subjunctive) E&S:47

maziko *n3-pl-red* hearths; households ☞ See: amaziko; See: iziko R36, R37.13.14

mba[1] *n2-sg-red* issue, case, problem ☞ See: umba R24.7=2, R27.10.11.12.13

-mba[2] *v-tr* dig (up), excavate; make a cutting; sink (a well); mine latent vowel verb ☞ Pass: -mbiwa; Cf: imba CGB:125, E&S:51, PCX:21, SXWU:32, XED:87

mbaleki *n5-sg-red* runner R33

-mbalwa *atr-root* few ☞ Opp: -ninzi CGB:172, E&S:30, XED:6, R28, R33

Mbeki *pn* Mbeki (family name) ☞ See: Govan Mbeki R32

mbhodamo *n2-sg-red* turmoil, confusion R26

-mbi *enum-pro-root* other, some other, another (of a different kind); [neg] no other Structure: RED noun form + ENUM / ENUM + FULL noun form ☞ Contrast: -nye (of the same kind) E&S:27, EXD:425, PCX:110, XED:88, R5, R6x

mbiza *n5-sg-red* pot ☞ See: imbiza R25

mbuze *v-obj-imp* ask him R6

-mdaka *atr-root* dirty, unclean, untidy, muddy; dun, mud-colored, dark earth brown; dark (of color); [fig] evil ☞ Cf: -ntsundu 'brown' AM-94:107, CGB:172, E&S:30, EXD:143, KED:233, RD-96:397, UEX:14, XED:27, R8, R25=3

meats *loan* meats ☞ See: inyama R1

-mela[1] *v-ben* stand at; stand for, represent; [ext] defend AXG:17, EXXE:56, XED:88, R33x

-mela[2] *v-aux* must, should VERB; ought to VERB ☞ See also: -mele, -melwe (-melwa) E&S:47

-mele *v-aux-perf* should have VERBed [active]; should have been VERBed [passive] • *zimele ukuphekwa 'they should have been cooked'* Structure: followed by uku- (infinitive) construction E&S:47

-melwe *v-aux-pass-perf* should have been VERBed [passive perfect auxiliary verb construction] • *zimelwe kukuphekwa 'they should have been cooked'* Structure: followed by kuku- + passive infinitive E&S:47

-mema *v-tr* invite, summon, call; cite, proclaim, exclaim ☞ Pass: -menywa EXXE:56, PCX:89; 103, XED:88

Memela *pn* Memela (personal name) R28

-menywa *v-pass* be invited ☞ rw: -mema PCX:103

Metuse *pn* Metuse (personal name) R26

Mfengu *clan* Mfengu (clan or ethnic group within the greater Xhosa community) CGB:1, MI:273

mfixi *ideophone* be stuffed up (of the nose), have a cold KED:235, XED:89, R30

mfo *n1-sg-red* a fellow, a man R32

-mfusa *atr-root* very dark, dark brown; [ext] purple, maroon, violet ☞ Cf: -fusa [v]; umfusa [n2] EXD:494, KED:235, RD-96:397;111, UEX:14, Uys:4, XED:41,89, R34.7.8

mgaqosiseko *n2-sg-cmp-red* Constitution ☞ See: umgaqosiseko R21

Mgudlwa *pn* Mgudlwa (author's surname) R37=2

mhla *conj-rel* when, the day that Structure: followed by relative construction E&S:36

mhlaba *n2-sg-red* the world R32

mhlawumbi *adv* perhaps [lit: another day] AM-94:115, E&S:59, XED:89, R17.6

mhle *adj-red* nice, pleasant, beautiful R29

mhleli *n1-sg-voc* editor! [vocative] term of address ☞ See: umhleli R17.1, R20

-mhlophe *atr-root* white; clear; clean; pure (water); bright • *amanzi amhlophe 'pure water'; izulu limhlophe 'the sky is clear'* ☞ Cf: -mnyama 'black' AM-94:107, CGB:172f, E&S:30, EXD:723, NDK-91:339, RD-96:397, UEX:14, Uys:4, XED:89;60, R34.11, R37

mhlotsheni *loc* in the light ☞ rw: -mhlophe XED:89

Mhonto *pn* Mhonto (personal name) R32.5

mi-[1] *n2-pl-red-prf* [group 2 plural reduced noun prefix] • *le minyaka 'these years'* Loss of article i- from imi- R20

mi-[2] *n2-pl-adj-pred* they are ADJ [group 2 plural adjective agreement prefix used predicatively] E&S:28, MI:248, PCX:118f

mibandela *n2-pl-red* amendments • *nale mibandela 'and these amendments'* R21.1

mibutho *n2-pl-red* organizations ☞ See: imibutho R37

midaka *n2-pl-red* common people ☞ Red: imidaka R17.7

mihla *n2-pl-red-time* days ☞ See: imihla (umhla) R9, R28, R31, R33, R37

mini *qw-n2-pl* what kind?, of what sort? • *mibuzo mini? 'what sort of questions?'* ☞ See: -ni PCX:28; 118

-minxa *v-tr* hold s.t. tight, press, squeeze, interlock, pinch, choke XED:89, R36.1

minyaka *n2-pl-red* years ☞ See: iminyaka R20, R28, R31.1

-misa *v-caus* make stand; institute, set up, erect; establish, ordain; appoint (to a position); restore, make restitution; stop (a vehicle) ☞ rw: -ma XED:89f, R4dx, R33

misebenzi *n2-pl-red* jobs ☞ See: imisebenzi R29

-misela *v-ben* set up, establish; appoint s.o. for / to (a position); restore, compensate for; substantiate ☞ rw: -ma XED:90, R4dx, R29x

mix *n5-sg-red* mix ☞ See: iJikelele Sishebo Mix R8=2

-mka *v-intr* leave, depart latent vowel verb ☞ Cf: imka CGB:42; 125, E&S:51

ml *abr* milliliters R8=4

mlawuli *n1-sg* ruler, governor R21

mlesi *loan* reader R20

mlimi *n1-sg-red* farmer R28

mna *pro-1sg-abs* I; myself; as for me • *ngokwendlela mna endibona 'the way I see it'* AM-94:92; 163, CGB:158, E&S:21, PCX:29, R4a, R4c, R4d, R11, R33=2

Mnamata *pn* Mnamata (family name) R5

-mnandi *atr-root* nice, good, pleasant, delightful; a pleasure; fine, smooth, soft; fun; sweet, delicious; refined, civil, polite ☞ Cf: -krakra 'bitter', -muncu 'sour' AM-94:107, CGB:121; 172, E&S:30, XED:90, R14, R23, R29, R31, R36

Mncedisi *pn* Mncedisi (personal name) R4a

mni[1] *qw-n1-sg* what kind?, of what sort? • *mntu mni? 'what sort of person?'* ☞ See: -ni PCX:28; 118

mni[2] *qw-n2-sg* what kind?, of what sort? • *mbuzo mni? 'what sort of question?'* ☞ See: -ni PCX:28; 118

mntu *n1-sg-red* person; someone R31=2

mntwana *n1-sg-red* child R19

-mnyama *atr-root* black; dark; low, base ☞ Cf: -mhlophe 'white' AM-94:107, CGB:172f, E&S:30, EXD:57; 143, NDK-91:30; 70, RD-96:398;60, UEX:14, Uys:4, XED:90, R5, R31, R34

Mofula *pn* Mofula (personal name) R33

molo *intj-sg* good morning!, hello! ☞ Pl: molweni E&S:59, XED:90, R23=2

molweni *intj-pl* good morning!, hello! [to a group] ☞ Sg: molo E&S:59, XED:90

-momoza *v-intr* increase, grow; bush out luxuriously • *imali imomoza 'money will grow astonishingly'* R34.10

motel *n5-sg-red-loan* motel R26

moya *n2-sg-red* wind, air, breath; spirit, ghost • *inqwelo-moya 'airplane'* reduced form is used in compounds KED:237, R13=2, R24

Mozambique *loan* Mozambique R15=2

mpawu *n6-pl-red* signs, indications, symptoms ☞ See: iimpawu R30=2

mpela *adv* entirely R36

mpengempenge *n-redup* half-clad person; open, airy place ☞ See: kwampenge-mpenge XED:90, R36.11

mphathi *n1-sg-red* director, manager R27.3

Mpilo *pn* (Xhosa personal name) • *u-Desmond Mpilo Tutu* R32.7

Mpondo *clan* Pondo, Mpondo (most remote clan or ethnic group within the greater Xhosa community, formerly had the least contact with Whites) ☞ See: umPondo, amamPondo AXG:20, CGB:1-4; 109, MI:273, XED:129

Mpondomise *clan* Mpondomise (clan or ethnic group within the greater Xhosa community) CGB:1, MI:273

Mrs. *abr* Mrs. R5

msebenzi *n2-sg-red* work, job, employment; labor, task; duty; trade, occupation; use, service ☞ See: umsebenzi R7, R29=6

msinya *adv-time* soon; quickly ☞ Alt: kamsinya XED:91; 67

msinyane *adv-time* soon; quickly ☞ Alt: kamsinyane XED:91; 67

-msulwa *atr-root* pure, innocent, faultless ☞ rw: -sula XED:91;155, R11

mthetho *n2-sg-red* law, rule, regulation ☞ See: umthetho R11=3, R21, R31, R36=2

mthethweni *loc-n2-sg* in the law; [atr] lawful R36.0

-mthubi *atr-root* yellow (as egg yolk); cream-colored; bright (of sun) (CGB:172f), (RD-96:398), EXD:737, XED:168, R34

Mthumele *pn* (personal name) R26.5

Mtika *pn* Mtika (family name) R18=2

mtsha *adj-red* new R25

-muncu *atr-root* sour ☞ Cf: -krakra 'bitter', -mnandi 'sweet' CGB:172

musa uku- -a *v-aux-neg-imp-sg* don't, do not VERB!, stop, refrain from VERBing [negative imperative singular] • *Musa ukulipha 'Don't give it!'; Musa ukuthetha! 'Don't speak!'* Structure: musa uku-Δ-a (followed by infinitive construction) ☞ Red: suku- -a E&S:47, PCX:43f, XED:91, R6

musa ukulipha *v-neg-imp* don't give it R6

musani uku- -a *v-aux-neg-imp-pl* do not VERB!, stop, refrain from VERBing [negative imperative singular] • *Musani ukuza! 'Don't go!'* Structure: musani uku-Δ-a PCX:43f

Musquito *loan* Mosquito (nickname) R33

mveliso *n5-sg-red* produce ☞ See: imveliso R29

Mxenge *pn* Mxenge (family name) ☞ See: Victoria Mxenge R32=2

mxhaka *n2-sg-red* ivory armband R32

Mxoli *pn* Mxoli (family name) R17.7

myalelo *n2-sg-red* instruction, direction ☞ See: umyalelo R6

-mzaba *atr-root* blue NDK-91:494

Mzantsi *n2-sg-red* South • *Mzantsi Afrika 'South Africa'* PCX:203, R10, R16, R22.1, R24.3

N

n-[1] *pro-2pl-S1-prf* you (all) [short form before vowel initial root] • *Nenza 'you are doing' = n(i)-enza* CGB:125

-n-[2] *pro-2pl-obj-prf* you (all) [short object form before vowel initial verb] ☞ Alt: -ni- E&S:18

N. H. Agencies *loan* N. H. Agencies (distributor of herbal medicines) R25

na-[1] *pro-2pl-S3b-pos* (and) you (all) VERBed [S3b past subjunctive positive subject pronoun] CGB:189, E&S:42, MI:247, SXWU:141

na-[2] *prep-comit-prf* with, along with, together with, accompanied by [comitative] • *nabahlobo 'with friends'* Structure: appears as a prefix before the noun; Note: undergoes sound changes ☞ See: ne-, nee-, no-, noo- AM-94:83, AXG:38f, CGB:149, E&S:21, R5, R8=2, R9, R11, R14

na-[3] *adv-prf* too, also, as well CGB:149, E&S:21, RD-96:398, R1

na-[4] *adv-prf* even [emphatic prefix] with appropriate sound changes ☞ See also: kwa na- EXD:196, R10

na-[5] *conj-prf* and • *abazali nabantwana 'parents and children'* Structure: appears as a prefix before the final noun in a linked series; Note: undergoes sound changes ☞ See: ne-, nee-, no-, noo- AM-94:80, CGB:120; 148, E&S:21, PCX:26, R2=2, R3=2, R4bx=3, R4c, R4d, R7=3, R9=2

na[6] *qw-particle* is it?, isn't it?, then? • *...sokuba ubagcine na abo bahlobo... '...whether you should keep those friends or not...' Also 'Ungubani na?', 'Who is it, then?'* particle often put after a verb or another question word, added for emphasis in questions CGB:129, E&S:33;59, XED91, R6, R9, R11, R14, R29, R30=2, R35, R36, R37=3

-na[7] *v-intr* rain ☞ Cf: imvula [n5-sg] AM-94:112, RD-96:398

na-[8] *v-poss-cmp* have, own, possess [when used with subject and object concord as a verb 'to be;' lit: 'be with'] • *ndinabantwana 'I have children'; ndinemali 'I have some money'* Structure: S1-na/VC-OBJ, i.e., appears as a prefix before the object possessed; Note: undergoes sound changes ☞ See: ne-, nee-, no-, noo- AM-94:84, CGB:150, R2, R3, R4a=2, R4b=2, R4c, R4d, R8, R10, R12=4, R33.9

na- -na *indef-pro* any-, -ever [indefinite pronoun circumfix] • *nakuwuphina 'to anyone'* R9

naba *deic-1-n1-pl-pred-loc* here are [group 1, 1a plural predicate locative] Agr: aba- / oo- AM-94:151, CGB:164, E&S:31, PCX:116, SXWU:153

nababeliqela *v-conj-rel-n1-pl-cop-n3-sg* and who were a gang ☞ See: iqela R36.2

nabacinezelwa *conj-v-rel-ben-pass* and those who are oppressed R32.4

nabahlobo[1] *comit-n1-pl* with friends R14

nabahlobo[2] *conj-n1-pl* and friends R33

nabakumgangatho *conj-n1-pl-comp* and those of the lower classes R37.13

nabangayisebenzisela *conj-n1-pl-pot-n5-sg-v-tr-caus-appl* and they may benefit by it R37.25

nabani *qw* with whom? CGB:129

nabanina *n1-pl* anyone, anybody • *uthe bafuna nabanina onolwazi... 'they said they want anyone with information...'* na +bani + na SZZ:22, R18.6

nabanolwazi *conj-v-poss-rel-n1-pl-rel+n6-sg-obj* and who have knowlege of • *nabanolwazi ngoMgaqo-Siseko 'and who have knowlege of the Constitution'* R37.11

nabantu[1] *comit-n1-pl* with people R29.1.2.5.18

nabantu[2] *n1-pl-conj* and people R9, R35.1

nabantwana *n1-pl-conj* and children R2, R37.24

nabanye[1] *adj-num-n1-pl-comit* with others • *ukudibana nabanye* R34

nabanye[2] *adj-num-n1-pl-conj* and others R3, R32

nabaseki *conj-n1-pl* and establishers R32

nabasetyhini *n3-sg-poss* and women • *amadoda nabasetyhini 'men and women'* R35

nabaya *deic-3-n1-pl-pred-loc* there (far, yonder) are CGB:164, E&S:31, PCX:116

nabazali *conj-n1-pl* and parents R18.1

nabe *preverb-past-pro-2pl* you (all) did VERB; you had VERBed [remote past compound tense preverb] Structure: nabe ni-Δ (participial verb form) ☞ Alt: naye E&S:39, GDX3:714, PCX:186

nabo[1] *comit-n1-pl* with them E&S:21, R5, R14

nabo[2] *n1-pl-conj* and they; and as for them CGB:158, E&S:21, R14=2, R23, R29=2, R36, R37

nabo[3] *n7-conj-pro* and he, she, it; and as for him, her, it CGB:158, E&S:21

nabo[4] *deic-2-n1-pl-pred-loc* there (not far, just mentioned) are CGB:164, E&S:31, PCX:116

nabo[5] *deic-2-n7-sg-pred-loc* there (not far, just mentioned) is CGB:164, E&S:31, PCX:116

nabu *deic-1-n7-sg-pred-loc* here is Agr: ubu- AM-94:151, CGB:164, E&S:31, PCX:116, SXWU:153

nabuya *deic-3-n7-sg-pred-loc* there (far, yonder) is CGB:164, E&S:31, PCX:116

-naka *v-tr* accuse s.o. falsely; get s.o. into trouble XED:92, R4dx

-nakana[1] *v-tr* glimpse, see from afar, have a distant view of s.t.; guess (at), form an idea of; get an inkling of, begin to comprehend, perceive, understand a little KED:242, XED:92, R4d

-nakana[2] *v-recip* accuse one another falsely; get each other into trouble R4dx

nakanjani *conj-adv* anyway R19

nakanjanina *adv* whatever, at all, whatsoever • *Andicingi nakanjanina ukuba ndirhoxe 'I have no intention whatever of resigning'* Structure: placed after a noun in a negative context EXD:721

-nakho uku-[1] *v-abil-cmp-prf* can VERB, be able to VERB [stressing ability to do] Structure: S1-nakho uku-Δ-a ☞ Neg: SNEG-nakho uku-Δ-a E&S:45

-nakho uku-[2] *v-neg-abil-cmp-prf* cannot VERB, not be able to VERB [stressing inability to do] Structure: SNEG-nakho uku-Δ-a ☞ Pos: S1-nakho uku-Δ-a E&S:45

nako[1] *n8-vn-conj-pro* and it; and as for it CGB:158, E&S:21, R37

nako[2] *deic-2-n8-vn-pred-loc* there (not far, just mentioned) is CGB:164, E&S:31, PCX:116

nako[3] *deic-2-n10-loc-pred-loc* there (not far, just mentioned) is PCX:116

-nako[4] *v-aux* can, able to Structure: takes a verb in the infinitive EXD:1

naku-[1] *pro-2pl-temp* when you (all) VERB / VERBed [temporal verb construction] • *Nakufika 'When you arrive...'* E&S:42, PCX:91f

naku[2] *deic-1-n8-vn-pred-loc* here is Agr: uku- AM-94:151, CGB:164, E&S:31, PCX:116, SXWU:153

naku[3] *deic-1-n10-loc-pred-loc* here is Agr: uku- PCX:116

-naku-[4] *v-neg-abil-cmp-prf* can not VERB, be unable / unwilling to VERB = na-(u)ku- (short infinitive); Structure: SNEG-naku-Δ-a ☞ Pos: S1-noku-Δ-a E&S:45

nakuba *conj* although, even though, despite Structure: followed by the participial AXG:151, E&S:41, EXD:196

nakuba kunjalo *conj-expr* even so, although that is the case EXD:196

nakubantu *loc-n1-pl* to the people • *Kwaye kwacaca ke nakubantu 'It had become clear to the people'* na- is bound to the verb -caca, thus nakubantu 'to the people,' not 'and to the people' R37.25

nakule *conj-deic* and at this, and to this [in the sense of 'moving on'] • *Nakule ke ngoku... 'Now moving on to this...'* R20

nakuluntu *loc-n6sg* and from people R35

nakumaziko *conj-loc-n3-pl* and in households R36

nakuwuphi na *pro-indef-n1-sg-loc* in anyone; in whomever R9

nakuya[1] *deic-3-n8-vn-pred-loc* there (far, yonder) is CGB:164, E&S:31, PCX:116

nakuya[2] *deic-3-n10-loc-pred-loc* there (far, yonder) is PCX:116

nakwaLobengula *pn-conj* as well as Lobengula R32

nakwaMzilikazi *pn-loc-conj* (place in Shona region of Zimbabwe, the former Rhodesia) R32

nakwaNdebele *pn-loc-conj* and Ndebele (province in South Africa) R20

nakwaNqabisile *pn-loc-conj* and of Nqabisile R26

nakwi *conj-loc* and in the R33=2

nakwimizi *conj-loc-n2-pl* in the homes • *...kungakhange kuvakale nomkhondo nakwimizi ekufutshane nesi sikolo '...without any visible trace or sound heard, not even by the householders living near the school'* na + kw + imizi R18.2

nakwizindlu *conj-loc-n5-pl* and in houses/buildings R36

nakwizinxiba *conj-loc-n4-pl* and from the wearers • *nakwizinxiba-mxhaka 'and from the wearers of the ivory armlet (i.e., royal councilors)'* R32.4

nalapho *conj-deic-loc* and there R26

nalawo *conj-deic* and those R37

nale *conj-deic* and this, these • *nale mibandela 'and these amendments'* R17.1, R21, R37.20

nali *deic-1-n3-sg-pred-loc* here (it) is Agr: ili- / i- AM-94:151, AXG:15, CGB:164, E&S:31, PCX:116, SXWU:153, XED:92, R34

nalinye *conj-cop-num* a single one R32

naliphina *pro-indef-n3-sg* whatever, whichever EXD:721; 724, R6

naliya *deic-3-n3-sg-pred-loc* there (far, yonder) is AXG:15, CGB:164, E&S:31, PCX:116

nalo[1] *n3-sg-conj-pro* and he, she, it; and as for him, her, it CGB:158, E&S:21

nalo[2] *n6-sg-conj-pro* and he, she, it; and as for him, her, it CGB:158, E&S:21

nalo[3] *deic-2-n3-sg-pred-loc* there (not far, just mentioned) is AXG:15, CGB:164, E&S:31, PCX:116

nalo[4] *deic-2-n6-sg-pred-loc* there (not far, just mentioned) is CGB:164, E&S:31, PCX:116

nalo[5] *deic-conj* with that • *...kunye nalo mntwana. 'together with that child'* agent copulative na- + deic-class1 R19, R27=2, R33, R36

nalu *deic-1-n6-sg-pred-loc* here is Agr: ulu- / u- AM-94:151, CGB:164, E&S:31, PCX:116, SXWU:153

naluloyiko *adv-n6-sg* with fear R36

nalulutsha *adv-n6-sg* by young people R36

naluya *deic-3-n6-sg-pred-loc* there (far, yonder) is CGB:164, E&S:31, PCX:116

nam *pro-1sg-conj* and I; and as for me AM-94:93, CGB:158, E&S:21, R4c, R23, R24

nama *n3-pl-conj-prefix* of [NUM] • *abamalunga nama-250 'a quantity of 250'* R35

-nama ... eminyaka *v-poss-expr* be aged, be NUM years old [lit: has NUM (20 or higher) of years] This is a fixed expression; Structure: SUBJ-nama-NUM eminyaka ☞ See also: -neminyaka engama-NUM R4b, R24=2

namadlagusha *conj-n3-pl* with the Afrikaner (Boer) government R20

namadoda *conj-n3-pl* and men R31, R36

namagorhakazi *conj-n3-pl* and brave women R32

namagumbi *n3-pl* with rooms R35

namahlaba *conj-n3-pl* and pains in the lungs R25

namakhwenkwana *conj-n3-pl* and the boys R36

namalaphu *conj-n3-pl* fabric, cloth R28

namalungelo *adv-n3-pl* with rights R35

namandla *v-poss-atr* strong, powerful, forcible [lit: having force] EXD:226, XED:97, R12

namantombazana *conj-n3-pl* and girls R36

namany *conn-enum-red* other R36

namanye *conn-enum* and others R32, R33

namanzi *comit-n3-pl* with water R8

namapolisa *conj-n3-pl* and the police R27, R28

namaqanda *conj-n3-pl* and the eggs R25

namaqhakuva *n3-pl* and pimples R25=2

namatshamba *conj-n3-pl* of a great feast R31

namatutu *comit-n3-pl* with cattle-rustlers R26.3

namava *n3-pl-conj* and experience R4d

namaxhwele *conj-n3-pl* and herbalists • *ilungu lombutho wamagqirha namaxhwele 'member of the association of witch doctors and herbalists'* ☞ rw: ixhwele R7

namhlanje *adv-time* today; nowadays, of the day, the present day • *imivuzo ephantsi nanamhlanje 'today's low wages'* AM-94:112, AXG:143, E&S:59, EXD:669, MI:231; 256, PCX:36f, R10, R17.3, R32.9, R37.19

Nampura *pn-geog* Nampura R15

nanamhlanje *adv-time-conj* and today R10

nandlela *n5-sg* with the way R32

nanga *deic-1-n3-pl-pred-loc* here are Agr: ama- AM-94:151, CGB:164, E&S:31, PCX:116, SXWU:153, XED:93

nangamanye *adv-enum* by others R36

nangaphandle *adv-loc-conj* and on the outside; and also outside R25, R36=2

nangaya *deic-3-n3-pl-pred-loc* there (far, yonder) are CGB:164, E&S:31, PCX:116, XED:93

nangeminqweno *conj-n2-pl* and through desires R34.3

nango[1] *deic-2-n2-sg-pred-loc* there (not far, just mentioned) is; here it is CGB:164, E&S:31, PCX:116, XED:93, R20.7

nango[2] *deic-2-n3-pl-pred-loc* there (not far, just mentioned) are CGB:164, E&S:31, PCX:116, XED:93

nangoko *adv-time* even then ☞ Contrast: nangoku 'even now' EXD:196

nangoku *adv-time* even now; and now ☞ Contrast: nangoko 'even then' EXD:196, R36=2

nangokuthi *conj-adv-v-inf-red* and by saying R27

nangomso *adv-time* even tomorrow R5

nangona[1] *conj* although, even if; even though; even supposing • *Nangona umthetho waseMzantsi-Afrika ukuchaza ukudlwengula njengo 'Although South African law defines rape thus'; Nangona kungathandabuzeki ukuba ngabafazi namantombazana abadlwengulwa 'Although it is not doubtful that it is women and girls who get raped'* Structure: followed by participial construction E&S:36, R10, R18.5, R23.6, R33.9, R36.00.08, R37.12

nangona[2] *conj* although, even if; even though; even supposing • *Nangona eli ilinyathelo eliya phambili 'Although this is a step forward'* Structure: followed by relative construction ☞ Alt: nangani, noko E&S:36, MI:257, XED:93, R10

nangu *deic-1-n2-sg-pred-loc* here is Agr: um- AM-94:151, CGB:164, E&S:31, PCX:116, SXWU:153, XED:93

nanguthathatha *n1a-sg-agent-adv* even by a kid • *Le nto yaziwa nanguthathatha 'Even a little child knows this' [Xhosa newspaper column]* GDX3:279, R10

nanguya *deic-3-n2-sg-pred-loc* there (far, yonder) is CGB:164, E&S:31, PCX:116, XED:93

nani[1] *pro-2pl-conj* and you; and as for you CGB:158, E&S:21, XED:93

nani-[2] *pro-2pl-remote-past* you (all) had VERBed [contracted remote past compound tense] AXG:93f, E&S:39, PCX:186

naninina *conj,-adv* whenever (at whatever time) EXD:722

nanje *conj* and R34.12

nanjengoko *adv-cmp* even as R36=3

nanko *deic-2-n1-sg-pred-loc* there (not far, just mentioned) is CGB:164, E&S:31, PCX:116, XED:93

nanku *deic-1-n1-sg-pred-loc* here is [group 1, 1a singular predicate locative] Agr: um- / u- AM-94:151, CGB:164, E&S:31, PCX:116, SXWU:153, XED:93

nankuya *deic-3-n1-sg-pred-loc* there (far, yonder) is CGB:164, E&S:31, PCX:116, XED:93

nantsi[1] *deic-1-n2-pl-pred-loc* here are Agr: imi- AM-94:151, CGB:164, E&S:31, PCX:116, SXWU:153, XED:93

nantsi[2] *deic-1-n5-sg-pred-loc* here is Agr: i- / iN- AM-94:151, CGB:164, E&S:31, PCX:116, SXWU:153, XED:93

nantsiya[1] *deic-3-n2-pl-pred-loc* there (far, yonder) are CGB:164, E&S:31, PCX:116, XED:93

nantsiya[2] *deic-3-n5-sg-pred-loc* there (far, yonder) is CGB:164, E&S:31, PCX:116, XED:93

nantso[1] *deic-2-n2-pl-pred-loc* there (not far, just mentioned) are CGB:164, E&S:31, PCX:116, XED:93

nantso[2] *deic-2-n5-sg-pred-loc* there (not far, just mentioned) is CGB:164, E&S:31, PCX:116, XED:93

-nanza *v-tr* like, approve of, be pleased with; care for, pay attention to; consider, look at with recognition; admire; [neg] dislike, not care for, care little for XED:93, R37.20.21

nanzi[1] *deic-1-n5-pl-pred-loc* here are Agr: iiN- / iziN- AM-94:151, CGB:164, E&S:31, PCX:116

nanzi[2] *deic-1-n6-pl-pred-loc* here are Agr: ii- / iziN- CGB:164

nanziya[1] *deic-3-n5-pl-pred-loc* there (far, yonder) are CGB:164, E&S:31, PCX:116

nanziya[2] *deic-3-n6-pl-pred-loc* there (far, yonder) are CGB:164

nanzo[1] *deic-2-n5-pl-pred-loc* there (not far, just mentioned) are CGB:164, E&S:31, PCX:116

nanzo[2] *deic-2-n6-pl-pred-loc* there (not far, just mentioned) are CGB:164

naphakade *adv-time* ever; [neg] never AXG:143; 214, CGB:178, XED:93

naphi na *adv-indef* everywhere; wherever ☞ Alt sp: naphina EXD:197, R30

naseColchester *n5-sg-pn-conj-loc* and in Colchester R24

naseHorseshoe Motel *n5-sg-conj-loc* and at the Horseshoe Motel R26

nasekulandiseni *n8-vn-conj-loc* and in expanding it loc. from -andis- to enlarge XED:3, R35

nasemadolweni *n3-pl-conj-loc* and on the knees ☞ See: idolo R32

nasemakhayeni *n3-pl-conj-loc* and to homes R9

nasemini *n5-sg-time-conj-loc* and during the day R2

nasemiphakathweni *n2-pl-conj-loc* and in the palms of the hands R30

nasemlonyeni *conj-loc-n2-sg* and in the mouth ☞ See: umlomo R36.21

nasezintsweni *n5-pl-conj-loc* and in the kidneys R25

nasi *deic-1-n4-sg-pred-loc* here is Agr: isi- AM-94:151, CGB:164, E&S:31, PCX:116, SXWU:153, XED:93

nasiphina *pro-indef-n4-sg* whatever, whichever EXD:721

nasiya *deic-3-n4-sg-pred-loc* there (far, yonder) is CGB:164, E&S:31, PCX:116, XED:93

naso[1] *n4-sg-conj-pro* and he, she, it; and as for him, her, it CGB:158, E&S:21, XED:93

naso[2] *deic-2-n4-sg-pred-loc* there (not far, just mentioned) is CGB:164, E&S:31, PCX:116, XED:93

nathe *v-aux* should be • *nathe akananzwa zibhodi 'should not be those preferred by the boards'* R37.20

nathi[1] *pro-1pl-comit* with us GDX3:293, R9

nathi[2] *pro-1pl-conj* and we; and as for us CGB:158, E&S:21

National *loan* National R37

nawe[1] *pro-2sg-comit* with you • *Baya kuba kunye nawe 'They will be together with you'; uthandane nawe 'she is in love with you'* R14, R19

nawe[2] *pro-2sg-conj* and you; and as for you AM-94:93, CGB:158, E&S:21

nawo[1] *n2-sg-conj-pro* and he, she, it; and as for him, her, it CGB:158, E&S:21

nawo[2] *n3-pl-conj-pro* and they; and as for them • *amapolisa ... nawo 'the police also...'* na + wo(na) [lit: and them - in the sense above has meaning of 'also'] CGB:158, E&S:21, R13, R26, R36=3

nawobunzima *conj-poss-n7-sg* and of difficulty R14

nawokuvala *conj-v-tr-inf* and the closing of (companies for Christmas) R31

nawuphina *pro-indef-n1-sg* anyone, whoever R37.2

naxa *conj-rel* and whenever R37=2

naye[1] *comit-n1-sg* with him R26

naye[2] *n1-sg-conj* and he, and she; and as for him, her CGB:158, E&S:21, R37

naye[3] *preverb-past-pro-2pl* you (all) did VERB; you had VERBed [remote past compound tense preverb] Structure: naye ni-Δ (participial verb form) ☞ Alt: nabe AXG:93f, E&S:39, GDX3:714

nayiphina *pro-indef-n5-sg* any, whatever, whichever • *Nayiphina into oyithethayo andikukholelwa 'Whatever you say, I don't believe you'; nayiphi na indoda 'any man'* ☞ Alt sp: nayiphi na EXD:721; 724, R30.7, R36.21

nayo[1] *n2-pl-conj-pro* and they; and as for them CGB:158, E&S:21

nayo[2] *n5-sg-conj-pro* and he, she, it; and as for him, her, it CGB:158, E&S:21, R37

nazi *deic-1-n4-pl-pred-loc* here are Agr: izi- AM-94:151, CGB:164, E&S:31, PCX:116, SXWU:153

naziphina[1] *pro-indef-n4-pl* whatever, whichever EXD:724

naziphina[2] *pro-indef-n5-pl* whatever, whichever EXD:724

naziya *deic-3-n4-pl-pred-loc* there (far, yonder) are CGB:164, E&S:31, PCX:116

nazo[1] *n4-pl-conj-pro* and they; also (them); and as for them CGB:158, E&S:21, R1

nazo[2] *comit-n4-pl* with them E&S:21, R34

nazo[3] *n5-pl-conj-pro* and they; also (them); and as for them CGB:158, E&S:21

nazo[4] *comit-n5-pl* with them E&S:21, R33

nazo[5] *n6-pl-conj-pro* and they; also (them); and as for them CGB:158

nazo[6] *deic-2-n4-pl-pred-loc* there (not far, just mentioned) are CGB:164, E&S:31, PCX:116

nazo[7] *deic-2-n5-pl-conn* of them, of those R30, R37

-nceda[1] *v-tr* help, aid, assist XED:94, R12

-nceda[2] *preverb* please • *bancede bangazihluphi 'they should please not waste their time'* Structure: nceda S3a Δ-e (used with the present subjunctive) CGB:170, R4c

-ncedakala *v-atr* be helped, get assisted KED:248, R33.9, R37.16

-ncikane *adj-root* little, small ☞ Alt: -ncinci, -ncinane PCX:120

-ncinane *adj-root* small (very small), little, slight, tiny; young ☞ Alt: -ncinci, -ncikane AXG:63, CGB:171; 179, E&S:30, PCX:120

-ncinci *adj-root* small ☞ Alt: -ncinane, -ncikane AXG:63, CGB:171, E&S:30, PCX:120

-ncipha *v-intr* reduce, grow less, diminish, become smaller, decline • *Caus: -nciphisa* XED:95

-nciphisa *v-tr* reduce, lessen, diminish, make smaller ☞ Pass: -ncitshiswa PCX:103, XED:95

-ncitshiswa *v-pass* be lessened, reduced ☞ rw: -ncipha PCX:103, XED:95

-ncoka *v-intr* chat, converse; joke (around) XED:95

-ncokola *v-ben* converse with; hold a friendly conversation, joke (around with); [ext] gossip PCX:36f, XED:95, R37.27

ncwadana *n5-sg-dim-red* booklet ☞ See: incwadana R22=4, R30

nd-[1] *pro-1sg-S1-prf* I [short form before vowel initial root] • *Ndazi 'I know' = nd(i)-azi* CGB:119; 125

-nd-[2] *pro-1sg-obj-prf* me [short object form before vowel initial verb] ☞ Alt: -ndi- E&S:18

nda- *pro-1sg-S3b-pos* (and) I VERBed [S3b past

subjunctive/Remote Past (see Note) positive subject pronoun] CGB:189, E&S:42, MI:247, SXWU:141, R4a

ndaba *n6-pl-red* news; information ☞ See: iindaba (udaba) R23.8, R29=2

ndabangela *v-tr-past* I caused R33

ndabanjwa *v-pass-past-sub* I was arrested R4a

ndabe *preverb-past-pro-1sg* I did VERB; I had VERBed [remote past compound tense preverb] Structure: ndabe ndi-Δ (participial verb form) ☞ Alt: ndaye E&S:39, GDX3:714, PCX:186

ndafunda *v-past-sub* and I learned R33

ndagqwesa *v-pro-1sg-past-sub* I won R33

ndaku- *pro-1sg-temp* when I VERB / VERBed [temporal verb construction] • *Ndakufika 'When I arrive'* E&S:42, PCX:91f

ndambhatala *v-tr-past* I paid him R26

ndandi- *pro-1sg-remote-past* I had VERBed [contracted remote past compound tense] • *Ndandimele uMzantsi Afrika kwiWorld Cross Country 'I had represented South Africa in the World Cross Country Race'* AXG:93f, E&S:39, PCX:185, R33=2, R36=5

ndandibaleka *v-remote-past* I had run R33

ndandijongene *v-remote-past* I had faced R36

ndandimele *v-remote-past* I had represented R33

ndandingabanqandayo *v-rel-remote-past* whereby I could stop them R36

ndandiqhokrekile *v-remote-past-perf* I had become paralyzed R36

ndandisazi *v-remote-past* I had known Note -sa- (-s-) aux prefix 'already' R36

ndandisithi *v-cmp-remote-past* I had thought = ndaba ndisithi (reduced to ndandisithi) R36.6

ndaphuma *v-intr-past* I came out R33

ndaqala *v-past-sub* I began R33

ndathandana *v-recip-1sg* I fell in love with R19.1

ndawo *n5-sg-red* place R20.6, R35, R36

ndaye *preverb-past-pro-1sg* I did VERB; I had VERBed [remote past compound tense preverb] Structure: ndaye ndi-Δ (participial verb form) ☞ Alt: ndabe AXG:93f, E&S:39, GDX3:714, R19.1

ndaza *aux.* and then (in the past) XED:189, R33

ndazalelwa *v-ben* I was born at R28

ndaziva *v-tr-past* I felt R36

ndedwa *pro-quan-1sg* I alone; just me; by myself Agr: ndi-, mna ☞ Alt: ndodwa E&S:27, PCX:62

ndenze *v-sub* I did, I have done • *bendifanele ukuba ndenze njalo 'I probably should have done that'* after complementizer ukuba, nd(i)enze is in the subjunctive mood ☞ rw: -enza 'do' R23.6

ndi-[1] *pro-1sg-S1-prf* I • *Ndifuna iqabanekazi 'I am looking for a female friend'* CGB:115; 158, E&S:18, RD-96:373, SXWU:29, XED:xvi, R3, R4a=4, R4c=3, R4d=4, R9, R12, R23

ndi-[2] *pro-1sg-S2-prf* I VERBing [S2 participial subject] AXG:89; 91, CGB:191, R36.6

ndi-[3] *pro-1sg-S3a-prf* (and) I VERB [S3a present subjunctive subject pronoun] CGB:167

ndi-[4] *pro-1sg-S4* I can VERB; I may VERB [first person singular potential / conditional verb subject (S4) agreement pronoun] E&S:45, PCX:166, SXWU:149

ndi-[5] *pro-1sg-pred-prf* I am [copulative or predicative prefix construction] • *ndim 'it is I'* E&S:21, PCX:97, XED:xvi, R4c

-ndi-[6] *pro-1sg-obj-prf* me E&S:18, SXWU:44, R4a, R4c, R12

ndi-[7] *pro-1sg-dir-rel2* I who [direct relative 2] • *mna ndivelayo 'I who see'* E&S:34n

ndi-[8] *pro-1sg-ind-rel2* me whom [indirect relative 2] E&S:35

ndibaleka *v-intr* I run R33

ndibaleke *v-intr-sub* that I run R33

ndibe *preverb-recent-pro-1sg* I was VERBing [recent past compound tense preverb] Structure: ndibe ndi-Δ (participial construction) AXG:91f, E&S:37f, PCX:183

ndibhalisele *v-caus-ben* I registered • *Andizange ndibhalisele irhafu ngaphambili 'I was never on the tax register before this'* R23.6

ndibongoza *v-tr* I beseech, implore, entreat R16

ndicela *v-pres-1sg* I request, I'm asking for R4a, R12

ndicinga *v-intr* I think R3, R33

ndifumane *v-tr-sub* that I get R33

ndifuna *v-pres-1sg* I want (to); I am looking for PCX:20, R4a, R4c, R4d=2, R23, R37.17

ndihamba *v-pres-1sg* I go R4a

ndikhathazwa *v-pass* I am troubled R9

ndikho *v-exis-pro-1sg* I am here / present E&S:29

ndikhuthazwa *v-pass-part* I having been encouraged R33.2

ndikuvile *v-tr-perf* I heard R23

ndikwave *v-tr-perf* I heard them R36

ndilusizi *expr* I am sorry!, Pardon me! [lit: I am sad] PCX:37

ndiluthumele *v-sub-pro-1sg-S3a+n6-sg-obj* that I send it R23.3

ndiluzalise *v-tr-sub* that I fill it (a form) R23

ndim *pro-1sg-pred* I am; it is I [copulative or predicative] AXG:44f, E&S:21, PCX:97

ndimbuna *1sg-atr* I'm docile R36

ndimele *v-intr-perf* I stood for R24

ndineminyaka *v-poss* I am NUM years old R4a, R28

ndinenkolo *cop-n5-sg* I have faith R33

ndinentlaninge *v-poss* I have plenty R33

ndinethemba *v-poss* I have hope R33

ndingavuya *v-pot* I would be glad, grateful R16

ndingawufezi *v-pot-neg* I do not accomplish it • *Akukho nto kundinqanda ndingawufezi umnqweno wam 'There is nothing to stop me from achieving my objective' [note double negative construction]* R33.11

ndingazange *v-aux-past* I never R23

ndingemntu *1sg-neg-n1-sg* I am not a person R36

ndingumfana *cop-n1-sg* I am a young man R19.1

ndingumyeni *pro-1sg-pred* I am a husband R4d

ndini *voc* oh!, hey! [emphatic vocative marker] • *mfo ndini 'my dear fellow!'* follows the noun in the vocative form AXG:28, XED:97; 37

ndinokufika *v-abil* I can reach R33.10

ndinomsindo *v-poss-n2-sg-obj* I had an outburst of anger R36

ndiqalise *v-caus* I made myself begin R33

ndisafunda *v-tr* I am still studying R33

ndisakopha *v-prog-part* whilst I still bled R36

ndisathandana *v-recip* I still fall in love R4d

ndisebenzisa *v-tr-caus* I use R33

ndiseke *v-sub* that I support R20

ndiselula *v-atr-past-prog* I was already easily R33.2

ndisesikolweni *cop-loc-n4-sg* I was still in school R19.1

ndishiya *v-tr* I passed R33

ndisoloko *atr-pro-1sg* I always R33=2

ndithanda *v-pres* I like; I want R4c

ndithandazela *v-tr-ben* I pray, I intercede for R33

ndithetha *v-tr* I say R11

ndithi *v-tr* I say R20

nditsho *v-intr* I say so R17.3

nditshoyo *v-pres-rel* I say so R17.7

ndiya *v-aux-fut* I will • *ndiya kwenza njalo 'I will do the same'* R4c, R33

ndiya kwenza *v-fut* I will do R4c

ndiyabazonda *v-pro-1sg-long-pres-n1-pl-obj* I feel strongly about them R11

ndiyayibamba *v-tr* I am keeping R23

ndiyazi *v-tr* I understand R23

ndiyigxininise *v-tr* I should emphasise R37

ndiyintombazana *pro-1sg-pred-expr* I am a single girl R4c

ndiyoyika *v-tr* I'm afraid R23=2

ndiza *v-aux-fut* I will R23.12

ndizakuhlawuliswa *v-tr-fut-pass* I will be fined R23

ndizalisa *v-tr-caus* I'm filling R23

ndizihlawule *v-tr-sub* I should pay R23

Ndlambe *pn* Ndlambe (Xhosa chief of Rharhabe clan who resisted the colonial forces during the Frontier Wars) ☞ Cf: Ngqika CGB:4

-ndle *root* out (in the open) ☞ See: indle, endle, phandle, ngaphandle PCX:70, XED:97, R3, R19.3.5, R21.3, R23.7, R26.7, R35.10

ndlela *n5-sg-red* path; way; means ☞ See: indlela R29, R36, R37

ndo- *v-pro-1sg-short-fut* I will VERB [contracted / short positive future pronoun prefix] CGB:165, E&S:20, R23

ndoda *n5-sg-red* man, male ☞ See: indoda R36

ndodwa *pro-quan-1sg* I alone; just me; by myself ☞ See: ndedwa E&S:27n, PCX:62

ndohlwaywe *v-sub-fut* and I will be punished R23.5

Ndondo *pn* Ndondo (family name) ☞ See: Bathandwa Ndondo R32

ndonke *pro-enum-1sg* all of me; the whole of me Agr: ndi-, mna E&S:27, PCX:62

ne-[1] *combo* and, as well as • *umbuzo nempendulo 'question and answer'; kunye ne-High Blood pressure 'as well as High Blood pressure'* indicates that the conjunctive prefix (na-) is linked to a noun prefixed with the article i-; part of kunye ne- ☞ See: na- + i-; kunye na- AM-94:80, CGB:120, PCX:27, R12, R25

ne-[2] *combo* with, together with • *baphe nerayisi 'serve them with rice'* indicates that the comitative prefix (na-) is linked to a noun prefixed with the article i- ☞ See: na- + i- R8

ne-[3] *combo* have OBJECT • *umntu onemali 'someone who has money'; neAIDS 'have AIDS'* indicates that the possessive verb (na-) has a n5 sg object (i-) ☞ See: na- + i- R4d, R12, R30=3

-ne[4] *adj-root* four AM-94:76, AXG:64, CGB:171, E&S:30, PCX:120

nebeleko *conj-n5-sg* and the uterus R25.2

nebezikade *conj-cop-adv-adj* and those of long ago R37

nebezikhona *v-aux-loc* as those which were there R37

nebhanki *conj-n5-sg* and the bank R37

neBrand Manager *loan* and Brand Manager R29

nedwa *pro-quan-2pl* you alone; just you (all) Agr: ni-, nina ☞ Alt: nodwa E&S:27, PCX:62

nee- *combo* and • *Galela iitumato, iminqathe, iitapile neegreen beans 'Mix in the tomatoes, carrots, potatoes and green beans'* indicates that the conjunctive prefix (na-) is linked to n5-pl (ii-) ☞ See: na- + ii- AM-94:80, CGB:120, R8, R9

neebhedi *n5-pl* and beds R35

neediphu *conj-n5-pl* and dippping tanks R27

neegreen beans *n5-pl-conj* and green beans R8

neelwimi *n5-pl* and languages R37.5

neembiza *conj-n5-pl* like pots R35

neeminyazi *conj-n2-pl* like rush baskets na + iminyazi ☞ umnyazi XED:116, R35

neemvakalelo *conj-n5-pl* and the emotions R14

neen- *combo* and; with; also • *neenguqu 'with the changes'; kukwakho neendawo 'there are also places'* indicates that the comitative preposition (na-) is linked to n5 pl (iin-) ☞ See: na- + iin- R28.4, R30, R32, R33.11, R35, R36.11

neendawo *conj-n5-pl* also places R36.11

neendebe *conj-n5-pl* and trophies R33.11

neenduli *conj-n5-pl* and hills R28.4

neengutyana *conj-n5-pl* and small blankets R35.6

neenkampu *conj-n5-pl* and camps R36.9

neenkqubo *adv-n5-pl* with procedures R35.5

neentsizi *conj-n5-pl* and grief R36

neenyawo *conj-n6-pl* and feet • *izandla neenyawo 'hands and feet'* R30.3, R32.4

neetitshala *conj-n5-pl* and teachers R9

neewardrobhu *loan* wardrobe R35

negalelo *conj-n5-sg* having a contribution R29.8, R35.14

negazi *comit-n3-sg* with blood R25

negqala *n3-sg-conj* and an observer R32

negqiza *n3-sg-conj* and a small group R17.6

negxobha *conj-n5-sg* and affect R36.24

nekhondom *comit-n5-sg* with a condom R30

nekhulu *conj-n3-sg* with a hundred R33

nekungakhange *conj-inf-neg-aux* that did not ever R18

nelayisensi *conj-n5-sg-loan* license R31

neLetaba After-Care Centre *n5-sg-cmp-pn-conj* and / with the Letaba After-Care Center R35

nelingumhlolokazi *conj-rel-n1-sg* and who is a widow R24.5

nelizwe *conj-n3-sg* and the [his] country R16

nelo *v-poss-deic* have that R36

Nelson *pn* (personal name) R32

nemeko *conj-n5-sg* and the quality R34.12

nemfundo *conj-n2-sg* and/with learning R22

nemfuno *conj-n5-sg* with the wants R37

nemfuyo *conj-n5-sg* and livestock R13

nemi-[1] *combo* have OBJECT; also had OBJECT • *iqabanekazi elineminyaka engama-20 'a female friend who is 20 years old'* indicates that the possessive verb (V + na-) has a n2 pl object (imi-) ☞ See: na- + imi- R4a=2, R4b, R4c, R4d

nemi-[2] *combo* here, like • *zifana nemizi yazo 'they are similar to their homes'* indicates that the preposition (na-) is linked to n2 pl (imi-) ☞ See: na- + imi- R11

nemibutho *conj-n2-pl* and organizations R37=2

nemibuzo *conj-n2-pl* and questions, or 'with questions' • *Kukho nemibuzo 'there are (many) questions'* na+ (i)mibuzo R22

neminyaka *v-poss* has / have years R4a=2, R4b, R4c, R4d

-neminyaka ... engama *v-poss-rel-n2-pl-pred-num-n3-pl-expr* be aged, be NUM years old Followed by a number in the fixed expression: -neminyaka engama-NUM ☞ See also: -nama-NUM eminyaka EXD:417, R4a=2, R4c, R19=2

neminye *conj-enum* and others R37=2

nemithandazo *conj-n2-pl* the prayers R13

nemithetho *v-poss-n2-pl-obj* having laws R11

nemithinjana *conj-n2-pl* and young people (of both sexes) R36

nemizi *conj-n2-pl* with homes • *zifana nemizi yazo 'they are similar to their homes'* R11

nemizuzwana *n2-pl-dim-conj* and seconds R33=3

nempahla *n5-sg* and clothes R35

nemveliso *conj-n5-sg* with produce R29

nemvisiswano *n5-sg-conj* and mutual understanding R13

nen- *combo* have OBJECT • *ukuze isizwe sibe nenkqubela 'so that the nation may have progress'* indicates that the possessive verb (na-) has a n5 sg object (in-) ☞ See: na- + in- R3

nenceba *conj-n5-sg* mercy R31

nendala *adj-n5-sg* and old R25

nendibano yesondo *v-poss-cmp* have sexual relations • *xa unendibano yesondo 'when you have sex'* R30

nendlela *conj-n5-sg-pred* and is the way R37=2

nene *n-root* right (side); truth ☞ See: inene, kanene, kunene, ngenene, okunene, ubunene, ukunene XED:98, R12

nengozi *n5-sg-poss-atr* dangerous [lit: having danger] EXD:143, XED:47

nengulo *conj-n5-sg* and the illness Note: ingulo is not normally found in either Xhosa or Zulu, but by productivity rules, we can interpret it as 'sickness' R25.7

nengxaki *conj-n5-sg* with problems; having trouble R36, R37

nenkantsi *v-poss-n5-sg-obj* numb, benumbed [lit: having numbness] XED:68, R25

nenkqubela *v-poss* have progress R3

nenkwenkwe *conj-n5-sg* and a boy R28

neNLP *pn-conj* and the NLP R37

nentlaninge *n5-sg-conj* and an abundance R32

nentombazana *conj-n5-sg* with a girl R19.1

nentsebenziswano *conj-n5-sg-recip* and working together R34

-nenxaxheba *v-poss-cmp* have a share / role in s.t.; show interest in s.t.; take part in (game, contest) EXD:311; 439, R22, R33, R37.19

nenye *conj-num* even one R26

nenzala *conj-n5-sg* and the interest R32

nepilisi *comit-n5-sg* with a pill R25

nepolisa *conj-n3-sg* with the police R27

neqabane *comit-n3-sg* with a partner R30

neqhayiya *conj-n3-sg* proud R29

nerayisi *comit-n5-sg* with rice R8

nerhashalala *n5-sg-conj* and a rash R30

nesi-[1] *combo* and • *nesiZulu 'and Zulu'* indicates that the conjunctive (na-) is linked to a n4 sg (isi-) ☞ See: na- + izi- R7

nesi[2] *deic-conj* in this R18

nesigulo *conn-n-4sg* to/with the sickness R37

nesiyezi *n4-sg-conj* and dizziness R25

nesiZulu *n4-sg-conj* and Zulu R7, R37

nesuntswana *conj-adj-dim* even a small (tiny) R32

nethi[1] *conj-aux* and so, let's say (no direct English equivalent) • *ePalamente nethi inike ingxelo 'by Parliament and, let's say, makes its reports...'* R37

Nethi[2] *pn* Nethi (family name) R4a

nexesh' *conj-n3-sg* have time • *nibe nexesh' elimnandi 'you have a good time'* R31

neyasekwa *conj-v-pass-past* and was established R37

neyeLetaba After-Care Centre *n5-sg-cmp-pn-conj-poss* and of the Letaba After-Care Center R35

neyobisi *conj-n6-sg* and also milk R28.6

neyokuhlawulwa *conj-poss-v-inf-pass* and of training R35

neyolawulo *conj-n6-sg* and administration / administrative R22

neyona *conj-pron-abs* with him, her; and he himself, and she herself R33.5

nezezinye *conj-cop-enum* and other R33

nezi- *combo* and • *nezifundo 'and lessons'* indicates that the conjunctive (na-) is linked to a n4 pl (izi-) ☞ See: na- + izi- R7

nezifo *conj-n4-pl* and illness R13

nezifundo *n4-pl-conj* and lessons R7

nezigqitho *n4-pl-conj* and the transgressions R13

nezihlunu *v-poss-n4-pl-obj* having muscles R12

nezikhundla *n4-pl-conj* and the situations, positions R22

neziko *conj-n3-sg* and a center R35.13

nezilonda *n4-pl-conj* and sores R25

nezinye *n4-pl-adj-conj* and other R11=2, R37

neziphumo *conj-n4-pl* and the results R24, R36

nezisasetyenziswayo *v-rel-conj-n5-pl* and the ones being utilized R35

nezono *conj-n4-pl* and sins R13

n g[1] *change* change of N to NG (before C, Q, X) • *iingcango 'doors' = iin-cango; iingxelo 'reports' = in-xel-o* E&S:51, PCX:195, R9

ng-[2] *pred-prf* is / are [predicative / copulative prefix] ☞ See: ngaba- [n1-pl], ngama- [n3-pl], ngoo- [n1a-pl], ngu- [n1a-sg], ngum- [n1-sg, n2-sg] PCX:96, TD, R3, R4a=2

-nga[1] *adj-root* so much, of such a number (unspecified) ☞ Contrast: -nje E&S:30, PCX:120

nga-[2] *adv-prf* -ly [adverb-forming prefix] • *ngakumbi 'especially', ngamandla 'strongly', ngamanye amaxesha 'sometimes', ngasese 'secretly'* related to instrumental preposition MI:256, R5, R14, R30

nga-[3] *adv-reiteration* by, after [indicating reiteration or variation] • *imihla ngemihla 'day by day, day after day', izinto ngezinto 'various things', ngasixhenxe 'by sevens'* AXG:39

nga-[4] *prep-relat-prf* about, over, concerning, regarding [relational, topical] • *ngantoni? 'what about'; ngesipho 'concerning the gift'* Structure: appears as a prefix before the noun; Note: undergoes sound changes ☞ See: nge-, ngee-, ngo- AM-94:89f, AXG:39, CGB:151, E&S:21, PCX:134, RD-96:398, R4d, R6, R10x

nga-[5] *prep-instr-prf* with, through, by means of [instrumental] • *ngamanzi 'with water', ngemoto 'by car'* Structure: appears as a prefix before the noun; Note: undergoes sound changes ☞ See: nge-, ngee-, ngo- AM-94:87, AXG:39, CGB:150, E&S:21, RD-96:398, R4b, R4d, R6, R7=3, R9x, R21

nga-[6] *prep-loc-prf* at, on, in, into [unspecified place, vague location] • *ngekhaya 'at home', ngaphambili 'in front', ngaphandle 'outside', ngaseKapa 'in the vicinity of Cape Town'* Structure: appears as a prefix before the location noun AM-94:90, AXG:39, CGB:151, E&S:21, R3, R15

nga-[7] *prep-time-prf* on, by [date]; at, in [time] • *ngabani ixesha? 'at what time?' ngokuhlwa 'in the evening'* Structure: appears as a prefix before the time noun; Note: undergoes sound changes ☞ See: nge-, ngee-, ngo- AM-94:90, AXG:39, CGB:151, E&S:21, R4a, R10, R14, R28=2

-nga-[8] *preverb* may, can, would [potential, conditional]; would you mind if? [permissive preverb expressing ability, permission, willingness, possibility] • *engathanda 'he would like'; SINGAZUZA sonke 'we can all benefit'* Structure: SC-nga-OBJ-Δ-a ☞ Neg: -nge- AM-94:90, AXG:128f, CGB:151, E&S:45, MI:255, RD-96:398, SXWU:149, R4b, R4c, R7=2, R37.0

-nga[9] *v-tr* wish; seem AXG:107

nga-[10] *v-cop* is, are [predicative copulative element] • *Ootitshala ngabona bantu babalulekileyo kuluntu 'Teachers are the people important to society'* R3

-nga-[11] *neg-inf-prf* not [negative infinitive prefix] • *ukungathethi 'not to speak'* CGB:121, PCX:104

-nga-[12] *neg-part-prf* not [negative participial prefix] • *angamaziyo 'whom he does not know'; ungahambi 'it not going'* Also used in relative constructions CGB:192, PCX:82f; 151, R4c, R6, R9, R14, R33.9, R37.14

-nga-[13] *neg-sub-pres-prf* not [negative present subjunctive prefix] • *ungaqhubi 'you should not drive'* CGB:168, R4c=2, R6, R10, R14

-nga- -anga *v-rel-neg-perf* who / which did not VERB [negative perfect relative construction] Structure: REL-nga-Δ-anga MI:257, PCX:150, R6

-nga- -i[1] *v-part-pres-neg* not VERBing [negative present participial verb construction] • *abangabahoyi 'who are not concerned about them,' ungahambi 'it not going'* Structure: S2-nga-Δ-i or REL-nga-Δ-i CGB:192, PCX:82f, R2, R9, R36.08, R37.14

-nga- -i[2] *v-sub-pres-neg* (that / should) not VERB [negative present subjunctive verb construction] • *angayixhasi 'and it does not support it'; ungazithandi 'that you not like yourself'* Structure: S3a-nga-Δ-i CGB:168, R4c=2, R6, R10, R14

nga ngokuba *conj-expr* as much as Structure: followed by the participial AXG:151

ngaba-[1] *n1-pl-pred-prf* they are [group 1 plural copulative or predicative prefix construction] • *ngabantwana 'they are children'* CGB:135, E&S:21; 25, PCX:96, XED:xvi, R11, R29

ngaba-[2] *n1-pl-agent-prf* by (done by, produced by) them [marker of group 1 plural agent of passive verb] E&S:25; 43, R37=11

ngaba[3] *deic-1-n1-pl-pred* these are; it is these E&S:26, PCX:99

ngaba[4] *deic-1-n1-pl-instr* by means of these, with (using) these E&S:26

ngaba[5] *deic-1-n1-pl-relat* about these, concerning these E&S:26

ngaba[6] *v-pred-pot* can be; is it possible that R33

ngabaa *deic-3-n1-pl-pred* those (far, yonder) are E&S:26

ngabafazi *cop-n1-pl* it is women R36

ngabahlali *n1-pl-agent* by residents R26=3, R27

ngabakwantsasana *adv-n1-pl* by the police R18

ngabaninzi *n3-pl-adj* they are many R36

ngabantsundu *cop-atr* they are brown / black R29

ngabantu[1] *n1-pl-agent* by people R17.1, R20.2, R29.5.8, R37=11

ngabantu[2] *n1-pl-atr* of people • *kwelijikayo ngabantu aba 'the turnaround of these people'* R20.1.2, R36.12

ngabantu[3] *n1-pl-pred* people are R14, R31.2, R37.5

ngabasemagunyeni *adv-n1-pl-loc-n3-pl* by those in power agentive copulative, hence adverbial R36

ngabazali *adv-n1-pl* by parents R33

ngabo[1] *n1-pl-pred* they are; it is they [group 1 plural copulative or predicative] AXG:44f, E&S:21, PCX:97

ngabo[2] *n1-pl-relat* about them, concerning them AM-94:93, E&S:21, R37

ngabo[3] *n7-sg-relat* about him, her, it; concerning him, her, it E&S:21

ngabo[4] *deic-2-n1-pl-pred* these are E&S:26

ngabo[5] *deic-2-n1-pl-relat* about these, concerning these E&S:26

ngabo[6] *deic-2-n1-pl-instr* by means of these, with (using) these E&S:26

ngabona *n1-pl-pred-emph* it is they who are; they are the ones who are • *ootitshala ngabona bantu babalulekileyo kuluntu 'It is teachers who are the people most important to society'* followed by REL2 construction TD, R3, R29

ngafane *adv-time* seldom RD-96:399

ngafanelanga *atr-neg* undeserved RD-96:399

ngafanelekanga *atr-neg* unfit, improper RD-96:399

ngafumanekiyo *atr-neg* unavailable RD-96:399

ngafundanga *atr-neg* uneducated RD-96:399

ngafuniyo *atr-neg* unwilling RD-96:399

ngagqibekanga *v-atr-neg* incomplete RD-96:399

ngagqibelelanga *atr-neg* imperfect RD-96:399

ngahle *preverb* possibly, maybe VERB • *Ngahle avume 'Maybe he'll* *agree'* Structure: followed by S3a + present subjunctive E&S:47

ngajikiyo *atr-neg* unalterable RD-96:399

-ngaka *atr-root* as big / large as, so great, such CGB:172; 179, E&S:30

-ngakanani *qw-atr-root* how big?, how large?; how much? CGB:129; 172, E&S:33

-ngakhathaleli *v-neg* neglect RD-96:399

ngakhathaliyo *atr-neg* careless RD-96:399

ngakhona *adv* thereabouts ☞ Syn: malunga khona EXD:659

ngako *n8-vn-relat* about it, concerning it E&S:21, R37=3

ngakuba *conj* because Structure: after a negative clause, followed by the participial AXG:151, E&S:41

ngakumbi *adv* chiefly, all the more, especially EXD:93, MI:256, XED:88, R5, R19.3, R36.5, R37.25

ngala[1] *deic-1-n3-pl-pred* these are; it is these E&S:26, PCX:99

ngala[2] *deic-1-n3-pl-relat* about these, concerning these E&S:26

ngala[3] *deic-1-n3-pl-instr* by means of these, with (using) these E&S:26

ngalaa *deic-3-n3-pl-pred* those (far, yonder) are E&S:26

ngale[1] *deic-1-n2-pl-relat* about these, concerning these • *uyafunda ngale misebenzi 'you are learning about these jobs'* E&S:26, XED:81; 98, R29

ngale[2] *deic-1-n2-pl-instr* by means of these, with (using) these E&S:26, XED:81; 98

ngale[3] *deic-1-n5-sg-relat* about this, concerning this • *ucacisa ngale bhodi yeelwimi 'she explains about this language board'* E&S:26, XED:81; 98, R37.01.05.24

ngale[4] *deic-1-n5-sg-instr* by means of this, with (using) this one • *ngale ndlela 'in this way, by means of this'* E&S:26, XED:81; 98, R15, R29

ngalibalekiyo *v-atr-neg-rel* unforgettable RD-96:399

ngalindelekanga *v-atr-neg-perf* unexpected RD-96:399

ngalinganiyo *atr-neg* uneven; unequal RD-96:399

ngalinye *adv-enum* each one R35

ngalo[1] *n3-sg-relat* about him, her, it; concerning him, her, it ☞ Agr: lona E&S:21

ngalo[2] *n3-sg-instr* by means of it ☞ Agr: lona E&S:21, XED:99

ngalo[3] *n6-sg-relat* about him, her, it; concerning him, her, it ☞ Agr: lona E&S:21, R37.11.26

ngalo[4] *n6-sg-instr* by means of it ☞ Agr: lona E&S:21, XED:99

ngalo[5] *deic-1-n1-sg-relat* about this, concerning this one E&S:26

ngalo[6] *deic-1-n1-sg-instr* by means of this, with (using) this one E&S:26

ngalo[7] *deic-1-n2-sg-relat* about this, concerning this one E&S:26, R24.7

ngalo[8] *deic-1-n2-sg-instr* by means of this, with (using) this one E&S:26

ngalo[9] *adv* thereby, therefore EXD:659, R31.1, R37.17

ngaloo[1] *deic-2-n1-sg-relat* about that, concerning that one E&S:26

ngaloo[2] *deic-2-n1-sg-instr* by means of that, with (using) that one E&S:26

ngaloo[3] *deic-2-n2-sg-relat* about that, concerning that one E&S:26

ngaloo[4] *deic-2-n2-sg-instr* by means of that, with (using) that one E&S:26

ngaloo[5] *deic-2-n2-pl-relat* about these, concerning these E&S:26

ngaloo[6] *deic-2-n2-pl-instr* by means of these, with (using) these E&S:26

ngaloo[7] *deic-2-n2-pl-time* in those (times) • *ngaloo minyaka 'in those years'* E&S:26, R28

ngaloo[8] *deic-2-n3-pl-relat* about these, concerning these • *ngaloo magama 'about these words'* E&S:26, R37.10

ngaloo[9] *deic-2-n3-pl-pred* these are E&S:26

ngaloo[10] *deic-2-n3-pl-instr* by means of these, with (using) these E&S:26

ngaloo[11] *deic-2-n5-sg-relat* about that, concerning that one E&S:26

ngaloo[12] *deic-2-n5-sg-instr* by means of that, with (using) that one E&S:26

ngalunganga *atr-neg* incorrect, wrong RD-96:399

ngam *pro-1sg-relat* about me, concerning me • *kuphandle ngam 'apart from anything about me' [following kupandle it should be kwam]* E&S:21, R36.5

ngama-[1] *n3-pl-pred-prf* they are [group 3 plural copulative or predicative prefix construction] • *ngamazwe 'they are countries'* CGB:135, E&S:21; 25, PCX:96, XED:xvi, R4a=2, R4c, R19.1, R26.1, R33.5.7.9, R35.2.3.6, R36.15

ngama-[2] *n3-pl-agent-prf* by (done by, produced by) them [marker of group 3 plural agent of passive verb] E&S:25; 43, XED:xvi, R4b, R20.3.4, R31.0, R32.3, R33.9, R36.9

ngamabhulu *n3-pl-agent* by the Afrikaners R32.9

ngamadlagusha *n3-pl-agent* by the sheep-eaters {slang name for the Afrikaners or Boers} • *kwakubanjwa ngamadlagusha 'when they were arrested by the Boers'* R20.3

ngamadoda *n3-pl-agent* by males R36.9

ngamagqiyazana *n3-pl-agent* by young single women R4b

ngamahamba *n3-pl-agent* by those who travel the road • *ngamahamba-nandlela 'by fellow travelers'* R32.3

ngamahashe *n3-pl-instr* on horses, on horseback R28.3

ngamakhosi *n3-pl-agent* by chiefs R20.4

ngamandla *adv-atr* strongly; [atr] vigorous [lit: with power] ☞ Cf: amandla 'power' MI:256, RD-96:399, R30, R31, R37

ngamanenekazi *cop-n3-pl* it is ladies; there are ladies (who) R36.14

ngamanye amaxesha *adv-cmp-time* sometimes EXD:604, MI:256, R14

ngamanyundululu *adv-n3-pl* about the corruptions R32

ngamanzi *n3-pl-adv,-atr* fluid, liquid [lit: with water] ☞ Cf: amanzi RD-96:399

ngamapolisa *n3-pl-agent* by the police R31.0

ngamatutu *n3-pl-pred* they are cattle-rustlers R26.1

ngamaveletshona *n3-pl-cmp* with Westerners = nga+(a)ma+vela+(i)tshona 'with those who come from the West' R20.7

ngamaxesha *n3-pl-time* in times, at times R14=2

ngamazwe *n3-pl-agent* by countries R33

ngamehlo *adv-n3-pl* with eyes R25

ngamnye *adv-enum* per individual R35

nganeno *adv-loc* on this side CGB:178

ngani *pro-2pl-relat* about you, concerning you (all) E&S:21

ngani na *qw* why? ☞ Alt: kungani na; Syn: kutheni E&S:33, R10x

ngantoni *qw-instr* how?, with what?, using what?, by means of what? • *Uhamba ngantoni? 'How did you travel?'* AM-94:87, CGB:131, E&S:33

nganye *adv-quant* each one, apiece R25, R35.8

ngapha *adv-loc* in this direction, hither AM-94:90

ngaphakathi[1] *adv-loc* inside, within; [atr] internal; inland AM-94:90, MI:256, RD-96:399, R25

ngaphakathi[2] *adv* including • *ngaphakathi ecela ukhuseleko 'including a request for protection'.* R25, R36=2

-ngaphakathi[3] *atr-neg* eternal, unending RD-96:399

ngaphambi *adv-time* before R30

ngaphambili[1] *adv-loc* ahead, in front; forward MI:256, RD-96:399, XED:123, R18.6, R27, R37=2

ngaphambili[2] *adv-time* before, formerly R23.3.6, R28.17

ngaphambili[3] *adv* outside of, apart from R36

ngaphandle[1] *adv-loc* on top; outside AM-94:90, MI:256, RD-96:399, R26.3, R35.3, R37

ngaphandle[2] *prep; conj* without; with the exception of; besides • *Ngaphandle kwentuthumbo yengqondo 'Besides the psychological trauma'* R3, R26.7, R35.10, R36.4

ngaphandle kwa- *prep-expr* except (for), apart from; without • *ngaphandle kootitshala 'without teachers'; ngaphandle kwezifundiswa eziziprofesa zaseziyunivesithi 'except for those well-read ones who are university professors'* RD-96:399, R3, R19.3.5, R23.7, R26.7, R35.10

ngaphantsi *adv-loc* below, under MI:256, RD-96:399

ngaphaya *deic-3-n9-expr* across; beyond; yonder; the other side of • *ngaphaya kwehlathi 'the other side of the forest'* Structure: usually with a possessive construction AXG:144, PCX:92, RD-96:399

ngaphezu *adv* over, exceeding; upon; than XED:127, R10, R36

ngaphezu koko *conj-expr* furthermore, moreover, in addition EXD:53; 390, MI:257, R10

ngaphezulu *adv-loc* outside MI:256

-ngaphi[1] *qw-loc-adv* where?, whereabouts?, which way?, in which direction?, from what direction? • *Uvela ngaphi na? 'Where are you coming from?'; Uya ngaphi na? 'Where are you going?'* AXG:142, CGB:129f, E&S:33

-ngaphi[2] *qw-adj-root* how many? AM-94:193, AXG:63;141f, CGB:129f, E&S:30; 33, PCX:117; 119, R28

ngase- *prep-cmp-prf* nearby, near, close to, in the vicinity of ☞ See: nga- + -s- + e- AXG:39, CGB:151, E&S:32, RD-96:399, SXWU:102, R18, R27

ngasekhohlo *n6-sg-adv* to the left, on the left ☞ Opp: ngasekunene AXG:144, EXD:339

ngasekunene *n10-loc-adv* to the right, on the right ☞ Opp: ngasekhohlo AXG:144, EXD:536, XED:98

ngasemlanjeni *loc-n2-sg* in the vicinity of the river ☞ Contrast: emlanjeni 'in the river' SXWU:102

ngaseMonti *n5-sg-pn-loc* near East London ☞ See: iMonti R27

ngaseQonce *loc-n3-sg* near Qonce (the Buffalo River) ☞ See: iQonce [n3] R18

-ngasese *adv-atr* secretly, out of sight AXG:145, EXD:566, XED:149, R30=2, R35

ngaso *n4-sg-relat* about him, her, it; concerning him, her, it E&S:21

ngathi[1] *pro-1pl-relat* about us, concerning us E&S:21

ngathi[2] *pro-1pl-instr* through us GDX3:293

ngathi[3] *v-aux* probably, perhaps; as if; it seems, it appears to be EXD:568, MI:257, PCX:115, XED:160, R12, R35

ngawakho *adv-pron* with yours, your own, by means of your • *ngawakho amazwi 'in your own words'* R21.0

ngawaphi *conj-pron-rel* whichever ones • *okanye ngawaphi na amagama asetyenziswa luluntu 'or whichever words are used by the community'* R37=2

ngawe *pro-2sg-relat* about you, concerning you E&S:21

ngawo[1] *n2-sg-relat* about him her it; concerning him, her, it • *umhla ezifanele zisetyenziswe ngawo iikhondom 'the day by which the condoms should be used' (lit: the date in respect of which the condoms should be used by it)* E&S:21, R30, R34

ngawo[2] *n3-pl-pred* they are; it is they [group 3 plural copulative or predicative] E&S:21, KED:260, PCX:98

ngawo[3] *n3-pl-relat* about them, concerning them E&S:21

ngawo[4] *n3-pl-agent* by them E&S:21, KED:260, PCX:98

ngawona *cop-pron-abs* it's them R36

ngaye *n1-sg-relat* about him, her, it; concerning him, her, it AM-94:93, E&S:21

ngayo[1] *n2-pl-relat* about them, concerning them E&S:21

ngayo[2] *n5-sg-relat* about him, her, it; concerning him, her, it • *ungayiboni into oyenzileyongayo ' you don't know what (thing) happened to it'* E&S:21, R15, R28, R29, R31, R36=3, R37=5

ngayo[3] *n5-sg-instr* through it, by (means of) it, using it AM-94:93, E&S:21, R11=2

ngayo[4] *adv* thereby EXD:659

ngazo[1] *n4-pl-relat* about them, concerning them E&S:21

ngazo[2] *n5-pl-relat* about them, concerning them E&S:21, R37

ngazo[3] *n6-pl-relat* about them, concerning them • *Iintlobo zezityo ezifanelekileyo ndibone ngazo 'I have seen kinds of meal which are suitable'* MQH1:17

ngazo[4] *adv* thereby EXD:659

nge-[1] *combo* with, by, using • *ngegama lokuba zinyusa ingxowa-mali yazo 'in the name of raising funds for them'* indicates that the instrumental preposition (nga-) is linked to polysyllabic roots of n3 sg (i-) ☞ See: nga- + i- R9

nge-[2] *combo* with, by, using • *ngeLiqui-Fruit 'with Liqui-Fruit'; nge fax 'by fax'* indicates that the instrumental preposition (nga-) is linked to n5 sg (i-) ☞ See: nga- + i- R10, R12, R21, R24

nge-[3] *preverb* would, should VERB; ought to VERB; might have been [preverb aspect marker indicating unlikelihood] • *Ngaphandle kootitshala, khawutsho ngebekho oogqirha, amagqwetha, abongikazi 'Without teachers could you say there would be doctors, lawyers, nurses?'; Ngendihamba 'I should be going'* Structure: followed by a participial construction; nge-S2-Δ-a (positive) and nge-S2-nga-Δ-i (negative) AXG:130, E&S:47, Pahl:103; 210, TD, XED:98, R3

-nge-[4] *neg-rel* not [negative marker in relative constructions] • *kungekho sizathu 'for no reason'; ongekhoyo 'who is not present'* E&S:28, PCX:83, XED:98; 100, R4d, R10, R14

-nge-[5] *preverb-neg* may not, cannot, would not [negative potential / conditional preverb expressing inability, lack of permission, unwillingness, impossibility] Structure: SNEG-nge-Δ-i ☞ Pos: -nga- (S4-nga-Δ-a) E&S:45, PCX:166, R11

ngebekho *preverb-+-v-exis* would they be TD, R3

ngebhaqo *adv* by surprise MI:256

ngebheyili *adv-n5-sg-loan* on bail R31

ngedemokhrasi *adv-n5-sg-loan* democratically R16

ngeebhokhwe *n5-pl-instr* with goats R26.7

ngeelwimi *n6-pl-instr* in languages R37.6

ngeemeko *adv-n5-pl* about conditions R28

ngeemfuno *n5-pl-relat* about the needs • *ngeemfuno zabantu 'about people's needs'* R37.12

ngeemveliso *n5-pl-instr* with produce R29

ngeendawo *n5-pl-adv* by those places R29

ngeengcinga *conj-n5-pl* and thoughts R14

ngeenkonzo *n5-pl-ee-change-k* by means of services R37

ngeenkophe *adv-n5-pl* with eyelashes R36

ngeenkwenkwezi *n5-pl-instr* by / through the stars R34

ngeentsimbi *n5-pl-instr* using iron, out of steel • *uninzi lwazo zenziwe ngeentsimbi 'the majority of them are made of steel'* R35

ngeenyawo *n6-pl-instr* on foot, by foot, afoot; [fig] in motion EXD:225, R28=2

ngegama *n3-sg-instr* in the name, using the name R9

ngehelikopta *n5-sg-instr* by helicopter R24

-ngeka- *v-prf-neg-punc* not yet VERBing [negative participial punctual aspect prefix] • *Bengekasebenzi 'they not yet working'* Structure: S2-nge-ka-Δ-i; Negative only PCX:83f

-ngekakhuli *atr* immature RD-96:399

-ngekasetyenziswa *atr* undeveloped RD-96:399

ngekhaya *loc-n3-sg* at home R15

-ngekho *v-exis-neg* be absent; not be there; there is not negative participial form of existential verb -kho E&S:49, EXD:3, RD-96:399, SXWU:127, R11, R28, R36

-ngekho mtethweni *atr-cmp* illegal EXD:289, RD-96:399

-ngekhoyo *v-exis-neg-rel* absent ☞ Alt: ngekho EXD:3, RD-96:399

ngeli[1] *deic-1-n3-sg-relat* about this, concerning this E&S:26, R34.10

ngeli[2] *deic-1-n3-sg-instr* by means of this, with (using) this one • *ngeli thuba 'by this opportunity'* E&S:26, R34.10

ngelishwa *adv* unfortunately MI:256

ngelithi *v-part-agent* by saying it R27

ngelithuba *n3-sg-instr* by means of this opportunity nga+(e)li+(i)thuba R34.4

ngelixa *conj* while, during, at the time ☞ Alt: ngexa GDX3:557, RD-96:399

ngelo[1] *deic-2-n3-sg-instr* by means of that, with (using) that one E&S:26

ngelo[2] *deic-2-n3-sg-relat* about that, concerning that E&S:26

ngelo[3] *deic-2-n3-sg-time* on that (date), during that (time) • *ngelo xesha 'at that time'* R28

ngem- *combo* with, by, using • *ngembalelwano 'by correspondence'* indicates that the instrumental preposition (nga-) is linked to n5 sg (im-) ☞ See: nga- + i- R7

ngembalelwano *n5-sg-instr* by correspondence [lit: by each other being written to] EXD:126, R7

ngemfakadolo *instr-n5-sg* with a breechloading rifle R32.4

ngemfazwe *adv+-N* about the civil war nga+imfazwe R24

ngemibandela *relat-n2-pl* about additional topics ☞ See: umbandela R16

ngemibutho *n2-pl-agent* by the organizations R37.5

ngemihla *adv-n2-pl* day after day R36

ngemini *adv-n5-sg* on a day R28.5

ngemizuzu *n2-pl-instr* by minutes R33=2

ngempazamo *adv* by mistake, in error MI:256

ngempilo *adv-n5-sg* with life R13

ngempumelelo *n5-sg-instr* with success; [adv] successfully R33

-ngena *v-tr* enter, go in / into, penetrate PCX:34, RD-96:399, XED:100, R28.5, R36.2, R35.7

-ngenabubele *atr-neg* unkind RD-96:399

-ngenabulungisa *atr-neg* unjust RD-96:399

ngenakunikelwa *v-neg-poss-rel-pass-ben* inalienable EXD:296

-ngenakwenzeka *v-atr-neg* impossible RD-96:399

-ngenaluncedo *atr-neg* helpless EXD:273, RD-96:399

-ngenambeko *atr-neg* impolite, rude, ill-mannered RD-96:399

ngenambulelo *atr-neg* ungrateful RD-96:399

-ngenamfesane *atr-neg* uncharitable [lit: not having an umbilical cord] RD-96:399

-ngenampilo *atr-neg* unhygienic, unhealthy RD-96:399

-ngenamsebenzi *atr-neg* useless, trivial RD-96:399

-ngenanceba *atr-neg* unmericful, merciless RD-96:400

ngenandlela *v-rel-atr* impracticable XED:31

-ngenanto *atr-neg* vacant, empty [lit: having nothing] RD-96:400

ngendebe *instr-n5-sg* with a cup R27.8

ngendima *adv-n5-sg* by the role R27.7

ngendlela *n5-sg-instr-adv* in the way, in the manner BS, R27, R37=3

ngenene *adv* truly, in truth, in reality; absolutely RD-96:400, XED:98, R12

ngengozi *n5-sg-instr-adv* dangerously [lit: with danger] EXD:143

ngengqondo *adv-n5-sg* through means of/with mind, intellect; understanding, reason; mental capacity, intelligence R34

ngenhla *adv-loc* above ☞ See Xhosa: ngentla DNZ:1, EZZE:189, R15=2

ngenjongo *n5-sg-instr-adv-purpose* on purpose, purposely; for the purpose (of) (EXD:494), R17.3, R34.1, R35.2

ngenkani *instr-n5-sg* with stubbornness R32.8

ngenkxaso *comit-n5-sg* with the support ☞ See: inkxaso R35.15

ngentla *adv-loc* on the upper side; to the North XED:100, R15x, R37

ngentloko *n5-sg-instr* by heart PCX:50

ngentsuku *adv-n5-sg* in days R25

ngenxa *prep* on account of Structure: followed by a possessive construction PCX:134, XED:100, R18, R19, R20=2, R24, R32, R35=2, R36, R37=2

ngenxa yoko *conj-expr* therefore ☞ Syn: ngoko EXD:659, R22x

ngenxa yokuba *conj-expr* therefore, on account of that ☞ Syn: ngenxa yoko R36=2

ngenyanga *prep-n5-sg* per month R28=2, R29

ngephepha *instr-n3-sg* with / in paper R30

ngephulo *adv-n3-sg* about the campaign ☞ See: iphulo R31.2

ngeregister *n5-sg-instr* by registered mail R7

ngerhafu *relat-n5-sg* about tax R23.0.9

ngesi-[1] *combo* in [language specified] • *ngesiXhosa 'in the Xhosa language'* indicates that the instrumental preposition (nga-) is linked to n4 sg (isi-) R4b, R7

ngesi[2] *deic-1-n4-sg-relat* about this, concerning this E&S:26

ngesi[3] *deic-1-n4-sg-instr* by means of this, with (using) this one ☞ See: nga- + isi- E&S:26

ngesisa *adv* freely, for nothing [lit: by benevolence] ☞ See: isisa XED:147

ngesiXhosa *n4-sg-instr* in the Xhosa language R4b, R7, R37

ngeso[1] *deic-2-n4-sg-instr* by means of that, with (using) that one E&S:26

ngeso[2] *deic-2-n4-sg-relat* about that, concerning that E&S:26

ngethamsanqa *adv-n5-sg* by good fortune R23

ngethuba *adv-n3-sg* on the occasion R26=2, R27

ngexa *conj* during, while ☞ Alt: ngelixa GDX3:557

ngexesha[1] *n3-sg-time* in time; at (the) time • *ngexesha elifutshane 'in a very short period of time'* R10, R19.1, R27, R32=2

ngexesha[2] *adv-time* early MI:256, R10x

ngezandla *adv-n4-pl* by hand R35

ngezantsi *loc-n3-sg* below, underneath R25, R37.6

ngezenzo *n4-pl-instr* for deeds R11

ngezesondo *adv-n5-pl* of sexuality R36

ngezi[1] *deic-1-n4-pl-relat* about these, concerning these • *ngezi ziganeko 'about these demonstrations'* E&S:26, MQH1:17

ngezi[2] *deic-1-n4-pl-instr* by means of these, with (using) these E&S:26

ngezi[3] *deic-1-n5-pl-relat* about these, concerning these E&S:26, R22, R26

ngezi[4] *deic-1-n5-pl-instr* by means of these, with (using) these E&S:26

ngezi[5] *deic-1-n6-pl-instr* by means of these, with (using) these • *Mbethe ngezi zinti ' beat him with these sticks'* MQH1:17

ngezimvo *adv-n5-pl* through, by means of opinions, ideas, feelings R34

ngezindlela *n5-pl-adv* by ways / means R15

ngezinto *adv-n5* about things • *izinto ngezinto 'many things'* R22

ngeziphumo *adv-n4-pl* with successes R33

ngezisu *adv-n4-pl* with a stomach R20

ngezithethe *adv-n4-pl* in a customary way isithethe 'way of doing things according to custom' R21

ngezo[1] *deic-2-n4-pl-relat* about these, concerning these E&S:26

ngezo[2] *deic-2-n4-pl-instr* by means of these, with (using) these E&S:26

ngezo[3] *deic-2-n5-pl-relat* about these, concerning these E&S:26

ngezo[4] *deic-2-n5-pl-instr* by means of these, with (using) these E&S:26

ngezo[5] *deic-2-n6-pl-relat* about these, concerning these • *ngezo ntsuku 'concerning those days'* CD2

ngezomsebenzi *adv-n2-sg* about work R28

ngingqi *n5-sg-red* river basin, valley, region R27.2.7.10

ngo-[1] *combo* on [day], in [month, year] • *ngoJuni 'in June', ngo-1955 'in 1955'* indicates that the temporal preposition (nga-) is linked to n1a sg (u-) ☞ See: nga- + u- CGB:46f, R4a, R24, R33, R35

ngo-[2] *combo* about, concerning • *ngothando 'about love'* indicates that the relational preposition (nga-) is linked to n6 sg (u-) ☞ See: nga- + u- R4d

ngo-[3] *combo* with, by means of • *ngocoselelo 'with care, carefully'* indicates that the instrumental preposition (nga-) is linked to n6 sg (u-) ☞ See: nga- + u- R6

NGO[4] *abr* Non-Governmental Organization R35

ngo-1995 *prep-time* in 1995 R33, R36

ngoba[1] *qw-adv* why? CGB:129, R23

ngoba[2] *conj* because Structure: followed by participial E&S:41

ngobo[1] *deic-2-n7-sg-instr* by means of that, with (using) that one E&S:26

ngobo[2] *deic-2-n7-sg-relat* about that, concerning that E&S:26

ngobo[3] *deic-2-n7-sg-time* on that (date), during that (time) • *ngobo busuku 'on that night'* E&S:26, R36

ngobu[1] *deic-1-n7-sg-relat* about this, concerning this E&S:26

ngobu[2] *deic-1-n7-sg-instr* by means of this, with (using) this one E&S:26

ngobukho *adv-loc* of the presence / existence of R37

ngocoselelo *n6-sg-instr* with care; [adv] carefully R6

ngohlobo *adv-n6-sg* of the manner; in a way R37.11.15.19.26

ngoJuni *n1a-sg-time* in June ☞ rw: uJuni CGB:47, R4a

ngoko[1] *deic-2-n8-vn-relat* about that VERBing, concerning that one (not far, just mentioned) E&S:26

ngoko[2] *deic-2-n8-vn-instr* by means of that VERBing, with (using) that one (not far, just mentioned) E&S:26

ngoko[3] *deic-2-10-loc-relat* about that VERBing, concerning that (time, place, situation not far, just mentioned) [not found in any references; cf: E&S:26]

ngoko[4] *deic-2-n10-loc-instr* by means of that VERBing, with (using) that (time, place, situation not far, just mentioned) [not found in any references; cf: E&S:26]

ngoko[5] *adv-time* then, at that time • *Wayekho ngoko 'He was present then'* AXG:143, E&S:59

ngoko[6] *conj* therefore, so EXD:659, XED:100, R12, R28=3, R29, R31, R34=3, R37.17

ngokokuba *conj* because Structure: followed by the participial AXG:151

ngokomthetho *adv-n2-sg* by the law R36

ngokomzekelo *adv-n2-sg* for example R29

ngoku[1] *deic-1-n8-vn-relat* about this, concerning this E&S:26

ngoku[2] *deic-1-n8-vn-instr* by means of this, with (using) this one E&S:26

ngoku[3] *deic-1-n10-loc-relat* about this (situation), concerning this (time, place) • *ngokungaphantsi 'much less'* XED:124

ngoku[4] *deic-1-n10-loc-instr* by means of this, with (using) this (time, place, situation) [not found in any references]

ngoku[5] *adv-time* now • *Bona ngoku bafuna 'Now they themselves want'* AXG:143, E&S:59, EXD:409, MI:256, PCX:29f, RD-96:400;373, R17.3, R20, R22, R23=2, R27, R29=3, R30=2, R33, R34=5, R35=2

ngokuba[1] *conj* because Structure: nga+ukuba; followed by the participial ☞ Alt: kuba AXG:88; 151; 148, E&S:41, RD-96:400, R24.8, R26.1.5, R28, R29.8.11 R34.12

ngokuba[2] *qw* why? RD-96:400

ngokubanzi *n8-vn-adv* at large; extensively, broadly • *nelizwe ngokubanzi liyamhlonipha 'and the country at large respects him'* EXD:332, R16, R22.3.4, R36.24

ngokubhekisele *adv-v-inf* concerning R37.12

ngokubonelela *adv-v-inf-ben* by making provision for R37.20

ngokubuyisa *adv-vn-caus* by returning R36

ngokuchaseneyo *adv-vn* by opposing R36.25

ngokuchazelwa *adv-vn-ben-pass* by being explained to R36

ngokudlwengula *adv-vn* for raping R36

ngokudlwengulwa *v-pass* and to be raped R36

ngokugxothwa *relat-v-pass* about the driving away R26.8

ngokujonga *v-inf-instr* by looking at R37

ngokukhawuleza *adv* right away, quickly, in a hurry R18, R25

ngokukhululekileyo *v-perf-rel* extremely, completely R34.11

ngokulandela *adv* by following • *by following* R34

ngokungaseli *inf-neg-relat* about not drinking R6

ngokungayihlawuli *v-tr-neg-inf-pass* without being fined R23

ngokungcungcuthekisa *adv-vn-caus* by making thin, by causing to lose weight R36.18

ngokungekho *adv* presently not, not being • *ngokungekho mthethweni 'unlawfully'* R36

ngokunjalo *adv* accordingly CGB:179, R35

ngokunokwakhe *adv-conj-pron* personally R27

ngokunyanga *adv-v-inf-red* for curing R26

ngokuphanda *adv-v-inf* by examining nga+uku+phanda R24

ngokuphatha *adv-v-inf-red* by the management R22

ngokupheleleyo *adv* completely EXD:112, R33, R34

ngokuphuculwa *adv-v-inf-pass* by being improved R37.19

ngokuqeqeshwa *adv-vn-pass* through training R35

ngokuqinisekileyo *v-perf-rel* for certain R34

ngokuseka *adv-v-inf* for establishing R32

ngokuthi *conj* because [lit: about which could be said] • *besi sikolo ngokuthi sivula nje '...of this school because it just opened...'* R18.1, R29.12, R31.3, R37.5.7.16

ngokutsha *adv* anew ☞ Cf: ukutsha XED:163

ngokutsho *adv-v-aux* according to, as is said by R36=4

ngokuwadlwengula *adv-vn* by raping them R36

ngokuwava *adv-vn* to hear R36

ngokuzilolonga *n8-vn-instr* by looking after yourself R34

ngokwa- *prep-cmp-prf* according to [lit: through that of] • *ngokwemiyalelo 'according to the directions'; ngokwendlela 'in such a way'* usually results in an adverb of manner EXD:5, NDK-91:509, XED:100, R6

ngokwalo *adv-deic-n2-sg* by this R36.14

ngokwaneleyo *adv* enough EXD:190, R4cx

ngokweli *deic-adv-loc* by the, at this R34

ngokwemiyalelo *n2-pl-prep* according to the directions R6

ngokwendalo *adv-n4-sg* by nature R36

ngokwendlela *n5-sg-prep* in such a way R11

ngokwenene *adv* actually R34

ngokwengxelo *adv-Phrase* according to the report ngokwa + ingxelo R26

ngokwenjongo *adv-n5-sg* with the purpose of R35

ngokwentetho *adv-n2-sg* by declaration R36

ngokwenza *n8-vn-instr* by doing R17.1

ngokwerhafu *adv-n3-sg* about tax R23=2

ngokwesondo *n5-sg-prep-adv-manner* sexually, in a sexual manner R36=3

ngokwezicelo *adv-n5-pl* by the requests R27

ngolo[1] *deic-2-n6-sg-instr* by means of that, with (using) that one E&S:26

ngolo[2] *deic-2-n6-sg-relat* about that, concerning that E&S:26

ngolonakalo *adv-n6-sg* about the damage nga + ulonakalo R26.7

ngolu[1] *deic-1-n6-sg-relat* about this, concerning this one E&S:26

ngolu[2] *deic-1-n6-sg-instr* by means of this, with (using) this one E&S:26, R30

ngolunya *adv-n6-sg* with malice R32

ngolwaa[1] *deic-3-n6-sg-instr* by means of that, with (using) that one • *ngolwaa thando 'by that love'* E&S:26, R4d

ngolwaa[2] *deic-3-n6-sg-relat* about that, concerning that one (far) E&S:26

ngolwimi *adv-n6-sg* in the language R23

ngom-[1] *combo* about, concerning • *ngomsebenzi wakhe 'in connection with her work'* indicates that the relational preposition (nga-) is linked to n2 sg (um-) ☞ See: nga- + um- R24

ngom-[2] *combo* with, by, using • *ngomsa ka Thixo 'with the love of God'* indicates that the instrumental preposition (nga-) is linked to n2 sg (um-) ☞ See: nga- + um- R4d

ngoMgaqo *adv-n2-sg* about the Constitution R37

ngomhla *prep-n2-sg* on the date R23

ngomnye *num-adj* is one R37

ngomnyobo *adv-n2-sg* (with, in) a model, design R31

ngomonde *adv-n6-sg* with perseverance R13

ngomoya *adv-n2-sg* with the spirit R13

ngompu *instr-n2-sg* by the gun (i.e., to take by force) R32

ngomsa *n2-sg-instr* in the love, with the affection R4d

ngomsebenzi *adv-n2-sg* for the work R24

ngomso *adv-time* tomorrow ☞ rw: -sa AXG:143, E&S:59, EXD:670, MI:231; 256, RD-96:400;373, XED:147

ngomthandazo *n2-sg-instr* with a prayer R36

ngonyaka *adv-n2-sg* by the year R35

ngoo-[1] *n1a-pl-pred-prf* they are [group 1a plural copulative or predicative prefix construction] • *ngoonyana 'they are sons'* E&S:25, PCX:96

ngoo-[2] *n1a-pl-agent-prf* by (done by, produced by) them [marker of group 1a plural agent of passive verb] CGB:187, E&S:25; 43

ngoo-[3] *adv-prefix* as R32

ngoobani *qw-n1a-pl* who (all) are they? ITX:14, SXWU:33

ngoonesi *n1a-pl-agent* by nurses R17.3.5

ngoozwilakhe *adv+n1a-pl* by dictators = nga + oo+ zwilakhe 'by (means of) dictators' [compound noun formed from u- + (ili)zwi+ l+akhe 'one who only follows his own voice'] R16

ngothando *n5-sg-relat* about love • *umntu ozimisele ngothando 'someone who is serious about love'* R4d

ngowokuba *adv-vn-aux* is that of R35

ngowona *adv-abs-2-sg* it is (the most) [lit: by itself] • *Ngumsebenzi omhle UMbulelo uthi ezentengiso ngowona msebenzi mhle onokuwukhetha ngoku.'It's a nice job,' Mbulelo says about sales, 'being one of the most pleasant you can choose nowadays.'* R29.13

ngqalelo *n5-sg-red* start, beginning, commencement ☞ See: ingqalelo R36.12

-ngqiba *v-tr* beg (s.t. from s.o.); ask alms (of s.o.); sponge (off s.o.) EXD:17; 50, XED:108, R9

Ngqika *pn* Ngqika (Xhosa chief of Rharhabe clan, who collaborated with the colonial forces during the Frontier Wars) ☞ Cf: Ndlambe AXG:20, CGB:4, MI:274

-ngqina *v-tr* testify, bear witness (to); attest EXXE:60, XED:108

ngqo *ideophone* go straight ahead; keep on, work steadily at; do right away; [adv] exactly E&S:59, EXD:197, XED:101, R37.16

ngqongqo *atr-root* hard, severe [atr]; [adv] hard, severely XED:101, R11, R34

ngu-[1] *n1a-sg-pred-prf* he, she, it is [group 1a singular copulative or predicative prefix construction] • *ngunyana 'he is a son'* E&S:25, PCX:96, R4d=2, R10x

ngu-[2] *n1a-sg-agent-prf* by (done by, produced by) him, her [marker of group 1a singular agent of passive verb] CGB:187, E&S:25; 43, R2, R3, R5=2, R9, R10, R11, R16, R31, R37.12

ngu-[3] *pro-2sg-pred-prf* you are [singular copulative or predicative prefix construction] • *nguwe 'it is you'* E&S:21, PCX:97, XED:xvi

ngubani *qw-n1a-sg* who is it? AXG:142, CGB:129, ITX:14, R29

ngubhishophu *loan* is the bishop R32

Ngudle *pn* (family name) • *Looksmart Solwandle Ngudle* R32.5

ngulaa[1] *deic-3-n1-sg-pred* that (far, yonder) is E&S:26

ngulaa[2] *deic-3-n2-sg-pred* that (far, yonder) is E&S:26

ngulo[1] *deic-1-n1-sg-pred* this is; it is this one E&S:26, PCX:99

ngulo[2] *deic-1-n2-sg-pred* this is; it is this one E&S:26, PCX:99, R27

nguloo[1] *deic-2-n1-sg-pred* that (not far, just mentioned) is E&S:26

nguloo[2] *deic-2-n2-sg-pred* that (not far, just mentioned) is E&S:26

ngulowo *deic-2-n2-sg-pred* that is [lit: it is that which] R29.2

ngum-[1] *n1-sg-pred-prf* he, she, it is [group 1 singular copulative or predicative prefix construction] • *ngumtwana 'he is a child'* CGB:135, E&S:21; 25, PCX:96, XED:xvi, R4d, R14, R16

ngum-[2] *n1-sg-agent-prf* by (done by, produced by) him, her [marker of group 1 singular agent of passive verb] E&S:25; 43

ngum-[3] *n2-sg-pred-prf* he, she, it is [group 2 singular copulative or predicative prefix construction] •

ngumxube 'it is a mixture' CGB:135, E&S:21; 25, PCX:96, XED:xvi, R12

ngum-[4] *n2-sg-agent-prf* by (done by, produced by) him, her, it [marker of group 2 singular agent of passive verb] E&S:25; 43, R10, R34

ngumakoti *n1a-sg-pred* be my wife KM, R4d

ngumama *n1a-sg-pred* she is a mother R4d

ngumhlobo *n1-sg-pred* he is a friend R14

ngummeli *n1-sg-pred* be a representative R24

ngumntu *n1-sg-cop-n1-sg* be a person; be someone (who) R29, R34

ngumongameli *n1-sg-agent* by the president R32

ngumothuko *n2-sg-agent* by the shock R34

ngumqobo *cop-n2-sg* it is an obstacle R33.9

ngumsebenzi *n2-sg-cop* it is a job R29

ngumthetho *n2-sg-agent* by the law R10=2

ngumvuzo *cop-n2-sg* wage, salary, earning R28

ngumxube *n2-sg-pred* it is a mixture R12

ngumzali *cop-n1-sg* by a parent R36

ngumzekelo *cop2-sg-n2-sg* it is an example R31

ngumzi *cop-n2-sg* by the household R15

ngunyaka *adv-n2-sg* year R31

nguqu *n5-sg-red* change; return, rally ☞ See: inguqu R22

ngurhulumente *n1a-sg-agent* by the government R32, R37.2

ngusihlalo *cop-n4-sg* be the chairperson R32

ngutata *n1a-sg-agent* by father R5

nguwe *pro-2sg-pred* you are; it is you [singular copulative or predicative] AXG:44f, E&S:21, PCX:97, R23, R29=2, R31

nguwo *n2-sg-pred* he, she, it is; it is he, she, it [group 2 singular copulative or predicative] E&S:21, PCX:97

nguye[1] *n1-sg-pred* he, she, it is; it is he, she, it [group 1 singular copulative or predicative] AXG:44f, E&S:21, PCX:97

nguye[2] *n1-sg-agent* by him, her, it R37.02

-ngwevu *atr-root* gray, grey AM-94:107, EXD:256, NDK-91:128, UEX:14, Uys:4

ngxaki *n5-sg-red* difficulty R18.4

-ngxama *v* rush, hurry, be impetuous • *sanukungxama, midaka yakowethu 'let's not be impetuous, my dark people'* EXD:549, R17

-ni-[1] *pro-2pl-obj-prf* you (all) E&S:18, SXWU:44

ni-[2] *pro-2pl-pred-prf* you are [plural copulative or predicative prefix construction] • *nini 'it is you'* E&S:21, PCX:97, XED:xvi

ni-[3] *pro-2pl-S1-prf* you (all) CGB:115; 158, E&S:18, SXWU:29, XED:xvi

ni-[4] *pro-2pl-S2-prf* you (all) VERBing [S2 participial subject] AXG:89; 91, CGB:191; R31

ni-[5] *pro-2pl-S3a-prf* (and) you (all) VERB [S3a present subjunctive subject pronoun] CGB:167, R4a, R4b=3, R9, R12

ni-[6] *pro-2pl-S4* you can VERB; you may VERB [first person plural potential / conditional verb subject (S4) agreement pronoun] PCX:166, SXWU:149

ni-[7] *pro-2pl-dir-rel2* you (all) who [direct relative 2] • *nina nivelayo 'you all who see'* E&S:34n

ni-[8] *pro-2pl-ind-rel2* you (all) whom [indirect relative 2] E&S:35

-ni[9] *qw-adj-root* what (kind)?, of what sort? • *ntoni 'what?'* ☞ See: #ni, bani, buni, kuni, lini, luni, mani, mini, mni, sini, zini AXG:63, E&S:30, E&S:33, PCX:27;118f, R9, R10

ni[10] *qw-n5-sg* what kind?, of what sort? • *nto ni? 'what sort of thing?'* ☞ See: -ni PCX:28; 118

-ni[11] *v-suf-imp-pl* do VERB! [positive imperative plural verb suffix] • *vukani 'you all get up!', yityani 'you all eat!', yitshoni 'you all say so!'* Structure: #-Δ-a-ni [added to imperative singular form] PCX:22f, R11, R17, R19

nibe[1] *preverb-recent-pro-2pl* you (all) were VERBing [recent past compound tense preverb] Structure: nibe ni-Δ (participial construction) AXG:91f, E&S:37f, PCX:183

nibe[2] *v-aux* you have (a good time) R31

nifake *v-sub* you should enclose R4b

-nika *v-tr* give, hand s.t. to s.o.; deliver; confer, bestow upon; supply with EXD:246, RD-96:400, XED:103, R6, R12, R14

-nika iinkcukacha *v-cmp* give the details, go into the particulars EXD:439

-nika imbeko *vp* honor RD-96:400

-nika ingxelo *vp* report, issue a report RD-96:400

-nikela *v-ditr* offer, give s.t. to or for s.o.; devote s.t. to s.o. EXD:246, RD-96:400

-nikezela *v* sacrifice; surrender RD-96:400

nikho *v-exis-pro-2pl* you are here / present E&S:29

nilumkile *v-intr-stative-sub* that you may be cautious/wise R31

nina *pro-2pl-abs* you; yourselves; as for you AM-94:92; 163, CGB:158, E&S:21, PCX:31, RD-96:400

nindithumelele *v-ben-sub* that you should send to me R12

ningabanjelwa *v-neg-ben-pass* you not being arrested for R31

nini[1] *pro-2pl-pred* you are; it is you [plural copulative or predicative] AXG:44f, E&S:21, PCX:97

nini[2] *qw-adv* when? CGB:129f, E&S:33, PCX:29, RD-96:400, R9x, R30

-ninji *adj-root* much, many ☞ See: -ninzi; Alt: -nintshi PCX:120

-nintshi *adj-root* much, many ☞ See: -ninzi; Alt: -ninji PCX:120

-ninzi *adj-root* many, a lot, plenty (of), much, abundant, plentiful ☞ Opp: -mbalwa; Alt: -nintshi, -ninji AM-94:193, AXG:63, CGB:171; 179, E&S:30, PCX:120, RD-96:400, XED:104, R10, R37=10

niphila *v-intr-part* you living R31.0

niphinde *v-aux* you again R20

niphulaphula *v-intr-part* you listen R31

niselile *v-tr-perf-part* you having drank R31

nivane *v-sub* you understand each other R25

niwazi *v-tr-sub* you know subjunctive R20

niya *v-aux-fut* you will R31

nize *v-aux-imp* you (all) should R4b

nj *change* change of MB to NJ • *banjwa 'be arrested' [= bamb/nj-w-a]* CGB:142, MI:147, PCX:69; 103; 196, R4a, R37.3

njalo[1] *atr-root* so, thus, like that, of that kind; in that way; the same • *see 'kunjalo'* old auxiliary verb 'nja'+demonstrative ☞ Cf: -nje; rw: -enza AM-94:112, CGB:172; 179, E&S:30, XED:104, R4c, R15, R23=2, R25, R37x

njalo[2] *adv-time* often RD-96:400

njalo njalo *adv* and so on, and so forth, etc. R25, R37.14.19

-njani *qw-atr-root* how?, like what?, of what kind? nja-ni compound form, not usually found in component parts AM-94:107, CGB:129f, E&S:30; 33, PCX:29, RD-96:400, SXWU:26, XED:104, R21=2, R22, R23, R31.1, R37.7.8.9

-nje[1] *adj-root* so much, so many, of this number (usually specified by raising the appropriate number of fingers) • *iigusha ezinje 'so many sheep'* AXG:63, KED:272, PCX:120

nje[2] *atr-root* thus, such, like this; in this way, in this manner, so [also used for marking emphasis] ☞ Cf: -njalo; rw: -enza AM-94:112, CGB:172; 179, E&S:30, KED:272, R9, R10, R11, R14, R18, R37=2

nje[3] *adv-clitic* then, just, only • *sifumanise imizi kububutyobo nje 'when we arrived at the houses, we just found chaos'* RD-96:401, R9, R17.5, R20, R26, R27, R31, R32=2, R33, R36=2

nje ngokuba *conj-expr* as, according to, just like • *Nje ngokuba bethanda 'as they wish'* Structure: followed by the participial AXG:151

njenga *conj-comp-prf* as, like, such as, just as [comparative] • *njengobuxhwele 'like a medicine man'* CGB:151, EXD:30, XED:104, R7, R11, R20, R24, R34

njengakwamanye *conj-comp-loc-n3-pl* just like in others R11

njengaseKapa *conj-comp-loc-n5-sg-geog* such as from Cape Town R35

njengawokulalana *v-conj-comp* like sleeping together R36

njengaxa *conj-comp-time* as when ☞ rw: xa XED:181

njengeenkokeli *conj-comp-n5-pl* as leaders R20

njengehlazo *conj-comp-n3-sg* as a disgrace R36

njengeminye *conj-comp-enum* like others R37

njengendawo *conj-comp-n5-sg* like a place R35

njengengcali *conj-comp-n5-sg* as an expert R24

njengenxalenye *conj-comp-n5-sg* as a single unit, a unified community R35

njengeqabane *conj-comp-n3-sg* as a friend R24

njengesikhokelo *conj-comp-n4-sg* as the lead R21.5

njengesitofu *conj-comp-n4-sg* like an injection R25

njengezakhiwo *conj-comp-n4-pl* as buildings R35

njengezisemthethweni *conj-comp-loc* like those which have been mentioned in speeches R37

njengo *conj* as a, as R36

njengobuxhwele *n7-comp* like a medicine man, such as being a herbalist R7

njengoko *conj* as, whereas; accordingly, like that ☞ Syn: njengokuba XED:104, R21, R28, R31, R36x, R37=2

njengokuba *conj* whereas, as, like; considering that {legal} Structure: followed by the participial ☞ Syn: njengoko E&S:41, EXD:346;722, XED:104, R34, R36

njengokungathi *adv* as if; as though XED:104; 160

njengombophi *-conj-comp* like one who binds wounds R36.21

njengomntu *n1-sg-comp* as a person R29, R36

nkcazelo *n5-sg-red* explanation • *le nkcazelo 'this explanation'* R27.11

-nke *pro-enum-root* all, every, the whole (of) ☞ See: -onke

CGB:176, E&S:27, PCX:62;24, R1=2, R5

nkokeli *n5-sg-red* leader ☞ See: inkokeli R16

Nkopo *pn* Nkopo (family name) R18

nkosi *n5-sg-red* chief; Lord ☞ See: inkosi R13=2

nkqu[1] *ideophone* even R28.3

nkqu[2] *ideophone* emphatic point • *baba nalo nkqu igila 'they made an emphatic point'* R36.6

nkqubo *n5-sg-red* procedure; program (radio, TV) ☞ See: inkqubo R37

nkwantya *v-intr* tremble with fear; be terrified R32

nkxaso *n5-sg-red* support ☞ See: inkxaso; rw: -xhas- R36.24

no-[1] *combo* and NOUN • *abantwana notata 'children and father'* indicates that the conjunctive prefix (na-) is linked to a noun prefixed with the article u- ☞ See: na- + u- AM-94:80, CGB:120, R4d, R5=2, R10

no-[2] *prep-prf* with • *noLizo 'with Lizo'; bonana no-Nompumelelo '(you) and Nompumelelo see one another'* Structure: appears as a prefix before the noun; Note: undergoes sound changes ☞ See: na- + u- PCX:36, R15

no-[3] *v-pro-2pl-short-fut* you (all) will VERB [contracted / short positive future pronoun prefix] E&S:20

nobamadoda *conj-poss7-n3pl* of people • *nobamadoda ubomi 'the lives of people'* R36

nobandlululo *n2-sg-agent* by Apartheid • *ukwahlukana nobandlululo 'to be divided by Apartheid'* R20.4 [not found in any references, but confirmed by mother-tongue speakers]

nobani *qw* with whom?, to whom? CGB:130

nobefanele *v-ben-perf-oblig* and it is probable; probably [when followed by ukuba] • *nobefanele ukuba wenze njalo 'and it is probable that you will do that'* R23.7

NoBible *n1a-red* Bible Holder (female helper associated with a church) [lit: mother of the Bible] ☞ See: uNoBible R5=2

nobugcisa *conj-n7-sg* with skill R34.8

nobume *n7-abs-conj* and the condition R34.2

nobusuku *n7-sg-time-conj* and night R28

nodwa *pro-quan-2pl* you alone; just you (all) ☞ See: nedwa E&S:27n, PCX:62

nohambo *conj-n6-sg* journey R28=2

-nok- *v-abil-cmp-prf* can, could VERB; be able, willing to VERB [form of noku- used before o verb] • *nokomelela 'can be healthy'* R12

nokholo *conj-n6-sg* and faith R36

noko *conj-rel* although, notwithstanding Structure: followed by relative construction ☞ Alt: nangona E&S:36, R26

nokokuba *conj* and so ☞ See: nokuba – several senses XED:106

nokomelela *v-st-abil* can be vigorous R12

nokophula *n8-vn-conj* and breaking R36.14

noku-[1] *combo* and to VERB; and VERBing • *Uthanda ukufunda nokubhala 'He likes reading and writing'* indicates that the conjunctive (na-) is linked to an infinitive or verbal noun (uku-) ☞ See: na- + uku- R4b=2, R4c, R10

-noku-[2] *v-abil-prf* can, could VERB; be able, willing to VERB • *umsebenzi unokukutyebisa 'a profession which can make you rich'* = na-uku-; Structure: S1-noku-Δ-a; Neg: SNEG-naku-Δ-a CGB:150, E&S:45, R2, R6, R7, R14, R28, R30

nokuba[1] *conj* even if, even though [calls attention to the extreme nature of what follows] usually followed by S1 and indicative mood EXD:196, MI:257, PCX:89, XED:106, R4c, R7

nokuba[2] *conj* and that XED:106

nokuba[3] *conj* and if XED:106

nokuba[4] *conj* than that [comparative] XED:106

nokuba[5] *conj* whether ☞ Alt: ukuba EXD:722, NDK-91:517, XED:106

nokuba[6] *conj* or XED:106

nokuba[7] *conj* because R11, R28, R29, R31, R36, R37

-nokuba nguwuphi *pro-expr* either RD-96:401

nokuba okanye *conj-expr* either ... or [cmp] RD-96:401

nokubhala *n8-vn-conj* and writing R4b

nokubila *n8-vn-conj* and sweating R30

nokubiwa *n8-vn-pass-conj* and the theft [lit: and the being stolen] R27.10

nokudinwa *n8-vn-conj* and being tired R30

nokufikelela *conj-v-inf* and to reach R37.17

nokufunda *conj-v-inf* and to read R24

nokufundisa *v-inf* for teaching R37

nokuhla *conj-v-inf* and losing R30

nokuhlonitshwa *conj-v-inf-pass* and to be respected R37=2

nokukholelwa *conj-v-inf-ben-pass* and to believe in R36

nokukhuselwa *conj-v-ben-pass* and to be protected R37.2

nokukuchazela *conj-v-inf* telling you R28

nokumamela *conj-v-inf* and to listen R4c

nokumiswa *conj-v-inf-pass* and setting up R29

nokungakwazi *conj-v-pot-neg* and not being able to know R30

nokungathandi *conj-v-inf-neg* and not to like R25

nokungavumelani *conj-v-neg-ben-recip* and not agreeing with R14

nokunye *conj* together with R25

nokuphosa *n8-vn* like throwing [comparative] R9

nokuphuculwa *conj-v-inf-pass* with the improvement R37.2

nokuphulukana *conj-v-tr-recip* lose, let slip away from R31

nokusebenzisa *conj-v-inf-caus* and to use R37.26

-nokusetyenziswa *v-rel-atr* useful, usable, that will be utilized EXD:699, RD-96:401;133, R16, R37.20

nokuthetha *conj-v-tr* and to speak; how to speak R34.11

nokuthi *conj-inf-aux* and how R22, R31

nokuthunyelwa *conj-v-inf-pass* with sending R29

nokutshoyo *conj-v-inf-rel* with what you say R14

nokuva *conj-v-inf-red* to even hear R26

nokuvula *conj-+-v-inf* and to open R10

nokuxabana *v-recip* above R14

nokuya *n8-vn-conj* and going R4b

nokuza *vn* come R35.11

nokuzakha *conj-v-inf+obj* and to build them R13

nokuzimela *conj-v-refl-ben* and to stand on one's own from -ma 'stand' R35.15

nokuzonyanya *conj-v-inf-refl* as to dread myself R36.5

nokwakhiwa *v-inf-pass* with the building of R37

nokwambatha *conj-v-tr* to put on some covering R36.26

nokwamkela *conj-v-inf* and to accept R14

noluntu *n6-sg-conj* and people; and the community; and society • *abazali noluntu lwasekuhlaleni 'parents and people in residence'* R22.3.4, R35.10.15

nolunye *conn-n6-sg-enum* have some • *Unokuba nolunye lwezi mpawu 'If you have some of these signs...'* R30

nolwazi *n6-sg-conj* and/with knowledge R34, R37

nom-[1] *combo* have OBJECT • *inyama ibe nombala omdaka 'the meat should have a brown color'* indicates that the possessive verb (na-) has a n2 sg object (um-) ☞ See: na- + um- R8

nom-[2] *combo* and • *uthando lwentliziyo nomoya 'love of the heart and spirit'* indicates that the conjunctive (na-) is linked to a n2 sg (um-) ☞ See: na- + um- R4d

nomabonakude *n1a-sg-conj* and television R26

nomakhenikha *n1a-sg-conj* and mechanic R26

nomama *conj-n1a-sg* with mother R28

Nomaxabiso *n1a-sg-red-pn-fem* Nomaxabiso (female personal name) [lit: priceless] SXWU:11

nombala *v-poss-n2-sg-obj* have a color R8

nombhali *conj-n1-sg* and author R37.27

nombolo *n5-sg-red* number (especially a telephone number) ☞ See: inombolo R15, R23

nomgangatho *conj-n2-sg* (and the) level, standard, class [rw: umgangatho] R37.17

nomgaqosiseko *n2-sg* of the constitution R21

nomgqwaliso *conj-n2-sg* one with discolored skin associated with lice infestation A Zulu variant, derived from the verb -gqwala 'become discolored' EZZE:269, R25.4

Nomhle *n1a-sg-red-pn-fem* Nomhle (female personal name) [lit: having beauty] SXWU:11

nomhlobo *conj-n1-sg* with a mate R25, R26

nomkhondo *conj-n2-sg* with a trace • *nekungakhange kuvakale nomkhondo 'without leaving a trace'* R18.2, R25.1

nomkhwezeli *conj-n2-sg* with the fire maker R36

nomntu *conj-n1-sg-red* of anyone, anybody • *wacela nomntu 'he asked anybody'* R27.6, R36.26

noMnu *conj-n1-sg-red* with Mr. R26

nomongameli *conj-n1-sg* with the ruler R32.7

nomoya[1] *conj-n2-sg* and soul R4d

nomoya[2] *conj-n2-sg* and air R25

Nompumelelo *n1a-sg-pn-red* Nompumelelo (personal name) ☞ See: uNompumelelo R15

nomqolo *conj-n2-sg* and the spine R25=2

nomyeni *comit-n1-sg* with a husband R19.2

Nomzamo *n1a-sg-red-pn-fem* Nomzamo (female personal name) [lit: struggle] SXWU:11

-nona *v-st* get fat; become rich XED:106

Nongqawuse *pn* Nongqawuse (girl whose dream and prophecy led to the Great Cattle Killing of 1856–1857) CGB:4

nonke *pro-enum-2pl* all of you; you together Agr: ni-, nina ☞ See: onke AM-94:151, E&S:27, PCX:62

Nonkululeko *n1a-sg-red-pn-fem* Nonkululeko (female personal name) [lit: freedom] SXWU:11

-nonophela *v-tr* interest, charm, delight XED:106

nontsumpa *n1a-sg-conj* of the principal, of the head of school R18

nonzima *atr-conj* heavy R36

noogqirha *comit-n1a-pl* with doctors R37.12

noomakad' enetha *conj-atr-red* with very experience people [idiom; lit: with those long rained upon] R36.5

noomatrasi *conj-n1a-pl-loan* with mattresses ☞ Usually: imatrasi [n5-sg] (EXD:372), R35.6

nootitshala *conj-n1a-pl* with teachers • *abafana nootitshala 'those like teachers'* R37.24

noqeqesho *conj-n6-sg* and training; also education R22.1, R35.3.12

norhulumente *conj-n1a-sg* and the government R35.15

nosapho *conj-n6-sg* and family R5

noSarah Jane *pn-conj* and Sarah Jane R33

noSekela Mphathi *conj-n1a-sg* with the Assistant Manager R27.3

nosisilumko *assoc-n4-sg* with wisdom; having wiseness R34.7

nosuku *comit-n6-sg* with a day • *ukujongana nosuku olude 'to face a long day'* R12

nothanda *conj-v-rel-tr* and who loves expresses a sense of possession of an attribute, e.g., unothanda 'one who has love' R16

nothando *conj-n6-sg* and the love R4d

noTokoyi *pn-conj* and Tokoyi R5

notyhefu *conj-n3-sg* and poison probably group 3 singular, thus after na- 'netyhefu' is expected (XED:172), R25.1.7

noVerwoerd *pn-conj* and Vervoerd (past Prime Minister of South Africa) R32

nowasweleka *conj-v-rel-intr* and who died R24

noxa *conj* even if, even when MI:257

nozidla *conj-v-refl* and who is proud of himself R26.4

-nqaba *v-inch* become fixed, imbedded, stuck fast; [perf] be secure, immobile, safe; be dear, expensive; difficult, impossibe; be scarce XED:106, R35x

Nqabisile *pn* Nqabisile (personal name) R26

nqanam *n5-sg-red* section of a post, capital of a pillar. In this context - objective, target, goal. XED -107 R34

-nqanda *v-tr* prevent EXD:480, R32x, R33x

-nqena *v-tr* be lethargic, feel lazy; be disinclined, indisposed (to do s.t.) PCX:37, XED:108

-nqumla *v-tr* cut (off), split; divide; cross (a mountain) XED:110, R26, R28

-nqunqa *v-tr* chop (up), mince, dice, cut fine; chop (firewood) XED:110, R8=2

nqweneleka *v-atr* be desirable R34

Nthulani *pn* (family name) R33

-ntinga *v-intr* go far (away, up), soar XED:111

Ntlangwini *clan* Ntlangwini (clan or ethnic group within the greater Xhosa community) MI:273

nto *n5-sg-red* thing; something ☞ See: into EXD:604, R11, R17.1.3.4, R28, R33=2, R36=3, R37=7

ntolongo *n5-sg-red* jail, prison R36

ntombazana *n5-sg-red* girl ☞ See: intombazana R19.2.3.4

-ntoni *qw-root* what?, what thing? Structure: comes sentence or clause final AM-94:84; 87, CGB:129f, E&S:33, PCX:26, SXWU:31, R14, R20, R23, R35, R37.12

ntsapho *n6-pl-red* families R26=7

ntsasana *n5-sg-red* ruffian, rogue KED:292

ntsh *change* change of MP to NTSH • *ampontshwe 'pumped up' [= a-mpomp/tsh-w-a]* CGB:142, MI:147, PCX:69; 103; 196

-ntsha *adj* modern ☞ See: -tsha 'new' RD-96:401

-ntsundu *atr-root* brown, dark brown (color); dark (skin); black (race) AM-94:107, CGB:172, E&S:30, EXD:143, NDK-91:35, PCX:156f, UEX:14, Uys:4, XED:112, R29=4, R34, R37

-ntu *n-root* person, individual ☞ See: umntu (abantu), umntwana R1, R2, R3, R4d=2, R9=7, R10, R11

-ntyontya *v-intr* whistle continuously XED:113, R8x

-ntyontyisa *v-caus* do s.t. for a while, do s.t. for a long time, prolong; simmer R8

-nuka *v-intr* smell, emit an aroma or odor EXD:598, XED:113, R32.3

-nxanwa *v-st* be, get, become thirsty ☞ Perf: -nxaniwe CGB:155f

nxaxheba *n5-sg-red* interest, share, participation in s.t. ☞ See: inxaxheba R37.10

nxeba *n3-sg-red* wound ☞ See: inxeba R36

-nxiba *v-tr* wear, dress (up in) AM-94:73, PCX:25

ny *change* change of M to NY • *bathunywa 'they are sent' [= ba-thum/ny-w-a], entanyeni 'on the neck' [= e-(i)ntam/ny-eni], emlonyeni 'in the mouth' [= e-(u)m-lom/ny-eni]* CGB:142, MI:147, PCX:69; 103; 196, R6, R9

nyaka *n1a-sg-red* year R18

nyakenye *adv-time* last year, a year ago; next year, in one year AXG:144

nyakomnye *adv-time* two years ago, the year before last; the year after next, two years from now AXG:144

nyanga[1] *n5-sg-red* month, moon • *Kule nyanga 'this month'* R22, R28

-nyanga[2] *v-tr* treat, heal, cure (by medicine or charms); repair, mend; [ext] prepare for war; [fig] deceive EXD:139, XED:116, R15, R25

-nyanisa *v-intr* speak the truth; be true; be sincere (in speech), correct, upright (in conduct) XED:116, R4dx

-nyanya *v-tr* fear, dread XED:116, R36.5.18.22

-nyanzela *v-tr* press, squeeze, crumple up; [ext] force, compel, constrain EXD:112; 226, XED:116, R10x=2, R19x

-nyanzelwa *v-pass* be forced, be compelled R10=2

-nyathela *v-tr* step on, tread upon, trample; run over XED:117, R10x

-nye[1] *adj-root* one; single, individual follows the noun it modifies AM-94:76, AXG:64, CGB:171, E&S:30; 59, EXD:425, PCX:120, R3, R6=2, R9, R11=4, R14, R33x

-nye[2] *atr-root* some; other, another (of the same kind); [cmp] some ... others • *eny'indlela 'another way'* precedes the noun it modifies or stands alone as a pronoun ☞ Contrast: -mbi (of a different kind) E&S:59, XED:117, R9, R36

-nyelisa *v* abuse, slander, revile XED:117, R17

-nyuka *v-intr* ascend, go up, go higher; [v-tr] mount, climb; attack latent vowel verb ☞ Caus: -nyusa; Cf: inyuka E&S:51, PCX:22f, XED:119, R9x

-nyula *v-tr* draw out / up; choose, select, elect XED:119, R16, R21

-nyusa *v-caus* raise; lift s.t. up, lead s.o. up; cause to rise, make ascend ☞ rw: -nyuka RD-96:401, XED:119, R9=3

nzame *n5-pl-red* efforts, attempts • *ezi nzame 'these efforts'* R35.5

-nzima *atr-root* heavy, weighty; difficult, hard; [ext] pregnant (of humans) • *wabuyela emyenini wakhe enzima umntwana ongowakho 'she returned to her husband being pregnant with your child'* AM-94:107f, CGB:172; 179, E&S:30, EXD:476-77, R14, R19.2, R28, R35x, R37=2

-nzulu *atr-root* deep E&S:30

O

o[1] *change* change (coalescence) of -A + U- to O • *notata 'and father' = na-u-tata* CGB:120, PCX:192, R14

o[2] *change* loss (elision) of -A before O- • *boja 'they roast' [= b(a)-oja]* PCX:192

o -[3] *emph-prf* [emphatic formative before noun groups starting with u] ☞ See: obona, okhona, okona, olona, owona, oyena TD

- o[4] *n-suf* [noun-forming suffix] • *amaxabiso 'prices', imidlalo 'sports', isifundo 'lesson', umculo 'music', uthando 'love'* -o denotes a derived noun relating to the theme of the root R1, R4a, R4b=2, R4c=2, R4d=4, R5, R6=3, R7=3, R10=4, R11, R30, R37.1=2

o -[5] *n1-sg-rel1* he, she who [group 1, 1a singular direct relative 1 attributive agreement prefix positive or negative construction] CGB:174, E&S:23; 28; 34, MI:153; 248, PCX:151, SXWU:155, XED:xv; 120, R4c, R4d=4, R33x

o -[6] *n2-sg-dir-rel1* that which [group 2 singular direct relative 1 attributive agreement prefix positive or negative construction] CGB:174, E&S:23; 28; 34, MI:153; 248, SXWU:155, XED:xv; 120, R8, R25, R30

o -[7] *n2-sg-ind-rel1* which [group 2 singular indirect relative 1 agreement prefix] E&S:35

o -[8] *poss-pro-prf* [possessive pronoun formative before noun groups starting with u] ☞ See: owam SXWU:84

o -[9] *pro-2sg-dir-rel1* you who [direct relative 1] MI:248, XED:xvi; 120, R34

o -[10] *pro-2sg-ind-rel1* that which you; you whom [indirect relative 1] E&S:35, R14

o -[11] *pro-3sg-dir-rel1* he, she, it who [direct relative 1] without antecedent MI:248, XED:xvi; 120

- o -[12] *v-fut-prf* will VERB [contracted / short future prefix] • *Bayongqiba imali 'they will beg for money'; Ndofunda 'I'll study'* ☞ See: bo-, ko-, lo-, ndo-, no-, #o-, so-, wo-, yo-, zo- CGB:165, E&S:20, XED:120, R9, R19, R23, R29, R31

o -[13] *v-n3-pl-short-fut* they will VERB [contracted / short positive future group 3 plural noun prefix] E&S:20

obaa *deic-3-n7* that (far, yonder) Agr: ubu- ☞ Alt: obuya CGB:163, E&S:26, MI:160, SXWU:157, XED:xvi; 120

obalasele *adj* eminent (EXD:187), R33

obalulekileyo *v-perf-rel* important R16

obefudula *v-aux-past* who used to be R33

obeluquka *v-rel-tr* which included, including R33

obeluseKapa *n5-sg-pn-geog-cop-loc* which was in Cape Town R33

obhinqileyo *v-perf-rel* female, woman [atr] relative verb construction used as noun EXD:731, R36.0x.22.26=2

obo *deic-2-n7* that (not far, just mentioned) CGB:163, E&S:26, PCX:86, SXWU:157, XED:xvi; 120

obona *n7-pro-emph* the real one, that very one; the most [group 7 singular emphatic pronoun] • *obona buso 'that very face'* E&S:23, PCX:165

obonakeleyo *v-rel-intr* which are left destitute R16

obu-[1] *n7-rel1* that which [group 7 singular noun direct relative 1 attributive agreement prefix positive or negative construction] CGB:174, E&S:23; 28; 34, MI:153; 248, SXWU:155, XED:xv, R8, R34

obu-[2] *n7-sg-ind-rel1* which [group 7 singular indirect relative 1 agreement prefix] E&S:35

obu-[3] *n7-adj* [group 7 singular adjective agreement prefix] CGB:174, E&S:28, MI:248, XED:xv

obu[4] *deic-1-n7* this Agr: ubu- ☞ Sole form (no alternate) CGB:163, E&S:26, MI:159, PCX:86, SXWU:157, XED:xvi; 120

obubaxelela *rel-cop-v-ben* telling them R29

obudlulileyo *rel-n7-sg-v-ben* the past R35

obumnandi *n7-poss-n3-pl* of joy • *ngamaxesha obumnandi 'in times of joy'* R14

obungebu- *n7-adj-neg* [group 7 singular negative adjective agreement prefix] • *obungebude 'not long'* E&S:28

obuphantsi *n7-rel-atr* which is low R8

obuphezulu *rel-loc* which is up, above R34

oburhalarhume *n7-poss-n3-pl* of rage R36

obuthe *v-aux* which is [lit: which says, used as auxiliary before an ideophone for purposes of conjugation] • *ubutyebi obuthe chatha 'wealth used sparingly'* R34.10

obuthweleyo *v-perf-rel* which is carried R34.1

obuya *deic-3-n7* that (far, yonder) Agr: ubu- ☞ Alt: obaa CGB:163, E&S:26, MI:160, PCX:86, SXWU:157, XED:120

odlwengulo *rel-n6-sg* of rape R36

-odola *v-tr* order (goods) • *Xa ufuna ukuyiodola le ncwadana 'If you want to order this pamphlet'* NDK-91:203, R22.6

-odwa[1] *pro-quan-root* only, alone, by oneself Structure: with the thematic consonant of each noun class ☞ See: bodwa, kodwa, lodwa, ndedwa, ndodwa, nedwa, nodwa, odwa, sedwa, sodwa, wedwa, wodwa, yedwa, yodwa, zodwa CGB:176, E&S:27, PCX:62, R12, R36

odwa[2] *pro-quan-n3-pl* only they; they alone • *amadoda odwa 'men only'* Agr: ama-, wona E&S:27, PCX:62, XED:120, R36

ofanele *v-rel-ben-perf* which is suitable, right, appropriate R22

ofisini *loan* office R31

ohloniphekileyo *v-rel-intr-perf* who is respected R32.7

-ohlwaya *v-tr* find fault with; rebuke, reprove; punish, fine EXD:215; 493, XED:120, R11=2, R23x=3

-ohlwaywa *v-pass* be punished R11=2, R23

-oja *v-tr* roast, bake; grill, broil PCX:20, XED:120

ojongene *v-rel-recip-perf* which is looked at R36.14

oka *poss-emph-n1a* of the family of R27

okaa *deic-3-n8-vn* that (far, yonder) Agr: uku- ☞ Alt: okwaa, okuya XED:xvi; 120

okade *n2-sg-rel* of long ago R15

okanye *conj* or; otherwise; [neg] nor • *Uzakufika namhlanje okanye ngomso? 'Will you arrive today or tomorrow?'* AXG:148, E&S:59, RD-96:401, XED:120, R4b, R6=3, R7, R8=3, R12, R14, R15x, R19, R21=3, R23, R27=4, R30=3, R31=4, R33=2, R34, R35, R36=9, R37=10

okhathazekileyo *v-rel-perf* one who is troubled R19.3

okhona *n10-loc-pro-emph* the real place, that very location / situation; the most [group 10 locative noun emphatic pronoun] • *okhona 'that very spot'* PCX:165

oko[1] *deic-2-n8-vn* that (not far, just mentioned) • *lokwenza oko 'of doing that'* Agr: uku- CGB:163, E&S:26, MI:159, PCX:86, SXWU:157, XED:xvi;120, R14=2, R23, R29=3, R30, R37

oko[2] *deic-2-n10-loc* that (time, place, situation not far, just mentioned) PCX:86, R10, R12

oko[3] *deic-adv* then, at that time XED:120

oko[4] *conj* when XED:120

okokuba *conj* that ☞ Cf: ukuba XED:120, R21, R34

okokuqala *v-rel-tr* to start with R19, R35

okomshologu *v-rel-n8-vn-n1-sg* which is like an evil spirit; [adv] nightmarishly • *bagxothiswe okomshologu 'nightmarishly expelled'* R26.1

okona *n8-vn-pro-emph* the real one, that very action; the most [group 8 verbal noun emphatic pronoun] • *okona kutya 'that very food'* E&S:23, EXD:391, PCX:165, XED:120

Oktober *n-time-month-loan* October R23

oku-[1] *n8-vn-adj* [group 8 verbal noun adjective agreement prefix] CGB:174, E&S:28, MI:248, XED:xv

oku-[2] *n8-vn-rel1* the VERBing which [group 8 verbal noun direct relative 1 attributive agreement prefix positive or negative construction] CGB:174, E&S:23; 28; 34, MI:153; 248, SXWU:155, XED:xv, R12=4

oku-[3] *n8-vn-ind-rel1* which VERBing [group 8 verbal noun indirect relative 1 agreement prefix] E&S:35

oku-[4] *n10-loc-rel1* the (time, place, situation) which [group 10 locative noun direct relative 1 attributive agreement prefix positive or negative construction] XED:120

oku[5] *deic-1-n8-vn* this • *oku kutya 'this food'; oku kuthetha 'this means, this is to say'* Agr: uku-; sole form (no alternate) CGB:163, E&S:26, MI:159, PCX:86, SXWU:157, XED:xvi;120, R11, R12, R18.2, R21.3=2, R24.3, R27.2, R31.1, R35.14, R36.7.18.26, R37=10

oku[6] *deic-1-n10-loc* this (place, situation, time) ☞ Sole form (no alternate) PCX:86, R9

okuba *n3-pl-poss-n8-vn* of being; [conj] that, so that • *okuba abantu bakwazi 'so that people know...'* ☞ See: ukuba R28, R37

okubalulekileyo *v-atr-perf-rel* what is important R37.7

okucacayo *v-rel* what is clear R26.5

okucingayo *v-rel* what you are thinking R14

okudlwengulwa *v-rel-pass* one who is raped R36

okufunayo *v-rel* what you want R29.5

okugqithisileyo *v-perf-rel* which has surpassed; beyond measure R12

okuhlupha *v-rel* of inconveniencing R32

okunene *adv* indeed, truly, in fact ☞ Alt: okwenene AXG:145, XED:98; 120

okungacacanga *v-rel-neg* which is not clear R37.19

okungamahlebo *v-rel-neg-n8-vn+n3-pl* without slanderers = oku- + -nga- + amahlebo R34.8

okungeku- *n8-vn-adj-neg* [group 8 verbal noun negative adjective agreement prefix] • *okungekude 'not long'* E&S:28

okungezona *rel-cop-pron-abs* that were not the very ones R26

okunokubangelwa *v-rel-abil-pass* which can be achieved • *Kuninzi okunokubangelwa 'there is much which can be done'* R36.23

okunokuhlala *v-rel-abil* which can stay with (them) R36.23

okunye *cop-n8-enum* there is another (thing) R37.19

okuphambili *n8-vn-rel1* that which is foremost R12

okusemandleni *rel-cop-loc* that is in its strength R37

okusisipesheli *n8-vn-rel1* special R12

okusithungela *v-rel-ben+pro-1pl-obj* to sew for us R28.6

okuthandayo *v-rel-tr* who likes R29

okuthethwa *v-rel-pass* what is being discussed R22.4

okuthile *n8-vn-rel1* certain, particular; some R12

okuthiwa *v-rel* that is said R26.6

okutshoyo *v-rel* that which is said R14

okuvuleleka *v-rel* which cause to open R37.1

okuya[1] *deic-3-n8-vn* that (far, yonder) Agr: uku- ☞ Alt: okwaa CGB:163, E&S:26, MI:160, PCX:86, SXWU:157, XED:120

okuya[2] *deic-3-n10-loc* that (far place, remote situation, distant in time, yonder) Agr: uku- ☞ Alt: okwaa PCX:86

okuya[3] *conj-rel* then when Structure: followed by relative construction E&S:36

okuzigcina *n8-vn-poss-n3-pl* of taking care of oneself R34.2

okwaa *deic-3-n8-vn* that (far, yonder) Agr: uku- ☞ Alt: okaa, okuya CGB:163, E&S:26, MI:160, SXWU:157

okwabantu *n8-vn-poss-emph-n1-pl* for people R36.23

okwamagwinya *rel-loc-n3-pl* like hot cakes [lit: fat cakes] R29

okwamakhanukanodwa *rel-n3-pl-comp* of gay people R36

okwesibini *rel-poss-n4-num* second R37.8

olaa *deic-3-n6-sg* that (far, yonder) Agr: ulu- ☞ Alt: oluya, olwaa CGB:163, XED:xvi; 120

Olimpiki *loan* Olympics R33=2

olo *deic-2-n6-sg* that (not far, just mentioned) CGB:163, E&S:26, PCX:86, SXWU:157, XED:xvi;120, R33.6

olona *n6-sg-pro-emph* the real one, that very one; the most [group 6 singular emphatic pronoun] • *olona luvo 'the real opinion'* E&S:23, PCX:165, XED:120

olu-[1] *n6-sg-rel1* that which [group 6 singular noun direct relative 1 attributive agreement prefix positive or negative construction] CGB:174, E&S:23; 28; 34, MI:153; 248, SXWU:155, XED:xv; 120

olu-[2] *n6-sg-ind-rel1* which [group 6 singular indirect relative 1 agreement prefix] E&S:35

olu-[3] *n6-sg-adj* [group 6 singular adjective agreement prefix] CGB:174, E&S:28, MI:248, XED:xv; 120, R12

olu[4] *deic-1-n6-sg* this Agr: ulu- ☞ Sole form (no alternate) CGB:163, E&S:26, MI:159,

PCX:86, SXWU:157, XED:xvi; 120, R24, R37.11

olubhalwe *rel-n6-sg-v-pass* that it is written R37.11

olude *adj-n6-sg* long R12

olufuneka *v-atr* that needs R37

olukhethwe *v-rel-pass* that is chosen; of your choice R23.9

olukhulekileyo *v-perf-rel* which are free R16

olukumgangatho *rel-cop-n2-sg* those who have a standard • *olukumgangatho wentlalo esezantsi. 'those who have a low standard of living'* R37.1.25

olumbalwa *rel-cop-adj* which are few R33

olungafikelela *rel-n6-sg-v-intens* in which it will be accessible R37.1

olungakhaliyo *v-rel-intr-neg* that does not cry R27.14

olungangqamenanga *v-rel-neg-perf* which was not in relation R37.15

olungapheliyo *v-rel-intr-neg* which does not stop R30.2

olungelu- *n6-sg-adj-neg* [group 6 singular negative adjective agreement prefix] • *olungelude 'not tall'* E&S:28

olungileyo *v-perf-rel* who is right, good, ready R14

oluninzi *adj-n6-sg* much, a lot (of) R37.25

oluqhutywayo *v-rel-pass* which was conducted R18

oluya *deic-3-n6-sg* that (far, yonder) Agr: ulu- ☞ Alt: olaa, olwaa CGB:163, E&S:26, MI:160, PCX:86, SXWU:157, XED:120, R37

oluyakuthi *rel-n6-sg-aux* of whom it can be said • *uluntu oluyakuthi luyazi 'the community will come to know'* R37

oluzibalekisa *v-rel-atr-caus* who will cause them to run R31.1

oluzithethe *v-rel-atr* which is traditional • *...uluntu oluzithethe 'traditional societies'* olu-zi-thethe relative agreement for class6 + class4-pl noun R21

olwaa *deic-3-n6-sg* that (far, yonder) Agr: ulu- ☞ Alt: olaa, oluya E&S:26, MI:160, SXWU:157, R4d

olwenziwa *v-rel-pass* that was done R36.7

olwenziwe *v-rel-pass-perf* which was done • *kuphando olwenziwe ngu Athalie Crawford ' according to the research by Athalie Crawford'* R18.3, R37.12

om-[1] *n1-sg-adj* [group 1, 1a singular adjective agreement prefix] CGB:174, E&S:28, MI:248, XED:xv

om-[2] *n2-sg-adj* [group 2 singular adjective agreement prefix] CGB:174, E&S:28, MI:248, XED:xv, R37.1

-oma *v-st* become dry, hard; get ripe; [perf] dried up, paralyzed XED:120, R12x

omdaka[1] *atr-n2-sg* dark brown [lit: which is dark brown] R8

omdaka[2] *atr-n2-sg* dirty R25

omde *atr-n2-sg* long • *umgama omde 'a long distance'; umzabalazo omde nonzima 'a long, hard struggle'* R28.4, R36.22

-omelela *v-st* dry out; harden; ripen; [perf] strong, vigorous, robust, healthy XED:120, R12=2

omhle *atr-n2-sg* beautiful, pleasant, nice • *ngumsebenzi omhle 'it is a nice job'* R29.13

ominyaka *n2-pl-rel* who is NUM years old • *UTakalani ominyaka eli-17 '17 year old Takalani'* R33.1

omkhulu[1] *adj-n1-sg* large, major, superior, chief • *Umhleli Omkhulu 'editor-in-chief'* R21, R31.0.5, R32.9

omkhulu[2] *adj-n2-sg* big, large, huge; major • *umonakalo omkhulu 'major damage'* R18.5

omphefumlo *rel-n2-sg* of the breath; of the soul R36.21

omtsha *adj-n2-sg* new R37.1.3

omzabalazo *n2-sg-poss-n3-pl* of the struggle R32.3

-ona *v-tr* injure, harm, hurt; spoil; wrong, do wrong / injustice to; sin, transgress; deflower ☞ Pass: -oniwa PCX:20f; 93, XED:121, R30x

onabo *rel-deic* and they; and as for them; and he, she, it; and as for him, her, it; there (not far, just mentioned) is R34.8

-onakala *v-atr* be spoiled, ruined; get worn out; suffer an injury PCX:93, XED:121

-onakalisa *v-atr-caus* injure, spoil, damage, ruin EXD:142, XED:121, R30.7

oncumisayo *v-rel-caus* satisfying, pleasing [lit: which makes you smile] R29.10

-ondla *v-tr* feed, nourish, provide for; bring up, rear; cherish RD-96:372, R20.3

onemali *v-poss-rel* who has money R4d

oneminyaka *v-poss+n2-pl-obj* who is NUM years old R19.1

onenkathalo *v-rel-poss-n5-sg* who has concern for ☞ See: inkathalo; -khathala R16

-onga *v-tr* use sparingly, frugally, economically; avoid waste; give food sparingly (to the sick); [ext] nurse, take care of the sick ☞ Pass: -ongiwa XED:121, R3, R24.6

ongama *n2-sg-pred-num-n3-pl-expr* which is NUM, that is NUM • *ikumgama ongama-20km 'which is a distance of 20 kilometres'* R35.3

ongaselanga *v-rel-past-neg* who did not drink R31.4

ongazange *v-rel-aux-neg* who never did R23.7

ongazenzisiyo *v-rel-tr-caus* not pretending R27.7

ongekazilungeli *v-rel-neg-refl* (things) which are not appropriate for you R14

ongem-[1] *n1-sg-adj-neg* [group 1, 1a singular negative adjective agreement prefix] • *ongemde 'not tall'* E&S:28

ongem-[2] *n2-sg-adj-neg* [group 2 singular negative adjective agreement prefix] • *ongemde 'not tall'* E&S:28

ongemhle *adj-neg-n1-sg* who is not pretty R4d

ongowakho *rel-poss-pro-2sg-n1-sg* which is yours R19

ongumthengisi *v-rel-caus* who is selling R29.1

onjani *rel-interr* a kind R31

onk' *Class3-pl-enum* all (reduced) R13

-onke[1] *pro-enum-root* all, every, the whole (of) Structure: with the thematic consonant of each noun class ☞ See: bonke, konke, lonke, onke, sonke, wonke, yonke, zonke AM-94:163, CGB:176, E&S:27, PCX:62, RD-96:402, XED:121, R1=2, R5

onke[2] *pro-enum-n3-pl* all; every • *onke amazwe 'all countries'* Agr: ama-, wona AM-94:163, E&S:27, PCX:62, R1, R32=2

onokuthetha *v-rel-abil* who can say R14

onokuwukhetha *v-rel-abil+n2-sg-obj* which you can choose R29.13

onokuzikhusela *v-rel-abil-refl-ben* who can protect themselves R36.12

onolwazi *rel-conj-n6-sg* who has knowledge R18.6

onomdla *v-poss-rel* whoever is interested [lit: who has interest] R4c

-onwaba *v-st* be at ease, relax; be comfortable, content, happy; [ext] be well off CGB:119;155f, PCX:20f, XED:121, R14, R36.18x

-onwabisa *v-caus* delight, cheer up, make s.o. happy; please s.o., gratify ☞ Pass: -onwatyiswa PCX:104, XED:121, R36.18

-onwatyiswa *v-pass* be cheered up, delighted, made happy ☞ rw: -onwaba PCX:104

o o[1] *change* loss (elision) of -A before OO- • *kwanootitshala 'and even teachers' [= kwa-n(a)-oo-titshala]* PCX:192, R3

o o-[2] *n1a-pl-prf* [group 1a (Bantu class 2a) plural noun prefix] • *ootata 'fathers'* Consists of article #- + classifier oo- ☞ Sg: u-; Orig: abo- AXG:17f, CGB:103, E&S:17, PCX:51f, RD-96:372, SXWU:14, R3=5

oobawo *n1a-pl-kin* our fathers ☞ Sg: ubawo E&S:17; 56, R32

oobawomkhulu *n1a-pl-cmp-kin* grandfathers (my, our) ☞ Sg: ubawomkhulu E&S:56, R32

oobhuti *n1a-pl-kin* brothers SXWU:14, R36.18

oogqirha *n1a-pl* doctors ☞ Sg: ugqirha E&S:56, R3, R37.12x

oomama *n1a-pl-kin* mothers (our) ☞ Sg: umama CGB:103, E&S:22; 56, EXD:391, PCX:52, SXWU:14

oomatshini *n1a-pl* machines ☞ Sg: umatshini CGB:103

oomnu *n1a-pl* misters, sirs ☞ Sg: umnu R32

oonina *n1a-pl-kin* mothers, their mothers ☞ Sg: unina CGB:103, EXD:391

oonomathotholo *n1a-pl* disembodied voices; [ext] radios ☞ See: unomathotholo [sg] CGB:103

oonompilo *rel-n2-sg* health workers R36

oononkala *n1a-pl* crabs ☞ Sg: unonkala CGB:103, PCX:50; 52

oonopopi *n1a-pl* dolls ☞ Sg: unopopi CGB:103

oonyoko *n1a-pl-kin* mothers, your mothers ☞ Sg: unyoko CGB:103, EXD:391

oorhulumente *n1a-pl* governments ☞ Sg: urhulumente R20

oosisi *n1a-pl* women [term of respect or endearment] ☞ See: usisi SXWU:14, R4d

oosomashishini *n1a-pl* businessmen R35.5

ootata *n1a-pl-kin* fathers ☞ Sg: utata E&S:56, RD-96:372, SXWU:14

ootitshala *n1a-pl* teachers ☞ Sg: utitshala CGB:103, R3, R37.24

ophantsi *rel-n2-sg-loc* lower R37

opheleleyo *v-perf-atr-rel* who is perfect R4d

ophezulu *rel-n2-sg-loc* upper, higher, of above R37

oqulunqwayo *v-rel-pass* that is smoothed rel formed from -qulunq- = tidy, smooth, comb [v-tr] R37

-orenji *atr-root* orange (UEX:14), CGB:172, EXD:422, NDK-91:203, RD-96:402;104, Uys:4, R34

osebenzisana *v-rel-caus-recip* that you work together R34.3

osemthethweni *rel-loc-n2-sg* within the law R31

osenokuba *v-rel-pred-abil* which may still be R30

osezantsi *n3-sg-rel-loc-n2-sg* which is low R37=6

osithandayo *v-rel* which you love R31

osuka *v-dir-rel1* which originates R25.5

-othuka *v-st* be shocked, startled ☞ Caus: -othusa XED:122, R34x

otyunjelwe *v-rel-ben-pass* who were carried off R32.7

ovela *v-rel-ben* that come from R35.14

owafumanayo *v-rel-tr* of you getting R29.10

owaya *v-rel-intr* who went R28.1

owayenguMongameli *rel-cop-n1-sg* who was the ruler R24

owayenguyise *v-rel-cop-n1-sg* who was the father R32.4

owentwala *n1-sg* that of a louse; for lice R25

owokhohlokhohlo *rel-n6-sg-redup* that of coughing ukhohlokhohlo 'cough', derived from -khohla 'embarrass' R25.5

owomeleleyo *v-rel-ben* who is strong, who is healthy R36.12

owona *n2-sg-pro-emph* the real one, that very one; the most [group 2 singular emphatic pronoun] • *owona mthi 'the real tree'* E&S:23, PCX:164, R29

owufaneleyo *v-rel* suitable R29

oxhotyiswe *v-rel-pass* that is armed, being armed ☞ See: -xhoba R34.8

oya *rel-aux* [it] is going R34

oye *v-rel-aux* that he be VERB • *oyewavavaniywa 'who has been examined'* part of compound, normally joined R16

oyena *n1-sg-pro-emph* the real one, that very one; the most [group 1, 1a singular emphatic pronoun] • *oyena mntwana 'the very child'; oyena nyana 'the real son'* E&S:23, PCX:164

oyenzileyo *v-perf-rel* which you do R15

oyiforensic *rel-cop-n5-sg-loan* which is forensic R36

-oyika *v-tr* fear, dread, be afraid of ☞ Caus: -oyisa AM-94:106, AXG:112, RD-96:402, SXWU:31, R11

-oyikayo *v-rel-atr* afraid RD-96:402

-oyikisa *v-caus* frighten, terrify, cause s.o. to be afraid ☞ Cf: -oyisa RD-96:402

-oyikisayo *v-caus-rel-atr* apprehensive RD-96:402

oyingcwele *rel-cop-atr* who is holy R13

oyintombazana *v-rel-cop-n5-sg* who is a girl R19.1

-oyisa *v-caus* frighten, make s.o. afraid; [ext] defeat, conquer, overcome, overpower, subdue ☞ rw: -oyika; Cf: -oyikisa AXG:112, RD-96:402, R10

ozayo *v-rel* coming R31

ozimeleyo *v-refl-perf-rel-atr* who is independent R34.5

ozimisele *v-refl-perf-rel* who is serious R4d

ozuzileyo *v-rel-tr-perf* who acquired, who were recipients (of) R35.7

P

p *change* change of PH to P • *impelo 'end' [= im-phel-o], impendulo 'answer' [= im-phendul-o], impilo 'health' [= im-phil-o], impatho 'treatment' [= im-phath-o]* E&S:51, PCX:195, R1, R30=3

pasport *n-loan* passport R37.14

Patensie *pn-geog* Patensie (town) [lit: resting place for cattle] CGB:41, R4b

-patha *v-tr* carry in the hands CGB:143

Paulos *pn-loan* Paul R20

Peterson *pn-loan* (personal name) • *Hector Peterson* R32.5

pha-[1] *n9-loc-prf* [group 9 (Bantu class 16) locative noun prefix] • *phandle 'outside'* Consists of article #- + classifier pha- AXG:200, Pahl, PCX:51; 56; 71, RD-96:372, R3, R36

-pha[2] *v-ditr* give s.t. to s.o., present to, bestow upon; serve (food to) ☞ Pass: -phiwa AXG:107, PCX:104, XED:122, R6, R8x

-pha[3] *v-tr* pluck, pull (up / out), gather (harvest), cut (grass) latent vowel verb ☞ Cf: -ipha XED:122

-phakama *v-intr* stand up, be erect, rise, be elevated; stand out PCX:34, XED:122, R10x, R37x

-phakamisa *v-tr* raise, elevate, erect ☞ Pass: -phakanyiswa PCX:103, XED:122, R13, R37x

-phakanyiswa *v-pass* be raised ☞ rw: -phakama PCX:103

phakathi *adv-loc* inside, within; middle, midst ☞ Opp: phandle AM-94:108, AXG:200, CGB:178, E&S:27, Pahl, PCX:56; 96, XED:122, R27, R30, R34, R36=2

phakathi kwa *prep-expr* between, among; inside of, within AM-94:112, CGB:140, E&S:27; 32, XED:122, R4b

Phalo *n1a-sg-red-pn* Phalo (chief who ruled during the 18th century; his sons, Rharhabe and Gcaleka, split the Xhosa nation in two) ☞ See: Gcaleka, Rharhabe CGB:4

phambi *n9-loc-red;-adv* ahead, in front (of) [spatial]; before [temporal] ☞ Red: phambili PCX:71, XED:123, R6, R16, R23, R33

phambi kokuba *conj-expr* before Structure: followed by present subjunctive (no matter what mood or tense of the main verb) PCX:124, R6

phambi kwa *prep-expr* in front of; before ☞ Red: phambili CGB:140, E&S:27; 32, PCX:71, XED:123, R23

phambile *adv-loc* ahead, in front CGB:178

phambili[1] *adv-loc* ahead, in front, in advance, foreward; [atr] foremost • *'qhubela phambili' to progress* ☞ Opp: emva 'behind, at the back' AM-94:108, AXG:200, E&S:32n, EXD:227, Pahl, PCX:56; 71, XED:123, R10, R12, R34=5

phambili[2] *adv-time* before [temporal] ☞ Contrast: phambili 'ahead, in front' [locational] AM-94:112, EXD:50, XED:123

phandle *n9-loc;-adv-loc* outside, outdoor; [adv] openly; [ext] downright ☞ Opp: phakathi AM-94:108, AXG:200, CGB:178, NDK-91:537, Pahl, PCX:56; 70, RD-96:402;372, R34

phandle kwa *prep-expr* outside of, beyond CGB:140

phando *n6-sg-red* investigation ☞ See: uphando R37.10

-phangela *v-ben* work for or at; outrun, run before; speak before one's turn; arrive before R35.4

-phantsa *preverb* nearly, almost VERBed ☞ See: -phantse E&S:47

-phantse *preverb* nearly, almost VERBed • *Ndiphantse ndawa 'I almost fell'* Structure: followed by S3b + past subjunctive construction E&S:47, EXD:391, SXWU:140

phantse -nke *adv-cmp* mostly, almost all • *phantse bonke abantu bemka 'almost everybody left'; Phantse zonke izindlu zale dolophu zakhiwe ngodaka 'The village consists mostly of mud houses'* EXD:391

phantsi *adv-loc* down, below; under; place on the ground; [atr] low, lower; elementary • *amabanga aphantsi, lower standards/grades. (i.e., those school grades concerned with earlier education)* ☞ Opp: phezulu AM-94:108, CGB:140, E&S:27, MI:256, Pahl, PCX:34; 56; 70, RD-96:402, R1, R8, R9, R10x=2, R17.2, R20, R29, R32, R34, R35, R36, R37

phantsi kwa *prep-expr* below, under (down, towards the ground) • *phantsi komthetho 'under the law'* Possessive locative compound CGB:140, E&S:32, R36.14.15=2

-phatha[1] *v-tr* touch, handle, feel; hold, carry in the hand; treat, deal with; take control, take charge of, manage; command, rule ☞ Perf: -phethe CGB:153, RD-96:402, XED:125, R9, R11x, R22, R30

-phatha[2] *v-aux* take turns VERBing, do by turns; do VERB alternatively; do partly; first VERB ... then VERB [when used in two clauses] • *Uphatha kuhleka, aphathe kulila 'First she laughed, then she cried'* Structure: followed by short infinitive construction (ku-) E&S:47

-phathela *v-ben* carry for; bring to; [fig] introduce XED:125, R22, R28, R30

phaya *deic-3-n9-loc* that place (far), over there, yonder ☞ Cf: apha 'here', apho 'there' AM-94:109, AXG:144; 213, CGB:178, E&S:59, EXD:737, PCX:86, R26, R37

-phefumla *v-intr* respire, take a breath, breathe (out); rest; speak out XED:125, R36.21, R37.6

-pheka *v-tr* cook PCX:29, RD-96:402;69

-phela *v-intr* stop, cease, finish, come to an end, terminate CGB:143, XED:126, R1x, R4dx, R7x, R24

-phelela[1] *v-ben* be complete, intact, entire, perfect; [ext] be a virgin ☞ Perf: phelele KED:328, XED:126, R4d, R7, R15x

-phelela[2] *v-ben* end (for), expire; be the last of s.t.; end in nothing KED:328, R15

-phelele *v-perf-atr* perfect; complete, intact; fully-; implicit • *Mna ndingumyeni opheleleyo 'I am a perfect husband'; inkcazelo epheleleyo 'a complete explanation'* XED:126, R4d, R7, R15

-phelelwa *v-ben-pass* be gone, get used up, exhausted; be bereft of KED:328, R25, R28, R30, R36.23

-phelile *v-perf-atr* finished, done; all gone E&S:30

phendula *v-tr* answer, reply; return ☞ Cf: impendulo 'answer' XED:126

phesheya *n9-loc;-adv* beyond, across, on the other side of; external; [ext] foreign [lit: further-side] AXG:200, CGB:140, E&S:27, Pahl, PCX:56, XED:127

phesheya kwa *prep-expr* beyond, across, on the other side of AXG:200, CGB:140, E&S:27; 32, Pahl, PCX:56, XED:127

-phethe *v-tr-past* touched; held; treated, dealt with; took charge of, managed; commanded, ruled ☞ rw: -phatha CGB:153, XED:125, R11x, R22, R30

phezolo *n9-loc-time;-adv* last evening, yesterday night Pahl, XED:192

phezu kwa- *prep-expr* above, on (top of); over • *linabantu abangaphezu kwama-70 'it has people who are over 70'* ☞ Red: phezulu CGB:140, E&S:27; 32, PCX:71, XED:127, R35=2, R36.6

phezulu *n9-loc;-adv* up, above [lit: sky-side] = pha-i-zulu ☞ Opp: phantsi AM-94:108, AXG:200, CGB:140, E&S:32n, Pahl, PCX:56; 71, XED:127, R34, R35x=2, R36x

-phi[1] *pro-indef-root* any- (as in anything, anyone); -ever (as in whatever, whichever) EXD:23f, R7, R9

-phi[2] *qw-enum-root* which? (of two or more) [enumerative interrogative root] with low tone concord prefix ☞ See: baphi, buphi, kuphi, liphi, luphi, siphi, waphi, wuphi, yiphi, ziphi AXG:141, E&S:27; 33, EXD:722, GDX3:703, PCX:110f, R7x, R9x

-phi[3] *qw-loc-adv-root* where? [adverbial interrogative root] with high tone concord prefix ☞ See: aphi, baphi, buphi, iphi, kuphi, liphi, luphi, siphi, uphi, ziphi AM-94:107, AXG:63;141f, CGB:129, E&S:31; 33, PCX:29; 111

-phila *v-st* be well, healthy; get well, recover; enjoy life; live ☞ Cf: impilo 'health' CGB:155, PCX:29, XED:128, R31, R34x

-phinda[1] *v-tr* fold, double, turn s.t. over upon itself; repeat XED:128

-phinda[2] *v-aux* do VERB again • *ukuba aniwazi amakhosi anisokuze niphinde niwazi 'if you do not know the chiefs, you will never again know (them)'* Structure: followed by S3a + present subjunctive E&S:47, XED:128, R20, R37.10.17.21.26

phindana *v-redupl* multiply part of reduplicated construct 'phinda-phindana' R34

phofu *conj / adv* then, in that case; why, how then; therefore, and yet [expressing astonishment – calls for reasons for a course of action that appears absurd or contrary to expectation] MI:257, R36

-phola *v-st* cool; abate, subside; heal CGB:155, XED:129, R30=2

phondo *n3-sg-red* province, region, administrative division • *weli phondo 'of this region'* R18, R35

phone *loan* phone R15

phonoshono *n9-loc;-adv* this side [lit: hither-side] Pahl, PCX:56

-phosa *v-tr* throw, hurl, cast, fling RD-96:402, XED:130, R9

-phoxa *v-tr* shame, put to shame, make a fool of s.o.; deride, mock KED:339, XED:130, R4c

-phucuka *v-intr* slip off, come completely out; get rubbed, abraded, chafed, bruised; become smooth, polished; [ext] become civilized; improve XED:130, R17, R37.17

-phucula *v-tr* improve, benefit; civilize, modernize BS, R37=9

-phulaphula *v-tr* listen (to) carefully, hearken; attend; obey PCX:26, XED:131, R4b, R14, R30

phulo *n3-sg-red* information; project • *eli phulo lenkqubela yoluntu 'this community development project'* ☞ See: iphulo R30.1, R31.2

-phuma *v-intr* go outside, come out, exit; come from; rise (celestial body) ☞ Pass: -phunywa PCX:34, XED:131, R30

-phumelela *v-intens* come out into view, be prominent, conspicuous; come through; speed; [ext] reach (by effort), succeed; pass (exam); win (race); prosper; [fig] utter, disclose • *Wafunda kakhulu, waphumelela 'She studied a lot and passed'* EXD:727, KED:341, SXWU:140, XED:131, R29.8, R33.5.11, R37.20

-phunga *v-tr* drink (s.t. hot) ☞ Contrast: -sela (s.t. cold) CGB:143, EXD:175, R4ax

-pinki *atr-root* pink (RD-96:107;389), CGB:172, EXD:458, NDK-91:220, UEX:14, Uys:4

Pisces *loan* Pisces R34.12

PO Box *abr* Post Office Box R4c, R4d, R7, R15, R20, R21, R22, R25

Policy *loan* Policy R37

Port Elizabeth *pn-geog* Port Elizabeth ☞ See: iBhayi R4c

pressure *loan* pressure ☞ See: high blood pressure R25

prison *loan* prison R4a

private bag *n5-sg-cmp-red* private R4b

Project *loan* Project R37

protection *loan* protection ☞ See: Child Protection Unit R27, R36

protein *n5-sg* protein R12

Q

-qaba *v-tr* smear the body with red clay or ochre mixed with fat; paint XED:133, R4ax

-qabana *v-recip* paint each other with red clay, smear one another with ochre mixed with fat; [ext] be intimate XED:133, R4ax, R4cx

-qakadula *v-intr* gallop, frolic, frisk, gambol, skip about (like calves, puppies, or children) ☞ Alt: -qakathula GDX3:5-6

-qakathula *v-intr* gallop, frolic, frisk, gambol, skip about (like calves, kids or children) ☞ Alt: -qakadula GDX3:5-6

-qala *v-tr* begin, start, commence; do s.t. for the first time; do s.t. ahead of s.o. else; be the first (to do), take the lead, pioneer; start (a fight) GDX3:6f, R4c, R7x, R24

-qalisa *v-caus* start anew, make a beginning; make s.o. begin s.t. XED:133, R34=4

-qapheleka *v-atr* get noticed, be paid attention (to); be obvious, get cleared up Note: The Zulu root (-qaphela) is not found in any Xhosa references (even GDX3); yet it is used three times (eyaqaphelekayo, zaqapheleka, ziqapheleke) in a Xhosa article on the role of the South African Language Board EZZE:689, R37.7.12.24

-qeqesha *v-tr* break in, train (draft animal); discipline (child); educate s.o. EXD:675, KED:352, XED:136, R22.1, R33=6, R35

qete *adv* completely, perfectly, totally; [atr] complete, total, perfect GDX3:26, R34.2

qha *adv* only, just ☞ Syn: kuphela AM-94:115, GDX3:26

-qhekeka *v-st* split (in two), crack, break (up, into pieces), fracture, rupture GDX3:38, XED:135, R25

-qheleka *v-atr* become familiar to one by custom KED:351

qho *ideophone* do VERB always, continually, persistently, frequently; keep on VERBing EXD:18, GDX3:47, XED:137, R30

-qhotsa *v-tr* cook s.t. dry; bake; fry EXD:235, XED:139, R8+x

-qhuba *v-tr* drive (animal, vehicle); push on with; operate, move s.t. along; press, urge, exhort, drive (people) on; make steady progress EXD:421, GDX3:53, XED:139, R3x, R6, R31x

-qhubeka *v-atr* happen, go on, continue, be in progress; advance, progress XED:139; GDX3:54; KED:361; RD-96:403, R28.1.7, R35.11, R36.6

-qhubela *v-ben* drive (animal, vehicle) for / to; make steady progress on XED:139, R3x, R30x, R34

qhubela phambili *v-cmp* progress, move forward; gain ground EXD:238; 485, R34=4

-qina[1] *v-st* harden, be fixed or firm; tighten, get tight CGB:155, XED:136

-qina[2] *v-tr* render, melt (fat); roast (coffee); [ext] examine by torture; testify to s.t. XED:137, R36.23

qiniseka *v-atr* be fixed firmly; get established; [perf] determined; sure; convinced XED:136, R34=3

qinisekile *v-perf* has been fixed firmly; [atr] determined, established; sure; convinced EXD:155, R34.8

-qinisekisa *v-tr* convince, guarantee, ascertain RD-96:403

-qonda *v-tr* understand, comprehend, grasp, realize; trust, be sure about; know, be acquainted with; be understanding, open-minded GDX3:79, PCX:93, SXWU:19, XED:138, R37.11

-qondakala *v-atr* be understandable PCX:93

Qualbert *loan* subdivision of Durban R25

quba *v-tr* urge, push forward, drive; push on with, proceed, go on with, ☞ Pass: qhutywa KED:361, R18x

-qubha *v-intr* swim (of human) ☞ Contrast: -dada (of animal ~ bird) CGB:143

-quka *v-tr* take together, include, comprise; comprehend; call together (elders) XED:140, R33x

-qulatha *v-tr* contain, hold; have s.t. inside; [fig] have (within oneself) • *Uqulathe ntoni*

emlonyeni? 'What do you have in your mouth?' ☞ Alt: -quletha GDX3:90, R12x

-quletha *v-st* contain, hold; [fig] have (within oneself) ☞ Usually: -qulatha GDX3:90, R12=3

-qwalasela *v-tr* watch, view, look at intently, observe attentively; consider, address (an issue) RD-96:403, XED:142, R21=2, R34.11, R37.5.6

-qwela *v-tr* finish, round off; confiscate entirely, empty completely, ruin, destroy GDX3:105, XED:142, R36.26

R

R *abr* Rand (unit of South African currency) R7, R18, R25=2, R28=2, R29

Rachel *pn-loan* Rachel R33

Rajah *n5-sg-red* curry powder (brand name) R8

Rawlings *pn* Gerry Rawlings R16

Raymond *pn-loan* (personal name) • *Raymond Mhlaba* R32.3

reformed *loan* reformed ☞ See: Dutch Reformed Church R35.2

rhafu *n5-sg-red* tax R23=2

-rhalarhuma *v-intr* rage; be violent, enraged, fierce EXD:503, XED:143, R36x

-rhanuga *v-intr* abandon one's traditional area (to search for work on a farm or in the city); [perf] lost all touch with Xhosa culture and traditions GDX3:117, XED:143

Rharhabe *clan* Rharhabe, Rharabe (people, ethnic group within the greater Xhosa community who bore the brunt of the Frontier Wars) ☞ Cf: amaRharhabe CGB:2; 4, MI:274

rh e *ideophone* be rumored ☞ Alt sp: re XED:144

rhoqo *preverb* do often, always, continually ☞ Alt sp: roqo EXD:18, XED:145, R12, R36

-rhwaphiliza *v-tr* cheat, defraud s.o.; [v-intr] be greedy, gluttonous; be selfish; be fraudulent ☞ See: urhwaphilizo GDX3:143, R37.26

Riebeeck *-pn* Riebeeck (family name) ☞ See: Van Riebeeck R32

Robben Island *n5-pn-cmp* Robben Island R32

S

s-[1] *n4-sg-them* [group 4 singular thematic consonant prefix] ☞ See: sonke XED:147

-s-[2] *n4-sg-obj-prf* him, her, it [group 4 singular short object form before vowel initial verb] ☞ Alt: -si- E&S:18, XED:147

s-[3] *pro-1pl-S1-prf* we [short form before vowel initial root] • *Senza 'we are doing' = s(i)-enza* CGB:125, XED:147

-s-[4] *pro-1pl-obj-prf* us [short object form before vowel initial verb] ☞ Alt: -si- E&S:18, XED:147

-s-[5] *loc-pred-prf* being in [copulative or predicative locative prefix] • *isikolo seenkokeli zaseAfrika 'school for the leaders of (those in) Africa'; nasemakhayeni 'and to homes'* Structure: occurs after the predicative prefix and before the e- locative prefix CGB:141, E&S:32, XED:147, R2, R4c, R9, R10, R16=3, R36.00

-s-[6] *v-prf* [consonant prefix added to positive participial form of vowel-initial verbs] Structure: S2-s-Δ (participial verb form), if no other prefix occurs (e.g., pronoun object, potential -nga-, etc.) AXG:107, CGB:192, E&S:40, SXWU:148, XED:147, R10

-s-[7] *v-suf-caus* make VERB, cause to VERB [causative verb suffix on verbs ending in -k-] • *-godusa 'send home' [= goduk/s-a], -nyusa 'raise' [= nyuk/s-a], -vusa 'awaken' [= vuk/s-a]* ☞ See: -is- AXG:112, R9

sa-[1] *n4-sg-poss* of [group 4 singular possessive agreement prefix] • *isidlo sa kusasa 'breakfast' [lit: meal of morning]* Agr: isi- AM-94:163, E&S:22, SXWU:35f, XED:xv; 147, R7x, R14, R16

sa[2] *n4-sg-poss-n5-sg* of • *Sesotho sa Leboa 'the variety of Sotho spoken in Leboa* R37

sa-[3] *n4-sg-S3b-pos* (and) he, she, it VERBed [group 4 singular past subjunctive positive verb subject (S3b) agreement prefix] (CGB:189), E&S:42, MI:247, SXWU:141

sa-[4] *pro-1pl-S3b-pos* (and) we VERBed [S3b past subjunctive positive subject pronoun] CGB:189, E&S:42, MI:247, SXWU:141

-sa-[5] *preverb-prog* still, yet; [neg] no longer, not anymore [progressive aspect preverb, expressing continuance of action or state] Becomes se before a suppressed u and before predicates other than verbs; becomes so in the short future ☞ See: -sa- -a, a- -sa- -i, se, so CGB:127, E&S:46, EXD:624, GDX3:149, PCX:83, RD-96:373, XED:147, R4d, R27, R33.7, R37.6

-sa[6] *v-intr* dawn, become light; break (of day); clear up (of weather) ☞ See: kusasa, ingomso, ngomso, umso AXG:107, XED:147

-sa[7] *v-tr* bring, carry, convey latent vowel verb ☞ Pass: siwa; Cf: isa E&S:51, XED:147

-sa- -a *v-prog* still [progressive aspect verb construction] • *Basasebenza 'they are still working', ndisathandana ngolwathando lwakudala 'I still fall in love the old-fashioned way'* Structure: S1-sa-Δ-a CGB:127, EXD:624, PCX:83, R4d, R27, R33.7, R37.6

saa *ideophone* scatter, strew ideophone follows aux 'ukuthi' R26.4

sabe[1] *preverb-past-n4-sg* he, she, it had VERBed; he, she, it did VERB [group 4 singular remote past compound tense preverb] Structure: sabe si-Δ (participial verb form) ☞ Alt: saye E&S:39, GDX3:714, PCX:186

sabe[2] *preverb-past-pro-1pl* we did VERB; we had VERBed [remote past compound tense preverb] Structure: sabe si-Δ (participial verb form) ☞ Alt: saye E&S:39, GDX3:714, PCX:186

sabo[1] *n1-pl-poss-n4-sg* of them; their (own); theirs CGB:183, E&S:22, GDX3:691, XED:147

sabo[2] *n7-poss-n4-sg* its; of it GDX3:691, XED:147

sabuya *v-past* it returned R36

sadinwa *v-intr-past* we got tired R28

safika *v-intr-past* we arrived R28

Sagittarius *loan* Sagittarius R34.9

sahamba *v-past-sub-pro-1pl-S3b* we walked R28=4

sahlala *v-past-sub-pro-1pl-S3b* we lived R28

sakhe *n1-sg-poss-n4-sg* his, her, its CGB:182, E&S:22, GDX3:691, XED:147, R33=2, R36

sakho *pro-2sg-poss-n4-sg* your, yours, thy; your own [singular] CGB:182, E&S:22, GDX3:691, XED:147, R31, R34

sako[1] *n8-vn-poss-n4-sg* its, of it GDX3:691, XED:147

sako[2] *n10-loc-poss-n4-sg* its, of it GDX3:691

saku-[1] *n4-sg-temp* when it VERBs / VERBed [group 4 singular temporal verb construction] • *Sakufika 'When it arrives...'* E&S:42

saku-[2] *pro-1pl-temp* when we VERB / VERBed [temporal verb construction] • *Sakufika 'When we arrive...'* E&S:42, PCX:91f

-sala *v-intr* stay, remain (behind), abide, tarry ☞ Perf: -sele GDX3:154, PCX:37, XED:148

sale *deic-1-n5-sg-poss* of this R19.4

salo[1] *n3-sg-poss-n4-sg* his, her, its GDX3:691, XED:147

salo[2] *n6-sg-poss-n4-sg* his, her, its GDX3:691, XED:147

saluqala *v-tr-past* we started it R28

sam *pro-1sg-poss-n4-sg* of me; my, mine; my own • *isandla sam 'my hand'* AM-94:151, CGB:181, E&S:22, GDX3:691, PCX:60; 72, SXWU:36, XED:147

samabanga *n3-pl-poss* of grades R33

samapolisa *n3-pl-poss* of the police R18.5, R27.1.11

samkelwa *v-pass-past* was welcomed R24

sanuku- -a *v-aux-neg-imp-pl* don't (you all) VERB! [negative imperative plural] • *Sanukwenza 'Don't (you all) work!'* Reduction of musani uku- -a (q.v.) ITX:33, R17

sanukungxama *v-imp-neg* don't (you all) rush R17.7

saphelelwa *v-ben-pass* we ran out of R28

saqala *v-past* it started R36

saqhubeka *v-atr-past* we continued R28.7

saseRobben Island *n5-pn-cmp-loan* those of Robben Island R32

sasi-[1] *n4-sg-remote-past* he, she, it had VERBed [group 4 singular contracted remote past compound tense] AXG:93f, E&S:39, PCX:186

sasi-[2] *pro-1pl-remote-past* we had VERBed [contracted remote past compound tense] AXG:93f, E&S:39, PCX:186, R28=3

sasingazi *v-remote-past-neg* we had not known R28

sasingekafiki *v-remote-past-neg* we had not yet arrived R28

sasinyuka *v-remote-past* we had climbed R28

saso *n4-sg-poss-n4-sg* his, her, its; of him, her, it GDX3:691, XED:147

sathethathethana *v-intr-recip-redup* we chattered R26

sawo[1] *n2-sg-poss-n4-sg* its, of it GDX3:691, XED:147

sawo[2] *n3-pl-poss-n4-sg* their, theirs, of them GDX3:691, XED:147, R36.26

saye[1] *preverb-past-n4-sg* he, she, it had VERBed; he, she, it did VERB [group 4 singular remote past compound tense preverb] Structure: saye si-Δ (participial verb form) ☞ Alt: sabe AXG:93f, E&S:39, GDX3:714

saye[2] *preverb-past-pro-1pl* we did VERB; we had VERBed [remote past compound tense preverb] Structure: saye si-Δ (participial verb form) ☞ Alt: sabe AXG:93f, E&S:39, GDX3:714

sayo[1] *n2-pl-poss-n4-sg* their, theirs GDX3:691, XED:147

sayo[2] *n5-sg-poss-n4-sg* his, her, its GDX3:691, XED:147

saza *v-aux* then aux based on ukuza 'to come' R28

sazo[1] *n4-pl-poss-n4-sg* their; of them GDX3:691, XED:147

sazo[2] *n5-pl-poss-n4-sg* their; of them GDX3:691, XED:147

Schools *loan* Schools R22

Scorpio *loan* Scorpio R34.8

se-[1] *preverb* already, now, by this time, by then Structure: contracted perfect form of sala followed by S2 + participial ☞ Alt: -sel- with n1-sg-S2 and n3-pl-S2 AXG:132, E&S:46, XED:148, R36.6, R37.24

-se-[2] *preverb-prog* still, yet • *Ndisekho 'I am still here'* Structure: used instead of sa before predicates other than verbs and before suppressed u ☞ See: -sa- AXG:132, XED:148;147, R30

-se-[3] *loc-pred-prf* [copulative or predicative locative prefix] • *ebesecaleni '(he) being at her side'* Possibly derived from contracted form of -sala 'remain' ☞ See: -s- + e- [locative] CGB:141, R24

sebe *n4-sg-red* branch, department R18

-sebenza *v-intr* work, labor (at); operate; use [usually with nga-] ☞ Perf: -sebenzile; Pass: -setyenziwa AM-94:155, CGB:143, PCX:20, RD-96:404;136; 373, XED:149, R6x=3, R9x=2, R10=2, R12x

sebenzayo *v-rel-atr* working, active RD-96:404

-sebenzisa *v-caus* make s.o. or s.t. work; employ, give work to; use, utilize, make use of; apply, make work; operate s.t. AXG:112, RD-96:404, XED:149, R6=2, R9x, R25, R30, R34

-sebenzisana *v-caus-recip* cooperate, work together RD-96:404, R9, R37

Sebiloane *pn* Sebiloane (family name) R33

sedwa *pro-quan-1pl* we only / alone; just us Agr: si-, thina ☞ Alt: sodwa E&S:27, PCX:62, XED:149

seebhedi *n5-pl* of beds R35

seen- *combo* of • *isikolo seenkokeli 'school of leaders'* indicates that n5 pl (iin-) is possessed by a n4 sg (sa-) ☞ See: sa- + iin- R16

seenkokeli *n5-pl-poss-n4-sg* of leaders R16

sehonours *loan* honors R24

-seka *v-tr* mark the circle for a hut wall; lay a foundation, found, establish; support (a pot on stones) NDK-91:563, XED:149, R16, R37.1

sel- *v-aux-perf* already, now, by this time Structure: contracted perfect form of sala followed by e- (S2 n1-sg and n3-pl) + participial ☞ See: se- AXG:132

-sela[1] *v-tr* drink (s.t. cold); take (medicine) ☞ Contrast: -phunga (s.t. hot) CGB:143, EXD:175, XED:149, R4a, R4c=2, R6=5, R31.4

-sela[2] *v-tr* steal, pilfer XED:149

-sela[3] *v-ben* light up; become light to / for XED:147

-sela[4] *v-ditr* bring s.t. to / for s.o. XED:148

-sele[1] *v-perf* remained, stayed behind Perfect form of -sala GDX3:154

sele[2] *v-aux-perf* already VERbed • *Sele bemkile 'They have already left'* Structure: followed by S2 + participial ☞ See: -sa- EXD:17, GDX3:165, R7, R30=2, R31, R33, R35, R36=2

selinengxaki *v-poss-n4-sg+n5-sg-obj* it already has difficulty R35.5

semfundo *n2-sg* of learning R18

semihla *n4-sg-poss-n2-pl* day by day R36

sendiqhelile *v-perf-part-pro-1sg-S2* (when) I am already accustomed R36

senditshilo *v-ir-perf* I have already said ☞ See: -tsho R37.24

-senga *v-tr* milk PCX:37, XED:149

senitye *v-aux-perf* you have eaten R31

senkqubela *n4-sg-poss-n5-sg* of progress R34

senu *pro-2pl-poss-n4-sg* of you; your, yours; your own [plural] • *isikolo senu 'your school'* CGB:182, E&S:22, GDX3:691, PCX:60, SXWU:36, XED:147

senyaniso *n4-sg-poss-n5-sg* of the truth R32

senyumoniya *n4-sg-poss-n5-sg-loan* of pneumonia R35

service *n-loan* service R36

services *n5-sg-red* services ☞ See: Correctional Services R4b

-sesa *v-tr* do s.t. underhand, out of sight; do through another; perform s.t. secretly XED:149

sesaa *deic-3-n4-sg-pred* that (far, yonder) is E&S:26

-sese *v-perf* done underhand; [atr] underhanded; out of sight; secret ☞ See: -ngasese XED:149

sesi *deic-1-n4-sg-pred* this is; it is this one E&S:26, PCX:99, R36

sesibini *num-n4-sg* second PCX:29

sesine *num-n4-sg* fourth PCX:36

sesithathu *num-n4-sg* third PCX:34

seso *deic-2-n4-sg-pred* that (not far, just mentioned) is E&S:26

sesokuba *v-pred-n4-sg* it is to become R29.12

Sesotho *n4-sg-red* Sotho (language) ☞ See: isiSuthu R37=2

sethu *pro-1pl-poss-n4-sg* of us; our, ours; our own [plural] • *isikolo sethu 'our school'* CGB:182, E&S:22, GDX3:691, PCX:60; 72, XED:147

Setswana *pn-loan* Tswana (language) R37

-setyenziswa *v-caus-pass* be used R9, R37.10.20.21

-seza *v-tr* give s.o. s.t. to drink; make drink; water (plants); drench Irreg caus of: sela XED:150, R6

sezi *deic-1-n6-pl-poss* of these • *isigama sezi lwimi 'the vocabulary of these languages'* R37.19.20

sezizathu *n4-sg-poss-n4-pl* of the reasons R36

-shaya ucingo *v-cmp* phone, reach by phone; send a telegram ☞ See Xhosa: -betha ucingo DNZ:477, R15x

-sheba *v-tr* eat a mixed meal; flavor (s.t. with sauce, etc.) R8

-shiya *v-tr* leave (behind), abandon, forsake, desert; omit, leave out XED:150, R5, R33

-shukuma *v-intr* shake, move; stir; live XED:150

-shumayela *v* preach XED 474, R20, R31

-shushu *atr-root* hot, warm AM-94:107f, AXG:64, CGB:172f, E&S:30, XED:150, R8+x

si-[1] *n4-sg-red-prf* [group 4 singular reduced noun prefix] Loss of article i- from isi- R12

-si-[2] *n4-sg-obj* [group 4 singular object agreement prefix] Agr: isi-, is- E&S:18, PCX:51, SXWU:44

si-[3] *n4-sg-adj-pred* he, she, it is ADJ [group 4 singular adjective agreement prefix used predicatively] E&S:28, MI:248, PCX:118f

si-[4] *n4-sg-enum-prf* [group 4 singular enumerative agreement prefix] ☞ See: simbi, siphi E&S:27, PCX:110f

si-[5] *n4-sg-S1* he, she, it [group 4 singular subject (S1) agreement prefix] Agr: isi- CGB:117; 158, E&S:17f, PCX:51, SXWU:28

si-[6] *n4-sg-S2* he, she, it [group 4 singular participial subject (S2) agreement prefix] AXG:91, CGB:191

si-[7] *n4-sg-S3a* (and) he, she, it VERBs [group 4 singular present subjunctive verb subject (S3a) agreement prefix] (CGB:167), R3

si-[8] *n4-sg-rel2* he, she who / that which [group 4 singular direct relative 2 construction, attributive agreement prefix used predicatively] E&S:34, MI:153; 248, PCX:151

si-[9] *n4-sg-ind-rel2* whom, which [group 4 singular indirect relative 2 agreement prefix] E&S:35

-si-[10] *pro-1pl-obj-prf* us • *usisikelele 'you should bless us'* E&S:18, SXWU:44, R13.1

si-[11] *pro-1pl-pred-prf* we are [copulative or predicative prefix construction] • *sithi 'it is we'* E&S:21, PCX:97, XED:xvi

si-[12] *pro-1pl-S1-prf* we CGB:115; 158, E&S:18, PCX:24f, RD-96:373, SXWU:29, XED:xvi, R1, R5

si-[13] *pro-1pl-S2-prf* we VERBing [S2 participial subject] AXG:89; 91, CGB:191, R33.9

si-[14] *pro-1pl-S3a-prf* (and) we VERB [S3a present subjunctive subject pronoun] CGB:167, R3, R4d=4, R9=2, R14

si-[15] *pro-1pl-S4* we can VERB; we may VERB [first person plural potential / conditional verb subject (S4) agreement pronoun] • *singazuza sonke 'we can all benefit'* PCX:166, SXWU:149, R7, R37.0

si-[16] *pro-1pl-dir-rel2* we who [direct relative 2] • *thina sivelayo 'we who see'* E&S:34n

si-[17] *pro-1pl-ind-rel2* us whom [indirect relative 2] E&S:35

-si-[18] *v-prf* [prefix added to positive participial form of monosyllabic verbs] • *esingathi 'which can be said', ndisiwa 'I falling'; xa usitya 'when you eat'* Structure: S2-si-Δ (participial verb form), if no other prefix occurs (e.g., pronoun object, reflexive, potential -nga-, etc.). It is more likely that the particle is omitted from polysyllabic verbs, as it is found in other Bantu langs. as an invariable participial marker (see Swahili, Venda) CGB:192, E&S:40, SXWU:148, R2, R10, R12=2

sibe[1] *preverb-recent-pro-n4-sg* he, she, it was VERBing [group 4 singular recent past compound tense preverb] Structure: sibe si-Δ (participial construction) AXG:91f, E&S:37, PCX:183

sibe[2] *v-pred-sub* that it might become R3, R35.13

sibe[3] *preverb-recent-pro-1pl* we were VERBing [recent past compound tense preverb] Structure: sibe si-Δ (participial construction) AXG:91f, E&S:37f, PCX:183

sibe nenkqubela *v-poss-sub* that it might have progress R3

sibona *v-tr-pro-1pl-S2* we see R20

sibumbe *v-tr-sub-pres* that we form R21

sichazele *v-imp* explain to us R21

sicinge *v-pres-sub* that we think R17.6

sifike *v-perf* we arrived R26

sifudukele *v-ben-perf* we moved to R28

sifumane *v-pres-sub* that we may find R33.9

sifumanise *v-caus-perf* we found that R26

sifuna *v-pro-1pl-S1* we want R31, R35

sigxininisa *v-tr* it refers to R37

sihamba *v-tr* we walk R28

sihambisane *v-pres-sub* and we would go out together R4d

sihelegu *n4-sg-red* disaster, catastrophe • *sihelegu-nasemlonyeni 'trauma, kick in the teeth'* R36.21

sihlonele *v-sub* we should respect R3

sijonge *v-pro-1pl-pres-sub* we should look (at) R14, R17.6

sika[1] *n4-sg-poss-prf* of [personal possessive prefix / marker for noun group 4 singular] Agr: isi- E&S:23f, PCX:109

-sika[2] *v-tr* cut (off / out); supplant; [ext] kill, murder XED:151, R8x=2

sikarhulumente *n1a-sg-poss* of the government R18

sikelel' *v-imp* bless! R13=6

-sikelela *v-tr* bless, confer favors on; cut into, for, on behalf of XED:151, R13=3

sikhangele *v-pres-sub* we should look at R17.6

sikho[1] *v-exis-n4-sg* it is here; he, she is present E&S:29, ITX:17

sikho[2] *v-exis-pro-1pl* we are here / present E&S:29

sikhulisane *v-pres-sub* and we would grow together R4d

sikhululo *cop-n4-sg* of the station R27

sikhundla *n4-sg-red* position ☞ See: isikhundla R29

sikhutshwa *v-pass* it is submitted R5

sikolo *n4-sg-red* school R18=4

sikubo *pro-1pl-loc* we are in R17.4

sikuphathele *v-ben* we have brought you R28

silibize *v-pres-sub* that we call it R17.5

silumkiso *n4-sg-red* warning R31

-simahla *atr-poss-root* free, gratis, for nothing • *incwadana yee resiphi yasimahla 'booklet of free recipes'* Structure: uses possessive agreement markers EXD:255; 409, GDX3:197, R12

simbi *enum-pro-n4-sg* other, some other, different Structure: RED noun form + ENUM / ENUM + FULL noun form ☞ See: -mbi E&S:27, PCX:110

simngcambazisa *v-caus-1pl-3-sg* we make him hobble along • *simngcambazisa ngezi gusha 'we make him speak (but reluctantly) about the sheep'* R26

simothulela *v-tr-ben* we take off (our hats) for R32

sinakane *v-pres-sub* we should meet R4d

sincede *v-imp* help us R21

sineendawo *cop-assoc-n5-pl* we have places R33

sinentlaninge *v-poss* we have plenty R16

sinexesha *v-poss-pro-1pl+n3-sg-obj* we have time R23

singafane *v-aux-neg-sub* we cannot just R17.5

singakufumanisa *pro-1pl-S1-v-caus-pro-2sg-obj* we can help you get R7

singamapolisa *pro-1pl-pred-n3-pl* we are the police R27

singamaqaba *cop1-pl-n3-pl* we are not educated R17.2

singanazo *v-poss-neg-pres-part* we not having them R33

singavunjululwanga *v-past-neg-pass* it has not been turned up R32

singazifumanaphi *v-pot-interr* where can we get R23

singazuza *v-pot-pres* we can benefit R37.0

singumlomo *cop-n2-sg* we are the mouthpiece ☞ See: umlomo R27.14

sini *qw-n4-sg* what kind?, of what sort? • *sizwe sini? 'what sort of nation?'* ☞ See: -ni PCX:28; 118

sinokukhwela *v-tr-pot* we could ride R28

sinqumla *v-pres-part* we crossing R28

sinyamezele *v-intr-sub* we must be patient R17.6

sinyelisa *v-tr-part* it is abusing, slandering us (XED:117), R17.4

siphezulu *cop-loc* highest R29

siphi[1] *qw-loc-adv-n4-sg* where is? ☞ See: -phi E&S:31, PCX:111

siphi[2] *qw-n4-sg* which (one)? E&S:27, GDX3:703, PCX:111

Siphokazi *n1a-sg-pn-fem* Siphokazi (female personal name) [lit: big gift] ☞ See: isipho AM-94:164, SXWU:11

siqhubeke *v-atr-past* we pushed on, we continued R28.7

sis *loan* sister R31.5

sisalamane *cop-n4-sg* sibling R36

sisaqhubeka *v-atr-prog* we are still continuing R28.1

siseko *n4-sg-red* it is the foundation ☞ See: umgaqo-siseko 'constitution' R16, R37=4

sisengxakini *n4-sg-cop-loc-n5-sg* it has problems [lit: it (the school) is in problems] R18.1

sisenzo *cop-n4-sg* an act R36

sishebo *n4-sg-red* flavoring, mix ☞ Zulu: isishebo 'mixed meal, mixed grill;' See: -sheba R8=3

sisi[1] *n-loan* sister R36.18

sisi-[2] *n4-sg-pred-prf* he, she, it is [group 4 singular copulative or predicative prefix construction] • *sisilo 'it is a wild animal'* CGB:135, E&S:21; 25, PCX:96, XED:xvi

sisi-[3] *n4-sg-agent-prf* by (done by, produced by) him, her, it [marker of group 4 singular agent of passive verb] E&S:25; 43

sisihlwele *n4-sg-agent* by a crowd • *siye samkelwa sisihlwelwe 'they were welcomed by a crowd'* R24.2

sisini *cop-n4-sg* a gap between their teeth R36

sisiqalo *n4-sg-cop-pred* it is the beginning R35, R36

sisitshixo *cop-n4-sg* it is the key R34

siso *n4-sg-pred* he, she, it is; it is he, she, it [group 4 singular copulative or predicative] E&S:21, PCX:98

sisonka *cop-n4-sg* the bread R36

Sisulu *pn* (family name) • *Walter Sisulu* R32

siSwati *pn-loan* Swazi (language) R37

sithembane *v-pres-sub* and we would rely on each other R4d

sithengisa *v-tr* we sell R1

sithi[1] *pro-1pl-pred* we are; it is we [copulative or predicative] AXG:44f, E&S:21, PCX:97, XED:160

sithi[2] *v-pres* we say R5, R32

sithini *v-qw-n4-sg-S1* what is it doing?; [dummy] what is it saying? • *Ingaba isazela sale ntombazana sona sithini? 'What might this girl's conscience be telling her?'* ☞ See: -thini R19.4

sitshiselwe *v-caus-ben-pass* it was burned R18

sityelele *v-perf* we visited R26

sivula *v-tr* it opens R18

siwakhankanye *v-tr-perf* we mentioned R37.13

-sixhenxe *num-atr-root* seven (7) SXWU:57

sixhuma-xhuma *v-part-pres* we rattling R17.2

siyabathanda *v-tr-pro-1pl-S1-long-pres-n1-pl-obj* we love them R11

siyazikhuthaza *v-tr-prog* we encourage them R37.4

siye *conj* (that) we go verb in subjunctive, following -kuba R24, R28

sizathu *n4-sg-red* reason ☞ See: isizathu EXD:510, R11

sizise *v-tr* we bring them R27

sizonda *v-pro-1pl-S1* we feel strongly (about, for, against) R11

sizwe[1] *n4-sg-red* nation ☞ See: isizwe PCX:25

Sizwe[2] *n1a-sg-pn-masc* Sizwe (male personal name) [lit: nation] SXWU:11

-so[1] *n4-sg-root* he, she, it; his, her, its [group 4 singular pronoun root] E&S:22

so-[2] *v-n4-sg-short-fut* he, she, it will VERB [contracted / short positive future group 4 singular noun prefix] E&S:20

so-[3] *v-pro-1pl-short-fut* we will VERB [contracted / short positive future pronoun prefix] CGB:165, E&S:20, R19

-so-[4] *preverb-prog* still, yet; [neg] no longer, not anymore [progressive preverb] • *Andisokubuya 'I will not return anymore'* Structure: used in short future constructions ☞ See: -sa- XED:147

sobe *preverb* will never VERB Structure: takes S3a + present subjunctive ☞ Alt: sokuze, soze E&S:47

sobonelelo *n6-sg-poss-n4-sg* of the concession R23.11

sodwa[1] *pro-quan-n4-sg* he, she, it alone; only him, her, it Agr: isi-, sona E&S:27, PCX:62

sodwa[2] *pro-quan-1pl* we only / alone; just us ☞ See: sedwa E&S:27n, PCX:62

sohlukane *v-fut-sub* that we would separate R19.2

soku- *combo* of indicates that n8 vn (uku-) is possessed by n4 sg (sa-) ☞ See: sa- + uku- R7, R35

sokuba *n8-vn-poss-n4-sg* of being; [conj] that, so that ☞ See: ukuba GDX3:475, R7, R14, R36

sokudlwengulwa *n8-vn-poss* (one) who is raped R36

sokufundisa *n8-vn-poss* of / for teaching • *isikolo sokufundisa 'a school for teaching'* R16

sokuhlonitshwa *n8-vn-poss* for honoring or respecting R24.1

sokunyusa *n8-vn-poss-n4-sg* of raising R35

sokuqala *n8-vn-poss* of starting; [atr] beginning, first PCX:20; 26, R24

sokuwa *n8-vn-poss-n4-sg* of fits R30

sokuze *preverb* never VERB, not ever VERB Structure: takes S3a + present subjunctive ☞ Alt: sobe, soze E&S:47, R20=2

sokuzibalula *n4-sg-poss-v-inf-refl* to select R21

sokwenene *rel-poss-n3-sg* rare; s.t. very rare XED:79, R33

-soloko *preverb* always VERB • *Akasoloko evuma 'She doesn't always agree'* Structure: followed by S2 + participial construction E&S:47, EXD:18, R29, R33=2, R37.17

Solwandle *pn* (personal name) • *Looksmart Solwandle Ngudle* R32

somsebenzi *n2-sg-poss* of work R22

somzabalazo *n2-sg-poss-n4-sg* of a struggle • *sisiqalo somzabalazo omde nonzima 'it is the beginning of a long, hard struggle'* R36.22

sona *pro-n4-sg-echo* he, she, it [group 4 singular echo / absolutive pronoun] AM-94:93; 163, CGB:158, E&S:21, PCX:57, R19.4

-sondela *v-ben* approach, come near to CGB:42, XED:154

-sondeza *v-caus* bring s.t. near CGB:42, XED:154

-songa *v-tr* roll up, wrap (up), fold; turn back, prevent, dissuade XED:154, R30

Sonjani *pn* (personal name) R5

sonke[1] *pro-enum-n4-sg* every; the whole (of) • *sonke isizwe 'the whole nation; every nation'* Agr: isi-, sona AM-94:163, E&S:27, PCX:62;24f

sonke[2] *pro-enum-1pl* all of us; we together Agr: si-, thina ☞ See: onke AM-94:115, E&S:27, PCX:62, RD-96:404, XED:154, R21, R28, R37.0

soshishino *n6-sg-poss-n4-sg* of business R34.6

South African Schools Act *n5-sg-cmp-red* The South African Schools Act R22

Southdale *pn-geog* Southdale R22

soze *preverb* will never VERB • *(Andi)soze ndihambe 'I will never go'* Structure: takes S3a + present subjunctive ☞ Alt: sobe, sokuze E&S:47, MI:257

Sparrow *pn* (personal name) • *Sparrow Mhonto* R32

square *loan* square R1

Steve Biko *pn* Steve Biko (Xhosa martyr) CGB:2, R32

stishi *n4-sg-red* station R27

Stutterheim *pn-geog* Stutterheim ☞ See: iCumakala R4a=2

-suka[1] *v-intr* start (off); go away, leave; rise, get up, arise; originate (from) latent vowel verb ☞ Caus: -susa; Cf: isuka AXG:112, E&S:51, XED:154, R4d, R25.5, R28.0, R29.8

-suka[2] *v-aux* then, thereupon, immediately VERB; start VERBing Structure: followed by S3a + present subjunctive E&S:42; 47, XED:154, R35.12

-suka[3] *v-aux* VERB on the contrary, on the other hand • *basuka balile 'on the contrary, they cry'* Structure: followed by S3a + present subjunctive E&S:47, XED:154, R35.1

-suke *preverb* merely VERB; just VERBed; VERBed thereupon, immediately • *Usuke wancuma 'He just smiled'* Structure: followed by S3b + past subjunctive E&S:47, R25.5

-sukela *v-ben* run after, chase, pursue; get up for; start from GDX3:229, XED:154, R4d, R33.10, R35

suku- -a *v-aux-neg-imp-sg* don't VERB! • *Sukutya! 'Don't eat!'* Reduction of musa uku- -a (q.v.) ITX:33

-sukuba *v-aux-rel* -ever [pronominal relative auxiliary verb] • *umntu osukuba efika 'whoever comes'* Structure: inflected with relative subject agreement forms and followed by a participial verb construction AXG:173

-sula *v-tr* wipe off / away, blot out; clean, polish; wipe out, obliterate XED:155, R1x, R11x

-susa *v-tr* send s.o. away ☞ rw: -suka AXG:112

-susela[1] *v-tr* start, begin, commence XED:155

-susela[2] *v-aux* begin VERBing, start to VERB (from a certain time); do VERB henceforth XED:155

-sweleka *v-intr* die (of a human) ☞ Syn: -bhubha; Contrast: -fa CGB:143

T

t *change* change of TH to T • *intetho 'speech' [= in-theth-o], iintuthu 'ashes' [= iin-thuthu], intobeko 'humility' [= in-thobek-o], izinti 'sticks' [= izin-thi]* E&S:51, PCX:195

tanci *adv-time* first; earlier AXG:143, CGB:178, R33

Taurus *loan* Taurus R34

TB *n5-sg-red* TB ☞ See: iTB R30

Tel *abr* telephone number R25

-tha *v-tr* pour into AXG:107

-thabatha *v-tr* take (s.t. from s.o.); take and hold; take over; assume, put on a quality or appearance ☞ Pass: -thatyathw-; Alt: -thatha EXD:647f, XED:156, R24, R34, R35=2, R36

-thamba *v-inch* soften, become soft, supple, pliant, tender; become tame, civilized; be gentle, submissive; lubricate CGB:155, XED:157, R8=2, R25x, R30x

-thambisa *v-caus* soften, make supple, pliant; oil, lubricate, anoint; [ext] subdue, tame XED:157, R30x

-thanda *v-tr* love, like; adore AM-94:155, CGB:114, NDK-91:574, PCX:37, RD-96:404;371, SXWU:20, R4b=2, R4c, R4d=4, R11, R14=2

-thandabuza *v-intr-cmp* doubt, hesitate; be undecided, in doubt [lit: like to ask] XED:157, R36.03

-thandabuzeka *v-atr-cmp* be doubtful, uncertain XED:157, R36.03

-thandana *v-recip* be in love with, fall in love with s.o. EXD:358, R4d

-thandathu *adj-root* six AM-94:76, AXG:64, CGB:171, E&S:30, PCX:120

-thandazela *v-tr-ben* pray, intercede for R33x

Thandeka[1] *n1a-sg-red-pn-fem* Thandeka (female personal name) [lit: beloved] SXWU:11

-thandeka[2] *v-atr* be lovable PCX:93

Thandi *n1a-sg-pn-masc/fem* Thandi (male / female personal name) [short form] ☞ Cf: Thandile [pn-m], Thandiwe [pn-f] AM-94:164, R19.1

Thandile *n1a-sg-pn-masc* Thandile (male personal name) [lit: loved one] AM-94:164

Thandiwe *n1a-sg-pn-fem* Thandiwe (female personal name) [lit: loved one] AM-94:164

thando *n6-sg-red* love ☞ See: uthando R4d

-thatha *v-tr* take EXD:647, R37.5.17.19.24.26

-thatha amanyathelo *v-cmp* take steps EXD:623, R34x

-thathu *adj-root* three AM-94:76, AXG:64, CGB:171, E&S:30, PCX:120, XED:158, R8x

-the[1] *v-tr-ir-perf* said ☞ Past of: -thi CGB:153, R5, R18=3

-the[2] *v-aux-fact-perf* did VERB [perfect tense form of factitive auxiliary verb] ☞ See: -thi TD, XED:160, R5

-theka *v-atr* happen, come to pass, be done • *Kuthekani ke ngoku apha? 'What is going on here?'* used with the impersonal construction (ku-) when enquiring what is happening ☞ rw: -thi GDX3:282, XED:160

theko *n3-sg-red* festivity, event, party, function, special occasion ☞ See: itheko R24, R31

Themba[1] *n1a-sg-pn-masc* Themba (male personal name) [lit: trust] AM-94:164, PCX:29f, SXWU:11

themba[2] *v-tr* expect, hope; trust, rely (on, upon) AM-94:164, XED:159, R4dx, R9

-thembana *v-recip* trust one another, rely on each other XED:159, R4d

Thembeka[1] *n1a-sg-pn-fem* Thembeka (female personal name) [lit: hopeful] AM-94:164

-thembeka[2] *v-st* be hopeful; be trusted; [perf] trustworthy, reliable ☞ Perf: -thembekile XED:159

-thembela *v-ben* hope for; trust in, rely upon; confide in RD-96:404, XED:159, R9

-thembisa *v-ditr* cause s.o. to hope in s.t.; [ext] promise s.t. to s.o. ☞ Pass: -thenjiswa PCX:103, XED:159

Thembu *clan* Thembu (clan or ethnic group within the greater Xhosa community) ☞ Cf: umThembu CGB:1; 2; 3, MI:273

-thenga *v-tr* buy, purchase AM-94:73, PCX:34, XED:159, R1x, R12, R29=11

-thengisa *v-caus* sell PCX:37, R1, R29=3

-thenjiswa *v-pass* be promised ☞ rw: -themba PCX:103

-thetha *v-tr* say, talk, speak; talk of; mean AM-94:155, CGB:114, PCX:26, RD-96:405;122; 373,

SXWU:19, XED:159, R9, R11=6, R12, R22, R37=2

-thethana *v-recip* talk to each other, speak to one another RD-96:373

-thethayo *v-rel-atr* talkative RD-96:405

-thetheka *v-atr* be speakable, utterable PCX:93

-thethela *v-ben* speak for, speak at; speak (in a specified manner); give a command to PCX:92, RD-96:373, XED:159

-thethile *v-perf* spoke, has spoken RD-96:373

-thethisa *v-caus* cause to speak RD-96:373

-thethisana *v-caus-recip* admonish each other RD-96:373

thi[1] *pro-1pl-root* we; us [first person plural pronoun root in copulative and prepositional expressions] • *kuthi 'to us', nathi 'with us', ngathi 'through us', sithi 'it is we'* GDX3:293, XED:160, R9

-thi[2] *v-tr-ir* say, mean; intend, think Never uses long present ☞ Perf: -the; Neg: -thanga; Pass: -thiwa CGB:123; 153, PCX:21, RD-96:405, XED:xvi; 160, R4b, R4d=2, R5+x, R10, R22=2

-thi[3] *v-aux-fact* do VERB [factitive auxiliary verb] TD, XED:160, R5x

-thi[4] *v-aux-fact* be ATR [emphatic pseudo verb] XED:160, R28x

-thi[5] *v-aux* be / do IDEOPHONE standard marker of ideophones E&S:59, PCX:173, XED:160

-thile *atr-root* certain, particular; some CGB:172, KED:412, RD-96:452, XED:160, R6, R12, R34

-thimba *v-tr* take, seize, capture; defend oneself (of domestic animal) XED:160

thina *pro-1pl-abs* we; ourselves; as for us • *Thina singamapolisa! 'We are the police!'* AM-94:92; 163, CGB:158, E&S:21, PCX:31, RD-96:405, XED:160, R17.2, R27.14, R28.3

-thini *v-intr* do something, do anything; [qw] do what?; [dummy] do VERB implied by context • *Andinakuthini 'I can't do anything'; Wayengazi umama ukuba uza kuthini 'My mother did not know what to do'; Ingaba isazela sale ntombazana sona sithini? 'What might this girl's conscience be telling her?'* XED:160, R19.4, R28.5, R37.10.19

thinjana *n-dim-root* young men, maidens XED:161, R13

-thoba *v-st* bend, bow, stoop down; [tr] depress, lower CGB:155, XED:162, R6x=2

Thobeka *n1a-sg-pn-fem* Thobeka (female personal name) [lit: humility] AM-94:164

-thobela *v-ben* bow to / under; submit to; obey XED:162, R6=2

Thobile *n1a-sg-pn-masc* Thobile (male personal name) [lit: humility] AM-94:164

-thola *v-tr* obtain, get, pick up, receive; come upon, find; adopt ☞ See Xhosa: -fumana DNZ:496, EZZE:799, R15x

-thola umntwana *v-cmp* give birth DNZ:496, R15x

-thomba *v-intr* shoot, sprout; [ext] initiate a young girl into womanhood XED:162

thuba *n3-sg-red* opportunity R34.10

-thuma *v-tr* send ☞ Pass: thunywa XED:169, R4ax, R7x, R9x, R12x

-thumela *v-ditr-ben* send s.t. to s.o., dispatch s.t. to or for s.o. XED:169, R4a, R7, R12, R21.11, R23.3, R25.7

-thunga *v-tr* sew AM-94:73

-thunywa *v-pass* be sent ☞ See: -thuma XED:169, R9

-thwala *v-tr* carry (on the head); bear (a burden, fruit); abduct, carry off, elope with s.o. ☞ Perf: -thwele CGB:143, XED:170

thwele *v-perf* bear (a burden, fruit); carry; abuct, elope with ☞ See: -thwala XED:170

thwesa *v-caus* crown, put on the head; supply with; instruct; initiate (a young doctor) XED:171, R13

t l *change* change of HL to TL • *intlumo 'growth' [= in-hlum-o], izintlu 'rows' [= izin-hlu], wentlalo 'of living' [= wa-in-hlal-o]* E&S:51, PCX:195, R37.1

Together *loan* together ☞ See: Leading Together R22=3

Tolo *clan* Tolo (clan name of the Dlangamandla family) MI:277

town *loan* town ☞ See: Cape Town, King William's Town R1, R21

training *n-loan* training ☞ See: Northern Training Trust R35

Transkei *pn-geog* Transkei (Xhosa region settled by the descendants of Gcaleka) CGB:4, R20

triangle *loan* triangle ☞ See: eVaal Triangle R33

trust *n-loan* trust ☞ See: Northern Training Trust R35

Truth Commission *loan* Truth Commission R32

t s *change* change of S to TS • *iintsiba 'pens' [= iin-siba], iintsuku 'full days' [= iin-suku]* E&S:51, PCX:195

-tsala umnxeba *v-cmp* phone, telephone s.o., dial (up) [lit: pull the cord] EXD:653, KM, R23

tsalela *v-ben* draw towards; long for; dial (telephone number) XED:163, R23

tsh[1] *change* change of PH to TSH • *-hlonitshwa 'be respected' [= hloniph/tsh-w-a]; futshane 'very short' [= fuph(i)/tsh-ane]; elusatsheni 'in the family' [= e-lu-saph/tsh-eni]* Palatalization occurs when a bilabial in the root encounters the passive form -w- (a velar labial): ph > tsh, b > j, mb > nj, and so on CGB:142, MI:147, PCX:69; 103; 196, R5, R10, R11

tsh[2] *change* change of SH to TSH • *intshukumo 'earthquake' [= in-tsh/shukum-o]* E&S:51, PCX:195

-tsha[1] *adj-root* new; young; fresh; recent; modern AXG:64, CGB:171, E&S:30, PCX:120, RD-96:405;102, XED:163, R33, R35, R37.0.1

-tsha[2] *v-intr* burn, be on fire; dry up; [fig] become hoarse (voice, throat); [ext] heal (wound) PCX:73, XED:164

-tshata *v-tr; v-st* marry; be married (said only of a woman) R19.1.2

Tshatshu *pn* Tshatshu (family name) Address is Isipingo - so possibly of Zulu origin R20

Tshawe *clan* Tshawe (original descent group of the Xhosa community) CGB:2f

-tshaya *v-intr* smoke (tobacco) EXD:598, XED:164, R4a, R4c=2

-tshayela *v-tr* sweep PCX:20ff, XED:165

-tshilo *v-ir-perf* said Irreg perf of -tsho ☞ See: -tsho XED:166, R33=2, R37.24

-tshintsha *v-tr* change, exchange; give s.t. as a substitute, replace; change (money) XED:166, R27.8, R36.3, R37.15

-tshiphu *atr-root* cheap ☞ Opp: -dulu AM-94:107

-tshisa *v-tr* burn, set s.t. on fire; scald; fire (gun); [fig] be very hot, be sweltering AM-94:112, EXD:75, XED:164, R18x, R25x

Tshivenda *pn-loan* Venda (language) R37

-tshiwo *v-ir-pass* be said, declared, affirmed ☞ rw: tsho XED:166

-tshixa *v-tr* lock, bolt, bar; turn the key XED:166, R6x

-tshixela *v-ben* lock s.t. up in; turn the key on XED:166, R6

-tshiza *v-intr* drizzle AM-94:112

-tsho *v-ir* assert, say so, declare; do thus (with gesture); how are you? [formula for a greeting, usually among males] Never uses long present; final vowel does not change in the present negative ☞ Perf: tshilo; Neg: tshongo; Pass: tshiwo CGB:123; 124, PCX:21f; 36, XED:xvi; 166, R3, R14, R17

-tshongo *v-ir-neg* not say, affirm, declare ☞ rw: tsho XED:166

tshotsho *interr* serves you or him right R32

-tsibela *v-ben* spring upon, jump at PCX:92

-tsolo *atr-root* sharp, pointed; keen (sight); quick, acute (mind); harsh, bitter, painful (words) • *ngamazwi atsolo 'with harsh words'* GDX3:424

tu *ideophone* be quiet, still; be none • *uvuthwe tu 'he is quietly enthusiastic'; Yithi tu! 'Be quiet!'* PCX:173, XED:168, R25.4, R32.2

Tutu *pn* (family name) • *u-Desmond Mpilo Tutu* R32.7

ty[1] *change* change of B to TY • *ekhatywayo 'which is kicked' [= e-khab/ty-w-a-yo]; ichutywe 'they should be peeled' [= i-chub/ty-w-e]; -setyenziswa 'be used' [= seb/tyenz-is-w-a]* CGB:142, MI:147, PCX:69; 103; 196, R4b, R6, R8, R9

ty[2] *change* change of TYH to TY • *intyafo 'weakness' [= in-tyhaf-o]* E&S:51, PCX:195

-tya *v-tr* eat, consume, devour; [ext] cheat s.o. out of s.t. ☞ Pass: -tyiwa AM-94:120, AXG:107, CGB:188, NDK-91:91, PCX:20f, RD-96:405, XED:171, R12=2, R20

-tyala *v-tr* plant (with the hand) EXD:461, XED:172, R12x=7

-tyatyamba *v-intr* flower, blossom, bloom; [fig] ache, throb, have a shooting pain; rumble (thunder) XED:172, R30x

-tyeba *v-inch* be fat; get / become rich; be valuable SXWU:18, XED:172, R7

-tyebile *v-perf-atr* fat; [ext] rich E&S:30

-tyebisa *v-caus* fatten, cause to become fat; enrich, make s.o. rich R7

-tyeka *v-atr* be edible, eatable PCX:93

-tyela *v-ben* eat at (place); eat from (dish); eat for (a reason); [ext] misappropriate, help oneself to s.t. belonging to another GDX3:450, R31

-tyelela *v-tr* visit, pay a visit to s.o. GDX3:450, XED:173, R26

tyelelo *n6-sg-red* visit ☞ See: utyelelo R24

-tyhafa *v-intr* be weak, delicate, feeble, without energy E&S:51, XED:171f, R25

-tyhefa *v-tr* poison EXD:466, GDX3:454, R25x

tyhefu *n5-sg-red* poison ☞ See: ityhefu R25

-tyheli *atr-root* yellow ☞ Syn: -lubhelu GDX3:455, NDK-91:344; 592, UEX:14, R34

-tyhila *v-tr* uncover, lay bare; reveal, disclose, expose; narrate RD-96:405; 114, XED:173, R14

-tyhileka *v-atr* be disclosed, get revealed; be open, manifest XED:173, R14

-tyhola *v-tr* accuse, blame, denounce; calumniate XED:174, R26=2

-tyisa *v-caus* feed, make eat; chew the cud XED:171, R35.12

-tyumba *v-tr* select, appropriate, pick out and carry off; raid (cattle) ☞ Pass: -tyunjwa XED:174, R37.3x

U

u-[1] *n1a-sg-prf* [group 1a (Bantu class 1a) singular noun prefix] • *urhulumente 'government', utata 'father', uNelson Mandela 'Nelson Mandela'* Consists of article u- + classifier # ☞ Pl: oo- AXG:17f, CGB:103, E&S:17, EXD:252, PCX:51f, RD-96:372, SXWU:14, R4b, R4c, R6, R10, R16

u-[2] *n1-sg-S1* he, she [group 1, 1a singular subject (S1) agreement prefix] Agr: um-, u- CGB:117; 158, E&S:17f, PCX:51, SXWU:28, R4b=2, R4c

u-[3] *n1-sg-rel2* he, she who [group 1, 1a singular direct relative 2 construction, attributive agreement prefix used predicatively] E&S:34, MI:153; 248, PCX:151, R5

u-[4] *n2-sg-prf* [group 2 (Bantu class 3) singular noun prefix on some roots beginning with m-] • *umoya 'wind' [= u(m)-moya]* AXG:18

u-[5] *n2-sg-S1* he, she, it [group 2 singular subject (S1) agreement prefix] Agr: um- CGB:117; 158, E&S:17f, PCX:51, SXWU:28

u-[6] *n2-sg-S2* he, she, it [group 2 singular participial subject (S2) agreement prefix] AXG:89; 91, CGB:191, R37.14

u-[7] *n2-sg-S3a* (and) he, she, it VERBs [group 2 singular present subjunctive verb subject (S3a) agreement prefix] CGB:167, R11

u-[8] *n2-sg-rel2* that which [group 2 singular direct relative 2 construction, attributive agreement prefix used predicatively] E&S:34, MI:153; 248, PCX:151, R7, R30

u-[9] *n2-sg-ind-rel2* which [group 2 singular indirect relative 2 agreement prefix] E&S:35

u-[10] *n6-sg-prf* [group 6 (Bantu class 11) singular noun prefix on polysyllabic roots] • *ucango 'door'; ucoselelo 'carefulness'* ☞ Pl: iiN- (e.g., iim-, iing-) CGB:106f, E&S:17, PCX:54f, RD-96:372, SXWU:20, R1, R4d, R6

u-[11] *n7-sg-prf* [group 7 (Bantu class 14) singular noun prefix on irregular roots] • *utyani 'grass', utywala 'alcoholic beverage'* PCX:55, SXWU:20

-u[12] *n-suf* [noun-forming suffix] • *amendu 'speed', isisulu 'towel; windfall, bargain', ityhefu 'poison'* R1

u-[13] *pro-2sg-S1-prf* you (singular = thou) CGB:115; 158, E&S:18, SXWU:28, XED:xvi, R3, R7, R12

u-[14] *pro-2sg-S2-prf* you (singular = thou) VERBing [S2 participial subject] AXG:89; 91, CGB:191, R6=3, R7, R12=3

u-[15] *pro-2sg-S3a-prf* (that) you (singular = thou) VERB [S3a present subjunctive subject pronoun] CGB:167, R6=6, R14, R25

u-[16] *pro-2sg-S4* you can VERB; you may VERB [second person singular potential / conditional verb subject (S4) agreement pronoun] • *Ungagoduka ngoku 'You can go home now'* E&S:45, PCX:166, SXWU:149, R7

u-[17] *pro-2sg-dir-rel2* you who [direct relative 2] • *wena uvelayo 'you who see'* E&S:34n

u-[18] *pro-2sg-ind-rel2* you whom [indirect relative 2] E&S:35

u-[19] *pro-3sg-S1* he, she • *usebenzile 'he/she worked'* Structure: when there is no direct antecedent AM-94:163, CGB:115, RD-96:373, SXWU:28, XED:xvi

uAgasti *n1a-sg-time* August ☞ Syn: eyeThupha AM-94:73, CGB:46, EXD:36, MI:232, RD-96:375

uApreli *n1a-sg-time* April ☞ Alt: uApril; Syn: uTshaz'iimpumzi CGB:45

uApril *n1a-sg-time* April ☞ Alt: uApreli; Syn: ekaTshaz'iipuzi EXD:27, MI:232

ub- *n7-prf* [group 7 (Bantu class 14) singular noun prefix before roots beginning with o-] • *ubomi 'life', ubongikazi 'nursing'* ☞ Alt: ubu- PCX:55, RD-96:372, SXWU:20

uba *v-part* you being, having R29

ubabalo *n6-sg* favor CGB:114

ubabona *v-tr* you see them R29

ubagcine *v-pro-2sg-S3a-n1-pl-obj-pres-sub* you should keep them R14

ubala *n6-sg* desert, wilderness (vast vacant area) • *ilizwe lilubala 'the country is a desert'* KED:20, XED:6

ubambo *n6-sg* rib ☞ Pl: iimbambo CGB:114, EXD:533

ubango *n6-sg* cause, reason, ground, rationale XED:8

ubani[1] *qw-n1a-sg* who? ☞ Pl: oobani AXG:18, E&S:56, PCX:37, RD-96:405, SXWU:14, XED:8

ubani[2] *pro-indef-n1a-sg* anyone, whoever; [neg] no one • *akukho bani 'there is no one'* XED:8, R27, R35

ubarman *n1a-sg* barman R31

ubasikelele *v-tr-sub* you bless them R13

ubathwese *v-imp* crown them with! R13

ubaw' *n1-sg-red* father R16=2

ubawo *n1a-sg-kin* father (my), our father; benefactor; master; [ext] Reverend ☞ Pl: oobawo AXG:18; 36; 215, CGB:109, E&S:17; 56, EXD:209, MI:262, XED:9, R17.5, R20x, R32

ubawokazi *n1a-sg-kin* uncle (my paternal), our father's brother ☞ Pl: oobawokazi; Cf: umalume (maternal) AXG:36; 215, E&S:33, EXD:689, MI:262, R36

ubawomkhulu *n1a-sg-cmp-kin* grandfather (my, our) ☞ Pl: oobawomkhulu AXG:215, E&S:56, EXD:254, RD-96:405, R32x

ubawozala *n1a-sg-kin* father-in-law (of a woman, husband's father) ☞ Pl: oobawozala AXG:215, EXD:209, RD-96:405

ube-[1] *v-n1-sg-recent-past* he was VERBing; she has been VERBing [group 1, 1a singular contracted near / recent past continuous prefix] Structure: ube-Δ (participial verb form) ☞ Alt: ebe- AXG:91f, E&S:37f, PCX:183, R24

ube[2] *preverb-recent-pro-n1-sg* he, she was VERBing [group 1, 1a singular recent past compound tense preverb] Structure: ube e-Δ (participial construction) AXG:91f, E&S:37f, PCX:183

ub e[3] *v-pred-sub-n2-sg* that it be, it should become R11

ube[4] *preverb-recent-pro-n2-sg* it was VERBing [group 2 singular recent past compound tense preverb] Structure: ube u-Δ (participial construction) AXG:91f, E&S:37f, PCX:183

ub e[5] *v-pred-sub-pro-2sg* that you become R25, R29=4, R34

ube[6] *preverb-recent-pro-2sg* you were VERBing [recent past compound tense preverb] Structure: ube u-Δ (participial construction) AXG:91f, E&S:37f, PCX:183

ubekho *cop-loc* you are here R32

uBelekazana *pn-geog* Hogsback Mountain CGB:40, XED:194

ubenakho *v-cop-loc-sub-pro-2sg-S3a* that you be there • *ukuze ubenakho ukufaka isicelo 'so you can be there to put in an application'* R23.9

ubenezwi *v-aux-conj-n3-sg* you have a voice R21

ubenze *v-tr* you make them R29

ubesecaleni *v-recent-past* he was at the side R24

ubeyimbaleki *v-aux-cop-n5-sg* she has been a runner R33

ubhalele *v-sub* you should write to R15

ubhelu *n6-sg* yellow (color); s.t. yellow; [ext] very handsome person XED:11

ubhontsi *n1a-sg* big toe, great toe EXD:669, RD-96:12, XED:15

ubhuti *n1a-sg-kin* brother ☞ Pl: oobhuti SXWU:14

ubisi *n6-sg-mass* milk No direct plural (iimbisi 'types / apportionments of milk') AM-94:100, E&S:58; 22, PCX:37; 196, RD-96:405, XED:13, R28.6

ubomi *n7-abs* life ☞ Loc: ebomini AM-94:101, CGB:107, PCX:55, RD-96:406;372, SXWU:20, R7x, R11, R24, R32, R34x, R36

ubomvu *atr* redness R26

ubona *v-tr* you see R29

ubonakalise *v-atr-caus* you show R19

ubone *v-pres-sub* you should see R25

ubonelelo *n7-sg* provision, providing for; advantage; [ext] concession R23.0.7.9.11

ubongameli *n7-abs* presidency PCX:55

ubongikazi *n7-sg* nursing PCX:55

uboni *n7-abs* depravity, injustice, sinfulness XED:121

uboya *n7-mass* wool; fur, hair (of animal); down (of bird) AM-94:101, AXG:200, CGB:107, E&S:58; 31, RD-96:406, XED:122

ubu-[1] *n7-prf* [group 7 (Bantu class 14) singular noun prefix] • *ububele 'hospitality', ubuso 'face'* Consists of article u- + classifier bu- ☞ Alt: ub- AXG:15, CGB:107, E&S:17; 33, PCX:51; 55, RD-96:372, SXWU:20, R2=2, R7=2, R8, R14=2, R30

ubu-[2] *v-n2-sg-recent-past* it was / it has been VERBing [group 2 singular contracted near / recent past continuous prefix] AXG:91f, E&S:37f, MI:247, PCX:183

ubu-[3] *v-pro-2sg-recent-past* you were / have been VERBing [contracted near / recent past continuous prefix] AXG:91f, E&S:37f, MI:247, PCX:183

ububanzi *n7-abs* breadth, width EXD:725, RD-96:406

ububele *n7-abs* kindness, benevolence; natural affection; hospitality AM-94:101, CGB:107, E&S:58, PCX:50; 55, RD-96:406;372, SXWU:20, XED:10

ububi *n7-abs* evil, badness; ugliness CGB:107, E&S:58, SXWU:20

ububovu *n7-sg* pus, matter (EXD:495), AXG:200, CGB:114, KED:44, XED:16

ubuchopho *n7-sg* brain ☞ Loc: ebuchotsheni AXG:200, CGB:114, EXD:67, PCX:69, RD-96:13, XED:24, R34

ubuchule *n7-abs* skill EXD:591, R33

ubudala *n7-abs* age AM-94:101, SXWU:20

ubude *n7-abs* length; height; depth SXWU:20, XED:28

ubudenge *n7-abs* foolishness CGB:107, E&S:58

ubudlelwane *n7-abs* friendship, fraternity ☞ - [doke & vilakazi:156] [Zulu-English Dictionary -- C.M. Doke & B.W. Vilakazi; Witwatersrand University Press, Johannesburg, 1972] R34

ubudoda *n7-abs* manliness, manhood SXWU:20

ubufazi *n7-abs* womanliness, womanhood SXWU:20

ubugcisa *n7-sg-abs* skill, expertise, proficiency AXG:200, XED:44, R34.8, R35.6.9

ubugqi *n7-abs* magic, sorcery, enchantment AXG:200, CGB:114, XED:48

ubugqwirha *n7-abs* sorcery, witchcraft, magic; unnatural crime ☞ Alt sp: ubugqwira AXG:200, EXD:605, XED:50

ubugwenxa *n7-sg-abs* wrongness, perversity, crookedness R13

ubuhlanti *n7-sg* corral, cattle-fold, kraal (place of great religious or social significance) ☞ Pl: iintlanti; Loc: ebuhlanti AM-94:103, AXG:200, CGB:107; 114, PCX:70

ubuhlaza *n7-abs* greenness; freshness, rawness ☞ Cf: -luhlaza 'green, blue' XED:59

ubuhle *n7-abs* beauty CGB:107, E&S:33; 58; 22, SXWU:20

ubuhlobo *n7-abs* friendship, intimacy, mutual attachment AM-94:101, KED:159, XED:60, R34

ubuhlungu *n7-sg* pain; grief, sorrow; poison, venom; [ext] cure, medicine, antidote XED:61, R30, R36

ubuhlwempu *n7-abs* poverty ☞ Loc: ebuhlwentshini CGB:107, EXD:473, PCX:69, XED:62

ubukhulu *n7-abs* greatness, largeness, bigness; size; amount; dignity R36=2

ubukrele-krele *n7-abs* brilliance, brightness MI:198, R12x

ubulali *n7-abs* meekness, gentleness, mildness XED:80

ubulawu *n7-mass* perfume, incense, sweet-smelling ointment AXG:200, CGB:107; 114, XED:81

ubulembu *n7-sg* lichen CGB:114, EXD:343

ubuliso *n6-sg* greeting, salutation XED:17

ubulongo *n7-sg* dung, manure (fresh cow dung) ☞ Alt: ubulongwe AXG:200, CGB:114, XED:83

ubulongwe *n7-sg* fresh cow dung ☞ Cf: amalongwe EXD:179, XED:83

ubulumko *n7-abs* caution; wisdom CGB:107, E&S:58

ubulungisa *n7-abs* justice, righteousness, rectitude; goodness, benevolence, kindness; a good deed No plural AXG:200, CGB:114, EXD:323, XED:85

ubulungu *n7-abs* membership XED:85

ubume *n7-abs* position, state, status, condition XED:86, R21.4, R34.2x

ubumfama *n7-abs* blindness CGB:107, EXD:59, XED:89

ubumhlophe *n7-abs* whiteness, brightness, clearness, purity AXG:200, CGB:114, XED:89

ubumnandi *n7-abs* sweetness; delight, pleasure, joy, jubilation XED:90, R14

ubumnyama *n7-abs* darkness; blackness; gloom, ignorance AXG:200, CGB:114, EXD:143, XED:90

ubunene *n7-abs* truth; rank; nobility XED:98

ubungozi *n7-abs* misfortune, state of being unfortunate; peril, state of danger EXD:143, KED:125; 264, XED:47, R6x

ubungqina *n7-sg* evidence; testimony NDK-91:510, XED:108, R19, R36

ubungwevu *n7-abs* gray (the color), greyness EXD:256

ubunina *n7-abs* motherhood, motherliness EXD:391

ubuninzi *n7-abs* plenty, abundance; sufficiency XED:104

ubunja *n7-abs* dog nature; [fig] surliness; baseness; wretchedness XED:104

ubunjengele *n7-abs* courage, bravery; heroism; generalship XED:104

ubunkokeli *n7-abs* leadership EXD:336, R16, R32x

ubuntu *n7-abs* humanity, human nature, quality of being human; virtue, human goodness AM-94:103, AXG:15; 200, CGB:107; 114, SXWU:20, XED:112

ubuntwana *n7-abs* childhood AM-94:101, AXG:15; 200, CGB:114

ubunye *n7-abs* oneness, unity, unanimity XED:117

ubunzima *n7-abs* difficulty, hardship R14, R35

uburhalarhume *n7-abs* rage, wrath R36x

ubushushu *n7-abs* heat; temperature AM-94:101, E&S:33, R8x

ubusi *n7-mass* honey No plural AM-94:101, AXG:200, CGB:114, E&S:58, SXWU:20

ubusika *n7-time* winter [lit: cutting time, reaping season] ☞ Loc: ebusika, kubusika AM-94:73; 101, AXG:200; 217, CGB:46; 114, E&S:58, PCX:70, SXWU:20; 102, XED:151, R35x

ubuso *n7-sg* face ☞ Loc: ebusweni AM-94:101, CGB:139, PCX:55; 68; 96, SXWU:20

ubusuku *n7-time* night, nighttime ☞ Loc: ebusuku AM-94:63; 101, AXG:200, CGB:114; 173, E&S:58; 17, EXD:404, MI:231, PCX:29; 55, SXWU:20, XED:155, R2=2, R27.5, R28.5, R30.2, R36.1

ubutata *n7-abs* fatherhood EXD:209

ubuthathaka *n7-abs* weakness, feebleness, softness, inefficiency XED:158, R30x

ubuthongo *n7-abs* sleep, slumber, weariness CGB:107, E&S:58, EXD:594, R25x

ubutsha *n7-abs* newness, freshness; youth XED:163, R14

ubutye *n7-abs* stoniness E&S:33

ubutyebi *n7-abs* wealth (wealthiness), richness; fatness EXD:717, XED:172, R34

ubuvila *n7-abs* laziness, sloth ☞ Pl: amavila EXD:336; 596, XED:177

ubuxhego *n7-abs* old age EXD:417, XED:183

ubuxhwele *n7-sg* herbal medicine; state of being a herbalist or medicine man R7+x

ubuxoki *n7-abs* falsehood, lying AXG:15

ubuzali *n7-abs* parenthood AM-94:101, XED:190

ubuzalwana *n7-abs* kinship, brotherhood, relationship by blood, (genetic) connection; [ext] friendship ☞ Alt: ubuzalwane EXD:72, GDX3:646

ubuzalwane *n7-abs* kinship ☞ See: ubuzalwana EXD:326, GDX3:646

ubuzele *n7-sg* mucus, mucous matter; chewed cane AXG:200, CGB:114, XED:191

ucacisa *v-n1a-sg-pres* he, she explains R37.1

ucando *n6-sg* survey EXD:642

ucango *n6-sg* door ☞ Pl: iingcango; Loc: elucangweni AM-94:100, CGB:107, E&S:58, PCX:34; 55; 69, RD-96:406;372

uchaza *v-tr* he explains R36

uchaze *v-tr-perf* she explained R35

uchazile *v-tr-perf* he explained R36

ucing *v-intr-red* think R36

ucinga *verb-tr]* you think R21

ucingo *n6-sg* wire (metal); wire fence; telegraph or telephone line; [ext] telegram • *Ungabetha ucingo 'You can phone'* ☞ Pl: iingcingo CGB:114, XED:23, R15

ucoselelo *n6-sg* care, carefulness, close attention, interest EXD:83, R6

ucwambu *n6-sg* cream RD-96:406, XED:26, R32x

udaba *n6-sg* report, message; matter, item of conversation, news ☞ Pl: iindaba XED:27, R18.6, R23x=2, R29, R33.7

udade *n1a-sg-kin* sister (my, our - used by men); sister-in-law (wife's sister) ☞ Pl: oodade AXG:18; 216, CGB:109, E&S:56, EXD:590, KED:70, XED:27

udade bobawo *n1a-sg-cmp-kin* aunt (my paternal), our father's sister ☞ Pl: oodade bobawo; Also: udadobawo AXG:216, EXD:36

udade boyihlo *n1a-sg-cmp-kin* aunt (your paternal), your father's sister ☞ Pl: oodade boyihlo AXG:216, EXD:36

udade boyise *n1a-sg-cmp-kin* aunt (his / her paternal), their father's sister ☞ Pl: oodade boyise AXG:216, EXD:36

udade wabo *n1a-sg-kin-cmp* his / her sister (said by a brother); their elder sister (said by sisters) AXG:216

udade wenu *n1a-sg-kin-cmp* your sister (said by a brother); your elder sister (said by sisters) AXG:216

udade wethu *n1a-sg-kin-cmp* my sister (said by a brother); our elder sister (said by sisters) AXG:216

udadobawo *n1a-sg-cmp-kin* aunt (my paternal), our father's sister ☞ Pl: oodadobawo; Also: udade bobawo SXWU:14

udaka *n6-sg-mass* mud, mire, dirt; mortar ☞ Pl: iindaka 'kinds ~ types of mud'; Loc: eludakeni; Cf: -mdaka 'mud-colored, dirty' AM-94:100, CGB:114; 142, E&S:58, XED:27

udakada *n1a-sg/n6-sg* spleen; milt (of vertebrate animals) ☞ Pl: oodakada AHD:1147, EXD:612, KED:71

udale *v-n2-sg-past* it created R37.1

udaliwe *n1a-sg* rock painting (left by the San on a cliff near the Thorn River) ☞ Pl: oodaliwe; Cf: iDaliwe CGB:40, XED:27

ude *v-aux* still, even aux formed from -de 'length' R37.14

uDesmond *n1a-pn* (personal name) • *u-Desmond Mpilo Tutu* R32.7

udidi *n6-sg* sort, kind, type, category; pedigree, breed; class; caste, rank; row; stamp ☞ Pl: iindidi EXD:687, NDK-91:401, XED:29, R1, R25.2

udino *n6-sg* fatigue EXD:209

uDisemba *n1a-sg-time* December ☞ Syn: eyomNga AM-94:73, CGB:46, EXD:146, MI:232

udlwengulo *n6-sg* rape EXD:506, R27, R36

udonga *n6-sg* wall, embankment, rampart; bank (of river); washed out gully ☞ Pl: iindonga; Loc: eludongeni AM-94:100, CGB:42, E&S:58, PCX:55, XED:32

udongwe *n6-sg* clay E&S:58, XED:32

ududumo *n6-sg* thunder AXG:218, XED:33

udumo *n6-sg* fame EXD:206, R33x

uEdward *n1a-sg-pn* Edward (personal name) R4b

ufake *v-tr-sub* you put in R23

ufakwe *v-pass* it is put, placed R31

uFebruwari *n1a-sg-time* February ☞ Syn: eyomDumba, eyoMdumba AM-94:73, CGB:45, EXD:210, MI:232

ufele *n6-sg* skin, hide, leather ☞ Pl: iimfele E&S:58, EXD:592

ufudo *n6-sg* tortoise ☞ Pl: iimfudo CGB:107; 190, E&S:58, RD-96:407;372

ufumana *v-pres* you find R12, R29

ufumane *v-sub-pro-2sg* you get • *ukuze ufumane inkonzo 'so that you get service'* R37

ufumanisa *v-tr-caus* he finds R36

ufuna *v-tr* you want • *Ingaba ufuna uncedo? 'Do you want help?'* R15, R22.6, R23.9, R28.5

Ufunde *pn* family name, surname R22

ufunisayo *v-caus-rel* who is searching R26

ufunyaniswe *v-caus-pass* you are found R31

uGeorge Sebiloane *n1a-sg-pn-loan* George Sebiloane R33

ugqatso *n6-sg* race XED:48, R33=3

ugqibo *n6-sg* decision, resolution XED:48

ugqirha *n1a-sg* doctor (medical), qualified doctor; medicine man; medical practitioner ☞ Pl: oogqirha E&S:56, MI:273, SXWU:14, XED:48, R3x, R6, R32=2, R36=2, R37.15=2

ugqithisile *v-caus* you have passed R31

uGraca *n1a-sg-pn* Graca R24

ugula *v-part* you (are)sick, infected participial after 'sele' R30

uhamba *v-intr-pro-2sg* you travel R31.2

uhambisana *v-caus-recip* he goes with R36

uhambise *v-tr-perf* he moved on R27

uhambo *n6-sg* journey, trip; visit NDK-91:435, RD-96:407, SXWU:20, R28

uhambo ngomoya *n6-sg-cmp* flight [lit: trip in air] RD-96:407

uhili *n1a-sg* a fabulous river-dwarf supposed to carry off children R32

uhlanganyelwano *n6-sg* a coming together R34.3

uhlawuliswe *v-caus-pass* you are made to pay R31.3

uhlaza *n6-sg* fresh green grass; [fig] spring ☞ Cf: -luhlaza 'green, blue' XED:59

uhlobo *n6-sg* sort, kind of s.t., (particular) type; [atr] choice, pedigree ☞ Pl: iintlobo KED:159, XED:60, R21, R30, R37.11.15.19.26

uhluthi *v-part-perf* you get full R12

uJanuwari *n1a-sg-time* January ☞ Loc: ngoJanuwari; Syn: eyomQungu, eyoMqungu AM-94:73, CGB:45, EXD:318, MI:232

uJohn Vorster *n1a-pn* John Vorster R32

uJojo *n1a-sg-pn* Jojo (personal name) AXG:18, E&S:24

uJulayi *n1a-sg-time* July ☞ Syn: eyeKhala AM-94:73, CGB:46, EXD:322, MI:232

uJuni *n1a-sg-time* June ☞ Syn: eyeSilimela AM-94:73, CGB:46, EXD:322, MI:232, R4a

uk- *n8-vn-prf* [group 8 (Bantu class 15) verbal noun prefix before roots beginning with o] • *ukondla 'feeding', ukoja 'roasting, baking', ukona 'wrongdoing'* Used with a verb that begins with o- ☞ See: uku- CGB:125, PCX:56;20, RD-96:372, SXWU:20

ukanina *n1a-sg-kin* cousin (where parents are sisters) ☞ Pl: ookanina; Contrast: umntakwethu, umza EXD:129

ukanti *conj* nevertheless R27=2

ukapteni *n1a-sg* captain ☞ Pl: ookapteni R27=2

ukhethwe *v-pass-perf* she was selected R24.7

ukhetshe *n1a-sg* hawk ☞ Pl: ookhetshe CGB:109, EXD:268

ukho[1] *v-exis-n1-sg* he is here, she is present E&S:29, ITX:17

ukho[2] *v-exis-n2-sg* it is here; he, she is present E&S:29, ITX:17

ukho[3] *v-exis-pro-2sg* you (thou) are here / present E&S:29

ukhohlele *v-intr-sub* you cough R25

ukhohlo *n6-sg* left (hand, direction, side) ☞ Opp: ukunene; Loc: ekhohlo AXG:144, PCX:70, XED:72

ukholelwa *v-tr* he believes R29

ukhombe *n6-sg* forefinger, index finger XED:73

ukhulelwe *v-pass-ben* (if) you are pregnant R6

ukhululwe *v-pass* be released R31.3

ukhuni *n6-sg* wood; log; [pl] firewood ☞ Pl: iinkuni XED:77, R11

ukhuphiswano *n6-sg* contest EXD:121, R33

ukhuselekile *v-st-atr-perf* it is protected R18.6

ukhuseleko *n6-sg-vn* protection, state of being protected R36.1

ukhuthazwa *v-pass* he is encouraged R36.17

ukohlwaywa *v-vowel-pass* to be punished R23.3

uKomani *pn-geog* Queenstown (so-named it is rumored after a works foreman shouted "Come on!" repeatedly) ☞ Loc: kuKomani, kwaKomani CGB:175, MI:246, XED:194

ukona *n8-vn* sin, sinning, wrongdoing PCX:56, SXWU:20

ukondla *n8-vn* feeding RD-96:372

ukonwaba *n8-vn* happiness (being happy); ease, comfort PCX:56, SXWU:20, XED:121

ukoyika *n8-vn* fear; fearing AM-94:102

ukrebe *n1a-sg* shark ☞ Pl: ookrebe CGB:109, EXD:578

uku-[1] *n8-vn-prf* [group 8 (Bantu class 15) verbal noun prefix] • *ukubhala 'writing'* Consists of article u- + classifier ku- CGB:108, E&S:17, PCX:51;55f, RD-96:372, SXWU:20, R3, R4c, R4d, R5, R6, R7, R9x

uku-[2] *n10-loc-prf* [group 10 (Bantu class 17) locative noun prefix] • *ukunene 'right-hand side'* Consists of article u- + classifier ku-; designates place, situation, or time RD-96:372

uku- -a *v-inf-pos* to VERB; VERBing [positive infinitive / gerund verb construction] • *ukufunda 'to learn; learning'* Structure: uku-Δ-a CGB:121, PCX:20, R4b=4, R4c=3, R5, R6, R7=2, R10=2, R12

ukuba[1] *n8-vn* being XED:5, R6x

ukuba[2] *v-inf* to be R33

ukuba[3] *conj* that [statement of fact] • *Ndicinga ukuba ootitshala ngabona bantu babalulekileyo kuluntu 'I think that teachers are people essential to society'; bathunywa ukuba bayongqiba imali 'They are sent so that they will collect money'* Structure: a complementizer, equivalent to English 'that', joining a main clause to a subordinate clause; in this meaning, followed by indicative ☞ Cf: bokuba, kokuba, lokuba, nokuba, okuba, sokuba, wokuba, yokuba, zokuba AXG:149, GDX3:475, XS-92:158f, R3, R9=2, R10, R11=2, R12=2, R18.4.5, R19.1.2.3.5, R20.4, R23.5, R26.5.6, R27.5.6.14, R28.4.5.7, R29.8, R30=4, R31.3.4, R32.2.4, R33.0.10, R34.6.10, R35.11.12, R36=13, R37=18

ukuba[4] *conj* that [statement of situation] • *Baphawula ukuba beza kufumana uchatha 'They note that they are going to get an increment'* Structure: followed by participial XS-92:158f, R9

ukuba[5] *conj* as long as, so long as, provided that [statement of condition] • *ukuba ngumama wekhaya 'so long as she is a housewife'* EXD:31, R4d

ukuba[6] *conj* if [conditional]; whether • *Ukuba nditsho 'If I may say so'; Ndingavuya ukuba ubaw' uNelson Mandela unokuvula isikolo esinje 'I would be grateful if father Mandela would be able to open such a school; Ukuba uyamthanda lo mfana, mtshate! 'If you love that young man, marry him!'* Structure: followed by indicative ☞ Alt: nokuba; See: xa AXG:149, E&S:59, EXD:722, GDX3:475, MI:257, PCX:21;26, RD-96:407, XED:175, R16, R17.3, R20.2, R21.3, R23.9, R27.3, R34.6, R37.17

ukuba[7] *conj* that, so that, in order to [statement of desire or purpose] • *Kwizilwanyana akuvumeleki ukuba amantshontsho ayabule ebusuku 'In the animal kingdom the young are not allowed to wander around at night'* Structure: followed by present subjunctive AXG:96; 152, E&S:42, GDX3:475, XED:175, XS-92:158f, R2, R14, R16, R18.5, R19.2, R23.6.7, R24.3.7, R25.4, R27.1, R28.5, R29.11, R32.6.7.9, R33.9, R34.12, R35.5.10, R36.16, R37.7.10.16.17.19.20.21.24

ukuba[8] *conj* that ... should, that ... must [hortative]; that ... may [optative] • *Ndafumana ukuba mandifunde isiXhosa 'I found that I must study Xhosa'* Structure: followed by ma- hortative construction XS-92:158f

ukubacutha *v-inf* to minimize R32

ukubahlawulisa *v-caus* to charge them • *ukubahlawulisa irhafu 'to charge them tax* R23

ukubaleka *v-inf* to run R33

ukubanako *vn8-sg* ability ☞ Syn: ukwazi EXD:1

ukubatshintsha *v-inf* to change them R37.15

ukubhala[1] *n8-vn* writing, handwriting AM-94:102, AXG:15; 200, CGB:114, RD-96:407;372

ukubhala[2] *v-inf* to write R24

ukubhalelwa *v-ben-pass-inf* to be written to R4b

ukubila *n8-vn* perspiring, condition of being covered with sweat EXD:643, R30=2

ukubiwa *v-tr-pass-inf* theft, thieving, to steal R27

ukubona *v-inf* to see R35

ukubukela *v-inf-ben* to watch (TV) • *Ndithanda ukubukela ezemidlalo kumabonakude 'I like to watch sports on television'* R4c

ukubulisa *n8-vn* greeting; salute (act of greeting) CGB:108

ukucela *v-inf-n8-vn* to ask; requesting, asking R35, R36

ukucenga *v-inf* to plead R29

ukuchaza *v-tr-n2-sg-S1+n8-vn-obj* it explains it R36.0

ukucula *n8-vn* singing, song (act of singing) E&S:58; 22, SXWU:20

ukudada *n8-vn* floating; swimming E&S:58

ukude *conj* until Structure: followed by present subjunctive E&S:42

ukudla[1] *n8-sg* food ☞ Syn: ukutya AXG:200, XED:30

ukudla[2] *v-inf* eat R27

ukudlala *v-inf* to play R4b

ukudlwengula *n8-vn* to rape; raping • *ukuchaza ukudlwengula njengo 'describes raping as'* R36=2

ukudlwengulwa *vn-pass* to be raped; being raped R36=4

ukudumba *v-inf* to swell; swelling R30

ukufa *n8-vn* death; dying AM-94:102, AXG:200, CGB:114, PCX:50; 55, SXWU:20, XED:37

ukufaka *v-inf* to put in R23

ukufakwa *vn-pass* to be put in R36

ukufika *n8-vn* arrival; arriving AM-94:102

ukufikelela *v-inf-intens* to arrive at, reach R34.3, R37.11

ukufumana *v-inf* to get, to find R7, R28

ukufuna *vn* to want R36

ukufunda[1] *n8-vn* learning AM-94:102, PCX:55

ukufunda[2] *v-inf* to read R4b

ukugcina *v-inf* to take care of; to preserve R34.5, R35.6

ukugula *v-intr* to become sick R30

ukuhamba *n8-vn* travel; walking AXG:15; 200, NDK-91:435, R28, R36

ukuhambisa *n8-vn* dispatching, sending off NDK-91:435

ukuhla[1] *n8-vn* loss, losing R30.2.3.4

ukuhla[2] *v-inf* to descend, come / go down XED:56, R30=2

ukuhla komzimba *n8-poss-cmp* weight loss [lit: losing of the body] R30=2

ukuhlala *v-inf* to live, stay, be among (people) R29

ukuhleka *n8-vn* laughing, laughter E&S:58

ukuhlwa *n10-time* nightfall, evening, decline of the day EXD:404, PCX:37, XED:61

ukujongana nosuku *v-cmp-expr* to face the day ☞ See: -jongana na- R12

ukukhanya *n8-vn* shining; light AXG:200

ukukhohlela *n8-vn* to have difficulty in breathing; coughing XED:72, R30

ukukhuphela *vn* to release R36=2

ukukhusela *v-inf* to protect R10

ukukhweliswa *vn-pass* to be given a lift, to be picked up R36

ukukufumana *v-inf* to find, get R29

ukulalana *vn-recip* the sleeping together R36

ukulesa *n8-vn* reading AXG:15

ukulibala *n8-vn* forgetting; loss of memory R30=2

ukulicaphukela *vn-ben* to be annoyed at R36

ukulima *n8-vn* plowing; farming, cultivation E&S:58

ukulumkisa *v-tr-caus* to warn R31

ukulungele *v-pro-2sg-n8-vn-obj* you are ready R29.4, R30.3

ukulungelelaniswa *conj-v-inf-ben-recip-caus-pass* and of preserving R37

ukuma *n8-vn* standing, state, condition ☞ rw: -ma XED:86

ukumamela *n8-vn* listening (act of listening) CGB:108

ukumbeka *vn-tr* to place R36

ukumeka *n8-vn* being ☞ Alt: umeko; rw: -ma XED:86

ukumkani *n1a-sg* king ☞ Pl: ookumkani AXG:35, EXD:327

ukumkanikazi *n1a-sg-fem* queen ☞ Pl: ookumkanikazi AXG:35, EXD:499

ukundixelela *v-inf-ben* to tell me, to mention to me R19.2

ukundlandlathekiswa *v-tr-inf-pass* to be frightened by R36

ukunene *n10-loc* right (hand, direction, side) n10-loc (not n8-vn) ☞ Opp: ukhohlo PCX:70, RD-96:408;372, SXWU:102, XED:98

ukunga *conj* to, that, so that • *Walangazelela ukunga angakubona 'He longed to see you' [lit: that he might see you]* AXG:149

ukunga- -i *v-inf-neg* not to VERB; not VERBing [negative infinitive / gerund verb construction] • *ukungaboni 'not to see; not seeing'* Structure: uku-nga-Δ-i CGB:121, R6=2

ukunga- -w- -a *v-inf-pass-neg* not to be VERBed; not VERBed [negative passive infinitive / gerund verb construction] • *ukungabonwa 'not to be seen'*

Structure: uku-nga-Δ-w-a; Note: the suffix is -a, not -i PCX:104

ukungabikho *v-cop-loc-inf-neg* the absence, shortage R27.9

ukungakwazi *v-inf-neg* ignorance, inability R24

ukungamchazeli *v-inf-neg* not to explain to him R37.15

ukungawuthobeli *v-inf-neg* not obeying it R6, R31

ukungenela *v-ben* entering (into) R33

ukunika *v-inf* to give R37

ukunqaba *n8-vn* difficulty, impossibility; scarcity • *ukunqaba kwemali 'scarcity of money'* EXD:557, XED:106, R35

ukunwenwa *vn-pass* to spread, spreading R36

ukunyusa *n8-vn* raising R9

ukuphanda *vn* dig up, scratch up, investigate XED:124

ukuphatha[1] *v-inf* to lead; leading R22

ukuphatha[2] *v-inf* to handle, to take charge of R36

ukuphathele *v-ben* she introduces you to R22

ukuphathwa *v-inf-pass* the management [lit: to be managed] • *ukuphathwa kwezikolo 'the management of the schools'* R22.2

ukuphazamisa *v-inf* hinder, impede, obstruct,interrupt; confuse XED:125, R17.3

ukuphelelelwa *n8-vn* complete exhaustion XED:126

ukuphelelwa *n8-vn* lack (of), being bereft of • *Ndapelelwa butongo 'I did not sleep at all'* KED:328, R25.6

ukuphelelwa bubuthongo *n8-vn-cmp* insomnia, sleeplessness KED:328, R25

ukuphila *v-inf* to be in good health R17.3

ukuphinda *v-aux-inf* to VERB again R37.17

ukuphuculwa *v-inf-pass* to be improved R37.8.18

ukuphulaphula *v-inf* to listen to R4b

ukuphuma *v-inf* to come out, to rise R37

ukuphumeza *v-inf* to bring out or over R34.9

ukuphunyezwa *v-inf-pass* to cause the promotion of R37

ukuqhuba *v-inf* driving R31

ukuqhubela *v-ben-inf* to drive for or to R34.1.4=2

ukuqinisekisa *v-inf-atr-caus* to make sure R27, R37

ukuqwalasele *v-inf* to observe attentively R21

ukuqwalaselwa *v-pass-inf* to be addressed; to be viewed R37.5

ukusa *n8-vn* dawn, daybreak ☞ Loc: ekuseni EXD:144, PCX:68, XED:147

ukusebenza *v-inf* to work R29

ukusebenzisa *v-inf-caus* to use R16, R34

ukusekwa *v-inf-pass* the establishment [lit: the being established] R32.2

ukusetyenziwa *v-inf-pass* usage [lit: to be used] ukusetyenzwa is correct form, but 'i' is often inserted in common usage GDX3, R6

ukusifukama *v-inf* to sit, to be in prison as understood in S. Africa R17.6

ukusiphucula *v-inf* to civilize us R17.4

ukususela *adv* from that time EXD:588, R33

ukuthanda *n8-vn* loving, liking E&S:58

ukuthatha *v-inf* to take R37.19

ukuthengisela *v-caus-ben* selling to R29

ukuthengwa *v-pass* to be bought R29

ukuthetha[1] *n8-vn* speaking, talking; speech AXG:200, CGB:108, E&S:58

ukuthetha[2] *v-inf* to speak, to talk CGB:108, R36

ukuthethe *v-tr-perf* he said it R27

ukuthi *conj* that complementizer used after cognitive verbs AXG:149, XED:160, R25

ukuthini *v-inf-qw* to do what? • *ithetha ukuthini le Bhodi 'what does the Board mean?' [dummy verb; note word order reversal]* R37.19

ukutsha *n8-vn* newness [lit: being new] XED:163

ukutshisa *v-caus-inf* to burn R25.1

ukutshoyo *v-inf* that which you said R23

ukutya[1] *n8-vn* food; groceries; eating (act of eating) AM-94:102, AXG:200, CGB:173, E&S:58; 17, NDK-91:114, PCX:55, RD-96:408;373, SXWU:20, R26, R35=2

ukutya[2] *v-inf* to eat R12, R25

ukutyeba *v-inf* to become rich R7

ukutyhafa *n8-vn* weakness R25

ukutyhileka *v-atr-inf* to be open, disclosed, revealed R14

ukuva *v-inf* to hear; hearing • *Besithanda ukuva kuwe 'We would like to hear from you'* AXG:200, R21

ukuvelisa *v-tr-inf* to produce R34

ukuvula *v-tr* to open • *livula 'it opens'* XED:178, R25

ukuwa *n8-vn* fits, seizure [lit: falling] R30

ukuwanceda *vn-tr* to help them R36

ukuwaxhasa *v-tr-inf* to support them R36

ukuwongwa *v-inf-pass* to be taken care of ☞ See: -onga R24.6

ukuxhalabela *vn-ben* the great fright R36

ukuxinana *v-i* congestion, to be congested R25=2

ukuxokozela *v-inf* make a loud, confused noise or din XED:185, R33

ukuxolisa *v-caus-inf* to appease, put at peace R14

ukuya[1] *n8-vn* to go to; going to; [prep] up to R4d, R8, R35=2

ukuya[2] *inf-aux* going to VERB, will VERB [aux for future tense] • *awukwazi ukuya kufota i-passport 'they don't issue passports'* R37.14

ukuyazisa *vn-tr-caus* make known R36

ukuyeka *v-inf* to abandon, leave alone R17.3

ukuyilondoloza *v-inf* to take care of it R31

ukuyiodola *v-inf* to order it R22

ukuyisebenzisa *v-inf* to use it R30, R37.17

ukuyo *n2-sg-rel-n5-sg-loc* which is in it R30

ukuza *v-inf-aux* to come • *ukuza kumamela 'to come to hear about...'* infinitive form of aux of future tense R37

ukuze *conj* that, so, in order that Structure: followed by present subjunctive AXG:95, E&S:42, MI:257, XED:175, R3, R11, R12, R21, R23=2, R29=4, R30=2, R31, R33=2, R35=2, R37=7

ukuzibalula *v-inf-refl* to select for oneself; to self-determine R21.1.2

ukuzikhululula *v-inf-refl* to relieve oneself of R36.17

ukuzikisa *v-inf* use to the best advantage, cut deep, plough, make quite plain R30=2

ukuzikisa ingqondo *v-inf-cmp* to concentrate; [vn] concentration EXD:114, R30=2

ukuzimisela *v-inf-refl-caus-ben* being serious R33, R34

ukuzisebenzisa *v-inf-caus* to use them R37.16

ukw-[1] *n8-vn-prf* [group 8 (Bantu class 15) verbal noun prefix before roots beginning with a, e, and i] • *ukwakha 'building', ukwenza 'doing'* Used with a verb that begins with a- or e- ☞ Alt: uku- AM-94:102, CGB:114, PCX:56;20, RD-96:372, SXWU:20

ukw-[2] *n10-loc-prf* [group 10 (Bantu class 17) locative noun prefix] • *ukwindla 'autumn'* Designates place, situation, or time ☞ See: uku- RD-96:372

ukwahlukana *v-inf-recip* to part with R20

ukwakha *n8-vn* building, construction (act of building) E&S:58, EXD:73, PCX:56, SXWU:20

ukwamkela *v-inf* to receive R36.19

ukwanelisa *v-caus-vowel* to satisfy R36.20

ukwathe *v-tr-past* (she) also said R18

ukwayanyaniswa *vn-caus-pass* to be associated with R36

ukwazi[1] *n8-vn* knowing; knowledge, intelligence, ability AM-94:102, AXG:200, CGB:114, EXD:1, XED:4

ukwazi[2] *v-inf* to know, to understand R29=2

ukwenda *n8-vn* marriage (getting married - of a woman) ☞ Alt: ulwendo [n6] PCX:56

ukwenza[1] *n8-vn* doing, making; performance AM-94:102, CGB:125, RD-96:408;372, SXWU:20

ukwenza[2] *v-inf* to do, to make (according to context) • *ukwenza ilizwe elinempilo 'to make a healthy nation'* R11, R14, R30, R35=2, R37

ukwenzela *v-inf* to enable R27

ukwenziwa *v-pass* to be done R35

ukwindla *n10-time* time of harvest [lit: eating season, when the first ripe grain is eaten]; [ext] autumn a locative (not n8-vn) ☞ Loc: ekwindla AM-94:102, AXG:200; 217, CGB:46; 138, E&S:58, EXD:37, Pahl, PCX:56, RD-96:408;372, XED:62

ukwisikhundla *cop-loc-n4-sg* you are in position R31

ul- *n6-sg-prf* [group 6 (Bantu class 11) singular noun prefix] • *ulonwabo 'happiness', uloyiso 'victory'* PCX:55, RD-96:372

ulibone *v-tr-sub* you should see it R25

ulifake *v-tr* you put it R30

uligqirha *n3-sg-pred* you being a witch doctor R7

ulikhupha *v-tr* you take it out, you withdraw it R30.6

ulikhuphe *v-tr-sub* that you take it out R30.6

ulimo *n-6-sg* the crops R13

ulisikelele *v-tr-imp* you bless it R13

ulithwal' *v-tr-red* carry R13

uloliwe *n1a-sg* train ☞ Pl: oololiwe CGB:103, E&S:56, SXWU:14

ulonakalo *n6-sg* damage R26.7

ulonwabo *n6-sg* pleasure, happiness, delight; comfort, ease CGB:114, EXD:265, PCX:55, RD-96:408;372, XED:121

ulonyulo *n6-sg* nomination TD

uloyiko *n6-sg-abs* fear, dread EXD:210, R36

uloyiso *n6-sg* conquest, victory EXD:118; 706, PCX:55

ulu- *n6-sg-prf* [group 6 (Bantu class 11) singular noun prefix on monosyllabic roots] • *uluthi 'stick'* Consists of article u- + classifier lu- CGB:106, E&S:17, PCX:51; 54, RD-96:372, SXWU:20

ulubethe *v-pres-sub* you should speak it R29

uluhlu *n6-sg* row, line, string (of things); rank (military); coil, convolution (of snake) ☞ Pl: izintlu CGB:114, E&S:58, PCX:54, XED:61

ulumvi *n6-sg* gray hair ☞ Alt: uluvi (q.v.); Pl: izimvi KED:240

ulundi *n6-sg-ir* horizon No plural CGB:114, EXD:281

ulungile *v-st-perf* he is OK R4c

ulungiselelo *n6-sg* provision, preparation (for future needs) ☞ Pl: amalungiselelo EXD:489, R28

ulungiswe *v-pass* be repaired R35

uluntu *n6-sg* people, population; community, society; humanity, mankind, the human race; the common people No plural ☞ Loc: eluntwini AM-94:100, CGB:114, E&S:58, RD-96:409, XED:112, R3x, R20, R30x, R32=2, R35+x=4, R36=2, R37=5

ulunya *n6-sg-abs* ill-will, malice XED:115

ulunyukiswa *v-pass* (if) you are warned ☞ rw: -lumkisa R6

ulurhe *n6-sg* rumor ☞ Alt sp: ulure XED:144

ulusu[1] *n6-sg* skin (of human or small animal) ☞ Pl: izintsu CGB:107, EXD:592, XED:154, R30x

ulusu[2] *n6-sg* paunch, (large) tripe ☞ Pl: izintsu PCX:54, XED:154

uluthi *n6-sg* stick, rod; wattle ☞ Pl: izinti AM-94:100f, CGB:183, E&S:58; 22, PCX:54, RD-96:372, SXWU:20

ulutsha *n6-sg-mass* youth, young people No plural AM-94:100, XED:163

uluvi *n6-sg* gray hair (single strand) ☞ Pl: izimvi PCX:54, XED:91

uluvo *n6-sg* idea, opinion, point of view, attitude; emotion, feeling, sensation; common sense ☞ Pl: izimvo AM-94:100, CGB:107, E&S:58; 17, NDK-91:202, PCX:50, RD-96:409;104, SXWU:20, XED:176, R32, R34

ulw- *n6-sg-prf* [group 6 (Bantu class 11) singular noun prefix] • *ulwandle 'sea', ulwazi 'knowledge'* ☞ See: ulu- PCX:55, RD-96:372, SXWU:20, R11

ulwa *v-tr* who fights R36

ulwakhiwo-zindlu *n6-sg-cmp* housing [lit: being built of houses] • *uMphathiswa woLwakhiwo-zindlu 'the Minister of Housing'* TD

ulwalo *n6-sg* refusal EXD:517

ulwandle *n6-sg* sea ☞ Pl: iilwandle; Loc: elwandle AM-94:63; 101, AXG:219, CGB:107; 139, E&S:58, MI:262, PCX:55; 70, RD-96:409;372

ulwandlekazi *n6-sg-aug* ocean MI:262

ulwaphulo-mthetho *n6-sg-cmp* crime, breaking the law EXD:134, RD-96:409, R11

ulwazi *n6-sg* knowledge, knowing EXD:329, PCX:55, SXWU:20, R34x

ulwendo *n6-sg* marriage (getting married - of a woman) ☞ Alt: ukwenda [n8] PCX:55

uLwesibini *n6-sg-time* Tuesday [lit: second day] AM-94:73, CGB:46, EXD:683, MI:232, PCX:47

uLwesihlanu *n6-sg-time* Friday [lit: fifth day] AM-94:73, CGB:46, EXD:233, MI:232, PCX:47

uLwesine *n6-sg-time* Thursday [lit: fourth day] AM-94:73, CGB:46, EXD:665, MI:232, PCX:47

uLwesithathu *n6-sg-time* Wednesday [lit: third day] AM-94:73, CGB:46, EXD:718, MI:232, PCX:47

ulwimi *n6-sg* tongue; language ☞ Pl: amalwimi 'tongues' vs. iilwimi 'languages' AM-94:101, CGB:107, NDK-91:486, PCX:55, RD-96:409;94, R29, R37.12.20

ulwimishe *n1-sg* talebearer Requires n1-sg agreement although derived from n6-sg NDK-91:486

um-[1] *n1-sg-prf* [group 1 (Bantu class 1) singular noun prefix] • *umntu 'person', umyeni 'husband'* Consists of article u- + classifier m- ☞ Pl: aba- AXG:17, CGB:102, E&S:17, PCX:51f;23f, RD-96:372, SXWU:15, R4d=3, R9, R10

um-[2] *n2-sg-prf* [group 2 (Bantu class 3) singular noun prefix] • *umthi 'tree', umculo 'music'* Consists of article u- + classifier m- ☞ Pl: imi- AXG:18f, CGB:104, E&S:17, PCX:51f;27, RD-96:372, SXWU:16, R4b, R4c=3, R4d, R5=2, R37.1

um- -i *n1-sg-doer* -er, -or [singular doer or agentive noun circumfix] • *umbulali 'murderer', umfundi 'student', umpheki 'cook'* E&S:33, R11x

uma[1] *n1a-sg-kin* mother (my); our mother ☞ Alt: umama; Pl: ooma AXG:18; 36; 216, EXD:391, MI:262, XED:86

uma[2] *conj* if ☞ See Xhosa: xa R15=2

umabonakude *n1a-sg* telescope, binoculars; [ext] television [lit: may see far] ☞ Pl: oomabonakude; Cf: isibonakude; Syn: itelevizhini AM-94:60, EXD:56; 653, RD-96:409, R4c

uMachel *n1a-sg-pn* Machel R24

uMadiba *n1a-sg-pn* Madiba (clan name of Nelson Rholihlahla Mandela) MI:275, R17.5, R32

umAfrika *n1-sg* African (person) ☞ Pl: amaAfrika EXD:11

umahlab *n2-sg-comp* part of compound - stabbing pain R25

umakazi *n1a-sg-kin* aunt (my maternal), our mother's sister ☞ Pl: oomakazi AXG:36; 216, EXD:36, MI:262, SXWU:14

umakheniki *n1a-sg* mechanic SXWU:14, R26x

umakhi *n1-sg* builder ☞ Pl: abakhi AXG:15; 17, PCX:52

umakhulu *n1a-sg-kin* grandmother (my, our) ☞ Pl: oomakhulu AXG:216, CGB:135, E&S:56, EXD:254, SXWU:14

umakoti *n1a-sg-kin* bride, wife ☞ Pl: oomakoti; See Xhosa: umtshakazi KM, R4d

umalume *n1a-sg-kin* uncle (my maternal), our mother's brother ☞ Pl: oomalume; Cf: ubawokazi (paternal) AXG:215, EXD:689, SXWU:14, R36

umama *n1a-sg-kin* mother (my); our mother ☞ Pl: oomama; Alt: uma; Contrast: unina (their mother), unyoko (your mother) AM-94:62; 65, CGB:103, E&S:22; 56, EXD:391, MI:262, PCX:52, SXWU:14, R4d, R28=8

uMandela *n1a-sg-pn* Nelson Mandela R16, R24

umanyano *n6-sg* union, association, combination ☞ Pl: iimanyano PCX:55, XED:87, R13.8

umanyisikazi *n1a-sg-kin* foster mother ☞ Pl: oomanyisikazi EXD:391

umaphuli *n1-sg* breaker (of s.t.) • *umaphuli-mthetho 'lawbreaker'* ☞ See: -aphula R36.17

uMatshi *n1a-sg-time* March ☞ Syn: eyoKwindla AM-94:73, CGB:45, EXD:368, MI:232

umatshini *n1a-sg* machine, machinery, plant ☞ Pl: oomatshini CGB:103, EXD:461, MI:273, SXWU:14, R6

umawokhulu *n1a-sg-kin* grandparent ☞ Pl: oomawokhulu EXD:254

umba *n2-sg* narrow ridge, dangerous pass; [fig] problem, case, issue ☞ Pl: imiba RD-96:409, XED:5, R24.7, R27.10.11.12.13, R37.6

umbala[1] *n2-sg* color ☞ Pl: imibala EXD:107, R8x, R34=12

umbala[2] *n2-sg* shin, shinbone, tibia KED:20, XED:7

umbandela *n2-sg* fibula (bone attached to the shinbone); addition, supplement; graft; amendment; crowd of hangers-on XED:7, R16, R21.1

umbane *n2-sg* lightning; [ext] electricity ☞ Pl: imibane AXG:19; 117; 218, CGB:110, MI:262, XED:8

umBashe *n2-sg-pn-geog* Bashee River AXG:19

umBhaca *n1-sg* Bhaca, Baca (person, member of an ethnic group within the greater Xhosa community) ☞ Pl: amaBhaca AXG:20

umbhali *n1-sg* writer; clerk, scribe; author ☞ Pl: ababhali; Loc: kumbhali CGB:109, PCX:71, XED:6, R37.27

umbhinqo *n2-sg* wraparound (any garment tied around the waist) XED:13

umbilo *n2-sg* perspiration, sweat; moisture on the surface of anything EXD:643

umbona *n1a-sg* maize ☞ Pl: oombona AXG:18, E&S:56

umboneleli *n1-sg* provider EXD:489

umbongo *n2-sg* lullaby ☞ Pl: imibongo EXD:359, XED:15

umboniso *n2-sg* show, exhibition; illustration ☞ Pl: imiboniso AXG:19, CGB:110, RD-96:409

umbono *n2-sg* sight, vision; perspective, point of view; view, scene; prospect; phenomenon ☞ Pl: imibono EXD:450, RD-96:409, XED:15, R30x

umbulali *n1-sg* killer, murderer ☞ Pl: ababulali XED:17, R11x

umbulelo[1] *n2-sg* thanks, gratitude, thankfulness; thanksgiving; [intj] thank you ☞ Pl: imibulelo CGB:110, XED:17, R5=2, R27

UMbulelo[2] *n1a-sg-pn* Mbulelo (Xhosa male personal name) [lit: gratitude] R29=2

umbuliso *n2-sg* greeting, salutation ☞ Pl: imibuliso CGB:110, EXD:256, XED:17

umbuthi *n1-sg* collector ☞ Pl: ababuthi XED:19

umbutho *n2-sg* assembly, gathering; organization, society, association ☞ Pl: imibutho; Alt: ibutho [n3-sg], ibutho [n5-sg] NDK-91:383, RD-96:409, XED:19, R7x

umbuzo *n2-sg* question, query; subject of inquiry ☞ Pl: imibuzo; Cf: impendulo 'answer' E&S:56, PCX:26; 52, SXWU:16, XED:19, R27x

umcebo *n2-sg* wealth, riches, possessions ☞ See Xhosa: utyebo, indyebo EZZE:104, R15

umcimbi *n2-sg* matter, subject (under discussion); affair, business, transaction KED:62, XED:23, R22x

umculo *n2-sg* singing, concert; [ext] music EXD:395, RD-96:410, XED:25, R4b, R4c

umda *n2-sg* boundary ☞ Pl: imida CGB:42; 110, EXD:66

umdaka *n2-sg* very dark person ☞ Pl: imidaka 'common people' [fig] XED:27, R17x

umdali *n1-sg* creator ☞ Pl: abadali XED:27, R13

umdla *n2-sg* appetite, relish (for); delight (in); [ext] interest, enthusiasm EXD:311, RD-96:410, XED:30, R4c, R16x

umdlali *n1-sg* player AM-94:155

umdlalo *n2-sg* play; game; sport ☞ Pl: imidlalo AM-94:155, CGB:110, E&S:56, EXD:613, SXWU:16, XED:30, R4cx, R12x

umdli *n1-sg* glutton, voracious eater XED:30

umeko *n6-sg* being ☞ Alt: ukumeka; rw: -ma XED:86

umendo *n2-sg* path, way; highway, road ☞ Pl: imendo AXG:19, CGB:42; 110, PCX:52, XED:36

umenzi *n1-sg* doer, maker, performer ☞ Pl: abenzi AXG:15; 17, PCX:52, XED:36

uMeyi *n1a-sg-time* May ☞ Syn: ekaCanzibe AM-94:73, CGB:45, EXD:373, MI:232

umfana *n1-sg-dim* young man, youth; son; servant ☞ Pl: abafana AXG:17; 36; 37, E&S:56, PCX:23, XED:37, R19

umfanekiso *n2-sg* picture ☞ Pl: imifanekiso SXWU:16

umfazi *n1-sg* woman; female; wife, married woman ☞ Pl: abafazi; Cf: umfo AXG:17; 35; 36, CGB:102; 109, E&S:17; 56, EXD:725, PCX:23, RD-96:410;373, XED:38, R31

umfazikazi *n2-sg-aug* huge woman, Amazon AXG:36

umfelandawonye *n1-sg-cmp* supporter, staunch member of a specific group [lit: one who (with others) dies at one place] ☞ See: -fa (-fela), ndawo, nye R20.6

umfixane *n6-sg* stuffiness of the nose KED:235, R30

umfo *n1-sg* guy, chap, man, fellow {colloq} ☞ Pl: abafo AXG:17;28;36f, CGB:109, EXD:211, XED:37

umfula *n2-sg* watercourse, brook, stream; [ext] valley ☞ Pl: imifula; Alt: imfula [n5] AXG:19, CGB:42, XED:40

umfundi *n1-sg* student, pupil, learner; reader (of a publication) ☞ Pl: abafundi AM-94:155, AXG:17, CGB:109, E&S:33; 56, SXWU:15, XED:40

umfundisi *n1-sg* teacher; minister, priest, preacher, clergyman; father {address} ☞ Pl: abafundisi AM-94:155, E&S:56, EXD:209, SXWU:15

umfuno *n2-sg* plant (any edible plant found growing wild); vegetable ☞ Pl: imifuno E&S:56, XED:40

umfusa *n2-sg* dark brown animal ☞ Pl: imifusa XED:41

umgama *n2-sg* distance EXD:166, R28.3.4

umgangatho *n2-sg* floor (mud, any other kind); deck (of ship); level; standard, quality ☞ Pl: imigangatho ITX:66, RD-96:410, XED:43, R33.9, R37=11

umgangatho wentlalo *n2-sg-cmp* standard of living R37.1.12.13=2

umgaqo *n2-sg* animal track; [ext] method; policy, rule, regulation MI:262, RD-96:410, R16, R37.1

umgaqo-siseko *n2-sg-cmp* constitution ☞ Alt sp: umgaqosiseko MI:262, RD-96:410, R16, R21x, R37.1

umgaqosiseko *n2-sg-cmp* constitution ☞ Alt sp: umgaqo-siseko R21=3

umgcobo *n2-sg* joy, gladness, merriment, rejoicing AXG:19, XED:44

uMgqibelo *n2-sg-time* Saturday [lit: closing day] AM-94:73, CGB:46, EXD:555, MI:232, PCX:47

umgqithi *n1-sg* transgressor, sinner XED:48

umgqomo *n2-sg* bin, barrel, tub, drum; [ext] garbage can, trash bin EXD:240; 545, EZZE:266, NDK-91:429, RD-96:410, R30

umgubho *n2-sg* initiation festival ☞ Loc: emgubheni PCX:68

umgubo *n2-sg* flour, meal (ground powdered food) ☞ Pl: imigubo E&S:31; 56, XED:50

uMgungundlovu *pn-geog* Pietermartizburg, Maritzburg (city) ☞ Loc: eMgungundlovu MI:246, XED:194

umguquli *n1-sg* translator, interpreter ☞ Pl: abaguquli EXD:677, R3x

umgwebi *n1-sg* judge ☞ Pl: abagwebi XED:52

umgxobhozo *n2-sg* swamp, marsh, bog ☞ Pl: imigxobhozo; Alt: igxobho CGB:42, EXD:369; 643, XED:54

umhadi *n2-sg* pit, deep hole; ant-bear hole ☞ Pl: imihadi CGB:110, XED:55

umhambi *n1-sg* traveler; passenger; visitor ☞ Pl: abahambi AXG:17, CGB:109, NDK-91:435, RD-96:410

umhambo *n2-sg* walk RD-96:410

umhla *n2-sg-time* day, date; point in time ☞ Pl: imihla AXG:19, CGB:110, E&S:56, EXD:143, PCX:27, XED:56, R9x, R10x, R30

umhlaba[1] *n2-sg* earth, ground, soil; world, the Earth ☞ Pl: imihlaba; Loc: emhlabeni AXG:19, CGB:42; 110, E&S:56, XED:56, R4cx, R32=2

umhlaba[2] *n2-sg* aloe (the common red aloe) ☞ Pl: imihlaba CGB:110, XED:56

umhlakulo *n2-sg* spade, shovel ☞ Pl: imihlakulo E&S:56

umhlali *n1-sg* resident ☞ Pl: abahlali R35

umhlana *n2-sg* back (anatomical) ☞ Pl: imihlana; Loc: emhlana AXG:19, CGB:110; 139, EXD:39

umhlaza *n2-sg* ulcer, a raw sore, cancer R26

umhlekazi *n1-sg* his excellency PCX:89

umhleli *n1-sg* editor ☞ Pl: abahleli R17, R20, R31

umhlobo *n1-sg* friend, intimate; relative, blood-relation ☞ Pl: abahlobo; Alt: isihlobo AXG:17, E&S:56, KED:159, SXWU:15, XED:60, R14x=6

umhlolo *n1-sg-masc-kin* widower ☞ Pl: abahlolokazi EXD:725, R28x

umhlolokazi *n1-sg-fem-kin* widow ☞ Pl: abahlolokazi EXD:725, XED:60, R24.5, R28

umhobe *n2-sg* poem, song of exultation (triumph after war, celebration at a wedding or circumcision ceremony) KED:164, NDK-91:446, XED:62

umjelo *n2-sg* water furrow ☞ Pl: imijelo CGB:110, XED:64

umka *n1-sg* wife (of), married woman AXG:18; 37, XED:66

umkabawokazi *n1a-sg-cmp-kin* aunt (wife of paternal uncle) ☞ Pl: oomkabawokazi EXD:36

umkamalume *n1a-sg-cmp-kin* aunt (wife of maternal uncle) ☞ Pl: oomkamalume EXD:36

umkhandi *n1-sg* smith, blacksmith ☞ Pl: abakhandi AXG:17

umkhiwane *n2-sg* fig tree (wild) ☞ Pl: imikhiwane; See: ikhiwane (fruit) AXG:19, CGB:110, SXWU:16

umkhoba *n2-sg* yellowwood tree ☞ Pl: imikhoba AXG:19, CGB:110

umkhokeli *n1-sg* guide; leader ☞ Alt: inkokeli XED:72, R16x

umkhombe[1] *n2-sg* hollowed out log, trough; kneading pan; [ext] canoe, boat umkhómbè (high-low tone) AXG:37, XED:73

umkhombe[2] *n2-sg* rhinoceros [lit: the pointing horn] umkhòmbé (low-high tone) XED:73

umkhomishinali *n1-sg* commissioner R23

umkhondo *n2-sg* footprint, track, trace, trail; lead, clue; class, row XED:73, R18x, R25x

umkhonjana *n2-sg-dim* small boat AXG:37, XED:73

umkhonto *n2-sg* spade, shovel ☞ Pl: imihlakulo E&S:56

umkhosi *n2-sg* military [also atr] ☞ Pl: imikhosi EXD:380, R16x

umkhuba *n2-sg* staff (walking stick); custom, practice, habit ☞ Pl: imikhuba XED:74, R34x

umkhulu *cop-n2-sg* is big • *Ngulowo ke owona msebenzi wakho umkhulu 'That is your biggest job'* ☞ Cf: omkhulu R29.2

umkhuluwa *n1-sg-kin* older brother (of a male); brother-in-law (husband's elder brother) ☞ Alt: umkhuluwe; Pl: abakhuluwa; Loc: kumkhuluwa; Cf: umninawa (younger) AXG:17; 215, E&S:56, EXD:72, PCX:70, R36

umkhuluwe *n1-sg-kin* older brother (of a male) ☞ See: umkhuluwa AXG:215

umkhuluwekazi *n1-sg-kin* sister-in-law (brother's wife) ☞ Alt: umninawekazi AXG:216

umkhwe *n1-sg-kin* brother-in-law (sister's husband; wife's brother) ☞ Pl: abakhwe AXG:17; 215, EXD:72

umkhwekazi *n1-sg-kin* mother-in-law (of a man, wife's mother) ☞ Pl: abakhwekazi AXG:216

umkhwenyana *n1-sg* son-in-law ☞ Pl: abakhwenyana AXG:215, EXD:605

umkondo *n2-sg* track, trace, trail KED:192, R34x

umlambo *n2-sg* river ☞ Pl: imilambo; Loc: emlanjeni, ngasemlanjeni AXG:19; 37, CGB:42; 104, E&S:33; 56, EXD:538, PCX:69, SXWU:102

umlambokazi *n2-sg-aug* big river E&S:33

umlanjana *n2-sg-dim* stream, brook, small river ☞ Pl: imilanjana AXG:37, CGB:42, E&S:33

umlanya *n1-sg-kin* brother-in-law (wife's brother) ☞ Pl: abalanya EXD:72

umlanyakazi *n1-sg-fem-kin* sister-in-law (of a man) ☞ Pl: abalanyakazi EXD:590

umlebe *n2-sg* lip ☞ Pl: imilebe EXD:350, R30x

umlenze *n2-sg* leg ☞ Pl: imilenze AXG:19, CGB:104; 110, E&S:56, SXWU:16

umlilo *n2-sg* fire ☞ Pl: imililo AXG:19, CGB:110, E&S:22; 56

umlimi *n1-sg* farmer ☞ Pl: abalimi CGB:102, E&S:22; 56, R28x

umlomo *n2-sg* mouth ☞ Pl: imilomo; Loc: emlonyeni AXG:19, CGB:104; 110, PCX:69; 196, SXWU:16, R27.14, R30.2, R36.9.21

umlonde *n2-sg* ancestral spirit, spirit guardian AXG:19, XED:83

umLungu *n1-sg* White (person) ☞ Pl: abeLungu AXG:17, PCX:52, SXWU:15, R28

umlwelwe *n2-sg* invalid, disabled person, sickly or infirm man AXG:19, XED:85

ummandla *n2-sg* area, district, division, zone, region; surroundings NDK-91:486f, RD-96:411, XED:86

ummango *n2-sg* ridge AXG:18

ummbi *n1-sg-ir* digger, excavator, miner PCX:52

ummeli *n1-sg* advocate, representative, defender ☞ Pl: abameli; rw: -ma AXG:17, EXD:10; 524, XED:88, R24x

ummelwana *n1-sg* neighbor E&S:56

ummi *n1-sg* inhabitant, occupant, resident ☞ Pl: abemi; rw: -(i)ma AXG:17, PCX:52, XED:86

ummiselo *n2-sg* appointment; ordinance, statute; law of nature XED:90

umnakwabo *n1-sg-kin* his / her brother (used by women only) ☞ Pl: abanakwabo AXG:215, PCX:116

umnakwenu *n1-sg-kin* your brother (used by women only) ☞ Pl: abanakwenu AXG:215, PCX:116

umnakwethu *n1-sg-kin* my brother; our brother (used by women only) • *Ngumnakwethu 'He is my brother'* ☞ Pl: abanakwethu AXG:215, PCX:116

umncedisi *n1-sg* assistant ☞ Pl: abancedisi ITX:66

umnga *n2-sg* mimosa thorn tree, thornwood tree ☞ Pl: iminga AXG:19, CGB:110, SXWU:16

umngcunube *n2-sg* willow tree ☞ Pl: imingcunube SXWU:16

umNgqika *n1-sg-pn* Gaika, Ngqika (person, member of an ethnic group within the greater Xhosa community) ☞ See: Ngqika AXG:20

umngqusho *n2-sg* cornmeal, mush, pounded meal, pulverized maize XED:110, R8

umNguni *n1-sg-ir* Nguni Bantu (person) ☞ Pl: abeNguni PCX:52

umnikazi *n1-sg-fem* owner (female) R26

umninawa *n1-sg-kin* younger brother (of a male); brother-in-law (husband's younger brother) ☞ Alt: umninawe; Pl: abaninawa; Loc: kumninawa; Cf: umkhuluwa (older) E&S:56, EXD:72, PCX:70, XED:104

umninawe *n1-sg-kin* younger brother ☞ See: umninawa AXG:17; 215, XED:104

umninawekazi *n1-sg-kin* sister-in-law (brother's wife) ☞ Alt: umkhuluwekazi AXG:216

umnini *n1-sg* owner, master (of) followed directly by noun object without article (i.e., without any possessive links) ☞ Pl: abanini E&S:56, EXD:431, XED:104, R28.5

umnqathe *n2-sg* carrot, wild carrot ☞ Pl: iminqathe XED:107, R8x=2

umnqwazi *n2-sg* headdress (woman's); [ext] hat, cap, bonnet ☞ Pl: iminqwazi AM-94:72, XED:110, R32

umnqweno *n2-sg* desire ☞ Pl: iminqweno EXD:154, R33, R34x

umnta *n1-sg* child ☞ Pl: banta; Red: umntwana XED:111, R11x

umntakwethu *n1-sg-kin* my brother (said by a sister); cousin (where parents are brothers) ☞ Pl: abantakwethu; Contrast: umza (umzala), ukanina E&S:56, EXD:72; 129, R11x

umntla *n2-sg* upper part; north ☞ Opp: umzantsi EXD:407, PCX:70, SXWU:102

umntu *n1-sg* person, individual, human being; [pro] someone, somebody ☞ Pl: abantu; Loc: emntwini AXG:17, CGB:102; 139, PCX:23; 68, RD-96:412;372, SXWU:15, XED:112, R4d=2, R9=5, R14, R23, R27=2, R28, R31, R36=3

umntwana *n1-sg-dim* baby, infant, child; young (person); pupil Dim of: umntu ☞ Pl: abantwana; Alt: umntana CGB:102, E&S:33, PCX:23, RD-96:412, SXWU:15, XED:112, R9=5, R10, R19=4, R36.19

uMnu. *n1a-sg-abr* Mr. ☞ Abr: uMnumzana EXD:385, R26=3, R27=2

uMnumzana *n1-sg* head of a village; person of breeding, gentleman; sir; Mister ☞ Pl: abanumzana; Abr: uMnu AXG:17, E&S:56, EXD:385, XED:113

umnwe *n2-sg* finger ☞ Pl: iminwe AXG:19, EXD:215, RD-96:12, SXWU:16

umnxeba *n2-sg* vine sp., cord; [ext] phone EXD:653, KM, XED:112, R23

umnxulumanisi *n2-sg* the correlator from inxulumana 'correlation EXD:126, R35

umnyaka *n2-sg-time* year ☞ Pl: iminyaka; Alt: unyaka [n1a], inyaka

[n5] AXG:19, CGB:110, E&S:56, EXD:737, SXWU:16, XED:115, R4ax

umnyama[1] *n2-sg* rainbow AXG:218, EXD:504, XED:116

umnyama[2] *n2-sg* darkness; eclipse AXG:218, XED:116; 90

umnyamazana *n2-sg-dim* dusk, twilight XED:116

umnyangi *n1-sg* diviner, tribal doctor, healer, herbalist ☞ Alt: inyangi XED:116, R25x

umnyango *n2-sg* doorway, entrance; porch ☞ Pl: iminyango; Loc: emnyango AXG:19, CGB:139, PCX:70, XED:116

umolokazana *n1a-sg-kin* daughter-in-law AXG:216, EXD:144

umona[1] *n1a-sg* envy, grudging, selfishness EXD:192, XED:90

umona[2] *v-pro-2sg-S1-n1-sg-obj* you wrong him, her; you hurt him, her R14

umonakalo *n2-sg* damage EXD:142, MI:262, R18.5

umonakalokazi *n2-sg-aug* disaster, great damage MI:262

umongameli *n1-sg* manager, overseer, ruler; supervisor, superintendent; chairman, president ☞ Pl: abongameli E&S:56, XED:121, R32=2

umongikazi *n1-sg-fem* nurse (for the sick), nursing sister ☞ Pl: abongikazi E&S:56, EXD:410; 590, XED:121, R3x

umoni *n1-sg* wrongdoer, one who injures or wrongs others; sinner ☞ Pl: aboni AXG:15; 17, PCX:52, XED:121

umothuko *n2-sg* shock EXD:580, R34x

umoya[1] *n1a-sg* spirit (of one who has died), ghost, apparition; air, wind ☞ Contrast: umoya [n2-sg] E&S:56, EXXE:57, XED:90

umoya[2] *n2-sg* air; wind; the atmosphere; breath; soul, spirit ☞ Pl: imimoya; Contrast: umoya [n1a-sg] AXG:18, CGB:42; 110, EXD:611, EXXE:57;2, RD-96:412;53, XED:90, R4d, R13, R25, R30, R34

umoyisi *n1-sg* conqueror, victor ☞ Pl: aboyisi EXD:118; 706

umpatsiya *n2-sg* bloated stomach • *uhluthi ngenene, kodwa ungengompatsiya 'you'll feel well satisfied, but you won't feel bloated'* AK, R12

umpesika *n2-sg* peach tree ☞ Pl: imipesika SXWU:16

umphakathi[1] *n1-sg-ir* middleman, agent, intermediary (between a chief and his people); councilor, advisor; headman ☞ Pl: amaphakathi AXG:20, XED:122

umphakathi[2] *n2-sg* palm, inside of the hand; sole (of foot) XED:122

umphakatho *n2-sg* side, flank; groin; [ext] pocket (in pants, trousers) ☞ Pl: imiphakatho XED:122, R30

umphandle *n2-sg* outside, exterior NDK-91:537, RD-96:412

umphathi *n1-sg* bearer; master; manager, director, ruler; (government) minister ☞ Pl: abapathi E&S:56, KED:325, SXWU:15, XED:125, R27.1.3.7, R37.27

umphathiswa *n1-sg* authority, s.o. put in charge, invested with authority; department head, minister (government) ☞ Pl: abaphathiswa XED:125, R37

umpheki *n1-sg* cook ☞ Pl: abapheki CGB:109, E&S:33; 56, SXWU:15

umphunga *n2-sg* lung ☞ Pl: imiphunga EXD:360, RD-96:13

umPondo *n1-sg* Pondo, Mpondo (member of an ethnic group within the greater Xhosa community) ☞ Pl: amaMpondo; See: Mpondo AXG:20, CGB:1; 109, XED:129

umpu *n2-sg* gun E&S:56, SXWU:16

umqa *n2-sg* porridge, mush; Kaffir-corn porridge XED:133, R8

umqala *n2-sg* throat ☞ Pl: imiqala CGB:110, EXD:662

umqeqeshi *n1-sg* trainer ☞ Pl: abaqeqeshi EXD:674, R33x

umqhaphu *n2-sg* cotton (plant) ☞ Loc: emqhaphini EXD:127, PCX:69

umqhubi *n1-sg* driver; one who drives or urges on ☞ Pl: abaqhubi CGB:109, XED:139

umqobo *n2-sg* s.t. long and thick; obstacle, hindrance GDX3:72, R33.9

umqolo *n2-sg* spine, backbone, back between the shoulders ☞ Pl: imiqolo; Loc: emqolo CGB:110; 139, SXWU:16, R25x

umqolomba *n2-sg* cave ☞ Pl: imiqolomba CGB:42; 110, EXD:87

umqulu *n2-sg* bundle ☞ Loc: emqulwini EXD:74, PCX:68

umRugwane *pn-geog* Caledon River ☞ Loc: emRugwane XED:194

umsa *n2-sg* kindness, love, affection, tenderness (of a mother) No plural AXG:18, MI:259, XED:147, R4dx

umsakwabo *n1-sg-kin* his / her / their younger sister (said by a female) ☞ Pl: abasakwabo AXG:216

umsakwenu *n1-sg-kin* your younger sister (said by a female) ☞ Pl: abasakwenu AXG:216

umsakwethu *n1-sg-kin* my younger sister (said by a female) ☞ Pl: abasakwethu AXG:216

umsebenzi[1] *n1-sg* worker, laborer ☞ Pl: abasebenzi AM-94:155, E&S:56, RD-96:136, XED:149, R37.14

umsebenzi[2] *n2-sg* work, job, employment; labor, task; duty; trade, occupation; use, service ☞ Pl: imisebenzi (R22), AM-94:24; 155, EXD:179, RD-96:412;136, XED:149, R7x, R10x, R12, R24, R28=2, R29, R31

umSebenzi[3] *pn-geog* Balfour (town) ☞ Loc: emSebenzi XED:194

umseki *n1-sg* founder, leader, establisher, founding father EXD:209

umsele *n2-sg* ditch ☞ Pl: imisele AXG:19, CGB:110, EXD:168

umshologu *n2-sg* ghost AXG:19, EXD:245

umsi *n2-sg* smoke; vapor, steam (from a kettle) No plural EXD:598, XED:151, R25

umsila *n2-sg* tail ☞ Pl: imisila PCX:140

umsindo *n2-sg* anger, wrath ☞ Pl: imisindo E&S:56, EXD:21, PCX:89; 93, R36=2+x

umsinga *n2-sg* current, stream, torrent AXG:36, XED:152

umsintsi *n2-sg* Kafferboom, Kaffir-tree (tree with gorgeous red flowers) ☞ Pl: imisintsi AXG:195, XED:153

umsipha *n2-sg* sinew, tendon; nerve XED:153

umso *n2-sg* dawn, daybreak, morning; morrow, tomorrow ☞ Pl: imiso CGB:110, XED:147, R5x

umsulwa *n1-sg* blameles, innocent person XED:155, R11x

umSuthu *n1-sg-ir* Sotho (person) ☞ Pl: abeSuthu AXG:17, PCX:52

umswane *n2-sg* chyme, stomach contents of a slaughtered animal; [ext] nonsense, rubbish GDX3:237f, KED:399, R31x

umthambo *n2-sg* vein, artery XED:157, R25

umthandazo *n2-sg* prayer ☞ Pl: imithandazo, from v-tr 'thandaza 'to pray' E&S;56, R36

umThatha *n2-sg-pn-geog* Umtata (town and river) ☞ Loc: eMthatha CGB:41, PCX:69

umThembu *n1-sg-clan* Thembu (clansman) ☞ See: Thembu AXG:17

umthethi *n1-sg* speaker XED:159

umthetho *n2-sg* law, rule, command, regulation, ordinance ☞ Pl: imithetho AM-94:155, AXG:19, CGB:110, RD-96:413;94, XED:159, R10, R11=4, R16, R21, R31.2.3, R32.3.6, R36.0.14.17

umthi *n2-sg* tree, shrub, plant; wood, timber; [ext] plant extract, drug obtained from plants ☞ Pl: imithi; Loc: emthini AM-94:108, AXG:19; 36, CGB:139, E&S:17; 56, PCX:50; 69, RD-96:413;372, XED:160

umthikazi *n2-sg-aug* large tree AXG:36

umthimbi *n1-sg* captor (s.o. who seizes in war), hostage-taker XED:160

umthinjana *n1-sg-dim* young man, maiden XED:161, R13

umthinjwa *n1-sg* captive, hostage, s.o. taken in war XED:160

umthombo *n2-sg* spring (of water); fountain ☞ Pl: imithombo; Loc: emthonjeni AXG:19, EXD:614, PCX:69

umthubi *n2-sg* beestings, beastings, colostrum, milk of a newly-calved cow; yolk (of an egg) ☞ Cf: -mthubi XED:168

umthungi *n1-sg* tailor ☞ Pl: abathungi CGB:109

umthungula *n2-sg* Natal plum (tree) ☞ Pl: imithungula; Cf: ithungula (fruit) XED:169

umthunzi *n2-sg* shade ☞ Pl: imithunzi E&S:56, SXWU:16

umThwa *n1-sg* San, Bushman (member of the ethnic group) ☞ Pl: abaThwa AXG:17

umtsalane *n2-sg* attraction, attractiveness EXD:35, R34

umtsha *n1-sg* youth, young person XED:163

umtshakazi *n1-sg-fem* bride [lit: young wife] ☞ Pl: abatshakazi AXG:18, XED:164

umtshana *n1-sg* nephew (sister's son); niece (sister's daughter) ☞ Cf: intombi AXG:215, EXD:401; 404

umTshwana *n1-sg* Chwana, Tshwana (person) ☞ Pl: abeTshwana AXG:17

umva *n2-sg* back (anatomical / away from the front); reverse side; [ext] whatever is behind in space or time EXD:39, XED:176, R30x, R35

umvi *n1-sg* examiner ☞ Pl: abevi AXG:17

uMvulo *n2-sg-time* Monday [lit: opening day, i.e., of work week] AM-94:73, AXG:19, CGB:46; 110, EXD:388, MI:232, PCX:47, XED:178

umvundla *n2-sg* hare E&S:56, SXWU:16

umvuzo *n2-sg* reward; payment, wage, salary ☞ Pl: imivuzo XED:179, R10x, R29=2, R34

umxhasi *n2-sg* one who or that which supports; a support KED:468, R33x

umxhentso *n2-sg* dance ☞ Pl: imixhentso SXWU:16

umXhosa *n1-sg* Xhosa (person) ☞ Pl: amaXhosa AM-94:22, AXG:17, CGB:105; 109, E&S:56, SXWU:17

umxolisi *n1-sg* peacemaker ☞ Pl: abaxolisi XED:185

umxube *n2-sg* mixture ☞ Pl: imixube XED:186, R12x

umyalelo *n2-sg* instruction, direction ☞ Pl: imiyalelo XED:187, R6x=3

umyalezo *n2-sg* order, instruction, command ☞ Pl: imiyalezo XED:187, R32, R35

umyeni *n1-sg* husband, bridegroom; male relative (by marriage) ☞ Pl: abayeni AXG:18;

215, E&S:31; 56, EXD:285, XED:188, R4d, R19=2, R31

umyinge *n2-sg* limit, size; degree GDX3:632, R31

umza *n1-sg-kin* cousin (where parents are brother and sister), first cousin (child of paternal aunt or of maternal aunt or uncle) ☞ Pl: abaza; Alt: umzala; Contrast: ukanina, umntakwethu EXD:129, GDX3:641, XED:190, R31x, R36x

umzabalazo *n2-sg* struggle, effort, endeavor, attempt ☞ Pl: imizabalazo GDX3:641, R32, R36.22

umzala *n1-sg-kin* cousin ☞ See: umza GDX3:641;644, R31, R36

umzali *n1-sg-masc* parent (male or generic), father, progenitor ☞ Pl: abazali AXG:17; 215, E&S:56, SXWU:15, XED:190, R2x

umzalikazi *n1-sg-fem* parent (female), mother AXG:216, EXD:391, XED:190, R2x

umzalwana *n1-sg-kin* kinsman, close relative (brother, cousin) ☞ Pl: abazalwana AXG:17; 215, XED:190

umzalwane *n1-sg* kinsman, relative, (genetic) connection ☞ Pl: abazalwane EXD:326, XED:190

umzantsi *n2-sg* lower part, base; bottom; southern part (of a region); [atr] south • *Mzantsi Afrika 'South Africa'* ☞ Opp: umntla GDX3:649, PCX:70, SXWU:102, XED:190, R10x, R11, R33, R36.00

uMzantsi-Afrika *n2-sg-pn-geog-cmp* South Africa ☞ Loc: eMzantsi-Afrika AM-94:63, GDX3:649, SXWU:101, R10x, R11, R33, R36.00

umzekelo *n2-sg* example, pattern EXD:197, XED:190f, R21, R36=2, R37.14.15

umzi[1] *n2-sg* home (institution), household; extended family; homestead, group of huts belonging to a single owner; village; kraal; [ext] tribe, nation, people umzì (low tone) ☞ Pl: imizi; Cf: ikhaya AXG:13, CGB:42; 104, E&S:56, EXD:279, SXWU:16, XED:191, R5, R11, R18.2

umzi[2] *n2-sg* reed, common rush (used for making mats) umzí (high tone) AXG:13, XED:191

umzimba *n2-sg* body ☞ Pl: imizimba AXG:19, CGB:110, EXD:62, GDX3:662, RD-96:413, SXWU:16, R25, R30x, R34x, R36

umZimvubu *n2-sg-pn-geog* Mt. Frere, Port St. Johns (town); the St. Johns (Zimvubu) River ☞ Loc: emZimvubu AXG:19, CGB:110, MI:246, XED:194

umZinyathi *pn-geog* Buffalo River (in Natal) ☞ Zulu - who use u- as place name prefix frequently XED:194

umzobi *n1-sg* artist ☞ Pl: abazobi SXWU:15

umzukulwana *n1-sg-kin* grandchild, grandson, granddaughter ☞ Pl: abazukulwana; Loc: kumzukulwana AXG:17;215f, EXD:254, PCX:70

umZulu *n1-sg* Zulu (person) ☞ Pl: amaZulu AM-94:22, AXG:17, CGB:109, XED:193

umzuzu *n2-sg* moment, while, short time; brief space; minute (60 seconds) ☞ Pl: imizuzu CGB:110, EXD:383, MI:262, SXWU:16, XED:193, R8x, R33x=4

umzuzwana *n2-sg-dim* moment, little while; second (unit of time) ☞ Pl: imizuzwana EXD:566, MI:262, XED:193, R33x=3

unako *v-aux-pot* you can R31

unama-27 eminyaka *v-poss-expr* he is 27 years old [lit: he has 27 of years] R4b

unamandla *v-poss* you have strength R12

unantoni *qw-expr* what do you have?, what have you got?; what is wrong with you?, what is troubling you? AM-94:84

unantsika *n1a-sg* whatchamacallit, thingamabob, thingamajig (AXG:18), AHD-Eng, SXWU:14

unaphakade *adv* for endless time R36

uncedisa *v-caus* you help R29

uncedo *n6-sg* help, aid, assistance; helpfulness ☞ Pl: amancedo; See also: -luncedo AM-94:100, CGB:114, E&S:58, EXD:273, XED:94, R27=2, R35, R36=2

uncipho *n6-sg* decline, reduction, decrease XED:95

undaba *n1a-sg* person or thing much talked about, subject of conversation or public discussion, hot (news) item; one who is often spoken of ☞ Contrast: udaba (iindaba) [n6] KED:252, XED:96, R33x

undlebende *n1a-sg* donkey, mule [lit: long ears] ☞ Pl: oondlebende CGB:109, PCX:89f

uNdlovukazi *pn-geog* Lesseyton (town) ☞ Loc: kwaNdlovukazi XED:194

uneAIDS *v-poss+n5-sg-obj* you have AIDS R30.1

uneliso *v-poss-idiom* he is an expert at, has a sharp eye for [lit: he has an eye] AM-94:87

uNelson *n1a-sg-pn* Nelson (Mandela) R16=3, R24

unendibano yesondo *v-poss-cmp-obj* you have sexual relations R30.6

unendlebe *v-poss+n5-sg-obj* you have an ear (i.e., you can hear) R31.4

unenkinga *v-poss+n5-sg-obj* you have a problem R15

unentloko *v-poss-n5-sg-obj* he is clever [lit: he has a head] AM-94:87

unentsholongwane *v-poss+n5-sg-obj* he has a virus R36.7

unesiphiwo *v-poss+n4-sg-obj* you have a gift R33.9, R34.6

unetyala *v-poss+n3-sg-obj* you have a fault (i.e., you are guilty) R31.4

ungahambi *v-n2-sg-S2-neg-part-pres* it not going R37.14

ungakanani *interr* how much R18

ungakwazi *v-tr-pot* you can know it R34

ungaqhubi *v-sub-pres-neg* you should not drive R6

ungasebenzisi *v-pot-neg* you should not use R30

ungashaya *v-pot* you can reach ☞ See Xhosa: -betha (ungabetha) R15

ungavumeli *v-imp-neg* you must not allow R30

ungayiboni *v-pot-sub* and you cannot see it R15

ungayilibali *v-pot-neg* do not forget R31

ungazilandela *v-pot* you can follow them R7

ungaziqhathi *v-refl-neg-imp* don't cheat yourself R31.3

ungazithandi *v-refl-pres-sub* that you not like yourself R14

ungengompatsiya *pro-2sg-pot-cop-n2-sg* you won't get bloated • *uhluthi ngenene, kodwa ungengompatsiya 'you'll feel well satisfied, but you won't feel bloated'* AK, R12

ungowam *rel-abs* who is mine R19

ungqinile *v-tr-perf* he, she testified (for) R18

ungum- *n1-sg-pred-exis* he, she is a NOUN • *ungumntu 'he is a person'; ungumphathi 'she is the director'* R16, R37.27

ungumamni *qw-expr* What is your clan (name)? [to a female] MI:277

ungumni *qw-expr* What is your clan (name)? [to a male] MI:277

ungumntu *n1-sg-pred* he is a person R16

ungumphathi *n1-sg-pred-n2-sg* she is the director or chairperson R37.27

unike *v-sub* that you give R21

unina *n1a-sg-kin* mother (his / her); their mother ☞ Pl: oonina; Contrast: umama (our mother), unyoko (your mother) AXG:18; 35; 216, CGB:103, E&S:56, EXD:391, R28

uninakazi *n1a-sg-kin* aunt (his / her maternal), their mother's sister ☞ Pl: ooninakazi AXG:216, EXD:36

uninakhulu *n1a-sg-kin* grandmother (his, her, their) ☞ Pl: ooninakhulu AXG:216

uninalume *n1a-sg-kin* uncle (his / her maternal), their mother's brother ☞ Pl: ooninalume; Cf: uyisekazi (paternal) AXG:215, EXD:689

uninazala *n1a-sg-kin* mother-in-law (of a woman, husband's mother) ☞ Pl: ooninazala AXG:216, EXD:391

uninzi *n6-sg* majority; the most XED:104, R10, R29=2, R31, R35, R36=2, R37

unit *loan* unit ☞ See: Child Protection Unit R27, R36

university *loan* university R24=2

unkosk *n1a-sg-abr* Mrs. ☞ Abr: Nkosikazi R18=2

uNksk *n1a-sg-abr* Mrs. ☞ Abr: Nkosikazi R24=2

uno- *n1a-sg-prf* [noun-forming prefix; lit: mother of] • *unobhala 'secretary, clerk' [lit: mother of writing], unoncwadi 'librarian' [lit: mother of books]* reduction of unina wo-, a female-personifying prefix, even if the noun so formed may have a masculine meaning MI:259, R5

unobhala *n1a-sg* secretary, clerk [lit: mother of writing] ☞ Pl: oonobhala CGB:109, MI:259

uNoBible *n1a-sg* Bible-Holder [lit: mother of the Bible] (usually older women in a church guild, who wear a uniform specific to that particular church; called NoBible not so much because they study the Bible, but because they are always seen carrying a Bible on their way to church, a funeral, a wake, etc.) R5=2

unobubele *cop-n7-sg* you are kind R34

unobuhle *n1a-sg* beauty queen EXD:49, R33x

unobumba *n1a-sg* letter (of the alphabet) ☞ Pl: oonobumba EXD:342, R34=12

unocanda *n1a-sg* surveyor ☞ Pl: oonocanda CGB:109, EXD:642

unogumbe *n1a-sg* flood; the Flood AXG:218, EXD:222

uNojoli *pn-geog* Somerset East (town) ☞ Loc: kwaNojoli MI:246

unokoyiswa *v-tr-caus* who is feared R36

unokuba *pro-conj* even if you R30.2.3

unokucinga *v-abil* you can think R20.4

unokufikelela *v-abil-intens* you can reach R29.12

unokukutyebisa *v-rel2-abil* which can make you rich R7

unokutsalela *v-abil* you can call R23.9

unokuvula *v-tr-abil* he is able to open R16

unokuxabana *v-abil-recip* you can quarrel with R14

unokwamkela *v-pot-tr* she can earn R28

unomadudwane *n1a-sg* scorpion ☞ Pl: oonomadudwane CGB:103, SXWU:14

unomathotholo *n1a-sg* spiritual or disembodied voice (heard by traditional healer); [ext] radio ☞ Pl: oonomathotholo; Loc: kunomathotholo; Syn: iradiyo, iwayilesi AM-94:60, CGB:103, EXD:502

unomeva *n1a-sg* wasp, hornet AXG:18

uNompumelelo *n1a-sg-pn* Nompumelelo (Nguni Bantu female personal name) R15

uNomsa *n1a-sg-pn-fem* Nomsa (female personal name) [lit: mother of motherly affection] CGB:109, MI:259, PCX:29f

uNomvula *n1a-sg-pn-fem* Nomvula (female personal name) [lit: mother of rain, i.e., born on a rainy day] AM-94:164

unomyayi *n1a-sg* crow ☞ Pl: oonomyayi CGB:103

unoncwadi *n1a-sg* librarian [lit: mother of books] MI:259

unonkala *n1a-sg* crab ☞ Pl: oononkala AXG:18, CGB:103, PCX:50; 52, SXWU:14

unopopi *n1a-sg* doll ☞ Pl: oonopopi CGB:103

unoqwalaselo *v-poss-n6-sg* you are perceptive R34.11

uNosisa *n1a-sg-pn-fem* Nosisa (female personal name) [lit: mother of benevolence] MI:259

uNovemba *n1a-sg-time* November ☞ Syn: eyeNkanga AM-94:73, CGB:46, EXD:409, MI:232

uNoxolo *n1a-sg-pn-fem* Noxolo (female personal name) [lit: mother of peace] R37=2

unwele *n6-sg* hair (single strand) ☞ Pl: iinwele AM-94:100, PCX:55

unxweme *n6-sg* shore ☞ Pl: iinxweme CGB:42

unyaka *n1a-sg-time* year ☞ Pl: oonyaka; Alt: umnyaka [n2], inyaka [n5] E&S:56, EXD:737, SXWU:16, XED:115, R18, R22

unyana *n1a-sg-kin* son; nephew (brother's child) ☞ Pl: oonyana AXG:18; 35; 95; 215, E&S:56, EXD:401; 605, PCX:96, XED:116, R31

unyanzelise *v-suf-caus* you force yourself R34

unyawo *n6-sg* foot ☞ Pl: iinyawo; Loc: elunyaweni AM-94:100, CGB:107; 114, E&S:58, EXD:225, PCX:55; 69, SXWU:20, R28x, R30x

unyoko *n1a-sg-kin* mother (your); your mother ☞ Pl: oonyoko; Contrast: umama (our mother), unina (your mother) AXG:18; 36; 216, CGB:103, EXD:391

unyokokazi *n1a-sg-kin* aunt (your maternal), your mother's sister ☞ Pl: oonyokokazi AXG:36; 216, EXD:36

unyokokhulu *n1a-sg-kin* grandmother (your) ☞ Pl: oonyokokhulu AXG:216

unyokolume *n1a-sg-kin* uncle (your maternal), your mother's brother ☞ Pl: oonyokolume; Cf: uyihlokazi (paternal) AXG:215, EXD:689

unyulo *n6-sg* choice, selection; election RD-96:414, XED:119, R16

unziphonde *n1a-sg* spring hare ☞ Pl: oonziphonde CGB:109

uOktobha *n1a-sg-time* October ☞ Syn: eyeDwarha AM-94:73, CGB:46, EXD:414, MI:232

uphakathi *n6-sg* middle finger ☞ Pl: iimpakathi CGB:114, XED:122

uphando *n6-sg* investigation, examination, inquest RD-96:414, R32, R37=3

uPhapha *n1a-sg* Pope, the Holy Father EXD:209

uphaphamile *v-intr* you are vigilant R34.11

uphatho[1] *n6-sg* rule, authority; conduct ☞ Pl: iimpatho CGB:114, XED:125

uPhatho[2] *n1a-sg-pn* Phatho (personal name) AXG:18

uphawu *n6-sg* brand (on animal), distinguishing mark; notch; sign, indication, symptom ☞ Pl: iimpawu EXD:587; 646, PCX:55, XED:125, R30x=3

uphendula *v-tr* she answers, she replies to R19.0

uphi[1] *qw-loc-adv-n1-sg* where is? ☞ See: -phi E&S:31, R31

uphi[2] *qw-loc-adv-n2-sg* where is? ☞ See: -phi E&S:31

uphila *v-part-pres* you being healthy R31

uphile *v-sub-pres* that you be healthy R34.2

uphile qete *vp-sub-pres* that you be bursting with good health GDX3:26, R34.2

uphinde *v-aux* he, she VERBed again [past tense aux] R33.7

uphondo *n6-sg* horn; tusk; tower, turret, steeple; wing (of an army) ☞ Pl: iimpondo CGB:114, XED:129, R13

uphume *v-intr-perf* she came out R33

uphuphu *n6-sg* hoof AXG:37, XED:133

uphuphwana *n6-sg-dim* small hoof No sound change (ph remains and does not change to tsh) AXG:37

uPrimrose Williams *pn* Primrose Williams R36

uqala *v-pres* you start R30=2

uqaqamba *v-intr* it throbs R36

uqeqesho *n6-sg* training, discipline, education KED:352, R22.1, R35=2

uqhube[1] *v-tr-sub* you should pass R29

uqhube[2] *v-tr-sub* that you drive R31

uqinisekile *v-st-perf* you are confident R34.8

uqobo *adv-loan* actually, really R37

uQoboqobo *pn-geog* Keiskammahoek, Keiskama Hoek (town) ☞ Loc: kuQoboqobo / eQoboqobo MI:246, XED:194

uqonde *v-tr-sub* you should understand R29

uqwalaselo *n6-sg* watching, observance Pahl:101, R34.11

uqwelile *v-tr-perf* she finished, she rounded off R36.26

uReginah *pn-loan* Reginah R35.4.11.12

uRene Kalmer *n1a-sg-pn-loan* Rene Kalmer R33.5

urhulumente *n1a-sg* government • *oburhulumente 'official'* ☞ Pl: oorhulumente; Alt: urulumente EXD:252, NDK-91:126, RD-96:377, XED:146, R10=2, R23=2, R24x, R37x

urhwaphilizo *n6-sg-vn* cheating ☞ See: -rhwaphiliza GDX3:143, R37.26

uSajini *n-1sg-loan* Sergeant R26

usana *n6-sg* baby, infant, little child ☞ Pl: iintsana; Loc: elusaneni AM-94:100, CGB:142, E&S:58; 17; 32, PCX:55; 69, SXWU:20, XED:148, R27

usapho *n6-sg* family; offspring ☞ Pl: iintsapho AM-94:100, CGB:107; 142, E&S:58, PCX:69, SXWU:20, XED:148, R5

usazi *v-tr* you know R31

usebenza[1] *v-pres-n1-sg* he, she works R37.27

usebenza[2] *v-pres-pro-2sg* you work • *Usebenza nabantu 'You work with people'* R29.2, R34.10

usebenze *v-tr-sub* you should work R29=2

usebenzele *v-sub-ben* that you work for R34.5

usebenzisa *v-part-pres* you using; (if) you use R6, R34.6

usebenzise *v-pres-sub-seq* and you should (not) operate denoting sequence R6

usele *v-pres-sub* you should drink R6=3

uselo *n6-sg* drink, beverage; draught ☞ Alt: isiselo [n4-sg], intselo [n5-sg] XED:149

uselusizini *cop-loc-n6-sg* you in sadness R14

uSeptemba *n1a-sg-time* September ☞ Syn: eyomSintsi ~ eyoMsintsi AM-94:73, CGB:46, EXD:571, MI:232

useze *v-pres-sub* you should give it to s.o. to drink R6

ushishino *n6-sg* trade, act of doing business • *ushishino lweTaxi 'the taxi business'; unesiphiwo soshishino 'you have a gift for business'* [not found in any references] R23.5, R34.6=2

usiba *n6-sg* feather, quill; [ext] pen ☞ Pl: iintsiba AM-94:100, E&S:58, MI:262, XED:151

usibalisela *v-caus-ben* she is telling us R28=2

usibonise *v-tr-perf* she showed it R33

usimele *v-tr* she represented R33

usini *n6-sg* gum (area above or below the teeth); [ext] smile, grin; laugh ☞ Pl: iintsini KED:392, XED:152

usinikwe *v-tr-pass* she was given it R24

uSipho *n1a-sg-pn-masc* Sipho (male personal name) [lit: gift] ☞ See: isipho AM-94:164, SXWU:14

usisi *n1a-sg* woman; sister [term of respect for a girl or woman older than oneself; term of endearment used by elders for a female of any age] ☞ Pl: oosisi; Loc: kusisi (koosisi) AM-94:65, GDX3:207, SXWU:14, R4dx

usisikelele *v-sub* you should bless us R13.1

usitya *v-part-pres* you eating R12

usizi *n6-sg* pity No plural AM-94:100

usizo *n6-sg* help ☞ Xhosa: uncedo EZZE:762, R15

uso- *n1a-sg-prf* [noun-forming prefix; lit: father of] • *uSobantu 'God' [lit: father of the people], usompempe 'referee' [lit: father of the whistle]* reduction of uyise wo-, a male-personifying prefix MI:259

uSobantu *n1a-sg* God [lit: father of the people] MI:259

usoloko *atr-n2-sg* you always R29

uSomandla *n1a-sg* God, the Almighty [lit: father of power] CGB:109, MI:259

usomashishini *n1a-sg* businessman, entrepreneur, manufacturer (one who is engaged in, owns, or operates a business or factory) ☞ Pl: oosomashishini GDX3:218, SXWU:14, R35.5.15

usombawo *n1a-sg* ancestor CGB:109

usomfazi *n1a-sg-kin* father-in-law (of a man, wife's father) ☞ Pl: oosomfazi AXG:215

usompempe *n1a-sg* referee [lit: father of the whistle] EXD:516, MI:259

usuka *v-intr* she started off R28.0

usuke *preverb* it (smoke) just VERBs R25.5

usukile *v-intr-perf* you moved R29.8

usuku *n6-sg-time* day (24 hour period), a day and a night ☞ Pl: iintsuku AM-94:100, E&S:58, EXD:144, MI:231, SXWU:20, XED:155, R2x, R12

usuluthollile *v-perf* you would already have received ☞ See Xhosa: usulufumene R15

uTakalani *n1a-sg-pn* Takalani (Tsonga male or female personal name) KM, R33=5

utata *n1a-sg-kin* father (my), our father; our daddy ☞ Pl: ootata; Contrast: uyihlo (your father), uyise (their father) E&S:56, EXD:209, RD-96:415;372, SXWU:14, R5, R31

utatomkhulu *n1a-sg-kin* grandfather (my, our) ☞ Pl: ootatomkhulu SXWU:14, R36

uthanda *v-pres* he likes R4b

uthandane *v-recip* she fell in love R19

uThandi *n1a-sg-pn-masc/fem* Thandi (male / female personal name) ☞ Alt: Thandi R19.0

uthando *n6-sg-abs* love, regard; favor, approval No plural AM-94:155, CGB:114, E&S:58, EXD:209, SXWU:20, R4dx=3, R34

uthathatha *n1a-sg* trifle, s.t. of little or no significance; simpleton, person of little intelligence; kid, small child who still has an immature mind • *Yinto eyaziwa nanguthathatha ukuba... 'It is common knowledge that ...'* ☞ Pl: oothathatha GDX3:279, R10

uthe[1] *v-ir-perf* he, she said R18.3.4.6, R26=5, R27=2

uthe[2] *v-aux* finally • *uthe wakuvela 'when he finally arrived'* as auxiliary has above meaning, emphasising the action of the main verb R26

uthembekile *v-st-atr-perf* you are trustworthy R34.8

uthenga *v-part-pres* you buying R12

uthethwano *n6-sg* communication NTM, R34.4

uthi *v-tr* he says R29, R36

uThixo *n1a-sg* God, the Deity, Heavenly Father ☞ Loc: kuThixo AM-94:65, CGB:189, EXD:209, XED:161, R4dx

uthuli *n6-sg-mass* dust, grain of dust • *uthuli eluthulini 'dust to dust'* No direct plural ☞ Pl: iintuli 'dust storm' AM-94:101, EXD:179, PCX:55, XED:168

uthuthu *n6-sg* ash; ashes • *uthuthu eluthuthwini 'ash to ash'* ☞ Pl: iintuthu CGB:114, PCX:54f, XED:170

utitshala *n1a-sg* teacher (male, generic) ☞ Pl: ootitshala; Alt: ititshala CGB:103, JPD:122, MI:262, SXWU:14, R3x

utitshalakazi *n1a-sg-fem* teacher (female) ☞ Pl: ootitshalakazi MI:262

uTokoyi *n1a-sg-pn* Tokoyi (personal name) R5

utshatile *v-st-perf* she is married, she was married ☞ See: -tshata R19.2

utshilo *v-ir-perf* so he, she said • *"Akunanto yakwenza nam," utshilo. "There's nothing for me to do here," said he.* R24.3.8, R26.7, R27.1.14, R33.9.10, R35.11

utsho *v-intr* say so ukutsho 'to say so' R36

utyani *n7-mass* grass (for grazing), pasture, pasturage; verdure ☞ Syn: ingca AXG:200, CGB:107; 114, MI:273, PCX:55, SXWU:20

utyatyambo *n6-sg* throbbing R30

utye *v-tr-pres-sub* that you eat R34.2

utyebo *n6-sg* wealth, riches ☞ Syn: indyebo XED:172, R15x

utyelelo *n6-sg* visit GDX3:450, R24x

uTyhila *n1a-sg-pn* Tyhila (personal name) R22

utyhole *v-tr-perf* he accused R26

utyumbe *v-tr-perf* he picked out R32

utywala *n7-mass* beer, brew, strong drink, alcoholic beverage ☞ Pl: iindywala, iintywala AM-94:101, AXG:200, CGB:107, EXD:50, PCX:55; 195, RD-96:59, SXWU:20, XED:175

uvalelwa *v-ben-pass* being locked up R31

uvalo *n6-sg* breastbone ☞ Pl: iimvalo PCX:55

uvavanyo *n6-sg* test, examination SXWU:20, R36

uVuma *n1a-sg-pn-masc* Vuma (male personal name) R36=4

uvumile *v-tr* he agreed R27

uvutho-ndaba *n6-cmp* hot news R29=2

uvuthulule *v-sub-pres* (that) you shake off R34

uvuthwe *v-intr-pass* he is enthusiastic R32

uvuyo *n6-sg* joy, delight, gladness; rejoicing CGB:121, E&S:58, XED:179

uwangawanga *n6-sg* very long, extensive or endless thing ☞ Pl: iinwangawanga CGB:114, XED:180

uwasikelele *v-tr-imp* you bless them R13

uwelwa *v-pass* you are fallen on • *uwelwa ngumzi 'your house is falling apart' {idiom} [lit: you are fallen upon by the household]* R15

uwusikelele *v-tr-imp* you bless it R13=2

uwuvuyele *v-tr-ben-perf* he was rejoicing R27

uxam *n1a-sg* iguana, leguaan, Cape monitor lizard ☞ Pl: ooxam AXG:18, CGB:109, GDX3:563, SXWU:14, XED:182

uxanduva *n6-sg* responsibility, duty; burden, trouble, difficulty GDX3:565, R35, R37.17

uxhulumane *v-tr-sub* you should contact R29

uxhulumene *v-recip-perf* you contact R29

uxinanisa *v-past-sub* it crowds together, gathers R25

uxolelo *n6-sg* forgiveness, pardon XED:185

uxolo *n6-sg* peace; pardon No plural AM-94:100; 164, CGB:114, E&S:58, PCX:24f, XED:185, R34x

uxomoyi *n1a-sg* kingfisher ☞ Pl: ooxomoyi CGB:109, EXD:327

uxwebhu *n6-sg* discourse, long discussion, treatment; [ext] document (official); form (to be filled in) ☞ Pl: amaxwebhu EXD:170, GDX3:613, RD-96:415, XED:186, R23.2.3, R37.7.11.19

uya *v-fut-aux* you will R29=2, R31, R34=3

uyafuna *v-pres-qw* you want to; do you want to? R7

uyafunda *v-tr* you are learning R29

uyakoyikisela *v-tr-caus-ben* fear R36

uyakufumanisa[1] *v-fut-n2-sg* it will find out R37.15

uyakufumanisa[2] *v-fut-pro-2sg* you will discover R12

uyakwazi *v-tr* you are able, you know R34.11

uyalumkisa *v-tr-caus* he warns R36

uyaphumelela *v-intens* you are succeeding R29.8

uyavalelwa *v-ben-pass* you are arrested ☞ -vala = close, shut (XED: 176) XED 176, R31

uyayingqina *v-tr* she renders it; she testifies R36.23

uyazi *v-tr-pro-2sg* you know • *Uyazi yintoni 'you know what?'* R25, R33.6, R36.6

uyazifuna *v-tr* he, she wants them R23

uyazinceda *v-refl* you are helping yourself R34.6

uye *v-aux* he, she went on to • *uye wacela 'he then asked...'* compound tense aux [3-sg + ye] R19, R27=2, R37.14

uyenze *v-tr-sub* you should make R29

uyiBrand Manager *loan* you are a Brand Manager R29

uyihlo *n1a-sg-kin* father (your) ☞ Pl: ooyihlo; Contrast: ubawo, utata (our father), uyise (their father) AXG:18; 215, E&S:56, EXD:209

uyihlokazi *n1a-sg-kin* uncle (your paternal), your father's brother ☞ Pl: ooyihlokazi; Cf: unyokolume (maternal) AXG:215, EXD:689

uyihlomkhulu *n1a-sg-cmp-kin* grandfather (your) ☞ Pl: ooyihlomkhulu AXG:215

uyindoda *cop-n5-sg* being a man R36

uyingqonyela *cop-n5-sg* she is the champion, the one who has achieved Copulative formed from n1-sg+SC+ngqonyela ☞ See: ingqonyela GBS, GDX2 (unpublished), NOM, R24.4

uyise *n1a-sg-kin* father (his, her); their father ☞ Pl: ooyise; Contrast: utata (our father), uyihlo (your father) AXG:18; 35; 36; 38; 215, E&S:56, EXD:209, MI:262

uyisebenzise *v-tr-sub* (that) you use it R30

uyisekazi *n1a-sg-kin* uncle (his / her paternal), their father's brother ☞ Pl: ooyisekazi; Cf: uninalume (maternal) AXG:36; 215, EXD:689, MI:262

uyisemkhulu *n1a-sg-cmp-kin* grandfather (his, her, their) ☞ Pl: ooyisemkhulu AXG:215

uyisikelele *v-tr-imp* you bless it R13

uza *pro-3sg-aux-fut* he, she will VERB • *akhuko mntu uza kusinda 'Nobody will escape from'* R23, R28, R29, R31=3, R32, R33

uzakubafaka *v-tr-fut* he will put them in aux and complement normally separated R26

uzame *v-tr-sub* you should try R29

uzazi *v-pro-2sg+n5-pl-obj* you know them R22.1, R29.19

uzenze *v-pres-sub* you should do them R22

uzibambe *v-tr-perf+n5-pl-obj* he held them R36.3

uzibuthe *n1a-sg* mercury, quicksilver [lit: that which gathers itself] GDX3:659, NDK-91:383

uzimisele *v-refl-perf* he, she is serious R33

uzingelo *n6-sg* hunt PCX:89f

uzipho *n6-sg* nail, fingernail, toenail ☞ Pl: iinzipho EXD:215; 669, RD-96:12

uziqhele *v-refl-imp* you get familiar!, familiarize yourself! R22.1

uZodwa *n1a-sg-pn-fem* Zodwa (female personal name) PCX:36f; 52

uZola *n1a-sg-pn* Zola (personal name) SXWU:14, R26

uzoyibhatala *v-fut* you will pay R25

uzu- -e *preverb* you [singular] ought to VERB Structure: uzu-Δ-e (present subjunctive) ☞ Neg: uzu-nga--i; Pl: zeni- CGB:168f

uzu-nga- -i *preverb-neg* you [singular] ought not to VERB Structure: uzu-nga-Δ-i (negative present subjunctive) ☞ Pos: uzu--e; Pl: zeni-nga--i CGB:169

uzuze *v-sub* that you obtain, acquire R34.6.9

uzwane *n6-sg* toe ☞ Pl: iinzwane; Alt: izwane [n3-sg] AM-94:100, XED:193

V

-va *v-ir* experience, perceive by sense: hear, taste, feel; understand; obey; be vigorous, be fruitful • *Andiva 'I do not hear'* latent vowel verb; final -a does not become -i in negative ☞ Cf: iva AM-94:115,

CGB:124; 126, E&S:51, PCX:21f; 40, SXWU:32, XED:175f, R4dx

-vakala *v-atr* be audible, perceptible, sensible, intelligible, sound ☞ rw: -va AXG:116, XED:176, R23.8

Van Riebeeck *pn* Van Riebeeck ☞ See: Van Riebeeck R32

vangeli *n6-sg* sermon R20

-vavanya *v-tr* test, try (out), examine, inspect, investigate; prove (a weapon) RD-96:415, SXWU:20, XED:176, R16, R36x

veki *n5-sg-red* week R32

-vela[1] *v-intr* appear, come into sight; come forth; come from E&S:17, XED:176, R32

-vela[2] *v-aux* naturally VERB; VERB from birth; VERBed long ago • *Uvela exoka 'He's a natural liar'* Structure: followed by S2 + participial construction E&S:47

-velisa *v-tr* bring out / forth, produce, yield; put up (proposal), propose, suggest; expose (error, wrongdoing) EXD:200, XED:177, R24, R32

veza *v-caus* produce, make appear, show, bring forth R21

Victoria Mxenge *-pn* Victoria Mxenge R32

Virgo *loan* Virgo R34

-visisana *v-caus-recip* agree, be in accord, come to an understanding ☞ rw: -va XED:176, R37.14

vitamin B *n5-sg* vitamin B R12

vokotheka *v-intr* of a speech: be perfectly explicit, leaving no doubt or query in the mind of the audience; be acceptable and satisfying; be persuaded by lengthy argument GDX3:509, XED 178, R32

Volkstaat *loan* Volkstaat [lit: a people's state, as visualized by Afrikaners desirous of retaining separate and cultural identity] R21=2

Vorster *pn* John Vorster • *uJohn Vorster* R32

-vuka *v-intr* get up, wake up, arise ☞ Caus: vusa AXG:112, PCX:20f

-vula *v-tr* open PCX:34, R10, R37.1

-vuleka *v-st* open (up), be open, stand open XED:178, R33.9x

-vuma *v-tr* consent, agree, accede; assent to; admit, confess; suit, agree with s.o.; fall in with the leader (in singing) XED:178, R2x

-vumela *v-ben* allow, agree to, approve of ☞ Pass: vunyelwa KED:456, XED:178, R2x, R30

-vumeleka *v-ben-atr* be approved of, allowable XED:178, R2

Vumile *n1a-sg-pn-masc* Vumile (male personal name) [lit: agreed] SXWU:11

-vusa *v-tr* awaken, arouse ☞ rw: -vuka AXG:112

-vuthiwe *v-perf-atr* ripe E&S:30

vuthulul *v-tr-red* shake off, shake out of, shake off from XED:179, R34

vuthulula *v-tr* shake off, shake out of, shake off from XED:179, R34

-vuya *v-intr* rise in boiling; [ext] rejoice, be glad, joyful, delighted XED:179, R16, R34

Vuyani *n1a-sg-pn-masc* Vuyani (male personal name) [lit: rejoice] SXWU:11

-vuyisa *v-tr* cheer s.o. up, delight, make s.o. happy or glad, give s.o. joy, cause to rejoice EXD:93, XED:179

-vuyisana *v-caus-recip* rejoice together; congratulate one another GDX3:533

-vuza[1] *v-tr* reward; pay XED:179, R10x, R29x

-vuza[2] *v-intr* leak, ooze out XED:179, R30

W

w[1] *change* change of O or U to W before another vowel • *abantwana 'children' [= aba-ntu-ana]; wenza 'you do' [= u-enz-a]; esikoweni 'to school'* CGB:119; 125, PCX:30; 193, R2=4, R4b, R9=7, R10=2, R11

w[2] *change* addition of W before U- after a vowel-final prefix • *khawutsho [= kha-w+u-tsho]* R3

w-[3] *n1-sg-them* [group 1 singular thematic consonant prefix] • *Umama wenza... 'Mother does...'* ☞ See: wonke R28

w-[4] *n2-sg-S1-prf* he, she, it [group 2 singular short subject (S1) agreement prefix before vowel initial verb] Agr: um- ☞ Alt: u- R5

-w-[5] *n2-sg-obj-prf* him, her, it [group 2 singular short object form before vowel initial verb] ☞ Alt: -wu- E&S:18

-w-[6] *n3-pl-obj-prf* them [group 3 plural short object form before vowel initial verb] ☞ Alt: -wa- E&S:18

w-[7] *pro-2sg-S1-prf* you [short form before vowel initial root] • *Wenza 'you are doing' = u-enza* CGB:125, R14

-w-[8] *v-suf-pass* be VERBed [passive verb suffix] Causes palatalization of bilabials in preceding verb root CGB:187, PCX:103f, R4a, R4b, R5, R6=4, R7=2, R8=5, R9, R10=5, R11=4, R12=7

wa-[1] *n1-sg-poss* of [group 1, 1a singular possessive agreement prefix] Agr: um-, u- AM-94:163, E&S:22, SXWU:35f, XED:xv, R4dx, R5

wa-[2] *n1-sg-S3b-pos* (and) he, she VERBed [group 1, 1a singular past subjunctive positive verb subject (S3b) agreement prefix] CGB:189, E&S:42, MI:247, SXWU:141, R16

wa-[3] *n2-sg-poss* of [group 2 singular possessive agreement prefix] Agr: um- AM-94:163, E&S:22, SXWU:35f, XED:xv, R4cx, R5, R7, R36.00, R37

wa-[4] *n2-sg-S3b-pos* (and) he, she, it VERBed [group 2 singular past subjunctive positive verb subject (S3b) agreement prefix] CGB:189, E&S:42, MI:247, SXWU:141

-wa-[5] *n3-pl-obj* them [group 3 plural object agreement prefix] Agr: ama- E&S:18, PCX:51, SXWU:44, R6

wa-[6] *n3-pl-enum-prf* [group 3 plural enumerative agreement prefix] ☞ See: wambi, waphi E&S:27, PCX:110, R14

wa-[7] *pro-2sg-S3b-pos* (and) you (singular = thou) VERBed [S3b past subjunctive positive subject pronoun] CGB:189, E&S:42, MI:247, SXWU:141

wa-[8] *pro-3sg-S3b-pos* (and) he, she VERBed [S3b past subjunctive positive subject pronoun] no direct antecedent CGB:189f, E&S:42, MI:247, SXWU:141

-wa[9] *v-suf-pass* be VERBed [passive verb suffix] • *ndiyabetwa 'I am beaten'* termination of the passive voice, with present, imperfect, and future tenses, and their compound forms ☞ See: -w- and -a CGB:187, KED:459, PCX:103f, R4a, R4b, R5, R6=4, R7=2, R8=5, R9, R10=5, R11=4, R12=7, R32

-wa[10] *v-intr* fall AXG:107, CGB:125, GDX3:535

wabaleka *v-past-sub-n1-sg-S3b* he, she ran R33

wabantu *n2-sg-poss-n1-pl* of the people • *singumlomo wabantu 'we are the mouthpiece of the people'* R27.14

wabe[1] *preverb-past-n1-sg* he, she, it had VERBed; he, she, it did VERB [group 1, 1a singular remote past compound tense preverb] Structure: wabe e-Δ (participial verb form) ☞ Alt: waye E&S:39, GDX3:714, PCX:186

wabe[2] *preverb-past-n2-sg* he, she, it had VERBed; he, she, it did VERB [group 2 singular remote past compound tense preverb] Structure: wabe u-Δ (participial verb form) ☞ Alt: waye E&S:39, GDX3:714, PCX:186

wabe[3] *preverb-past-pro-2sg* you did VERB; you had VERBed [remote past compound tense preverb] Structure: wabe u-Δ (participial verb form) ☞ Alt: waye E&S:39, GDX3:714, PCX:186

wabo[1] *n1-pl-poss-n1-sg* of them; their (own); theirs E&S:22, GDX3:691

wabo[2] *n1-pl-poss-n2-sg* of them; their (own); theirs E&S:22, GDX3:691

wabo[3] *n7-poss-n1-sg* its; of it GDX3:691

wabo[4] *n7-poss-n2-sg* its; of it GDX3:691

wabona *v-tr* he saw u+a+bona R26, R28

wabubeka *v-tr-past* she put it 3-sg-past-N7-agr-verb R24

wabuyela *v-intr-past* she returned R19=2

wabuza *v-tr-past* she asked R28

wacacisa *v-tr-past* he clarified R27.11

wacela *v-tr-past* he requested R27=2

wacinga *v-tr-past* she thought R28

wagqiba *v-past* she concluded R28

wakhe[1] *n1-sg-poss-n1-sg* his, her, its E&S:22, GDX3:691, R19.2.3.4.5.6, R26.6, R28.5

wakhe[2] *n1-sg-poss-n2-sg* his, her, its • *ngomsebenzi wakhe 'for her work'* E&S:22, GDX3:691, R24.1, R28

wakhe[3] *v-sub-pro-2sg* that you may build • *wakhe ingqondo 'so that you may build your mind'* = u- + -akh- + -e; with vowel verb u > w R34

wakho[1] *pro-2sg-poss-n1-sg* your, yours; your own [singular] E&S:22, GDX3:691, R25, R31

wakho[2] *pro-2sg-poss-n2-sg* your, yours; your own [singular] CGB:182, E&S:22, GDX3:691, R6, R13, R29=2, R31, R34=2

wako[1] *n8-vn-poss-n1-sg* its, of it GDX3:691

wako[2] *n8-vn-poss-n2-sg* its, of it GDX3:691

wako[3] *n10-loc-poss-n1-sg* its, of it GDX3:691

wako[4] *n10-loc-poss-n2-sg* its, of it GDX3:691

waku-[1] *n2-sg-temp* when it VERBs / VERBed [group 2 singular temporal verb construction] • *Wakufika 'When it arrives'* E&S:42

waku-[2] *pro-2sg-temp* when you VERB / VERBed [temporal verb construction] • *Wakufika 'When you arrive'* E&S:42, PCX:91f

wakuba *v-cop-temp* if it is to be R21.10

wakuvela *v-temp* when he appeared R26

wakwa-Mabhele *n2-sg-poss-loc* of the Mabhele family R5

wale[1] *deic-1-n2-pl-poss* of those • *IPANSALB ngomnye wale mibutho. 'PANSALB is one such assembly.'* R37.1

wale[2] *deic-1-n5-sg-poss-n1-sg* of this • *nguSihlalo wale Khomishoni yeNyaniso 'He is the chairman of this Truth Commission'* R32

wale[3] *deic-1-n5-sg-poss-n2-sg* of this • *umsila wale nja 'the tail of this dog'* PCX:140

walifuna *v-tr-past* you wanted it R15

walo[1] *n1-sg-poss-n1-sg* his, hers, its, of his, hers, its • *kumqeqeshi walo '...to his trainer'* R33, R35

walo[2] *n3-sg-poss-n1-sg* his, her, its; of him, her, it GDX3:691

walo[3] *n3-sg-poss-n2-sg* his, her, its; of him, her, it GDX3:691

walo[4] *n6-sg-poss-n1-sg* his, her, its; of him, her, it GDX3:691

walo[5] *n6-sg-poss-n2-sg* his, her, its; of him, her, it GDX3:691

waloo *n1-sg-poss-deic* of that R28

Walter Sisulu *-pn* Walter Sisulu R32

wam[1] *pro-1sg-poss-n1-sg* of me; my, mine; my own • *umntwana wam 'my child', unyana wam 'my son'* AM-94:151, CGB:181, E&S:22, GDX3:691, PCX:60; 72, SXWU:36, R9, R19.2=2

wam[2] *pro-1sg-poss-n2-sg* of me; my, mine; my own AM-94:151, CGB:181, E&S:22, GDX3:691, PCX:60; 72, R33

wama-[1] *combo* of • *ngummeli wamalungelo abantwana 'she is a representative of children's rights'* indicates that n3 pl (ama-) is possessed by a n1 sg (wa-) R24, R32

wama-[2] *combo* of • *umhlaba wama-Afrika 'the world of Africans'; lilungu lombutho wamagqirha 'be a member of the association of witch doctors'* indicates that n3 pl (ama-) is possessed by a n2 sg (wa-) R7, R32

wamaAfrika *n3-pl-poss* of the Africans R32

wamagqirha *n3-pl-poss* of witch doctors R7

wamalungelo *n3-pl-poss* of the rights • *ngummeli wamalungelo abantwana 'she is a representative of children's rights'* R24

wamamkela *v-past-sub* he accepted her R28

wamaPhuthukezi *n1-sg-poss-n3-pl* of the Portuguese R24

wamatshetshi *n3-pl-poss* of the churches R32

wambi *enum-pro-n3-pl* others, some others (of a different kind) Structure: RED noun form + ENUM / ENUM + FULL noun form ☞ See: -mbi E&S:27, PCX:110, R14=2, R35

wamisa *v-tr-past* she set R33

wamkelwe *v-pass* it be received R21.10

wangena *v-tr-past* she entered R28.5

wangumphathiswa *cop-n1-sg* she became a minister R24.6

wangumqeqeshi *cop-n1-sg* he, she is a trainer R33

waphi *qw-n3-pl* which (ones)? E&S:27, GDX3:703, PCX:110f

waphuma *v-intr-past* she came R33

waphumelela *v-past-sub* he, she won • *Waphumelela nakwi-3,000m kwi South African Championships 'She won in the 3,000 m South African Championships.'* R33

waqala *v-tr-past* she began R19.2

waqonda *v-tr* he realized R26

Warrenton *pn-geog* Warrenton (small town in the Northern Cape, near Welkom / Uppington area) TD, R4d

waseGhana *pn-geog-rel-poss* those people of Ghana R16

waseMozambique *n1-sg-poss-loan* of Mozambique R24

waseMzantsi *atr* of (those) in the south; [atr] southern RD-96:121, R36.00, R37

waseMzantsi Afrika *n2-sg-pn-cmp-poss* of (those) in South Africa RD-96:121, R36.00, R37

wasezindabeni *v-n1-sg-S3b-n6-pl-loc* she was still in the news ☞ See: udaba R33.7

washiya *v-tr-past* she left behind, abandoned R33

wasithengela *v-tr-past* bought us R28

waso[1] *n4-sg-poss-n1-sg* his, her, its; of him, her, it GDX3:691

waso[2] *n4-sg-poss-n2-sg* his, her, its; of him, her, it GDX3:691

wathatha *v-tr-past* he took R19

wathi *v-intr* he, she said R27, R36

watshixele *v-obj-imp* lock them up! R6

watsho *v-tr-past* she said R28

wavalelisa *v-tr-past* she took leave of R28

wavavanywa *v-pass-past-sub* he has been tested R16

wawo[1] *n2-sg-poss-n1-sg* its; of it GDX3:691

wawo[2] *n2-sg-poss-n2-sg* its; of it GDX3:691

wawo[3] *n3-pl-poss-n1-sg* their; of them GDX3:691, R31

wawo[4] *n3-pl-poss-n2-sg* their; of them • *Amabhinqa namadoda akuyo enza umsebenzi wawo! 'They are men and women who are doing their job!'* GDX3:691, R31

wawu-[1] *n2-sg-remote-past* he, she, it had VERBed [group 2 singular contracted remote past compound tense] AXG:93f, E&S:39, PCX:186

wawu-[2] *pro-2sg-remote-past* you had VERBed [contracted remote past compound tense] AXG:93f, E&S:39, PCX:186

waye-[1] *n1-sg-remote-past* he, she, it had VERBed [group 1, 1a singular contracted remote past compound tense] AXG:93f, E&S:39, PCX:186, R28=9, R33

waye[2] *preverb-past-n1-sg* he, she, it had VERBed; he, she, it did VERB [group 1, 1a singular remote past compound tense preverb] Structure: waye e-Δ (participial verb form) ☞ Alt: wabe AXG:93f, E&S:39, GDX3:714

waye[3] *preverb-past-n2-sg* he, she, it had VERBed; he, she, it did VERB [group 2 singular remote past compound tense preverb] Structure: waye u-Δ (participial verb form) ☞ Alt: wabe AXG:93f, E&S:39, GDX3:714

waye[4] *preverb-past-pro-2sg* you did VERB; you had VERBed [remote past compound tense preverb] Structure: waye u-Δ (participial verb form) ☞ Alt: wabe AXG:93f, E&S:39, GDX3:714

wayekhuphisana *v-remote-past* she had overtaken / passed R33

wayenabantwana *v-poss-remote-past* she had had children R28

wayeneentombi *v-poss-remote-past* she had had girls R28

wayenefama *v-poss-remote-past* she had had a farm R28

wayenelisekile *v-aux-conn-stative* she was satisfied R28

wayengayigcini *v-remote-past-neg* she had not kept them R28

wayengazi *v-remote-past-neg* she did not know R28

wayenobubele *v-poss-remote-past* she had had kindness R28

wayenokwamkela *v-abil-remote-past* she could have earned R28.6

wayenoloyiko *v-aux-cop-n6-sg* he, she had fear R36

wayesamkela *v-remote-past* she had earned (already) Derived from -sala 'already'; -s- is remnant of -sa- R28.6

wayesinika *v-remote-past* she had given it to us R28

wayeve *v-remote-past-perf* she had heard wa + yiv(a) + e yiva > yeve by assimilation R28

wayeyinkwenkwana *v-aux-cop-n5-sg-dim* he was a little boy past aux + cop+ noun +dim-suffix R36

wayo[1] *n1-sg-poss-n1-sg* to her • *umyeni lo wayo, 'that husband of hers'* R19

wayo[2] *n2-pl-poss-n1-sg* of them; their (own); theirs GDX3:691

wayo[3] *n2-pl-poss-n2-sg* of them; their (own); theirs GDX3:691

wayo[4] *n5-sg-poss-n1-sg* his, her, its GDX3:691

wayo[5] *n5-sg-poss-n2-sg* its; of it GDX3:691

waza *v-aux* he, she went / came to • *waza wabuza 'she went to ask...'* sc+past+za R24, R28=3, R33=2

wazi *v-tr* you (sg) know R29

wazithandazela *v-refl-past* he prayed for himself R36.1

wazo[1] *n4-pl-poss-n1-sg* their; of them GDX3:691

wazo[2] *n4-pl-poss-n2-sg* their; of them GDX3:691

wazo[3] *n5-pl-poss-n1-sg* their; of them GDX3:691, R13

wazo[4] *n5-pl-poss-n2-sg* their; of them GDX3:691

we-[1] *combo* of • *ngutata wekhaya 'by the father of the family'* indicates that n3 sg (i-) is possessed by a n1a sg (wa-) ☞ See: wa- + i- R4d, R5

we-[2] *combo* of • *umculo wegosipile 'gospel music'* indicates that n5 sg (i-) is possessed by a n2 sg (wa-) ☞ See: wa- + i- R4c

we[3] *n1-sg-poss* of wa + i- > we R23=2, R29

-we[4] *v-suf-pass-past* was / were VERBed [short form passive past verb suffix] ☞ Contrast: -iwe CGB:188, R6=2, R7, R12=7, R37

weANC *-abr* of the African National Congress R32

wedwa *pro-quan-2sg* you alone; thou only Agr: u-, wena E&S:27, PCX:62, XED:180, R36

wee-[1] *combo* of • *umxube wee carbohydrate 'a mixture of carbohydrates'* indicates that n5 pl (ii-) is possessed by a n2 sg (wa-) R12

wee-[2] *v-aux* called, they say it is • *ngumxube wee carbohydrate 'it is a mixture they call carbohydrates'* auxiliary use of ukuthi, abbreviated form of wathi R12

weembacu *n1-sg-poss-n5-pl* of the destitute wanderers R32

weemoto *n1-sg-poss-n5-pl* of cars R26

wefama *n1-sg-poss-n5-sg* of the farm R28

wegosipile *n5-sg-poss* of the gospel R4c

wekhaya *n3-sg-poss* of the home • *ngumama wekhaya 'she is the mother of the home'* R4d, R5

wekomiti *n5-sg* of the committee R22

-wela *v-tr* fall (on, into, over); pass, overtake; ford (river), cross (sea); take a voyage CGB:42, XED:180

weli[1] *deic-1-n1-sg-poss-n3-sg* of this • *sikarhulumente weli phondo 'of the government of this region'* R18

weli[2] *deic-1-n3-sg-poss* of this • *ngokomthetho weli 'under the law of this (land)'* R36

Welkom *pn-geog* Welkom R17.7

wembiza *n2-sg-poss-n5-sg* of the pot R25

wemfundo *n1-sg-poss-n2-sg* of education R24

wena *pro-2sg-abs* you; yourself; as for you AM-94:92; 163, CGB:158, E&S:21, PCX:29, RD-96:415, R6, R14x, R19

wenene *n1-sg* close, intimate • *umhlobo wenene 'a true friend'* wa +-i- > -e- +nene EXD:101, R25, R34

wenkqubo *n1-sg-poss-n5sg* progress, advancement Derived from -qhuba 'drive' R37

wentlalo *n2-sg-poss-n5-sg* of living • *umgangatho wentlalo 'standard of living'* R37.1.12.13=2

wenu[1] *pro-2pl-poss-n1-sg* of you; your, yours; your own [plural] E&S:22, GDX3:691

wenu[2] *pro-2pl-poss-n2-sg* of you; your, yours; your own [plural] E&S:22, GDX3:691

wenza[1] *v-inf* to do R23, R24, R28

wenza[2] *v-pres* it is making R5

wenzantoni *interr* what are you doing? u+enza+ntoni elided R23

wenze[1] *v-pro-2sg-pres* you do R15, R23

wenze[2] *v-pro-2sg-sub* that you might do R14

wesikhululo *n4-sg* of the release (from jail) R18

Western Holdings *pn-geog-loan* Western Holdings ☞ See: intshonalanga R17.7

wethu[1] *pro-1pl-poss-n1-sg* of us; our, ours; our own [plural] E&S:22, GDX3:691, R10

wethu[2] *pro-1pl-poss-n2-sg* of us; our, ours; our own [plural] E&S:22, GDX3:691

weVosloorus *n1-sg-poss-pn* of Vosloorus R33

wezi[1] *deic-1-n4-pl-poss* of these R26

wezi[2] *deic-1-n5-pl-poss* of these • *umnikazi wezi gusha 'the owner of these sheep'* R26

wezi[3] *deic-1-n6-pl-poss* of these • *umgangatho wezi lwimi 'a standard for these languages'* R37.17.20

wezibi *n1-sg-poss-pn* of Zibi (a cartoon character used in an anti-litter campaign) • *kumgqomo wezibi 'into a waste disposal bin'* R30.6

with *prep* with • *60 ml yeJikelele Sishebo Mix with Rajah* R8

wo-[1] *v-n1-sg-short-fut* he, she, it will VERB [contracted / short positive future group 1, 1a singular noun prefix] E&S:20, R19

-wo[2] *n2-sg-root* it; its [group 2 singular pronoun root] absolute pronoun with suffix -na deleted E&S:22, GDX3:551

wo-[3] *v-n2-sg-short-fut* it will VERB [contracted / short positive future group 2 singular noun prefix] E&S:20

-wo[4] *n3-pl-root* they; their [group 3 plural pronoun root] E&S:22

wo-[5] *v-pro-2sg-short-fut* you will VERB [contracted / short positive future pronoun prefix] E&S:20

wobumbano *n2-sg-poss-n7-sg-abs* of the form, moulded together, hence 'National' R32

wocalulo *n2-sg-poss-n6-sg* of discrimination R32

wodwa *pro-quan-n2-sg* it alone; only it Agr: um-, wona E&S:27, PCX:62

wohlukane *v-short-fut* and she would separate R19

woku[1] *n2-sg-poss-deic-1* of this • *umzekelo woku 'another example of this'* R37.15

woku[2] *deic-1-n8-vn-poss-n1-sg* of this VERBing R21, R31

woku[3] *deic-1-n8-vn-poss-n2-sg* of this VERBing • *umzekelo woku 'as an example of this...'* R37.15

woku[4] *deic-1-n10-loc-poss-n1-sg* of this (place, time, situation) [not found in any references; see deic-1-n8-loc]

woku[5] *deic-1-n10-loc-poss-n2-sg* of this (place, time, situation) • *Umzekelo woku 'using this example'* R37

wokuba *n2-sg-poss-n8-vn* of being; [conj] that, so that • *ngumzekelo kwabanye wokuba akulunganga 'be an example to others that it is not OK'* ☞ See: ukuba R24.1, R31.2

wokufumanisa *n2-sg-poss-v-inf-caus* of making or helping to find R34

wokugqibela *n2-sg-poss-v-inf* to end R21

wokukhulula *n2-sg-poss-v-inf* of setting free R32.3

wokumela *n1-sg-poss-v-inf* of representing R33

womzantsi *n1-sg-poss-n2-sg* of south R32

wona[1] *pro-n2-sg-echo* it [group 2 singular echo / absolutive pronoun] AM-94:93; 163, CGB:158, E&S:21, PCX:57, R26

wona[2] *pro-n3-pl-echo* they [group 3 plural echo / absolutive pronoun] AM-94:93; 163, CGB:158, E&S:21, PCX:57

wonga *n3-sg-red* degree ☞ See: iwonga R24.8

wongeze *v-tr-past* he added R27

wonk' *enum* all R13

wonke[1] *pro-enum-n1-sg* every; all, the whole (of) • *wonke umntu 'every person; the whole person'; wonke ubani 'everyone, each and everybody'* Agr: um-, yena AM-94:163, CGB:176, E&S:27, PCX:62f, R23, R27, R30, R35=2

wonke[2] *pro-enum-n2-sg* every; all, the whole (of) Agr: um-, wona AM-94:163, E&S:27, PCX:62

wonke[3] *pro-enum-2sg* all of you; the whole of you Agr: u-, wena E&S:27, PCX:62

wonwabile *v-st-perf* you are injured R14

wophula *v-tr-past* he, she broke R33.4

wovisiswano *n6-sg* of agreement, harmony • *umoya wovisiswano 'a spirit of harmony'* R34.4

woyisakele *v-n1-sg-atr* it is fearful of • *urhulumente wethu woyisakele 'our government is afraid'* R10

wu-[1] *n1-sg-enum-prf* [group 1, 1a singular enumerative agreement prefix] ☞ See: wumbi, wuphi E&S:27, PCX:110f, R9

-wu-[2] *n2-sg-obj* [group 2 singular object agreement prefix] Agr: um- E&S:18, PCX:51, SXWU:44, R6=2, R11x

wu-[3] *n2-sg-enum-prf* [group 2 singular enumerative agreement prefix] ☞ See: wumbi, wuphi E&S:27, PCX:110

-wu-[4] *pro-2sg-SNEG* you • *Awundiboni na? 'Don't you see me?'; Awukho kulo mcimbi 'This matter does not concern you'* often used instead of -ku- after the negative formative a- ☞ GDX3:553, R15

wumbi[1] *enum-pro-n1-sg* other, some other, different Structure: RED noun form + ENUM / ENUM + FULL noun form ☞ See: -mbi E&S:27, PCX:110

wumbi[2] *enum-pro-n2-sg* other, some other, different Structure: RED noun form + ENUM / ENUM + FULL noun form ☞ See: -mbi E&S:27, PCX:110

wuphi[1] *qw-n1-sg* which (one)? E&S:27, EXD:722, GDX3:703, PCX:110f, R9x

wuphi[2] *qw-n2-sg* which (one)? E&S:27, EXD:722, GDX3:703

wuthobele *v-obj-imp* obey it! R6

X

x *intj* stop it! ☞ Alt: xa XED:181

xa[1] *conj-time* when, whenever; while, as [temporal] • *xa bebe kwilifu elimnyama 'when they were in the dark cloud'; Xa ulunyikiswa ngokungaseli 'when you are warned about not drinking'* Structure: followed by participial construction E&S:36, EXD:288, GDX3:556, SXWU:164, XED:181, XS-92:184, R5, R7, R12=2, R14=2, R17.3, R18, R20.6.7, R24.0.1.8, R25.7, R26.6, R27.3, R29.2.8, R30=6, R31.3.4=3, R32.3, R33.4.6.7=2.9, R35, R36.3.6, R37.19

xa[2] *conj-time* if [conditional] • *xa ulunyikiswa ngokungaseli 'if you are* *warned about not drinking'; xa ukhulelwe 'if you are pregnant'; xa inkampani izimisele ukuthengisela abantu abantsundu imveliso yayo 'if a company is serious about selling its product to black people'* Structure: followed by participial construction E&S:36, EXD:288, GDX3:556, XED:181, XS-92:184, R6=3, R17.7, R20.2.4, R22.6=2, R29.14, R31.4, R33.10, R36.7.12.19

xa[3] *conj-time* when, whenever; if • *Phulaphula xa ndithethayo 'Listen when I speak'; Ndimbone xa afikayo 'I saw him arriving'* Structure: followed by relative construction (in Tshiwo dialect) E&S:36, EXD:288, GDX3:556, XED:181, XS-92:184

xa[4] *intj* stop it! ☞ Alt: x XED:181

xa limbi *adv-time* now; then; [cmp] now ... then GDX3:556, XED:181

xa sele *conj-expr* whenever, at such time that [lit: when already] Structure: followed by S2 + participial ☞ See: -sa- R7, R30=2, R31

xa sukuba *conj-expr* whenever, on any occasion, as often as, every time that EXD:722

-xaba *v-tr* lay across, bar (entrance); thwart, hinder, obstruct; oppose; reprove XED:181, R1x, R14x=2

-xabana *v-recip* obstruct one another, be at cross-purposes; [ext] disagree, quarrel XED:181, R14=2

-xabana na *vp-recip* quarrel with one another XED:181, R14

-xabisa *v-tr* set across, set awry; reach the mark; make hostile; be worth XED:182, R1x

xabiseka *v-atr* make valuable; have value, be of value EXD:701, RD-96:415

-xakekile *v-perf-atr* busy E&S:30

Xayiya *pn* Xayiya (name) R5

-xela *v-tr* tell, say, mention; order, command; be like, resemble XED:183, R14x

-xelela *v-ditr* inform, tell s.o. s.t.; mention, say s.t. to s.o. XED:183f, R14x

xenikweni[1] *conj* when Structure: followed by relative construction ☞ Alt: xeshikweni; rw: xa E&S:36, XED:181, XS-92:184

xenikweni[2] *conj* when Structure: followed by participial (situative) construction ☞ Alt: xeshikweni; rw: xa E&S:36, XED:181, XS-92:184

xesha *n3-sg-red* time R19.2, R26, R28

xeshikweni[1] *conj* when Structure: followed by relative construction ☞ Alt: xenikweni; rw: xexha XS-92:184

xeshikweni[2] *conj* when Structure: followed by participial (situative) construction ☞ Alt: xenikweni; rw: xexha XS-92:184

Xesibe *clan* Xesibe (clan or ethnic group within the greater Xhosa community) CGB:1, MI:273

-xhamla *v-tr* overdo, overwork; overeat; use up, squander, waste ☞ Pass: -xhanyulwa XED:183

-xhapha[1] *v-tr* lap up (as a dog); eat carelessly; [v-st] be smeared around the mouth (with food, fat, blood, foam); boil over, bubble up (when boiling) GDX3:576, XED:183, R9x

xhapha[2] *ideophone* bubble (up, when boiling); boil over; froth, foam at the mouth; sound of animal lapping up (water) (XED:183), GDX3:575, R9x

-xhaphaka *v-st* be plentiful, abundant; be present in great numbers, quantities; be all over the place; be regular, occur often; frequent, be a frequent visitor (to a place) GDX3:576, R9

-xhasa *v-tr* prop, stay up; support, maintain, assist ☞ Cf: inkxaso SXWU:19, XED:183, R10=2, R14x, R33x, R37.7

-xhoba *v-tr* take, pick up, prepare (provisions for a journey); take (arms), arm oneself XED:184, R34.8

-xhomekeka *v-st* depend upon; be dependent on s.o. (for support, help, etc.) GDX3:589, R27, R29, R34

Xhosa *clan* Xhosa (specific clan or ethnic group as well as the greater Xhosa community) ☞ See: umXhosa (amaXhosa), isiXhosa CGB:1, MI:273, R37

xhuma-xhuma *v-intr* clank, rattle; prance, gambol XED:186, R17

Xitsonga *pn-loan* Tsonga R37

-xoka *v-intr* lie, fib, tell an untruth PCX:37, XED:185

Xola[1] *n1a-sg-pn-masc* Xola (male personal name) [lit: peace] AM-94:164

-xola[2] *v-st* become satisfied, appeased, reconciled; [perf] be at peace, content AM-94:164, XED:185, R14

-xola[3] *v-tr* repair, mend, patch up XED:185

-xolela *v-ben* be appeased towards; forgive, pardon; be satisfied, content with XED:185, R14

-xolisa *v-caus* satisfy, appease, pacify, put at peace XED:185, R14

Xoliswa *n1a-sg-pn-fem* Xoliswa (female personal name) [lit: peace was made] AM-94:164

-xuba *v-tr* mix (s.t. up); [perf st] be different, be of different sorts ☞ Pass: -xutywa XED:186, R12x

xwebhu *n6-sg-red* discussion, discourse; document ☞ See: uxwebhu R37.7.11.19

Y

y[1] *change* change of I to Y before a vowel • *yoyika 'it fears' [= i-oyika]* CGB:119, PCX:192

y[2] *change* addition of Y before I- after a vowel-final prefix • *mayinyanzelwe [= ma-y+i-nyanz-el-w-e]* R4c, R10

y-[3] *n2-pl-them* [group 2 plural thematic consonant prefix] ☞ See: yonke XED:187

-y-[4] *n2-pl-obj-prf* them [group 2 plural short object form before vowel initial verb] ☞ Alt: -yi- E&S:18, R31

y-[5] *n5-sg-them* [group 5 singular thematic consonant prefix] ☞ See: yonke R1

-y-[6] *n5-sg-obj-prf* him, her, it [group 5 singular short object form before vowel initial verb] ☞ Alt: -yi- E&S:18, R9

y-[7] *v-pres-long* is / are VERBing [long present verb prefix on vowel-initial verb stems] • *ziyazi 'they know'* Structure: S1-y-Δ-a ☞ See: -ya- -a PCX:30, R11

y- -a[1] *v-pres-long* is / are VERBing [long present verb construction, on vowel-initial verb stems] • *ndiyazi 'I know'* Structure: S1-y-Δ-a ☞ See: -ya- -a PCX:30, R11

y- -a[2] *v-imp-sg* do VERB! [positive imperative singular verb construction, on vowel-initial verb stems and latent-I monosyllabic stems] • *Yenza shushu ioyile 'Heat the oil!'; Yakha 'build!'; yona 'do wrong!'; yiza 'come!'* Structure: y-Δ-a PCX:22, R8

ya-[1] *n2-pl-poss* of [group 2 plural possessive agreement prefix] Agr: imi- AM-94:163, E&S:22, RD-96:416, SXWU:35f, XED:xv, R11, R22x

ya-[2] *n2-pl-S3b-pos* (and) they VERBed [group 2 plural past subjunctive positive verb subject (S3b) agreement prefix] (CGB:189), E&S:42, MI:247, SXWU:141, R37.6

ya-[3] *n5-sg-poss* of [group 5 singular possessive agreement prefix] Agr: i-, iN- AM-94:163, E&S:22, RD-96:416, SXWU:35f, XED:xv, R1x=2, R4c, R8, R9=3, R12

ya-[4] *n5-sg-S3b-pos* (and) he, she, it VERBed [group 5 singular past subjunctive positive verb subject (S3b) agreement prefix] (CGB:189), E&S:42, MI:247, SXWU:141, R37.5

-ya-[5] *v-pres-prf* does VERB, is / are VERBing [long present verb prefix] • *ndiyafuna 'I want'* Structure: S1-ya-Δ-a, but avoid the concept that -ya- differentiates between Present and Present Continuous tenses (see grammar section for further discussion). ☞ See: -ya- -a CGB:122, E&S:17, PCX:30, R7, R11=2

-ya-[6] *preverb-fut* will, shall VERB [proposed / remote future positive preverb] Structure: S1-ya ku-Δ-a ☞ Neg: -yi-; See also: -za- CGB:165, E&S:20, R4c, R12, R14=4, R17, R37.15

-ya[7] *v-intr* go (to), travel • *Uya phi? 'Where are you going?'* ☞ Contrast: -hamba 'go (from)' CGB:130; 143, PCX:29; 32, R4b, R4d, R8x, R10

-ya[8] *v-aux* go to (do s.t.); go and VERB [andative auxiliary] XED:187

-ya[9] *v-aux* do VERB [factitive auxiliary] Structure: takes present subjunctive ☞ See also: -ye E&S:47, R7

-ya- -a *v-pres-long* does VERB, is / are VERBing [long indicative present tense verb construction] • *abantwana bayahamba 'the children are walking', umama uyapheka 'mother is cooking', uyalesa 'are you reading?'* Structure: S1-ya-Δ-a; used on a verb when it stands alone (no object or adverb is expressed) or when the verb is final, otherwise emphasizes either the action or a following adverb (has an assertive implication) CGB:122, E&S:17, PCX:30f, R11=2

-ya-ku- -a *v-fut* will VERB Structure: S1-ya-ku-Δ-a E&S:20

yaba *v-aux* it is R37

yabafazi *n1-pl-poss* of women R37

yabantu *n5-sg-poss-n1-pl* of the people R35.4, R37.10.16.17

yabasetyhini *n3-sg-poss* of women • *kwi-5,000m yabasetyhini kwiRegional Championships 'in the women's 5000m Regional Championships'* R33

yabazali *n5-sg-poss-n1-pl* of parents R18

yabe[1] *preverb-past-n2-pl* they had VERBed; they did VERB [group 2 plural remote past compound tense preverb] Structure: yabe i-Δ (participial verb form) ☞ Alt: yaye E&S:39, GDX3:714, PCX:186

yabe[2] *preverb-past-n5-sg* he, she, it had VERBed; he, she, it did VERB [group 5 singular remote past compound tense preverb] Structure: yabe i-Δ (participial verb form) ☞ Alt: yaye E&S:39, GDX3:714, PCX:186

yabemi *n5-sg-poss-n1-pl* of the residents R27

yabo[1] *n1-pl-poss-n2-pl* of them; their (own); theirs E&S:22, GDX3:691

yabo[2] *n1-pl-poss-n5-sg* of them; their (own); theirs • *impahla yabo 'their belongings'* E&S:22, GDX3:691, R20, R22, R26

yabo[3] *n7-poss-n2-pl* its; of it GDX3:691

yabo[4] *n7-poss-n5-sg* its; of it GDX3:691

-yabula *v-intr* roam about aimlessly, wander (around); talk nonsense, be off topic GDX3:617, R2=3

yakhe[1] *n1-sg-poss-n2-pl* his, her, its E&S:22, GDX3:691, R24

yakhe[2] *n1-sg-poss-n5-sg* his, her, its E&S:22, GDX3:691, R4b, R4c, R37

yakho[1] *pro-2sg-poss-n2-pl* your, yours; your own [singular] E&S:22, GDX3:691

yakho[2] *pro-2sg-poss-n5-sg* your, yours; your own [singular] E&S:22, GDX3:691, R29=3, R31, R34=5

yako[1] *n8-vn-poss-n2-pl* its, of it GDX3:691

yako[2] *n8-vn-poss-n5-sg* its, of it GDX3:691

yako[3] *n10-loc-poss-n2-pl* its, of it GDX3:691

yako[4] *n10-loc-poss-n5-sg* its, of it GDX3:691

yakowethu *n5-sg-poss-n1-pl-pro* our; of ours R17.7

yaku-[1] *n2-pl-temp* when they VERB / VERBed [group 2 plural temporal verb construction] • *Yakufika 'When they arrive'* E&S:42

yaku-[2] *n5-sg-temp* when it VERBs / VERBed [group 5 singular temporal verb construction] • *Yakufika 'When it arrives'* E&S:42

-yakwazi uku- *v-pot-cmp* can VERB, know how to VERB [implying skill at doing] Structure: S1-yakwazi uku-Δ-a E&S:45

yakwaZwelitsha *n5-sg-poss-pn-loc* of Zwelitsha (a place) R18

yakwenza *n5-sg-poss-v-inf* to do with R24

-yala *v-tr* instruct (a novice in his duties), exhort, admonish, warn, charge, command XED:187, R6x=3

-yalela *v-ben* direct, instruct, order, command; warn s.o. regarding s.t. RD-96:416, XED:187, R6x=3

yalo[1] *n3-sg-poss-n2-pl* his, her, its; of him, her, it GDX3:691

yalo[2] *n3-sg-poss-n5-sg* his, her, its; of him, her, it • *Iholo yalo ikwasetyenziswa 'The hall of it (the center) was used...'* GDX3:691, R35=2

yalo[3] *n6-sg-poss-n2-pl* its; of it GDX3:691

yalo[4] *n6-sg-poss-n5-sg* its; of it GDX3:691

yalo[5] *deic-1-n1-sg-poss* of this • *inja yalo mntu 'this person's dog'* PCX:140

yam[1] *pro-1sg-poss-n2-pl* of me; my, mine; my own • *imithi yam 'my trees'* AM-94:151, CGB:181, E&S:22, GDX3:691, PCX:60; 72, RD-96:416

yam[2] *pro-1sg-poss-n5-sg* of me; my, mine; my own • *inja yam 'my dog'* AM-94:151, CGB:181, E&S:22, GDX3:691, PCX:60, SXWU:36, R19.1

yama-[1] *combo* of • *imfundo yamabanga ephakamileyo 'education at higher levels'* indicates that n3 pl (ama-) is possessed by a n5 sg (ya-) ☞ See: ya- + ama- R10

yama[2] *num-poss* of the [NUM] • *yama-62 'sixty-second'* R33

yamabanga *n3-pl-poss* of grades R10

yamaBhulu *n2-pl-poss-n3-pl* of the Whites R32

yamagorha *n3-pl-poss* of heroes R32

yamagqiyazana *n3-pl-poss* of young women R33

yamanzi *n3-pl-poss* of water R8

yamaphandle *n5-sg-poss-n3-pl* the country outside, external R21

yamapolisa *n3-pl-poss* of the police R26=2, R27

yamazwe *n5-sg-poss-n3-pl* of countries R16

yamcela *v=tr-past* it requested her R24

yamkeleke *v-atr* be received R37

yangasese *atr-n5-sg* out of sight, far away from, secret, private • *indlu yangasese 'toilet' (euphemism)* R30

yangcali *n5-sg-poss* of an expert R36.24

yanto *n5-sg-poss-n5-sg* of nothing R36

yantoni *qw* of what? CGB:129

yaphefumla *v-intr-past* it breathed out; it spoke out R37.6

yaqaliswa *v-pass* it was started R22

yaqwalaselwa *v-pass-past-sub* they were addressed R37.6

yase *n5-sg-poss+loc* from • *yaseQuzini 'of Quzi town'* R15=2

yaseEssex *pn-loan* of Essex R24

yaseka *v-tr-past* it established R35

yasekuhlaleni *n5-sg-poss-loc* of those who are lying down (i.e., marginalized minorities) R37.26

yasekwa *v-pass-past* it was established R37.2

yaseMzantsi *n1-sg-pred-loc* of (those) in the south R16, R24

yasentolongweni *loc-n5-sg* of those in prison R36.2

yasephalaborwa *n5-sg-poss-loc-n-prop* (a town in the Northern Province) R35

yaseQuzini *n5-sg-poss-loc-n-prop* of Quzini (a name of a place) R26=2

yasimahla *atr-poss-n5-sg* free, gratis, for nothing EXD:255; 409, GDX3:197, R12

yaso[1] *n4-sg-poss-n2-pl* his, her, its; of him, her, it GDX3:691

yaso[2] *n4-sg-poss-n5-sg* his, her, its; of him, her, it GDX3:691

yathatha *v-tr-past* it took R37.5

yathi *v-aux* it is said aux verb, used with verbs indicating action of speech R37

-yawa- *preverb* yet again [implying disapproval or censure] • *Umpheki uyawanxila 'The cook is drunk again'* E&S:46

yawo[1] *n2-sg-poss-n2-pl* its, of it GDX3:691

yawo[2] *n2-sg-poss-n5-sg* its, of it GDX3:691

yawo[3] *n3-pl-poss-n2-pl* their, of them GDX3:691

yawo[4] *n3-pl-poss-n5-sg* their, of them • *ngenxa yawo amakhosi 'on account of their chiefs'* GDX3:691, R19, R20

yaye[1] *preverb-past-n2-pl* they had VERBed; they did VERB [group 2 plural remote past compound tense preverb] Structure: yaye i-Δ (participial verb form) ☞ Alt: yabe AXG:93f, E&S:39, GDX3:623; 714

yaye[2] *preverb-past-n5-sg* he, she, it had VERBed; he, she, it did VERB [group 5 singular remote past compound tense preverb] Structure: yaye i-Δ (participial verb form) ☞ Alt: yabe AXG:93f, E&S:39; 49, GDX3:623; 714, R37.5

yaye[3] *conj-v-aux* and; (and) also, thus [lit: let it be] Structure: links coordinate verb clauses together ☞ Contrast: kanti; Alt: kwaye KM, Pahl-1983:102, R14, R22=3, R28.6, R29=5, R31=3, R37=6

yaye yayila *v-remote-past* it had designed R37.5

yayi-[1] *n2-pl-remote-past* they had VERBed [group 2 plural contracted remote past compound tense] AXG:93f, E&S:39, PCX:186

yayi-[2] *n5-sg-remote-past* he, she, it had VERBed [group 5 singular contracted remote past compound tense] AXG:93f, E&S:39, PCX:186, R36.1, R37.24

yayibalulekile *v-remote-past-perf* it had been important R37

yayikokokuqala *v-remote-past* it had been the first time R36.1

yayiza *v-past* it was going to happen R36

yayo[1] *n2-pl-poss-n2-pl* their, of them GDX3:691, XED:9

yayo[2] *n2-pl-poss-n5-sg* their, of them GDX3:691, XED:9

yayo[3] *n5-sg-poss-n2-pl* its, of it GDX3:691

yayo[4] *n5-sg-poss-n5-sg* its, of it • *Xa inkampani izimisele ukuthengisela abantu abantsundu imveliso yayo 'If a company is serious about selling its products to black people...'* GDX3:691, R29

yaza *aux* therefore R24

yaziwayo *v-rel-pass* who is (well) known R33

yazo[1] *n4-pl-poss-n2-pl* their; of them GDX3:691

yazo[2] *n4-pl-poss-n5-sg* their; of them, for them GDX3:691, R9

yazo[3] *n5-pl-poss-n2-pl* their; of them, for them • *iintolongo zifana nemizi yazo 'prisons are just like their homes'* GDX3:691, R11, R26

yazo[4] *n5-pl-poss-n5-sg* their; of them, for them GDX3:691

yazo[5] *n6-pl-poss-n5-sg* their, of them, for them • *ezi ntsapho zigxothwe elalini yazo ngabahlali 'these families were expelled from their village by the residents'; ezi ntsapho zilayisha impahla yazo kuyo 'these families are loading their goods'* R26=2

ye-[1] *combo* of • *yemi godi 'of the mines'* indicates that n5 sg (i-) is possessed by a n2 pl (ya-) ☞ See: ya- + i- R35

ye-[2] *combo* of • *500 g yelamb chops '500 grams of lamb chops'* indicates that n5 sg (i-) is possessed by a n5 sg (ya-) ☞ See: ya- + i- R8=4, R12=2

ye[3] *n3-sg-abs-red* he, him, she, her • *nguye 'it is he/she'* R25

-ye[4] *preverb* had VERBed; did VERB [remote past compound tense preverb] • *Ndaye ndifuna 'I had wanted'; Baye bebuzile 'They had asked'* Structure: S3b-ye S2-Δ (followed by participial verb form); frozen perfect tense form of andative verb -ya ☞ Alt: -be AXG:90;93f, E&S:39, GDX3:714

-ye[5] *v-aux-perf* did do VERB [factitive auxiliary] • *Uye wafika 'He did arrive'* Structure: takes S3b + past subjunctive ☞ See also: -ya E&S:47

-ye[6] *conj-root* and; (and) also ☞ See: kwaye, yaye AXG:174, Pahl-1983:102, R4a, (R33)

ye- -a *v-pres-long* is / are VERBing [long present verb construction, on latent I- verb stems] • *ndiyeza 'I am coming', ndiyeva 'I hear';* Structure: S1-ye-Δ-a [= ya-i-Δ-a] ☞ See: -ya- -a PCX:30

yeAIDS *loan* of AIDS R36

yebronze *loan* of bronze R33

yechopped green beans *n5-sg-cmp-poss-n5-sg* of chopped green beans R8

yeDemocratic Language Policy *n5-sg-poss-loan* of a Democratic Language Policy R37.27

yedliso *n5-sg-poss-n3-sg* of poisoning R25

yedrop *loan* of drop R25

yedwa *pro-quan-n1-sg* he, she, it alone; only him, her, it Agr: um-, yena E&S:27, PCX:62

yee *combo* of indicates that n5 pl (ii-) is possessed by a n5 sg (ya-) ☞ See: ya- + ii- R12, R22.2, R33.11

yeekomiti *n5-sg-poss-n5-pl* of the committees R22.2

yeelwimi *n5-sg-poss-n6-pl* of languages • *iBhodi entsha yeelwimi 'the new language Board'* R37.0.1.12

yeembasa *n5-sg-poss-n5-pl* of medals R33.11

yeen- *combo* of • *inkoliso yeenkokeli 'the majority of leaders'* indicates that n5 pl (iin-) is possessed by a n5 sg (ya-) ☞ See: ya- + iin- R16

yeengqondi *n5-sg-poss-n5-pl* of minds R16

yeenkokeli *n5-sg-poss-n5-pl* of leaders R16

yeeOlimpiki *n5-sg-poss-n5-pl-loan* of the Olympics R33=2

yeeresiphi *n5-sg-poss-n5-pl* of receipes • *incwadana yeeresiphi 'booklet of receipes'* ☞ See: iresiphi R12

yegusha *n5-sg-poss-n5-sg* of sheep • *inyama yegusha 'mutton, lamb' [lit: meat of sheep]* R26.8

yeHIV *n5-sg-poss-n-loan* of HIV R30

yeJikelele Sishebo Mix *n5-sg-cmp-poss-n5-sg* of Jikelele Sishebo Mix (brand name) ☞ See: -jikelele; sishebo < -sheba {Zulu} R8

-yeka *v-tr* leave (off, alone); cease, stop; spare; give in, yield; relax (one's body) XED:188, R16

yekamva *n3-sg-poss* of the future ☞ See: umva R34

yekhondom *n5-sg-poss* of the condom R30

yekhwalithi *n5-sg-poss-n5-sg* of quality ya + i- > ye. Strictly speaking there are three morphemes, i- + -a- + -i. R12=2

yelahleko *n5-sg-poss-n5-sg* of the loss R18.3

yelamb chops *n5-sg-cmp-poss-n5-sg* of lamb chops • *500 g yelamb chops okanye iiknuckles '500 grams of lamb chops or knuckles'* R8

yelapha *v-pres* he, she cures R15

yeli *n5-sg-poss-deic* of this R35

yemali *n5-sg-poss-n2-pl* of money R22

yemigodi *n2-pl* of the mines ☞ umgodi (sg) R35

yemizuzu *n2-pl-poss* of minutes R33

yena[1] *pro-n1-sg-echo* he, she; himself, herself; as for him, her [group 1, 1a singular echo / absolutive pronoun] • *UTakalani Rachel "Musquito" Nthulani yena 'Takalani Rachel "Mosquito" Nthulani herself'* AM-94:92; 163, CGB:158, E&S:21, PCX:57, R4cx, R26, R27, R33, R36

yena[2] *pro-3sg-echo* he, she; himself, herself; as for him, her [third person singular echo or absolutive pronoun] without antecedent AM-94:92; 163, CGB:158, PCX:57, RD-96:416, R4c, R19

yendlela *n2-pl-poss-n5-sg* of the road • *imithetho yendlela 'the rules of the road'* R31.1

yengqolowa *n5-sg-poss-n5-sg* wheat R28

yengqondo *n5-sg-poss-n5-sg* of the mind R36

yentloko *n5-sg-poss* of head R25=2

yentonga *n5-sg-poss-n5-sg* of the stick R25.3

yenu[1] *pro-2pl-poss-n2-pl* of you; your, yours; your own [plural] E&S:22, GDX3:691, PCX:73

yenu[2] *pro-2pl-poss-n5-sg* of you; your, yours; your own [plural] CGB:182, E&S:22, GDX3:691

yenyanga *n5-sg-poss-n5-sg* each month, monthly R35

yenyaniso *n5-sg-poss-n5-sg* of the truth R32=3

yenye *n5-sg* of another ya + enye R36

yenza *v-imp-sg* make! i coalesces with e- to give 'y' R8

yenze *v-tr* doing, making R37=2

yenzeke *v-atr* it might happen R37.21

yenziwa *v-pass* it is done R35.9

yeoyile *n5-sg-poss-n5-sg* of oil • *30 ml yeoyile '30 ml of oil'* R8

yePANSALB *loan* of PANSALB (the Language Board) R37

yeqaqa *n5-sg-poss-n3-sg* of a smelling creature; [atr] smelly, stinking • *kwemithetho yeqaqa 'laws that stink'* ☞ See: iqaqa R32.3

yesi-[1] *combo* of • *imali yesikolo 'money for school'* indicates that n4 sg (isi-) is possessed by a n5 sg (ya-) ☞ See: ya- + isi- R10

yesi[2] *n5-sg-poss-deic* of this R18

yesidoda *n4-sg-poss-n5-sg* of a man; [atr] male R30

yesikolo *n4-sg-poss-n5-sg* of / for school R10, R36

yesilivere *n5-sg-poss-n5-sg-loan* of silver R33

yesine *n5-sg-poss-num* four R28

yesithathu *n5-sg-poss-n4-num* third [lit: of three] R33

yesondo *n5-sg-poss-n3-sg* of sex R30=5

yethu[1] *pro-1pl-poss-n2-pl* of us; our, ours; our own [plural] E&S:22, GDX3:691, PCX:72

yethu[2] *pro-1pl-poss-n5-sg* of us; our, ours; our own [plural] E&S:22, GDX3:691, SXWU:36, R1, R13, R21

yexhwele *n5-sg-poss-n3-sg* apprentice witch doctor • *inkuntsela yexhwele 'the apprentice master'* poss + xhwele XED182, R26.1

yeyokuba *cop-n5-sg-conj* it is that R36.26

yeza *n3-sg-red* medicine R25=2

yezi-[1] *combo* of • *imali yezikolo 'money for schools'* indicates that n4 pl (izi-) is possessed by a n5 sg (ya-) ☞ See: ya- + izi- R9

yezi[2] *deic-1-n5-pl-poss* of these • *imisila yezi zinja 'the tails of these dogs'* PCX:140

yezikolo *n4-pl-poss-n5-sg* of / for schools R9

yezinto *n5-sg* of things R21, R36, R37

yezizizathu *n5-sg-cop-n4-pl* of reasons R36

-yi-[1] *n2-pl-obj* them [group 2 plural object agreement prefix] Agr: imi- E&S:18, PCX:51, SXWU:44, R6

yi-[2] *n2-pl-enum-prf* [group 2 plural enumerative agreement prefix] ☞ See: yimbi, yiphi E&S:27, PCX:110

-yi-[3] *n5-sg-obj* him, her, it [group 5 singular object agreement prefix] • *mayiyanzelwe 'let it be forced...'* Agr: i-, iN- E&S:18, PCX:51, SXWU:44, R10, R30, R37.17

yi-[4] *n5-sg-agent-prf* by (done by, produced by) him, her, it [marker of group 5 singular agent of passive verb] E&S:25; 43

yi-[5] *n5-sg-enum-prf* [group 5 singular enumerative agreement prefix] ☞ See: yimbi, yiphi E&S:27, PCX:110

yi-[6] *n5-sg-pred-prf* he, she, it is [group 5 singular copulative or predicative prefix construction] • *yinja 'it is a dog'; yi-"Arrive Alive" (Fika Uphila) [copulative form preceding borrowed slogan]* CGB:135, E&S:21; 25, PCX:96, XED:xvi, R10, R14, R25, R31.2

-yi-[7] *preverb-fut-neg* will not VERB [proposed / remote future negative preverb] Structure: a-SNEG-yi-ku-Δ-a ☞ Pos: -ya-; See also: -zi- CGB:166, E&S:20, R14

yi- -a *v-imp-sg* do VERB! [positive imperative singular verb construction, on monosyllabic consonant stems] • *Yitya 'eat!'* Structure: yi-Δ-a ☞ Note: yitsho 'say so!' PCX:22

yibambe *v-imp-obj* hold it! R30

yibhodi[1] *n5-sg-pred* it is a board R37.2

yibhodi[2] *n5-sg-agent* by the board R37.6

yicinezele *v-imp-obj* press it! R30

yifake *v-imp* put it R30

yifunde *v-obj-imp* read them! R6

yihla *v-imp* go down, come down R13=3

yikhuphe *v-imp* withdraw it R30

-yila *v-tr* plan, design; devise, invent; mark out (a site); shape, mold, fashion NDK-91:609, XED:188, R37.5

yilaa[1] *deic-3-n2-pl-pred* those (far, yonder) are E&S:26

yilaa[2] *deic-3-n5-sg-pred* that (far, yonder) is E&S:26

yilahle *v-imp-obj* throw it away! R30

yile[1] *deic-1-n2-pl-pred* these are; it is these E&S:26, PCX:99, R37.6

yile[2] *deic-1-n5-sg-pred* this is E&S:26

yile[3] *deic-1-n5-sg-agent* by this R37.7.19

yiLife Line *loan* it is Life Line R36

yiloo[1] *deic-2-n2-pl-pred* these are E&S:26, R11

yiloo[2] *deic-2-n5-sg-pred* that is E&S:26, R11

-yilwa *v-tr* fight RD-96:416

yimarketing *loan* marketing R29

yimbi[1] *enum-pro-n2-pl* others, some others (of a different kind) Structure: RED noun form + ENUM / ENUM + FULL noun form ☞ See: -mbi E&S:27, PCX:110

yimbi[2] *enum-pro-n5-sg* other, some other, different Structure: RED noun form + ENUM / ENUM + FULL noun form ☞ See: -mbi E&S:27, PCX:110

yimi-[1] *n2-pl-pred-prf* they are [group 2 plural copulative or predicative prefix construction] • *yimithi 'they are trees'* CGB:135, E&S:21; 25, PCX:96, XED:xvi, R32.4, R33.0.7

yimi-[2] *n2-pl-agent-prf* by (done by, produced by) them [marker of group 2 plural agent of passive verb] E&S:25;43, R37.26

yimibutho *n2-pl-agent* by organizations R37.26

yimilonjikazi *cop-n2-pl* they are singers R33.0

yimini *cop-n5-sg* it is a day R24.4

yimithetho *cop-n2-pl* it is the laws R32.4

yimizuzu *cop-n2-pl* they are minutes R33.7

yindibanisela *cop-v-tr-caus-ben* is a combination R34.7

yindima *n5-sg-cop-n5-sg* it is the land of a day's ploughing; [fig] it is something obvious • *ukwenza indima 'to do something visible or obvious'* copulative of the noun indima 'the amount of ploughing expected in one day' ☞ See Mesatywa 1954:114 XED:29, R37.26

yindlela *c5-n5sg* it is the way R37.7

yindoda *cop-n5-sg* by a man R36.14.16

yingqele *n5-sg-pred* it is cold ☞ ingqele 'frost, cold' XED48, R35.7

yingxaki *cop-n5-sg* it is a problem R36.24

yinjuze *n5-sg-pred* he, she is a champion (EXD:90), R33

yinkcazelo *cop-n5-sg* by the explanation R27.3

yinkosi *cop-n5-sg* it is a chief agent copulative after 'ibe' R20.2

yiNLP *pn-poss* of the NLP (National Language Project) R37.5.6

yinto *n5-sg-pred* it is a thing R10, R32.2, R37.21

yintoni *qw-n5-sg-pred* what is it?; [indef pro] it is something

CGB:129, R11, R14, R19, R20.4, R36=2

yiphi[1] *qw-n2-pl* which (ones)? E&S:27, GDX3:703

yiphi[2] *qw-n5-sg* which (one)? E&S:27, EXD:722, GDX3:703, RD-96:416, XED:189, R30

yisonge *v-imp-obj* wrap it up R30.6

yitsho *v-imp-sg* say so; how are you? [formula for a greeting, usually among males] ☞ Pl: yitshoni PCX:36f

yitshoni *v-imp-pl* say so; how are you? [formula for a greeting, usually among males] ☞ Sg: yitsho PCX:37

yiUN *-abr* by the UN R24.7

yiva *v-imp* hear • *yiva nemithandazo yethu (hear our prayers)* R13.1

yiyo[1] *n2-pl-pred* they are; it is they [group 2 plural copulative or predicative] E&S:21, PCX:97

yiyo[2] *n5-sg-pred* he, she, it is; it is he, she, it / that [group 5 singular copulative or predicative] E&S:21, PCX:98, R36, R37=3

yo-[1] *combo* of indicates that n6 sg (u-) is possessed by a n5 sg (ya-) ☞ See: ya- + u- R1

-yo[2] *n2-pl-root* they; their [group 2 plural pronoun root] E&S:22, XED:189

yo-[3] *v-n2-pl-short-fut* they will VERB [contracted / short positive future group 2 plural noun prefix] E&S:20, XED:189

-yo[4] *n5-sg-root* he, she, it; his, her, its [group 5 singular pronoun root] E&S:22, XED:189

yo-[5] *v-n5-sg-short-fut* he, she, it will VERB [contracted / short positive future group 5 singular noun prefix] E&S:20, XED:189

-yo[6] *v-suf-rel* [relative verb suffix, used attributively] • *angamaziyo 'whom he does not know', hambayo 'mobile, moving', sebenzayo 'working, active'* PCX:152, XED:189, R2, R3=2, R4b, R4c, R4d, R7, R9, R10=2, R12, R14, R22, R37

yobandlululo *n5-sg-poss-n6-sg* of Apartheid KM, R20.5

yobonelelo *n6-sg-poss-n5-sg* of the concession R23.9

yobu *deic-1-n7-sg-poss* of this • *incasa yobu tywala 'the taste of this beer'* PCX:140

yobudoda *n5-sg-poss-n7-sg* of a male R30.6

yocingo *n5-sg-poss-n6-sg* of telephone R15

yodidi *n5-sg-poss-n6-sg* of a kind R1

yodwa[1] *pro-quan-n2-pl* only they; they alone Agr: imi-, yona E&S:27, PCX:62

yodwa[2] *pro-quan-n5-sg* he, she, it alone; only him, her, it Agr: i(N)-, yona E&S:27, PCX:62

yoko *n5-sg* of that ya + oko (Demonstrative) KED:188, R22.4, R35.1

yokophuka *n5-sg-poss-vn* of the breaking R35.9

yoku-[1] *combo* of VERBing • *indlela yokunyusa imali 'a way of raising money'* indicates that n8 vn (uku-) is possessed by a n5 sg (ya-) ☞ See: ya- + uku- R4c, R9, R37

yoku[2] *deic-1-n8-vn-poss* of this • *incasa yoku kutya 'the taste of this food'* PCX:140

yokuba *n5-sg-poss-n8-vn* of being; [conj] that, so that ☞ See: ukuba GDX3:475, R27.11=2, R33.9, R35.9, R36.12.13, R37=3

yokufunda *n5-sg-poss-vn* for learning R35.9

yokugcina *n5-sg-poss-vn* for taking care of R35.2

yokuhlala *n5-sg-poss-vn* for living R35.3

yokujongana *n5-sg-poss-vn-recip* for looking at together (i.e., having common interests) R37.1

yokulala *n5-sg-poss-vn* for sleeping from ukulala 'to sleep' R35.7

yokulondoloza *n8-vn-poss* for taking care of R35.12

yokungabikho *v-cop-loc-n5-sg-neg* there is no R35.5

yokungalandeli *vn-neg-ben* of not following R37.12

yokungenwa *n5-sg-poss-vn-pass* of being entered R35.7

yokunqongophala *n5-sg-poss-v-inf* scarcity R28.2

yokunyusa *n8-vn-poss-n5-sg* of raising R9

yokuphazamiseka *v-atr* to be disturbed R37.14

yokuphelelwa *n8-vn-poss-n5-sg* of being expired; [atr] expiration R30.4

yokuphila *n8-vn-poss* of living • *indlela yokuphila kwabo 'their way of living'* R37.17

yokuphuhlisa *n5-sg-poss-v-inf* come up well R21.3

yokuqala *n8-vn-poss* of starting; [atr] beginning, first R4c, R37.7

yokuqhuba *n5-sg-poss-v-inf* for driving R31.3

yokusebenza *n5-sg-poss-vn* of work R29.9

yokuthenga *n5-sg-poss-vn* for purchasing R35.4

yokuthintela *n5-sg-poss-vn* to prevent R30.5

yokuyila *n8-vn-poss-n5-sg* of planning, designing R22.5

yokuzama *n5-sg-poss-v-inf* of trying R32.9

yokwenza *n5-sg-poss-vn* for making R35.6

yolawulo *n5-sg-poss-n6-sg* administrative R22.5

yoluntu *n6-sg-poss-n5-sg* of the community; of society • *inkqubela yoluntu 'society's progress'; inkxaso yoluntu 'the maintenance of the community'* R21.5, R30.1, R35.1=2

yomlungu *n5-sg-poss-n1-sg* of the European R28.5

yompu *n5-sg-poss-n2-sg* of a gun (i.e., a type of gun) R32.4

yomsebenzi *n5-sg-poss-n2-sg* of the work R24.7

yomthetho *n5-sg-poss-n2-sg* of the law ☞ See: inkqubo yomthetho R16, R31.2

yona[1] *pro-n2-pl-echo* they [group 2 plural echo / absolutive pronoun] AM-94:93; 163, CGB:158, E&S:21, PCX:57

yona[2] *pro-n5-sg-echo* himself AM-94:92; 163, CGB:158, E&S:21, PCX:57, RD-96:416, R24.3, R36.22, R37=2

yona[3] *v-imp-sg* do wrong! PCX:22

yonk' *enum-red* all R25.2

yonke[1] *pro-enum-n2-pl* all; every Agr: imi-, yona AM-94:163, E&S:27, PCX:62;26, R20.7, R31.1

yonke[2] *pro-enum-n5-sg* every; all, the whole (of) Agr: i(N)-, yona AM-94:163, E&S:27, PCX:62, RD-96:416, R25.2, R37.17

yonke imihla *time-expr* every day [lit: all days] E&S:59, MI:231, PCX:26f

yonyulo *n5-sg-poss-n5-sg* of the election R21.6.8

yoosomashishini *n5-sg-poss-n1a-pl* of the business owners R35.15

yophando *n6-sg* of the investigation R18.5

yowiso *n5-sg-poss-n6-sg* make fall ☞ See: yowisomthetho R21.11

yowisomthetho *n5-sg-poss-cmp-n2-sg* of administering laws [lit: of dropping laws] ☞ Cf: -wisa 'cause to fall' R37.2

yoxolo *n5-sg-poss-n6-sg* of peace R34.12

Z

z-[1] *n4-pl-them* [group 4 plural thematic consonant prefix] ☞ See: zonke XED:189

z-[2] *n4-pl-S1* they VERB [group 4 plural subject (S1) agreement prefix before vowel-initial verb] Agr: izi- R11

z-[3] *n4-pl-S3a* (and) they VERB [group 4 plural present subjunctive verb subject (S3a) agreement prefix before vowel-initial verb] R11=2

-z-[4] *n4-pl-obj-prf* them [group 4 plural short object form before vowel initial verb] ☞ Alt: -zi- E&S:18

z-[5] *n5-pl-them* [group 5 plural thematic consonant prefix] ☞ See: zonke XED:189

-z-[6] *n5-pl-obj-prf* them [group 5 plural short object form before vowel initial verb] ☞ Alt: -zi- E&S:18

z-[7] *v-refl-prf* -self, -selves, VERB oneself [reflexive verb prefix] Structure: placed immediately before a vowel verb root in the same position as OBJ agreement prefixes, and mutually exclusive thereto ☞ See: zi- R36

-z-[8] *v-suf-caus* make VERB, cause to VERB [causative verb suffix on verbs ending in -la] • *-khathaza 'bother s.o.' [= khathal/z-a], -khumbuza 'remind' [= khumbul/z-a]* ☞ See: -is- AXG:112, R2, R9

za-[1] *n4-pl-poss* of [group 4 plural possessive agreement prefix] Agr: izi- AM-94:163, E&S:22, SXWU:35f, XED:189;xv, R1, R9, R11

za-[2] *n4-pl-S3b-pos* (and) they VERBed [group 4 plural past subjunctive positive verb subject (S3b) agreement prefix] (CGB:189), E&S:42, MI:247, SXWU:141, XED:189

za-[3] *n5-pl-poss* of [group 5 plural possessive agreement prefix] Agr: ii-, iiN-, izin- AM-94:163, E&S:22, SXWU:35f, XED:189;xv, R4c=2, R16, R20

za-[4] *n5-pl-S3b-pos* (and) they VERBed [group 5 plural past subjunctive positive verb subject (S3b) agreement prefix] (CGB:189), E&S:42, MI:247, SXWU:141, XED:189

za-[5] *n6-pl-poss* of [group 6 plural possessive agreement prefix] • *zalapha 'of those (languages) here'* Agr: iiN-, iziN- XED:189;xv, R37.2

za-[6] *n6-pl-S3b-pos* (and) they VERBed [group 6 plural past subjunctive positive verb subject (S3b) agreement prefix] (CGB:189), MI:247, XED:189

-za[7] *v-intr* come; [ext] come after (a preceding child) latent vowel verb ☞ Cf: iza CGB:125f, E&S:51, PCX:21f, RD-96:394, SXWU:32, XED:189, R5x

-za[8] *v-aux* come to (do s.t.); come and VERB [venitive auxiliary] Structure: followed by verb with reduced infinitive prefix DFG, TD, R5

-za[9] *v-aux* then, and then • *waza wapendula kubo 'then he answered them'; waza wati kuye 'and he said to him'* Structure: S3b-za S3b-Δ-a; expresses sequence in time, one event following the other E&S:47, KED:483, R33x

-za-[10] *v-aux-fut* will / shall VERB; going to VERB [near future positive preverb] Structure: S1-za ku-Δ-a ☞ Neg: -zi-; See also: -ya- CGB:165, E&S:20, R4d, R32=2

-za[11] *v-aux-imp* should, shalt • *nize nifake ifoto 'you should enclose a picture'* Structure: S3a-ze S3a Δ-e E&S:47, XED:190;189, R4bx

-za-ku- -a *v-fut-near* will VERB, going to VERB Structure: S1-za-ku-Δ-a E&S:20

zaba[2] *deic-1-n1-pl-poss-n5-pl* of these (people) PCX:140

zaba[3] *deic-1-n1-pl-poss-n6-pl* of these (people) R17.0

-zabalaza *v-tr* endeavor, struggle (to free oneself), make an all-out effort, attempt; wrestle with • *Indoda izabalaza de kulunge 'A man struggles until he succeeds'* GDX3:641, R32, R36.22

zabantu *n5-pl-poss-n1-pl* of the people R16, R23.4, R27.6, R37=6

zabantwana[1] *n4-pl-poss-n1-pl* of children R24.8

zabantwana[2] *n5-pl-poss-n1-pl* of children R25.7

zabe[1] *preverb-past-n4-pl* they had VERBed; they did VERB [group 4 plural remote past compound tense preverb] Structure: zabe zi-Δ (participial verb form) ☞ Alt: zaye E&S:39, GDX3:714, PCX:186

zabe[2] *preverb-past-n5-pl* they had VERBed; they did VERB [group 5 plural remote past compound tense preverb] Structure: zabe zi-Δ (participial verb form) ☞ Alt: zaye E&S:39, GDX3:714, PCX:186

zabe[3] *preverb-past-n6-pl* they had VERBed; they did VERB [group 6 plural remote past compound tense preverb] Structure: zabe zi-Δ (participial verb form) ☞ Alt: zaye SG-3:119;124

zabo[1] *n1-pl-poss-n4-pl* of them; their (own); theirs CGB:183, E&S:22, GDX3:691, XED:189, R27

zabo[2] *n1-pl-poss-n5-pl* of them; their (own); theirs za- Possessive formative + -bo, from 'bona', the absolute pronoun for Class1(PL) CGB:183, E&S:22, GDX3:691, XED:189, R19, R20=2, R31

zabo[3] *n7-poss-n4-pl* its; of it GDX3:691

zabo[4] *n7-poss-n5-pl* its; of it GDX3:691

zakhe[1] *n1-sg-poss-n4-pl* his, her, its CGB:182, E&S:22, GDX3:691, XED:189

zakhe[2] *n1-sg-poss-n5-pl* his, her, its CGB:182, E&S:22, GDX3:691, XED:189

zakho[1] *pro-2sg-poss-n4-pl* your, yours; thy; your own [singular] CGB:182, E&S:22, GDX3:691, XED:189, R7, R31, R34

zakho[2] *pro-2sg-poss-n5-pl* your, yours; thy; your own [singular] E&S:22, GDX3:691, PCX:60, R14=2, R19.0, R21.11, R29.5, R31.3, R34.12=2

zakho[3] *pro-2sg-poss-n6-pl* your, yours; thy; your own [singular] R21

zako[1] *n8-vn-poss-n4-pl* its, of it GDX3:691

zako[2] *n8-vn-poss-n5-pl* its, of it GDX3:691

zako[3] *n10-loc-poss-n4-pl* its, of it GDX3:691

zako[4] *n10-loc-poss-n5-pl* its, of it GDX3:691

zaku-[1] *n4-pl-temp* when they VERB / VERBed [group 4 plural temporal verb construction] • *Zakufika 'When they arrive'* E&S:42, PCX:89; 91

zaku-[2] *n5-pl-temp* when they VERB / VERBed [group 5 plural temporal verb construction] • *Zakufika 'When they arrive'* E&S:42

zaku-[3] *n6-pl-temp* when they VERB / VERBed [group 6 plural temporal verb construction] • *nazintsuku zakubuya 'when those days return'* MQH1:29

zakufika *v-temp* upon their arrival PCX:91, R32.4

zakwaGoniwe *n5-pl-poss-loc-n-prop* of Goniwe R26.2

zakwamkhozi *n5-pl-poss-loc-n2-sg* confidentially [lit: of confidence] • *indaba zakwamkhozi 'confidential information'* R18.6

zakwaPhalo *n5-pl-poss-loc-pn* of Phalo (place of Chief Phalo in the Xhosa region) R32.4

-zala[1] *v-tr* beget, generate, bear / father (child); lay (eggs) AXG:17, EXD:209, PCX:50, XED:190, R2x

-zala[2] *v-st* become full; grow, increase ☞ Perf: -zele XED:190, R18x

zalapha[1] *deic-1-n9-loc-poss-n4-pl* of this place (here) • *kwizibhedlele zalapha eKapa 'in the hospitals here in Cape Town'* R37.12

zalapha[2] *deic-1-n9-loc-poss-n5-pl* of this place (here) • *Le ntombazana yayisebenza kwenye yeevenkile ezinkulu zalapha eDikeni 'This girl was working in the big shops here in Alice'* CD:39

zalapha[3] *deic-1-n9-loc-poss-n6-pl* of this place (here) • *iilwimi zonke zalapha 'all the languages of this area'* R37.2

zale *deic-1-n2-pl-poss* of these • *iingcambu zale mithi 'the roots of these trees'* PCX:140

-zalelwa *v-ben* be born at / in KED:485, R28

zalisa *v-tr* help in childbirth (generate), cause to become full XED:190, R13.7

zalo[1] *n3-sg-poss-n4-pl* his, her, its; of him, her, it GDX3:691

zalo[2] *n3-sg-poss-n5-pl* his, her, its; of him, her, it GDX3:691

zalo[3] *n6-sg-poss-n4-pl* its; of it GDX3:691

zalo[4] *n6-sg-poss-n5-pl* its; of it GDX3:691

zalo[5] *deic-1-n2-sg-poss* of this • *iingcambu zalo mthi 'the roots of this tree'* PCX:140

zam[1] *pro-1sg-poss-n4-pl* of me; my, mine; my own • *izandla zam 'my hands'* AM-94:151, E&S:22, GDX3:691, PCX:60; 72, XED:189, R33.2

zam[2] *pro-1sg-poss-n5-pl* of me; my, mine; my own • *iincwadi zam 'my books'* AM-94:151, E&S:22, GDX3:691, PCX:60; 72, SXWU:36, XED:189

zam[3] *pro-1sg-poss-n6-pl* of me; my, mine; my own • *ezi ntshaba zam 'these enemies of mine'* MQH1:11

zama-[1] *combo* of • *izikolo zamabanga aphantsi 'elementary schools' [lit: schools of lower grades]* indicates that n3 pl (ama-) is possessed by a n4 pl (za-) ☞ See: za- + ama- R9

zama-[2] *combo* of • *iinkokeli zamazwe 'the leaders of countries'* indicates that n3 pl (ama-) is possessed by a n5 pl (za-) ☞ See: za- + ama- R16

-zama[3] *v-tr* shake, move (as tree in wind); struggle (with), exert oneself, strain; strive, try; persevere; urge, press RD-96:416, XED:190, R9, R35x=2, R36.21, R37.16

zamabanga *n3-pl-poss* of grades R9

zamabanjwa *n5-sg-poss-n3-pl* of prisoners R31.4

zamajoni *n5-pl-poss-n3-pl* of soldiers from Eng. "John" name used by British troops for other troops R36.9

zamakhwenkwe *n3-pl-poss* of boys R36.9

zamashishini *n3-pl-poss* of businesses R35.13

zamasoka *n5-pl-poss-n3-pl* of the bachelors R36.9

zamazwe *n3-pl-poss* of countries R16, R33.6

zamkelwe *v-pass-short-past* accepted R29.5

zamva *n2-sg-poss-n5-pl* of later; [atr] subsequent ☞ See: umva R30.3

-zanga *preverb* never VERB ☞ See: zange E&S:47

zangasese *n5-pl-poss-adv* secret R36.11

zange *preverb-neg* never VERBed • *Abazange basebenze 'They never* *worked'* Structure: followed by a present subjunctive construction to form the remote past negative E&S:19; 47, EXD:402, R23.3.6.7

zango *n5-pl-poss-adv* of / in NUM [followed by year] R33.11

-zantsi *n-root* low; south, southern ☞ See: izantsi, umzantsi RD-96:416;121, XED:190, R10, R16, R37

zaphuli *n4-pl-red* breakers ☞ See: -aphula R31.2

zaqapheleka *v-intr-past* that were obvious • *enye yezinto ezathi zaqapheleka 'one of the things which was obvious'* ☞ See: -qapheleka R37.12

zaqhubeka *v-atr-past* they continued R36.6

zaseAfrika *n5-sg-pred-loc* African, of those in Africa R16=2

zaseYurophu *n5-pl-poss-pn* those of Europe R32.4

zaseziyunivesithi *n5-pl-poss-loc-n5-sg* of the university R37.10

zaso[1] *n4-sg-poss-n4-pl* his, her, its; of him, her, it GDX3:691

zaso[2] *n4-sg-poss-n5-pl* his, her, its; of him, her, it GDX3:691

zavakala *v-atr-past* be clear R23.8

zawo[1] *n2-sg-poss-n4-pl* its; of it GDX3:691

zawo[2] *n2-sg-poss-n5-pl* its; of it GDX3:691

zawo[3] *n3-pl-poss-n4-pl* their, of them GDX3:691

zawo[4] *n3-pl-poss-n5-pl* their, of them GDX3:691

zaye[1] *preverb-past-n4-pl* they had VERBed; they did VERB [group 4 plural remote past compound tense preverb] Structure: zaye zi-Δ (participial verb form) ☞ Alt: zabe AXG:93f, E&S:39, GDX3:714

zaye[2] *preverb-past-n5-pl* they had VERBed; they did VERB [group 5 plural remote past compound tense preverb] Structure: zaye zi-Δ (participial verb form) ☞ Alt: zabe AXG:93f, E&S:39, GDX3:714

zaye[3] *preverb-past-n6-pl* they had VERBed; they did VERB [group 6 plural remote past compound tense preverb] Structure: zaye zi-Δ (participial verb form) ☞ Alt: zabe AXG:93f

zayeka *v-tr-past* they leave rem past za + yeka 'to leave off, desist' R36.6

zayo[1] *n2-pl-poss-n4-pl* their; of them GDX3:691

zayo[2] *n2-pl-poss-n5-pl* their; of them GDX3:691

zayo[3] *n5-sg-poss-n4-pl* his, her, its; of him, her, it GDX3:691, XED:189, R13.9

zayo[4] *n5-sg-poss-n5-pl* his, her, its; of him, her, it GDX3:691, XED:189

zayo[5] *n5-pl-poss-n5-sg* of it • *inika izimvo zayo '...give opinions of it...'* R24.7, R37.5

zazi-[1] *n4-pl-remote-past* they had VERBed [group 4 plural contracted remote past compound tense] used in compound tenses AXG:93f, E&S:39, PCX:186

zazi-[2] *n5-pl-remote-past* they had VERBed [group 5 plural contracted remote past compound tense] AXG:93f, E&S:39, PCX:186

zazi-[3] *n6-pl-remote-past* they had VERBed [group 6 plural contracted remote past compound tense] AXG:93f

zazinqongophele *v-aux-part* they were scarce za-(past) +Participial form zinqongophele R28.3

zazo[1] *n4-pl-poss-n4-pl* their; of them • *Izaphuli-mthetho ziyazi ukuba azohlwaywa ngezenzo zazo 'Criminals know they won't be punished for their deeds'* GDX3:691, R11

zazo[2] *n4-pl-poss-n5-pl* their; of them GDX3:691

zazo[3] *n5-pl-poss-n4-pl* their; of them GDX3:691

zazo[4] *n5-pl-poss-n5-pl* their; of them GDX3:691

ze[1] *n5-pl-poss* of, belonging to • *Iimpawu zamva zeAIDS 'advanced signs of AIDS'* za + i- R23.1, R27.9, R30.3

-ze[2] *v-aux-imp* should, shalt [used to suggest or exhort action, e.g., expressing a command, giving emphatic form to such a command]; never [in some negatives]; just [in other expressions] • *nize nifake ifoto 'you should enclose a picture'; uz' ungebi 'Thou shall not steal'; aze angayikhasi 'They never support'* used as an auxiliary to add color to other verb phrases, it is derived from ukuza 'to come' ☞ Contrast: the adj/atr -ze 'naked, bare' with which there exists no relationship E&S:42; 47, EXD:403, XED:189, XED:190;189, R4b, R10

zedrop *loan* of drop R25.2

zeenkomo *n5-pl* of cows R27.9

zehagu *n5-sg-poss* of the pig • *...iintwala zehagu 'swine lice'* R25.4=2

-zeka *v-tr* take to oneself; marry; obtain, receive, incur; grip, hold fast to also source of nouns such as umzekelo 'example' XED:190, R10x

zekomiti *n4-pl-poss-n5-sg* of the committee R22.5

zeKrismesi *n5-pl-poss-n5-loan* of Christmas R31.1

zeli-[1] *combo* of • *iimbono zelizwe 'the views of the nation'* indicates that n3 sg (ili-) is possessed by a n5 pl (za-) ☞ See: za- + ili- R30

zeli[2] *deic-1-n3-sg-poss* of this R13.6, R32.7

zelizwe *n3-sg-poss* of the country R30

zem- *combo* of • *izisulu zempela-veki 'weekend specials'* indicates that n5 sg (im-) is possessed by a n4 pl (za-) ☞ See: za- + im- TD, R1

zemfundo *n5-sg-poss* of education R22

zemi- *combo* of • *iinkqubo zemidlalo 'sports programs'* indicates that n2 pl (imi-) is possessed by a n5 pl (za-) ☞ See: za- + imi- R4c, R12

zempela-veki *n4-pl-poss-time-n5-sg* of the weekend TD, R1

zemveli *n5-pl-poss-n5-sg* of the time R20.1

zendlela *n5-sg-poss* of the road R31.1

zeni- -e *preverb* you [plural] ought to VERB Structure: zeni-Δ-e (present subjunctive) ☞ Neg: zeni-nga--i; Sg: uzu- CGB:168f, R4bx

zeni-nga- -i *preverb-neg* you [plural] ought not to VERB Structure: zeni-nga-Δ-i (negative present subjunctive) ☞ Pos: zeni--e; Sg: zeni- CGB:169

zenkcenkce *n5-pl-poss-n5-sg* of zinc, tin, corrugated sheeting R35.6

zenu[1] *pro-2pl-poss-n4-pl* of you; your, yours; your own [plural] • *izifundo zenu 'your lessons'* E&S:22, GDX3:691, PCX:60

zenu[2] *pro-2pl-poss-n5-pl* of you; your, yours; your own [plural] • *iincwadi zenu 'your books'* CGB:182, E&S:22, GDX3:691, PCX:60, R31.4

zenu[3] *pro-2pl-poss-n6-pl* of you; your, yours; your own [plural] • *phantsi kweenyawo zenu 'down at your feet'* MQH1:69

zenza *v-pres-n4-pl* they do R11

zenze *v-perf* done, made R37.10

zenziwe *v-pass-perf* which are made, done R21.10, R35.6

zesikolo *n5-pl-poss-n4-sg* of school R18.0

zesondo *n5-pl-poss-n3-sg* of sex R30.5, R36.18.20

zethu[1] *pro-1pl-poss-n4-pl* of us; our, ours; our own [plural] • *izifundo zethu 'our lessons'* CGB:182, E&S:22, GDX3:691, PCX:60, R7=2

zethu[2] *pro-1pl-poss-n5-pl* of us; our, ours; our own [plural] • *iincwadi zethu 'our books'* CGB:182, E&S:22, GDX3:691, PCX:60; 72, R13.3, R23.4

zethu[3] *pro-1pl-poss-n6-pl* of us; our, ours; our own [plural] • *ziintshaba zethu 'they are our enemies'* MQH1:12

zexesha *n5-pl-poss-n3-sg* time R35.12

zezaa[1] *deic-3-n4-pl-pred* those (far, yonder) are E&S:26

zezaa[2] *deic-3-n5-pl-pred* those (far, yonder) are E&S:26

zezemhlonele *rel-cop-v-tr* those who revere him R13.3

zezi[1] *n5-pl-poss-n5-pl* of these R30.3

zezi[2] *deic-1-n4-pl-pred* these are; it is these E&S:26, PCX:99

zezi[3] *deic-1-n5-pl-pred* these are E&S:26

zezigebenga *n5-pl-poss-n5-pl* by the murderers ☞ -gebeng- = fall upon, kill and rob R32.5

zezikolo *n5-pl-poss-n4-pl* of schools R22.4

zeziphi *rel-enum* which of R23.5

zezo[1] *pro-rel* those which R37.3

zezo[2] *deic-2-n4-pl-pred* these are E&S:26

zezo[3] *deic-2-n5-pl-pred* these are E&S:26

zezokuba *cop-conj* they are for R36.25

zi-[1] *n4-pl-red-prf* [group 4 plural reduced noun prefix] • *ezi zikhalazo 'these causes for complaint'* Loss of article i- from izi- R27

-zi-[2] *n4-pl-obj* them [group 4 plural object agreement prefix] Agr: izi-, iz- E&S:18, PCX:51, SXWU:44, XED:191, R7

zi-[3] *n4-pl-adj-pred* they are ADJ [group 4 plural adjective agreement prefix used predicatively] E&S:28, MI:248, PCX:118f

zi-[4] *n4-pl-enum-prf* [group 4 plural enumerative agreement prefix] ☞ See: zimbi, ziphi E&S:27, PCX:110f

zi-[5] *n4-pl-voc-prf* oh!, hey! [group 4 plural vocative noun prefix] • *zihlobo 'friends!'* Agr: izi- TD, R5

zi-[6] *n4-pl-S1* they VERB [group 4 plural subject (S1) agreement prefix] Agr: izi- CGB:117; 158, E&S:17f, PCX:51;24f, SXWU:28, XED:191, R1, R7, R11

zi-[7] *n4-pl-S2* they [group 4 plural participial subject (S2) agreement prefix] AXG:91, CGB:191

zi-[8] *n4-pl-S3a* (and) they VERB [group 4 plural present subjunctive verb subject (S3a) agreement prefix] (CGB:167), R11x

zi-[9] *n4-pl-rel2* they who / those which [group 4 plural direct relative 2 construction, attributive agreement prefix used predicatively] E&S:34, MI:153; 248, PCX:151, R7

zi-[10] *n4-pl-ind-rel2* whom, which [group 4 plural indirect relative 2 agreement prefix] E&S:35

zi-[11] *n5-pl-red-prf* [group 5 plural reduced noun prefix] • *ezi zinto 'these things'* Loss of article i- from izi- R36

-zi-[12] *n5-pl-obj* them [group 5 plural object agreement prefix] Agr: ii-, iiN-, iziN- E&S:18, PCX:51, SXWU:44, XED:191

zi-[13] *n5-pl-enum-prf* [group 5 plural enumerative agreement prefix] ☞ See: zimbi, ziphi E&S:27, PCX:110f

zi-[14] *n5-pl-S1* they [group 5 plural subject (S1) agreement prefix] Agr: ii-, iiN-, izi- CGB:117; 158,

E&S:17f, PCX:51, SXWU:28, XED:191

zi-[15] *n5-pl-S2* they [group 5 plural participial subject (S2) agreement prefix] AXG:91, CGB:191

zi-[16] *n5-pl-S3a* (and) they VERB [group 5 plural present subjunctive verb subject (S3a) agreement prefix] (CGB:167), R8=2

zi-[17] *n5-pl-rel2* they who / those which [group 5 plural direct relative 2 construction, attributive agreement prefix used predicatively] E&S:34, MI:153; 248, PCX:151

zi-[18] *n5-pl-ind-rel2* whom, which [group 5 plural indirect relative 2 agreement prefix] E&S:35

zi-[19] *n6-pl-S1* they [group 6 plural subject (S1) agreement prefix] Agr: ii-, iziN- CGB:117; 158

zi-[20] *n6-pl-S2* they [group 6 plural participial subject (S2) agreement prefix] AXG:91, CGB:191

zi-[21] *n6-pl-S3a* (and) they VERB [group 6 plural present subjunctive verb subject (S3a) agreement prefix] (CGB:167)

zi-[22] *n6-pl-rel2* they who / those which [group 6 plural direct relative 2 construction, attributive agreement prefix used predicatively] MI:248

zi-[23] *n6-pl-ind-rel2* which [group 6 plural indirect relative 2 agreement prefix] (E&S:35)

-zi-[24] *preverb-fut-neg* will not VERB; not going to VERB [near future negative preverb] Structure: a-SNEG-zi-ku-Δ-a ☞ Pos: -za-; See also: -yi- CGB:166, E&S:20

zi-[25] *v-refl-prf* -self, -selves, VERB oneself [reflexive verb prefix] • *zithanda 'like oneself'* Structure: placed immediately before the verb root in the same position as OBJ agreement prefixes, and mutually exclusive thereto ☞ Alt: z- [before a vowel verb] CGB:134, E&S:59, SXWU:45, XED:191, R2, R4c, R4d, R11, R14, R22

ziba *v-aux* they are, they become R37.16

zibandakanya *n5-pl-VERB* they include, bind together, unite R35.8, R36.11

zibe[1] *preverb-recent-pro-n4-pl* they were VERBing [group 4 plural recent past compound tense preverb] Structure: zibe zi-Δ (participial construction) AXG:91f, E&S:37, PCX:183

zibe[2] *preverb-recent-pro-n5-pl* they were VERBing [group 5 plural recent past compound tense preverb] Structure: zibe zi-Δ (participial construction) AXG:91f, E&S:37, PCX:183

zibe[3] *preverb-recent-pro-n6-pl* they were VERBing [group 6 plural recent past compound tense preverb] Structure: zibe zi-Δ (participial construction) AXG:91f

zibe[4] *v-aux-sub* that they should be R37.19

zibhalwe *v-pass-perf* they were written R7

zibhodi *n5-pl-agent* by the boards • *akananzwa zibhodi ezidlulileyo 'perceived by the boards of the past'* R37.20

zibukeka *v-atr* they are admired / liked R11

zicaciswe *v-caus-pass-short-past* they have been explained R37.7

zidilizelwe *v-ben-pass-perf* they were demolished to their disadvantage • *zidilizelwe imzi yazo 'they have their houses demolished'* Passive benefactive reflects action against subject - here the families have their houses demolished [lit: are demolished of their houses] R26.3

-zifaka e- *v-refl-cmp* get oneself involved in, meddle with Structure: reflexive verb with locative noun construction XED:37, R2

zifana *v-pres* they are like / similar to R11

zifanayo *v-rel-recip* alike R21.2

zife *v-pres-sub* they should die R25.4

zifumane *v-tr-sub* they find R26.8

zifunde *v-n5-pl-pres-sub* that they should learn R16

zifundo *n4-pl-red* lessons, subjects ☞ See: izifundo R29.17

zifunwa *v-pass* they are wanted R31.2

zifunyanwa *v-pass* they are found ☞ rw: -fuman- R25.7

zigwetywe *v-pass-perf* they were condemned ☞ See: -gweba R32.7

zigxothwe *v-pass-perf* they were expelled R26.8

zihamba *v-intr-pres* they go R27.6

zihambe *v-intr-sub* they should go R34.12

zihleka *v-part* they laughing R36.6

zihlobo *n4-pl-voc* friends! [vocative] term of address TD, R5

-zihlupha *v-refl* trouble oneself; get anxious; waste one's own time R4c

ziiMarketing Assistants *cop-n5-pl-loan* they are Marketing Assistants R29.11

ziiN-[1] *n5-pl-pred-prf* they are [group 5 plural copulative or predicative prefix construction on polysyllabic roots] • *ziintombi 'they are girls'* PCX:96, R18

ziiN-[2] *n5-pl-agent* by them [group 5 plural passive agent prefix construction on polysyllabic roots] • *amagumbi elizaliswe ziincwadi 'rooms filled by books'* R18.2

ziincwadi[1] *n5-pl-pred* they are books R18.4

ziincwadi[2] *n5-pl-agent* by books R18.2

ziindaba *n6-pl-pred* they are news R18.6, R23.12

ziinkanuko *n5-pl-agent* by lust, out of desires R36.18

zijinga *v-intr-part* them swinging R32.8

zijongelwe *v-ben-pass-short-past* who/which were looked on as R37.8

zika[1] *n4-pl-poss-prf* of [personal possessive prefix / marker for noun group 4 plural] Agr: izi- E&S:23f, PCX:109

zika[2] *n5-pl-poss-prf* of [personal possessive prefix / marker for noun group 5 plural] Agr: izi- E&S:23f, PCX:109, R20.2

zikabawo *n5-pl-poss-n1a-sg* of our father • *hayi zinto zikabawo 'now then, children of our father' (figuratively, my brothers and sisters)* R20.2

zikandabazabantu *n5-pl-poss-n5-sg-poss-n1-pl-comp* of the affairs of the people; [atr] governmental • *iiofisi zikandabazabantu 'the government offices'* R37.13.14

zikawonkewonke *n5-sg-poss-n-redupl-enum* for everbody R35.8, R36.11

zikhalazo *n4-pl-red* the cause of complaint, complaints rel formed from verb R27.14

zikhethe *v-sub* that they choose R22.3

zikho[1] *v-exis-n4-pl* they are here / present E&S:29, ITX:17

zikho[2] *v-exis-n5-pl* they are here / present E&S:29, ITX:17

zikhona *v-exis-n4-pl* there are R1

zikhumbule *v-tr-imp* keep in mind, remember R13.3

zikhuphe *v-tr-perf* they released, issued R37.10

-zikisa *v-tr* cut deep, hoe, plough; make quite plain; [ext] use to the best advantage; [fig] ponder RD-96:416, XED:191

ziko *n3-sg-red* hearth; center ☞ See: iziko R35=8

zikumgangatho *n5-pl-n2-sg-comp* of a (relegated) status R37.19

zilandelayo *v-rel-ben* which are the following R22.5, R29.17, R37.3.5

zilayisha *v-part* they being loaded R26.8

zilula *atr-n4-pl* they are easy R7

zimanzi *cop-atr* they being wet R26.8

-zimasa *v-tr* support, fix firmly, establish, confirm; frequent, support by one's presence or company XED:192, R36.09x

zimbi[1] *enum-pro-n4-pl* others, some others (of a different kind) Structure: RED noun form + ENUM or ENUM + FULL noun form ☞ See: -mbi E&S:27, PCX:110

zimbi[2] *enum-pro-n5-pl* others, some others (of a different kind) Structure: RED noun form + ENUM or ENUM + FULL noun form ☞ See: -mbi E&S:27, PCX:110

zimbini *n5-pl-num* two [lit: who are two] • *Ezi nkokeli zimbini 'these two leaders'* R16, R26.2.8, R37.7

-zimeleyo *v-refl-perf-rel-atr* having stood on one's own, independent, self-governing, free (from control) (EXD:299), (GDX3:663), R34.5, R37.2

-zimisele *v-refl-perf-atr* be sincere, serious ☞ See: -misela; rw: -ma EXD:572, R4d, R29, R33, R34.5.9

zimoyika *v-n5-pl-S1* they fear R13.3

ziN-[1] *n5-pl-voc-prf* oh!, hey! [group 5 plural vocative noun prefix] • *zinqununu 'principals!'* Agr: iziN- AXG:28, E&S:32, PCX:54, R9

ziN-[2] *n5-pl-adj-pred* they are ADJ [group 5 plural adjective agreement prefix used predicatively] E&S:28, MI:248, PCX:118f

-zin-[3] *loc-n5-pl-prf* in, on, at [contracted form of group 5 plural affix used after the locative e-] • *ezinyaweni 'on one's feet', bezifaka ezinkathazweni 'getting themselves into troubles'* ☞ See: e- + iziN- PCX:69, R2

ziN-[4] *n6-pl-voc-prf* oh!, hey! [group 6 plural vocative noun prefix] • *zintsana 'babies!'* Agr: iiN- E&S:32, PCX:55

zin-[5] *n6-pl-adj-pred* they are ADJ [group 6 plural adjective agreement prefix used predicatively] MI:248

-zin-[6] *loc-n6-pl-prf* in, on, at [contracted form of group 6 plural affix used after the locative e-] • *Uphinde wasezindabeni 'She was again in the news'* ☞ See: e- + iziN- PCX:69, R33

zingabikho *v-cop-loc-neg* they are not present R37.13

zingakhange *v-aux-neg* without having ever VERBed R37.10

zingama *n5-pl-pred-num-n3-pl-expr* they are NUM R33.9

-zingela *v-tr* hunt, pursue, prey; scout PCX:90, RD-96:416, XED:192

zingungqikana *v-intr-recip* they were wandering aimlessly from -gungqa 'move back and forth' with neuter and reciprocal extensions - the latter adds to the expressive description of aimless wandering R26.6

zini[1] *qw-n4-pl* what kind?, of what sort? • *zizwe zini? 'what sort of nations?'* ☞ See: -ni PCX:28;118

zini[2] *qw-n5-pl* what kind?, of what sort? • *zinto zini? 'what sort of things?'* ☞ See: -ni PCX:28;118

zininzi *n5pl-cop-atr* there are many R29.4, R37.13

zinomdla *v-poss* they are interested in [lit: have interest] R16

zinqunqwe *v-pass-pres-sub* they should be chopped R8

zinqununu *n5-pl-voc* principals! [vocative] term of address ☞ Sg: inqununu R9

zintle *atr-n5-pl* they are pretty R11

zinto *n5-pl-red* things, items ☞ See: izinto PCX:28, R20.2, R22.5, R36.23

zinyusa *v-pres* they raising • *lokuba zinyusa ingxowa-mali yazo 'the way they are raising their funds'* R9

zinzileyo *v-perf-rel* firm; stable ☞ Alt: zinzile RD-96:416

-zinzisa *v-tr* fix, make firm; establish; bed (a stone) RD-96:416, XED:192

-ziphatha *v-refl* behave, carry oneself, handle oneself ☞ Perf: -ziphethe XED:125, R11, R36.20

-ziphethe *v-refl-perf* behaved R11

ziphi[1] *qw-n4-pl* which (ones)? E&S:27, GDX3:703, PCX:111

ziphi[2] *qw-loc-adv-n4-pl* where are? ☞ See: -phi E&S:31, PCX:111

ziphi[3] *qw-n5-pl* which (ones)? E&S:27, GDX3:703, PCX:111

ziphi[4] *qw-loc-adv-n5-pl* where are? ☞ See: -phi E&S:31, PCX:111

zipho *n4-pl-red* gifts R35.7

ziphuculiwe *v-pass-perf* it is improved ☞ Cf: ziphuculwe R28.1

ziphuculwe *v-pass-short-past* that they be uplifted ☞ Cf: ziphuculiwe R37.19

ziqapheleke *v-atr-sub* they should get noticed ☞ See: -qapheleka R37.7

ziqhuba *v-tr* they drive, press on R37.26

-ziqhubele *v-refl* move oneself ahead R34.9

ziqokelela *v-tr-ben* they were gathering R26.4

zirhalarhume *n4-pl-red* violent men R36.6

-zisa *v-tr* bring; make come ☞ rw: -za RD-96:416, XED:190

zisafuna *v-prog-tr* they still need R37.5

zisejele *cop-loc-n5-sg-loan* they were in jail R32.7

zisenabantu *v-poss-n1-pl* they have people (i.e., are staffed by...) R37.13

zisetyenziselwa *v-caus-ben-pass* they are used for R35.6

zisetyenziswa *v-caus-pass-n5-pl* they are used R35.6

zisetyenziswe *v-pass-pres-sub* they should be used R30.7, R37.20

ziseziseleni *cop-loc-n4-pl* they are in cells R20.7

zisikwe *v-pass-pres-sub* they should be cut (up) R8

zisithi *v-part* they saying R36.6

zitshintshile *v-perf* they have changed R27.8

zitshise *v-caus* they burned R18.0

zityunjwe *v-pass-past* they were selected ☞ rw: -tyumba R37.3

zivuke *v-pres-sub* and they rise R25.4

zivuliwe *v-pass* they are open R27

zixhomekeke *v-st* they should depend on R29.15

ziya *v-aux-fut* they are going R34.12

ziyakuba *v-aux-fut* they will be R37.11

ziyakupheza *v-intr-fut* they will stop -pheza 'desist' R36.6

ziyathengiswa *v-caus-pass* they are sold R35.5

ziyayazi *n5-pl-pres-n5-sg-v* they know it R37.11

ziyazi *v-irreg-vowel-n4-pl-S1* they know R11

ziyi- *n5-pl-pred* they are (a price of) • *Xa zizonke iimbiza ziyi-50 yi-R40 'For quantities of 50, it's R40.00'* R25.7

ziyingozi *n5-pl-pred* they are dangerous R30.7

zizakukhutshwa *v-rel-fut* that will be released R18.4

zizangqa *n4-pl-pred* they are circles ☞ See: isangqa R8

zizazela *n4-pl-agent* by conscience R36.22.23

zizi-[1] *n4-pl-pred-prf* they are [group 4 plural copulative or predicative prefix construction] • *zizilo 'they are wild animals'* CGB:135, E&S:21; 25, PCX:96, XED:xvi, R8

zizi-[2] *n4-pl-agent-prf* by (done by, produced by) them [marker of group 4 plural agent of passive verb] E&S:25; 43, R9

zizi-[3] *n5-pl-pred-prf* they are [group 5 plural copulative or predicative prefix construction on monosyllabic roots] • *zizinja 'they are dogs'* E&S:21; 25, PCX:96, XED:xvi

zizi-[4] *n5-pl-agent-prf* by (done by, produced by) them [marker of group 5 plural agent of passive verb] E&S:25; 43, R4c

zizi-[5] *n6-pl-pred-prf* they are [group 6 plural copulative or predicative prefix construction] XED:xvi

zizikolo *n4-pl-agent* by schools R9

zizikrelemnqa *cop-n4-pl* by vandals R18.1

zizilambi *n4-pl-pred* they become sufferers of starvation ☞ Sg: isilambi; Cf: -lamba R26.5

zizinto *n5-pl-agent* by the things R4c

ziziphakamiso *n4-pl-pred* motions are R37.5

zizixhiphothi *n4-pl-agent* by the robust, bearded people zizi agentive copulative followed by N ☞ GDX3:585 R32.5

zizo[1] *n4-pl-pred* they are; it is they [group 4 plural copulative or predicative] E&S:21, PCX:98, XED:192

zizo[2] *n4-pl-agent* by them [group 4 plural agent of passive verb] XED:192

zizo[3] *n5-pl-pred* they are; it is they [group 5 plural copulative or predicative] E&S:21, PCX:98, XED:192

zizo[4] *n5-pl-agent* by them [group 5 plural agent of passive verb] XED:192

zizo[5] *n6-pl-pred* they are; it is they [group 6 plural copulative or predicative] XED:192

zizo[6] *n6-pl-agent* by them [group 6 plural agent of passive verb] XED:192

zizonke *v-pred* they are all R25.7

zizwe *n4-pl-red* nations ☞ See: izizwe PCX:25

-zo[1] *n4-pl-root* they; their [group 4 plural pronoun root] ☞ See: nazo, yazo, zazo E&S:22, R1, R9, R11

-zo[2] *n5-pl-root* they; their [group 5 plural pronoun root] E&S:22, R11, R33=3

zo-[3] *v-n4-pl-short-fut* they will VERB [contracted / short positive future group 4 plural noun prefix] E&S:20

zo-[4] *v-n5-pl-short-fut* they will VERB [contracted / short positive future group 5 plural noun prefix] E&S:20

zo-[5] *v-n6-pl-short-fut* they will VERB [contracted / short positive future group 6 plural noun prefix] (E&S:20)

zobugcisa *n5-pl-poss-n7-sg* of skill R35.6

zodumo *n5-pl-poss-n6-sg* of the famous (plural) R33.6

zodwa[1] *pro-quan-n4-pl* only they; they alone Agr: izi-, zona E&S:27, PCX:62

zodwa[2] *pro-quan-n5-pl* only they; they alone Agr: izi(N)-, zona E&S:27, PCX:62

-zohlwaya *v-refl* repent [lit: rebuke oneself] RD-96:416

zohlwaywe *v-pass-vowel-sub-pres-n4-pl* they should be punished R11

zoku- *combo* of • *izifundo zakho zokuqala 'your first lessons'* indicates that n8 vn (uku-) is possessed by n4 pl (za-) R7

zokuba *n5-pl-poss-n8-vn* of being; [conj] that, so that • *iimpawu zokuba neTB 'signs that one has TB'* = za-u-ku-ba ☞ See: ukuba R30.2=2

zokubaleka *n5-pl-poss-vn* of running R33.2

zokudlwengulwa *n5-pl-poss-vn-pass* of being raped R36.23

zokufuna *n5-pl-poss-v-inf* of wanting R17.3

zokugcina *n5-pl-vn* for keeping R35.5

zokuhlala *n5-pl-vn* for residing R35.6

zokuhlamba *n8-vn-poss* for washing R35.8=2

zokuhombisa *n5-pl-vn* for adorning za + uku + hombisa ☞ ukuhombisa XED:62, R35.5

zokungavisisani *n5-pl-poss-vn-neg-inf* of not agreeing, of not coming to an understanding R37.14

zokungawuzisi *n4-pl-poss-vn-neg-caus* of not bringing R36.13

zokuphelisa *n5-pl-poss-v-inf-caus* of ending R24.6

zokuqala[1] *n8-vn-poss-n4-pl* first • *izifundo zakho zokuqala 'your first lessons'* R7

zokuqala[2] *n8-vn-poss-n5-pl* first • *iimpawu zokuqala 'the first signs'* R30.2

zokuqalisa *n5-pl* of starting anew, making a beginning R34.1

zokuqokelela *n5-pl-vn* of collecting R35.5

zokusebenza *n5-pl-poss-n2-sg* of employment R28.1=2

zokusixhasa *n5-pl* of supporting us R17.4

zokuveliswa *v-caus-pass* of growing R29.19

zokuziqeqesha *n8-vn-refl-poss-n5-pl* of self-training R33.9.10=2

Zola[1] *n1a-sg-pn* Zola (personal name) R26.8

-zola[2] *v-st* become calm CGB:155

zole *ideophone* subside; become tranquil E&S:59

zom- *combo* of • *iqabane elidiniweyo zizinto zomhlaba 'a companion who is tired of the things of the world'* indicates that n2 sg (um-) is possessed by a n5 pl (za-) ☞ See: za- + um- R4c

zomhlaba *n2-sg-poss* of the world R4c

zomthetho *n5-pl-poss-n2-sg* of the law; in the law R32.6

zomthonyama *n2-sg-cmp* of the kraal; [ext atr] traditional compound formed from um- (in)to > tho + (i)nyama R32.4

zomzimba *n2-sg-poss-n5-pl* of the body • *iinkanuko zomzimba 'lusts of the flesh'* R36.17

zona[1] *pro-n4-pl-echo* they [group 4 plural echo / absolutive pronoun] AM-94:93; 163, CGB:158, E&S:21, PCX:57

zona[2] *pro-n5-pl-echo* they [group 5 plural echo / absolutive pronoun] AM-94:92; 163, CGB:158, E&S:21, PCX:57, R28.1, R37.11

zona[3] *pro-n6-pl-echo* they [group 6 plural echo / absolutive pronoun] CGB:158, PCX:57

-zonda *v-tr* have a strong feeling (for / against); desire, long for, dote on, be very fond of; hate, loathe, abhor, detest XED:192, R11=2

zonk' *pron-quant* all ☞ See: zonke R13.7

zonke[1] *pro-enum-n4-pl* all; every • *zonke izizwe 'all the nations'* Agr: izi-, zona AM-94:163, E&S:27, PCX:62f;24f

zonke[2] *pro-enum-n5-pl* all; every • *abefundisi bemvaba zonke 'preachers from all missionary societies'* Agr: izi(N)-, zona AM-94:163, CGB:176, E&S:27, PCX:62, R13.6, R25.7, R27.6

zonke[3] *pro-enum-n6-pl* all; every Agr: izi(N)-, zona CGB:176, R37.2

-zotha *v-tr* nauseate RD-96:416

zoyike *v-sub-n4-pl-S3a* they should fear R11

-zuza *v-tr* obtain, acquire; earn, achieve, reach; gain, benefit, profit; reclaim (land); hit (an opponent); win RD-96:416, XED:193, R27.1, R33.6, R34.6.7.9, R35.2.3.7, R37.0